Unless Recalled Earlier

IMF Essays from a Time of Crisis

IMF Essays from a Time of Crisis

The International Financial System, Stabilization, and Development

Stanley Fischer

The MIT Press
Cambridge, Massachusetts
London, England

This book was set in Palatino on 3B2 by Asco Typesetters, Hong Kong, and was printed and bound in the United States of America.

Library of Congress Cataloging-in-Publication Data

Fischer, Stanley.
  IMF essays from a time of crisis: the international financial system, stabilization, and development / Stanley Fischer.
    p. cm.
  Includes bibliographical references and index.
  ISBN 0-262-06237-2 (hc. : alk. paper)
  1. International Monetary Fund. 2. Monetary policy—Developing countries.
3. Economic stabilization—Developing countries. 4. Foreign exchange rates—Developing countries. I. Title.

HG3881.5.I58F55   2004
332'.042—dc21   2003051251

10 9 8 7 6 5 4 3 2 1

Contents

Contents

Preface

The papers collected in this book date from the period 1994–2001, during which I served as First Deputy Managing Director of the International Monetary Fund. They reflect many of the issues that confronted the Fund during those years—among them monetary policy and central bank independence, exchange rate regimes, inflation and how to end it, the transition process in the former members of the Soviet bloc, the role of the Fund, the Asian crisis, capital account liberalization, and poverty and development. All but two (chapters 2 and 7) were written while I was at the Fund, and the two exceptions were published after I joined the IMF.

During these years, particularly during the Asian crisis and its aftermath, the Fund came under severe attack, and there were numerous suggestions for reforming the international financial system. The chapters in section I, on the role of the IMF and the reform of the international system, discuss many of those issues. Chapter 1, on the need for an international lender of last resort, reflects on the fundamental case for the existence of an agency like the IMF. Chapter 4, on the role of the IMF, is a presentation made to the Meltzer Commission (the International Financial Institution Advisory Commission) that explains what the IMF does, why it is needed, and how it changed in response to events and critiques. Chapter 3, on the IMF and the Asian crisis, was an early response to critics of the policy responses of the Fund in the Asian crisis. Chapter 5, on capital account liberalization, examines a central issue in the financial crises of the last decade. And Chapter 6 discusses the reform of the international financial system.

The controversies over the Fund are a mark of its importance to the international system and to the well-being of its developing country members. The Fund's decisions mattered to the countries that came to it for assistance, and they matter for the behavior of the international financial system. And when decisions are required, decision-makers must commit one way or the other on possibly close-cut issues. Because the Fund makes decisions, because those decisions frequently come at a time of crisis in a member country, and because opinions on those decisions differ, the Fund inevitably will be at the center of controversy. This controversy is a fact of life that those with the responsibility for making decisions—the Fund's management and the responsible officials in its member countries—must accept.

The Fund's member countries, and certainly its management, paid close attention to the criticisms we received—for mistakes are inevitable, especially when policy decisions have to be made in the heat of a crisis, when the Fund is engaged in battlefield medicine. We modified some policy positions as a result, remained open to further changes, and tried to engage intellectually with the critics, to left and right. But we could not please them all, both because many of the criticisms were mutually inconsistent, and because in some cases we believed—on the basis of economic analysis—that they were wrong.

Criticism is both necessary and healthy, so the management of the Fund did not object to the controversies. We would have preferred to receive more public support from the governments that had voted for programs that came under attack. Some of our members did support us in public; others preferred to remain silent. That was disappointing. But what was objectionable were the attacks on our dedicated, talented, and hard-working staff, who were in no position to fight back.

All the chapters in this book are policy-related, and by the standards of the journals, they are relatively nontechnical. Some originally were published in professional journals; some were speeches aimed at more general audiences. I have included both types because of their subject matter, which encompasses the major issues that confronted the Fund during the period, and so that readers—and I hope students in economics will be among them—will see the different levels at which economics is deployed in policy work.

In each section of the book, I comment on the papers[1] to set them in context, and, where relevant, to reflect on changes in my views. Although the basic set of policy beliefs I brought to the job—that a sound macroeconomic framework is essential for the stability and sustained growth of the economy, that for many economies inflation targeting is a good way of conducting monetary policy, that market-friendly structural policies are good for growth, and that policies should explicitly target poverty reduction—did not change, some of my specific policy views did. For instance, I was more favorably inclined towards the temporary use of a pegged exchange rate as a means of reducing inflation in 1994 than I was when I left the Fund. And, as I explain at some length in the introduction to chapter 2, my views on the Fund's role in dealing with poverty changed while I was at the Fund. These changes resulted from not only fresh evidence but also the vigorous debate about the policies and programs the IMF has supported.

Ratna Sahay of the IMF, and Carlos Végh, who was at the Fund but later moved to UCLA, are my coauthors on three of the chapters in this book. I am extremely grateful to them for many enjoyable and fruitful collaborations. I also owe thanks to my coauthors and friends David Burton of the IMF, on moderate inflation, and Bill Easterly, then of the World Bank, on inflation and the poor. On one or more papers, I also benefited from the assistance of Claire Hughes Adams, Robert Chote, and Mary Elizabeth Hansen. And I am grateful to Prachi Mishra of Columbia University for her essential contribution to bringing this volume to press.

I am immensely grateful to many other colleagues inside the IMF and out, for their direct assistance on some of the papers, and for their support—including sometimes their criticism. I learned a great deal from Michel Camdessus about the substance of what the Fund does, but I learned even more by seeing him in action, understanding that a leader has to make decisions, fight to get them carried out, accept the responsibility for them, and stand behind the staff that implements them. I benefited from and enjoyed working with my fellow deputy managing directors, my close friend Alassane Ouattara, P. R. Narvekar, Shige Sugisaki, and Eduardo Aninat. I also learned a great deal from members of the Executive Board of the IMF (the representatives of the Fund's member countries), both in board meetings, and outside. I had many policy discussions with officials of member governments, not least those in the United States Treasury, especially Larry Summers; I also learned much during discussions and program negotiations with members who were seeking IMF financial assistance. I would like also to thank friends in academe—especially the late Rudi Dornbusch—and policy research institutions who wrote about what the Fund was doing, or called to express views, or were available for confidential discussion when issues were particularly difficult.

After seven years as First Deputy Managing Director, I stepped down with enormous admiration for the IMF. It is a superb organization, very small relative to the tasks that it undertakes, highly disciplined, which time after time has delivered what the international community has asked of it. That is in no small part a result of the quality of its Executive Board.

Even more it is due to the quality of the staff. They are dedicated, effective, first-rate professionals, upon whom the international community and the international financial system rely. I am tempted to name some of them with whom I worked most closely, but if I started, I would not know where to stop.

This book is dedicated to the staff of the IMF.

Note

1. Chapter 9, "Modern Hyper- and High Inflations," has been published so recently that I have not yet had time to view it from a fresh perspective.

Sources

1. Fischer, Stanley. 1999. "On the Need for an International Lender of Last Resort," *Journal of Economic Perspectives*, vol. 13, no. 4, Fall 1999, 85–104. Reprinted with permission from the American Economic Association.

2. Fischer, Stanley. 1995. "The IMF and the World Bank at Fifty," in *The International Monetary System*, H. Genberg (ed.). Heidelberg: Springer-Verlag, 171–200. Reprinted with permission from Springer-Verlag.

3. Fischer, Stanley. 1998. "The IMF and the Asian Crisis," Forum Funds Lecture, UCLA, March 20, 1998. Reprinted with permission from the International Monetary Fund.

4. Fischer, Stanley. 2000. "The Role of the IMF," presentation to the International Financial Institution Advisory Commission (Meltzer Commission), Washington, D.C., February 2, 2000. Reprinted with permission from the International Monetary Fund.

5. Fischer, Stanley. 1998. "Capital Account Liberalization and the Role of the IMF," in *Essays in International Finance*, Stanley Fischer, Richard N. Cooper, Rudiger Dornbusch, Peter M. Garber, Carlos Massad, Jacques J. Polak, Dani Rodrik, and Savak S. Tarapore. Princeton: Princeton University, no. 207, May 1998, 1–10. Reprinted with permission from Princeton University.

6. Fischer, Stanley. 1999. "Reforming the International Financial System," *Economic Journal*, vol. 109, no. 459, November 1999, F557–576. Reprinted with permission from Blackwell Publishing.

7. Fischer, Stanley. 1994. "Modern Central Banking," in *The Future of Central Banking: The Tercentenary Symposium of the Bank of England*, Forrest Capie, Stanley Fischer, Charles Goodhart, and Norbert

Schnadt (eds.). Cambridge: Cambridge University Press, 262–308. Reprinted with the permission of Cambridge University Press.

8. Fischer, Stanley. 2001. "Exchange Rate Regimes: Is the Bipolar View Correct?" *Journal of Economic Perspectives*, vol. 15, no. 2, Spring 2001, 3–24. Reprinted with the permission of the American Economic Association.

9. Fischer, Stanley, Ratna Sahay, and Carlos A. Végh. 2002. "Modern Hyper- and High Inflations," *Journal of Economic Literature*, vol. XL, September 2002, 837–880. Reprinted with the permission of the American Economic Association.

10. Burton, David, and Stanley Fischer. 1998. "Ending Moderate Inflations," in *Moderate Inflation: The Experience of Transition Economies*, C. Cottarelli and G. Szapáry (eds.). Washington, D.C.: IMF and National Bank of Hungary, 15–96. Reprinted with permission from the International Monetary Fund.

11. Fischer, Stanley. 1995. "Recollections of the United States' Role in the Israeli Stabilization," presented at the Israeli Economic Association's Conference on the Tenth Anniversary of the Israeli Stabilization Program, November 1995. Also published in *Rivon Lecalcala* (*Economic Quarterly*, Hebrew), vol. 42, no. 4, December 1995, 589–597.

12. Fischer, Stanley, Ratna Sahay, and Carlos A. Végh. 1996. "Stabilization and Growth in Transition Economies: The Early Experience," *Journal of Economic Perspectives*, vol. 10, no. 2, Spring 1996, 45–66. Reprinted with permission from the American Economic Association.

13. Fischer, Stanley, Ratna Sahay, and Carlos A. Végh. 1997. "How Far is Eastern Europe from Brussels?" in *Quo Vadis Europe?*, H. Siebert (ed.). Tübingen: J.C.B. Mohr, 97–145. Reprinted with permission from J.C.B. Mohr.

14. Easterly, William, and Stanley Fischer. 2001. "Inflation and the Poor," *Journal of Money, Credit, and Banking*, vol. 33, no. 2, part 1, May 2001, 160–178. Reprinted with permission. © 2001 The Ohio State University. All rights reserved.

15. Fischer, Stanley. 1999. "ABCDE: Past Ten Years, Next Ten Years," in *Annual World Bank Conference on Development Economics 1998*, Pleskovic, Boris and Joseph E. Stiglitz (eds.). Washington, D.C.: World Bank, 77–86.

16. Fischer, Stanley. 1995. "Economic Reform and the Poor," Exim Bank Commemorative Lecture, Bombay, March 27, 1995.

I

The Role of the IMF and Reform of the International Financial System

1   *Introduction*

The argument set out in "On the Need for an International Lender of Last Resort" had been forming for a long time before I wrote the chapter. I first heard about the issue in Charles Kindleberger's international economics lectures at MIT in the late 1960s. Kindleberger's notion was that one or a few of the major central banks needs to take responsibility for the operation of the international system, and in that sense act as international lender of last resort. Inside the IMF, Alexandre Kafka, the venerable representative of Brazil, kept insisting that the Fund should operate as a lender of last resort, and the Managing Director, Michel Camdessus, would privately say that it was already operating in that way.

The main impetus to the writing of this paper was provided by the need to reflect on the IMF's role in dealing with the crises in Mexico, Asia, and Russia. When the U.S. government failed in February 1995 to come up with the full $40 billion it had led the markets to believe it would lend Mexico, and turned to the IMF for financing, the Fund was acting in an important sense as a lender of last resort. And when the Fund (with the sometimes heavy involvement of its major shareholders) took a leading role in managing the Asian crises, including in assembling financing packages, it felt as though it was acting as a lender of last resort.

In the chapter, I define the lender of last resort (LOLR) as carrying out two functions, those of crisis lender and crisis manager. In discussing the LOLR, some focus on the lending function, on the ability of the central bank to provide unlimited amounts of credit, and thus to stay a panic. For these analysts, the IMF by definition cannot operate as the international lender of last resort since it cannot provide unlimited amounts of foreign exchange to a country suffering from a run on its currency.

In the chapter I argue in some detail that *while it is advantageous for the lender of last resort to be able to create money, that is not an essential attribute of the LOLR*. However, there is no point in getting tied up in arguments over definitions. Accordingly, those who insist on the definition of LOLR as applying only to institutions that have the ability to create money in unlimited amounts should interpret the argument of the paper as being that there is a useful role in the international system for an institution that can act as both crisis lender and crisis manager—even if such an institution does not meet their definition of lender of last resort.

I believe the chapter provides a convincing argument to that effect. It also argues that the IMF is increasingly playing that role, and that it could play it more effectively. That is not to deny that the primary responsibility for ensuring the stability of the international financial system lies with the central banks of the major economies; it is to argue that those central banks are not and should not be charged with resolving the foreign exchange crises of other countries, especially the emerging market countries.

In discussing the role of the IMF as crisis lender and crisis manager, I emphasize private sector involvement in the resolution of crises. I did not use the distinction between *liquidity* and *solvency* crises in the chapter, because there is no clear definition of insolvency for a sovereign government: it is a matter of political judgment as to whether a country can and should pay its debts. Nonetheless, the distinction is conceptually useful, because a pure liquidity crisis can be resolved by the provision of sufficiently large loans, whereas real burdens have to be borne in an insolvency crisis. In a liquidity crisis, all lenders can emerge whole, whereas in a solvency crisis they should not. However, it is never clear until later whether a particular crisis is a liquidity or a solvency crisis. That is one reason for seeking to spell out in advance the rules of burden sharing in international financial crises, which is part of the framework for private sector involvement.

Those rules are essential also to reduce the moral hazard that results from the existence of a lender of last resort, a crisis lender. Moral hazard is an important problem that has to be taken into account in both the design of the international system and in resolving individual crises. But, as I argue in the chapter, there is no perfect solution to the moral hazard problem—because moral hazard is always present when insurance is being provided, managing moral hazard requires balancing the benefits of the insurance against the costs of the adverse incentives such insurance may create. I sometimes felt during crises that the moral hazard problem was being overplayed, and that we were in effect being asked to impose severe costs on a particular country to serve as an example to others. Because that should not be done, it is critical to try to define the principles and rules of crisis management in advance—while recognizing that it will never be possible to spell out all future actions precisely.

After this chapter was written, it became clear that several members of the Executive Board of the IMF objected to the characterization of the Fund as an international lender of last resort. Their main analytic argument was that since the Fund could not create money, it could not be an international LOLR. But another factor may have been in the background, the fear that to discuss the Fund's role in these terms would create more moral hazard—in other words, the view that constructive ambiguity about the role of the lender of last resort is useful in limiting moral hazard. I discuss that view in the chapter, and I disagree with it.

I believe it useful for the discussion on the role of the Fund as international lender of last resort to continue, for international financial crises and panics will continue to occur and will on occasion punish relatively innocent countries and their citizens. If we can mitigate them, we should.

1

On the Need for an International Lender of Last Resort

Stanley Fischer

The frequency, virulence, and global spread of financial crises in emerging market countries in the last five years—Mexico in 1994, with the subsequent tequila contagion in Latin America and for a day or two in east Asia; east Asia in 1997 and 1998, with contagion spreading crisis within the region; Russia in 1998, itself affected by Asian contagion, with the Russian contagion spreading to Latin America in addition to eastern Europe and the rest of the former Soviet Union—has led to the most serious rethinking of the structure of the international financial system since the breakdown of the Bretton Woods system in 1971. In the coming months and years, governments and international institutions will be putting in place a series of changes designed to strengthen the international financial system.

The vision that underlies most proposals for reform of the international financial system is that the international capital markets should operate as well as the better domestic capital markets. To express the goal in this way is to drive home the point that volatility and contagion cannot be banished, for asset prices inevitably move sharply, and in ways that are significantly intercorrelated. But while volatility and contagion will always be with us, we can surely do better in reducing the frequency and intensity of emerging market financial crises, and the extent of contagion, than we have in the last five years.

As we consider how to make the global capital markets operate better and how to reduce the frequency and virulence of financial crises, I would like to revisit a literature that emerged out of the financial crises of the last century, that on the lender of last resort. The best-known classic writing on the lender of last resort is Walter Bagehot's (1873) *Lombard Street*.[1] The most famous lesson from

Bagehot is that *in a crisis, the lender of last resort should lend freely, at a penalty rate, on the basis of collateral that is marketable in the ordinary course of business when there is no panic.*

I will start by reviewing the case for a lender of last resort in the domestic economy, and the set of rules that the lender of last resort is supposed to follow. I will then discuss the moral hazard problem that is created by the existence of a lender of last resort—that is, the problem that the existence of a lender of last resort may create incentives for risky behavior which raise the chances of financial crises—and measures to mitigate it. I then turn to the international system and will argue that it too needs a lender of last resort. I will argue that the International Monetary Fund, although it is not an international central bank, has undertaken certain important lender of last resort functions in the current system, generally acting in concert with other official agencies—and that its role can be made more effective in a reformed international financial system.[2]

The Domestic Lender of Last Resort

The role of lender of last resort for the central bank is associated with the prevention and mitigation of financial crises. Financial crises and panics have been taking place for centuries (Kindleberger, 1996; MacKay, 1841). They are typically associated with a sudden loss of confidence in the standing of some financial institutions or assets. Because the chain of credit is based on tightly interlinked expectations of the ability of many different debtors to meet payments, a sense of panic can spread rapidly, contagiously, through the financial system, and if unchecked, have significant effects on the behavior of the real economy. The role of the lender of last resort is to offer an assurance of credit, given under certain limited conditions, which will stop a financial panic from spreading—or better still, stop it from even getting started.[3]

While there is considerable agreement on the need for a domestic lender of last resort, some disagreements persist about what the lender of last resort should do. I will start with the traditional Bagehot (1873) conception, as summarized and developed by Meltzer (1986, p. 83):

The central bank is called the lender of last resort because it is capable of lending—and to prevent failures of solvent banks must lend—in periods

when no other lender is either capable of lending or willing to lend in sufficient volume to prevent or end a financial panic.

Meltzer lists (pp. 83–84) five main points concerning a lender of last
resort, the first four derived from Bagehot:

The central bank is the only lender of last resort in a monetary system such
as [that of the United States].

To prevent illiquid banks from closing, the central bank should lend on
any collateral that is marketable *in the ordinary course of business when there is
no panic* [emphasis added]. It should not restrict lending to paper eligible for
discount at the central bank in normal periods.

Central bank loans, or advances, should be made in large amounts, on
demand, at a rate of interest above the market rate. This discourages borrowing by those who can obtain accommodation in the market.

The above three principles should be stated in advance and followed in a
crisis.

Insolvent financial institutions should be sold at the market price or liquidated if there are no bids for the firm as an integral unit. The losses should
be borne by owners of equity, subordinated debentures, and debt, uninsured
depositors, and the deposit insurance corporations, as in any bankruptcy
proceeding.

Meltzer's (1986) statement for the most part agrees with other
formulations, but does not emphasize the view, summarized for
instance by Humphrey (1975) and attributed to Thornton (1802), that
the overriding objective of the lender of last resort should be to prevent panic-induced declines in the aggregate money stock, and thus
that the lender of last resort role can be viewed as part of a central
bank's overall task of monetary control. In some more recent formulations, this view has been extended to what could be considered
a sixth precept, which could be added to the above list: "In the event
of a panic, the central bank should assure liquidity to the market, but
not necessarily to individual institutions."[4]

With this notion of the lender of last resort in mind, I will take up
six questions about the role of the domestic lender of last resort.

Is the Central Bank the Only Lender of Last Resort?

Lenders of last resort have generally undertaken two roles: *crisis
lender* and *crisis manager*. The crisis lender provides financing to deal
with a crisis. The crisis manager takes responsibility for dealing with
a crisis or potential crisis, whether or not the institution itself lends

for that purpose. In the midst of a financial crisis, there is often a potential managerial (or facilitating or coordinating) role in which other agents or institutions may be encouraged to act in the right way, for instance by extending a loan to an institution whose failure could have systemic consequences.

While historically the central bank has generally been both the crisis manager and the crisis lender, neither role has to be carried out by the central bank. If a certain authority, and access to resources, are necessary for taking this coordinating role, then a Treasury may be able to do it as well as a central bank. At various times in U.S. history, institutions other than the central bank have played one or both of these roles, including: the U.S. Treasury; private institutions, such as clearinghouses; and in 1907, J. P. Morgan (Kindleberger, 1996, pp. 133–135).[5] Indeed, the separation of the roles of crisis lender and crisis manager could become more frequent as the task of supervision of the financial sector is separated from the central bank, as it has been in the United Kingdom and elsewhere.

Does the Lender of Last Resort Need the Ability to Create Money?

There is no question that a lender of last resort will often find it useful to have the power to create money. The clearest example is when a panic takes the form of a run from bank deposits into currency. Then the central bank is well-positioned to create quickly the currency needed to deal with the panic, and at no first-round cost to the taxpayer.[6]

However, panics caused by a demand for currency are rare (Kaufman, 1988; Schwartz, 1988). More generally, a panic may take the form of a run, possibly enhanced by contagion, in which deposits shift from those banks and financial institutions deemed unsound to those thought to be healthy. In these cases, creating additional money may be unnecessary. At least in principle, the liquidity can simply recirculate from the institutions gaining money back to those losing it. Again in principle, the market can accomplish this shift, if it is able to distinguish the merely illiquid from the insolvent companies.

But—and this is the critical point—*the line between solvency and liquidity is not determinate during a crisis.* If a crisis is well-managed, the number of bankruptcies may remain small; if it is badly managed, it may end in general illiquidity and insolvency. A skilled lender of last resort, able to assure the markets that credit can and will be made available to institutions that would be solvent in normal times, can help stem a panic and reduce the extent of the crisis.

All this is straightforward, provided the central bank is free to create money. However, at the time that Bagehot (1873) wrote *Lombard Street*, the Bank of England was bound by gold standard rules; that is, money could only be created in accordance with the amount of gold held by the Bank, and the Bank did not have the ability to create gold. Nonetheless, Bagehot enjoined the Bank to act as lender of last resort. In the three financial crises preceding the writing of *Lombard Street*, the Bank of England was given permission to break the gold standard rule, and since Bank of England credit was accepted as being as good as gold, it managed to stay the panics. The key was not the legal right to create money, but the effective ability to provide liquidity to the market.

A similar question, of whether there can be a lender of last resort when the central bank is constrained in the creation of money, arises today in countries with currency boards, where foreign exchange holdings constrain the domestic money supply. If the question is how to deal with domestic financial institutions that may suffer liquidity problems, one solution adopted in Bulgaria, where the banking department of the central bank is assigned the task of (limited) lender of last resort, is to set up an agency that is endowed with sufficient resources to lend in the event of a panic or banking sector problems. If the problem is how to deal with a potential external shock that puts pressure on the domestic banking system, then the country may either hold excess foreign exchange reserves, or as in the case of Argentina, borrow from the markets and the official sector and put in place international lines of credit. In these cases, the private and public sector lenders to the central bank are acting as the crisis lender, while the central bank is acting as crisis manager.[7]

These examples make the point that lender of last resort need not have the power to create money, as long as it can provide credit to the market or to institutions in trouble. It is possible to set up an agency to deal with potential banking sector problems and endow it with sufficient funds—perhaps from the Treasury—to cover the anticipated costs of normal crises. In dealing with banking crises, the lender of last resort has more often acted as crisis manager, as coordinator, without putting up its own funds, than as outright lender.

In the 20-year period ending in 1993, taxpayer or deposit insurance money was used in over half the 120 banking rescue packages studied by Goodhart and Schoenmaker (1995), in part because the central bank simply did not have the real resources that were required to deal with the banking problem. In any case, the costs of major financial system difficulties will one way or another be borne by the fiscal authority, either explicitly or implicitly, in the form of lower central bank profits over an extended period of time.[8]

This point—that while it is advantageous for the lender of last resort to be able to create money, it is not an essential attribute of the lender of last resort—is both central to the argument of this paper, and controversial. I make the argument on logical and historical grounds, namely, that it is possible to conceive of an institution that does not have the ability to create money acting usefully as both crisis manager and crisis lender and that as a historical matter, such institutions have usefully undertaken such roles. Others would argue that without the ability to create unlimited amounts of money, the would-be lender of last resort lacks credibility and thus cannot stabilize a panic. Those who take the latter view should interpret the argument of this paper as being that there is a useful role to be played by an institution that can be both crisis manager and crisis lender, even if—according to their own definition—it cannot be a lender of last resort.

Why Should a Lender of Last Resort Lend Only against Collateral, Especially Collateral Evaluated at its Value in Noncrisis Times?

By basing the decision to lend on the availability of acceptable collateral, the lender of last resort applies a rough but robust test of whether the institution is in trouble because of the immediate panic, or because of an insolvency that will persist even after the panic. Moreover, when financial institutions know that the lender of last resort will demand collateral, they have an incentive to reduce risks in their portfolios by holding assets that would be accepted as collateral.

The requirement that the collateral be good in normal times is the critical insight. The implicit view behind the requirement that the lender of last resort require collateral, and that the collateral be valued at noncrisis levels, is that there is a good equilibrium towards which the lender of last resort is trying to steer the system. By lending on the basis of the value of collateral in normal times, the lender of last resort helps prevent the panic in the market from becoming self-fulfilling.

More broadly, this rule also suggests that the lender of last resort should apply the rules of collateral generously. In a famous passage bearing on this point, Bagehot (1873 [1924 edition, p. 52]) quotes the Bank of England in 1825:

"We lent it by every possible means and in modes we had never adopted before; we took in stock on security, we purchased Exchequer bills, we made advances on Exchequer bills, we not only discounted outright but we made advances on the deposit of bills of exchange to an immense amount, in short by every possible means consistent with the safety of the bank, and we were not on some occasions over-nice."

In a similar spirit, the Governor of the Bank of England described the Bank's reaction to the Overend financial crisis in May 1866 (as quoted in Clapham, 1944, volume II, pp. 283–284): "We did not flinch from our post ... we made advances which would hardly have been credited ... before the Chancellor of the Exchequer was perhaps out of his bed we had advanced one-half of our reserves ... I am not aware that any legitimate application for assistance made to this house was refused."

Why Should the Lender of Last Resort Charge a Penalty Interest Rate?

The penalty interest rate serves several functions. It limits the demand for credit by institutions that are not in trouble. It reduces the risk that financial institutions will take excessive risks in normal times, secure in the knowledge that they will be able to borrow cheaply in tough times. It encourages institutions to repay the lender of last resort as soon as possible after the crisis, in preference to other outstanding loans.[9]

But just as the requirement for collateral is not intended to stifle the lender of last resort, neither is the application of penalty interest rates. The penalty rate need not be defined relative to the rate at which institutions would lend to each other in the market during a panic. Instead, the penalty must be relative to the interest rate during normal times. In practice, the lender of last resort has frequently lent at a nonpenalty rate (Giannini, 1998).

Should the Lender of Last Resort Lend Only to the Market, and Not to Individual Institutions?

This view holds that, given the provision of sufficient liquidity to the markets, the private sector will be able to decide which institutions should be saved. Moreover, by providing liquidity to the market, the lender of last resort avoids the political hazards of lending to individual institutions.

This idea is a worthy one that should be followed when possible. But given the uncertainties in the midst of a panic over what market conditions will exist in the future, and thus over which institutions should survive, the precept cannot be accepted as a general rule of conduct for the lender of last resort. Almost by definition of a financial panic, a market in the throes of a panic will not do a sound job of allocating credit across institutions. Indeed, Goodhart and Huang (1998) argue that adopting the view that the lender of last resort should lend only to the market is to reject the notion of the lender of last resort.

Should the Principles on Which the Lender of Last Resort Would Lend Be Clearly Stated in Advance?

During a crisis, the knowledge that there is an effective lender of last resort should tend to reduce the incentive for runs on otherwise healthy institutions. However some, who fear that market participants will have an incentive to take excessive risks if they believe a lender of last resort will always be available to stem panics, argue for *constructive ambiguity* about the circumstances in which a lender of last resort will step in to seek to stabilize a crisis. The uncertainty generated by such ambiguity should encourage market participants to take fewer risks.[10]

Some ambiguity is simply unavoidable: no central bank or lender of last resort will ever be able to spell out precisely in advance the circumstances under which it would act as either a crisis lender or crisis manager and the conditions it will lay down at that time. But unnecessary ambiguity is not constructive, for it implies that occasions will occur when the putative lender of last resort is expected to deliver, but does not—for example in the Russian crisis of August 1998, when many market participants expected the official sector to prevent a Russian devaluation. In such a setting, ambiguity makes the economic costs of a given financial crisis worse; indeed, Gutten-tag and Herring (1983, p. 24) describe as the worst possible system one in which a lender of last resort is expected to take action, but the relevant institution cannot or does not provide the function.

There are three reasons for a lender of last resort to spell out its rules to the extent possible. First, by specifying a good set of rules, the central bank reduces the likelihood of unnecessary self-justifying crises. This was Bagehot's (1873) justification. Second, by announc-ing and implementing a particular set of rules, the lender of last resort provides incentives for other stabilizing private sector behav-ior; for instance, in the holding of assets good for collateral. Third, by spelling out the rules in advance, the lender of last resort somewhat limits its own freedom of action after the event, which reduces risks of politically motivated or spur-of-the-moment actions. Of course, *in extremis* the rules could be broken as they were by the Bank of England when it violated the gold standard rules to provide addi-tional credit during crises in the 19th century. Spelling out the rules would nonetheless serve a useful purpose, since the lender of last resort would hesitate before incurring the cost of breaking them.

Much of the discussion of these six questions revolves around a common topic, the issue of moral hazard, to which I will now turn.

Moral Hazard

"Moral hazard," notes Guesnerie (1987, p. 646), "refers to the adverse effects, from the insurance company's point of view, that insurance may have on the insuree's behaviour." The standard but extreme example is that of an individual with fire insurance who burns down the property; the less extreme example is of a fire insurance holder who, after becoming insured, takes less care to prevent a fire. More generally, the idea of moral hazard applies to any situation where a perceived reduction in the risk it faces leads a party to take riskier actions, or to neglect precautionary measures.

In the case of the domestic lender of last resort, moral hazard problems could arise with respect to both the actions of managers of financial institutions who believe they are better protected against risk because they would receive loans from the lender of last resort during a crisis, and the actions of investors in those financial insti-tutions (Hirsch, 1977). If the lender of last resort was able to inter-vene only to stop unwarranted panics, leaving institutions that would be insolvent in normal times to fail, the managers of these institutions and their investors would face the right incentives and there would be no moral hazard created by the existence of the lender of last resort. But the lender of last resort is unlikely to be able to distinguish perfectly between warranted and unwarranted crises. Moreover, financial institutions already know that because of the existence of deposit insurance and the too-big-to-fail doctrine, the government has an incentive to prevent them from failing, and thus already have a moral hazard motivation to believe that a government rescue of some sort will be forthcoming. For all these reasons, measures to offset the moral hazard of both managers of financial institutions and investors would be helpful.

In considering how to reduce moral hazard, it is important to recognize that the problem has no perfect solution. Instead, appropriate policies will generally combine the provision of insurance with measures to limit moral hazard. In the case of moral hazard resulting from the existence of a lender of last resort (as well as resulting from deposit insurance and too-big-to-fail provisions), there are three categories of measures to limit moral hazard: official regulation; encouragement for private sector monitoring and self-regulation; and the imposition of costs on those who make mistakes, including enforcement of bankruptcy procedures when appropriate (Stern, 1999). I consider these in turn.

First, to be eligible for loans from a lender of last resort, banks' portfolio activities are regulated. The regulations are intended to limit the likelihood of panics and the need for a lender of last resort, while not preventing well-informed risk taking by investors.

Second, the system seeks to encourage private sector monitoring of financial institutions, particularly by sophisticated investors. Requirements for the provision of information to investors are helpful in this regard. The limit on the size of bank accounts covered by deposit insurance is intended to provide an incentive for large depositors to monitor banks (along with limiting government liability in the case of a bank failure); however, because of concerns that large institutions are too big to fail without threatening financial contagion, these limits rarely operate when large institutions get into trouble. In addition, when the lender of last resort, acting as crisis manager, arranges a bank rescue package financed by the private sector, it encourages more careful monitoring by such institutions in the future.

Third, the lender of last resort should seek to limit moral hazard by imposing costs on those who have made mistakes. Lending at a penalty rate is one way to impose such costs. Changes in management of an institution that is being helped should typically occur, and, as specified in Meltzer's fifth law stated above, equity-holders and holders of subordinated claims on the firm should suffer losses. In the case of insolvency, institutions should be sold or liquidated under the provisions of well-defined bankruptcy laws, which help ensure that workouts for insolvent firms are carried out in an orderly way.

How well do these devices work to limit moral hazard work? A first judgment, based on the frequency of financial crises around the world during the last two decades, is this: Not very well. But this answer is too sweeping. Moral hazard is something to be lived with and controlled, rather than fully eliminated; some crises are bound to happen in any system that provides appropriate scope for private sector risk taking; and many financial crises have been caused by waves of euphoria and depression, not by the existence of a lender of last resort—for after all, the long history of financial crises predates lenders of last resort and deposit insurance. The right comparison is not between the real world and a hypothetical world with no financial crises, but rather between the operation of a system with a lender of last resort (and deposit insurance) and one without them. I am not aware of careful studies that have attempted to make this more sophisticated judgment. However, I suspect that such a study, while likely to absolve the presence of various official forms of financial insurance, including the assumption that there is a lender of last resort, from blame for much financial instability, would conclude that it is important to do a better job of controlling moral hazard in the domestic financial system.

An International Lender of Last Resort?

The case for a domestic lender of last resort is broadly accepted. In the aftermath of the global financial turmoil of the last five years, the question arises of whether the international financial system needs a lender of last resort.

The issue is whether there is a useful role for an institution that takes responsibility for dealing with potential and actual crises, either as a crisis lender, or as a crisis manager, or both. This differs from the question that is sometimes asked as to whether leading central banks should accept some responsibility for the performance of the global economy, along with their national economy. For instance, when Kindleberger (1986) blames the Great Depression on the absence of an international lender of last resort, he means that no agency—and the natural candidates were the Bank of England, the Banque de France, and the U.S. Federal Reserve—pursued a monetary policy that took account of the international dimensions of the crisis in which it found itself. Kindleberger would probably say, approvingly, that in the late 1990s, the Fed *has* acted as international lender of last resort in that sense, even though it was taking actions in the interests of the United States.

I will focus specifically on the case for an international agency to act as lender of last resort for countries facing an external financing crisis. In such a crisis, a country—and by this I mean both the official and private sectors within the country—faces a typically massive demand for foreign exchange. The domestic central bank cannot produce this currency. Thus, the fact that the country may have its own central bank capable of creating the domestic currency is typically irrelevant to the solution of an external financing problem.

There is a potential need for such assistance to a country both because international capital flows are not only extremely volatile but also contagious, exhibiting the classic signs of financial panics,[11] and because an international lender of last resort can help mitigate the effects of this instability and perhaps the instability itself. At the macroeconomic level, a country faced with a sudden demand for foreign exchange can permit its exchange rate to adjust and/or can restrict domestic demand to generate a current account surplus. At the microeconomic level, foreign creditors can attempt to collect on obligations and financial institutions and corporations can—if necessary, and if the domestic legal system is adequate—be put into bankruptcy. However, all such measures are likely in a panic to result in a considerable overshooting of the needed adjustment, and there is accordingly a case for the public sector both to provide emergency foreign exchange loans and to assist the domestic authorities in attempting to manage the crisis.

The argument rests also on the view that international capital mobility is potentially beneficial for the world economy, including for the emerging market and developing countries. Critics of this view argue that neither the theoretical nor empirical evidence supports a positive link between openness to international capital markets and growth. Indeed, both China and India have grown rapidly during the 1990s with only limited openness to international capital markets and appeared relatively immune from the east Asian financial crisis. It is true that there is as yet little convincing econometric evidence bearing on the benefits or costs of open capital markets. However, all the economically most advanced countries are open to international flows of capital, which suggests that this should be the eventual goal for other countries. In addition, countries that close themselves off to international flows of capital also thereby protect the financial sector from foreign competition, which reduces the efficiency of this important industry. Finally, I suspect, but cannot of course establish, that with regard to empirical work on the benefits of capital account liberalization, the economics profession is a little behind where we were a decade ago on trade liberalization, when empirical work showing its benefits was widely regarded as highly suspect, too.

But the critics of international capital mobility are correct to this extent: its potential for economic benefit can only be realized if the frequency and scale of financial crises can be reduced. The founders of the Bretton Woods system provided for the use of controls on international capital flows to reduce the likelihood of such crises. Some controls—particularly controls that seek to limit short-term capital *inflows*—can be envisaged as a useful part of a transitional regime while the macroeconomic framework and financial structure of an economy are strengthened. The use of controls to limit capital *outflows* has been advocated in the recent crises by several academics and adopted by Malaysia. But it is surprising and impressive how few countries have enacted capital controls in recent years. Indeed, policymakers in Latin American countries that often had such controls in the 1980s have rejected them this time around, emphasizing that the controls were inefficient, widely avoided, and had cost them dearly in terms of capital market access. It remains an open question whether more countries will turn to capital controls in the next few years, either in normal times or in the midst of crises. The answer will depend to an important extent on the success of other financial reforms that are implemented in the next few years.

I will argue not only that the international system needs a lender of last resort, so that the global economy can reap greater net benefits from international capital mobility, but also that the IMF has increasingly been playing the role of crisis manager for the last two decades (Boughton, 1998). Changes in the international system now under consideration—particularly those relating to efforts to bail in the private sector—should make it possible for the IMF to exercise the lender of last resort function more effectively.

In focusing on the Fund's potential role as lender of last resort, I leave aside its other important functions. For example, Article I(i) of the Articles of Agreement, as enacted in 1944, describes the first of its fundamental purposes as being: "[t]o promote international monetary cooperation through a permanent institution which provides the machinery for consultation and collaboration on international monetary problems." Other functions of the Fund include lending for current account purposes to countries that lack market access; surveillance and the associated provision of information; and technical assistance, including policy advice and monitoring.

Let me immediately turn to the argument that the IMF cannot act as a lender of last resort because it is not an international central bank and cannot freely create international money. As discussed earlier, even the domestic lender of last resort—whether as crisis lender or as crisis manager—is not necessarily the central bank. The IMF has resources to act as a crisis lender, because its financial structure, close to that of a credit union,[12] gives it access to a pool of resources which it can lend to member countries. The IMF also has been assigned the lead as crisis manager in negotiating with member countries in a crisis and helping to arrange financing packages. Finally, as will be discussed below, it also has the ability—not so far used—to create international reserves in a crisis.

The question arises whether the IMF, as crisis lender, has sufficient resources to do the job. The Fund has reached its present size as a result of a series of increases in countries' quotas—that is, the amount which members of the IMF agree to deposit in the Fund in their own currencies. Relative to the size of the world economy, the IMF has shrunk significantly since 1945. If the Fund were today the same size relative to the output of its member states as it was in 1945, it would be more than three times larger.[13] If the quota formula applied in 1945 were used to calculate actual quotas today, the Fund would be five times its present size. If the size of the Fund had been maintained relative to the volume of world trade, it would be more than nine times larger; that is, the size of the Fund would be over $2.5 trillion. Since the Fund was set up at a time when private capital flows were very small, its scale relative to private capital flows has declined even more than its size relative to trade flows.

Despite this significant shrinkage relative to the original conception, the Fund as lender of last resort is still able to assemble a sizeable financial package in response to a crisis. In case of systemic problems, the Fund can augment the use of its own resources by borrowing. Further, as demonstrated in the recent Brazilian and east Asian financial rescue packages, member governments and other international financial institutions may add significantly to these packages in cases they deem to be of particular importance. Whether the Fund will in future be large enough relative to the scale of problems will depend on the future scale and volatility of international capital flows, which will in turn depend on the effectiveness of reforms, including measures to deal with problems of moral hazard.

The earlier discussion noted in the domestic case that while it is not essential that the lender of last resort be the central bank, it is helpful. Would it be useful for the IMF to be able to create reserves? Under Article XVIII of the Articles of Agreement, the Executive Board of the Fund can by an 85 percent majority allocate Special Drawing Rights (SDRs) "to meet the long-term global need, as and when it arises, to supplement existing reserve assets." These SDRs would augment the reserves of member countries. It is easy to envisage circumstances under which a targeted increase in reserves would be useful to prevent a seizing up of flows of credit in the world economy; indeed, for a short period that seemed to be the case in the fall of 1998. However, a general allocation of SDRs has to be made in proportion to quota holdings and so this mechanism would not in its current form be well-suited to dealing with a problem that affects a specific group of countries.

The IMF thus has the capacity to act as crisis lender to individual countries, and in specified circumstances, through an issue of Special Drawing Rights, could lend more broadly. It also acts as crisis manager. Kindleberger (1996, p. 188) complains that the Fund is too slow in emergencies, but in Korea in late 1997 the IMF has demonstrated an ability to move very rapidly, using the Emergency Financing Mechanism introduced after the Mexican crisis in 1994. The main constraint on the IMF's ability to react speedily in a crisis is that governments suffering a financial crisis delay too long in approaching it, in part because excessive delay is a common characteristic of governments that experience financial crises, but also because they hope to avoid taking the actions that would be needed in a Fund program.

The Evolving Context of the International Financial System

The IMF already acts in important respects as international lender of last resort, but the job can surely be done better. However, before addressing that issue directly, I will discuss four central elements in the ongoing evolution of the international financial system: exchange rate systems; reserve holdings; measures to bail in the private sector; and international standards.

In regard to the first subject, over a century of controversy has produced no clear answer to the question of which exchange rate system or monetary regime is best. The best exchange rate for a country seems to depend on the country's economic history, particularly its history of inflation. Nonetheless, it is striking that the major external financial crises of the last three years—in Thailand, Korea, Indonesia, Russia, and Brazil—have affected countries with more or less pegged exchange rates. Further, the assumption within these countries that the exchange rate was stable profoundly affected economic behavior and certain kinds of risk taking, especially in the banking system, and contributed to the severity of the post-devaluation crises.

The link between pegged exchange rates and susceptibility to crisis is far from ironclad, however. Several countries with very hard pegs, particularly Argentina and Hong Kong, have succeeded with fixed exchange rates. Some countries with flexible rates, among them Mexico, South Africa, and Turkey, have been severely affected by the global economic crisis. Nor should we forget that many countries benefitted from using a pegged or fixed exchange rate as a nominal anchor in disinflation efforts and that the fear of devaluation is often a vital discipline for weak governments. Nonetheless, the virulence of the recent crises is likely to shift the balance towards the choice of more flexible exchange rate systems, including crawling exchange rate pegs with wide bands.

But while the number of nominal exchange rate pegs may decline in the coming years, the world is unlikely to move to a system in which exchange rates for all countries float freely. If countries desire to fix their exchange rates, they may well want to do so definitively, through a currency board. In the longer run, if Europe's move to a single currency succeeds, the result may be additional currency unions and fewer currencies. Because sharp shifts in international investor sentiment regarding even a country with a floating rate can set off a panic and contagion, and because some countries will continue to peg their rates, the need will still exist for an international lender of last resort.

Second, regarding the issue of reserves, there has been surprisingly little emphasis on the fact that countries with very large foreign exchange reserves have generally fared better in the recent economic crises than those with small reserves. However, a number of countries, particularly Korea, have recognized that the ratio of reserves to short-term external liabilities is an important factor determining the likelihood of a financial crisis (Calvo, 1995), and are accumulating reserves accordingly.[14]

Foreign exchange reserves can be built up in several ways. The most obvious approach is to run a current account surplus; indeed, it is likely that a general desire by emerging market countries to build up reserves by running current account surpluses will impart a deflationary impact to the world economy in the next few years. Reserves can be borrowed, although the interest costs are typically well above the return on reserves. Argentina and a few other countries have put into place a variation on the idea of borrowing reserves, which is to arrange for precautionary or contingent lines of credit, which can be drawn on at short notice if needed. International reserves might also be increased by international agreement on, for example, an issue of Special Drawing Rights. It is not possible without a more detailed analysis to decide which approach is preferable: the approaches differ in terms of effects on aggregate demand, the distribution of seigniorage and other variables. However, I expect that one way or another, the recent experience of crises will lead to larger holdings of reserves.

Third, no topic in the new international financial architecture has received as much public attention as the need to involve the private sector in the resolution of financial crises. The arguments are simple and compelling. At the economic level, as the role of private capital flows in the international economy increases, the public sector should not take upon itself the full responsibility for financing countries from which the private sector is withdrawing, for to do so is to court moral hazard on a major scale, to set the wrong incentives for private sector investors and to accept an impossible task—since the public sector will not in the end have enough resources to carry out such a commitment. At the political level, elected officials are unwilling to make public money available for unlimited bailouts of previously incautious private investors.

One approach, just mentioned, is to put in place precautionary lines of credit from private sector lenders. Such lines of credit can serve as a useful supplement to the holding of reserves, and might well be cheaper than actually increasing reserves. A second approach, suggested in a report by the G-10 deputies after the Mexican crisis, is the proposal that bond contracts should be modified to facilitate the rescheduling of payments in the event of a crisis, including by permitting creditors to make decisions by majority rather than unanimity.[15] Yet another suggestion, associated with Jeffrey Sachs, is the possibility of a mechanism which would formally impose or allow a stay on payments by a country in financial crisis, a proposal which is sometimes referred to as international bankruptcy. Some developing countries object that such measures would make it more expensive for them to borrow, but most likely that would reflect a more appropriate pricing of risks.

Private sector involvement in external financing crises needs to be approached carefully, lest proposed solutions increase the frequency of crises. For instance, it is sometimes proposed that banks (or other creditors) should always be forced to share in the financing of IMF programs. But if such a condition were insisted on, the creditors would have a greater incentive to rush for the exits at the mere hint of a crisis. This problem suggests that even with private sector involvement, a lender of last resort will continue to be necessary. It also suggests that the involvement of the private sector should differ according to the circumstances of each country: sometimes a formal approach may be necessary, as in Korea at the end of 1997; at other times less formal discussions could serve better; and on occasion, if a country enters an IMF program sufficiently early, perhaps private creditors need not be approached at all.

Fourth, because weaknesses in financial sectors and in the provision of information were such an important factor in the recent crises, a major effort is now underway to encourage emerging market countries to meet agreed international standards of financial and corporate sector behavior, as well as the provision of information. The best-known standards are those for banking, defined by the Basel Committee on Banking Supervision. The IMF's Special Data

Dissemination Standard has just gone into full operation. Codes of fiscal practice and monetary and financial transparency are also being prepared by the IMF in cooperation with other institutions. A major international effort will be undertaken to improve banking standards, in part through international monitoring and IMF surveillance in cooperation with the World Bank. Among other important international standards already developed or in the process of development are international accounting standards, International Organization of Securities Commissions (IOSCO) standards for the operation of securities markets, and an international standard for bankruptcy regulations.

The main incentives for a country to adopt any of these standards are the expectation that the economy would operate more efficiently and the hope that international investors would treat the economy more favorably. In fact, most leading emerging market countries have subscribed to the IMF's Special Data Dissemination Standard, which suggests that these incentives may suffice to encourage participation in international standards. Nonetheless, further incentives may prove useful; for instance, the risk weights assigned by regulators in creditor countries could reflect the recipient country's observance of the standards. Further incentives can be provided by the appropriate design of official lending facilities.

Improving the Functioning of the International Lender of Last Resort

At the end of 1997, the IMF introduced the Supplemental Reserve Facility (SRF), which can make short-term loans in large amounts at penalty rates to countries in crisis. SRF loans have been made to Korea, Russia, and Brazil, subject to conditions that certain economic policies be followed. In addition, in April 1999, the Executive Board of the IMF established the Contingent Credit Line (CCL) facility, designed to provide countries with a line of credit that can be drawn on in the event they are struck by contagion from an external crisis. To qualify for a CCL, a country must be pursuing good macroeconomic policies, have a strong financial sector and either meet or be moving towards meeting international standards in a variety of areas. The CCL is thus intended to provide an element of insurance and reassurance for countries with good policies, and incentives for others to pursue good policies, rather than to come to the assistance of countries that are already in trouble. The lending terms for the CCL are similar to those for the SRF. No CCLs have yet been arranged.

Calomiris (1998) and Calomiris and Meltzer (1998) recommend that the IMF act only as lender of last resort, under Bagehot rules, and only to countries that meet a stiff set of requirements, most importantly on the banking system. Among these conditions is the requirement that foreign banks be allowed to operate in the country, a reform that countries should adopt in any case. Loans would be made to qualifying countries on the basis of collateral, and without policy conditionality. Without going into the overall merits of their analysis,[16] I would like to note that the CCL goes some way towards meeting their proposals. It would further be desirable if the rate charged for access to the CCL and the SRF depended on the extent to which countries meet the relevant international standards. For example, a nonqualifying country might pay a higher penalty interest rate, or be subject to tougher policy conditionality, or in extreme cases, be denied access to the lender of last resort funds.

IMF lending under the Supplemental Reserve Facility incorporates the classic Bagehot (1873) prescription that crisis lending should be at a penalty rate. Policy conditionality can be interpreted as a further element of the penalty, as seen from the viewpoint of the borrower country's policymakers. But what about the Bagehot prescriptions that lending should take place on good collateral, and that institutions that would be bankrupt in normal times should not be saved?

The Articles of Agreement permit the Fund to ask for collateral, but it has rarely done so. The Fund and the World Bank are regarded as preferred creditors, who have a first claim on payments made by countries in debt to them, and their collateral is thus the threat of denying access to global capital markets to countries that default. That is the main, and a powerful and effective, incentive for countries to repay—which is almost always done, in full and on time. While collateralized lending should remain a possibility for the Fund, it does not seem to be essential given the Fund's preferred creditor status.

The more general Bagehot prescription that institutions which are truly bankrupt should not be saved by a lender of last resort is difficult to apply in the international context. To the extent that foreign creditors have claims on private sector corporations in a debtor country, the bankruptcy rules for the debtor country should apply and the Bagehot prescription would be relevant. But it has to be recognized that bankruptcy regulations in many emerging market countries have been ineffective, which is why an effort is now underway to develop an international standard for a domestic bankruptcy code. For a sovereign debtor, the ability to generate repayments is more a matter of political than of economic feasibility. There is no bankruptcy status for a sovereign, but workout procedures, including those of the Paris and London Clubs, and possibly those to be developed as private sector bail-ins are considered further, play a similar role.

The one Bagehot prescription that does not apply in an international crisis is that of lending freely, if by freely is meant without limit. As already discussed, such a policy would create too much moral hazard.[17] How can an international crisis lender and manager deal with moral hazard problems? Charging a penalty rate of interest should help discourage borrower moral hazard, but moral hazard for borrowers is of much less concern than for investors. Borrower moral hazard is already deterred by the requirements of policy conditionality. Governments try to avoid going to the IMF— indeed they frequently delay too long—and policymakers who preside over a crisis and then have to turn to the IMF generally lose office, as witness the Asian crisis countries and Russia.

Investor moral hazard—that a lender of last resort would encourage investors to loan unwisely—is a more serious concern. In considering this issue, it is important to distinguish the hazards associated with different types of international capital flows.[18] In the case of equity investment, for example, the investor needs to be held responsible—and they have been, for equity investors have taken large losses in the recent crises. In the case of interbank lines of credit, however, the responsibility for addressing the risk of unwise lending because of moral hazard lies as much with the government of the lender as with the borrower government, for it is the former which supervises and tends to protect its banks. Lender supervisory authorities will have to recognize the responsibilities of their institutions to participate in workout procedures and private sector bail-ins when necessary.

The single most important change in the international system that will tend to limit moral hazard by encouraging better monitoring and self-regulation by capital market participants is the adoption of better methods of involving the private sector in financing the resolution of crises. As discussed above, the issues here are immensely difficult; they are also immensely important. Unless better ways of involving the private sector are found, the IMF will not be able to perform its proper function as international lender of last resort, both as crisis lender and crisis manager. At present, the official sector is seeking to involve private sector lenders in several countries in crisis; as this experience is analyzed within the coming months, some general principles for how to involve the private sector should be distilled and begun to be implemented in cases of crisis lending by the IMF and other official institutions.

The crises of the last five years have revealed major weaknesses in the structure of the international economy. It is urgent to start developing and implementing the constructive solutions that have been proposed, among them improvements in transparency, the adoption of appropriate exchange rate systems, the development and monitoring of international standards, including a bankruptcy standard, the development of precautionary lines of credit, and methods to involve the private sector in financing the resolution of emerging market crises. Important progress has been made during the last twelve months. As these changes continue to be implemented, the role of the international lender of last resort will become both better defined and more effective.

Notes

This chapter is a revised version of a paper delivered at the joint luncheon of the American Economic Association and the American Finance Association, New York, January 3, 1999. A longer version of the paper was published in the Princeton Series in International Finance. I am grateful to my MIT colleague Charles Kindleberger for sparking my interest in this question many years ago, for his support and for the pleasure provided by a fresh reading of *Manias, Panics, and Crashes*; to Mervyn King for helpful discussions during the writing of the paper; to Allan Meltzer, Olivier Blanchard, Jack Boorman, Guillermo Calvo, J. Bradford De Long, Peter Diamond, Eduardo Fernandez-Arias, Curzio Giannini, Charles Goodhart, Stephen Grenville, Bengt Holmstrom, Alexandre Kafka, Arend Kapteyn, Peter Kenen, Martin Mayer, Frederic Mishkin, Jacques Polak, Andrei Shleifer, Robert Solow, John Spraos, Onno Wijnholds, and David Williams for helpful comments and discussions; to Timothy Taylor for his editing; and to Claire Adams for excellent research assistance. The views expressed in this paper are those of the author, and are not necessarily those of the International Monetary Fund; indeed, it may safely be said that they are not the views of some members of the International Monetary Fund.

1. Henry Thornton's (1802) analysis of the role of lender of last resort is also remarkably sophisticated. For an historical discussion of the lender of last resort, see Humphrey and Keleher (1984).

2. Among those who have sought to build on and develop the analysis of the role of lender of last resort in recent years, see Benston et al. (1986), Freixas (1999), Garcia and Plautz (1988), Goodhart (1995), Goodhart and Huang (1998), Goodfriend and Lacker (1999), Holmstrom and Tirole (1998), Kindleberger (1996, first edition 1978), Meltzer (1986), Mundell (1983), Schwartz (1988), Solow (1982), and Wijnholds and Kapteyn (1999). Claassen (1985) provides an interesting discussion of the role of international and domestic lenders of last resort in an international context. Recent discussions of the potential role of the IMF as an international lender of last resort include Calomiris (1998), Calomiris and Meltzer (1998), Capie (1998), Chari and Kehoe (1999), Giannini (1998), Jeanne (1998), and Meltzer (1998). Mishkin (1999) and Radelet and Sachs (1998) take up lender of last resort issues in the context of the Asian crisis.

3. In economic theory panics can be modeled as cases of multiple equilibria, possibly dependent on herd behavior. The classic reference is Diamond and Dybvig (1983). For a related model in the international context, see Chang and Velasco (1998).

4. In private conversation, Meltzer has indicated that he sees no advantage to the rule that the central bank should lend only to the market rather than on occasion if necessary also to individual institutions.

5. Although some have pointed with approval to the role of clearinghouses in financial panics, note Kindleberger's quotation (1996, p. 134) from Jacob Schiff in 1907: "The one lesson we should learn from recent experience is that the issuing of clearinghouse certificates in the different bank centers has also worked considerable harm. It has broken down domestic exchange and paralyzed to a large extent the business of the country."

6. Accordingly, Schwartz (1988) argues that the central bank should act as lender of last resort only in the event of a run from banks into currency.

7. Of course, the question arises why any external financing is needed in response to a currency shock if the rules of the currency board are strictly applied. The answer is that the monetary authority may want to mitigate the adverse effects of an external shock on the banking system and the economy.

8. Not all financial crises need ultimately to be costly to the public sector; indeed, if the lender of last resort intervenes in a pure panic and manages to stabilize the situation, it should expect to come out ahead when its lending is repaid. Apparently both the Swedish and Norwegian bank restructuring agencies that were set up in the crises of the early 1990s have come close to meeting this criterion. (I am indebted to my colleague Stefan Ingves for this information.)

9. Mints (1945, p. 191) attributes Bagehot's advocacy of a high lending rate to his view that internal and external drains typically accompany each other; that is, an internal financial panic under a gold standard was often accompanied by gold leaving the country. The high interest rate was designed to stop the external drain of gold, and lending freely would stop the internal drain—a reading that is consistent with Bagehot.

10. Freixas (1999) develops a theoretical case for constructive ambiguity by the lender of last resort.

11. For models with multiple equilibria in an international context, see Chang and Velasco (1998) and Zettelmeyer (1998).

12. The analogy is due to Kenen (1986).

13. Total quotas are approximately $300 billion. The effective availability of resources to lend is smaller, since the weaker currencies held by the Fund are not in practice usable for lending.

14. The focus in the text is on the numerator of the ratio of reserves to short-term debt; however, countries need also to ensure that the denominator stays under control. This element plays an important role in the evolving international architecture, but I shall not pursue it here.

15. This possibility is developed in the report of the [G-22] Working Group on *International Financial Crises*. See also the speech by Gordon Brown (1998).

16. I note for the record that the suggestion that the IMF should operate only as lender of last resort either overlooks or grossly undervalues the other functions carried out by the IMF, which were noted earlier in this discussion.

17. To say this does not, however, determine the optimal size of crisis loans.

18. I am grateful to Mervyn King for emphasizing this point.

References

Bagehot, Walter. 1873, *Lombard Street: A Description of the Money Market*. London: William Clowes and Sons.

Benston, George, Robert Eisenbeis, Paul Horvitz, Edward Kane, and George Kaufman. 1986. *Perspectives on Safe and Sound Banking: Past, Present, and Future*. Cambridge, Massachusetts: MIT Press.

Boughton, James. 1998. "From Suez to Tequila: The IMF as Crisis Manager." Unpublished; Washington: International Monetary Fund.

Brown, Gordon. 1998. "Rediscovering Public Purpose in the Global Economy." Speech delivered at the Kennedy School, December 15.

Calomiris, Charles. 1998. "Blueprints for a New Global Financial Architecture." Unpublished; New York: Columbia Business School.

Calomiris, Charles, and Allan H. Meltzer. 1998. "Reforming the IMF." Unpublished; New York: Columbia Business School.

Calvo, Guillermo. 1995. "Varieties of Capital Market Crises." University of Maryland Center for International Economics, Working Paper 15.

Capie, Forrest. 1998. "Can there be an International Lender of Last Resort?" Unpublished; London: City University Business School.

Chari, V. V., and Patrick J. Kehoe. 1999. "Asking the Right Questions about the IMF," in *The Region*, 1998 Annual Report of the Federal Reserve Bank of Minneapolis, pp. 3–26.

Claassen, Emil-Maria. 1985. "The Lender-of-Last-Resort Function in the Context of National and International Financial Crises." *Weltwirtschaftliches Archiv*. 121:2, pp. 217–237.

Clapham, Sir John. 1944. *The Bank of England*. Cambridge: Cambridge University Press.

Chang, Roberto, and Andres Velasco. 1998. "The Asian Liquidity Crisis." NBER Working Paper 6796, November.

Diamond, Douglas, and Philip Dybvig. 1983. "Bank Runs, Deposit Insurance, and Liquidity." *Journal of Political Economy.* June, 91:3, pp. 401–419.

Freixas, Xavier. 1999. "Optimal Bail Out Policy, Conditionality and Creative Ambiguity." Unpublished; Bank of England.

Garcia, Gillian, and Elizabeth Plautz. 1988. *The Federal Reserve: Lender of Last Resort.* Cambridge, Massachusetts: Ballinger.

Giannini, Curzio. 1998. "Enemy of None but a Common Friend to All? An International Perspective on the Lender-of-Last-Resort Function." Unpublished; Washington: International Monetary Fund.

Goodfriend, Marvin, and Jeffrey M. Lacker. 1999. "Limited Commitment and Central Bank Lending." Federal Reserve Bank of Richmond, Working Paper January, 99:2.

Goodhart, Charles A. E. 1995. *The Central Bank and the Financial System.* Cambridge, Massachusetts: MIT Press.

Goodhart, Charles A. E., and Haizhou Huang. 1998. "A Model of the Lender of Last Resort." Unpublished; Washington: International Monetary Fund.

Goodhart, Charles A. E., and Dirk Schoenmaker. 1995. "Should the Functions of Monetary Policy and Bank Supervision Be Separated?" *Oxford Economic Papers.* 47, pp. 539–560.

Guesnerie, Roger. 1987. "Hidden Actions, Moral Hazard, and Contract Theory." in *The New Palgrave: A Dictionary of Economics.* Eatwell, John, Murray Milgate, and Peter Newman, eds. Volume II, pp. 646–651. London: The Macmillan Press.

Guttentag, Jack, and Richard Herring. 1983. "The Lender-of-Last-Resort Function in an International Context." *Princeton University Essay in International Finance.* No. 151, May.

Hirsch, Fred. 1977. "The Bagehot Problem." *The Manchester School.* September, 45:3, pp. 241–257.

Holmstrom, Bengt, and Jean Tirole. 1998. "Private and Public Supply of Liquidity." *Journal of Political Economy.* February, 106:1, pp. 1–40.

Humphrey, Thomas. 1975. "The Classical Concept of the Lender of Last Resort." *Federal Reserve Bank of Richmond Economic Review.* February, 61, pp. 2–9.

Humphrey, Thomas, and Robert Keleher. 1984. "Lender of Last Resort: An Historical Perspective." *Cato Journal.* 4:1, pp. 275–321.

Jeanne, Olivier. 1998. "The International Liquidity Mismatch and the New Architecture." Unpublished; Washington: International Monetary Fund.

Kaufman, George. 1988. "The Truth about Bank Runs," in *The Financial Services Revolution: Policy Directions for the Future.* England, C., and T. Huertas, eds. Boston: Kluwer Academic Publishers.

Kenen, Peter. 1986. *Financing, Adjustment, and the International Monetary Fund.* Washington: Brookings Institution.

Kindleberger, Charles. 1996. *Manias, Panics, and Crashes: A History of Financial Crisis (Wiley Investment Classics Series)*. New York: John Wiley & Sons, 3rd edition. (First edition, 1978).

Kindleberger, Charles. 1986. *The World in Depression, 1929–1939*. Revised and enlarged edition. Berkeley: University of California Press.

MacKay, Charles. 1841. *Extraordinary Popular Delusions and the Madness of Crowds*. New York: Farrar, Straus and Giroux (reprint, 1932).

Meltzer, Allan. 1986. "Financial Failures and Financial Policies," in *Deregulating Financial Services: Public Policy in Flux*. Kaufman, G. G., and R. C. Kormendi, eds. Cambridge, Massachusetts: Ballinger.

Meltzer, Allan. 1998. "What's Wrong with the IMF? What Would Be Better?" Paper prepared for Federal Reserve Bank of Chicago Conference: *Asia: An Analysis of Financial Crisis*. October 8–10.

Mints, Lloyd W. 1945. *A History of Banking Theory*. Chicago: University of Chicago Press.

Mishkin, Frederic S. 1999. "Lessons from the Asian Crisis." National Bureau of Economic Research Working Paper 7102, April.

Mundell, Robert. 1983. "International Monetary Options." *Cato Journal*. 3:1, pp. 189–210.

Radelet, Steven, and Jeffrey D. Sachs. 1998. "The East Asian Financial Crisis: Diagnosis, Remedies, Prospects." *Brookings Papers on Economic Activity*. 1, pp. 1–74.

Schwartz, Anna. 1988. "Financial Stability and the Federal Safety Net," in *Restructuring Banking and Financial Services in America*. Haraf, W. S., and G. E. Kushmeider, eds. Washington: American Enterprise Institute.

Solow, Robert. 1982. "On the Lender of Last Resort," in Kindleberger, C. P., and J. P. Laffargue, eds. *Financial Crisis: Theory, History, and Policy*. New York: Cambridge University Press.

Stern, Gary. 1999. "Managing Moral Hazard." *The Region*. Federal Reserve Bank of Minneapolis, June, 13:2.

Thornton, Henry. 1802. *An Enquiry into the Nature and Effects of the Paper Credit of Great Britain*, Hayek, F. A., ed. Fairfield: Augustus M. Kelley Publishers (reprint, 1978).

Wijnholds, Onno, and Arend Kapteyn. 1999. "The IMF: Lender of Last Resort or Indispensable Lender." Unpublished; International Monetary Fund, June.

Zettelmeyer, Jeromin. 1998. "International Financial Crises and Last Resort Lending: Some Issues." Unpublished. Washington: International Monetary Fund.

2 *Introduction*

This chapter was written shortly before I knew I would be joining the IMF, and I include it as a baseline, to show how my views on the role of the Fund evolved while I was there.

On several issues my basic views did not change, even if they evolved somewhat during the next seven years:

• The importance of the Fund's Articles—its constitution—and especially Article I, as guiding principles for its operation. (Michel Camdessus used to carry a dog-eared version of Article I in his pocket; I once asked to borrow it and discovered that it was in French and barely legible. Thereafter I carried around my own laminated English version, which came in handy on many an occasion.) Fund Economic Counselor Michael Mussa used to argue that Article IV—which includes the surveillance mandate, and sets out growth and reasonable price stability as policy goals—is as important as Article I.

• The central importance of the Fund's lending for stabilization, and the judgment that it was frequently, but not always, successful; and some skepticism about the success of lending to the poorest developing countries.

• The importance of greater transparency and greater self-evaluation by the Fund. The transparency theme is pervasive in this chapter, and it is the area in which I believe the greatest progress was made during the time I was at the Fund. The change in the Fund's attitude to transparency in the second half of the 1990s was revolutionary.

• The potential importance of technical assistance, and the need to evaluate it better—something that was done while I was at the Fund.

• The need for the Bank and Fund to more truly represent the interests of all their members, as discussed in the third-last paragraph.

What I said there is not the whole story on this very complicated question, but it is an important part of the story.

• The opposition to a merger between the Fund and the Bank, on the grounds that the joint institution would be too large to manage well, and would be too powerful for developing member countries to deal with. That is a position that I still hold very strongly.

I changed my views on some issues:

• I was more approving of adjustable exchange rate pegs then than I am now.

• I blundered in expressing my views about the Executive Directors. I said that "Executive Directors of the large countries tend to be middle level government officials rather than independent decision-makers." At a Board meeting before I left the Fund, this was quoted back to me by a veteran Board member who had demonstrated more independence than implied in the preceding quote. In fact, the Executive Board of the IMF is a remarkably successful institution, which is essential to the effectiveness of the Fund.[1]

• Before joining the Fund I shared the view common among academics that the Fund should leave the poorest countries, whose problems are mainly those of development, to the World Bank. I now think that view is wrong, as explained in the following lengthy quote from a talk I gave at the Fund in April 2001.

Some observers question whether we should remain involved in the poorest countries, and in poverty reduction at all. I disagree, for several compelling reasons.

First, the IMF must be active in all of its 183 member countries. Much of the strength and cohesion of this institution and of its Executive Board derives from the fact that it is a universal institution in which all member countries have rights and obligations. Most of the countries the IMF lends to are poor countries, where the problem of poverty reduction is central to the entire policy debate. So, in conducting surveillance of those countries, and in lending to them, the IMF has to analyze the impact of policies on poverty.

But shouldn't the IMF concentrate on helping countries achieve macroeconomic stabilization and leave it to others to worry about poverty reduction? After all, isn't stabilization good for everyone? Stabilization is ultimately good for everyone, but its effects are not spread uniformly. Cuts in fiscal expenditures or changes in tax policy, for instance, have different effects on different groups. We need to know what these effects are likely to be and to make sure that the policies we support are, as far as possible, helping to reduce poverty and increase social welfare.

Similarly, it has taken many years of argument about the impact of inflation on poverty to get to the point where it is now generally accepted that high inflation is bad for the poor. So our advice on monetary and fiscal policies also requires some knowledge of the impact of those policies on poverty.

In any country with a well-developed capacity for policy analysis, it can be left to the government to figure out and take into account the distributional impacts of policies. But the IMF is also involved in many countries that do not have that capacity, and we need to have the analytical and empirical bases to provide the right advice and technical assistance.

A second, closely related point was driven home during the Asian crisis: the impact of stabilization policies on poverty depends on the institutional structures in place. For example, if a stabilization program is going to have a particularly adverse impact on unemployment, health, or the access of the poor to basic foods, the IMF staff needs to know how to advise the country what to do when the program goes into effect. Typically, if the country needs help in developing institutions, others—such as the World Bank or the regional development banks—will provide that assistance. But the IMF cannot be ignorant of what is needed, nor avoid some of the responsibility for helping ensure that what is needed gets done.

Third, we know that sustained poverty reduction requires sustained growth. But the links between growth and poverty are complicated. So it is not enough to leave it at "growth is good for the poor," even though that is true. We need to know which pro-growth macro policies are most effective in reducing poverty, and we need to promote them.

That is the intellectual basis for why we should be centrally involved in the war on poverty. But for those who are not persuaded, let me offer a political and pragmatic argument. First, policies will not be sustainable—in all countries, rich or poor—if they are not perceived as broadly equitable. So, if we want the stabilization policies we support to be sustained, we need to take account of their distributional impact. Second, the IMF will not enjoy public support in the countries that finance our lending if we are seen to be supporting policies that damage the poor.

Of course there is another reason to focus on the poverty aspects of macroeconomic policies: it is the right thing to do. But since some people are more comfortable with arguments grounded in realpolitik than in morality, it is worth establishing that both considerations point in the same direction.

Note

1. I expanded on this point at some length in my August 30, 2001, farewell speech to the Board, which is available on the Fund website.

2

The IMF and the World Bank at Fifty

Stanley Fischer

The vitality of the International Monetary Fund and World Bank Group and their central roles in the world economy testify to the foresight of the founding fathers who designed them as two of the three bulwarks of the postwar international monetary system. This remains true even though neither institution operates as planned at Bretton Woods in 1944, and even though the third institution, the International Trade Organization, was stillborn—not to reappear until fifty years later, as the impending World Trade Organization.

The IMF was set up to police an adjustable peg exchange rate system which disappeared in 1973 and it has had no effective responsibility for the international monetary system since then. The Fund's last loan to a high income industrialized country was made in 1977. Increasingly it has become a specialized development agency, one that was in danger of losing its rationale during the debt crisis but that has been revived by its new mission in the reforming formerly centrally planned economies.

The IBRD has remained closer to its original design. Originally it was thought that the Bank would channel funds to the developing countries by guaranteeing their obligations, but for good reasons it has rather lent to them directly, placing its own bonds in the international capital markets. The World Bank Group has grown beyond its original design, first by the addition in 1956 of an affiliate, the International Finance Corporation (IFC), which helps finance the private sector in developing countries, and then through the creation—at the initiative of the United States—in 1960 of the International Development Association (IDA). IDA lends on concessional terms to the poorest countries. In most years loan commitments made by IDA amount to one third to one quarter of the commitments made by the IBRD; net disbursements made by IDA are usually

more than half those of the IBRD, and in some years exceed those of
the IBRD. IDA plays a key role in enabling the Bank Group to continue lending to the poorest countries. Another affiliate, the Multilateral Investment Guarantee Agency (MIGA), was set up in 1988.[1]

Fifty years after Bretton Woods it is natural to review the role
and performance of the international institutions, and to discuss the
major questions about their futures. Among the big issues are:[2]

• Is there a demand for the services the agencies provide?

• If so, should these services be provided by the Fund and the Bank?

• Should the goals of the agencies be redirected, for instance by
requiring the IMF to take more responsibility for the international
monetary system, and the Bank to return to its roots as a project
lender?

• Should the overlap of activities between the agencies be reduced
by sharpening the division of responsibilities between them?

• Should the Bank and the Fund be merged?

There is also a host of more specific questions about each agency.
For instance, in the case of the Bank, whether it should be down-
sized, whether it should put more people in the field, and how to
enhance its interactions with the regional development banks.

Of course the Bank, the Fund, and the international economy have
been evolving and reforming over the past fifty years. A host of
interlocking agencies and groupings, among them the GATT (soon
to become the WTO), the FAO, other UN agencies, the G-7, the G-10,
the G-24, the regional development banks, the OECD, the European
Community, and other regional trade blocs have grown up and help
run the international economy. A full review of the institutional
structure of the world economy would take all these organizations
into account, ask why and whether they should exist, and whether
there is a better way of achieving their goals. Such a review would
have to distinguish between an optimal institutional structure
designed from the ground up, which we can safely assume would
not look like the present system, and the best improvements that can
be made starting from the current structure rather than from the near
tabula rasa of 1944.

In this chapter I focus narrowly, on the World Bank Group and the
IMF, and refer to other agencies and institutions only as they relate
to the functions of the Bretton Woods twins. I start by describing the

initial functions, current structures and operations of the IMF and the World Bank. In these sections I discuss questions and make suggestions about current modes of operation. I then go on in section 3 to discuss the major issues set out above. Readers familiar with the current structures of the Fund and the Bank should concentrate on section 3.

1 The International Monetary Fund

Table 2.1 sets out the six functions of the Fund specified in Article I of its Articles of Agreement. There has been substantial progress in several of these areas since 1945. Trade has expanded more rapidly than output almost every year in that period; payments restrictions have essentially disappeared among the major countries, and have been greatly reduced even among many developing countries;[3] and Fund resources are indeed routinely utilized by developing country members. Progress in expanding trade owes more to other institutions than to the Fund; the Fund has been too accepting of current account restrictions for several major members, such as India; but its role in promoting current account convertibility has generally been constructive.

To a considerable extent, the Fund does serve as specified in clause (i), as an institution through which countries consult on international

Table 2.1
Purposes of the IMF, Article I of the Articles of Agreement

(i)	To promote international monetary cooperation through a permanent institution which provides the machinery for consultation and collaboration on international monetary problems.
(ii)	To facilitate the expansion and balanced growth of international trade ...
(iii)	To promote exchange stability, to maintain orderly exchange arrangements among members, and to avoid competitive exchange depreciation.
(iv)	To assist in the establishment of a multilateral system of payments in respect of current transactions between members and in the elimination of foreign exchange restrictions which hamper the growth of world trade.
(v)	To give confidence to members by making the general resources of the Fund temporarily available to them under adequate safeguards, thus providing them with the opportunity to correct maladjustments in their balance of payments without resorting to measures destructive of national or international prosperity.
(vi)	In accordance with the above, to shorten the duration and lessen the degree of disequilibrium in the international balances of payments of members.

monetary problems. There is probably no forum in which more serious regular discussion of international financial issues takes place
than the Fund's Executive Board. However, the important decisions
are made elsewhere, through consultations by the G-7.[4] This should
not be a surprise, for the Fund Board is an unwieldy group in which
to negotiate. Because the big decisions are made outside the Fund,
Executive Directors of the large countries tend to be middle level
government officials rather than independent decision-makers.

Discussions in the Fund Board are confidential. While this gives
the Executive Directors the freedom to speak frankly, the Fund keeps
far too much of its information from the public. Some discussions, of
problems such as devaluations and the debt strategy where expectations of a policy change can become self-justifying, have to remain
confidential. But background papers prepared for the great majority of Board discussions, including the Fund's reports on *Recent
Economic Developments* in member countries, should be made available to the public within a few weeks of the Board discussion. This
would enhance the quality of economic policy discussion in member
countries. Publication of the *World Economic Outlook* represents an
important step forward, but publication and public provision of
information should become the rule rather than the exception.

There is an important issue of whether the Fund management and
staff should be taking more of the initiative in identifying and pro-
posing solutions to problems in the international system. Two considerations should be noted. First, the management of the Fund or
the Bank is ultimately controlled by the Board, and needs to retain
the confidence of the governments they represent; thus management
cannot lead where it knows the Board is certain not to follow. But
there is a great deal of space for leadership between playing the role
of Don Quixote and the passive acceptance of prevailing G-7 views.

Second, the Fund may not have a solution. Consider for instance
the reform of the international monetary system, a topic which is
central to the Fund's mission. Ultimately Fund staff would probably
like to return to a fixed or adjustable peg system, but there is absolutely no prospect that the major countries will move in that direction soon; nor does the recent European experience commend that
course unless policies and the structure of economies become far
more coordinated than they are now. The Fund is also generally
anxious to strengthen the role of the SDR in the international system.

While the SDR serves as a convenient composite unit of account, the Fund has not presented any persuasive argument in favor of expanding its role in the current international system.[5] Thus at this time the Fund staff appears to have little to contribute in the area of international monetary reform.[6]

In the international debt crisis, the Fund first helped form and then dutifully followed the G-7's policy line from 1982 until at least 1987. Then the Managing Director began to speak out with increasing bluntness, contributing to the general change in attitude and approach that led to the Brady Plan in 1989. In this case, the Managing Director timed his dissent so as to get ahead of the official strategy, but only when the strategy clearly was not working. Since it was obvious to many by 1986 that the Baker Plan was not succeeding, the Managing Director could have moved earlier. Indeed, he may have, for we do not know what his confidential advice to G-7 policymakers was at the time.

Turning now to the current structure of the Fund, a simplified balance sheet is presented in table 2.2, and the administrative budget in table 2.3. With total assets of $140 billion, the Fund is large as international agencies go. However, it is difficult to appraise its size relative to potential demands for resources, since only a subset of countries are potential borrowers, and only a subset of the Fund's

Table 2.2
Fund balance sheet, April 30, 1992 ($ billion)*

Assets		Liabilities	
Currencies and securities	129.8	Quotas	127.7
SDR holdings	1.0	Borrowing	5.2
Gold[+]	5.1	Special disbursement a/c	3.6
SAF loans	2.6	Other	5.3
Other	3.3		
Total	141.8	Total	141.8

Source: *International Monetary Fund Annual Report*, 1992, p145.
*Original data in SDR's; calculated at an exchange rate of $1.40/SDR.
[+]Gold valued at 35 SDR/oz ($49/oz).
SAF ≡ Structural Adjustment Facility; Special Disbursement Account contains funds available for SAF lending.
The Fund also has potential access to SDR18.5 billion ($26 billion) of borrowing under the GAB (General Arrangements to Borrow), which have been in existence since 1962. The GAB are currently set to expire in December 1993, but are expected to be renewed.

Table 2.3
Fund administrative budget, year ending April 30, 1993 ($ million)

Expenses	
Personnel expenses	236.0
Travel expenses	54.4
Data processing	18.3
Communications	7.5
Other	38.9
Total	355.1
Income	
Net operating income	451.0

Source: *International Monetary Fund Annual Report*, 1992, pp. 143, 146.
*Net operating income data specified in SDR's; calculated at an exchange rate of $1.40/SDR.

resources are likely to be available to be borrowed.[7] Note that the Fund has relied almost entirely on its own resources for lending to its members: borrowing by the Fund from member countries has been small relative to the scale of its assets, but it has potential access under the GAB (General Arrangements to Borrow) to $26 billion of borrowed resources. Note also the attraction of Fund gold sales, which are perenially advanced as a solution to some shortage of funds:[8] with its gold valued at SDR35 per oz, the Fund would on paper make a capital gain of over $30 billion if it could sell all its gold at $350 per oz.[9]

The Fund is generally thought of as running a tight ship. Administrative expenses in financial year 1992 were $350 million, for a staff of about 1750.[10] Most of these expenses were for personnel, with travel expenses accounting for 15 percent of costs. The Fund's net income amply covers expenses.

The Fund's resources are deployed in three main lines of activity: surveillance and analysis of the economies of member countries and the international system; lending; and technical assistance and training.

1.1 Surveillance

The term surveillance derives from the Fund's responsibility under Article IV to exercise "firm surveillance over the exchange rate policies of its members." On the argument that domestic policies affect exchange rates, the Fund staff conducts annual Article IV consultations with members that cover the full range of domestic macroeconomic policies. The resultant Article IV report typically provides a highly competent, informative, data-packed, macroeconomic analysis of the economy. These reports are discussed by the Board either annually or every second year.

The importance of the exercise varies from country to country. In the smaller and less developed countries, the Fund's analysis may well be not only the best, but also the only, thorough analysis of the macroeconomy.[11] It is not uncommon in such countries for the Fund's report to be leaked by one agency or the other (the central bank or the finance ministry) either because that agency has been commended, or in support of a particular policy view. Article IV consultations receive less attention in the more developed countries. That is a pity, because the Fund's analysis could contribute to improving the domestic policy debate.

To increase the influence of the reports in both developing and industrialized countries, the Fund should work towards making them available to the public within a short time of their being written. No doubt it will be argued that publication will affect the frankness of the reports. While that danger exists, the professional quality of the staff should ensure that the basic message gets across—certainly the *World Economic Outlook* (WEO) manages to say what it wants on the major issues. It should be possible even now to find some countries that are both self-confident enough and that sufficiently value informed public discussion to agree to the timely publication of the Article IV report on their country. Once a few countries take the lead, others will follow.

In addition to the Article IV reports, the Fund staff twice a year presents the WEO to the Board. This is the opportunity for the Fund to discuss the global economy, both the policies of the major countries individually, and systemic problems such as the debt crisis and the economics of socialist transition. Staff papers on special topics are also discussed from time to time.

How effective are these surveillance and analytic exercises? The Fund Board is quoted on this issue in the 1992 *Annual Report* (p. 15): "the effectiveness of Fund Surveillance has less to do with strengthening the principles of surveillance and more to do with the willingness of member countries to consider fully the views expressed by the international community—through the forum of the Fund—

in formulating and adopting their macroeconomic and structural policies."

Powerful countries have shown little overt inclination to change their basic economic policies because of the views of the international community. Continued complaints by the rest of the G-7 seem to have had very little impact on the United States' willingness to deal with its twin deficits; the wishes of its ERM partners had little visible effect on German monetary policy; and the examples could be multiplied.

However, it is far too absolutist a position to argue that the Fund's analytic exercises therefore have no impact on individual country policies and on systemic problems, such as the debt crisis. Peer pressure, "arm twisting by public exposure," "pointing the finger of public shame,"[12] does have some impact. Continued international pressure on the United States to cut its deficit helped keep that issue in public view; Germany in fact tried to keep the ERM alive for longer than its own preferences would have dictated; and academic analyses as well as brute facts helped bring about a change in the debt strategy. And even if finger pointing were ineffective, it is better to speak up than to acquiesce in error.

The influence of Fund surveillance on policy will have as much to do with the quality of the analysis as with the forum in which it is presented. The WEO is generally well regarded. Most Article IV reports are well regarded, though there is a view that reports on some countries are unduly responsive to the views of the authorities. By presenting analyses of unquestionably high quality, and objectivity, on individual countries and other issues, and by making its reports public, the Fund will increase its influence on policy. To do that it has to ensure that the analytic quality of its staff remains very high, and is indeed enhanced, and that the staff receives the backing of management for presenting its own views. The Fund could further increase the quality of its analysis and its influence by engaging in more public interchange with academics and others who analyze policy in member countries.

To increase the effectiveness of surveillance, the Fund should pursue two goals: it should ensure that it becomes the world's premier macroeconomic policy analysis institution; and it should ensure that it is seen and understood to be the best such unit. It cannot do the latter while hiding behind the shelter of confidentiality.

1.2 Lending

For over a decade the Fund has lent exclusively to developing countries. Lending exploded during the debt crisis of the early 1980s, with the outstanding stock of Fund credit rising from SDR10 billion in 1980 to over SDR37 billion in 1985; the outstanding stock then declined through 1990, and has subsequently risen somewhat.

Tables 2.4–2.6 provide information on Fund lending, both the volume, and the different forms in which assistance is provided. The Structural Adjustment Facility (SAF) and Extended SAF (ESAF) both lend at highly subsidized terms, with an interest charge similar to that of IDA. However, since the term of the lending is much shorter than that of IDA, the repayment burden from loans through these facilities is greater than for IDA loans. While the volume of lending under SAF and ESAF is relatively small (table 2.4), these facilities make it possible for the poorest countries to borrow from the Fund

Table 2.4
Fund lending, year ending April 30, 1992 ($ billion)

Total disbursements			8.3
Purchases from General Resources Account		7.4	
Standby and first credit tranche	3.3		
Compensatory financing facility	1.9		
Extended Fund Facility	2.2		
Loans		0.9	
Special disbursement account	0.2		
ESAF Trust resources	0.7		
Repurchases and repayments			6.7
Repurchases		6.7	
Loan repayments		0.0	
Outstanding Fund credit			37.4
Standby arrangements		13.3	
Extended Fund Facility arrangements		12.1	
CCFF		7.5	
SAF		2.1	
ESAF		2.3	
Trust fund		0.2	
Number of indebted countries	82		

Source: *International Monetary Fund Annual Report*, 1992, pp. 74,102.
*Data in source specified in SDR's; calculated at an exchange rate of $1.40/SDR.

Table 2.5
Fund lending facilities, policies, and terminology

General Resources Account: Fund account that holds member country currencies, the Fund's SDR holdings, and gold.

Purchases: Borrowing.

Tranche policies: Access to the Fund's regular credit comes in four tranches of 25 percent of the country's quota in the Fund. First credit tranche purchases are provided if the country demonstrates a reasonable effort to solve its balance of payments problem, and without performance criteria. Upper credit tranche purchases are usually associated with a *standby*, a negotiated loan from the Fund to the member, based on the country's economic program, with specified performance criteria. Purchases are made in installments. Repayments are made over 3.5–5 years.

Extended arrangements: These provide financing for medium term economic programs, generally for 3 years. The program spells out objectives for the entire period, and policy actions for the first year, with subsequent policy changes to be agreed on in annual reviews. Repayments are made over 4.5–10 years.

Compensatory and contingency financing facility (CCFF): Lends to members to cover temporary balance of payments needs arising from factors beyond the control of the member.

Structural adjustment facility (SAF): Concessional loans (at an interest rate of 0.5 percent) to support medium-term adjustment programs in low-income countries facing sustained balance of payments problems. Repayments are made over 5.5–10 years.

Enhanced structural adjustment facility (ESAF): This facility was created in 1987, and has similar conditions to those of the SAF.

Source: *International Monetary Fund Annual Report*, 1992, pp. 50–51, Appendix IX.

Table 2.6
Details of fund lending, year ending April 30, 1992

Shares of total disbursements (%)		
To industrialized countries	0.0	
By region:		
Africa	12.5	
Asia	25.0	
Europe	25.7	
Middle East	5.6	
Western Hemisphere	31.1	

Number of arrangements	Made in 1991/92	Total outstanding
Standby arrangements	21	22
Extended arrangements	2	7
CCFF	7	na
SAF	1	8
ESAF	5	16

Source: *International Monetary Fund Annual Report*, 1992, pp. 72–74.

at a low interest rate and for a longer period than under a normal standby.

Net resource flows to the developing countries in 1991 amounted to $131 billion,[13] $73 billion of that in the form of official development finance. This is a base against which to scale the Fund's net disbursements of $1.6 billion seen in table 2.4. However, disbursements understate the significance of some Fund loans, for in many cases the availability of that portion of the loan which is not yet disbursed gives the borrower the confidence to proceed with adjustment measures. It is also true that the Fund can make a crucial difference with a very big loan to a country that has decided to stabilize; for instance, in March 1992 the Fund reached an extended agreement for $3 billion with Argentina; in 1989 it made a loan in excess of $5 billion to Venezuela. Loans of this size, whether drawn or not, are not available other than through the Fund.

In addition, the Fund's loans come with a stabilization and often a reform program, and with conditionality. The conditionality usually relates to monetary, fiscal, and exchange rate policy, and is often criticized for being mindlessly contractionary. This criticism has to be evaluated on a case-by-case basis. Certainly in many cases the Fund is only trying to get a country to stabilize the macroeconomy while living within its budget constraint. But in some circumstances, the description of the budget constraint may be too unimaginative. For example, during the debt crisis, debt relief came onto the Fund's agenda very late.

One description of the difference between the Fund's financial programming approach to stabilization, and the World Bank's two-gap model approach, is that the Fund asks what resources are available and tailors the program to that availability, whereas Bank economists ask what resources are needed to achieve a target growth rate, and then go out to find the money.[14] Needless to say, this is a caricature, but is does capture a subtle difference in attitude that affects the two institutions.

What is the record of success of Fund loans? Khan (1990) evaluated the effects of Fund programs between 1973 and 1988. He concluded that Fund programs unambiguously reduced the current account deficit,[15] and tended to reduce inflation, though the inflation effect was not statistically significant. The programs reduced the growth rate in the year they went into operation, but this effect was moderated (though not reversed) over time.

Despite this very mixed verdict, I judge that the Fund's lending activities to developing countries are frequently productive. Further, the Fund's ability to move large amounts of funding quickly is extremely valuable to a country seeking to stabilize, as it was to Poland, and may yet be to Russia.

It has also to be recorded that the Fund's lending to countries with deep-seated structural problems, many of them in Africa, has not been successful. The notion underlying a standby, that the balance of payments will be corrected within a few years, is not relevant to these countries. It is for that reason that the Fund has had steadily to lengthen the term of its loans. Because countries in Africa, and some of the heavily indebted countries, did not return to equilibrium quickly, the Fund's loans were in effect repaid by the World Bank.

There is a strong case for the Fund to concentrate on short-term macroeconomic stabilization, and to stay away from the long-run development problems that should be the focus of World Bank activities. The Fund itself seems to have drawn this conclusion, as it has slowed the pace of its lending to Africa.

1.3   Technical Assistance

The Fund provides a broad range of technical assistance to its members.[16] The IMF Institute runs regular courses and seminars in Washington for middle- and senior-level officials. In 1991–1992, 639 participants took part in the Washington courses. Most of the courses are on financial programming and policy, i.e. on the Fund's approach to balance of payments and monetary policy issues, with an admixture of material on adjustment. Other courses covered money and banking statistics, balance of payments methodology, and government finance statistics. The Institute also conducted courses abroad, the majority of them in the last few years in the reforming formerly centrally planned economies.

Technical assistance was provided to member countries by the Departments of Monetary and Exchange Affairs (formerly Central Banking), Fiscal Affairs, Legal, and Statistics. A variety of statistics suggests that this is a major activity: in 1991–1992 68 person-years of assistance to 79 countries and 3 regional organizations were provided by the Monetary and Exchange Affairs Department; Fiscal Affairs helped 82 countries; Legal helped 29 countries; and Statistics 37 countries. Much of the assistance has been sent to Eastern Europe and the former Soviet Union.

Evaluation of these programs is not publicly available.[17] One criticism that has been levied, especially with regard to the former Soviet republics, is that the Fund's technical experts do not spend enough time with the recipients to leave a deep imprint on their systems. Certainly in many developing countries there is a deep need for longer term technical assistance, for experts who remain in the country for at least a year, to try to ensure that the methods they teach take hold.

As international development continues on two tracks, with much of the world's population in Asia enjoying the fruits of rapid growth, and with others, in South Asia and especially in Africa, growing more slowly or not at all, the need for technical assistance for the countries with impaired institutional capacity becomes more urgent. It is likely that the international community and agencies will increasingly contribute to the slower-growing economies through technical assistance. It is therefore a serious priority to begin to evaluate these programs and their effects more systematically.

1.4 Summary

The Fund undertakes three main lines of activity, surveillance and analysis, lending, and technical assistance. Evaluation of the effectiveness of each has at best been partial. Given that the Fund does not now lend to industrialized countries, and that it should be cutting back its lending to countries whose problems are not short-term, its lending is likely to continue at a lower level than in the early 1980s.[18] Increasingly, in future, the Fund is likely to assist members through its surveillance or analytic activities, and through technical assistance. In both these areas, it can make a major contribution to the efficient operation of individual economies and the international system. While the quality of the Fund's analytic and policy-advising contributions appears on average to be high, there is a need for more openness and more daring in these areas. Not enough is known at present about the quality of the Fund's technical assistance programs.

2 The World Bank Group

The purposes of the World Bank as set out in the Articles of Agreement lack the crispness of those stated for the Fund. The emphasis is on the promotion of reconstruction and development by encouraging

Table 2.7
Purposes of the IBRD, Article I of the Articles of Agreement (as amended, December 1965)

(i)	To assist in the reconstruction and development of territories of members by facilitating the investment of capital for productive purposes, including ... the encouragement of the development of productive facilities and resources in less developed countries.
(ii)	To promote private foreign investment by means of guarantees or participations in loans and other investments made by private investors; and when private capital is not available on reasonable terms, to supplement private investment by providing, on suitable conditions, finance for productive purposes out of its own capital, funds raised by it and its other resources.
(iii)	To promote the long-range balanced growth of international trade and the maintenance of equilibrium in balances of payments by encouraging international investment for the development of the productive resources of members ...
(iv)	...
(v)	...

Source: Mason and Asher (1973), pp. 759–760.

international investment, private if possible, but public if necessary. Since the great bulk of lending has been for projects, and since the Bank finances the foreign exchange costs of projects, it can be said to have promoted development by encouraging international investment, though most of the investment has been by the public sector. IFC loans and investments more directly support the private sector in developing countries. Adjustment loans, formally introduced in 1980, and since then accounting for about 20–25 percent of lending, are less directly linked to international investment—though policy changes that improve economic performance in a country are likely to lead to greater foreign investment.

The IBRD's balance sheet (table 2.7) shows assets of $140 billion, almost identical to those of the Fund. This is however a misleading figure, for IDA has assets in excess of $80 billion (table 2.8),[19] so that IBRD/IDA assets exceed $220 billion. IFC assets, less than $10 billion, have to be added to obtain the asset value of the World Bank Group, which a year ago were about $230 billion.

By contrast with the Fund, the IBRD is a market borrower, which jealously guards its AAA rating. The Bank does not borrow more than its callable capital, so the question of whether the rating derives from the guarantees provided by the callable capital or from the quality of the portfolio cannot be answered. However, the experi-

Table 2.8
IBRD balance sheet, June 30, 1992 ($ billion)

Assets		Liabilities	
Investments and cash collateral	29.5	Short-term borrowing	5.4
Loans outstanding*	100.8	Long-term borrowing	91.7
Other	10.1	Loan-loss provisions	2.5
		Other liabilities	17.1
		Equity	
		Subscribed capital	10.1
		Retained earnings	13.2
		Other	0.4
Total	140.4	Total	140.4

Source: *World Bank Annual Report*, 1992, pp. 198–199.
*Total loans approved ($154.9 b) minus loans approved but not yet effective ($11.2 b) minus undisbursed balance of effective loans ($42.9 b).

ence of the IFIs (international financial institutions) with arrears in the last few years suggests that their portfolios are quite secure. This is not because their borrowers are safe bets, but because the major donors have made certain that arrears with the IFIs are cleared immediately when a formerly recalcitrant country returns to the fold. It has also become clear that developing countries cannot stay out of the international system; in the end, all the defaulters want to come back into the system, and the system has been sufficiently imaginative to help them come back in on condition of good behavior.[20]

About a third of Bank lending is through IDA. These funds are contributed by the donors, the wealthier countries, with IDA being replenished on a three year cycle. Mason and Asher wrote in 1973 that the Bank would have to find a more secure way of financing IDA, but now, as the tenth replenishment struggles to closure, it is clear that the donors prefer the short leash of the three year cycle to a longer cycle. The present arrangement enables the donors to pressure the Bank more effectively on issues such as the environment and poverty than appears to be possible through the regular Board channel.

IDA can be thought of as an efficient way for donors to provide conditional aid to developing countries, using the expertize of the World Bank to try to ensure that the aid is used productively. However, as the pressure on aid budgets increases, countries seeking to preserve bilateral aid programs may cut back on IDA contributions.

Table 2.9
IDA resources, June 30, 1992 ($ billion)

Development Resources			Funding		
Available net assets		29.5	Member subscriptions &		73.1
Credits outstanding	75.6		contributions		
less undisbursed balances	23.3		Other contributions*		3.4
Net outstanding credits		52.3	Other		5.3
Total		81.8	Total		81.8

Source: *World Bank Annual Report*, 1992, p. 220.
*From Switzerland and IBRD.

Table 2.10
World Bank administrative budget, year ending June 30, 1992 ($ million)

Expenses	
Personnel	791.2
Travel	113.5
Other	269.8
Reimbursements	(100.5)
Total	1074.0
Income	
Net operating income	1645.0

Source: *World Bank Annual Report*, 1992, pp. 104, 200.

Because IDA credits are very long-term, the flow of repayments has so far been small. Less than a decade from now, reflows will increase to more than $2 billion a year, making possible a substantial nominal increase in IDA lending—provided the donors do not take the opportunity to reduce their contributions correspondingly. Indeed, IDA has already precommitted SDR one billion of reflows to be relent in the next IDA period. These reflows, together with contributions of profits from the IBRD, have made an increase in IDA resources possible at a time when direct donor contributions have not risen.

The Bank has three times as many staff members as the Fund. In June 1992 there were 6000 staff members, 766 long-term consultants, and over 500 other employees. As table 2.10 shows, Bank personnel costs are almost three times those of the Fund, though its travel budget is relatively smaller. Despite the general impression that the Bank staff is too big (presumably for the work that it does), it would be difficult to establish that the Bank suffers from more than the usual levels of bureaucratic waste and inefficiency. The 1987 reorganization did downsize the Bank somewhat and increases in staff size have been kept small since then, though it has expanded to deal with the challenges of the formerly centrally planned economies. As in the case of the Fund, the Bank's income more than covers its expenses.

The Bank's activities can be categorized into lending, technical assistance, analysis and research, and aid coordination.

2.1 Lending

In recent years the Bank has lent about $20 billion per annum, a sizable amount relative to the flow of resources to the developing countries. But net flows from the Bank have been smaller, with net disbursements in fiscal year 1991–1992 being $10 billion, while net transfers in that year were negative (table 2.11). The negative net transfers were accounted for mainly by large repayments from Latin America. It is also the case that in real terms, IBRD lending has barely increased over the past five years, despite the opening up of lending to Eastern Europe and the former Soviet Union.

Through 1980, almost all Bank lending was for projects, although program lending was permitted, and had indeed taken place, for instance to India in 1965. The Bank lends for an enormous range of projects. Whereas the Fund made 36 loans in 1992, the Bank made 222. The projects are classified under 12 major headings, including agriculture and rural development, industry, education, energy, telecommunications, and so forth. This range of projects demands that the Bank maintain either a high level of expertize in a variety of areas, or access to a wide range of consultants.

Even before the debt crisis broke, the Bank moved to introduce adjustment lending—policy-based, rapidly disbursing loans. The Bank justified this form of lending as responding to the needs of the borrowers at a time when private flows were declining, and as a way for the Bank to have a say about the macroeconomic policies issues that were affecting the outcomes of its projects. During the 1980s adjustment loans played an important role in the debt crisis and accounted for an important share of bank lending. Because the loans disburse fast, adjustment lending in some years accounted for as much as 50 percent of disbursements to Latin America.

Adjustment lending was needed to deal with the debt crisis, and was supported by the G-7. But since the conditionality for adjustment

Table 2.11
Bank lending, year ending June 30, 1992 ($ billion)

Total loans		21.7
IBRD	15.2	
IDA	6.5	
Project loans	18.3	
Adjustment loans	3.4	
Gross disbursements		16.4
Net disbursements		6.3
Net transfers		−1.9

Loans by region		Number of loans
Africa		
IBRD	0.7	10
IDA	3.2	67
East Asia		
IBRD	4.4	33
IDA	1.1	13
South Asia		
IBRD	1.3	6
IDA	1.6	17
Europe and Central Asia		
IBRD	2.1	13
IDA	0.0	1
Latin America & Caribbean		
IBRD	5.3	37
IDA	0.4	8
Middle East & North Africa		
IBRD	1.3	13
IDA	0.2	4
Total	21.7	222

Source: *World Bank Annual Report*, 1992.

lending had to relate to macroeconomic policies, the Bank's role brought it into potential conflict with the Fund and its conditionality. The Fund, ever fearful to being dominated by the much larger Bank, sought to establish its primacy in dealing with macroeconomic policy conditionality in member countries. The conflict burst into the open when, at U.S. urging, the World Bank made an adjustment loan to Argentina in September 1988, at a time when the Fund was not willing to lend. With a G-10 report on the roles of the Bank and the Fund in the debt crisis in preparation, the two agencies reached an accord in March 1989 that set out procedures for dealing with conflicts, and that murkily divided responsibilities for short- and long-term macroeconomic policies between the Fund and the Bank. There have been few reports of conflicts since then, but that may be more because Eastern Europe and the FSU came along and provided enough work for everyone than because the accord provided the right formulae for cooperation.[21]

As in the case of the Fund, the potential importance of the Bank's lending depends on its ability to affect member countries' policies and growth. The Bank has carried out three major studies of the effectiveness of adjustment lending,[22] and a recent important study (the Wapenhans report) of the effectiveness of its project lending. The evaluations of adjustment lending have shown it to have an overall positive effect on exports and on growth, and a negative effect on investment.[23] Concerns over adjustment lending have more recently shifted to the question of whether adjustment, as defined in the mid-1980s, is sufficient for the restoration of growth, or whether it is necessary also to focus more on longer-term growth determinants that are not entirely market determined, such as institution building and the creation of human capital, as well as directly on poverty alleviation.

The Wapenhans report was critical of the declining quality trend that it saw in Bank projects, the success rate of which had fallen from more than 80 to 70 percent during the 1980s. It attributed this to the loss of Bank technical expertize (equivalently to the excessive increase in the number of economists) and to inadequate attention to project supervision. Bank management has promised the Board that it will remedy the situation, and is beginning to change the composition of the staff and supervisory practices to this end. It has also shifted the focus of Bank activities from new lending to the management of the entire portfolio, and to the overall contribution of the Bank to the country's development.

The optimal success rate for projects must be less than 100 percent, and too many resources can be put into project supervision. Thus the mere fact that success rates have declined is not conclusive evidence that Bank project lending needs to be reformed. But given that it is the borrowers who are left to pay off the loans, a failure rate of 30 percent does seem too high, and the Bank is justified in moving resolutely on this front.

It has to be recorded that the Bank's openness makes it vulnerable to criticism that other agencies, including the Fund, avoid. The Bank is continually engaged in evaluating its activities, not only through special reports such as those discussed above, but also through the Operations Evaluation Department, which reports directly to the Board. The solution is not for the Bank to scale back these evaluations, but for other agencies, including the Fund, to be required to undertake them.

2.2 Technical Assistance

The Bank lends to countries to finance technical assistance, provides training for developing country officials through the Economic Development Institute (EDI), and makes its own experts available for technical assistance to members.

In 1992 EDI put on a total of 117 seminars and courses, attended by over 2,900 participants. The largest number of courses and participants were in Africa, a special target of EDI. EDI runs two major scholarship programs for students from developing countries. It has also been seeking to build up research institutions in developing countries, in part by creating networks of institutions within each region.

In 1992 a Bank task force examined technical assistance (TA), charged with the goal of improving its effectiveness and the specific tasks of recommending how to organize the Bank's TA activities, and to improve coordination with other agencies, especially the UNDP. The task force recommended, among other things, the establishment of an Institutional Development Fund to provide grant support for TA. The Fund was set up, and given a budget of $25 million for its first year of operation.

This amount pales against the total of technical assistance provisions in Bank loans and credits, which in fiscal year 1992 amounted to more than $1.8 billion. Technical assistance is big business. Given its potential for good, the TA industry needs an overall evaluation of the type undertaken by the Bank in studying its own TA activities.

2.3 Analysis and Research

The Bank budget shows total spending of $90 million on research, policy, and dissemination. A vast amount of policy work on individual countries is undertaken in the course of operations. Each adjustment loan is accompanied by an analysis of the macroeconomy. In addition, the Bank prepares a "Country Economic Memorandum" for each country, generally every two years. The Bank has recently changed its public disclosure policy, and now makes most of its analytic work, much project information, and project reports available to the public.[24]

Bank research has many outlets, including working paper series and journals. The *World Development Report* receives worldwide attention, and also helps set the Bank's internal policy agenda. Other publications that come out of the Bank's research departments, such as the *World Debt Tables*, provide an outlet for staff opinions as well as valuable data for researchers and policymakers.

How influential is all this research and publication? I know of no systematic study, but have the impression that it is quite influential in many developing countries, and that it has had an increasing impact on the academic community in the United States in recent years.

2.4 Aid Coordination

The World Bank chairs the consultative groups for many countries, at which the donors meet to discuss a country's economic program and financing needs, and to pledge their contributions to meeting those needs. The Bank thereby helps coordinate aid. It coordinates aid also through IDA, taking the contributions of donor countries, and lending them in a coherent fashion dictated by Bank policy.

Cofinancing with the Bank by donors is another form of aid coordination. Some countries, especially Japan, will piggyback on a Bank loan to a country, thereby increasing the amount of aid provided through the loan, and increasing the leverage of the Bank in its loan negotiations. In fiscal year 1992, there was cofinancing on 115 loans (out of a total of 222), and the cofinancing on average almost doubled the amount of lending.

The aid coordination function is a highly valuable one, which increases the effectiveness of national aid programs at the same time as it in effect increases the Bank's financial resources.

2.5 International Finance Corporation

Since the World Bank demands government guarantees on its loans to member countries, it has great difficulty in financing the private sector directly. This does not of course mean that its activities do not contribute to the development of the private sector, because many of the structural changes supported by the Bank—for example in the financial sector, or in trade reform—are crucial to the efficient operation of the private sector.

The IFC was set up to lend directly to the private sector. It is an affiliate of the World Bank, and shares the Bank's president, but it is effectively run by an Executive Vice-President. The anomaly of the IFC's status as a public institution devoted to promoting the private sector has not kept it from being very active. While its own operations amount to less than $1 billion per year, it is typically involved as a co-financier or in a syndicate, and can therefore claim to be having a larger effect than the volume of its own operations indicates. It appears that many private sector lenders and investors want the comfort that is offered by the participation of a member of the World Bank group. The IFC's presence must be seen by others investors as a signal that their rights will be vigorously protected.

The IFC has recently had a major capital increase. Some of the shareholders see a much larger future role for the IFC, as World Bank borrowers graduate, and move into the commercial markets for their financing. We return to these issues below.

2.6 Summary

The Bank engages in a very wide range of activities. Its adjustment lending appears on the whole to have been successful, but there is a perception that the quality of projects has declined. It is a major provider of technical assistance, and has recently examined its record and recommended changes in the provision of TA. Its analytic work is on average good, and its aid coordination provides a valuable service to donor countries. While the Bank is a very large organization, so are the activities that it undertakes.

3   Reforms and a Possible Merger

Both agencies undertake similar functions: lending, almost entirely to governments; analysis of systemic and national economic issues; and the provision of technical assistance. In addition, the World Bank plays an important role in coordinating aid.

Each of these services except aid coordination is also provided by the private sector. The question is whether there is any case for continuing public sector provision. We start with lending, where there is a difference between the IMF and the IBRD. IMF stabilization loans are frequently very large, and come with policy conditionality; further, they are by definition made to governments in trouble. Could the private sector make stabilization loans? Certainly some large stabilization loans were made to major governments in trouble by the House of Morgan before World War I. But given the decline of gunboat diplomacy, it is doubtful that the private sector would make stabilization loans to governments on which no effective conditionality could be imposed. To be sure, the private sector participated in financing packages during the debt crisis, but that was always under official leadership. And it is hard to see the official sector leading if it was not itself lending.

Thus it is likely that lending for stabilization with conditionality will continue through official channels. Of course, the Fund has not lent to any member of the G-7 since 1977. That is largely because exchange rates have been flexible during that period (except within the EC), and governments have been willing to let the exchange rate take the strain.[25] Developing member countries are likely to continue to maintain an exchange rate peg. This implies a need for stabilization loans, and therefore for a Fund role.[26]

Successful countries such as Spain, Japan, and Korea, graduate from IBRD borrowing and go into the capital markets on their own. Even successful countries that have not yet graduated, such as Thailand, may decide to borrow directly from the capital markets. Many of the remaining countries must be borrowing from the IBRD because it is cheaper to do that than to go to the market; and in some cases they could probably not borrow in the markets at all.

If so, we have to ask whether the IBRD is mispricing its loans to the latter classes of borrowers, or whether there is some externality in the international capital markets which justifies such pricing. The externality may be the difficulties private sector lenders have in imposing conditionality on their borrowers. It is clear that private sector lenders prefer the comfort of a governmental (IMF or IBRD) presence when they lend to developing countries that have not yet achieved easy market access. There would then be a case for IBRD lending to weaker borrowers, as a catalyst for private sector lending.

Note though that this argument implies a diminishing future role for direct IBRD lending, and possibly a declining average quality of IBRD loans. Whether that is so depends on whether certain economies are doomed never to grow, something which we do not know, but which the convergence literature suggests is unlikely.

The argument that IBRD lending catalyses private lending returns us to the view of the Bank's founders that it should serve mainly as a guarantor rather than a lending agency. The IBRD itself is exploring the possibility of expanding its guarantee role. The major issue is whether a public sector agency should provide this function. Private lenders often express a wish for such guarantees from the public sector, for example in lending to the former Soviet Union, but it would have to be seen whether they are prepared to pay the unsubsidized price. Once again, the case for a public agency's involvement would be its greater ability to collect on loans, and to impose conditionality.[27] Since these advantages of the IBRD relate to lending to governments rather than the private sector, the case is mainly one for its guaranteeing loans to the public sector. Nonetheless, public sector involvement in guaranteeing private lending at an early stage is likely to speed the development of international capital flows. I would thus argue that the IBRD or IFC should develop the capacity to provide some form of guarantee, for example against political risk, of private sector lending, for a limited period, say five to ten years.

Both agencies have also served an important emergency lending role, in the debt crisis, and there is an argument for retaining that capacity for future unforeseen events—though it is hard to see that the emergency lending role alone would justify the existence of both agencies.

To sum up on lending: there is a case for the Fund to continue to make stabilization loans, and for the Bank to continue lending to countries that do not have market access. However Bank lending is likely to decline in relative importance in coming years, particularly since there are so few countries that are not now members. There is also a case for the Bank to expand its guarantee activities.

The arguments made here do not, strictly speaking, lead directly to a role for the Bank and the Fund. Perhaps some existing or new agency would do the job better. That is a theoretical possibility, but the costs of setting up a new organization or reorganizing functions argue for the continued use of the nineteenth street twins.

The analytic and systemic analysis functions carried out by the agencies could be done by the private sector if it had the same access to information and feedback. It is doubtful that it does, for much of what is most useful in Fund and Bank research is the unique combination of theory and worldwide experience on which it draws. There are real advantages to doing research and analysis in organizations where the data and experience are generated as part of the lending activities of the agencies. The Fund's lead role in analyzing the international monetary system is also unique, and would be hard to duplicate in another type of organization.

For all their advantages in carrying out research, the international agencies still need to adopt a far more open policy on information. It is encouraging that the World Bank has been moving in this direction.

Technical assistance can be and is provided by the private sector—often by people with experience in the international agencies. It is not certain that the agencies have a natural advantage in this area, except in bringing the fruits of their experience to member countries through EDI and the IMF Institute. In particular, IFI staff does not provide resident technical assistance for long periods, for example a year. It will not be possible to judge whether the IFIs should continue providing technical assistance until they start charging for their services. I would guess that there would still be a demand for their services, at least because of their brand name (or reputation).

Finally, the World Bank's aid coordination function is important, also an offshoot of its lending activities. We should identify IDA as part of the aid coordination function. To the extent that industrialized countries provide aid to foster economic growth, it is probably better done through the World Bank than bilaterally, because of the economies of information that reside in the Bank's deep involvement in many countries.

Should these agencies exist at all? The answer is yes. Without the Fund, the poorer countries would have a much more difficult and costly adjustment process to shocks. The private capital markets have not yet done a good job of lending to countries. Even when they do lend, they typically want the comfort of an official presence. This the Fund provides. It is also singularly well-placed to take the lead in analyzing and suggesting solutions to the problems of the international financial system.

The Bank plays a valuable role in lending to member countries that are not commercially credit-worthy, in coordinating aid, in technical assistance, and in its research and policy analysis. Absent the Bank, we would invent another institution like it.

But doesn't the existence of these agencies prolong adjustment, and create aid dependence. That is true, but that is why conditionality and clear analysis are needed. I believe that the debt crisis would have been over sooner if the official agencies had not been involved. But I also believe that the adjustment crisis—which was very deep—would have been much worse without these agencies.

I conclude that the activities of the Bank and Fund would be needed even if they did not exist, and that there is a case for continued public sector involvement in providing these activities. Combined with the transaction costs of setting up new agencies, that leads to the view that there is a continuing role for both agencies, with the possibility that Bank lending will decline over time, and that its guarantee function should expand.

Assuming that both agencies will continue in existence, what reforms should be made in each? There is a strong case for the Fund to stick to two main subjects: the international monetary system; and for member countries, short-term macroeconomic policy. The Fund is relatively small, feels that it is elite, and should become elite. This means it should stop trying to compete with the World Bank in fighting poverty, improving the environment, and similar good causes not inherently related to the Fund's purposes.

The reason to focus is that both topics are inherently important, and need to be done well. The more the Fund dissipates its efforts, the less it will have influence in the key areas. No doubt the Fund wishes the G-7 would give it more of a role in their own interactions, but that role will have to be earned by the creation and publication of evidence that the Fund has something to offer them. In Africa, the Fund seems to be retreating from its longer-term activities, and that is as well. It should make sure that it concentrates on short-run macroeconomic policy in Eastern Europe and the FSU as well. That is a crucial job, which needs all the Fund's attention. It can contribute through its lending, its surveillance, and its technical assistance.

The Bank engages in more self-examination than the Fund, and reorganizes itself more frequently. Nonetheless, it has a clear idea of what its basic activities should be, and until recently appears to have carried them out well. In some areas, such as Africa, it is less sure of what to do, but so is everyone else.

The Bank should not give up adjustment lending, and should of course continue to try to improve the quality of its projects. It may do that by providing longer-term technical assistance to the technically less well-equipped borrowers. The Bank should pay more attention to the environment, to poverty, and to the role of women in development than it did a few years ago and it is. In general, the Bank should be looking ahead to new issues—to the next popular wave, whatever it may be, rather than reacting defensively when criticized for neglecting a newly popular issue.

Looking ahead would mean greater involvement for the Bank with domestic interest groups in member countries. As such orgnizations become more important, not only in the United States but also elsewhere, the Bank will have to continue to expand its non-governmental interactions, talking directly to the public in member countries rather than only through the governments.[28]

There is no compelling case for downsizing the Bank. It takes on an immense range of tasks that would have to be done anyway. There is an argument for some decentralization, for building up resident missions, for better coordination with the regional banks, and for providing more longer-term technical assistance to poorer members. There is a good case for encouraging Bank (and Fund) staffers to spend a year or two in a developing country as part of their career development within the agencies. Certainly it would give them a better idea of the difficulties confronting developing countries than they are likely to get from Washington.

It is often argued that the Bank and Fund should more truly represent the interests of all their members. The idea sounds appealing. In its research and analysis, the staff has an obligation to be fair to the truth and therefore to all members; that is part of the leadership role of the institutions. But to ask the Boards to more truly represent the interests of all raises complicated questions: industrialized country Board members are quite likely to assert that their view are in the long-run real interests of all members, and that much of the criticism is pure rhetoric. If the appeal is directed to anyone, it must be to management, and if management is to be effective, it cannot afford to engage in unproductive rhetoric. To a considerable extent, the Boards of both institutions in practice recognize that.

Finally, should the agencies be merged? That is a superficially attractive suggestion, which should be rejected. Already the Bank stretches the capacity of management's control. The merged institution would be larger and more difficult to control. It would also be extremely costly to make the change.

However, the most important reason to reject a merger is that it would make the successor institution too powerful. Both the Bank and the Fund are now extraordinarily powerful in the smaller member countries. What they say goes. Staff in both institutions is quite self-confident that it has the right answers, even when they disagree with outsiders. The main check on each agency is the presence of the other, across the street, working on a similar issue. That check should remain in place. And it should be strengthened, by subjecting the analyses and arguments of the agencies, even with regard to proposed policies in individual countries, to far wider public scrutiny.

Notes

I am grateful to Jacques Polak, Max Schieler, Alfred Steinherr, and Jürgen von Hagen for comments. I have also benefitted greatly from suggestions by Johannes Linn of the World Bank.

1. ICSID, the International Center for the Settlement of Investment Disputes, was set up in 1966, but has not been very active.

2. Several of these issues and related proposals are discussed in *The Economist*'s 1991 survey of the IMF and the World Bank; see also Dell (1990), de Vries (1987), Feinberg, et al. (1986), Finch (1989), Neu (1993), and Polak (1993).

3. As of April 30, 1992, 71 countries, including 43 developing countries, had accepted the Fund's Article VIII obligations for current account convertibility. Nine, including Indonesia, Korea, Portugal, Thailand, and Turkey, had joined the list since 1987. Several countries on the list clearly violated Article VIII at times after joining; for example Nicaragua accepted the obligation in 1964.

4. The declining cost of communications and travel have increased the centralization of power, tending to reduce the power of representatives such as ambassadors and executive directors.

5. An SDR issue is often suggested to meet a special need for aid funds, for example for the heavily indebted African countries, or for the reforming formerly socialist economies.

6. This is not to say that others do.

7. To quote from a letter from Jacques Polak, "The balance sheet of the Fund is a curious tabulation ... It mixes its outstanding credits with its ability to give new credits—both being called currencies, which is technically correct but economically meaningless."

8. See also the discussion above of a potential SDR issue.

9. In 1975, the Fund sold one-sixth (25 million ounces) of its gold holdings to finance a Trust Fund for the benefit of developing country members (the resources from that fund are recorded in table 2.2 in the special disbursement account); another one-sixth was returned to member countries at the price they had received when subscribing the gold.

10. By August 1993 the Fund staff had grown to more than 2100, to deal with the expansion of membership from the reforming centrally planned economies.

11. Further, the Fund's data requirements may constitute the main incentive for these countries to collect data.

12. The first quoted phrase is from Jacques Polak, the second from Morris Goldstein.

13. Data from the Development Assistance Committee's 1992 Report, *Development Co-Operation*, (OECD, Paris, 1992) Chapter IV.

14. This description is due to a Bank staffer.

15. Khan's results show an improvement in the balance of payments, but this becomes statistically significant only when the period of evaluation is extended beyond the program year.

16. The information provided here is from the Fund's 1992 *Annual Report*, pp. 114–117.

17. The Fiscal Affairs Department has prepared a useful review of its technical assistance work, which summarizes the types of assistance the Fund provides, and attempts to assess its impact by discussing the extent to which the advice is embodied in legislation. See "Technical Assistance on Tax Policy: A Review," IMF Working Paper, WP/93/65, August 1993.

18. However there is likely to be a bulge in Fund lending as the reforming formerly centrally planned economies begin to stabilize.

19. Note that IDA is careful not to describe its balance sheet as such.

20. Another interpretation would be that the industrialized countries fear the costs of a generalized default to the IFIs, and therefore provide incentives for the defaulters to return to the fold.

21. Polak (1993) provides a more detailed account of the dispute, largely as seen from the viewpoint of the Fund, but which does not differ in its essentials.

22. These studies were published in 1988, 1990, and 1992 respectively.

23. The Bank reconciles these results by arguing that adjustment policies must have made investment more efficient.

24. Project reports become public after the Board has approved the project.

25. Stabilization loans have been made within the European system (e.g. to Italy).

26. To support this view, one has also to argue that an adjustable peg rather than floating exchange rate system is preferable for some countries. I would make the argument by referring to the need for a nominal anchor to provide self-discipline for the monetary and fiscal authorities.

27. The argument thus ends up turning on the inability of private lenders to impose penalties on defaulting governments, or equivalently on the absence of a bankruptcy mechanism for governments. These issues were discussed in the international debt crisis.

28. I owe this point to Johannes Linn.

References

Dell, Sidney (1990). "Reforming the World Bank for the Tasks of the 1990s," Exim Bank Annual Lecture, Bombay.

de Vries, Barend A. (1987). *Remaking the World Bank*. Washington, DC: Seven Locks Press.

de Vries, Margaret G. (1986). *The IMF in a Changing World*. Washington, DC: International Monetary Fund.

Economist, The (1991). "Sisters in the Wood," survey, October 12.

Feinberg, Richard E. (1986). *Between Two Worlds: The World Bank's Next Decade*. Washington, DC: Overseas Development Council.

Finch, C. David (1989). "The IMF: The Record and the Prospect," Essays in International Finance, no. 175, International Finance Section, Princeton University.

Khan, Mohsin S. (1990). "The Macroeconomic Effects of Fund-Supported Adjustment Programs," *IMF Staff Papers*, 37, 2 (June), 195–231.

Mason, Edward S. and Robert E. Asher (1973). *The World Bank since Bretton Woods*. Washington, DC: Brookings Institution.

Neu, C. R. (1993). *A New Bretton Woods*. Santa Monica, CA: Rand.

Polak, Jacques J. (1993). "The World Bank and the IMF: The Future of their Coexistence," mimeo, IMF.

World Bank (1988). *Adjustment Lending: An Evaluation of Ten Years of Experience*. Policy and Research Series Paper 1.

——— (1990). *Adjustment Lending Policies for Sustainable Growth*. Policy and Research Series Paper 14.

——— (1992). *Adjustment Lending and Mobilization of Private and Public Resources for Growth*. Policy and Research Series Paper 22.

3   *Introduction*

This chapter was delivered as a public lecture at UCLA in 1998, during the height of the controversy over the Fund's role in the Asian crisis.

The first half is devoted to an exposition of the Fund's purposes and its role. Once again, I use Article I of the Articles of Agreement as the basis for organizing the argument, noting that Article I has stayed essentially unchanged despite several amendments to the Articles.[1] I argue there that the Fund's role has stayed close to its original purposes despite the profound changes in the global financial system since the end of World War II.

At the time of the lecture, the Executive Board of the IMF still had not agreed to allow countries to publish the annual Article IV consultation report. Some progress had been made in that members were allowed to publish the PIN, the Chairman's summing up of the Board discussion of the report. In 2000, following an experimental pilot project, the decision was taken to allow countries that want to do so to publish the Article IV report. The only changes permitted in the published version of the report are to remove market-sensitive information. As noted in the lecture, the management of the Fund welcomed the trend of increased publication and supported it—in fact, enthusiastically, but as management chairs the Board, it could not move too far beyond the Board's center of gravity.

The lecture also contains a discussion of the thorny issue of whether the Fund should go public with warnings of impending crises. The issue is thorny because the Fund staff has privileged access to information, which it could lose if it revealed that information. There is a second, more important, reason to hesitate over issuing warnings of impending crises, namely that the Fund could be wrong. If these warnings became self-fulfilling prophecies, the Fund would then have caused a crisis that otherwise would not have occurred. I believe that there *are* occasions on which the Fund should go public, but only when it is virtually certain of its prediction.

In the second half of the lecture, I turned to some of the criticisms of Fund-supported programs in Asia. I argued that the interest rate defenses of currencies were by and large correct. I was more nuanced on fiscal policies in the crisis countries. The Fund at that point had agreed with the crisis countries on a widening of the fiscal deficit, essentially allowing the automatic stabilizers to work. Later we concluded that the initial fiscal adjustments in Asia had probably been too strong.[2] However, as we emphasized, these adjustments had been reversed within a few months and cannot have had a significant impact.

The chapter contains a strong defense of the central structural elements included in the programs, especially financial and corporate sector reforms, which I argue were essential to the revival of growth. Later analysis by Fund staff concluded that there was probably too much detailed structural conditionality in the Indonesian program. This may be so, but the Fund was in a virtually impossible situation in Indonesia, since the detailed structural conditionality was aimed squarely at well-known elements of corruption in Indonesia—and had the program not addressed those issues, the Fund would have been criticized for its support of corruption.

In discussing moral hazard, I grappled with an interesting issue that I have had trouble explaining. Specifically, the existence of moral hazard as a result of Fund lending does not imply that the Fund should not be lending in crises. Rather the marginal cost of the distortions in private capital flows created by moral hazard needs to be balanced against the marginal benefit of the reduction in the costs of crises that the Fund's loans provide.[3] This has to be true not only on a case-by-case basis, but also about the behavior of the system in its steady-state equilibrium. For that reason Fund lending has to be on a limited scale, and methods have to be found to ensure private sector involvement when needed.

The lecture ends with a discussion of the reform of the international financial architecture, a topic that was then high on the agenda, and which is discussed at greater length in chapter 6.

As is clear from the last three paragraphs, the lecture was also intended to make the case for the quota increase that was then under consideration by the U.S. Congress. The quota increase was eventually voted (in October 1998), but that was only after the Russian crisis and the alarm created by the failure of Long Term Capital Management and the first round of the Brazilian crisis.

Notes

1. The most significant changes took place following the collapse of the Bretton Woods system in the early 1970s, and the shift to a system of floating rates among the major currencies. They are embodied in the second amendment to the articles, ratified in 1978.

2. See for instance Boorman et al., "Managing Financial Crisis: The Experience in East Asia," *Carnegie-Rochester Conference Series on Public Policy*, No. 53. Amsterdam: North-Holland, 2000.

3. Obviously I am assuming here that Fund lending is effective in reducing the costs of crises.

3   The IMF and the Asian Crisis

Stanley Fischer

The Asian crisis and the Administration's request to Congress for IMF funding have focused unprecedented attention on the Fund. The ensuing debate should be a healthy part of the process by which the institution is held accountable to its member countries and governments. But the spotlight on the Fund has also revealed a number of critical misconceptions, relating both to its role in the international monetary system and to its recent activities in Asia.

On the role of the Fund: it is often stated that the Fund was established to manage the system of fixed exchange rates set up at the end of World War II, and that since the breakdown of that system in 1973, it has been searching for a rationale. The Fund has of course evolved and adapted since it began operating in 1946. Nonetheless, its current activities are closely consistent with its initial purposes— testimony to the remarkable foresight of the founders of the international economic system set up after World War II, a system which has helped produce more growth and more prosperity for more people than in any previous fifty year period.

In Asia it has been charged, among others by Martin Feldstein in the March/April 1998 issue of *Foreign Affairs*, that the Fund is applying traditional austerity remedies; that it is intervening excessively in borrowers' economies, thereby making countries increasingly reluctant to request financial assistance from the Fund; and that its activities bail out unwise lenders and lay the seeds for future excesses of private sector lending—the moral hazard argument. I will argue that the Fund's macroeconomic advice in Asia is appropriate to the circumstances of individual countries; that the structural changes in these economies supported by IMF programs are necessary for the sustainable return of growth; that IMF lending should be conditional on changes in policy and not too easily available; and that while the existence of any insurance—and the IMF's provision of backstop financing does provide insurance to its members and the markets—produces moral hazard, most lenders to the Asian countries in crisis have taken large losses. It will always be true, though, that the international community needs to find better ways of preventing crises and of dealing with the crises that inevitably will occur, and I will conclude by briefly discussing changes in the architecture of the international system now on the agenda.

The Purposes and Role of the IMF

The goal of the representatives of the 44 countries who met in Bretton Woods, New Hampshire in 1944 was to rebuild the international economic system, whose collapse had contributed to the Great Depression and the outbreak of war. To this end they proposed setting up the International Monetary Fund, the World Bank, and what much later became the World Trade Organization.

The primary purposes of the Fund are set out in Article I of the charter, which has remained essentially unchanged over the past fifty years. They include:

To promote international monetary cooperation through a permanent institution which provides the machinery for consultation and collaboration on international monetary problems;

To facilitate the expansion and balanced growth of international trade, and to contribute thereby to the promotion and maintenance of high levels of employment and real income . . . ;

To promote exchange stability, to maintain orderly exchange arrangements among members, and to avoid competitive exchange depreciation;

To assist in the establishment of a multilateral system of payments in respect of current transactions . . . and in the elimination of foreign exchange restrictions which hamper the growth of world trade; and

To give confidence to members by making the general resources of the Fund temporarily available to them under adequate safeguards, thus providing them with opportunity to correct maladjustments in their balance of payments without resorting to measures destructive of national or international prosperity.

The world economy has prospered mightily and changed dramatically since 1944, but the approach laid out at Bretton Woods has stood the test of time. The IMF too has changed, but its original purposes remain valid on the verge of the twenty-first century.

International Economic Cooperation

The Fund, with its 182 member countries, is the premier forum for international economic cooperation and consultation. Issues relating to the organization and functioning of the international system are generally discussed and, when decisions are needed, decided on in the Fund—by the Executive Board,[1] and by the Finance Ministers and Central Bank governors who constitute the Board of Governors of the Fund. Often the initiative may come from elsewhere, for example the G-7, or a member government, but it is the Fund that "provides the machinery for consultation and collaboration on international monetary problems" that is used to examine and make these suggestions operational. The Fund's highly professional staff, including 1,000 economists (450 of them with Ph.D.s), prepares the analysis that forms the basis for the discussion.

Almost every major international economic problem of recent years has been discussed and usually acted on (often together with other institutions, especially our Bretton Woods non-identical twin, the World Bank) by the IMF: the Mexican and Asian crises; technical and financial assistance to the economies in transition, including Russia; the debt problems of the poorest countries (in close cooperation with the World Bank); the attempt to improve international banking standards; economic assistance to Bosnia-Herzegovina; the ongoing effort, initiated following the Mexican crisis, to improve the quality and public provision of data, which has led to the Fund's Special and General Data Dissemination Standards; the unfortunately long-running problems of the Japanese economy this decade; the activities of hedge funds and their role in the Asian crisis; and the list goes on and will go on.[2]

Much of what the Fund does consists of *surveillance*, reporting by the staff to the Executive Board and thus to member governments on developments and problems in the international economy and in individual economies. The staff's surveillance of the international economy is published, after discussion by the Board, in the semiannual *World Economic Report* and in the annual *International Capital Markets* report. In addition, the staff reports regularly to the Board on world economic and market developments. Drawing on its continuous surveillance of the world economy, the Fund staff provides briefings on the international economy for meetings of the G-7 and other G's and organizations, including APEC.

Approximately once a year, the Fund staff prepares an *Article IV Report* for each country, an in-depth analysis of the country's economic policies and performance. In its discussion of the paper, the Board conveys its views—encouraging or critical—to the policymakers of the country. Through this process, policymakers seek to encourage their colleagues in other countries to improve policies. In addition, the staff reports regularly to the Board on countries facing particular economic difficulties or whose programs with the Fund may be off track.

Article IV reports are not published: most member governments say they would not be willing to discuss their economic problems frankly with the Fund if the reports were to be published. However, last year the Board agreed to allow countries that want to do so, to publish the Chairman's summing-up of the Board discussion. So far 60 PINs (Press Information Notices) containing the summing-up and other information on the economy, about half the number of Article IVs discussed during the period, have been published and are available on the Fund's website. In addition, at the end of its Article IV mission to each country, the Fund staff presents to the government a concluding statement, summarizing its views. The concluding statement generally foreshadows the conclusions of the Article IV report. Countries may, if they wish, publish these concluding statements, and an increasing number are doing so. Thus, gradually, the Fund's membership is moving to make public the conclusions of the Article IV consultation, a trend that is welcomed by Fund management.

In recent years, especially in the wake of the Mexican crisis, the IMF has strengthened and broadened its surveillance, paying particular attention to, among other factors, the quality and timeliness of the data it receives from member countries, the strength of their domestic financial systems, and the sustainability of private capital inflows. By providing warnings of impending problems, Fund surveillance should help prevent crises. When it does so, when a crisis is averted, surveillance has succeeded and is unlikely to be noticed— and there are many cases in which Fund warnings were given and action taken that averted a crisis. But surveillance may fail, either because warnings are given and not heeded, or because the problem was not anticipated.

In the Asian crisis, the Fund warned Thailand of an impending crisis but action was not taken. Fund staff also warned about financial sector weaknesses in several of the countries subsequently badly hit in the crisis. But we failed to foresee the virulence of the contagion effects produced by the widening crisis.

In drawing the lessons of this crisis, the Fund will have to seek both to make warnings more effective and to improve the quality of Fund economic forecasts, particularly of crises. Many have suggested that crises could be prevented, or at least mitigated, if the Fund went public with its fears. Two factors make this difficult. First, the Fund's access to information and its ability to act as a confidential advisor to governments would be lost if it made that information public; and absent such information, there is no good reason to think this is particularly a task for the public sector. Second, the Fund could by going public with its concerns create a crisis that otherwise would not have happened—a responsibility that should not lightly be assumed. As to forecasts of potential crises, there should be no illusion that forecasting of this type will ever be perfect. Some impending crises will be missed. For this reason, and because in any case not all warnings are heeded, we shall have to continue to improve our capacity to deal with crises even as we strive to improve surveillance to prevent crises.

Promoting International Trade

The Fund promotes international trade directly, by encouraging trade liberalization, both through surveillance and in its lending programs with member countries. It has always done so, and the purposes of the Fund require it to continue to do so. It is therefore a surprise that our Asian programs are criticized for including conditionality on trade liberalization measures. Although trade liberalization was at one time controversial, and import-substituting industrialization a popular prescription, the weight of experience, as well as more formal econometric evidence, have conclusively established the benefits of trade liberalization and integration into the world economy.

Even more important, the Fund promotes international trade indirectly, by encouraging countries to liberalize foreign exchange controls on trade in goods and services ("the establishment of a system of multilateral payments in respect of current transactions"). These controls were pervasive at the end of World War II, but by now 142 member countries have accepted Article VIII status with the Fund, which certifies that they allow full convertibility of their currency for current account transactions. Remarkably, most of the transition economies moved to Article VIII status within a few years, a contrast with many of today's advanced economies which took well over a decade to get rid of these restrictions after the end of World War II.

Currency Fluctuations

The pegged exchange rate system set up at the end of World War II lasted until 1973. In principle the IMF was assigned a major role in approving exchange rate changes, but in practice major countries tended to devalue first and seek approval immediately after. The fixed exchange rate system was a means of promoting exchange rate stability, not a goal. Once it lost its viability—a result of the incompatibility of fixed exchange rates, capital mobility, and policies focused on domestic objectives—there was no choice but to move to a more flexible system.

Exchange rates among the major countries, particularly between Japan and the United States, have fluctuated more than was expected by proponents of floating exchange rates, but no acceptable alternative is available for countries that—unlike future members of the European Monetary Union—are not willing to subordinate economic policy to the goal of stabilizing the exchange rate. Fluctuations such as those in the yen–dollar rate between 81 in the spring of 1995 and 133 late last year are so large that the search for a better way to promote exchange stability is bound to return to the agenda. Smaller countries, more dependent on the international economy than the United States, Europe, and Japan, do not have the luxury of ignoring the behavior of the exchange rate, and have tended either to choose some form of exchange rate peg or at least to adjust macroeconomic policies when the exchange rate threatens to move out of line. The peg of most ASEAN exchange rates to the appreciating dollar contributed to the Asian currency crisis.

The concern over competitive devaluations reflected in the Fund's charter, and the systemwide implications of changes in exchange rates, still motivate Fund policy recommendations. A major Fund concern in the Asian crisis has been the fear that Asian currencies would become so undervalued and current account surpluses so large as to damage the economies of other countries, developing countries included. This is one reason the Fund has stressed the need first to stabilize and then to strengthen exchange rates in the Asian countries now in crisis—and for this purpose, not to cut interest rates until the currency stabilizes and begins to appreciate.

Fund Lending

Despite its other activities—surveillance, information provision, and technical assistance—the IMF is best known for its lending. The Fund operates much like a credit union, with countries placing deposits in the Fund, which are then available to loan to members who need to borrow and who meet the necessary conditions. Members' *quotas* in the Fund determine both the amount they have to subscribe, and their voting shares. The size of a member's quota reflects, but typically with a lag, the size of its economy and its role in the world economy.[3]

Total quotas now amount to a bit under $200 billion. Countries have to pay in 25 percent of their quota (the so-called reserve tranche) in any of the five major currencies in the Special Drawing Right; the remainder can be paid in the country's own currency. This means that not all the quotas can be used for lending. Countries can have virtually automatic access to their reserve tranche, and the United States has drawn on its reserve tranche more than twenty times, most recently in defense of the dollar in 1978.

In September 1997 the members agreed to increase quotas by 45 percent, about $90 billion, with the United States's share of the increase amounting to nearly $14.5 billion. The Congress has before it at present both the Administration's request for the quota increase, and a request for $3.5 billion for the U.S. contribution to the New Arrangements to Borrow (NAB). The NAB will allow the IMF to borrow from a group of 25 participants with strong economies in the event of a risk to the international monetary system.[4] It would thus provide backup financing that could be available if the Fund runs short of regular quota-based resources. The NAB doubled the resources available to the Fund under the General Arrangements to Borrow established in the 1960s.

When a member in crisis approaches the Fund for a loan, the Fund seeks to negotiate an economic program to restore macroeconomic stability and lay the conditions for sustainable and equitable growth, paying careful regard to the social costs of adjustment. The decision whether to support the country will be taken by the Executive Board, based largely on the strength of the reform program the country is willing to undertake. The loan is typically *tranched*, paid out in installments, each conditional on the country's meeting the conditions to which it has agreed. These procedures, especially *conditionality*, constitute the adequate safeguards required by the Articles of Agreement.

The policies agreed on in a Fund-supported program typically include fiscal and monetary policies designed to restore viability to the balance of payments, help restore growth, and reduce inflation. Where appropriate, they also include structural policies designed to remedy the problems that led to the need to borrow from the Fund. When a country's problem is purely balance of payments related, and can be expected to be reversed in a short time, the Fund loan will typically cover policies for a year, with repayment starting after three years and concluding within five years. When the country's economic problems are more deep-seated and will take longer to deal with, the arrangement will last longer, covering policies for up to three or four years. In these cases, the program will contain, along with monetary and fiscal policy changes, more structural measures, such as reform of the financial system, the pension system, labor markets, agriculture, and the energy sector. Such extended arrangements typically include reforms that will be financed during the period of the program by World Bank loans. Such is also the case with the financial sector and other structural reforms in Asian countries.

Despite the common usage, "IMF program," the Fund itself is careful to speak of a "Fund-supported program." Ideally the program should be that of the country, and one that its government is committed to carrying out. Of course, in the loan negotiations, the Fund will usually ask the government to do more than it initially wanted. But because a program is unlikely to succeed unless those who have agreed to it intend to carry it out, a key element in the evaluation of any agreement is the degree of the government's commitment to the economic program which it has signed—a conclusion which is reinforced by the recent Asian experience, in which the Korean and Thai financial markets both turned around when new governments, strongly committed to carrying out the programs, came into office. The government's commitment may be difficult to judge, especially if it is divided, and if, as happens not rarely, the program is being used by those who favor reform as a vehicle to implement changes that some of their colleagues oppose. Although a Fund-supported program is often seen in the press as the international community's way of imposing changes on a country's economy, it is more often the international community's way of supporting a government or a group within the government that wants to bring about desirable economic reforms conducive to long-term growth.

But why then are programs so often unpopular? The main reason is that the Fund is typically called in only in a crisis, generally a result of the government's having been unwilling to take action earlier. If the medicine to cure the crisis had been tasty, the country would have taken it long ago. Rather the medicine will usually be unpleasant, in essence requiring the country to live within its means or undertake changes with short-term political costs. Probably the government knew what had to be done, but rather than take the responsibility, finds it convenient to blame the Fund when it has to act. Similarly, when structural changes have to be made, the losses are often immediate and the gains some way off. Despite all this, there are countries where the Fund is popular, among them transition economies that have seen hyperinflation defeated and growth begin during Fund-supported programs.

The secrecy that until recently has often attended Fund-supported programs may well have contributed to their unpopularity. A public that does not know what is being done, nor why, is less likely to support measures that are difficult in the short-run but that promise longer-run benefits. Governments have often been reluctant to publish their agreements with the Fund, disliking to give the impression that their policies were in any way affected by outsiders. Recently, in the Korean, Thai, and Indonesian programs, the government's Letter of Intent, its letter to the management of the Fund describing its program, has been published—another change welcomed by the management of the Fund.

Evolution of the World Economy and the IMF

While the purposes of the IMF have not changed, it has over the years been called upon to advise and assist an ever wider array of countries facing an ever greater diversity of problems and circumstances—not only industrial economies with temporary balance of payments problems, but also low-income countries with protracted balance of payments difficulties; transition countries struggling to establish the institutional infrastructure of full-fledged market economies; and emerging market countries seeking to secure the private capital inflows needed to maintain high rates of economic and human development.

Of course, the IMF has maintained its primary focus on sound money, prudent fiscal policies, and open markets as preconditions for macroeconomic stability and growth. But increasingly, the scope of its policy concerns has broadened to include other elements that also contribute to economic stability and growth. Thus, to different degrees in different countries, the IMF is also pressing, generally together with the World Bank, for sound domestic financial systems; for improvements in the quality of public expenditure, so that spending on primary health and education is not squeezed out by costly military build-ups and large infrastructure projects that benefit the few at the expense of many; for increased transparency and accountability in government and corporate affairs to avoid costly policy mistakes and the waste of national resources; for adequate and affordable social safety nets to cushion the impact of economic adjustment and reform on the most vulnerable members of society; and in some countries for deregulation and demonopolization to create a more level playing field for private sector activity.

This broadening of the scope of IMF policy concerns has met with mixed reactions. Some applaud the Fund for tackling the structural problems and governance issues that, in many countries, stand in the way of macroeconomic stability and sustained growth. But others roundly criticize the IMF, either for intruding too far in what they see as the domestic affairs of sovereign nations, or for failing to go far enough.

Finally, the diversity of its membership and the problems they face has led the IMF to establish a wider array of facilities and policies through which the Fund can provide financial support to its members. In addition to the traditional standby arrangement that usually lasts twelve to eighteen months and is designed to help finance temporary or cyclical balance of payments deficits, the Extended Fund Facility (EFF) supports three- to four-year programs aimed at overcoming more deep-seated macroeconomic and structural problems. The Enhanced Structural Adjustment Facility (ESAF) also finances longer-term programs, but at a concessional interest rate for low-income countries. At other times in the IMF's history, new facilities have been established to address particular problems. The most recent of these is the Supplemental Reserve Facility (SRF), which was created in December 1997 to assist emerging market economies facing crises of market confidence, while providing strong incentives for them to return to market financing as soon as possible: it allows the Fund to make large short-term loans at higher rates than it normally charges. The first borrower under the SRF was Korea.

What is the net effect of all these changes? Certainly, the IMF has not been completely transformed. One important feature that remains the same is the emphasis on sound policies at the national level and effective monetary cooperation at the international level. The corollary of this is that the IMF is not just a source of financing or a mechanism for crisis management, as is commonly believed, but mostly, in its daily business, a cooperative institution for multilateral surveillance. It must also be acknowledged, however, that from its relatively simple origins, the IMF has evolved into a complex institution with complex tasks to fulfill. So even if the IMF continues to look at all its member countries through the same prism—the requirements for economic stability and growth—it has to deal in a differentiated way with the full spectrum of problems and possibilities in 182 distinctive member countries.

The IMF and the Crisis in Asia

Among the many questions raised by the Asian economic crisis, I will focus on a set of issues about the nature of IMF-supported programs that have been raised by several critics, among them Martin Feldstein in *Foreign Affairs*. Before doing so, I will briefly discuss the origins of the crisis. I will not deal in any detail with the question of whether the Asian miracle is dead, beyond saying that I believe it is not, and that within a year or two the countries now in crisis will once again be growing at rates well above the world average.

Origins of the Crisis

The economic crisis in Asia unfolded against the backdrop of several decades of outstanding economic performance. Annual GDP growth in the ASEAN-5 (Indonesia, Malaysia, the Philippines, Singapore, and Thailand) averaged close to 8 percent over the last decade. Moreover, during the 30 years preceding the crisis, per capita income levels had increased tenfold in Korea, fivefold in Thailand, and fourfold in Malaysia. Indeed, per capita income levels in Hong Kong and Singapore now exceed those in some Western industrial countries. And until the current crisis, Asia attracted almost half of total capital inflows to developing countries—nearly $100 billion in 1996.

Nevertheless, there were problems on the horizon. First, signs of overheating had become increasingly evident in Thailand and other countries in the region in the form of large external deficits and property and stock market bubbles. Second, pegged exchange rate regimes had been maintained for too long, encouraging heavy external borrowing, which led, in turn, to excessive exposure to foreign exchange risk by domestic financial institutions and corporations. Third, lax prudential rules and financial oversight had permitted the quality of banks' loan portfolios to deteriorate sharply.

Developments in the advanced economies and global financial markets contributed significantly to the buildup of the crisis. In particular, weak growth in Europe and Japan since the beginning of the 1990s had left a shortage of attractive investment opportunities in those economies and kept interest rates low. Large private capital flows to emerging markets, including the so-called carry trade, were driven to an important degree by these phenomena, along with an imprudent search for high yields by international investors without due regard for the potential risks. Also contributing to the crisis were the wide swings in the yen/dollar exchange rate over the previous three years.

In the case of Thailand, the crisis, if not its exact timing, was predicted. Beginning in early 1996, a confluence of domestic and external shocks revealed vulnerabilities in the Thai economy that, until then, had been masked by rapid economic growth and the weakness of the U.S. dollar to which the Thai baht was pegged. But in the following 18 months leading up to the floating of the Thai baht in July 1997, neither the IMF in its continuous dialogue with the Thai authorities nor increasing market pressure could overcome their sense of denial about the severity of their country's economic problems. Finally, in the absence of convincing policy action, and after a desperate defense of the currency by the central bank, the crisis in Thailand broke.

Should the IMF have gone public with its fears of impending crisis? While we knew that Thailand was extremely vulnerable, we could not predict with certainty whether, or when, crisis would actually strike. For the IMF to arrive on the scene like the fire brigade with lights flashing and sirens wailing before a crisis occurs would risk provoking a crisis that never might have occurred. Short of that, IMF management and staff did do everything possible to convince Thailand to take timely, forceful action—but without success.

Once the crisis hit Thailand, the contagion to other economies in the region appeared relentless. Some of the contagion reflected rational market behavior. The depreciation of the baht could be expected to erode the competitiveness of Thailand's trade competitors, and this put downward pressure on their currencies. Moreover, after their experience in Thailand, markets began to take a closer look at the problems in Indonesia, Korea, and other neighboring countries. And what they saw, to differing degrees in different countries, were some of the same problems as in Thailand, particularly in the financial sector. Added to this, the debt service costs of the domestic private sector increased as currencies continued to slide. Fearful about how far this process might go, domestic residents rushed to hedge their external liabilities, thereby intensifying exchange rate pressures. But even if individual market participants behaved rationally, the degree of currency depreciation that has taken place exceeds by a wide margin any reasonable estimate of what might have been required to correct the initial overvaluation of the Thai baht, the Indonesian rupiah, and the Korean won, among other currencies. To put it bluntly, markets overreacted.

Thailand, Indonesia, and Korea face a number of similar problems, including the loss of market confidence, deep currency depreciation, weak financial systems, and excessive unhedged foreign borrowing by the domestic private sector. Moreover, all suffered from a lack of transparency about the ties between government, business, and banks, which has both contributed to the crisis and complicated efforts to defuse it. But the countries also differ in important ways, notably in the initial size of their current account deficits and the stages of their respective crises when they requested IMF support.

The design of the programs that the IMF is supporting in Thailand, Indonesia, and Korea reflects these similarities and these differences.[5] These programs have sparked considerable controversy on a range of issues. First, some have argued that they are merely the same old IMF austerity medicine, inappropriately dispensed to countries suffering from a different disease. Second is the criticism that by attempting to do more than restore macroeconomic balance—for instance in the measures to restructure the financial systems and improve corporate governance—the programs intrude inappropriately on matters that should be left to the country to handle. Further, it is argued that by doing so, the Fund discourages others from coming to the Fund for financial assistance before they have absolutely no choice. Yet others criticize the programs for not intervening enough, for instance for failing to tackle further reforms in such areas as workers' rights and environmental protection. Third, many people are troubled by questions of moral hazard, especially as regards foreign commercial lenders.

Are the Programs Too Tough?

In weighing this question, it is important to recall that when they approached the IMF, the reserves of Thailand and Korea were perilously low, and the Indonesian rupiah was excessively depreciated. Thus, the first order of business was, and still is, to restore confidence in the currency. To achieve this, countries have to make it more attractive to hold domestic currency, which, in turn, requires increasing interest rates temporarily, even if higher interest costs complicate the situation of weak banks and corporations. This is a key lesson of the tequila crisis in Latin America 1994–1995, as well as from the more recent experience of Brazil, the Czech Republic, Hong Kong, and Russia, all of which have fended off attacks on their currencies in recent months with a timely and forceful tightening of interest rates along with other supporting policy measures. Once confidence is restored, interest rates can return to more normal levels.

Why not operate with lower interest rates and a greater devaluation? This is a relevant tradeoff, but there can be no question that the degree of devaluation in the Asian crisis countries is excessive, both from the viewpoint of the individual countries and from the viewpoint of the international system.

Looking first to the individual country, companies with substantial foreign currency debts, as so many companies in these countries have, stand to suffer far more from a steep slide in the value of their domestic currency than from a temporary rise in domestic interest rates. Moreover, when interest rate action is delayed, confidence continues to erode. Thus, the increase in interest rates needed to stabilize the situation is likely to be far larger than if decisive action had been taken at the outset. Indeed, the reluctance to tighten interest rates forcefully at the beginning has been an important factor in perpetuating the crisis.

From the viewpoint of the international system, the devaluations in Asia will lead to large current account surpluses in those countries, damaging the competitive positions of other countries and requiring them to run current account deficits. Although not by the intention of the authorities in the crisis countries, these are excessive competitive devaluations, not good for the system, not good for other countries, indeed a way of spreading the crisis—precisely the type of devaluation the IMF has the obligation to seek to prevent.

On the question of the appropriate degree of fiscal tightening, the balance is a particularly fine one. At the outset of the crisis, countries needed to firm their fiscal positions, both to make room in their budgets for the future costs of financial restructuring, and—depending on the balance of payments situation—to reduce the current account deficit. In calculating the amount of fiscal tightening needed to offset the costs of financial sector restructuring, the programs include the expected *interest* costs of the intervention, not the capital costs. For example, if the cost of cleaning up the financial sector is expected to amount to 15 percent of GDP—a realistic estimate for some countries in the region—then the corresponding fiscal adjustment would be about 1.5 percent of GDP. This is an attempt to spread the costs of the adjustment over time rather than concentrate them at the time of the crisis. Among the three Asian crisis programs, the balance of payments factor was important only in Thailand, which had been running a current account deficit of about 8 percent of GDP.

The amount of fiscal adjustment in Indonesia was one percent of GDP; in Korea it was 1.5 percent of GDP; and in Thailand—reflecting its large current account deficit—the initial adjustment was 3 percent of GDP. After these initial adjustments, if the economic situation in the country weakened more than expected, as it has in the three Asian crisis countries, the IMF has generally agreed with the country to let the deficit widen somewhat, that is, to let automatic stabilizers operate. However, the level of the fiscal deficit cannot be a matter of indifference, particularly since a country in crisis typically has only limited access to borrowing and the alternative of printing money would be potentially disastrous in these circumstances. Nor does the IMF need to persuade Asian countries of the virtues of fiscal prudence—indeed, in two of the crisis countries, the government has insisted on a tighter fiscal policy than the Fund had suggested.

Thus, on macroeconomics the answer to the critics is that monetary policy has to be kept tight to restore confidence in the currency, and that fiscal policy was tightened appropriately but not excessively at the start of each program, with automatic stabilizers subsequently being allowed to do their work. That is as it should be. Moreover, these policies are showing increasing signs of success in Thailand and Korea, and interest rates could begin to come down if market confidence and the currencies continue to strengthen.

Structural Policies

Macroeconomic adjustment is not the main element in the programs of Thailand, Indonesia, and Korea. Rather, financial sector restructuring and other structural reforms lie at the heart of each program—because the problems they deal with (weak financial institutions, inadequate bank regulation and supervision, and the complicated and nontransparent relations among governments, banks, and corporations) lie at the heart of the economic crisis in each country.

It would not serve any lasting purpose for the IMF to lend to these countries unless these problems were addressed. Nor would it be in the countries' interest to leave the structural and governance issues aside: markets have remained skeptical where reform efforts are perceived to be incomplete or half-hearted, and market confidence has not returned. Similarly, the Fund has been accused of encouraging countries to move too quickly on banking sector restructuring: we have been urged to support regulatory forbearance, leaving the solution of the banking sector problems for later. This would only have perpetuated these countries' economic problems, as experience in Japan has shown. The best course is to recapitalize or close insolvent banks, protect small depositors, require shareholders to take their losses, and take steps to improve banking regulation and supervision. Of course, the programs take individual country circumstances into account in determining how quickly all of this—including the recapitalization of banks—can be accomplished.

Martin Feldstein proposes three questions the IMF should apply in deciding whether to ask for the inclusion of any particular measure in a program. First, is it really necessary to restore the country's access to the international capital markets? The answer in the case of the Asian programs is yes. Second, is this a technical matter that does not interfere unnecessarily with the proper jurisdiction of a sovereign government? The answer here is complicated, because we have no accepted definitions of what is technical, or what is improper interference. Banking sector reform is a highly technical issue, far more than the size of the budget deficit—a policy criterion Feldstein is apparently willing to accept as fit for inclusion in a Fund program. Nor is it clear why trade liberalization—which has long been part of IMF and World Bank programs—is any less an intrusion on a sovereign government than banking sector reform. Nor does Feldstein explain why the programs supported by the Fund in the transition economies, including Russia—which are far more detailed, far more structural, and in many countries as controversial as in Asia—are acceptable, but those in Asia are not. Third, if these policies were practiced in the major industrial economies of Europe, would the IMF think it appropriate to ask for similar changes in those countries if they had a Fund program? The answer here is a straightforward yes.

Interesting as they are, Feldstein's three criteria omit the most important question that should be asked. Does this program address the underlying causes of the crisis? There is neither point nor excuse for the international community to provide financial assistance to a country unless that country takes measures to prevent future crises. That is the fundamental reason for the inclusion of structural measures in Fund-supported programs. Of course, many of these measures take a long time to implement, and many of them are in the purview of the World Bank, which is why the overall framework for longer-term programs, such as those in Asia, typically include a series of World Bank loans to deal with structural issues.

Moral Hazard

The charge that by coming to the assistance of countries in crisis, the IMF creates moral hazard has been heard from all points of the political compass. The argument has two parts: first, that officials in member countries may take excessive risks because they know the IMF will be there to bail them out if they get into serious trouble; and second, that because the IMF will come to the rescue, investors do not appraise—indeed do not even bother to appraise—risks accurately, and are too willing to lend to countries with weak economies.

It would be far-fetched to think that policymakers embarking on a risky course of action do so because the IMF safety net will save them if things go badly. All the evidence shows many countries do their best to avoid going to the Fund. Nor have individual policymakers whose countries end in trouble generally survived politically. In this regard, Fund conditionality provides the right incentives for policymakers to do the right thing—indeed, these incentives have been evident in the preemptive actions taken by some countries during the present crisis. These incentives may even be too strong, and I agree with Martin Feldstein that it generally would be better if countries were willing to come to the Fund sooner rather than later. But I do not believe countries should have too easy access to the Fund: the Fund should not be the lender of first resort; that is the role of the private markets.

The thornier issues arise on the side of investors. Economists tend to point to the problems of moral hazard and the inappropriate appraisal of risks; others are more concerned that some investors who should have paid a penalty—and typically they refer to the banks—may be bailed out by Fund lending. These are two sides of the same coin: if investors are bailed our inappropriately, then they will be less careful than they should be in future.

First the facts. Most investors in the Asian crisis countries have taken very heavy losses. This applies to equity investors, and to many of those who have lent to corporations and banks. With stock markets and exchange rates plunging, foreign equity investors had by the end of 1997 lost nearly three quarters of the value of their equity holdings in some Asian markets—though, to be sure, those with the courage to hold on have done better since the turn of the year. Many firms and financial institutions in these countries will unfortunately go bankrupt, and their foreign and domestic lenders will share in the losses.

Some short-term creditors, notably those lending in the inter-bank market, were protected for a while, in that policies aimed to ensure that these credits would continue to be rolled over. In the case of Korea, where bank exposure is largest, the creditor banks have now been bailed *in*, with the operation to roll over and lengthen their loans having been successfully completed earlier this week. Further, we should not exaggerate the extent to which banks have avoided damage in the Asian crisis: fourth-quarter earnings reports indicate that, overall, the Asian crisis has been costly for foreign commercial banks.

None of this is to deny the problem of moral hazard. It exists, it always has to be borne in mind, and we need to find better ways of dealing with it. But surely investors will not conclude from this crisis that they need not worry about the risks of their lending because the IMF will come to their rescue. Investors have been hit hard. They should have been, for they lent unwisely. But there remains the question: if it was not mainly moral hazard that led to the unwise lending that underlies the Asian crisis, what was it? The answer is irrational exuberance.

Financial crises based on swings in investor confidence—on irrational exuberance and also on irrational depression, not really irrational in lacking some foundation in fact but sometimes representing an excessive reaction—far predate the creation of the IMF, and would not be avoided even if the IMF did not exist. This is not something to applaud. Rather we have to do everything we can to provide the information and incentives that will encourage rational investor behavior. We *do* need, as I will discuss shortly, to find better ways to bail in the private sector more systematically. But we cannot build a system on the assumption that crises will not happen. There *will* be times at which countries are faced with a massive reversal of capital flows and potentially devastating loss of investor confidence. Thus we need in the system the capacity to respond to crises that would otherwise force countries to take measures unduly "destructive of national or international prosperity."

The IMF is part of that system of response, to help countries when markets overreact. Here I would like to discuss briefly the role of IMF lending—and I emphasize that the IMF *lends* money and gets repaid, it does not give it away—and the issue of bailouts on a more fundamental level.

When the IMF lends in a crisis, it helps moderate the recession that the country inevitably faces. That means that the residents of that country, its corporations, and some of the lenders to that country, do better than they otherwise would have. That is not in any meaningful sense a bailout, provided lending of this type can be sustained in future crises. Rather, if properly designed to avoid as far as possible creating the wrong incentives for the private sector, it represents rational lending—not grants or handouts—in conditions when markets appear to have overreacted.

To ensure that lending of this type can be sustained in future crises, we have to be sure that the required size of Fund loans does not keep rising, which means that in seeking to improve the architecture of the international system, we will have to find ways of discouraging unwise private lending—that is, to help ensure that risk is properly priced, and to limit the required scale of official lending, in part by finding ways of sharing the burden between the official and private sectors.

The alternative proposed by those who would abolish the IMF is to leave countries and their creditors to sort out the country's inability to service its debts. That sounds simple, but it has rarely been so in practice. That is one reason that the IMF assisted the Asian crisis countries to avoid defaults or debt moratoria. In the absence of an accepted bankruptcy procedure for dealing with such cases, given that the debts involved generally include both sovereign and private obligations, and given the free rider problem, the experience—from the inter-War period and the 1980s—is that workouts have been protracted, and that countries have been denied market access for a long time, at a significant cost to growth. By contrast, in the Mexican crisis of 1994–1995, market access was lost for only a few months, and Mexico returned within a year to impressive growth assisted by its ability to tap the international capital markets. Similarly, in the present Asian crisis, it is quite likely that both Korea and Thailand will be back to the international markets within a few months. That surely bodes well for their recoveries, which it is reasonable to expect will begin later this year.

The second reason that the IMF tried to help countries avoid a standstill was the fear of contagion. We believed, and continue to believe, that a standstill by one country, at a time when markets were highly sensitive, would have spread to other countries and possibly other continents. That nearly happened in October but, due to prompt and courageous action by Brazil, did not.

Of course, we cannot know what would have happened had there been no official lending in the Asian crisis. But we do know that the crisis has been contained, and it is reasonable to believe that, deep and unfortunate as the crises in individual countries have been, growth in those economies can resume soon.

Architecture of the International Financial System

After every crisis, the international community reflects on what needs to be done to reduce the probability of future crises, and to ensure that crises that do occur can be handled more effectively. After the Mexican crisis the emphasis was on better provision of information to the market. Now the focus is on the architecture of the international system, specifically *crisis prevention* through the arrangements for monitoring and regulating flows of international capital, and *crisis response* to improve the system's response when a crisis occurs.

Let me make five points on crisis prevention. First, there is a need to increase the flow of timely, accurate, and comprehensive data to the public. Through the Special Data Dissemination Standard, the IMF is encouraging countries to move toward greater transparency and fuller disclosure; and it will be necessary to strengthen the standard, for instance by providing data on forward transactions by central banks. Better data provision should lead not only to better informed investor decisions, but also to better policies by governments, for some of the off-balance-sheet activities of central banks that were instrumental in the recent crisis could not have continued for as long as they did had they been public knowledge. It is also clear from the present crisis that we need better and more timely data on short term debt exposures, not only of banks, but also of corporations. The Bank for International Settlements is already working hard to improve the short-term debt data. At the same time as we work to improve the coverage, quality, and timeliness of data, we need to recognize that data do not provide information until they are processed by human intelligence—which means we need to improve our ability to read the meaning of the data, through research into crisis indicators, and through official and private sector surveillance of the international system.

Thus, second, ways need to be found to enhance the effectiveness of Fund surveillance—by ensuring, among other things, that all the relevant data is being supplied to the Fund, that countries' exchange rate regimes are consistent with other policies, and that capital inflows are sustainable. The question, already discussed, of whether the Fund should provide more public information, and if necessary issue public warnings, is sure to be on the agenda. Many have argued that the efficient functioning of the international system requires greater transparency at the IMF itself. This is happening, and the trend should continue.

The international system also needs to monitor international capital flows far more actively, to seek to identify potential trouble spots. The provision of better data on short-term debt flows and exposures will be critical to this effort. Henry Kaufman, who has written convincingly on the need for such monitoring, has suggested we consider setting up a separate international institution for this purpose, but we are not short of international institutions and do not need another one to do this.

Third, since crises are often provoked by problems in the financial sector or intensified by them, much more needs to be done to strengthen domestic financial systems. The IMF has been working in this direction by helping to develop and disseminate a set of best practices in the banking area, so that standards and practices that have worked well in some countries can be adapted and applied in others. These standards are codified in the Basle Committee on Banking Supervision's twenty-five core principles, introduced last year. This standard-setting effort is extremely important. But the international system also needs to develop mechanisms to monitor the implementation of the standards, to help ensure that countries meet the standards to which they have subscribed. IMF surveillance will play an important role in this regard.

Fourth, we need to improve the way capital markets operate, in both advanced and emerging market countries. One possibility would be to encourage countries to adopt international standards in areas needed for the smooth operation of financial markets, such as bankruptcy codes, securities trading, and corporate governance, including accounting. Market participants would then have a clearer basis for making their lending decisions. Once again the international system would need to find a way of monitoring the implementation of these standards, and this is a formidable task. Observance of these standards would be encouraged if the risk weightings on international loans applied by bank regulators in the lending countries reflected compliance of the borrowing countries with the standards.

Fifth, the opening of countries' capital accounts should be handled prudently. This means neither a return to pervasive capital controls, nor a rush to full immediate liberalization, regardless of the risks; the need is for properly sequenced and careful liberalization, so that a larger number of countries can benefit from access to the international capital markets. In particular, macroeconomic balance and a strong and well-supervised financial system are prerequisites for successful liberalization. To facilitate this process—to encourage the *orderly* liberalization of the capital account—the IMF is at work on an amendment of its charter that will make the liberalization of capital movements a purpose of the Fund.

Some steps have been taken in the direction of crisis response. Through the creation of the Emergency Financing Mechanisms, the IMF's internal procedures for dealing with crisis situations have been streamlined, an initiative that allowed the program for Korea to be negotiated, signed, and approved in less than two weeks. The IMF has also tailored the new Supplemental Reserve Facility to fit the special circumstances of financial crises in emerging markets.

Considerable thought is also being given to finding a mechanism for involving the private sector in the resolution of financial crises in a timely way—the bail-in question, an issue that was intensively discussed after the Mexican crisis, and to which there is no easy solution. There have been many suggestions, among them that we need the equivalent of an international bankruptcy court or code, and that the international system needs to find a way to authorize a temporary stay on payments in an external financial crisis. There are formidable legal problems in this area, but the search for ways to deal with this problem must continue. Whatever solutions may be suggested, it will be important to bear in mind the dangers of contagion, the possibility that an effort to involve the private sector in solving the problems of one country will lead to capital outflows from others, thus spreading the crisis even as it may be contained in the originating country.

Finally, it should be apparent that the IMF cannot perform a central role in crisis prevention and crisis management without adequate resources, including in particular the increase in IMF quotas now being considered by the Congress.

The new architecture of the international financial system is still on the drawing board, and it remains to be seen how the international community will decide to deal with these issues, and what precisely the role of the IMF will be. But even if the IMF has its shortcomings —and like all of us, it does—it provides a flexible framework for the international community to address global economic and financial problems that exceed the capacity of individual countries to resolve alone, and for sharing fairly the burden of managing the international system. That has been the source of the strength of the IMF, an institution established more than half a century ago to help restore an international economic system ravaged by depression and war.

Under the steadfast leadership of the United States during this long period, that goal has been achieved, and we again have a truly global international system. Its benefits in improved living standards in the United States and around the world far outweigh the costs that have been evident in recent crises. But we can do better yet, and for that purpose U.S. leadership remains indispensable.

Notes

I am grateful to Mary Elizabeth Hansen for assistance. This paper was prepared for delivery as the Forum Funds Lecture at UCLA on March 20, 1998.

1. The Executive Board has 24 members, called Executive Directors, appointed by and representing the 182 member countries. Eight Executive Directors, those for the largest countries, represent only their own countries; the 16 other chairs are organized into constituencies, each representing several countries. Each country's vote is proportional to its share in the Fund, with the United States currently holding about 18 percent of the shares. A majority of 85 percent is required for most major decisions.

2. Information about Fund activities and publications is available on the Fund's website (www.imf.org).

3. Because of the lag, fast-growing countries tend to have relatively low quotas, one of the reasons that the November 1997 loan to Korea was so big relative to the country's quota.

4. Among the countries that joined the NAB when it was set up in the wake of the Mexican crisis were Korea and Thailand. They are not now in a position to lend to the Fund.

5. The full texts of the most recent letters of intent outlining their program objectives and commitments are publicly available via the IMF's web-site.

Introduction

The International Financial Institution Advisory Commission was set up as part of the agreement on an IMF quota increase reached in October 1998. The Commission, which was to report to the Congress, was chaired by Professor Allan Meltzer of Carnegie-Mellon University and the American Enterprise Institute. It was expected to make recommendations on changes in the ways the IFIs (international financial institutions) do business. Meltzer and Professor Charles Calomiris of Columbia University had already written a paper, "Reforming the IMF," arguing that the bulk of the Fund's lending should be to countries that had prequalified for loans by meeting specified criteria, especially on the strength of the banking system. If a prequalified country got into trouble, the loans would be virtually automatic.

In preparing the testimony I wanted to emphasize the frequently overlooked fact that the IMF is a cooperative institution, reform of which has to be agreed to by the membership, and cannot in any simple way be imposed by the United States. Hence the plea early in the testimony, "[I]n considering the reform of the IMF, it is important to bear in mind its cooperative nature. It is an institution with nearly universal membership, dedicated to sound economic principles that the United States has long promoted and valued. All members have an interest in the future of the Fund...."

The cooperative nature of the Fund is of fundamental importance to the way the institution works. It means, for instance, that decisions are very rarely forced through the Executive Board, and that countries seeking change are willing to go quite far to seek a Board consensus on an issue. Inevitably this means compromise on many issues. It helps explain, for instance, why the countries in favor of greater transparency did not simply force their views through the

Board once they were in a majority, but rather agreed to a period of experimentation to see whether the concerns of those opposed to greater transparency could be dealt with.

I also wanted to emphasize two other points, summarized in the first two bullet points at the start of the testimony. First, that the principles of economic policy set out in the Fund's charter are good ones, which are in the interests of all the Fund's members, and which have contributed to the unprecedented prosperity of the global economy in the last half of the twentieth century. And second, that the Fund is much more than a crisis lender. It is, in the words of Article I of the Articles of Agreement, "a permanent institution which provides the machinery for consultation and collaboration on international monetary problems." In addition to lending, the Fund undertakes surveillance of the global economy and of the economies of its member countries, and it provides technical assistance to its members, including its advanced member countries. In the testimony, I give several examples of useful surveillance and policy advice, and of technical assistance that has been provided to members. As pointed out in the chapter, the Fund spends more than twice as much on surveillance and technical assistance as it does on its lending activities.

The argument that "The IMF is one of the most effective mechanisms through which the international community promotes good macroeconomic and financial sector policies among its members" is one that I believe deeply.

I believe that Meltzer and Calomiris were right to emphasize the benefits of prequalification for loans, for this is a way of enhancing the Fund's crisis prevention role. To prequalify to obtain IMF funds in a future crisis, a country would have to strengthen its policies and its financial system in advance—rather than as now more often happens, after a crisis has already occurred. This would mean that the Fund would be using its resources to prevent crises rather than to manage them after they have already occurred. That is surely a better idea.

In 1999 the Fund set up the CCL (Contingent Credit Line) facility, which does embody the notion of prequalification. However, there have been no takers for the CCL. This must be due to design flaws. The CCL is still on the books of the Fund, and it seems the Fund may be willing to try to redesign it. But even the optimists about the CCL, of which I was one, did not believe it would ever become the predominant vehicle for Fund lending. That is because when countries get into trouble, the international community will not leave them to founder because they have not prequalified. Recognizing that, incentives need to be created for signing up for the CCL, for instance that lending rates in the event of a crisis be significantly lower for CCL countries than for countries using the other facilities of the Fund.

The report of the International Financial Institution Advisory Commission did recommend that most of the Fund's lending be done through prequalification, and it made a series of other recommendations for Fund reform, some of them covered near the end of my testimony. But while the Commission believed further major reforms were needed, it was clear from the report and the comments on it made by the members, that they believed the Fund was a necessary institution that treats its role with appropriate seriousness, that has studied the lessons of recent experience, and that continually seeks to reform itself.

4

The Role of the IMF: Presentation to the International Financial Institution Advisory Commission

Stanley Fischer

Introduction

I am grateful for this opportunity to meet with you today to discuss the reform of the international financial institutions.... I will of course focus on the role of the IMF. I would like to make four main points:

• In joining the IMF, governments subscribe to a set of principles about the operation of the international economic system that are in their mutual interest. This confers legitimacy on the pursuit of these principles by the Fund and its members. The principles include policies to promote economic growth and reasonable price stability, the desirability of an open trading system and currency convertibility, and the need to avoid competitive devaluations. The application of these principles has helped create a period of unprecedented growth and prosperity in the world economy in the last half century.

• The IMF is much more than a crisis lender. Through surveillance and technical assistance, as well as through lending, it is a powerful force for good macroeconomic policies and the prevention of crises around the world.

• The IMF also plays a role, necessarily limited, as crisis lender to governments in temporary need of foreign exchange. Recent crises have made clear the need for some changes in the way this function is carried out.

• In the wake of these crises, the IMF is being reformed and modernized, the better to carry out its functions in a rapidly changing international financial system dominated by large scale private capital flows. But the Fund is still regarded by almost all its 182 member governments as an essential component of the international financial system. So in reforming the institution, it will be important to ensure that it remains capable of carrying out the purposes for which it was established.

The Purposes of the IMF and Its Articles of Agreement

Article I of the Articles of Agreement of the IMF (see the appendix), the institution's constitution, sets out its purposes: to create a permanent institution for consultation on international monetary problems; to promote the growth of international trade, and thereby full employment and economic growth; to promote exchange stability and avoid competitive devaluations; to promote current account convertibility; and to lend under adequate safeguards to member countries, to enable them to adjust to balance of payments difficulties "without resorting to measures destructive of national or international prosperity."

The wording of this article has not changed since the founding of the Fund. Our purposes today are indeed the same as they were more than half a century ago. It is sometimes said that the Fund was set up to administer the Bretton Woods system of pegged exchange rates, and that it has been struggling to find a role for itself since that system collapsed in 1973. But the purposes of the Fund were always broader than that, and the institution has demonstrated its ability to adapt effectively to changes in the international economy. This has been true of the shift towards flexible exchange rates among the major countries after the collapse of Bretton Woods, as well as the massive increases in private international capital flows. In doing so, the Fund has remained faithful to the purposes originally laid down for it by its members.

The IMF, as originally designed and as it has evolved, is effective because its governance structure combines legitimacy, accountability, and efficiency. The Fund's legitimacy is underpinned by its near-universal membership, with every member enjoying the same rights and accepting the same responsibilities. Its legitimacy is enhanced by the cooperative working relations that exist among the 24 members of its Executive Board, who represent the 182 member countries.

The Fund is accountable to its member governments through their representatives on the Executive Board, a discipline which is strengthened by the growing transparency of its activities and decisions to the general public. And it is efficient in part because the

Executive Board has remained relatively small. This helps ensure that the Fund can act very rapidly when necessary. Weighted voting ensures that the countries which contribute most to the Fund have the greatest say in its operation.

In considering the reform of the IMF, it is important to bear in mind its cooperative nature. It is an institution with nearly universal membership, dedicated to sound economic principles that the United States has long promoted and valued. All members have an interest in the future of the Fund. All members, including the United States, have benefited from the economic growth produced by the policies that the IMF promotes around the world.

Promoting Good Policies

The IMF is one of the most effective mechanisms through which the international community promotes good macroeconomic and financial sector policies among its members. We do this in several ways.

First, there is our regular *surveillance* of economic policies and prospects. At a national level, this is undertaken through our regular Article IV consultations with member authorities. These reports present a highly professional view of the economic situation and of policy options to the country's policymakers, a view that is also commented on by the Executive Board and thus by the Fund's member governments. Article IV reports are also valuable to other members of the Fund, providing basic information on developments in individual countries. And for many countries they are virtually the only professional appraisal of their economies and economic policies.

Until recently, these reports were not published. But, with the support of the management of the Fund, that is changing. A pilot study of the publication of these reports is now under way and will be evaluated by the Executive Board as it considers whether to allow countries to publish their Article IV reports. Publication would contribute to the domestic policy debate, as well as providing information to actual and potential investors. The growing transparency of the IMF is not only desirable in its own right; it is an essential means to increasing the effectiveness of the Fund.

Surveillance also has a regional dimension, for example in dialogue with the institutions of the European or West African monetary unions. At the global level, we publish twice-annual assessments in our *World Economic Outlook* and brief the Board every few weeks. We also present appraisals of the world or regional economic situations to G-7 Finance Ministers meetings and to regional economic meetings, such as APEC and the Western Hemisphere Finance Ministers Meeting. The Fund's *International Capital Markets Report* is published annually.

Surveillance can help prevent economic problems escalating into crises. This is a vital, but often thankless, task. As with banking supervision, the failures are obvious to everyone, while the successes usually pass without notice. But there are many cases in which the Fund has provided valuable policy advice to countries without necessarily lending to them. Let me give you a few examples:

• In the mid-1990s, we worked with the Swedish authorities under our "strengthened surveillance procedures," helping them resolve a deep fiscal crisis. The cooperation between the authorities and the Fund was particularly important in securing a strengthening of their budget process.

• The current Canadian government found the IMF's analysis of its budgetary options very useful when it embarked on an aggressive fiscal consolidation in the mid-1990s. Canada continues to value its Article IV consultations, in part because they bring a perspective more sensitive to global economic developments and better informed by cross-country experience than most other analyses.

• The Fund has helped the Palestinian Authority develop a fiscal administration and procedures from scratch. We have also provided guidance on banking policies and have been instrumental in encouraging transparency and budget accountability. The Fund is now helping the Authority develop a medium-term economic and financial strategy.

• The Fund's assistance is valued in places as far afield as the small economies of the Pacific. From time to time, in addition to regular Article IV consultations, the Fund has been asked by the authorities in this region to assess their macroeconomic frameworks, to assist them in repositioning economic policy, and to establish financial stability as a precondition for aid flows. Without an ongoing supportive relationship with the Fund, it would also have been impossible for many of the small central banks in the region to adopt market-based methods of monetary management.

Second, in addition to surveillance, we provide *technical assistance* to governments and central banks, not all of them Fund borrowers. We help countries develop and maintain an effective policy-making capacity. The advanced industrialized countries take this type of infrastructure for granted, but its absence is a critical hindrance to good policy-making in many other IMF member countries.

Again, let me give you a few examples:

• We helped set up modern statistical systems in the transition economies, an essential foundation for economic monitoring and policy-making. Through technical assistance associated with the Special Data Dissemination Standard (SDDS), we have helped many industrialized and emerging market countries upgrade the quality and presentation of their data systems.

• The Fund is providing technical assistance in the areas of banking regulation, supervision, and payments systems to the countries of the Southern African Development Community, led in this case by the South African Reserve Bank.

• The Fund recently provided a technical assistance mission in Chile to facilitate reform of public expenditure management. It identified directions for reform in several areas, such as transparency, accounting, and reporting systems.

• In Bulgaria, following the collapse of the country's financial system, the Fund helped strengthen banking supervision, to restore health to the banking system as the currency board system was introduced. The Fund also helped in other areas, such as fiscal policy and the mechanics of monetary policy.

• In Brazil, we helped the authorities develop and implement a sound inflation targeting regime. Last spring, for example, we helped organize a seminar with the Central Bank of Brazil, gathering experts on inflation targeting from around the world. We played a similar role in Colombia and maintain close relationships with many central banks to exchange ideas on how this sort of regime can be made to work better.

IMF surveillance and technical assistance make a valuable contribution to the well-being of the world economy. They are generally greatly appreciated by our members, but rarely get sufficient recognition outside the policy-making community. The IMF devotes more than twice as many staff resources to surveillance and technical assistance, taken together, as it does to the operation of its lending programs. In my view, this is time and money well spent. The increasing trend towards publishing Article IV reports and other IMF surveillance reports should enhance not only the effectiveness of surveillance but also public appreciation of its importance.

The IMF also promotes good policies through the conditions that we attach to our loans. I will turn shortly to our crisis lending. Before that I would like to discuss loans that we may make to countries that are not in financial crisis. It may be useful to distinguish three categories of these countries: the poorest, including those now receiving debt relief under the Heavily-Indebted Poor Countries (HIPC) initiative; the post-Communist transition economies; and other countries in difficulty but not in a financial crisis.

First, the IMF lends to the poorest countries on concessional terms, originally under the Enhanced Structural Adjustment Facility (ESAF), and now under the Poverty Reduction and Growth Facility (PRGF). The PRGF has recently been introduced in conjunction with the enhanced debt reduction scheme for heavily indebted poor countries. In these cases direct anti-poverty measures are to play a central role in programs supported by the World Bank, the IMF, and other lenders. In preparing these programs, member governments are expected to consult widely with relevant stakeholders, to help ensure widespread support, and hence country ownership, for them. Country ownership has proven to be a vital factor in determining the success of stabilization and reform efforts supported by the international organizations.

In the context of the enhanced HIPC initiative, PRGF programs provide a framework to ensure macroeconomic stability and medium-term viability. Such a framework is needed for at least two reasons. First, macroeconomic stability is necessary for sustained growth and the efficient use of resources—all the more essential in very poor countries where the very few resources available need to be used efficiently. Second, since the international community will be providing large amounts of assistance to these countries—in debt relief or other aid—the creditor countries need assurance that the resources they provide will be used in a stable macroeconomic environment. The IMF can help provide these assurances. The IMF will have to certify that a country's macroeconomic policies are satisfactory before debt relief can be granted or new concessional lending provided. Otherwise the country might not make a lasting exit from its debt problems into sustained growth and poverty reduction.

Close coordination and a clear delineation of responsibilities between the IMF and the World Bank is essential. The World Bank will take the lead in helping countries formulate their poverty reduction strategies and in lending for those purposes. For its part, the IMF has to take into account the fiscal implications of anti-poverty programs when designing the macroeconomic framework. Together with the World Bank, it needs to ensure that the impact of the necessary macroeconomic measures on the poor has been properly analyzed and the potential adverse effects minimized—the latter typically by means of World Bank–supported programs.

Second, the IMF lends to the transition economies: The collapse of the Soviet Bloc created an unprecedented situation in which it was necessary to transform the economies of over twenty-five countries, which had turned to the rest of the world for support. Within the official sector, the IMF and the World Bank were asked to take the lead in assisting the transition economies, both in designing programs and providing financial assistance. The European Bank for Reconstruction and Development was created to strengthen that effort and to encourage private sector investment.

The Bretton Woods institutions were given the primary role in these countries only in part because of their financial resources. More importantly, they had the right combination of institutional procedures—program preparation, missions, policy discussions and agreements with the country, then discussion and approval of programs by their boards, followed by periodic review. It would have been necessary to reinvent these procedures had the task been given to any other organization.

Although there was little precedent for an effort of this type, a professional consensus developed rapidly. The transition countries needed both macroeconomic stabilization and massive structural reform. This included the development of essential institutions, including an effective financial sector and an appropriate legal framework. It was recognized that the structural reform process was bound to take a long time.

Analysis of the first ten years of the transition process confirms these conclusions. The leading transition economies, such as the Czech Republic, Estonia, Hungary, and Poland, followed this path and are well on their ways to becoming developed market economies and joining the European Union. All countries except Slovenia had programs with the IMF. As macroeconomic stabilization and structural reforms took hold, the need for IMF financial involvement declined. Even so, Estonia and Latvia have continued to have pre-cautionary Fund arrangements. Though they do not intend to draw on Fund resources, they value the framework offered by a program supported by the IMF and the reassurance the markets find in knowing the countries have such a framework in place.

Progress in other transition countries varies greatly. In many countries, especially in the Commonwealth of Independent States, reform and growth has been held back. Progress has been impeded by the absence of an effective political consensus on the way ahead, as well as struggles over the control of national resources (which have often involved corruption). It is far more difficult to assist such countries effectively.

The international organizations, as well as individual member governments, have sought to support reformist policies. We have tried to help countries develop the necessary institutional frame-works, including measures to strengthen legal systems and to en-hance transparency and thereby fight corruption. There has been some progress in almost all transition countries, including impor-tantly Russia and Ukraine. But much remains to be done, and important questions remain about the most effective ways to support economic reform in these countries. The Bretton Woods institutions are likely to remain heavily involved in trying to help the lagging economies move more rapidly along the path of transition. But that will only be possible if the countries pursue reform programs and stick to their commitments.

Third, the IMF sometimes lends to countries not in a crisis but experiencing significant economic difficulties. Why should the Fund lend to countries that, while in difficulty, are not in an immedi-ate crisis? Either to prevent a potential crisis or to provide a framework—agreed with the country—in which policy will be con-ducted for some period ahead. In these cases the IMF provides an external constraint on policy that is useful to domestic policymakers in implementing necessary but often painful reforms. The Fund's involvement instills confidence in both domestic residents and for-eign investors that the policy framework will be implemented. In more technical language, such programs serve as both commitment and signaling devices.

Why is this possible? Because an IMF program provides a mecha-nism that ensures that policy commitments will be monitored and reviewed, in the first instance by the staff and then by the Board of the IMF, representing the international community. To return to the theme of transparency, this function is bound to be more effective if the details of the program are publicly known. This is one of the reasons why recent progress in securing the publication of country agreements with the IMF—their Letters of Intent—is so important.

This type of lending is exemplified by the programs that the IMF has recently agreed to support in Turkey and Colombia. In cases like these the Fund provides financial support to countries that have shown themselves prepared to implement sound policies. Sometimes countries find that an IMF-supported program provides the framework for a coherent attack on long-standing problems that had hitherto appeared intractable. This appears to be the case in the recent program with Turkey. Of course, the use of constraints on the policy process is not unusual, for instance balanced budget laws or the accession process for European Monetary Union.

Could one not rely on IMF certification to achieve this, without lending? The Fund does use the certification approach on occasion. Staff-monitored programs are sometimes used to establish a track record of performance before a loan agreement is negotiated. But governments and markets alike appear to place greater value on financial agreements with the Fund, possibly because the provision of resources is still seen to represent a greater commitment by the official sector. Precautionary arrangements—and a modified Contingent Credit Line facility—also offer the scope to provide effective international support for a policy framework, without necessarily lending.

It might be asked that if the Fund is lending in non-crisis situations, what prevents it lending to too many countries? The Fund is constrained by its Articles of Agreement only to lend to countries with a balance-of-payments need. In addition, countries generally seek to avoid getting into IMF arrangements, or to get out of them as soon as possible, because they typically dislike operating under the constraints of policy conditionality. Nonetheless, a few countries have become repeated borrowers. The issue of repeated borrowing needs to be dealt with. Countries need to be encouraged to move towards dependence on the markets rather than the official sector.

Do IMF-supported programs work? Attempts to assess their impact definitively have long been hampered by the problem of the counterfactual—our inability to know how a program country would have performed had it not come to the Fund. Recent studies try to address this issue by estimating policy-reaction functions for program and non-program countries.

These analyses indicate that IMF programs have been more successful than earlier empirical studies suggested. The consensus view now seems to be that in a typical program, economic activity will be depressed in the short term as macroeconomic policies are tightened, but that growth subsequently revives as structural reforms take root. Meanwhile the balance of payments improves, removing the need for further Fund financing. The impact on inflation is usually favorable (although in general not large enough to be statistically significant).

Crisis Lending

Let me now turn to the question of the IMF's role in crisis situations. I believe the world *does* need an official sector lender to countries facing an external payments crisis. This is necessary because international capital flows have proven extremely volatile and contagious. In many cases capital outflows from particular emerging markets have been an understandable response to the sudden revelation or gradual development of poor economic fundamentals. But the scale and sometimes indiscriminate character of these outflows are also classic signs of financial panic.

One option would be to impose extensive controls on capital flows. But while the Fund has supported the use of some Chilean-style market-based controls on capital inflows for countries whose financial systems are not yet sufficiently robust, the imposition of extensive controls would sacrifice most of the potential benefits of international capital mobility. Despite the recent crises, almost all emerging market countries have rejected the comprehensive capital control approach.

This enhances the need for an institution that can lend foreign exchange to countries experiencing an external payments crisis. The Fund already plays this role. But the experience of the recent crises has revealed the need to strengthen the Fund's approach in this area—particularly in reforming its lending facilities, and in seeking appropriate private sector involvement in the resolution of crises.

The Supplemental Reserve Facility was introduced in 1997, and the Contingent Credit Line (CCL) facility last year. The SRF is intended for countries experiencing exceptional balance-of-payments problems created by a large short-term financing need, arising from a sudden loss of market confidence. The SRF is likely to be used when a country's outflows are large enough to create a risk of contagion that could threaten the international monetary system. To minimize moral hazard, a member using the SRF is encouraged to maintain the participation of both official and private creditors.

Countries drawing under the SRF are expected to repay within 12–18 months, although the Board can extend this repayment period by up to one year. For the first year, members are subject to a surcharge of 300 basis points above the regular rate of charge on IMF loans. This surcharge is increased by 50 basis points at the end of that period and every six months thereafter until it reaches 500 basis points.

The CCL is intended as a preventative measure for countries concerned about their vulnerability to contagion, but not facing an imminent crisis. The cost and repayment terms of drawing on the CCL are the same as for loans under the SRF. The facility, like the SRF, is not subject to normal access access limits, although the amount available will normally be between three and five times the country's quota.

These facilities move in the direction of Bagehot's classic prescriptions for the lender of last resort, lending large amounts on relatively short term at penalty rates. The SRF was used in lending to Korea, Russia, and Brazil. No country has yet applied for a CCL.

The question frequently arises of whether the IMF operates as an international lender of last resort. In acting as a crisis lender, and crisis manager, the IMF does fulfill critical lender-of-last-resort functions. But unlike a domestic central bank that operates as lender of last resort in its own currency, the Fund's resources available for lending are strictly limited. For this reason, and to reduce moral hazard to the extent possible, it will be necessary in some circumstances to ensure that the private sector contributes to crisis resolution.

Private sector involvement in the prevention and resolution of financial crises remains one of the most difficult issues in the reform of the international system. On prevention, it has been suggested that in the future, international bond and other financial contracts should be designed to make it easier to restructure external obligations in the event of a crisis. The British government has recently included a collective action clause in one of its foreign currency bond issues, and it is to be hoped that this example encourages others to follow.

Measures to involve the private sector together with the official sector in the financing of the balance of payments were included in the responses to the Korean, Thai, and Brazilian crises. Further experience has been gained in the very different cases of Ecuador, Pakistan, Romania, and Ukraine. In the next few months, the IMF staff will seek to draw the lessons of these experiences for the consideration of the Executive Board on how best to deal with this difficult but critical issue.

The Bagehot rules of course also require loans to be made on the basis of good collateral. The Articles of Agreement permit the Fund to ask for collateral, but it has rarely done so. In an important sense, the Fund gets collateral through its preferred creditor status. It gains added reassurance from the adjustment programs to which countries commit themselves when borrowing from the Fund, which should improve the balance of payments and enable the country to repay.

Professors Calomiris and Meltzer address the question of collateral in their paper, *Reforming the IMF*. Their suggestions would require countries to hold larger amounts of short-term foreign assets, which is typically very expensive, and could possibly be substituted for by contingent credit lines, private or public. Nonetheless they are certainly right to suggest that some countries would be better off holding larger usable reserves, a conclusion that Korea for example has clearly drawn from its recent experiences.

They also raise the related question of whether countries should be required to prequalify for the IMF's financial support in crisis situations. This important idea is incorporated in the design of the CCL. Countries wishing to secure credit lines through this mechanism have to meet a variety of conditions in advance. These include a favorable review from its latest Article IV consultation, progress in adhering to international standards, good relations with creditors, and sound management of its external debt and reserves. To draw on the credit line, the country will also have to demonstrate its willingness to adjust its policies as necessary.

While prequalification provides important incentives for the adoption of good policies, is it realistic to make all other countries ineligible for any type of lender-of-last-resort financing? It is doubtful that the international community would be indifferent to the fate of countries that do not meet the prequalification requirements, or to the instability that might be generated when they get into trouble and are denied help. In practice, in such circumstances the large industrial countries would probably find another, less transparent, way to help a country in crisis. An alternative approach to pre-qualification would be to differentiate the terms on which assistance is provided, for instance by charging a premium to countries that fail to meet certain standards or requirements.

Reforming the IMF

The international community has learned many lessons from the turbulent events that have taken place in emerging markets over the last three years. With the support and encouragement of our members, the IMF has already been taking important steps to reform itself in the light of those lessons. Let me briefly mention some of the reforms under way in four areas: efforts to strengthen macro-economic policies and financial sectors; strengthening surveillance and increasing transparency—both central to increasing the effective-ness of the Fund; restructuring IMF lending facilities; and sharpen-ing the focus of IMF activities.

On macroeconomic policies, the recent crises have thrown a sharp light on the key role of the exchange rate system. It is a fact that all the countries that had major international crises had relied on a pegged or fixed exchange rate system before the crisis; and it is also true that some countries that appeared vulnerable but that had flex-ible exchange rates avoided such crises. Countries with very hard pegs have been able to sustain them. Accordingly, we are likely to see emerging market countries moving towards the two extremes, of either a flexible rate or a very hard peg—and in the long run, the trend is most likely to be toward fewer currencies.

The central importance of the strength of the financial sector is another lesson of the crisis. That is one reason why the economic cost of Brazil's crisis was smaller than that of the Asian crisis coun-tries. Together with the World Bank, generally with the assistance of experts from central banks and financial regulatory agencies in other countries, the IMF has begun to undertake assessments of the strength of financial systems in member countries. These include an evaluation of the extent to which the relevant international stan-dards, including the Basel core principles, are being observed. The assessments are presented to the country as a guide to the measures needed to strengthen the financial system. The conclusions are also incorporated in Article IV reports. So far twelve such assessments have been completed or are under way, for countries ranging from Canada to Cameroon.

Surveillance and transparency are keys to enhancing Fund effectiveness, both because they will encourage better informed policy debates and therefore better policy, and because in improving information to investors, they will help make capital markets more efficient.

As I noted earlier, the fruits of IMF surveillance are disseminated much more widely than they used to be. Public Information Notices summarizing the outcome of Article IV consultations with member countries are now published in around 80 percent of cases. More than fifty countries also have agreed to participate in a pilot project to publish the staff reports that are prepared as background for Article IV consultations in the Fund board.

More information is also being published on the policy programs that IMF lending supports. Letters of Intent are now being published for around 80 percent of requests for or reviews of the use of Fund resources. We are also publishing more staff papers on policy issues—for example, the use of capital controls—as well as regular data on the Fund's liquidity and available resources.

On the substance of surveillance, the Fund is placing greater emphasis on a number of policy areas shown to be especially important by the emerging market crisis. These include capital account and financial sector issues, the sustainability of exchange rate regimes, debt and reserve management practices, and vulnerability analyses. We are also focussing more on the regional dimension of surveillance and exploiting more effectively the Fund's comparative advantage in cross-country comparisons.

The Fund is more effectively integrating international standards and codes of conduct into its surveillance. These standards cover areas such as statistical dissemination, banking supervision and the transparency of monetary and fiscal policies. Several countries have already taken part in an experiment to collate information on compliance in these areas into Reports on the Observance of Standards and Codes (ROSCs), formerly known as transparency reports.

As I noted earlier, since the outbreak of the Asian crisis, the Fund has adopted two facilities that incorporate elements of lender-of-last-resort lending: the Supplemental Reserve Facility (SRF) and the Contingent Credit Line (CCL) facility.

Although the SRF has been used, the CCL has not, and it is clear that it will need to be redesigned when it is reviewed during the spring. There are two key areas for reform. First, since the interest rates are the same for the CCL as for the SRF, there is no financial incentive to prequalify for the CCL rather than await the potential use of the SRF if a crisis were to break out. Second, there may be a need to make access to the line of credit more automatic when a crisis breaks out.

In addition to creating new facilities appropriate to a world of large and volatile capital flows, the Fund needs to reduce the number of its facilities and reconsider the design of the remainder. The executive board agreed last month to eliminate the Buffer Stock Financing Facility. There was also a broad consensus in favor of eliminating the contingency element of the Compensatory and Contingency Financing Facility. The appropriateness of all the Fund's lending mechanisms will be scrutinized in a review getting under way in the run-up to our spring meetings.

The IMF's focus must be on macroeconomic policies and the accompanying structural areas—on monetary, fiscal, and exchange rate policies, and on the banking and financial sectors. In the financial sector, there is considerable overlap with the activities of the World Bank, and we have in the last few years cooperated extremely effectively with the Bank in this area.

Those must remain the areas of our lending activities, and the prime focus of our surveillance. But the recent crises have also driven home the lesson that the IMF must take into account the social consequences of the macroeconomic policies it recommends, and the fiscal and other macroeconomic consequences of the social policies its members need to implement. Lending and the design of programs in these areas remains the responsibility of the World Bank and other agencies.

Conclusion

I will conclude, as you would expect, by arguing that the IMF has and will continue to have a vital role in the international financial system. The purposes for which the Fund was established remain valid, and we have proved to be a valuable instrument through which the international community has improved macroeconomic policies, encouraged the growth of international trade, and assisted countries in difficulties.

The recent crises have posed difficult new challenges, to which we responded swiftly; we are now seeing the benefits of most of the policies we recommended. But the crises also revealed the need for reform of the Fund and its activities. The process of reform is now well under way, but far from complete.

Appendix: Articles of Agreement of the International Monetary Fund, Article I

Purposes

The purposes of the International Monetary Fund are:

(i) To promote international monetary cooperation through a permanent institution which provides the machinery for consultation and collaboration on international monetary problems.

(ii) To facilitate the expansion and balanced growth of international trade, and to contribute thereby to the promotion and maintenance of high levels of employment and real income and to the development of the productive resources of all members as primary objectives of economic policy.

(iii) To promote exchange stability, to maintain orderly exchange arrangements among members, and to avoid competitive exchange depreciation.

(iv) To assist in the establishment of a multilateral system of payments in respect of current transactions between members and in the elimination of foreign exchange restrictions which hamper the growth of world trade.

(v) To give confidence to members by making the general resources of the Fund temporarily available to them under adequate safeguards, thus providing them with opportunity to correct maladjustments in their balance of payments without resorting to measures destructive of national or international prosperity.

(vi) In accordance with the above, to shorten the duration and lessen the degree of disequilibrium in the international balances of payments of members.

The Fund shall be guided in all its policies and decisions by the purposes set forth in this Article.

5   *Introduction*

In April 1997 the Interim Committee of the IMF agreed that the Fund's Articles of Agreement should be amended to make the liberalization of international capital movements a central purpose of the Fund, and to extend the Fund's jurisdiction to capital movements. The original Articles of Agreement put current account convertibility and trade liberalization at the center of the Fund's mandate, and the intention of the amendment was to broaden the mandate.

The timing could hardly have been worse. A few months later the Asian crisis erupted, wreaking havoc on economies that had to that point been growing very fast. Massive capital flow reversals played a precipitating role in the crisis, and contagion among capital flows transmitted the crisis from Thailand to its ASEAN neighbors and Korea. Amendment of the Articles would have required parliamentary action by nearly all the Fund's member countries, and with capital flows widely seen as the villain of the crisis, the appetite of the IMF's members for the capital flow amendment disappeared. It shows no sign of reappearing.

Nonetheless, I believe that the concept of the capital account amendment was a good one. For, as emphasized in this chapter, the goal was to ensure *orderly* capital account liberalization. By this the IMF meant that capital account liberalization should be well sequenced, and occur only when the necessary preconditions are in place. The preconditions are spelled out in this chapter: strong macroeconomic policies, a strong banking and financial system, and adequate transparency and provision of information. In terms of sequencing, the general recommendation is to open at the long end first, starting with foreign direct investment, and to open to short term capital movements only when the macroeconomic and financial sector preconditions are met.

In both Thailand and Korea, capital account liberalization had not been done well; rather, each country had opened up at the short end without having the necessary preconditions in place. This type of liberalization would have been discouraged had the capital account amendment and the approach to capital account liberalization laid out in this chapter been in place.

Critics of the capital account amendment believe it would lead the Fund to press relentlessly for capital account liberalization. That was not the conception we had inside the Fund. Rather, the Fund in recent years has argued for the slow liberalization of the capital account, and has supported controls on inflows under some circumstances.

We believed that we would have to develop the analogues for the capital account of the present Articles VIII and XIV that apply to the current account. A country that has current account restrictions in place may maintain them under Article XIV. When it is ready, it declares that it accepts Article VIII, which prohibits the imposition of controls on current account transactions. After nearly sixty years, some countries still have not accepted Article VIII. If there were a capital account liberalization amendment, a country could maintain restrictions under the equivalent of Article XIV. When it was ready to begin liberalizing capital movements, it could declare acceptance of some interim state; and eventually it would accept the equivalent of Article VIII.

Of course, capital account liberalization is only a suitable aim for the Fund if it brings benefits to countries that implement it. I make the argument for capital account liberalization in this chapter. I believe the empirical evidence on its benefits gradually is becoming more solidly in favor of liberalization, provided it is done correctly.[1]

This chapter starts by predicting that the slowdown of international capital flows associated with the Asian crisis would probably be temporary. That has not happened. Flows did recover quite quickly in 1999 and 2000 but never reached their previous peak levels. They are not likely to do so until global growth recovers.

Note

1. See for instance Hali J. Edison, Michael W. Klein, Luca Ricci, and Torsten Sloek, "Capital Account Liberalization and Economic Performance: Survey and Synthesis," NBER Working Paper 9100, August 2002.

5 Capital Account Liberalization and the Role of the IMF

Stanley Fischer

This Fifty-Second Annual Meeting of the IMF and World Bank is taking place at a time of profound change in East Asia, propelled by an astonishing record of sustained economic growth, which within less than two decades has improved the living standards of more people, more rapidly, than at any other time or place in history. For the IMF, Hong Kong has for months appeared likely to be the meeting of the capital account and of Fund resources—the annual meeting at which our Executive Board would be given the mandate to complete its work on an amendment of the Articles of Agreement to promote capital account liberalization, and at which agreement could be reached on a quota increase and a special issue of SDRs. Coming a little over fifty years after the original Articles of Agreement put current account convertibility and trade liberalization at the center of the Fund's mandate, and at a time when the globalization of capital markets proceeds apace, the capital account amendment and the increase in resources would enable the Fund to play its full part in promoting the orderly liberalization of international capital markets.

But the recent market turmoil in the region has raised two fundamental sets of questions: the first, about the sustainability of the Asian miracle; and the second, about the risks of capital account liberalization. I will not discuss the Asian miracle, except to record my firm belief that, after a relatively brief pause, rapid growth will resume in those economies now adjusting to recent shocks, home- and foreign-made. And there is no reason that growth in other parts of Asia, most notably in India, should not increase to and be sustained in the range of 6–8 percent per annum. It is just a matter of policy—of the right macroeconomic policies, of accelerating market-oriented structural reforms, of improving education, and of opening up to trade and foreign investment.

My main focus today will be on the capital account. The question is whether the recent market turbulence in the region—the attacks on the Thai baht and its devaluation, the subsequent devaluations of other currencies in the region, and the contagion effects that have been present in East Asia in 1997, just as they were in Latin America in 1995, and perhaps also in Europe in 1993—does not suggest that the capital account is more often the source of economic difficulties and risk rather than benefit, and therefore that capital account liberalization should be put off as long as possible. If that were so, perhaps the proposed capital account amendment of the Fund's Articles of Agreement would be unnecessary, and everybody—not least the Fund's overworked Legal Department—could be saved a great deal of effort.

You will not be surprised to hear that I emphatically reject this view. But the concerns of those policymakers who fear some of the consequences of capital account liberalization cannot and should not be lightly dismissed. What I would like to do is to persuade those of you who remain skeptical about capital account liberalization of three things:

• that the benefits of liberalizing the capital account outweigh the potential costs;

• that countries need to prepare well for capital account liberalization: economic policies and institutions, particularly the financial system, need to be adapted to operate in a world of liberalized capital markets; and

• that an amendment of the IMF's Articles of Agreement is the best way of ensuring that capital account liberalization is carried out in an orderly, nondisruptive way that minimizes the risks that premature liberalization could pose for an economy and its policymakers.

In making this argument, I will also touch on several critical issues about international capital movements that recent crises have put on the policy agenda. I must, though, apologize in advance for raising more questions than I can answer.

The Growth of Capital Movements

First, some background facts and forecasts: Both gross and net international capital flows have increased markedly in recent years, and for many countries capital movements have been a critical factor in the balance of payments. Average annual net capital inflows to developing countries exceeded $150 billion in 1990–1996. After a pause in the first half of 1995 following the Mexican crisis, the pace of inflows to developing countries recovered, and has continued to increase since then. A net total of $235 billion in foreign capital flowed to developing countries in 1996, and this rate of flow appears to have been sustained in the first half of 1997. This is not a small amount: it is nearly 0.8 percent of world GDP, and well above 2 percent of developing country GDP.

Asia, in particular, has benefited from recent capital inflows, receiving more than $60 billion a year in 1990–1996, and a total of $107 billion in 1996. Asia has received a higher proportion of foreign direct investment, 55 percent of total capital inflows, than other regions. Net inflows to some countries in this region have averaged 5–8 percent of GDP over long periods, often with much of that taking the form of foreign direct investment.

Why have global capital flows increased so much? Let me mention four factors:

• first, rates of return in recipient countries. Capital inflows have responded favorably to successful stabilization and reform efforts. In some cases, especially where the flexibility of the exchange rate has been limited by policy, short-term capital has been attracted by high interest rates needed to fight inflation;

• second, the liberalization of international capital transactions by both industrial and developing countries. Indeed, in some cases the liberalization of capital outflows has strengthened the capital account by encouraging both foreign investment and a return of flight capital;

• third, the development of stronger financial systems in recipient countries; and

• fourth, external factors—including the declining trend in longer-term interest rates in the advanced economies over the last decade, and the emergence of large institutional investors in industrial countries.

International capital flows have by no means reached their peak. Portfolios in the advanced countries are still insufficiently diversified

internationally; and the residents of developing countries likewise
have much to gain from investing in capital markets in other countries. We can be sure that the volume of gross international capital
flows will continue to increase, as information about the potential of
developing country markets spreads, as transaction costs continue to
decline, and as the liberalization and sophistication of capital markets in developing and advanced countries continue to grow.

Benefits and Risks of Capital Account Liberalization

There are two arguments in favor of capital account liberalization.
The first is that it is an inevitable step on the path of development,
which cannot be avoided and therefore should be adapted to. In
support of this view, we may note that all the most advanced
economies have open capital accounts. This is a powerful argument,
and a correct one, even if it begs the question of how rapidly the
inevitable has to be accepted. But while sufficient, it is not as satisfactory as the second argument, that on balance the benefits of capital account liberalization outweigh its costs.

Put abstractly, free capital movements facilitate a more efficient
global allocation of savings and help channel resources into their
most productive uses, thus increasing economic growth and welfare.
From the individual country's perspective, the benefits take the form
of increases in both the potential pool of investable funds and the
access of domestic residents to foreign capital markets. From the
viewpoint of the international economy, open capital accounts support the multilateral trading system by broadening the channels
through which developed and developing countries alike can finance
trade and investment and attain higher levels of income. International capital flows have expanded the opportunities for portfolio
diversification, and thereby provided investors with a potential to
achieve higher risk-adjusted rates of returns. And just as current
account liberalization promotes growth by increasing access to
sophisticated technology, and export competition has improved
domestic technology, so capital account liberalization can increase
the efficiency of the domestic financial system.

Abstract as these arguments may sound, they have concrete coun-
terparts in the real world. Access to global savings means in part
foreign direct investment, about the benefits of which there is no
longer any serious controversy. Governments all over the world

borrow in the Euro-markets, gaining access to cheaper financing than they might be able to obtain domestically. Domestic corporations likewise can obtain cheaper and more sophisticated financing by borrowing abroad. The new financial technologies that accompany the entry of foreign participants in domestic markets can upgrade the entire financial system. Residents of countries that permit portfolio investment abroad can hold more diversified, less risky portfolios. These are not abstract concepts, but benefits that every country represented in this room has enjoyed as a result of its access to the international capital markets.

Still, what about the risks? International capital flows tend to be highly sensitive to the conduct of macroeconomic policies, the perceived soundness of the domestic banking system, and unforeseen economic and political developments. Accordingly, market forces should be expected to exert a disciplining influence on countries' macroeconomic policies. Normally, when the market's judgment is right, this discipline is a valuable one, which improves overall economic performance by rewarding good policies and penalizing bad. Of course, policymakers do not always welcome discipline of which they are the object, even if it is appropriate; nor are they likely to admit when trouble comes that the capital markets were only the messenger, delivering a verdict on their performance. Rather they may be tempted to shoot the messenger.

However, markets are not always right. Sometimes inflows are excessive, and sometimes they may be sustained too long. Markets tend to react late; but then they tend to react fast, and sometimes excessively. Of most concern, market overreactions sometimes take the form of contagion effects, spillovers from a crisis in one market to other, related, markets. Some spillovers are entirely rational and efficient—for instance, when a country devalues, the equilibrium exchange rate for its competitors may also depreciate. But sometimes, including to some extent in the recent East Asian crisis, and certainly in the attack on Argentina in 1995, contagion effects seem to be overreactions, perhaps based on incomplete information, perhaps a result of herd behavior, perhaps based on an inaccurate appraisal of the underlying economic situation. Contagion effects are all the more worrying in light of the possibility that attacks become self-fulfilling prophecies, for instance, because the banking system weakens in the face of an attack that forces a devaluation and higher interest rates.[1]

While I believe we sometimes see examples of market overreactions and unjustified contagion effects, I also believe that capital movements are mostly appropriate: currency crises do not blow up out of a clear blue sky, but rather start as rational reactions to policy mistakes or external shocks. The problem is that once started, they may sometimes go too far.

To sum up: Liberalization of the capital account can bring major benefits to countries whose residents and governments are able to borrow and lend on more favorable terms, in more sophisticated markets, whose own financial markets will become more efficient as a result of the introduction of advanced financial technologies—and who for all those reasons will attain a better allocation of both saving and investment, and will therefore grow more rapidly in a more sustainable manner. These gains have been seen all over the world where countries have accessed the international capital markets and allowed foreign competition in their own capital markets—and they have certainly been seen in Asia in the last two decades. At the same time, capital account liberalization increases the vulnerability of the economy to swings in market sentiment. Almost always these swings are rationally based, but they may on occasion be excessive, and they may sometimes reflect contagion effects, which may themselves be excessive on occasion. This is a valid concern to those contemplating capital account liberalization, and for the international community.

Managing a Liberalized System

What is the right response to operating in a system that offers major benefits, but that may penalize mistakes severely, and occasionally burden the economy with inappropriate shocks? The prime need obviously is to avoid policies that can cause rapid capital flow reversals, and to strengthen the structure of the economy and its policy framework so as minimize its vulnerability to sudden changes in market sentiment. Some of what needs to be done is well known and uncontroversial, in particular:

• to pursue sound macroeconomic policies;

• to strengthen the domestic financial system; and

• to phase capital account liberalization appropriately—which means retaining some capital controls in the transition.

There are also more controversial questions about:

- the provision of information to the markets;
- the role of surveillance; and
- the potential need for financing.

Let me take these topics up in turn, touching lightly on those elements on which there is a well-understood consensus, emphasizing rather the more novel or controversial points.

The Macroeconomic Policy Framework

A sound macroeconomic policy framework is one that promotes growth by keeping inflation low, the budget deficit small, and the current account sustainable. As a formal matter of debt dynamics, the sustainability of the current account depends on the economy's growth rate and the real interest rate at which the country can borrow. But sustainability has another sense, of the ability to withstand shocks, and that is less susceptible to formal analysis. In any case, large current account deficits—depending on the growth rate of the economy, in the range of 5–8 percent of GDP, and certainly any higher—should be cause for concern. Current account deficits financed by longer-term borrowing and in particular by foreign direct investment are more sustainable; sizable deficits financed in large part by short-term capital flows are a cause for alarm.

It is sometimes difficult to deal with short-term capital inflows that are a response to high domestic interest rates, particularly in a context in which policy limits exchange rate flexibility. This is the famous capital inflows problem that so many countries seeking to stabilize from moderate rates of inflation have faced. There is no easy answer to this problem, but a tightening of fiscal policy is the first line of defense. A second response is to increase the flexibility of the exchange rate.

How flexible should exchange rates be? The recent experience of East Asia has reopened the question of whether any form of fixed exchange rate system is consistent with free capital mobility. The Group of Seven countries, except for those intending to join the European Economic and Monetary Union (EMU), long ago decided on flexible rates. But freely floating rates, even among the major currencies, have moved excessively, and no developing country

seeking growth through integration into the world economy would
want to live with such fluctuations. East Asian countries were well
served over a long period by exchange rate systems that either fixed
the exchange rate or limited its flexibility, thus providing exporters
and importers with a measure of exchange rate certainty that facili-
tated their participation in the international economy. Nonetheless,
those countries that allowed the rate to float when threatened by an
imminent speculative attack made the right choice.

As more normal conditions return, the question of the optimal
exchange rate system will be back on the agenda. There is no generally agreed answer to that question. Some conclusions are easy: if
the exchange rate is pegged, it is almost certainly better to peg to a
basket of currencies rather than a single currency. Beyond that, it
may be that countries will return to some form of exchange rate
band, with very wide margins, perhaps—depending on domestic
inflation—a crawling band. If they do, they should stand ready if
circumstances warrant, to move the band. In any case, the level of
the exchange rate is bound to be a concern for policymakers, particularly in developing countries relying on export-led growth, and
macroeconomic policy needs to be adjusted when the exchange rate
(equivalently the balance of payments) shows signs of moving out of
desired ranges.

Strengthening the Financial Sector

The critical role of the strength of the financial system was becoming
clear before the Mexican crisis; it was crystal clear in that crisis and
its aftermath; and it has been equally clear in the Thai crisis and
its aftermath. The Fund staff's important paper, "Toward a Framework for Financial Stability," provides a detailed analysis of what
is required for a healthy banking and financial system. By now, policymakers have a good idea of what needs to be done to strengthen
financial systems, by improving supervision and prudential standards, by ensuring that banks meet capital requirements, provision
for bad loans, limit connected lending, publish informative financial
information, and by ensuring that insolvent institutions are dealt
with rapidly. Implementing those changes, particularly in a banking
system already in trouble, is frequently difficult, especially where
political pressures hamper the supervisory authorities. The task is
nonetheless urgent, both in countries now seeking to recover from

recent crises, and those that seek to avoid future crises: it cannot be emphasized strongly enough that a healthy banking and financial system is essential for the growth of the economy, and that a weak banking system is both a standing invitation to a macroeconomic crisis and a guarantee of the severity of any such crisis.

Phasing and the Use of Controls

There are obvious dangers in liberalizing capital movements in an economy in which the macroeconomic framework and the financial sector are weak. There is thus a case for phasing capital account liberalization, paying due regard to the country's macroeconomic situation (including the balance of payments), the stage of development of its financial markets and institutions, and the impact of existing controls. But in this area, as in the case of more familiar structural reforms, there are few hard and fast rules, and some countries—notably Indonesia—successfully liberalized the capital account very early in the reform process.

Absent the coordination of capital account liberalization and financial sector reform, there may be regulatory distortions and regulatory incentives for capital movements that are unrelated to underlying economic conditions. Both factors could risk instability in capital movements. Weak domestic financial institutions may be incapable of efficiently intermediating large flows of funds to which they obtain access as a result of capital account liberalization; they may in addition be adversely affected by movements in asset prices that result from international capital flows. Most important, weak financial institutions are especially vulnerable to potential reversals of capital flows.

The obverse side of the phasing of liberalization is the continued use of capital controls. Let me first offer a general perspective on the use of controls. Controls, except for prudential controls, are generally inefficient and costly for the economy. They are viewed by markets as an additional country risk factor, and their prolonged use has often been associated with capital flight. Countries that have already removed controls are unlikely to reimpose them except perhaps on a limited basis, temporarily, for emergency purposes. Countries that now have nonprudential controls in place will remove them, generally gradually, perhaps in a big bang. Countries that retain some controls may seek to refine them, removing those that cause the greatest distortions, perhaps replacing them with less distortionary controls—just as tariffs often replace quotas at the start of trade liberalization. Against the background of a general trend of progressive capital account liberalization, we need to consider the controls that are likely to be in place during transitional periods.

A theoretical case can be made for countries whose financial systems are not sufficiently robust to restrict selected forms of capital inflow, for instance the short-term inflows that produce the capital inflows problem. A judgment on whether any particular restriction in a particular country is desirable would have to take into account the costs of such restrictions, their effectiveness or lack thereof, the speed with which they will lose effectiveness, as well as their potential benefits if any. Whatever controls might be imposed, they are likely to do less damage if they are market-based, for instance taking the form of reserve requirements on foreign deposits, rather than quantitative. Controls on outflows may have been imposed for balance of payments reasons and retained both for that reason and because they provide a captive source of funds for domestic financial institutions. Their gradual removal is generally desirable.

Prudential controls on foreign capital are already in place in many countries, for instance restrictions on the open positions domestic banks can take in foreign currency. Similar restrictions could be contemplated on open positions taken by corporations. Such controls, intended to reduce the vulnerability of domestic institutions to shifts in foreign capital flows, could well form part of internationally accepted prudential standards.

Every currency crisis produces demands to do something about hedge funds and speculators. Usually the anger at the speculators would better be aimed closer to home, and in practice nothing much has yet been done to tame them. Still, occasional cases of market overreaction raise the question of whether better provision of information to and by market participants, as well as improved prudential regulations, could increase the efficiency of the markets. Since speculative positions have counterpart transactions in the domestic economy, we need to ask whether prudential regulation of the domestic economy could reduce the occasional excesses of speculative attacks, perhaps thereby also increasing the efficiency of the international capital markets. These are issues that deserve serious analysis.

Information Provision

One of the many lessons drawn from Mexico was that the extent of the crisis was worsened by the poor quality of information supplied to both the official sector (including the IMF) and the markets. Specifically, information on reserves was provided with a long lag, and information on the structure of the external debt was not readily available. As a result, the IMF's data standards initiative was initiated and the Special Data Dissemination Standard was established in early 1996. Considerable progress has been made with the development of the associated Dissemination Standards Bulletin Board.[2] The Thai crisis reinforces the argument for better and more timely provision of information, including information on central bank forward operations. There are two arguments for the provision of such information. First, better informed markets are likely to make better decisions. In each of the Mexican and Thai crises, this would have meant that the markets would have withdrawn funds sooner than they did, thereby hastening adjustments that needed to be made in each of those cases. Second, the obligation to publish information on certain interventions would affect the extent and nature of those interventions, and help prevent some unwise decisions.

There is much work to be done in thinking through the question of the optimal extent and timing of information provision. If the policy game is thought of as a battle between the authorities and hostile markets, then the official penchant for secrecy is easy to understand. If instead, the problem is thought of as one of designing a framework to influence both the choice of policies and the effectiveness of markets in responding to and disciplining policies, then the case for more information provision is strengthened. As that framework is developed, we will also have to consider the information that market participants need to make public in order to discipline their own actions and increase the efficiency of markets. These issues will surely be on the agenda in the next few years.

The Role of Surveillance

Since the Mexican crisis, the IMF has placed increased emphasis on timely surveillance of market developments. It is fair to say that the Fund's new surveillance procedures worked well in the case of Thailand, and reasonable to expect they will work well in future. But it would be a mistake to imagine that the Fund or any other surveillance could ever be made perfect. The Fund will surely miss the warning signs of some future crisis, and just as surely will predict some crises that do not happen. The international system cannot be built on the assumption that improved surveillance, or the increased provision of information to markets, will prevent all future crises, even though they should reduce the frequency of crises. The effectiveness of Fund surveillance is also limited by the fact that a country may be warned but not take action. Because the Fund's ability to conduct its surveillance depends on its privileged access to information, it is not in a position to enlist the markets in the cause of surveillance by making its concerns fully public. That is a limitation that we will have to accept.

IMF surveillance operates at the global level. There is in addition room for mutual surveillance within smaller groups of countries, such as those in the Organization for Economic Cooperation and Development (OECD), or in the European Union. Such mutual surveillance enables countries with similar experiences, or likely to be affected by what their neighbors do—for instance different groups of Asian countries—to become more familiar with the policies of fellow group members, and to exert mutual pressures for good policies. To be effective, such surveillance should be based on a sound analysis of the economic situation, and here the Fund is willing to play its part in supporting regional and other groups.

After a crisis, we in the Fund sometimes hear the refrain, generally from policymakers but sometimes from the markets, "But no-one—including the Fund—warned us of the dangers we faced." When such a complaint is accurate, and after every crisis, we need to draw the lessons and seek to improve our performance. At the same time, it is important not to lose sight of where the primary responsibilities lie. The prime responsibility for pursuing the right policies rests with the national authorities; the Fund and neighbors can provide information, analyze, suggest, seek to persuade, and cajole. But, ultimately, it is the government that has the duty to evaluate the situation and make the right decisions. There is also a responsibility on market participants to appraise the underlying economic situation accurately; if they do so, market incentives will ensure that markets operate efficiently. The prime responsibility for correctly evaluating the economic situation rests with market players, provided they are given the information they need.

The Need for Financing

No matter how much information is provided to markets, surveillance is strengthened, prudential regulations are refined, and government policies improve, crises will happen. In a crisis, private sector financing evaporates, and countries are forced to take painful adjustment measures. One of the purposes of the IMF set out in the first Article of Agreement is "To give confidence to members by making the general resources of the Fund temporarily available to them under appropriate safeguards, thus providing them with opportunity to correct maladjustments in their balance of payments without resorting to measures destructive of national or international prosperity." The Fund—that is, the international community—has shown its willingness to act in this way in many crises. The Fund will continue to act in accordance with its purposes, and to provide financing, with the conditionality that provides the safeguards referred to in Article I (v), to countries faced with the need to take actions to stem the destructive effects of an external crisis.

The Mexican and Thai crises, and the proposed capital account amendment of the Articles of Agreement have raised two important interrelated questions about Fund lending: first, whether the increased scale of international capital flows requires a reexamination of the criteria that determine the size of Fund loans; second, whether the Fund's willingness to lend in such circumstances creates a moral hazard. The answer to both questions is yes. As the efficiency of the international capital markets improves, it is reasonable to expect that there will be fewer crises requiring official funding in future, but it is also likely that they will be on a larger scale than typical in the past. In both the Mexican and Thai crises, the Fund was able to provide very large loans relative to the country's quota by invoking the "exceptional circumstances" clause, and such a route will be available in the future. But if capital account liberalization increases the likelihood of larger, even if fewer, crises, it would also be appropriate to review Fund lending criteria, to ensure that Fund loans—in some cases together with supporting funding—will remain adequate to their task.

There is no question that the Fund's willingness to lend to countries in trouble creates a moral hazard. The hazard is not that the availability of Fund financing in emergencies encourages countries to behave recklessly, for Fund conditionality is such that governments in trouble are usually too slow rather than too fast to come to the Fund. Instead the hazard is that the private sector may be too willing to lend because it knows that a country in trouble will go to the Fund rather than default. Spreads in some markets are so low as to support this view. The international community has struggled with the question of how to reduce this moral hazard, but has not yet found a good solution. We need to find one, a way of ensuring that the private sector shares in the financial costs of dealing with crises.

The regional roles in financing in both the Mexican and Thai crises raise the question of whether more permanent regional financing arrangements need to be put in place, to provide reassurance to countries that they will receive adequate help in crises. We see an important role for regional groups in the prevention of crises, by improving surveillance. We are more skeptical about the establishment of large regional funds for crisis financing, especially when their creation runs the risk of reducing the conditionality attached to crisis financing. The existence of such funds would also increase moral hazard, by making it clear to speculators that more official financing is available if a crisis hits.

One classic rule of lender-of-last-resort financing, intended to reduce moral hazard, is not to be too clear about the circumstances and amounts in which such lending will be available. There is thus a tradeoff between the volume of funds known to be available to deal with crises, and the likely size of crises. This is a consideration that has to be weighed in considering both the size of Fund lending limits, and the desirability of prepositioning regional support funds rather than leaving them to be arranged on an ad hoc basis.

The Role of the IMF and the Capital Account Amendment

Finally, let me turn briefly to the proposed amendment to the Articles of Agreement to extend the Fund's jurisdiction to capital movements. Against the background of the increased importance of capital movements for the operation of the international financial system, many countries have been liberalizing the capital account. Such decisions have potentially important effects on the balance of payments and on the demand for Fund resources. De facto, the Fund has become increasingly involved in helping member countries liberalize in a manner that does not undermine economic and financial stability. Yet the only formal jurisdiction the Fund has in this area is the right to require countries to impose capital controls in certain contexts.

In April 1997, the Interim Committee of the IMF agreed that there would be a number of benefits from amending the Fund's Articles of Agreement to make the liberalization of international capital movements a central purpose of the Fund and to extend the Fund's jurisdiction to capital movements. In a nutshell, *the prime goal of the amendment would be to enable the Fund to promote the orderly liberalization of capital movements.*

In doing so, it is likely that the Fund will develop the analogies for the capital account of the present Articles VIII and XIV that apply to the current account. When they are ready, members accept the obligation under Article VIII to refrain from imposing restrictions on the making of payments and transfers for current international transactions. In accepting the obligations of Article VIII, a country provides confidence to the international community that it will not impose restrictions on the making of payments and transfers for current international transactions without Fund approval and will, therefore, pursue policies that will obviate the need for such restrictions. Until a country is ready to accept Article VIII, it may, under Article XIV, maintain and "adapt to changing circumstances" existing restrictions that were in place when it joined the Fund, until its balance of payments position is sufficiently strong that reliance on exchange restrictions is no longer warranted. This framework has allowed the Fund to take account of the different starting positions of its members and has, at the same time, provided a basis for dialogue between the Fund and the member on the appropriateness of its restrictions and the policies and reforms that would be necessary to allow for their elimination.

Similarly, in the case of the capital account, we can envisage members eventually accepting the obligation to liberalize the capital account fully—though what precisely that means will have to be worked out. Until they are ready to do so, they would avail themselves of transitional arrangements that would be approved by the Fund. Members would be able to adapt to changing circumstances the controls in place when the amendment comes into force. New restrictions could be approved to reflect considerations of market and institutional evolution and for prudential reasons. The

Fund might also have provision to approve temporarily restrictions needed to address macroeconomic and balance of payments problems. Similar to the acceptance of Article VIII, a member's acceptance of the new obligations with respect to capital movements would send a clear signal of its intentions to the international financial community, and could serve to strengthen its access to international capital markets.

If this framework is adopted, the Fund will have to develop its analysis and evaluation of different types of capital controls, to advise countries on which types of controls are most likely to help them attain their goals, and on optimal methods of liberalization. In doing so, we will need to distinguish between controls on capital inflows and capital outflows; between general and selective controls; between market-based and quantitative controls; between prudential controls and those imposed for balance of payments or macroeconomic reasons; and among controls on different types of capital flow—and no doubt among other categories of controls too.

A capital account amendment that provides for a transitional period during which capital controls could remain in place would make it possible for the Fund to encourage the liberalization of capital flows while paying due regard to the varying circumstances of members. It would facilitate the establishment and application of a universally applied code of good behavior in the application of capital controls, enabling the Fund to determine when macroeconomic, structural, and balance of payments considerations require adherence to—or permit exemptions from—obligations relating to capital account liberalization. This is of particular importance in light of the fact that the Fund may also be called upon to finance the balance of payments problems that are caused by capital movements. And by giving the Fund jurisdiction in the area of capital movements, it would strengthen the Fund's surveillance role over international capital flows. The extension of Fund jurisdiction would thus complement rather than duplicate existing bilateral, regional, and multilateral agreements and initiatives in this area.

Concluding Remarks

I hope I have explained why we believe a capital account amendment along these lines, including transitional arrangements, will be in the interests of all Fund members. We all recognize that an international environment of free international capital movements provides enormous opportunities, but also entails significant challenges and risks for countries and the international monetary system. Recent developments in this region remind us of these risks. But the many benefits countries in this region have derived from capital inflows also remind us that no country can afford to cut itself off from the international capital markets. The increasing importance of international capital flows is a fact, which needs to be better reflected in the laws and agreements that help bring order to the international economy, and to the process by which individual countries liberalize their capital accounts. The proposed amendment to the Articles of Agreement will serve this purpose and our member countries well.

Notes

This chapter was presented at the seminar "Asia and the IMF" held in Hong Kong, China, on September 19, 1997. I am grateful to Barry Johnston for his assistance.

1. These are cases of so-called multiple equilibria.

2. This electronic bulletin board on the Internet provides information concerning countries' economic and financial data systems. As of September 1997, there were 43 subscribers, including Hong Kong, China.

Introduction

This chapter was first delivered as the David Finch Lecture at the University of Melbourne. It was a particular pleasure for me to deliver the lecture because it was David Finch, then Director of the Fund's central ETR Department (Exchange and Trade Restrictions, later to become PDR, Policy Development and Research) and a staunch believer in the importance of the Fund, who in 1984 first interested me in the possibility of working at the Fund. David had retired by the time I joined the Fund, but I benefited a good deal from meeting with him from time to time, running problems by him, and getting feedback on the issues with which we had to deal. David died in 2001.

Let me comment on a few points that arise in reading the chapter. First, I would like to emphasize one point made in the introduction—"that excessive volatility in the capital markets can push countries into bad equilibria. Simply put, when a country's institutions are subjected to massive pressure by a reversal of capital flows, they may crack, thereby seeming to justify the reversal of the flows that produced the crisis." Many times in crises I felt that the country we were trying to help was in a bad equilibrium, in which pessimism about its prospects justified the very high spreads and depreciated exchange rates that are typical in such circumstances, and that make the bad equilibrium self-sustaining. It also often seemed there was another equilibrium, a good one, in which optimism would justify lower interest rates and a more appreciated exchange rate, which would also be consistent with equilibrium. The question then was what could be done to move from the bad to the good equilibrium. And the answer, unfortunately, was usually that there was no simple and quick way of making that change. Rather, the country, with the Fund's help, would have to work hard to strengthen policies to persuade the markets that they were underestimating the strength of the country's underlying economic situation.

Second, the chapter supports the use of either flexible exchange rates or hard pegs by countries integrated into the international capital markets, with an explicit reference to Argentina. It was clear already then that hard peg regimes are very demanding; that, and the terrible consequences of the loss of Argentina's hard peg, reinforces the case for flexible exchange rates by emerging market countries. But flexible exchange rates do not guard against all types of crisis: as Brazil's difficulties in 2002 demonstrate, a country with a flexible exchange rate may still get into an external crisis because of doubts about its debt sustainability.

Third, in this chapter as in others, I emphasize the importance of strong domestic banking and financial systems. There has been a great deal of progress in this regard, particularly through the introduction of the FSAP, or Financial Sector Assessment Program. FSAPs are joint ventures of the IMF and the World Bank, with the participation of experts from governments of member countries. The FSAP team visits a country and provides a comprehensive report on the strengths and weaknesses of the financial sector. Many member countries have found these reports very useful in diagnosing problems in their financial sectors and in suggesting ways to deal with them.

The issue of how to deal with hedge funds and other highly leveraged institutions is raised more than once in this chapter. Asian crisis countries, as well as Australia, were convinced that hedge funds had been instrumental in the creation and propagation of the crisis; the collapse of Long Term Capital Management exacerbated these concerns. Despite several studies, not much has been done to change the behavior of these funds and other highly leveraged institutions.

The chapter also expresses support for the further consideration and elaboration of the proposal for some type of international bankruptcy mechanism. My successor at the Fund, Anne Krueger, has developed such a proposal, which now goes by the acronym of SDRM, or Sovereign Debt Restructuring Mechanism. The proposal is now receiving public attention. There are still formidable obstacles to its eventual adoption, since adoption will likely require the approval of the parliaments of the Fund's member countries, and both the emerging market issuers and private sector participants oppose the SDRM. But the public discussion serves the very useful purpose of stimulating thinking about how better to handle sovereign debt crises, and the official support for the SDRM was probably instrumental in leading private sector participants to welcome the adoption of CACs (collective action clauses) in bond contracts.

6   Reforming the International Financial System

Stanley Fischer

Few propositions about the international financial system command as much assent as the view that it should be reformed. Or, in familiar if inelegant language, we need a new international financial architecture.[1] But why? There are two main reasons:

• Because international capital flows to emerging markets are too volatile, subjecting recipient countries to shocks and crises that are excessively frequent and excessively large, as witnessed by the massive recessions in the East Asian crisis countries in 1998;[2]

• Because there is too much contagion in the system—a point that was argued by many during the East Asian crisis, but which became uncontestable after the Russian devaluation and unilateral debt restructuring spread the crisis to Latin America.

Whatever reforms are undertaken should cure—or at least substantially mitigate—both the excess volatility that affects individual countries and the contagion that is one of the mechanisms through which excess volatility is propagated.

It is reasonable to ask how we know that capital flows are too volatile and that contagion is excessive.

• The volatility of flows is remarkable (see figures 6.1 and 6.2) and so is the volatility of spreads (see figure 6.3). Could we establish that these levels of volatility are excessive? As we know from the work on excess volatility of the stock market (see Campbell et al. 1997, chapter 7), it is difficult to establish that proposition definitively. But the charts go a long way towards making the case.

• Excessive contagion is even harder to establish, particularly because when contagion strikes, there is typically method in the madness, namely, the contagion usually hits weaker economies harder

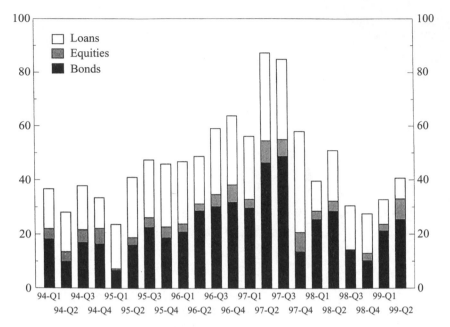

Figure 6.1
Private market financing for emerging markets, 1994 Q1 to 1999 Q2 in billions of U.S. dollars. Source: Capital Data, Ltd. Note: 1999 Q2 figures are estimated based on data for April and May 1999.

than stronger economies—so that it is always possible and generally accurate to argue that the countries most affected by contagion deserve it more than countries less affected.[3,4]

There seems to be a particular problem in establishing excess volatility and contagion if there are multiple equilibria, as I believe there are. One reason to worry about volatility then is that excessive volatility in the capital markets can push countries into bad equilibria. Simply put, when a country's institutions are subjected to massive pressure by a reversal of capital flows, they may crack, thereby seeming to justify the reversal of flows that produced the crisis.

It should be noted that in hoping to reduce the excesses in international capital flows, we are implicitly arguing that at times—for instance in mid-1997—foreign capital inflows to some emerging market countries have been too large and spreads too low. It is likely that many of the reforms that should be introduced in the next few years will raise the average level of spreads, and make foreign borrowing on average more expensive for emerging market borrowers.

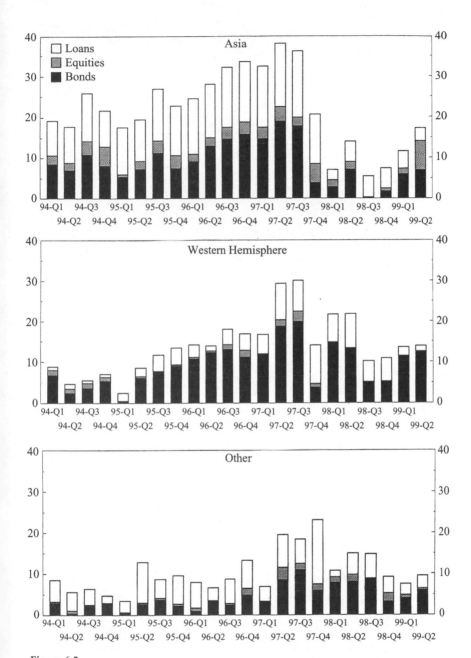

Figure 6.2
Private market financing for emerging markets, 1994 Q1 to 1999 Q2 in billions of U.S. dollars. Source: Capital Data, Ltd. Note: 1992 Q2 figures are estimated based on data for April and May 1999.

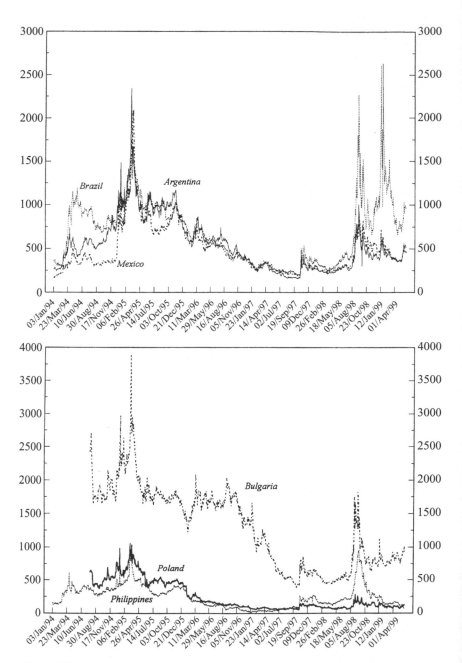

Figure 6.3
Stripped yield spreads for selected Brady Bonds, January 3, 1994, to June 4, 1999, in basis points. Sources: Reuters, Salomon Smith Barney, and IMF staff estimates.

That will not necessarily be a bad thing if it more accurately reflects the risks of such lending.

The reforms that are being considered at present will not create an entirely new system. Rather they consist of a number of measures to be implemented by the different participants in the international system which, taken together, should modify the existing system and make it perform more efficiently. The proposed changes will require action by three key sets of players in the international system: first, *governments and the private sector in emerging market countries*; second, *governments and the private sector in the leading industrialised countries where the capital flows originate*; and third, *international institutions*. These changes, which lie mainly in the area of *crisis prevention*, are designed to influence the behaviour of borrowers and lenders in the international system, and help reduce the frequency and extent of crises. But crises will nonetheless inevitably occur, and we need to consider reforms to lending practices and steps to improve *crisis management*—how to do better when crises break out. I will deal with these four issues in turn, and then present brief concluding remarks.

The Recipient Countries

In discussing what the recipient countries—the emerging market countries—need to do to make the system operate better, I will focus on five key elements: first, macroeconomic policies, including the choice of exchange rate system; second, provision of better information; third, strengthening the banking system and the financial system more generally; fourth, strengthening corporate finance including bankruptcy laws; and fifth, measures to deal with potential reversals of capital flows. We need also to ask what incentives can be put in place to induce countries to make the required changes.

First is the basics, sound macroeconomic policies. There is not much controversy over what constitutes sound macroeconomic policies in normal times, even if we recognise that it is much easier to recommend virtue than to practise it, and also that policies that are suitable under normal market conditions may rapidly become unsustainable when the markets turn hostile.

However there is a major question about the exchange rate regime that countries should adopt. A century of controversy has produced no clear answer to the question of which exchange rate or monetary regime is best. While the theory of the optimal currency area provides some clues, a country's history—particularly its history of inflation—is a critical consideration in determining its choice of regime. And whatever exchange rate system a country has, it is likely at some time to wish it had a different one.

The major external crises that have taken place in the last two years—in Thailand, Korea, and Indonesia, and in Russia and Brazil—have affected countries that had a fixed or more or less pegged exchange rate in the period leading up to the crisis. Further, the assumption that the exchange rate was stable profoundly affected economic behaviour in these countries, especially in the banking system, and contributed to the severity of the post-devaluation crises. It is also the case that several countries with flexible rates, among them Mexico, South Africa, and Turkey, although severely affected by the external crisis, nonetheless avoided a massive crisis. These facts of recent history have pushed the balance in the direction of floating rates. At the same time, the currency board countries, Argentina and Hong Kong, have succeeded in holding the line. Nor should it be forgotten that many countries benefitted from fixing the exchange rate as part of the process of stabilising inflation, and that the fear of devaluation is often the best discipline on weak governments.

Nonetheless, we are probably entering a period in which the greater risks of a clearly defined external financial crisis presented by a fixed exchange rate, will lead to the choice of more flexible exchange rate systems for countries that have open capital accounts. If countries choose to fix, they may well want to do so definitively, through a currency board, rather than through a less credible normal peg. For countries less open to short-term international capital flows, various forms of crawling peg, most likely with wide bands around the peg, could be the preferred choice. In the longer run, if EMU succeeds, as I expect, we are likely to see a shift towards currency blocs, with more currency unions and fewer currencies.

Second is steps to strengthen domestic banking and financial systems. Except in Brazil, a weak banking system has been at the centre of the most recent financial crises. IMF-supported programmes in Asia have placed their major structural emphasis on bank restructuring and recapitalisation. Thanks in part to the Basle Committee's *Core Principles* (1997) and to the IMF's *Toward a Framework for Financial Stability* (Folkerts-Landau and Lindgren, 1997), we know much of what it takes to produce a sound banking system, including both good bankers and a strong supervisory system. But it is not only regulations and supervision that are needed, so is competition, particularly foreign competition. This point is increasingly understood in Latin America, where the entry of foreign banks has been welcomed in this decade as a way of strengthening the domestic banking system. And at the same time as they work on their banking systems, countries need also to be strengthening the rest of the financial system, including equity and bond markets.

Third is provision of better information. After the Mexican crisis, many argued that the markets would have worked much better had they had the right information, including information on Mexico's reserves. This argument led to the creation of the IMF's SDDS—special data dissemination standard—a system which, after a two-year trial period, is now in operation.[5] The information contained in the SDDS would not have included a key fact in the Thai crisis, the central bank's forward commitments, and the SDDS will now be supplemented to include such data as well as information on external debt.

The recent crises owe some of their intensity to a general lack of transparency about the sizes of positions that had been built up by both borrowers and lenders. Domestic borrowers in many cases had highly leveraged and unhedged exposures, while the creditors were highly leveraged and in form hedged but in substance vulnerable to a major shock to the economy. Many of the relevant positions were off-balance-sheet. Lack of transparency vis-à-vis such exposure reflected a number of factors including the opaque nature of the markets where off-balance-sheet trading takes place, and difficulties in assessing complex positions in off-balance-sheet instruments.

Improvements in information require efforts by the private sector to adopt sound accounting practices and appropriate standards of disclosure to investors, financial institutions and official agencies. Governments in both debtor and creditor countries should promote and indeed enforce adequate practices and standards and then collect and disseminate economic and financial data on the private sector on a timely basis—but work needs also to be done to define what data need to be produced. It goes without saying that governments should provide comprehensive and transparent data on their own activities. Of course, better data will never be sufficient, and are not a substitute for good policies or good analysis, but it remains true that better information on a country's policies, on the state of the economy, and on individual firms, should make the private financial markets more efficient and less prone to disruption. It is also true that requirements to provide data are likely to lead to better policies, by both private sector agents and the government, since some of the practices and policies responsible for the depth of the recent crises would not have been undertaken had they been required to be made public.

Fourth is actions to strengthen corporate finance, including bankruptcy laws and their implementation. The virulence of the Asian crisis owes even more to excessive leverage by Asian corporations than it does to excessive leverage on the part of lenders. So long as the good times roll, high leverage is a winning strategy. If it is believed that borrowers are implicitly backed by government commitments, as must have been believed by many lenders in the Asian crisis countries, there is no great incentive for lenders to exercise caution. And then, if crisis strikes, heavy leverage increases the costs of finding a way out of the crisis, especially in the absence of good bankruptcy procedures. All this of course has become clear in the Asian crisis countries. It is thus critical to strengthen corporate governance and finance around the world. This includes the adoption of appropriate auditing and accounting standards, principles of good corporate governance, and efficient bankruptcy procedures—both laws and the courts to enforce them.

Fifth is dealing with potential capital flow reversals. The first line of defence in dealing with capital flow reversals, aside from macroeconomic policy and exchange rate responses, is to use the foreign exchange reserves. Countries with very large reserves have done better in dealing with the current crisis than those with small reserves. It is very likely that countries seeking to draw the lessons of the present crisis will decide they should hold much larger reserves than before. An alternative approach has been taken by several countries, most notably Argentina, that have put in place precautionary lines of credit from private sector lenders. This is a useful supplement to the holding of reserves, and could possibly be cheaper than increasing reserves.[6] The Contingent Credit Line facility recently opened by the IMF, to be discussed in more detail below, will also make additional resources available on a contingency basis, if countries that have pre-qualified are hit by contagion.

How about using capital controls to moderate capital flows? This approach has been taken by Malaysia, and has had support from leading academics. But it is surprising how few countries have reversed course on capital controls in the present crisis. The IMF's attitude to controls on outflows has been that these should be removed gradually, as a country's macroeconomy, balance of payments, and financial system strengthen. The most advanced countries have fully liberalised capital flows, and that is where all countries should ultimately be heading—but not prematurely. With regard to inflows, we see no case for controlling long-term inflows, particularly of foreign direct investment, but recognise the disadvantages of surges of short-term capital, both inflows and outflows, and therefore support market-based controls, along Chilean lines, that are intended to moderate the pace of short-term inflows and consequently of short-term outlows. While it may be tempting to impose capital outflow controls to deal with a short-term crisis, as Malaysia did in 1998, the longer-term consequences are likely to be adverse. Indeed, policymakers in Latin American countries that generally had capital controls in the 1980s have all rejected that approach this time around, emphasising that controls were inefficient, widely circumscribed, and had cost them dearly in terms of capital market access.

What can be done to encourage emerging market countries to implement the recommended measures? In the first instance, countries should see it as in their own interests to undertake measures to increase the efficiency of their capital markets and the resilience of their economies to external shocks. Second, the development of international standards, which will be discussed below, should give countries both the information about what needs doing and a further incentive to adopt them. Third, access to the IMF Contingent Credit Line will depend on the extent to which a country's policies are strong and on whether it is attempting to meet the relevant international standards.

It would be an important incentive for the adoption of these measures if the terms of foreign lending depended on the extent to which companies and countries have implemented the recommended policies. While the risk aversion of market participants can be relied on to make that happen in the next few years, when the memory of this crisis is fresh, it cannot be guaranteed to continue when the exuberant phase of the next cycle is reached. Regulators in the capital exporting countries could contribute by basing provisioning requirements for lenders on the extent to which recipient countries and companies are meeting the international standards.

The Originating Countries

The advanced industrial countries that established the international economic system in which the world has operated and prospered for the last fifty years, have the primary obligation to maintain and improve it. That commitment was put to a major test during 1998, when for some time it was uncertain whether the United States Congress would support the IMF quota increase. Fortunately the outcome was positive. And as the flurry of proposals and suggestions that are emerging from various G's, including the G-7 and G-22, proves, the industrialised countries are seized with the problem of reform of the international system. Most of these proposals involve actions that would need to be taken by emerging market countries and the international financial institutions. However, there are also a number of actions required of the industrial countries.

First, global prosperity is impossible if the industrialised economies, which account for over two-thirds of world output, are not prospering. Thus it is critical for them to pursue policies that will achieve sustained growth with low inflation. In the most recent period, the United States clearly, and Europe mostly, have met that obligation. The cuts in United States interest rates in October and November 1998 were critical in reversing a panic in the global economy, and cuts in European interest rates also contributed to the revival of confidence. However economic and financial weaknesses in Japan contributed to the crisis in Asia, both by weakening exports from the crisis-affected countries, and because Japanese banks, under pressure to strenghten their balance sheets, were withdrawing funds.

Second, the industrialised economies, like the emerging market countries, need to ensure that they maintain healthy financial, and especially banking, systems. The Basle capital adequacy standards in effect until mid-1999 have been widely accepted, but their preferential treatment of short-term interbank lines probably contributed to the volatility of capital flows by making it relatively more profitable for banks to lend short rather than long.[7] The strengthening of prudential regulations governing short-term positions warrants urgent consideration. In considering the strength of industrialised country banking systems, we should not take too much comfort from the absence of major banking sector difficulties in the United States and Europe in the last few years of macroeconomic stability and asset market booms, for these are not the circumstances that test the strength of bank balance sheets and management. And we should be worried by the extent of losses suffered even by highly respected banks following the Russian meltdown.

Indeed, the contagion following the Russian crisis undoubtedly owes much to the heavily leveraged positions taken by many participants in the Russian financial markets. Financial regulators need to examine ways to ensure that highly leveraged positions across many institutions are better monitored and controlled, possibly through higher margin requirements or controls on off-balance-sheet activities. As a result of the controversy over the role of hedge funds in the Asian crisis and the case of Long Term Capital Management, regulators are reexamining the adequacy of the regulations governing hedge funds and highly leveraged institutions (HLIs) more generally.[8] Among the aspects of the LTCM case that stand out are: the extent of the company's leverage; the extent of its use of derivatives; and the fact that leading banks lent to LTCM apparently without being well informed of either its activities or its other sources of financing. Accordingly consideration is being given to the relative benefits and scope for either direct controls of hedge fund-like activities, and/or for encouraging stronger bank oversight of their positions vis-a-vis such institutions.

We should not underestimate the difficulties of regulating the activities of highly leveraged institutions, even if only by requiring them to provide more information about the positions they take, particularly given the existence of offshore banking and financial centres. The activities of offshore centres is another topic that is receiving further attention as the international financial architecture is redesigned.[9]

The International Financial Institutions

The role of the IFIs is to help member countries implement the measures described above to strengthen their economies and improve the quality of international capital flows. In particular, work is ongoing (i) to strengthen financial systems and economic policies by encouraging the design and adoption of banking and other relevant standards; (ii) to encourage the provision of better information to the markets and to the public more generally; (iii) to improve surveillance of economic and financial developments and policies; and (iv) to consider changes in IFI lending practices.

As discussed above, weaknesses in the economic governance of the financial and corporate sectors in emerging market countries have contributed to the severity of the recent crises. As one step to improve this situation, the international community is placing particular emphasis on the development and implementation of *international standards* and principles. In the banking area, the Basle Committee on Banking Supervision (BCBS) has developed the *Core Principles for Effective Banking Supervision*, which will serve as the basic reference and minimum standard for supervisory authorities.

International standards exist or are being developed in other areas as well. The International Organisation of Securities Commissions (IOSCO) is working to establish universal principles for securities market regulation and to improve disclosure standards. The International Accounting Standards Committee has published a series of *International Accounting Standards* aimed at achieving uniformity in international accounting practices, while international auditing standards have been established by the International Federation of Accountants. Initiatives, in which the World Bank is taking a lead role, to harmonise domestic bankruptcy laws are also under way. The OECD, the Basle Committee, the World Bank, and the EBRD are all involved in the development of principles in the area of corporate governance; the OECD has developed a set of *Principles of Corporate Governance*, which were endorsed in May 1999. In addition to the SDDS mentioned above, the IMF has developed a Code of Good Practices on Fiscal Transparency to guide member countries in enhancing the accountability and credibility of fiscal policy; members will be encouraged to implement the Code on a voluntary basis. A similar code on the transparency of monetary and financial policies, prepared in consultation with central banks and multilateral financial supervisory authorities has also been agreed.

The development of the standards is the easier part of the process; ensuring their implementation the harder part. This will require both international monitoring, and appropriate incentives. The international monitoring will likely be undertaken mostly in the context of IMF surveillance, but with the assistance of experts in the relevant areas from national and international regulatory bodies. Financial sector specialists in the World Bank and the IMF have developed a framework for undertaking joint assessments of financial sectors, which are now getting under way. The presentation of the results of these assessments to member countries should help them strengthen their financial systems. The IMF has also begun an experiment of producing *transparency reports*, which describe the extent to which a country meets the various standards for data and policy transparency that now exist. Reports have already been prepared for Argentina, Australia (where the report was prepared mainly by the Australian treasury), and the United Kingdom, and more will be done and published in the coming year.

As part of the effort to strengthen financial systems, and improve coordination among the agencies responsible for them, the *Financial Stability Forum* (FSF) was established in April 1999. Membership of the FSF consists of: three members from each G-7 country, in each case representing the finance ministry, the central bank, and a financial sector supervisory body; representatives of the international financial supervisory bodies—the Basle Committee on Banking Supervision, IOSCO, International Association of Insurance Supervisors (IAIS); and representatives of the BIS, the IMF, and the World Bank. At its first meeting the FSF agreed to set up three working groups, including participants from non-G7 and emerging market countries, to study: HLIs; offshore financial centres; and short-term capital flows. This is the first time all the international bodies that deal with financial systems have been brought together, and it is reasonable to hope that the FSF will succeed in ensuring better coordination among them, in identifying regulatory gaps, and help bring together information on weaknesses in financial systems that can then be dealt with by national authorities and the IFIs.

The best incentives for the adoption of standards would be provided by the markets, if spreads would reflect the extent to which standards are being implemented. Another set of incentives could be provided by the public sector, both through regulation in the originating countries, for instance by requiring risk ratings for bank lending to reflect the extent to which a country meets the relevant standards, and by making the provision or the terms of IFI financing likewise dependent on the adoption of standards.

Private capital flows are more likely accurately to reflect underlying risks, the better the available information. There are also considerable international efforts under way to improve the provision of economic and financial data to the public by emerging market countries. Currently 47 countries are subscribers of the Special Data Dissemination Standard (SDDS). Both in the context of the SDDS and otherwise, the IMF is undertaking several initiatives to improve its coverage of financial sector vulnerabilities.

At the same time, the Eurocurrency Standing Committee is reviewing its current data collection and dissemination efforts, and the BIS is set to begin collecting information on over-the-counter derivatives while also working to improve its recording and publication of information on international bank lending and the exernal debts of emerging market countries.[10] Until recently, the BIS data on short-term international capital flows were available only twice a year, with a six month lag. This meant that a foreign exchange crisis could arrive and depart before these data would even have provided a warning sign. The BIS is now moving to quarterly data, with a one-month lag, which will contribute to better monitoring of short-term flows, although it would be preferable to have the data available monthly.

The third broad way in which the IFIs can contribute to reducing the risk and costs of financial crises is by strengthening the process of surveillance. Such surveillance can facilitate the diagnosis of vulnerabilities to potential crises and the prescription of suitable corrective policy actions. In addition, it would help monitor the adoption of the various international standards and codes of conduct and help enforce adherence to them.

IMF surveillance of member countries takes place mainly through the annual Article IV consultation with each member on the state of its economy. Article IV reports prepared by the staff are then discussed by the IMF's Executive Board, but have not themselves been made public. In the last two years, information on the consultation has been increasingly made public through the issuance of public information notices (PINs), which are based on the Chairman's summing-up of the Board discussion of Article IV reports.[11] A member country can block the publication of the PIN, but it cannot edit it except for market-sensitive material. In the two years since the PINs were introduced, a growing percentage of countries have agreed to their publication, with over two-thirds of countries now agreeing. Another important aspect of IMF surveillance is the regular analysis of the global economy and capital markets, which is reflected in the twice a year *World Economic Outlook* and the annual *International Capital Markets Report*. The IMF staff reports more regularly to the Executive Board, and thus to member governments, on world economic and market developments.

Surveillance needs to be strengthened in two key respects. First, the monitoring of international capital flows needs to be improved. Improvements in the BIS data on international capital flows will help make this possible. At the same time, within the IMF, a separate data base is used to monitor medium and long-term international capital flows monthly, and we need to consider how best to use the results and make them publicly available. Further, if the decision is made to require hedge funds and others to publish more information on their activities, the IMF in its surveillance function will need to report frequently on aggregate movements in hedge fund positions. More generally, in monitoring international capital markets, the IMF needs to continue to develop better contacts with market participants worldwide. While some in the private sector have suggested that such meetings should be regarded as an opportunity to exchange information and impressions, the main role of the public sector on such occasions is to listen carefully.

Second, to make surveillance more effective, it is essential to increase the incentives for national authorities to pay serious attention to the policy messages and recommendations that result from surveillance activities. While peer pressure exerted in the context of Executive Board meetings and perhaps through regional groups is one avenue, the effectiveness of surveillance would be improved if more IMF staff reports, especially Article IV reports, were to be published. This would not only provide more information to the public, it would also improve the product by ensuring that Fund analyses become subject to external appraisal. However the issue is not straightforward. Board members opposed to publication are typically from non-industrialised countries. They argue that they are far more vulnerable to Fund criticisms than are the advanced industrialised countries, and that they would accordingly be less willing to be fully frank in their discussions with staff during the Article IV consultation if the reports were to be published.

One approach, which the management of the Fund favours, is to allow countries that want to publish their Article IV reports to do so. As in the case of PINs, they could be edited only for market-sensitive information. An experimental pilot project involving at least 20 countries, which will be able to choose whether to publish the Article IV report, will be conducted over the next 18 months. Evaluation of the pilot study will begin within a year after its start. The pilot study should help decide whether the concerns of those opposed to publication, particularly that the reports will become less frank, are justified and whether such concerns should prevent adoption of a policy allowing Article IV publication by countries wanting to do so.

Strengthening surveillance procedures is no small task, particularly as it will require the building up of substantial information and expertise in a host of new areas. At the same time, it is necessary to be realistic about what can be achieved through enhanced surveillance. Sometimes what is missing is not information, but the recognition of what that information means. Financial sector problems have emerged even in countries with the most sophisticated data and supervisory systems, and we should not expect that better information and better monitoring will work wonders in preventing and minimising the potential costs of crises—but it should help.

Fourth, we consider potential changes in IFI lending practices. Inspired by the massive contagion in the international system in recent years, the IMF introduced the Contingent Credit Line (CCL) facility in April 1999.[12] The CCL will be available only to well performing countries, those whose policies are generally good, that are attempting to meet relevant international standards, whose external debt is well managed, and that are seeking to put in place private sector contingent credit lines. For such countries the CCL will establish credit lines that will be available in the event the country is affected by contagion. There is a presumption that a significant amount of the credit line will be available virtually automatically, with the remainder of the CCL becoming available subject to the normal IMF conditionality.

At the end of 1997, the IMF introduced the Supplementary Reserve Facility (SRF), which makes short-term loans in large amounts at penalty rates to countries in crisis, subject to policy conditionality. Financing under the CCL will be on the same terms. The critical difference is that the CCL will enable the IMF for the first time to use its financing in a *preventive mode and to help good performers*, seeking to prevent crises both by providing extra incentives for countries to pursue good policies—rather than having as always in the past to react to a crisis once it has happened—and by in effect supplementing their reserves at a relatively low cost.[13] In several respects, the design of the Supplemental Reserve Facility and the CCL reflect the time-honoured principles of the lender of last resort.

There has also been a good deal of attention in this crisis to the possible use of guarantees from the multilateral development banks to enhance the access of countries to the international capital markets. The World Bank and ADB have already provided such guarantees to Asian countries. The use of guarantees makes sense in a crisis when capital market access dries up, but should not become a regular feature of borrowing by emerging market countries—normally private capital flows should not have to rely on an official guarantee. Some consideration is also being given to using MDB guarantees to help countries put in place private sector credit lines of the Argentine type.

Crisis Management

Most of the changes discussed so far relate to the behaviour of the system in normal or pre-crisis times. They are intended to make capital flows less volatile, and to help make asset prices better reflect underlying returns and risks. If they succeed, the system will become less crisis prone; and quite likely spreads will on average be higher. But however well the international system works, crises inevitably will occur. And we need to strengthen the capacity of member countries and the system to deal with crises.

How? In the first instance, countries should pursue responsible policies and defend their economies in the face of adverse external developments before a crisis strikes. If policymakers do not take action, and turn to the IMF for help only when the country is already deep in crisis, for instance with its reserves almost totally depleted, they cannot expect a smooth landing. Precisely how to defend the economy as the external environment deteriorates will vary according to the circumstances, including the exchange rate regime, but it is typically necessary to raise interest rates and, if the exchange rate is flexible, to allow it to take some of the strain; a contractionary fiscal policy may also have to contribute. Many of these changes, especially of fiscal policy, should have been made well before crisis threatens. But a country under attack and willing to defend the economy should not be expected to bear the entire burden of adjustment. That is one of the critical agreed rules of participation in the international economy: among the purposes of the International Monetary Fund, set out in Article I (v) is

To give confidence to members by making the general resources of the Fund temporarily available to them under adequate safeguards, thus providing them with opportunity to correct maladjustments in their balance of payments without resorting to measures destructive of national or international prosperity.

IMF lending is most likely to be effective when a country turns to the Fund relatively early, with time to develop a programme, preferably one that has been formulated by the country itself. In IFI language, the most successful programmes are those *owned* by the country. Of course, country ownership is the ideal. But there have unfortunately been many cases in which a country gets into trouble because its policymakers are weak (either politically or technically or both) and then turns to the Fund for help. The IMF cannot refuse to help in these circumstances, at a minimum by offering advice, sometimes by lending. Sometimes policymakers are clearly unwilling or unable to take needed actions and the Fund should not lend, for failure is inevitable; but there are also circumstances in which policymakers seem committed to a programme that looks likely to succeed, and it may be wise to lend even though success is not guaranteed. In all circumstances the Fund needs to take as many precautions as possible to ensure the success of a programme, for instance by lending only after critical policy actions have been implemented, and by backloading the financial support. But there is a tradeoff between not lending until conditions are perfect and 'providing reassurance to countries' by lending.

Over the years the IMF has continued to reform and refine the design of the programmes it supports, and its lending instruments. That process will continue as the new contingency facility is introduced, and as the lessons of experience under recent programmes are drawn. The greater role of the capital account in recent than in earlier crises is already shaping this thinking, for instance in designing programmes and facilities that will reassure the markets that a country can have access to liquidity providing it stays on track with its programme.

In the last few years, no question in crisis management has received greater attention than that of how to bail in the private sector.[14] Both moral hazard and the insufficiency of public funding make this essential. The moral hazard concern is that a successful Fund loan—a bailout, in language that is often as misleading as it is vivid—will lead investors to exercise less caution than they should, in the belief that the Fund will always be there to ensure that they are repaid. The language is misleading in implying that the primary purpose of a Fund loan is to bail out the investors rather than help the country deal with a crisis "without resorting to measures destructive of national or international prosperity." It is also misleading in that most investors in all the recent crises have suffered very large losses. Nonetheless, the moral hazard concern is valid, and it is one good reason to seek to bail in the private sector. Economic necessity is an equally valid reason: the plain fact is that capital flows have become so large that the official sector often does not have enough resources to stabilise an economy without private sector participation.

A number of approaches that have been taken in the past, and some new ones, are being considered for use in future crises. First, in the debt crisis of the 1980s, IMF financing was generally not provided until a critical mass of financing was available from the commercial banks. The authorities in creditor countries generally made it clear to the banks that they were expected to agree on a reasonable financing package.[15] This approach was easier when the banks were the main creditors and when the country did not have market access, which was the situation that confronted Latin American countries for much of the 1980s. When there are other creditors, an appeal to the banks, or anticipated friendly persuasion by the official sector, could lead to more rather than less outflows as the non-banks pull out.

As we draw the lessons of the 1980s, we should not forget that the debt strategy took most of that decade to succeed, and that countries did not generally regain market access until the end of the decade when the Brady Plan was introduced. Further, we should note much greater reluctance by regulatory authorities in this decade to put pressure on banks to take actions that could weaken their balance sheets, an action that regulators see as inconsistent with their primary responsibility of maintaining the soundness of the financial system. Of course, if all that is being done by coordinating a bank response is to deal with the free rider problem or the problem of collective action—that all banks together would be better off by agreeing to roll over their loans than if each separately tried to pull out—then this particular objection would carry less weight.

However we should take into account the risk that the formalisation of a requirement that the banks, or any other set of creditors, always be forced to share the financing of IMF programmes, would be destabilising for the international system. If such a condition were insisted on, the creditors would have greater incentive to run at the mere possibility of a crisis. This is a case where a measure that would make it easier to deal with a crisis that has already broken out, would also make crises more likely. In the present crisis, countries that have approached the IMF have been concerned that a formalised rollover could hinder future market access, at a time when they believe the adjustment policies they are pursuing, with official support, should be sufficient to reassure investors and lead them to roll over credits voluntarily. This is a real dilemma, one that suggests we should not conclude that the banks will have formally to agree to roll over their debts as an accompaniment to every IMF loan. Rather, we need a differentiated case-by-case approach that depends on the circumstances of each country.

A number of different methods of involving the private sector have been pursued during the past year. In March 1999, as part of the reformulated Brazilian programme, Brazil reached a voluntary agreement with its bank creditors that they would maintain their exposure to the country. In Ukraine, at the end of 1998, private creditors whose bonds were maturing agreed to roll over most of the principal into a new bond. In Romania, the IMF and the government agreed on reserve targets that required the government to find new money to replace maturing Eurobonds. There is a general principle in this cases, that official money cannot be used primarily to replace private credit, but the details vary among countries. Possibly some set of more detailed principles could emerge after more experience is gained, but that is unlikely.

A second approach to involving the private sector would be along the lines already discussed, i.e. precautionary guarantee arrangements, possibly involving the international development banks, as have been provided in Argentina.

Third, after the Mexican crisis, the G-10 deputies suggested that bond contracts should be modified to make it easier to reschedule payments in the event of a crisis, for instance by allowing majority decision making, as opposed to the current unanimity requirement. A crisis could be defined either by a set of objective indicators (including possibly an approach by the country to the IMF for assistance) or by a formal declaration by the IMF. This approach could be extended to other contracts as well. Some developing countries object that changes in bond contracts would make borrowing more expensive for them, but that would in this case reflect a more appropriate pricing of risks. It turns out that this type of bond—a so-called British Trust Deed instrument—already exists, and has been used in some Eurobond issues.

Closely related is a fourth approach, the suggestion associated with Jeffrey Sachs, that the system needs the ability in effect to declare a country bankrupt, and to provide an orderly framework for a debt workout. For instance the IMF, representing through its Executive Board the governments of all 182 members, could be given the power—no doubt with a special majority—to declare a stay on payments by a member in difficulty. This would provide time for the country to work out a restructuring of its debts with its creditors. There is a certain ambiguity in saying "the country" in this formulation. If the government is the debtor, then it is the government that would work out the restructuring with its creditors. If the debtors are in the private sector, then they would be expected to operate within the bankruptcy regulations of their country; if they were able to make payments in local currency, the stay could permit a delay in the transfer of those payments into foreign currency. There has been a tendency in foreign exchange crises for the government to take over private sector debts. That happened in the Korean crisis and in the 1982 debt crisis, also in Chile. But that is a potent source of moral hazard that should be strongly discouraged.

The bankruptcy approach deserves further consideration and elaboration. A few years ago it seemed doubtful that legislatures of some industrialised countries would give an international organisation the power to interpose itself between the creditors and foreign debtors, in effect to change the terms of contracts. For instance, in some recent crises, the creditors have had a powerful legal weapon in the form of cross-default clauses on loans. If a stay were imposed, the cross-default clause would lose its sting. These are weighty changes, but legislatures might be more receptive to change after the experience of the last few years.

Fifth, and also related, the Executive Board of the IMF has recently decided that the Fund may make loans to countries in arrears to private creditors holding securitised debt (beyond just commercial bank lenders), provided the country is trying to resolve the problem, including through appropriate adjustment policies.

Of the proposed changes to the international system, those to bail in the private sector are probably the most consequential. Something has to be done, and is indeed gradually being done in a case-by-case way in recent IMF programmes. But we must beware of two tensions in the process. First, there is a tension between the desire to involve the private sector and the likelihood of contagion. The more certain it is that the private sector will be bailed in a compulsory way, the greater the incentive creditors will have to run—and this change would tend to produce more rather than fewer crises. A partial solution is the current approach of seeking to ensure that private sector participation varies according to the circumstances of each case. The second tension is between two views of the current situation: the lender of last resort view that implicitly underlies the development of the possible contingency financing facility, that contagion and investor panic (heading for the exits) is an important cause of crises, but one that can be resolved by providing the assurance that creditors pursuing good policies and with reasonable external financial positions, will have the resources they need to reassure creditors; and the view that moral hazard is the critical issue.

Concluding Remarks

Taken together, the proposed changes would reform but not revolutionise the international system.[16] Nor is revolution necessary, for the present system has been instrumental in producing more prosperity for more people than ever before. By improving the quality of information, strengthening banking and financial systems, improving macroeconomic policies, and increasing the resiliency of economies, the proposed reforms should reduce the frequency and size of crises. In addition, the changes, specifically measures to regulate hedge fund-type activities, the contingency facility, and better information that should lead to greater differentiation among countries, should reduce—but will not be able to eliminate—contagion.

The new machinery will be put in place gradually in the coming months and years. Some of the changes are already coming on stream, among them the *Basle Core Standards*, the SDDS, other standards, the Fund's Supplemental Reserve Facility, the CCL, the FSF, transparency reports, improved surveillance of the financial sector, greater IMF transparency, and the emerging policy on involving the private sector. Other changes can be introduced only after further work has been completed, including work on the banking sector, the creation, implementation, and monitoring of standards, and the regulation of hedge fund-type activities. The international community has before it a formidable work programme, to evaluate the many proposals for reform fully, and to act on those that should be implemented. But the process is now well under way.

Notes

This a revised and updated (as of June 1999) version of the David Finch Lecture delivered at the University of Melbourne, November 9, 1998. I am grateful to Claire Adams for research assistance, and to Dan Citrin, David Finch, and George Soros for their helpful comments, not all of which have been adequately reflected in this paper. Views expressed are those of the author, and not necessarily of the International Monetary Fund.

1. For a comprehensive and balanced view, see Eichengreen (1999); see also Council on Foreign Relations (1999). A guide to official sector literature on the new architecture is presented in IMF (1999b).

2. In 1998, GDP is estimated to have declined by 13.7% in Indonesia, 5.5% in Korea, 6.8% in Malaysia, 0.5% in the Philippines, and 8.0% in Thailand.

3. It is frequently argued after a crisis that there was no contagion, because after all the countries most badly affected had major policy or structural weaknesses. This fact should not be allowed to obscure the existence of contagion. By analogy, a medical epidemic is more likely to strike those with weaker health, but it is nonetheless an epidemic. A further factor contributing to the view frequently expressed after a crisis that there was no or little contagion is that history has a habit, ex post, of looking inevitable.

4. On the existence of contagion, see for instance Eichengreen et al. (1997); in this study, contagion is defined as existing if a country is more likely, ceteris paribus, to be experiencing a crisis if there is a crisis in another country or countries. For a review of the recent literature on contagion, see Dornbusch et al. (1999).

5. The SDDS can be accessed on the IMF's Dissemination Standards Bulletin Board, on http://dsbb.imf.org.

6. Reserve holding can be quite expensive: for a country borrowing at, say 500 basis points above LIBOR, the cost of holding an additional dollar in reserves is approximately 5% per annum, which is high. The fee for holding a contingent line of credit is likely to be well below this rate.

7. The Basle Committee recommended changes in the approach to capital adequacy in June 1999. See for instance, Financial Times, June 4, 1999.

8. Late in 1997 the IMF undertook a study of the role of the hedge funds in the East Asian crisis and concluded that many other institutions, including some investment banks, were engaged in the same activities. Hence the reference to HLI's, or Highly Leveraged Institutions. The Financial Stability Forum (FSF), established in April 1999, which will be discussed below, is undertaking a study of HLIs.

9. The Financial Stability Forum is also undertaking a study of offshore financial centres.

10. The 1998 G-22 report, *Transparency and Accountability*, contains suggestions for improving data provision by both private and public sectors.

11. PINs and other IMF information are available on www.imf.org.

12. See IMF Press Release 99/14, (http://ww.imf.org/external/np/sec/pr/1999/PR9914.htm) for a detailed description of the CCL.

13. Borrowers from the IMF have had the option in the past of treating their arrangement as precautionary, by not drawing the funds to which they are entitled. The difference between precautionary arrangements and the CCL is that a country has to have an existing balance of payments problem that would justify a normal lending programme in order for it to have a precautionary arrangement, whereas CCLs would be made available to those in a strong position.

14. See IMF (1999a).

15. This policy tilted the balance of bargaining between countries and creditors in favour of the creditors, for the country in effect could not obtain IMF financing until the private creditors had agreed to their part of the deal. The policy of lending into arrears developed as a response to this difficulty.

16. Critics of this approach describe it as interior decoration rather than architecture.

References

Basle Committee on Banking Supervision (1997). *Core Principles for Effective Banking Supervision: Consultative Paper*. (http://www.bis.org/publ/index/html).

Campbell, John Y., Lo, Andrew, W., and MacKinlay, Archie C. (1997). *The Econometrics of Financial Markets*. Princeton: Princeton University Press.

Council on Foreign Relations (1999). *Report of the Commission on Future International Architecture*. New York (August).

Dornbusch, Rudiger, Park, Y. C., and Claessens, Stijn (1999). "Contagion: How It Spreads and How It Can Be Stopped." Mimeo, World Bank.

Eichengreen, Barry (1999). *Toward a New International Financial Architecture*. Washington, DC: Institute for International Economics.

Eichengreen, Barry, Rose, Andrew, and Wyplosz, Charles (1997). "Contagious Currency Crises: First Tests," *Scandinavian Journal of Economics*, vol. 98, pp. 1–22.

Folkerts-Landau, David, and Lindgren, Carl (1997). *Toward a Framework for Financial Stability*. Washington, DC: International Monetary Fund.

Group of Twenty-Two (1998). *Report of the Working Group on Transparency and Accountability*. (http//www.imf.org/external/np/g22).

International Monetary Fund (1999a). *Involving the Private Sector in Forestalling and Resolving Financial Crises*. (http://www.imf.org/external/pubs/ft/series/01/index.html)

International Monetary Fund (1999b). *A Guide to Progress in Strengthening the Architecture of the International Financial System*. (http://www.imf.org/external/np/exr/facts/arch.htm)

II

Macroeconomic Policy, Stabilization, and Transition

7 *Introduction*

I wrote "Modern Central Banking" for the tercentenary celebration of the Bank of England in June 1994, a time when the bank still had not received its independence and interest rate decisions were made by the Treasury. The paper ends with a plea for the independence of the bank. Three years later, almost the first act of the newly-elected Labor government was to grant that independence and to set monetary policy the task of ensuring price stability. British monetary policy since then has been remarkably successful in bringing inflation down to around the long-run target level of 2.5% and keeping it there without any adverse consequences for growth.

This chapter makes the case for central bank independence with inflation targeting as the preferred approach to monetary policy. That approach has been accepted increasingly around the world, particularly in emerging market countries—among them Brazil, Chile, Israel, Korea, Mexico, Poland, and South Africa—and in the smaller industrial countries—among them Australia, Canada, New Zealand, and Sweden.

For different reasons, it has not been accepted by the Federal Reserve System, the European Central Bank, and the Bank of Japan. The Fed makes the argument that "if it ain't broke, don't fix it," especially since any attempt to change the legal basis for its operation could open a Pandora's box. Fed monetary policy since the early 1980s has been remarkably successful. But that happened under two outstanding chairmen, Paul Volcker and Alan Greenspan. Not all Fed chairmen will be that good, and it is primarily for that reason that the United States would benefit from a more coherent framework for monetary policy.

The ECB operates a so-called two pillar approach to monetary policy, the pillars being money growth and inflation targets. This approach reflects the historical opposition of the Bundesbank to inflation targeting and its devotion to monetary targeting. In practice the Bundesbank was far more pragmatic than its rhetoric about monetary targeting, and in practice the ECB comes as close to operating an inflation targeting approach to monetary policy—probably excessively so—as any central bank. However the ECB appears to operate an asymmetric inflation targeting approach, being willing to accept inflation rates below its targeted two percent. This fails to recognize that low inflation can also be bad for an economy, something which the Japanese experience makes clear.

Advocates of inflation targeting for Japan argue that the economy cannot recover while deflation continues, and that the Bank of Japan should be charged with achieving a positive inflation rate. The Bank of Japan responds that it cannot operate an inflation-targeting regime with a positive inflation target when, despite its best efforts, the country suffers from deflation. The argument turns on whether the Bank of Japan is doing all it can to reverse the deflation. The answer is no, for the Bank refuses to expand its purchases of government assets or foreign exchange as much as it could. Sometimes the Governor has argued that doing so could produce hyperinflation. A real constraint on the Bank of Japan *does* exist, namely that monetary expansion gains its effectiveness in part from exchange rate depreciation, and the rest of the world probably is unwilling to accept a massive real depreciation of the yen. However the BOJ could have done more than it has to run an expansionary monetary policy. I am not convinced that under current circumstances (the end of 2002) any major gain could come from the formal adoption of an inflation targeting regime in Japan, and failure to achieve the inflation target could further damage the BOJ's reputation. Rather, I believe that the Bank of Japan should define and carry out a more expansionary monetary policy, with the stated goal of producing positive inflation, and that it should introduce a formal inflation-targeting regime as soon as deflation is abating.

In one or two matters I have changed my views since writing this chapter in 1994. In particular, it argues that the central bank should choose the inflation targets, after consultation with the government. That view was based on the existence of an underlying inflationary bias in government policy-making. I would now reverse the presumption and say that the government should set the inflation targets, after consultation with the central bank. That is because the question of the democratic legitimacy and accountability of the central bank is important—as emphasized in the second sentence of the paper. More pragmatically, I now believe that precisely how each country determines the targets cannot be prescribed a priori and should be determined in light of the country's own traditions and legal structure.

The chapter emphasizes that any monetary policy framework must contend with the short-run tradeoff between inflation and output growth, and deplores the practice of some central bank governors of denying the tradeoff. But it does not present a clear solution to the problem. Subsequent experience has persuaded me that the Bank of England's approach of targeting the inflation rate two years out is probably the best way of dealing with the tradeoff. It allows the bank to take into account the short-run impacts of monetary policy on output while ensuring that the longer-run effects of monetary policy on inflation are kept center-stage.

Several inflation-targeting central banks have had to contend with the impact of monetary policy on the real exchange rate. A tightening of monetary policy to fight inflation often leads to a real appreciation of the exchange rate. In principle this effect should dissipate over time. Consistent with the spirit of inflation targeting, some have argued that exchange rate behavior should be taken into account only to the extent that it affects inflation. That implies that the value of the exchange rate and the current account should not independently affect monetary policy decisions. Alternatively, since one policy tool cannot achieve much more than one target, one can argue that if the real exchange rate matters, because the current account and export performance matter, then fiscal policy should be deployed to deal with the exchange rate. But if the deployment does not occur, the central bank is left to deal with the dilemma. In some inflation-targeting countries, central banks from time to time intervene in the foreign exchange markets to that end. Nonetheless, we do not yet have a good systematic way of thinking about how to deal with the exchange rate in an inflation-targeting monetary policy regime.

During the 1990s, the IMF frequently recommended the adoption of inflation targeting for countries that had lost their exchange rate anchor for monetary policy. This required a great deal of preparation, including the development of inflation forecasting models in the central bank, and changes in the legal framework. The question also arose, for instance in Turkey in 2001–2002, of whether an inflation-targeting approach could be adopted before inflation had reached the low double digit range. I believe that it is useful to indicate a target range for inflation even when inflation is higher, even up to 30–50 percent, but that approach risks the central bank's losing credibility at a time when policy credibility is in short supply. That problem can be addressed by indicating a wider range for the inflation target than would be needed when inflation is low, and by deferring the introduction of a formal inflation-targeting regime until the inflation rate comes down to below the 25–30 percent per annum range.

At inflation rates above the 30–50 percent range, inflation is extremely difficult to predict and control. If a country needed to stabilize from triple-digit inflation (and fortunately there are now very few countries in that situation), then it probably would have to use a very temporary exchange rate peg to help itself down from that level and put a very broad band around its inflation targets. The country should not stay with that peg for very long, since doing so would be likely to lead to a crisis. Even though a government cannot institute a formal inflation-targeting regime at high rates of inflation, it should provide some indication of an inflation target range as a way of helping the private sector focus its own expectations and price decisions.

The development of the inflation-targeting approach to monetary policy is a real case of progress in economics, a result of the interaction of theory and empirical evidence. In the 1950s, Milton Friedman made the case for the use of a simple money-growth rule rather than allowing the central bank to carry out discretionary policy. The nature of the tradeoff between inflation and output was clarified in the 1960s, with one of the key contributions here also being made by Milton Friedman, along with Edmund Phelps. The rational-expectations revolution and the development of the game-theory approach to economic policy in the 1970s clarified both the distinction between rules and discretion in economic policy, and the reasons for the difference between the short- and long-run tradeoffs between inflation and output. As these developments were absorbed into economics, the case for the inflation-targeting approach to monetary policy clarified. The approach combines discretion in the day-to-day conduct of policy with a rule for the goals of policy. And it works well.

7 Modern Central Banking

Stanley Fischer

Introduction

The practice and theory of modern central banking revolve around the inflationary tendencies inherent in the conflict between the short- and long-run effects of monetary expansion and in the temptations of monetary financing of government spending.[1] They should also revolve around the conflict between the benefits of shielding the central bank from political pressures and the principle of accountability to the public of those who make critically important policy decisions.

The earliest central banks were set up to provide financing for governments, and to help develop the financial system, often by bringing order to the note issue.[2] As the practice of central banking developed during the nineteenth century, the central bank took on the primary responsibility for protecting the stability of the financial system and the external value of the currency. The mandate given to the central bank in legislation passed during the 1930s and 1940s—in the Great Depression and the heyday of the Keynesian revolution—typically included both monetary stability and the promotion of full employment and maximum levels of production. Then, as the inflationary forces that destroyed the Bretton Woods system gathered strength in the 1960s and 1970s, the focus of monetary policy shifted to the maintenance of the domestic value of the currency.

The trend is summarised by the contrast between the absence of a specific mandate for the Bank of England in the Bank Act of 1946[3] and the very specific goals set out for the Reserve Bank of New Zealand in the Act of 1989, "The primary function of the Bank is to formulate and implement monetary policy directed to the economic objective of achieving and maintaining stability in the general level of prices."

I start this chapter by briefly reviewing the functions and goals of central banks—the mandates set out for them in legislation, and in some cases the mandates they have chosen in interpreting conflicting legislative goals. In recent years, central banks have increasingly come to emphasise the fight against inflation and to deemphasise the possibility that monetary policy can affect the level of output; I therefore turn next to the changing views of the Phillips curve trade-off, and economic analysis of the costs of inflation.

The rational expectations revolution in macroeconomics and the growing sophistication of game-theoretic models have radically changed the academic analysis of policy-making. For the first time, economists can talk analytically about such key issues as credibility, rules versus discretion, and central bank independence. I will briefly describe some of the relevant analysis of credibility and of rules versus discretion, and draw practical lessons for policy.

In the remainder of the chapter I concentrate on the key issue of central bank independence, its analytics, and the empirical evidence. I conclude by describing the charter of a modern central bank.

Central Bank Functions and Mandates

Central banks around the world perform a variety of functions. Through their control over the monetary base—their role as "bank of issue" in an earlier terminology—all have the responsibility for managing the supply of credit and money and correspondingly determining market interest rates. Sometimes, as in Britain, the Treasury or the finance ministry makes the decisions on interest rates, and leaves only their implementation to the central bank. The central bank may be fully or jointly responsible for determining the exchange rate and managing the foreign exchange reserves. Central banks hold the reserves of the commercial banks and play a role in managing the payments system. Most are given responsibility for promoting the stability of the financial system, by supervising the banks and other financial institutions, by serving as lender of last resort, and in some countries by administering deposit insurance. The central bank is usually the government's banker; central banks often administer foreign exchange controls; in some countries they manage all or part of the national debt; the research department of the central bank may often be the best and sometimes the only policy research group in the country; the central bank may have a development banking function.

A country, particularly a developing country, derives many benefits from having a highly professional, highly respected central bank. The capacity and the reputations of, for examples, the central banks of Israel, Italy, and Mexico have all played a key role in helping bring about stabilisation and stability in their countries. But I will take a narrow perspective on central banking in this paper, by concentrating on the essential central bank function, monetary policy—management of the supply of credit and money, and thus of money market interest rates. The lender of last resort function typically accompanies this responsibility. Exchange rate and foreign reserve management can hardly be divorced from interest rate determination, though the treasury frequently shares or is responsible for these tasks.[4] Commercial bank supervision is generally the responsibility of the central bank, but in some countries is carried out in a separate agency.[5] To avoid creating a conflict between the government's desire to keep debt service low and the goals of monetary policy, management of the national debt is best left to the treasury or another agency. Whether or not the central bank is the government's banker, there is a need for coordination between the fiscal authority's management of government cash flow, and the central bank.

Control over the supply of money and credit gives the central bank potentially enormous power. In countries where the central bank has sufficient independence to determine interest rates, the goals towards which that power should be deployed are often specified in legislation. The Bundesbank is directed to conduct monetary policy "with the aim of safeguarding the currency"; it is also required to support the general economic policy of the Federal Government, but only to the extent that this is consistent with its primary goal of safeguarding the currency.[6] The Act of August 4 1993, amended 31 December 1993, gives the Banque de France the aim of ensuring price stability, within the framework of the Government's overall economic policy. This is similar to the Bundesbank mandate, but without the provision that the price stability mandate overrides the obligation to support government economic policy. Like the Bundesbank, the Reserve Bank of New Zealand is charged with producing price stability. The Federal Reserve is given a more general charge,[7] to "maintain long-run growth of the monetary and credit aggregates commensurate with the economy's long run potential to increase production, so as to promote effectively the goals of maximum employment, stable prices, and moderate long-term interest rates." There are no clearly set out goals for the Bank of

England; indeed there is a logical difficulty in specifying independent policy goals for a non-independent agency.

Where goals are either unclear or multiple, central banks may succeed in setting their own priorities. For instance the Swiss National Bank is required "to regulate the country's money circulation, to facilitate payment transactions, and to pursue a credit and monetary policy serving the interests of the country as a whole." As the SNB explained to the House of Commons Treasury and Civil Service Committee last year,[8] "The SNB understands this ... primarily as a mandate for ensuring price stability with the instruments at its disposal." Similarly, the Bank of Japan, whose 1942 legislation requires it to enhance the nation's general economic activities, states that "its objectives are commonly described as 'to maintain price stability' and 'to foster the soundness and stability of the financial system.'"[9]

Table 7.1 presents a tabulation of the legally-specified objectives of seventy-two central banks, whose charters have been studied by Cukierman, Webb and Neyapti (1992). The objectives are scaled by the degree to which they emphasise price stability relative to

Table 7.1
Central bank objectives

Description	Value of objective	Full sample		Industrial countries
		Number of countries	Percent of total	
Only price stability (can override government)	1	2	3	Germany
Only price stability	0.8	6	8	Finland, Greece Ireland, Netherlands
Price stability and compatible objective	0.6	17	24	Austria, Denmark, Luxembourg, Spain
Price stability and incompatible objectives	0.4	22	31	Australia, Iceland, New Zealand, U.S.
No objectives	0.2	10	14	Canada, Italy, Sweden, U.K.
Objectives but not price stability	0.0	15	21	Belgium, France, Japan, Norway
Total		72		21

Source: Cukierman et al., 1992, table A.1.
Note: Data are for the 1980s.

other goals. These are the goals that existed in legislation as of the 1980s.[10] Two-thirds of the countries in both the overall sample and the industrialised country group include price stability among the goals of the central bank; it is also true that two-thirds of the central banks are either not given an explicit price stability mandate or are given one that is mentioned together with a conflicting goal, for example the maintenance of full employment.

In the period since the data were tabulated, several central banks have moved up in the table, among them the central banks of France and others that plan to join the European System of Central Banks, New Zealand, and Mexico. And, as we have seen, several of the central banks which do not have explicit or sole price stability targets, interpret their mandates as emphasising price stability. Increasingly, the debate over the role and mandate of central banks focuses on the question of whether the central bank should be given the sole or primary task of assuring price stability or low inflation.

Why should this be, when monetary policy affects both output and prices in the short run? The answer starts from the well-known history of the Phillips curve.

The Phillips Curve

The original 1958 Phillips curve showed a century-long relationship between wage inflation and unemployment in the United Kingdom. A century surely qualifies as a long run, and so it should not be surprising that some economists of the time concluded that the curve represented a trade-off menu of choices facing the government, in which the benefits of lower inflation have to be balanced against their costs in terms of higher unemployment. The Phillips curve was brought to the United States by Paul Samuelson and Robert Solow (1960), who after presenting the menu view of the curve, warned that their discussion dealt only with the short run, and that it would be wrong to think that the same trade-off would be maintained in the longer run.[11]

None the less, United States experience through the 1960s presented the appearance of a simple Phillips curve trade-off, as unemployment steadily declined and inflation gradually increased (figure 7.1). But that of course was only the beginning of the story. As the textbooks tell us,[12] even before the end of the 1960s Edmund Phelps (1967) and Milton Friedman (1968) predicted that the Phillips curve

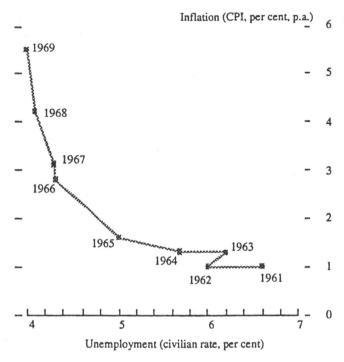

Figure 7.1
Inflation and unemployment, United States, 1961–1969.

would shift as expectations of inflation adjusted to actual inflationary experience. Unemployment could not be kept permanently
below its natural rate, and attempts to do so would lead only to
accelerating inflation. The experience of the next two decades, shown
in figure 7.2, certainly supported their prediction that the curve
would shift.

The Phillips curve had been presented as an empirical phenomenon, and rationalised as an example of the law of supply and demand which asserts that excess demand causes the price of a good to
rise. Friedman and Phelps pointed out that wage negotiators bargain
about the real wage, and that nominal wage increases would therefore be adjusted to reflect expectations of inflation. This destroyed
the theoretical basis for assuming a long-run trade-off between inflation and unemployment; the facts seen in figure 7.2 destroyed the
empirical basis for assuming that there is any simple form of long-
run trade-off. We shall return to the question of the long-run trade-
off below.

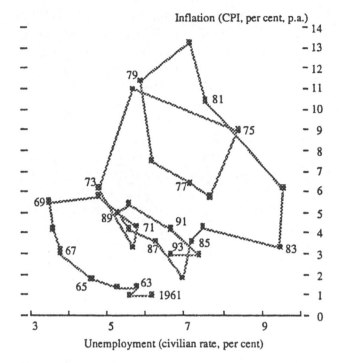

Figure 7.2
Inflation and unemployment, United States, 1961–1993.

In the Friedman-Phelps Phillips curve, it is only errors in expectations that permit unemployment to differ from the natural rate. Friedman and Phelps assumed that expectations were formed adaptively,[13] so that the monetary authority could for a time keep unemployment low by accelerating the inflation rate. As inflation accelerated, workers—forming their expectations with a lag—would continually underpredict inflation, the real wage would remain below its equilibrium level, and employment would exceed its equilibrium level. With the addition of the assumption of rational expectations, Lucas (1973) destroyed even the short-run Phillips curve trade-off. In his model, no predictable monetary policy has any effects on output, because the private sector takes the monetary policy into account, adjusts its expectations accordingly, and there is no possibility of a systematic gap between expected and actual inflation.

The Lucas no short-run trade-off view would, if correct, imply that systematic monetary policy can only affect the inflation rate, and should therefore be deployed to that end. But while the view that there is no long-run trade-off between inflation and unemployment is widely accepted, the no short-run trade-off view is not. The most obvious reason not to accept the no short-run trade-off proposition is that central banks have demonstrated repeatedly that they can create recessions by tightening monetary policy. It does not take sophisticated econometric analysis to recognize that the Fed produced a recession in 1981–1982 as is successfully reduced inflation. Romer and Romer (1989) have more systematically shown that Fed policy decisions to tighten monetary policy have been followed by recessions. A second reason not to accept the no short-run trade-off view is the econometric evidence that predictable monetary policy affects output and not only prices.[14]

The question remains of why there is a short-run Phillips curve trade-off. The short-run trade-off in the Lucas (1973) model is the result of confusion by buyers and sellers about the meaning of changes in nominal prices; in that model, even unpredictable monetary policy would have no real effect of any kind if there were perfect information about the current money stock or aggregate price level. A more plausible explanation is that monetary policy gets its short-run leverage from the existence of sticky wages and prices, resulting for instance from long-term and perhaps overlapping wage contracts.[15] The stickiness may result more fundamentally from costs of changing individual prices[16] or renegotiating wages.

The terms of the short-run trade-off between output and inflation may depend on the average rate of inflation. Because prices in a high inflation economy have to be changed frequently, any excess monetary expansion is likely to be taken into account in a price change within a short time. In a low inflation economy, by contrast, prices need not be changed very often, and so prices are likely to respond less rapidly to a monetary expansion. This would mean that the short-run Phillips curve is flatter in a low inflation economy than in a high inflation economy.[17]

The existence of a short-run trade-off between output and inflation is central to the day-to-day decisions confronting monetary policy-makers. There is no escaping the fact that it is almost always possible to increase output by accelerating money growth,[18] or to cause a recession by tightening credit sufficiently. Even if there is no long-run trade-off between inflation and real output, there is a short-run trade-off.

The social benefits of one part of that trade-off, the increase in output and decline in unemployment brought about by expansionary policy, appear to be obvious.[19] We need to consider the other part of the trade-off, the social costs of higher inflation, in more detail.

The Costs of Inflation

Reporting to the House of Commons in 1810, the Select Committee on the High Price of Gold Bullion dealt summarily with the costs of inflation (in this case high prices): "Your committee conceive that it would be superfluous to point out, in detail, the disadvantages which must result to the country from any such general excess of currency as lowers its value."[20] Almost two centuries later, it is still often said we lack an account of the costs of inflation that matches the intensity with which inflation is denounced by policymakers and disliked by the general public. It is more accurate to say that while there are convincing accounts of the many costs of inflation, especially in a society that has not adapted to its existence, the costs have been difficult to quantify.[21]

Table 7.2 presents a reasonably complete listing of the costs of inflation, which depend on the institutional structure of the economy and on the extent to which the inflation has been anticipated. Rather than work through the table in detail, I will summarise the major categories of costs, and then go on to discuss recent work relating the growth of output and productivity to inflation.

The most analysed cost of inflation is the money triangle or shoe-leather costs,[22] the social cost of economising on the use of non-interest bearing money. The area of the triangle depends on the magnitude of the relevant money stock and on the elasticity of money demand with respect to the nominal interest rate. For simplicity, we take currency to be the relevant concept of money. The average ratio of currency to GNP in the G-7 in 1992 was 5.2 percent. The average inflation rate (CPI) for these seven countries for the period 1989–1992 was 4.5 percent.[23] Assuming an interest elasticity of 0.25, and that the nominal interest rate is 2 percent when the inflation rate is zero, a reduction in the inflation rate to zero would increase the stock of currency to 7 percent of GNP. The welfare gained as a result of that decline in inflation would amount only to 0.03 percent of GDP.

Table 7.2
The real effects of inflation

Source of effect	Direct effect	Indirect (general equilibrium) effects
Fully indexed economy		
No interest paid on currency, a government (outside) liability	1. Increase in government revenue (inflation tax) 2. Economising on currency 3. Reduction in private net wealth 4. Resource costs of price change ('menu costs')	G1 Reduction in other taxes or increases in government spending. G2 Diversion of resources to transactions (shoe-leather costs) G3 Offsetting increase in capital stock, lowering real interest rate
Real effects of nominal government institutions		
Progressive taxation of nominal income	5. Increased real income tax bill	G5 See G1
Nominal tax base		
1. Taxation of nominal interest income received by persons	6. Reduction of net of tax return on lending relative to pretax real rate	G6–10 Potential effects on cost of capital to corporations and individuals, with resultant effects on capital accumulation; changes in patterns of financing
2. Deductibility of nominal interest paid by persons		G9 See also G1
3. Deductibility of nominal interest paid by corporations	7. Reduction of net real cost of borrowing relative to pretax real rate 8. Return to equity holders in levered corporations rises given constant debt-equity ratios, constant real pretax interest rate on bonds, and constant marginal product of capital 9. Changes in government tax receipts; net effect depends on induced changes in pretax real interest rate on bonds, differences in tax rates between debtors (including corporations) and creditors	

Table 7.2
(continued)

Source of effect	Direct effect	Indirect (general equilibrium) effects
4. Depreciation at original cost Costs of goods sold measured at original costs	10. Return to equity holders declines 11. Tax revenue increases	G10–11 See also G1 Combined effects vary among firms, depending on nature of assets; likely shift away from use of long-lived assets; shift in inventory accounting methods from FIFO to LIFO
5. Taxation of nominal capital gains	12. Post-tax return to equity owners on realized gains declines if pre-tax return remains constant 13. Lock in effects	
Nominal accounting methods used by government	14. Distortions in interpretations of economic situation, e.g., nominal interest share in GNP rises, savings rate misinterpreted since both income and savings measured incorrectly; overstatement of government deficit	
Real effects of nominal private institutions and habits		
Continued reliance on nominal annuity contracts, mortgages	15. Declining real repayment streams relative to nominal streams	G15 Possible effects on real interest rates, and therefore investment
Nominal accounting methods	16. Distortion of reports of profits; other money illusions based on confusion between real and nominal interest rates possible	G16 Effects on stock market valuation of firms; investment decisions
Real effects of unanticipated inflation through existing nominal contracts		
Existing contracts for goods or services fixed in money terms or otherwise sticky	17. Redistribution between buyer and seller if quantity of services fixed by contract 18. Effects on quantity of services provided 19. Distortions of relative prices fixed at different times	G17–19 Effects on level of economic activity (Phillips curve); short-run functional income redistribution by income size

Table 7.2
(continued)

Source of effect	Direct effect	Indirect (general equilibrium) effects
Existing debt contracts fixed in nominal terms	20. Redistribution from private to public sector 21. Redistribution between private debtors and creditors	G19 Misallocations of resources arising particularly from need to search for relative price information G20 Ultimately inter-generational transfers
Real effects of uncertainty of future inflation		
Need to make decisions without knowledge of future prices	22. Reluctance to make future commitments without knowledge of prices; absence of safe asset	G22 Changes in patterns of asset accumulation
	23. Shortening of nominal contracts	G23 Increased transactions costs of making frequent contracts, and loss of planning ability
Real effects of government endeavors to suppress symptoms of inflation		
Public dissatisfaction over inflation, and governmental reactions	24. Wage and price controls	G24 Shortages, possibly pervasive; misallocations of resources
Government concern over potential bankruptcies and other financial losses resulting from a rise in interest rates	25. Control of interest rates, intervention in bond markets	G25 Instability of financial flows, with possible effects on direction and level of investment activity

Of course, these small welfare costs apply only at low inflation rates.[24] When inflation reaches the triple digit range, the social costs of attempting to economise on currency become high. Financial departments of firms expand at the expense of production, consumers spend time and resources delaying payments, and this social cost of inflation rises—approximately with the square of the inflation rate.

The money triangle calculation implicitly assumes the existence of non-distorting taxes to compensate for revenues lost by reducing inflation. If lump-sum taxes are available, then Friedman (1969) showed that the optimal inflation rate is not zero but rather that inflation rate which satiates the economy with real balances by driving the nominal interest rate to zero. Absent lump-sum taxes, the inflation tax may form part of an optimal tax package, so that the optimal inflation rate could be positive. However, the fiscal approach to inflation provides no clear theoretical presumption as to whether the optimal inflation tax is positive.[25]

There are two other potential effects of even a fully anticipated inflation. First, savers may substitute capital for real balances in their portfolio as inflation increases.[26] This would offset the steady state costs of the inflation. The portfolio substitution effect is bound to be small at low inflation rates, because the money displacement effect is itself small. In addition, inflation would generate menu costs—the costs of more frequent changes of prices. Menu costs have not been measured, but it is hard to believe they would amount to much in a low inflation economy.

The familiar conclusion so far is that the costs of any fully anticipated inflation rate below say 5 percent, in an economy whose institutions have adapted to inflation, must be moderate indeed. If inflation has significant costs, they must arise from the non-adaptation of institutions to inflation, and because inflation is often not anticipated.

The most important source of institutional non-neutrality to inflation is the tax system; within the tax system it is the taxation of capital that is most distorted by inflation. The deductibility of nominal interest and the taxation of nominal capital gains are the two main distortions. Assuming that the effective tax rate on saving rises with inflation, and making a host of subsidiary assumptions, it is possible to calculate the costs of lower rates of capital accumulation implied by higher inflation.[27] In addition, rising rates of taxation associated with inflation cause misallocations of capital among sectors, and affect corporate financing decisions. In the presence of bracket creep, rising inflation would also affect labour supply.

Taken together, such inflation-caused distortions could easily have a social cost amounting to 2–3 percent of GNP at an inflation rate of 10 percent.[28] However, there is a very real question of whether these costs should be attributed to inflation, for most of them could be removed by indexing the tax system. Income tax brackets have been indexed in the United States but indexation of capital taxation is generally more cumbersome and rare.

The assumption of a constant value of money is also built into private sector institutions, including the typical level-payment nominal mortgage in the United States, and accounting practices. There has been an increasing recognition of inflation in both areas in the last two decades, with a corresponding reduction in the costs of inflation. It has also become more common to recognise the effects of inflation-caused increases in interest rates on government fiscal data, with the notion of the operational deficit gaining increasing usage in moderate-to-high inflation countries.[29]

Unanticipated inflations are associated with redistributions of income and wealth, the latter of which may be massive. Keynes (1924) argued that entrepreneurs gain from inflation, and it is often believed that labor loses. However, the direction of any redistribution of income must depend on the source of the inflationary shock and, at least in the moderate inflations in the United States, the estimated redistributions are small.

Inflation-induced wealth redistributions are larger, both between the private and public sectors, and within the private sector between debtors and creditors. Taking the Maastricht norm, at a debt to GDP ratio of 60 percent an increase in the price level by 1 percent reduces the value of government debt by 0.6 percent of GDP. Unanticipated changes in the price level thus have potentially large impacts on private sector wealth. However because a reduction in the value of government debt reduces future taxes, these redistributions should be viewed as intergenerational within the private sector rather than between public and private sectors, with unanticipated inflation reducing the wealth of the old and increasing that of the young. This is certainly one source of the political unpopularity of inflation. Within the private sector, unanticipated inflation benefits the debtors. Corporations appear to gain at the expense of their lenders, though equities do not generally benefit from inflation—so that unanticipated inflation benefits neither bondholders nor equityholders. Mortgage borrowers gain at the expense of depositors and other lenders.

The wealth redistributions associated with even moderate rates of unanticipated inflation are likely to be economically and politically significant. That is all the more so when unanticipated changes in the price level are large, as they have been in the aftermath of wars. It is however difficult to estimate the social costs of such redistributions, for one group gains what another loses.

A considerable body of evidence establishes that the variability of relative prices rises with the inflation rate, for both anticipated and unanticipated inflation. In both cases, it is likely that the increased variability of relative prices distorts the allocation of resources.[30] These inflation-related distortions must be part of the explanation for the negative association between growth and inflation to be documented below.

Finally, high inflation is also more uncertain inflation.[31] There are several possible reasons for this relationship: inflation is often associated with real shocks; the higher the inflation rate, the more likely it is that the government will want to reduce the inflation rate at some point; higher inflation is a signal of a government that is losing control over the economy. Whatever the cause, the higher uncertainty is costly, potentially reducing investment,[32] and also reducing the welfare of savers forced to contend with it. The welfare costs for savers of greater uncertainty are related to the potential benefits of the introduction of indexed bonds. Sample calculations in Fischer (1981) suggest that an increase in the uncertainty of inflation typically associated with a rise in inflation within the range of recent United States experience would create no more than a modest social cost.

This long list establishes the many ramifications of inflation, anticipated and unanticipated, in a modern economy even at moderate rates of inflation. Adding together those elements in the list that can be quantified would provide an estimate of the costs of a 10 percent inflation at 2–5 percent of GNP. That is a sizable social cost, albeit one that could be significantly reduced by indexation.

But it remains true that such an enumeration does not capture the very strong feelings about inflation that are evident even in the less inflation-averse industrialised economies. Some of the popular attitude must derive from the belief that inflation unfairly takes away the fruits of inflation-caused nominal income increases that people incorrectly attribute to their own merit and hard work.[33] Another factor must be the disorientation of having to deal with price increases in the face of the surprisingly deeply inbuilt belief that money values are stable, a form of money illusion.[34] A further cause of the popular view must be the fear that the disorders of hyperinflation lie just over the horizon of any inflation, a fear that is more vivid in countries that have suffered hyperinflations.

Most important, the experience of inflation is rarely that of a simple steady rate of growth of prices at sustained full employment. Rather, inflation is usually associated with other problems, supply shocks or a lack of fiscal control. Yet another cause of the popular attitude must be the generally negative association between output growth and inflation.

Indexation

Many of the costs of inflation would be reduced by the introduction of indexation. This applies to the tax system, to inflation-caused wealth redistributions on debt, and to the losses to savers from the greater uncertainty associated with higher inflation. Here lies the essential case for government introduction of indexed bonds, to reduce the uncertainties confronting those saving for retirement.[35] Indexation of wages would reduce the redistribution of income associated with demand-caused inflation in the presence of long-term labour contracts, and would also make the Phillips curve steeper.

Many governments, and particularly central bankers, have long opposed indexation, on the grounds that its introduction would be a confession of failure in the battle against inflation, and would weaken the will to continue the fight.[36] In the words of Arthur Burns (1978, p. 148):

This [indexation] is a counsel of despair ... I doubt if there is any practical way of redesigning economic contracts to deal with this problem satisfactorily. In any event, if a nation with our traditions attempted to make it easy to live with inflation, rather than resist its corrosive influence, we would slowly but steadily lose the sense of discipline needed to pursue governmental policies with an eye to the permanent welfare of our people.

Game theoretic models provide some support for this view (Fischer and Summers 1989). In models in which monetary policy has an inflationary bias because of dynamic inconsistency,[37] any change that reduces the social costs of inflation increases the equilibrium inflation rate, *and tends to worsen social welfare*,[38] essentially for the reasons given by the Radcliffe Committee and by Arthur Burns. However, it is necessary to distinguish different types of indexation. Indexing that increases the costs of unanticipated inflation to the government tends to reduce the inflation rate. Thus, indexation of taxes and of bonds that reduces the government's gains from unanticipated inflation would not necessarily cause higher inflation: the net effect depends on the relative extents to which such indexation reduces the social costs of inflation compared with the extent to which it reduces the government's gains from unanticipated inflation. Not all central bankers have opposed bond indexation;[39] nor has the introduction of index bonds in Britain had any obviously adverse effects on the government's will to fight inflation.

The extent of indexation in an economy is a measure of how much inflation that economy has experienced. It would thus be difficult to establish empirically whether indexation generally weakens the will to fight inflation. However, it is certainly clear from the cases of Israel and Brazil in the early 1980s that the view that the country had learned to live with inflation was instrumental in both the increases in inflation in each and the deterioration of their economic situations.

Widespread indexation that reduces the social costs of inflation for society is likely to increase inflation and quite possibly make the society worse off. Indexation that reduces the government's incentives to inflate by reducing its gains from inflation can make society better off.

Inflation, Growth, and Productivity

At least since the time of David Hume ([1752] 1955), it has been argued that a little inflation is good for growth:

The good policy of the magistrate consists only in keeping it [the money stock], if possible, still increasing; because by that means he keeps alive a spirit of industry in the nation, and increases the stock of labour in which consists all real power and riches.

Early models of money and growth likewise suggested that an increase in inflation would temporarily increase growth, and increase the steady state capital stock as investors substitute capital for real balances in their portfolio. More recent models allow for a negative association between inflation and growth, for example because inflation is associated with greater price variability and greater uncertainty, thereby reducing both the effectiveness of the price mechanism, and investment.

The context here is not the short-run Phillips curve trade-off, but rather the longer-term relationship between inflation and growth. The evidence points strongly to a predominantly *negative* longer-term relationship between growth and inflation.[40] Cross-country regressions reported in Fischer (1993) show a consistently negative association between inflation and growth. Based on a panel regression for eighty countries over the period 1961–1988, it is estimated that an increase in the inflation rate by 10 percentage points (e.g. from 5 to 15 percent per annum) is associated with a decline in output growth of 0.4 percent per annum. Estimation of a spline regression shows that these inflation effects are non-linear, the marginal effect on growth associated with an increase in inflation declining as inflation rises. The spline regression shows a larger though barely statistically significant effect of higher inflation on growth for inflation in the range of 0–15 percent per annum: in this range, a 10 percentage point increase in the inflation rate is associated with a reduction in the growth rate of output by 1.25 percent per annum.

Decomposing growth into its components due to capital accumulation, productivity growth, and an increase in the growth rate of the labour force, the negative association between inflation and growth can be traced to strong negative relationships between inflation and capital accumulation, and inflation and productivity growth, respectively. A 10 percentage point increase in the inflation rate is associated with a decline in productivity growth of 0.18 percent per annum.

These negative associations do not, of course, establish that increases in inflation cause lower growth. If higher inflation is caused by adverse supply shocks, then the negative correlation between inflation and growth merely reflects the common impact of supply shocks. Fischer (1993) attempts to deal with this possibility by breaking the period into two at 1973, the date after which supply shocks became prominent. It turns out that the negative association between growth and inflation exists for both sub-periods. While this result is suggestive, it does not entirely dispose of the causation issue; indeed, given that policymakers do not create inflation out of a clear blue sky, it is almost certain that countries with high inflation rates are countries that are already in trouble for fiscal or other reasons, and thus that it will be either impossible or extremely difficult to deal definitively with the issue of causation.

The association between growth and inflation has also been examined for individual countries. In the Canadian case, Jarrett and Selody (1982) found that a one percentage point reduction in inflation was associated with a 0.3 percent increase in the growth rate. The effect is too large to be causal: if it were, a decline in the inflation rate from 5 percent to zero would increase the growth rate by 1.5 percent, surely a trade-off anyone would be happy to make.

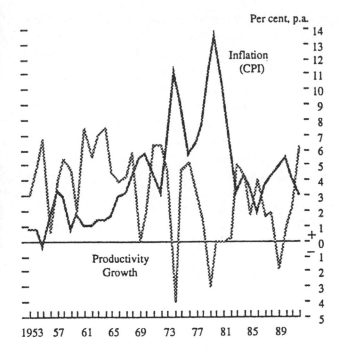

Figure 7.3
Inflation and productivity, United States, 1953–1992.

Rudebusch and Wilcox (1994) examine the closely related issue of the relationship between the rate of productivity growth and inflation. Using United States data, they find that an increase in inflation of 1 percent is associated with a 0.35 percent decline in productivity growth, an even bigger coefficient than in the Canadian case. Figure 7.3 shows United States data. The estimated coefficient for Canada and the UK is almost the same as that for the United States; it is significantly smaller and sometimes insignificant for other members of the G-7.

Rudebusch and Wilcox attempt to pin down whether the relationship is causal. One possibility is that the relationship reflects cyclical timing patterns: productivity growth is low near the peak of the cycle, when inflation is high, and high during the early part of the recovery, when inflation is typically still low. Figure 7.3 certainly suggests a strong cyclical element in the relationship. Making an adjustment for the cycle reduces the regression coefficient. Attempting to deal with the simultaneity issue econometrically, by the use of instrumental variables, Rudebusch and Wilcox find that the coefficient on inflation typically becomes insignificant. While these two approaches suggest the relationship is not causal, Granger causality tests point in the opposite direction, implying that inflation Granger-causes productivity growth rather than vice versa.

In summary, while there is a strong and suggestive negative relation between longer-term growth and inflation, and productivity growth and inflation, the statistical evidence has not yet established that the relationship is causal. One reason to suspect that the relationship is not causal is that the coefficient on inflation in the productivity growth equation is too large. Another is that the relationship does not appear particularly robust.[41]

However weak the evidence, one strong conclusion can be drawn: inflation is not good for longer-term growth.

The Optimal Inflation Rate: Zero Inflation versus Price Level Stability

The fiscal view of inflation presents one approach to determining the optimal rate of inflation. However, it is hard to believe that seigniorage can be a significant determinant of the optimal inflation rate in an industrialised economy with a sophisticated tax system. Rather the optimal inflation rate should be determined on the basis of all the costs of inflation, and of any benefits it might have.

The many costs of inflation are manifest. If there is no long-run trade-off between inflation and unemployment, or inflation and growth, at any positive inflation rate, and absent a fiscal motive for inflation, it is hard to see any benefits.[42] This would suggest a target inflation rate of zero.

Reinforcing this view is the argument that zero is the only credible target, that once the monetary authority agrees to allow some inflation, it cannot plausibly commit to fighting higher inflation. Phelps (1972, p. xvi) characterises this view[43] as

Compare "Price Stability, Right or Wrong," which has a nice ring to it, with "If I have but one job to give to my economy, let me give it for 5.5 percent inflation, as against higher numbers," which is absurd.

Let me for the moment accept that the target inflation rate should be zero. The important distinction then has to be drawn between a zero inflation target and the target of price level stability.[44] With a target

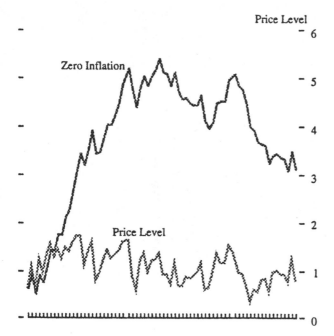

Figure 7.4
Price level, zero inflation vs. price-level targeting.

inflation rate of zero, the central bank aims to achieve zero inflation each period, that is, to keep the price level at its current level. A central bank committed to price level stability would aim to undo the consequences of past failures to achieve the target price level. With a zero inflation target each period, there is considerable uncertainty about price levels in the distant future. With a price level stability target, there should be much less uncertainty about price levels in the distant future.

Figure 7.4, one realisation of a stochastic simulation, illustrates the difference.[45] Each period the monetary authority achieves its target price level for that period, up to a random error. With a zero inflation target, the price level is a random walk. This means that the variance of future price levels increases linearly with their distance from the current period. With a price level target, the monetary authority is assumed each period to aim to close half the gap between the current price level and the target price level. This ensures that the actual price level stays close to the target level, and that uncertainty about future price levels is small.

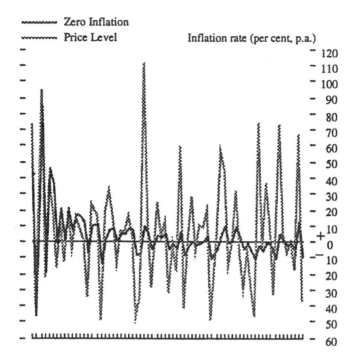

Figure 7.5
Inflation rates, zero inflation vs. price-level targeting.

The chief benefit of a price level target is that it keeps uncertainty about price levels in the distant future much smaller than it would be with a zero inflation target. The chief disadvantage is that the monetary authority with a price level target is attempting to deflate the economy half the time: the short-run target inflation rate will be negative half the time. For reasons to be discussed shortly, there are good reasons not to target negative inflation. Price level targeting is thus a bad idea, one that would add unnecessary short-term fluctuations to the economy. It is also true, as can be been in figure 7.5, that there is more variability and uncertainty about short-term inflation rates with a price level target than with a target inflation rate.

It is sometimes said that price level stability is desirable because it would once again make long-term nominal contracting more attractive. Reference is made in this context to 99-year nominal leases, or the 100-year railroad bonds issued during the nineteenth century, a period in which a substantial measure of price level stability was achieved: in Britain, the same level of prices prevailed in 1914 as in

1881 as in 1844; setting that level at 100, prices ranged only between 70 and 130 in the period 1826 to 1914.[46] It is difficult to see much benefit from 99-year nominal leases or to make the case that 100-year bonds are an economically significant improvement over 50-year bonds, or 30-year bonds. And besides, some 100-year bonds have recently been sold in the United States.

Price level predictability is desirable for those saving for retirement. But it is far easier to provide for a stable real income stream in retirement by issuing index bonds than by trying to maintain a constant value of money.

Uncertainty about future price levels is unlikely to be much greater if the monetary authority targets a small positive inflation rate rather than a zero inflation rate. Thus there is no significant benefit from the viewpoint of the predictability of future price levels between choosing a zero inflation target and a 2–3 percent inflation target.

So far I have accepted the zero inflation target. There are however three good reasons not to aim for zero inflation. First, it may sometimes be useful for the real interest rate to be negative. The real interest rate on bills cannot be negative if the inflation rate is zero and the nominal yield on currency, which sets a lower bound to the bill rate, is also zero.[47] The real rate has been negative during recessions, and there is no good reason to deprive monetary policy of the possibility of having an *ex ante* negative real yield at times. Second, any downward price inflexibility would increase the output costs of negative inflation rates, which would be more frequent with a zero inflation goal.[48] Third, our measures of inflation are biased upwards. Estimates of the bias in the United States are as high as 1.5–2 percent per annum.[49] It is very hard to see why the central bank should struggle to achieve a measured inflation rate of zero when true inflation would at that point be significantly negative.[50]

These arguments suggest that a positive though low target rate of inflation, around 1–3 percent, would be optimal. This is in practice the range that the Bundesbank has set for itself over the years, and it is similar to the ranges specified by both the Reserve Bank of New Zealand and the Bank of Canada in recent years.[51]

The issue of a target price level versus target inflation rate none the less remains. Compare the goal of being close to a target price level that is growing at 2 percent per annum from a given date, say January 1995, with the goal of achieving a 2 percent inflation rate each year from 1995 on. The argument about price level versus zero inflation targeting is easily reformulated to apply to this case. With a target price path, the monetary authority attempts to offset past errors, thus creating more uncertainty about short-term inflation rates than with an inflation target. The gain is more certainty about the long-term price level. My present view is that the inflation target with its greater short-term inflation rate certainty is preferable, despite its greater long-term price level uncertainty.

Dynamic Inconsistency and Inflationary Bias

Inflation in most of the G-7 countries ratcheted up in the 1960s and 1970s. In the four business cycles completed in the United States between 1960 and 1981, the average inflation rate rose from 2.8 percent to 9.9 percent. By the end of the 1970s, the inflation rate in the United States, like that in France, the United Kingdom, Italy and Canada was higher than any conceivable account of the costs and benefits of inflation could justify. No wonder that economists felt called upon to explain the apparent inflationary bias of economic policy.

Before we proceed, it is worth asking for a moment whether there is indeed an inflationary bias to economic policy. The simple answer is yes: inflation in most countries has exceeded the optimal rate of 1–3 percent. It was not always thus: at the ends of the Napoleonic and Civil Wars, and after World War I, Britain and the United States disinflated to get back to fixed gold parities. Certainly after World War I, this was not a wise policy and the disinflationary bias of monetary policy would have had to be explained. The price level was stable for nearly a century until 1914, and it is only in the era of fiduciary money that the inflationary bias has emerged in most countries.

The most obvious explanation for an inflationary bias in economic policy is seigniorage. As already discussed, inflation is a tax, and under certain conditions, should be used in an optimal fiscal program. But because the tax is not an explicit one, it tends to be used to excess: in Keynes's (1924, p. 46) much quoted words,

A Government can live for a long time, even the German Government or the Russian Government, by printing paper money ... The method is condemned, but its efficacy, up to a point, must be admitted. A Government can live by this means when it can live by no other. It is the form of taxation which the public finds hardest to evade and even the weakest Government can enforce, when it can enforce nothing else.

Seigniorage helps explain why inflation is on average higher in countries with less developed tax systems than in those that succeed in collecting taxes. The inflation tax is also central to the analysis of hyperinflations. But because seigniorage revenues in the major industrialised countries are relatively small as a share of GNP,[52] and perhaps because of the institutional separation between the Treasury and the central bank (the inflation tax rate is not set in the budget), seigniorage appears not to receive explicit weight in the policy calculus that produces the inflation rate.[53]

The fiscal aspects of inflation should nonetheless be taken more seriously as a source of inflationary bias. Inflation tax revenues of course constitute a larger share of tax revenues than of GNP; in the 1960s and 1970s, seigniorage accounted for more than six percent of tax (including seigniorage) revenues for several of the industrialised countries. Seigniorage considerations could help account for the increase in inflation during the 1960s and 1970s as government spending and taxes in general increased during that period. Further, a broader concept of the inflation tax, one that includes the gains that governments receive from unindexed tax brackets, and—if the inflation was unanticipated—from the devaluation of nominal government debt, renders the inflation tax explanation for an inflationary bias more plausible, especially if the inflation is unanticipated.

Nominal interest rate targeting provides a related explanation for the inflationary trends of the 1960s and 1970s. If monetary policy targets the nominal interest rate, and has no nominal anchor—that is, no monetary or price level target to tie down the price *level*—then the price level becomes indeterminate, and may move in any direction, including upwards at an increasing rate. The explanation appears straightforward: the central bank automatically accommodates any shock to money demand, including for instance one arising from an increase in output that tends to raise inflation through the Phillips curve, or an increase in the expected inflation rate. In so doing it may validate the original shock. However, this argument encounters difficulties on closer examination. Formally, it can be shown that nominal interest rate targeting may produce an indeterminate inflation rate if inflation expectations are adaptive, but will not do so if expectations are rational. More important, combining any nominal anchor with a nominal interest rate target keeps the price level determinate.[54] To put the same point less formally, a central bank that keeps its nominal interest rate constant no matter what, may produce an accelerating inflation; a central bank that raises the target nominal rate when inflation increases, need not suffer the same fate.

It is a third explanation of inflationary bias that forms the basis of most recent models of central bank independence. That is the notion of *dynamic inconsistency*. Dynamic inconsistency is the inconsistency between the optimal policies that a policy authority would announce if its announcements were believed by the public, and the policies the authority would carry out once the public had acted on the basis of those expectations. The simplest example of dynamic inconsistency arises in the case of capital taxation. In order to encourage growth, the government should promise to tax capital at a low rate. But once the capital is in place, the government is tempted to tax it, promising all the while that this will not happen again. In the case of inflation, the government will announce that it is committed to fighting inflation. If the private sector responds by signing contracts that embody a low expected rate of inflation, the central bank is tempted to produce higher output through surprise inflation. But in a rational world, the private sector will understand the temptations that face the monetary authority, and discount its pronouncements accordingly.

Equilibrium in this game theoretic model, due to Kydland and Prescott (1977) and Barro and Gordon (1983), occurs at that point where the inflation rate is sufficiently high that the marginal cost of higher (surprise) inflation is just equal to the marginal benefit of the lower unemployment it will produce. But this equilibrium inflation rate is higher than it needs to be. It is too high because output is at the same level (the natural rate) as it would be at a lower inflation rate. All that keeps inflation from being lower is the central bank's inability credibly to promise not to create surprise inflation at lower inflation rates—to precommit, in the language of game theory. Any device or institutional change that persuades the private sector that the government will not create surprise inflation at lower inflation rates will reduce the equilibrium inflation rate.[55]

The tension between the direct benefits of lower inflation and the benefits of surprise inflation[56] that lies at the heart of these models is fundamental to modern analyses of monetary policy in general and central banking in particular. The model provides not only the basis for a theory of the role of monetary policy, but also a clear definition of credibility: a policy is credible when the private sector believes it will be carried out, and when it is correspondingly in the interest of the public sector to carry out the policy once the private sector has acted on its beliefs. Equivalently, a policy is credible if it is not dynamically inconsistent. The term credibility is of course used less precisely in other contexts: for instance, a central bank is said to be credible if its announcements are believed.[57]

In practice, societies find ways of dealing with dynamic inconsistency. Despite the temptations of taxing capital in place heavily, just once, capital levies are rare. Some countries had low inflation rates well before the notion of dynamic inconsistency was formalised. The patent system deals with a similar problem in the creation of knowledge.[58]

An independent central bank is one of the mechanisms that can deal with the inflationary bias of monetary policy.

Rules, Discretion and Central Bank Independence

Kydland and Prescott (1977) and Barro and Gordon (1983) saw their demonstration of the inflationary bias of discretionary monetary policy as making the case for a monetary rule, along Friedman lines. With a monetary rule firmly in place, the central bank would not be able to create surprise inflation, and the problem of dynamic inconsistency would disappear. However a monetary rule is a far cry from an independent central bank.

Friedman's (1959) argument for a constant growth rate of money rule, based on the potentially destabilising effects of active monetary policy when its effects have long and variable lags, may have led to the view that a money rule must be a constant growth rate rule. But activist feedback monetary rules are possible. The Barro-Gordon argument for a money rule would carry over to a model in which there is a potential role for an active monetary policy in offsetting shocks, thereby helping to stabilize at least inflation and perhaps also output. Given the structure of the economy, the optimal monetary feedback rule could be legislated into place and dynamic inconsistency and its inflationary bias would be prevented.[59]

More sophisticated monetary feedback rules that take account of changes in the velocity of circulation have been proposed. For instance, McCallum (1994) proposes a rule that sets the growth rate of the money base at 3 percent per annum, with adjustments for the change in base velocity over the past four years[60] and also for the deviation of nominal GNP from a target path. This rule is shown to produce good inflation and output performance in several small econometric models.

Note that there are two different arguments for a monetary rule in preference to discretionary monetary policy. Friedman's view is that policy-makers not bound by a constant growth rate rule would be tempted into excess activism, destabilising rather than stabilising the economy. Barro and Gordon argue that discretionary policy has an inflationary bias, but do not dispute the possibility of a stabilising activist feedback policy. Once the latter possibility is admitted, the case for a monetary rule—a rule that rigidly prescribes the behavior of a monetary aggregate—must rest on dynamic inconsistency. But there is then a trade-off between the benefits of avoiding the inflationary bias of discretionary policy and the potential cost of being bound to follow a monetary rule that is no longer appropriate.

Goodhart's law and much recent experience suggest that any monetary rule will eventually break down; in the words of Richard Sayers (1958, p. 7), "we are doomed to disappointment if we look for rules applicable to all times and all places." The money demand instability manifested in many countries in the 1970s and 1980s, and in Germany in the last year, has put paid to the notion of relying on any simple monetary feedback rule, much less to legislating such a rule into existence. There cannot be a case now for dealing with the problem of dynamic inconsistency by putting in place any rule that prescribes by a fixed formula the growth rate of any monetary aggregate or the behaviour of interest rates. Rather, the monetary authorities need to be given some flexibility to decide on day to day monetary policy. In this context, rules of the McCallum type can provide a useful benchmark against which to judge policy.

A fixed exchange rate peg is a form of monetary rule, one that leaves very little room for discretionary policy if the peg is taken seriously. A country that pegs to a reasonably stable currency can solve its inflationary problem. But exchange rate pegging is not danger-free: because non-traded goods prices can increase relative to traded goods prices, countries that peg frequently find themselves with overvalued currencies. In any fixed exchange rate system, the key countries need to find a way of solving their own inflationary bias problem. And as the experience of the Bretton Woods system and the European Monetary System shows, sometimes the key country acts in a way that makes it impossible to maintain the peg.[61]

Because the fixed versus flexible exchange rate issue has been extensively investigated, and because the need remains to set overall monetary policy within a fixed exchange rate system, I shall not continue the discussion of the fixed exchange rate regime.

To retain flexibility in monetary policy while dealing with the inflationary bias of discretionary policy, Rogoff (1985) proposed the appointment of a conservative central banker, who is more averse to inflation than is society as a whole.[62] The central banker's aversion to inflation reduces the average inflation rate, but he still has the discretion to conduct stabilising counter-cylical policy.

There are two important points about the solution in the Rogoff model. First, it represents a trade-off between the reduction in the average inflation rate and the increase in the variability of output (relative to that attainable under a socially optimal policy) that is implied by the conservatism of the central banker. Second, there is an optimal degree of inflation aversion on the part of the central banker, which means that the central banker can be excessively inflation averse.

Rogoff's model provides one rationalisation for an independent central bank. The bank is given the independence to pursue activist policy, but it is expected to be more inflation averse than is society. Central banks that are given strong powers and a mandate to secure price stability, perhaps "within the framework of the Government's overall economic policy,"[63] seem to fit the Rogoff model. Based on this model, the convention has developed in empirical work of calibrating the independence of the central bank by the weight it places on inflation relative to output in its objective function.[64] By this measure of independence, a central bank can be too independent by being too monomaniacal about inflation.

Lohmann (1992) extends the Rogoff rule to allow the conservative central banker to be overruled by the government, at a cost. This produces a non-linear rule in which the central bank responds proportionately more strongly to large than to small disturbances, in such a way such that the government never actually overrules the bank.[65] The outcome under this rule is better than that under the simple Rogoff rule.

One of the reasons for central bank independence is to remove the inflation tax from the control of the fiscal authority. Debelle (1994a) extends the Rogoff model to add a fiscal authority, which puts more weight on government spending than does the central bank or society. The central bank is responsible for setting the inflation rate, but the government receives the seigniorage revenue. Debelle shows that the inflation rate will be higher the greater the weight the government puts on its spending. Extending these results, Debelle and Fischer (1994) show that the inflation rate tends to be higher when the fiscal authority makes its decisions before the central bank.[66] Inflation is also likely to be higher in a situation of fiscal dominance, when the fiscal authority chooses the deficit and forces the central bank to finance it. This is a situation in which the central bank has no effective independence.

Models that include the possibility of developing a reputation present an alternative way out of the dynamic inconsistency problem. With a sufficiently long horizon, and a sufficiently low discount rate, the monetary policymaker may find it optimal to develop a reputation for anti-inflationary zeal by pursuing the dynamically consistent low inflation policy.[67]

The most important recent development in the game theory approach to monetary policy has come from applications of the principal-agent model. In this model, a principal (society) with well-defined goals has to design a contract that will motivate an agent (the central bank) to act in the principal's interests. In general the agent has access to some information that the principal does not.

Walsh (1993) and Persson and Tabellini (1993) have shown that a contract between the government and the central banker in which the central banker's remuneration declines in proportion to inflation can attain the first best equilibrium.[68] Not only does this contract remove the inflationary bias of monetary policy, but the central bank's countercyclical policy is optimally active. Accordingly, appointing a central banker who has the same loss function as society, and penalising him or her by an amount proportional to the inflation rate, enables society to obtain the first best solution.[69] This result is based on the assumption that the central bank has the same loss function as society, and that the only problem that the contract has to deal with is the inflationary bias resulting from dynamic inconsistency.

The target inflation rate in this contracting approach should be made to depend on any shocks that affect the optimal dynamically consistent inflation rate. This is done in both Canada and New Zealand, where a formula is provided to adjust the inflation target if there are supply shocks, and if indirect taxes are imposed.

Walsh and Persson-Tabellini assume that the contract will be carried out. Of course, the principal faces the temptation to behave in a dynamically inconsistent way by changing the contract *ex post*. The model therefore carries an implicit assumption that it is costly to change the contract.

The targeting approach to monetary policy that emerges from the contracting model has been implemented in New Zealand and Canada. It contrasts with the approach taken in Germany and in the new statutes of the Banque de France, where the central bank is given a more general mandate for price stability. Both the Reserve Bank of New Zealand and the Bundesbank are described as independent, but they differ in the degree of independence they have to specify short-run policy goals. The Bundesbank decides on its own on the inflation path it seeks to attain, while the Reserve Bank of New Zealand has to negotiate a target path with the government. Each central bank has full independence or discretion about the monetary policy tactics it follows to achieve these goals.

Because the term independence is not precise, some prefer to describe a central bank as autonomous,[70] or "somewhat apart from government."[71] Rather than fight the inevitable, I shall continue to use the term independence, but draw a distinction between *goal independence* and *instrument independence*. A central bank whose goals are imprecisely defined has goal independence: at an extreme, one could imagine endowing a central bank with the power to conduct monetary policy and giving it the goal of doing good. At the other extreme, the goal may be as precisely specified as those in New Zealand, where there is no goal independence. A central bank with a mandate for price stability but no numerical targets has more goal independence. A central bank has instrument independence when it has full discretion and power to deploy monetary policy to attain its goals. A central bank bound by a monetary rule would not have instrument independence, nor would a central bank which was required to finance the budget deficit.

The concept of *accountability* can be addressed within the contracting approach. The general notion of accountability is that there be adverse consequences for the central bank or the central banker of not meeting targets. In the optimal contract, the central banker is responsible for achieving the target inflation rate, and is penalised for failing to do so. While the penalty in the formal models appears to be monetary, public obliquy would serve as well.[72] Thus even a

central bank with a more general mandate could be held accountable, for instance by being required to publish a monetary policy
report, or through public hearings on its performance such as the
Humphrey-Hawkins hearings at which the Chairman of the Fed
testifies twice a year. A central bank that is not held accountable
is more likely to behave in a dynamically inconsistent way than an
accountable bank—indeed any organisation that is not accountable
is likely to perform worse than one that is accountable.

A subsidiary question is to whom the central bank is accountable:
who is to judge whether targets were met, and to take the specified
actions if they were not met. The answer implicit in the contracting
approach is whoever makes the contract with the central bank. The
more general answer is that the central bank should be accountable
in some public forum, preferably to well-informed elected officials.
An important reason to expose central bankers to elected officials
is that, just as the latter may have an inflationary bias, the former
may easily develop a deflationary bias. Shielded as they are from
public opinion, cocooned within an anti-inflationary temple, central bankers can all too easily deny—and perhaps even convince
themselves—that there is a short-run trade-off between inflation and
unemployment, and that cyclical unemployment can be reduced by
easing monetary policy.

Another subsidiary question is who in the central bank should be
accountable. The answer must be primarily the Governor. It would
also be possible to penalise the entire board for failing to meet targets, by reducing their pay. There is no reason that should not be
done, for instance by fixing their salaries in nominal terms for the
length of their tenure.[73]

There is an interesting contrast between the accountability of the
Bundesbank and the planned European Central Bank and that of
the Fed or the Reserve Bank of New Zealand. The Bundesbank is
not formally accountable to any other body, whereas the Fed is.
The Bundesbank arrangement, where the policy goal is not precise,
and there is no formal accountability, poses a potential danger:
there is very little to prevent it from pursuing a socially excessive
anti-inflationary policy. While the Bundesbank holds regular press
conferences, these events are not the right forum to probe the basis
of monetary policy. In practice, the Bundesbank has been very careful to take public opinion with it, and to publish a serious *Monthly
Report*, but the danger remains.

Before turning to the empirical evidence on central bank independence, I want to re-emphasise the fact that every central bank continually faces the short-run trade-off between inflation and output. To illustrate, by 1991 the Bundesbank knew that it faced rising inflation. It could at that point have tightened money and raised short term interest rates to, say, 15 percent. Such a decision would have prevented some of the subsequent inflation, at a cost in terms of forgone output. Instead it chose to fight the inflation more gradually. In the fall of 1993, it faced another decision, of whether to cut interest rates more rapidly, tending to increase output but at the cost of a slower decline in the inflation rate. It chose not to cut interest rates rapidly, thereby disinflating more rapidly at the expense of slowing the recovery.

The Bundesbank's policy mandate to maintain the value of the currency is a far from complete guide to the crucial policy choices it has to make. Nor is a price stability mandate a sufficient guide for any central bank. That is why central banks cannot merely be given the task of keeping inflation low: they have also to be made accountable for their performance, especially their counter-cyclical performance, to be asked whether they are making the right judgement about the speed at which to reduce inflation, or to return to full employment. They cannot take refuge in the claim that there is no long-run trade-off. Again quoting Keynes (1924, p. 88). "Economists set themselves too easy, too useless a task if in tempestuous seasons they can only tell us that when the storm is long past the ocean is flat again."

Empirical Evidence on Central Bank Independence (CBI)

There are several empirical measures of legal central bank independence (CBI).[74] I use the Grilli, Masciandaro and Tabellini (1991) or GMT index, calculated for eighteen industrialised countries as a simple sum of fifteen different legal provisions, grouped under five headings: appointments; relationship with government; constitution; monetary financing of the budget deficit; and monetary instruments. Under appointments, the central bank is more independent if the government does not appoint the governor, the longer the term of the governor, and so forth. Two provisions appear under the constitution heading: whether there is a statutory requirement that the central bank pursue monetary stability among its goals; and whether

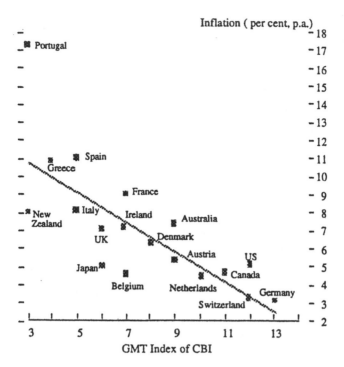

Figure 7.6
Inflation and CBI, GMT index.

there is any legal provision that strengthens the hand of the central bank in disputes with the government. There are also two criteria under the monetary instruments head: whether the central bank sets the discount rate; and whether the central bank supervises commercial banks.

Figure 7.6 shows the key empirical result in this literature. For the period 1960–1992, there is a significant negative relationship between the average rate of inflation and central bank independence.[75]

This relationship is very robust for the industrialised countries. But it does not extend to a larger sample of seventy-two countries examined in Cukierman et al. (1992). For these countries, those included in table 7.1, there is a slightly positive relationship between inflation and legal CBI. For this group, Cukierman et al. find that inflation is positively and significantly correlated with the rate of turnover of central bank governors. The contrast between the results for the industrialised countries and the larger group must be due to the difference between actual and legal independence.[76]

Table 7.3
Inflation and the components of central bank independence

Variable	(1)	(2)	(3)	(4)	(5)
INFOBJ	−1.76	−2.28	−4.27		
	(1.72)	(1.61)	(1.30)		
EC6	−1.02	−1.02		−1.53	
	(0.55)	(0.55)		(0.42)	
POL7	0.41				−0.94
	(0.45)				(0.51)
$\bar{R}^2$	0.44	0.44	0.37	0.42	0.12

Notes: Dependent variable is mean inflation rate, 1960–1992. Data definitions in text. Standard errors in parentheses.

The preceding analysis pointed most strongly to the central bank's mandate (lack of goal independence) and instrument independence as key factors in determining the inflationary bias of policy. To try to isolate these effects, I break down the GMT index of CBI into three components.[77] The first is the presence of a statutory requirement that the central bank pursue monetary stability among its goals; this is called INFOBJ. The second, EC6, consists of those measures relating to the central bank's right not to finance the government, and to set the discount rate.[78] The third is a combination of legal provisions relating to appointments and the central bank's relationship with the government; this is called POL7.

Table 7.3 shows that the two variables most closely tied to inflation performance are INFOBJ and EC6. EC6, a measure of the central bank's ability to use its instruments freely, is the single variable most highly correlated with inflation. The variables grouped into POL7, which relate to appointment procedures, are not significantly related to inflation.

The most striking result of the empirical work is that CBI seems to have *no* adverse consequences. GMT (1991) and Alesina and Summers (1993) show that the improved inflation performance associated with increased CBI for industrialised countries does not come at a cost in terms of foregone growth. Similarly, for a cross-section of countries including LDCs, Cukierman et al. (1993) find that while legal independence is negatively related to growth, the coefficient is not significant; an alternative (inverse) measure of central bank independence, the frequency of turnover of the central bank governor, is negatively related to growth (and positively related to

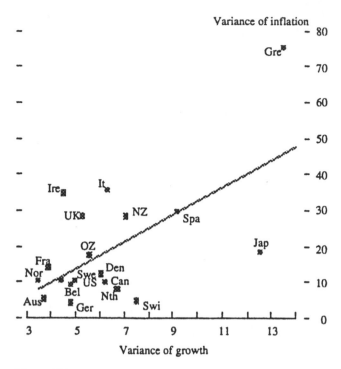

Figure 7.7
Inflation and output variability, 1960–1992.

inflation). Thus improved inflation performance does not seem to come at a cost in terms of lower growth.

Figure 7.7 shows the relationship between the variability of inflation and the variability of GDP growth over the period 1960–1992, for the countries for which GMT have constructed measures of CBI.[79] The association between these measures of variability is positive and significant, though the statistical significance disappears if Greece is excluded from the sample.[80]

These results could reflect either reverse causation from inflation aversion to CBI, or, closely related, the presence of a third factor that produces both economic stability and CBI. Cukierman et al. (1992) have investigated the reverse causation issue econometrically and still find a negative correlation between inflation and CBI. Havrilesky and Granato (1993) include both measures of the extent of corporatism[81] and the CBI index in a regression for the rate of inflation, and find that none of the measures of corporatism separately, nor all of them together, enter significantly. By contrast, Hall (1994) argues that centralised collective bargaining at the industry level (with IG Metall setting the pattern) is at least as much responsible for low inflation in Germany as is the independence of the Bunsdesbank.

The possibility of reverse causation is sometimes used to argue that the legal position of the central bank is hardly relevant to inflation performance: if a country is inflation averse, then it will have low inflation whatever the legal status of the central bank; if the country is not inflation averse, then the political system will always be able to get around the legal status of the central bank—as the results for the seventy-two-country Cukierman et al. (1992) sample establish. The implicit recommendation is that educating people about the costs of inflation is the best way of reducing inflation.

This is too extreme a position. In the first instance, the evidence on the costs of inflation and the relationship between inflation and growth suggests that countries benefit from being inflation averse. Even if reverse causation exists, it is probably optimal for those who want to reduce inflation to propose legislation setting up an independent central bank. There can be no better way of forcing public opinion to think about the inflation issue. And, if the country is one in which the laws are obeyed, successful legislation will lead to a different monetary policy.

While the empirical results show the gains from central bank independence, there remains an important anomaly. The Rogoff model implies that we should find a negative relationship in figure 7.7 if countries were being hit by the same shocks, and if the central banks were efficient but differed in their relative tastes for inflation and output variability. At least three factors could account for the positive relationship. If the variance of shocks differs systematically by country, then we would expect to find a positive relationship, with countries that are hit by bigger shocks[82] having greater variability of both inflation and GDP growth. Or, if some central banks are more efficient than others, they would do better at stabilising on both dimensions. Or, if more independent central banks are also more credible on inflation, they may obtain a "credibility bonus" which makes the economy respond more rapidly to monetary policy changes.[83]

Most likely, the positive relationship between output and inflation variability in figure 7.7 reflects both differences in the magnitude of shocks affecting different economies, and differences in the efficiency

Table 7.4
Inflation and output, United States and Germany

Quarterly data	United States	Germany
Mean inflation	1.19	0.83
Variance of inflation	0.69	0.43
Mean growth rate	0.73	0.73
Variance of growth rate	0.88	1.42
Sum of squared residuals of log output against:		
	Annual data	
Linear trend	0.0487	0.08
Quadratic trend	0.023	0.0292
	Quarterly data	
Linear trend	0.208	0.347
Quadratic trend	0.101	0.128

Note: Data are for 1960–1992/3.

with which policymakers respond to those shocks. Countries with independent central banks are likely to be countries with more disciplined governments, and thus to suffer smaller self-imposed shocks. It is also likely that more independent central banks are more efficient: they are likely to have better research staffs, and more able and experienced decision makers. I suspect that the credibility bonus explanation would also receive strong support, but return to the issue below.

Despite figure 7.7, I want to argue that, for the most sophisticated central banks, there remains a trade-off between price level and output stability. Consider for instance Germany and the United States. Table 7.4 presents the mean inflation rates and growth rates, as well as the variability of inflation and growth[84] for the United States and Germany for the period 1960–1992. German inflation was lower than that of the United States over the period, and growth rates were the same. The United States has more stable output and less stable inflation. No doubt the United States could have had more stable inflation, if its central bank had been more devoted to fighting inflation. Should it have had such a central bank? While the empirical results on CBI seem to say yes, since greater CBI comes with lower inflation and no evident costs, the comparison with German performance suggests there is a trade-off, and that countries have to decide how inflation averse they want their central bank to be.

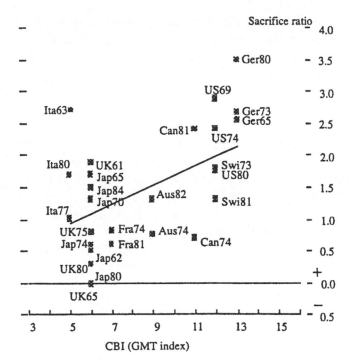

Figure 7.8
Sacrifice ratio and CBI, GMT index.

We return now to the credibility bonus. In figure 7.8, we show the sacrifice ratio in recessions since 1962 against the GMT measure of central bank independence.[85] The overall relationship is positive; it is also statistically significant. This implies that more independent central banks on average pay a *higher* output price per percentage point of inflation to reduce the inflation rate. A similar though weaker positive relationship holds between the output loss in recessions and central bank independence.[86]

This result is consistent with the Phillips curve being flatter in low inflation than in high inflation economies.[87] But it is none the less puzzling, because a more independent central bank should be more credible, and the public should more readily believe its anti-inflationary pronouncements. Figure 7.8 suggests that there is no credibility bonus in the labor markets for more independent central banks: they have to prove their toughness repeatedly, by being tough.

The evidence leaves little doubt that, on average, economic performance is better in countries with more independent central banks. The relationship between inflation and the elements of CBI is attributable mainly to the central bank's ability to use its policy instruments freely (instrument independence) and to the presence of a price stability goal (lack of goal independence). We further tentatively conclude that the causation in industrialised countries, where legal provisions are likely to have more force, runs at least in part from legal independence to lower inflation. As an analytic matter, we expect less price variability and greater output variability in countries with more independent central banks. Such a relationship is not visible in the aggregate data. The elements of a trade-off are present in comparing United States and German data, and there must be such a trade-off for an efficient central bank. Finally, central bank independence does not appear to bring a credibility bonus in the labour markets: even independent central banks have to fight hard and long to bring inflation down after an inflationary shock has struck.

The Charter of a Modern Central Bank

The case we have set out for an independent central bank is becoming increasingly accepted. Within the last decade, the central banks of Chile, France, Mexico, New Zealand, and Venezuela have all had their legal independence enhanced, and the Maastricht treaty requires national central banks participating in the European System of Central Banks to meet a prescribed standard of independence. And of course, there is a lively debate in Britain over the desirability of making the Bank of England, now explicitly subservient to the Treasury, independent.[88]

The argument for greater independence for the Bank of England is based on three foundations. The first is the theoretical literature on the inflationary bias of discretionary policy-making. The second is the empirical literature on central bank independence. Closely related is the third argument for greater independence, the success of the Bundesbank and the German economy over the past forty years. The Reserve Bank of New Zealand's success in reducing inflation provides further support for independence. However, the New Zealand experience has come at a time of general disinflation, and it remains to be seen how well the Bank operates as worldwide inflationary pressures build.[89]

The lessons that should be drawn from the theoretical and empirical evidence presented here are:[90]

• The central bank should have a clearly defined mandate, which includes price stability;

• The central bank should publicly announce its intermediate-term policy goals;

• The central bank should be accountable, in two senses: it should be held responsible for meeting its announced goals; and it should be required to explain and justify its policies to the legislature and the public;

• The government should have the authority to override the Bank's decisions, but the override decision should carry a cost for the government;

• The central bank should be given the authority to set interest rates and other monetary policy variables in order to achieve its policy goals;

• The central bank should not be required to finance the government deficit, and should not manage the public debt;

• There cannot be a separate responsibility for setting interest rates and the exchange rate so long as the exchange rate floats.

Let me expand briefly on each point.[91] The Bank's primary mandate should be to establish price stability, by which is meant a low (1–3 percent) average rate of inflation. The legislation should not deny the short-run Phillips curve trade-off: hence the need for a qualifier such as "primary," which leaves the short-run trade-off implicit; alternatively, the legislation can follow the Netherlands route and state that the mandate is for price stability "with a view to promoting the nation's prosperity and welfare."[92]

The Bank's inflation goals for the next three years should be announced, after consultation with the Treasury, and relative to a long-term target of, say, 2 percent. The announcement should describe the allowances that will be made for changes in the terms of trade, interest rates, and indirect taxes in judging whether the target has been met.[93]

The Governor of the Bank should be held responsible for meeting the targets. He should be required to testify on the performance of monetary policy in meeting its preannounced goals, in public, before a House of Commons Committee, twice a year.[94] The testimony should be accompanied by the publication of a report, along the lines of the *Inflation Report*. The most difficult issue is the sanctions that should be imposed on the Bank for failing to meet its targets. Sharp public questioning is the only sanction that is now applied in the United States, and there is no explicit sanction in most countries. Public reprimand and loss of reputation is probably a sufficient sanction.

Although the point has not been discussed so far, it is clear that monetary policy should be the responsibility of a Monetary Policy Board or Council. Some British observers claim that a Board has worked best in federal countries such as Germany, Switzerland, and the United States, where the geographic basis for Board representation gives its members independent standing. That result is more likely to be coincidental than causal; the performance of the Monetary Policy Council of the Banque de France will shed light on this issue. This is not the place to describe detailed procedures for choosing the Board, but the French requirement that the Board be drawn from "persons of recognised standing and professional experience in monetary, financial and economic matters" commends itself. Board members should be appointed for a lengthy term, more than five years, but well short of fourteen.

The undemocratic nature of independent central banking requires a procedure for overriding the Bank's decisions. In New Zealand, the government has the right to override the Bank's policy targets, by means of an Order in Council that lasts no more than a year. The more general Canadian provision whereby "the Minister of Finance, with the approval of ... the Cabinet ... may issue a directive to the Governor as to the monetary policy the Bank is to follow"[95] is a good precedent for Britain. The directive has to be made public. This procedure has never been used in Canada, and it is clear that if it were, the Governor would have to resign. While the procedure seems to give the government an easy means of controlling the Bank, any Chancellor contemplating firing the Governor would realise that most of the Board would remain in place, and that monetary policy could not therefore be easily manipulated by the government. At the same time, the threat of the use of the directive would give the Bank pause before it set out on a policy at odds with that of the government. This gives the right balance of power.

There is one important difference between the procedures recommended here and those in New Zealand. In New Zealand the Bank has to agree on inflation targets with the government. The recommendation here is that the Bank only consult with the government in setting the inflation targets. That gives the Bank a slightly greater measure of independence, but one which is constrained by the override procedures.[96]

It goes almost without saying that the central bank needs the monetary policy tools that will enable it to meet its responsibilities. The Bank of England has them at present, but management of government financing presents a conflict of interest of which the Bank would best be rid.

The final point concerns the interactions of exchange and interest rates. Monetary and exchange rate policies cannot be independent. Under floating rates, monetary policy affects the exchange rate. There is no other short-run policy that can affect the exchange rate. Thus the government cannot have control over exchange rate policy while the central bank has control over monetary policy. The government should have the authority to choose the exchange rate regime. If it chooses a fixed exchange rate regime, it has then essentially—though not completely—determined monetary policy. While a central bank can be more or less independent of the government in a fixed exchange rate system, its independent ability to determine the rate of inflation and interest rates is sharply curtailed.

On her 300th birthday, it is time to allow the Old Lady to take on the responsibilities of independence.

Notes

1. I am grateful to my discussants at the Bank of England Tercentenary Conference, Don Brash, Miguel Mancera, and Josef Tosovsky for useful comments, to Guy Debelle for research assistance, and to Michael Bruno, John Crow, Charles Freedman, and Mervyn King for discussions and the provision of literature.

2. See de Kock (1974) for the historical development of central banking, as well as the interesting companion paper for this conference by Capie, Goodhart, and Schnadt (1994).

3. The Bank of England's 1694 Charter starts "Now know ye, That we being desirous to promote the publick Good and Benefit of our People"; this section was embodied in the 1946 Bank of England Act.

4. The choice of the exchange rate system, as opposed to the management of the chosen system, is normally a central government rather than a central bank decision.

5. The question of whether the central bank or another agency should supervise the commercial banks has been extensively discussed (see for example paragraphs 83–103 of Volume I of the Treasury and Civil Service Committee report *The Role of the Bank of England*, London: HMSO, 1993; this report is referred to henceforth as *The Role of the Bank of England*). The weight of the evidence supports the view that the supervisory function should remain with the central bank, but the issue is not crucial.

6. I focus most directly on four central banks: the Bundesbank, the Reserve Bank of New Zealand, the Federal Reserve System, and the Bank of England.

7. This the goal of monetary policy set out in the Humphrey-Hawkins Act of 1978.

8. *The Role of the Bank of England*, Volume II, p. 175.

9. *The Role of the Bank of England*, Volume II, p. 165.

10. In the overall sample, the second country whose central bank has an overriding price stability goal is that of the Philippines.

11. Samuelson and Solow gave two examples of how the curve would shift: first, that low inflation might shift the curve down because of its impact on expectations; second, that structural unemployment might rise as a result of higher unemployment, so that the curve would shift up. Both these possibilities have been central to subsequent discussions, the first as the expectations-augmented Phillips curve, the second as the phenomenon of hysteresis (Blanchard and Summers, 1986).

12. See for example, Dornbusch and Fischer (1994), chapter 16.

13. That is, expectations of inflation are assumed to adjust on the basis of the gap between actual and expected inflation.

14. See for example Mishkin (1983).

15. See for instance, Fischer (1977); Blanchard (1986) shows how even quite short-term overlapping contracts may generate lengthy adjustment processes to nominal shocks.

16. However, Caplin and Spulber (1987) show that in some conditions, stickiness of prices at the level of the individual firm does not translate into stickiness at the aggregate level; Caplin and Leahy (1991) examine conditions in which the Caplin-Spulber neutrality result does not hold.

17. This theory is developed by Ball, Mankiw, and Romer (1988), who present supporting evidence. The short-run Phillips curve derived by Lucas (1973) is flatter the lower the variance of the aggregate inflation rate; and since the level of the inflation rate and its variance are in practice positively correlated, the Lucas model can also be seen as predicting that the short-run Phillips curve is flatter at lower inflation rates.

18. The qualifier takes care of the possibility that extra monetary expansions have no effect in extreme hyperinflations.

19. However the issue is not as analytically straightforward as it seems. If the economy is at an undistorted equilibrium, with the marginal value of leisure equal to the real wage, an expansion in output brought about by fooling workers as in the Friedman-Lucas model, does not increase their welfare. In the presence of distortions

that make the natural rate of unemployment exceed the socially optimal level, or at a monopolistic competition equilibrium, an increase in output beyond the equilibrium level will be socially beneficial.

20. Pp. cclviii–cclvix, reprinted by Arno Press, New York, 1978.

21. Keynes (1924) provides one of the earliest analyses. I draw here on Fischer and Modigliani (1978), and Fischer (1981). See also Driffill et al. (1990).

22. The classic reference is Bailey (1956).

23. These are unweighted averages, based on data in the International Financial Statistics. The relevant base for the inflation tax includes non-interest bearing bank reserves, but since interest is paid on some bank reserves in the G-7, for instance in Italy, I work with the currency stock. The average ratio of high-powered money to GNP in the G-7 in 1992 was 7.8 percent, and the social costs would rise proportionately if this were the relevant money stock.

24. Lucas (1994) shows that the welfare loss depends significantly on the functional form of the demand for money.

25. Phelps (1973) initiated the optimal tax analysis of inflation. For more recent general equilibrium analyses, see Cooley and Hansen (1991), and Chari et al. (1991). The optimal inflation tax is zero in the latter model. Faig (1988) also establishes conditions under which it is optimal not to tax money holdings.

26. Theory makes no unambiguous predictions in this case either: in infinite horizon maximising models, such as that of Sidrauski (1967), inflation would not affect the steady state capital stock; in an overlapping generations model, or a model with a cash-in-advance constraint, it can.

27. Fischer (1981) contains one such calculation, in which an increase in the inflation rate from zero to 10 percent has a social cost of 0.7 percent of GNP as a result of its impact on saving.

28. See Fischer (1981).

29. The operational or inflation-adjusted deficit deducts the decline in the real value of government debt caused by inflation from the nominal deficit. In analysing inflation stabilisations, there is also a case for calculating a "zero-inflation deficit," an estimate of what the deficit would be if inflation were reduced to zero. This would differ from the operational deficit because inflation affects other components of the budget, for example through the Tanzi effect, and because the real interest rate might change if inflation were stabilised. The zero-inflation deficit provides information about the extra fiscal effort that would be needed for a stabilisation programme to succeed.

30. For recent theoretical treatments, see Reagan and Stulz (1993) and Tommasi (1994).

31. See Fischer (1981) and Taylor (1981).

32. Huizinga (1991) presents a model in which uncertainty reduces investment as entrepreneurs wait for its resolution before committing themselves. It should be noted though that the general equilibrium effects of greater uncertainty on investment may differ from the partial equilibrium effects, since asset prices and interest rates can adjust in general equilibrium.

33. Fischer and Huizinga (1982) examine public opinion polls on attitudes to inflation, but are unable to substantiate this inflation illusion hypothesis.

34. Such money illusion appears to remain in economies that experience single digit inflation, but does not survive in prolonged moderate (15–30 percent) inflations, where a foreign currency is often used as a unit of account and store of value.

35. For discussion of the welfare economics of the introduction of indexed bonds, see Fischer (1983).

36. Report of the Committee on the Working of the Monetary System (the Radcliffe Committee), 1959, para 573.

37. The concept of dynamic inconsistency is discussed in more detail below.

38. This result holds for the usual quadratic loss function, but may be reversed for other loss functions.

39. In his 22 February 1994 Humphrey-Hawkins testimony, Fed Chairman Greenspan indicated support for the introduction of index bonds, mainly on informational grounds.

40. Neoclassical growth models imply that inflation would affect the level of output, but not the steady state growth rate. The new growth theory could generate a growth rate effect of inflation.

41. It is also puzzling that the coefficient is large and significant only for the English-speaking countries among the G-7.

42. I do not want to rule out the possibility that the revenue motive may justify positive inflation in countries that have difficulty raising revenues in other ways.

43. Despite the persuasiveness of the quote, Phelps does not share the view.

44. This issue has been discussed intensively in the Bank of Canada, which will produce a conference volume on the topic shortly.

45. With a zero inflation target, the price level is given by $p_t = p_{t-1} + \varepsilon_t$, where ε_t is a serially uncorrelated disturbance term. With a price level target, the price level is given by $p_t = p_{t-1} - 0.5(p_{t-1} - p^*) + \varepsilon_t$.

46. Data are from Keynes (1924).

47. This argument is due to Summers (1991). There may be a small convenience yield that would allow slightly negative nominal interest rates on large denomination bills; it is also well known that nominal rates were negative at some points during the great depression, but that was a result of special tax features of bills.

48. This argument implies money illusion.

49. The three sources of bias are the failure to correct systematically for quality change (estimated to yield a bias of about 1 percent per annum), "outlet substitution bias" (the bias resulting from the inappropriate treatment of a gradual shift to lower price stores), and most remarkably the "logarithm bias." The last bias is caused by the practice of recording a decline in price from, say $2 to $1 as a 50 percent decline, and a subsequent increase to $2 as a 100 percent rise. The price of the good would be shown as having risen 50 percent, even though it has not changed. Each of the last

two sources are estimated to account for a bias of 0.3–0.4 percent per annum. (I am indebted to Robert J. Gordon for discussion of this point.)

50. Duguay (1993) states that the measurement bias in Canada is only 0.5 percent per annum.

51. In arguing for a 1–3 percent inflation target, I am implicitly rejecting the view that a reduction in the inflation rate from 3 to 1 percent would increase the growth rate of output by any significant amount. The regression results above do not address the relationship between inflation and growth at very low inflation rates. And in the presence of downward price inflexibility, there is reason to believe that growth would be lower at very low inflation rates.

52. For most industrialised countries, seigniorage revenue, defined as the real value of the increase in the stock of high-powered money, is less than 1 percent of GNP. For a few countries, including Italy in the 1970s, it sometimes amounts to more than 3 percent of GNP.

53. Nor, as argued above, should it receive much weight in a country with a sophisticated tax system.

54. See Blanchard and Fischer (1989, pp. 577–580) on nominal interest rate targeting; the argument traces back to Wicksell ([1898] 1965) and was developed by Friedman (1968).

55. In his important work on the modern theory of central banking, Cukierman (1992), chapter 2, offers four reasons for an inflationary bias: the employment or short-run Phillips curve motive, a fiscal revenue motive, interest rate smoothing, and a balance of payments motive (under fixed exchange rates). Cukierman emphasises those motives that lead to dynamic inconsistency, whereas the argument here treats the revenue motive as a potentially separate cause of inflationary bias.

56. These benefits include both the higher output available through the Phillips curve and the fiscal gains discussed above.

57. This is close to the formal definition, since announcements will not continue to be believed if they are inconsistent with reality. The more general informal definition goes beyond that emerging from the formal analysis, because it allows for credibility about policy announcements and decisions that were not anticipated at the time the private sector was making its decisions.

58. In this case, incentives have to be provided for the creation of new knowledge, but it is in society's interests to allow the general use of the knowledge once it has been created.

59. Friedman's (1959) argument for a constant growth rate rule is formally independent of the problem of dynamic inconsistency or the inflationary bias of monetary policy; rather, the argument is that there is no feedback in the optimal feedback rule.

60. McCallum states that a four-year period is used to avoid adjusting for cyclical changes in velocity.

61. Fixed exchange rates within a monetary union are potentially different from fixed exchange rates among countries whose central banks can make independent monetary policy decisions.

62. Formally, both the central banker and society are assumed to prefer inflation and output levels that are close to (the same) target levels, but the central banker weights deviations of inflation from target relative to output deviations more heavily than society does.

63. The quote is from a translation of the 1993 Act on the Status of the Banque de France.

64. This convention is followed, for instance, in table 7.1.

65. This result fits with experience in countries such as Canada and the Netherlands where the government has the right to overrule the central bank but has to publish its reasons for doing so—and has not so far exercised its option.

66. Technically, the assumption is that the fiscal authority acts as a Stackelberg leader, moving first, but taking into account the central bank's response to its choice of policy variables.

67. Several reputational models are discussed in Fischer (1990).

68. One example of such a contract occurs when the salary of the governor is fixed in nominal terms during his or her term of office, as for the Bank of England and the Reserve Bank of New Zealand.

69. This result is obtained by Walsh (1993) and also by Persson and Tabellini (1993). Walsh shows that the first best can also be obtained by penalising the central bank by an amount proportional to the money stock—which is stochastically related to the inflation rate.

70. See for instance the evidence by Charles Goodhart in *The Role of the Bank of England*, Volume II, paragraph 3.

71. Freedman 1993, p. 91.

72. As Persson and Tabellini (1993) point out, the announcement of targets, for money or inflation, makes sense as a device to help ensure accountability.

73. As was pointed out in New Zealand, this contract would not survive a protracted deflation, since the central bankers would then be seen as benefitting from the misery that was being inflicted on the rest of the country.

74. See Cukierman (1992), chapter 19.

75. The t-statistic on CBI in the regression line shown in figure 8.6 is -4.6; R^2 is 0.54.

76. Cukierman et al. (1992) also create a questionnaire-based index of CBI for twenty-six countries. The questionnaires were answered by central bank officials. The rank correlation between the legally and questionnaire based indexes was very low for the entire group, and a bit higher (0.33) for the industrialised countries.

77. I draw here on Debelle and Fischer (1994).

78. GMT break their overall index down into a measure of political independence, which is (POL7 + INFOBJ), and one of economic independence, which is EC6 + the dummy variable that indicates whether the central bank supervises the commercial banks.

79. Eijffinger and Schaling (1993) examine the relationship between alternative measures of CBI (Bade-Parkin (1988), Alesina (1988), GMT, and their own index) and inflation and output growth variability. They find that inflation variability is significantly negatively related only to the GMT index (in two out of three decades), and that output growth variability is not significantly related to any of the measures of CBI.

80. The standard loss function in this literature penalises deviations of the level of output from its target level, rather than the variability of output growth. Using measures of output deviations from linear and quadratic trends (of log output), we still find a positive but insignificant correlation between output and inflation variability.

81. They include three measures of the power of organised labour, two measures of the leftward leaning of the government, and two measures of the size of the public sector.

82. These shocks could be self-imposed, for instance greater variability of government spending.

83. Kenneth Rogoff has pointed out that the relationship would also be positive if countries differ only in the wedge between the natural rate of unemployment and the socially optimal rate.

84. Similar results hold for the variability of output around linear or quadratic trends.

85. This relationship was discovered independently by Adam Posen (1993). The output loss and inflation measures that underlie the sacrifice ratios are from Ball (1993).

86. The t-statistic on the CBI measure is 3.8 in figure 7.8, and 1.96 when the output loss is regressed on CBI.

87. See note 17 and the paragraph to which it is attached.

88. See for instance Roll et al. (1993), Vibert (1993), and House of Commons (1993).

89. Australia, whose central bank is much less independent than that of New Zealand, was almost as successful in disinflating as New Zealand; however inflationary expectations in New Zealand at the end of 1993 were more favorable than those in Australia. See Debelle 1994b.

90. The recommendations here are essentially the same as those in Roll et al. 1993.

91. I am not taking into account here the need to conform with the Maastricht Treaty if Britain is to become a member of the EMU.

92. The fact that monetary policy can affect output in the short-run should not be ignored. Thus I disagree with the otherwise excellent report by Roll et al. (1993) when it states (p. 9) "Because monetary policy eventually affects only inflation, it should be the prime instrument to deal with inflation; and this long-run effort must be sustained. [Correct, so far]. Fiscal policy therefore seems the natural countercyclical tool to mitigate short-run fluctuations in demand." The last sentence is a *non sequitur*. Creating arrangements that prevent the use of countercyclical monetary policy will worsen economic performance.

93. The adjustments may take the form of using a special price index for measuring inflation, such as RPIX. See for example the Bank of England's *Inflation Report*, February 1994, p. 5.

94. It is sometimes claimed that the British system does not give House of Commons Committees the standing that Congressional committees have in the United States. That can surely change if the legislature decides it wants the change—and it should want the authority to question the Bank if it gains independence.

95. *The Role of the Bank of England*, Volume II, p. 161.

96. It is sometimes claimed that the British parliamentary tradition make it impossible to set up arrangements of the type discussed here. Countries with similar traditions, such as Canada and New Zealand, have done so successfully, and there is no reason Britain could not follow suit.

References

Alesina, Alberto (1988) "Macroeconomics and politics," *NBER Macroeconomics Annual*, 13–51.

Alesina, Alberto, and Guido Tabellini (1987) "Rules and discretion with non-coordinated monetary and fiscal policies," *Economic Inquiry*, 25, 619–630.

Alesina, Alberto, and Lawrence H. Summers (1988) "Central bank independence and macroeconomic performances: Some comparative evidence," *Journal of Money, Credit and Banking*, 25, 2 (May), 151–162.

Bade, Robin, and Michael Parkin (1988) "Central bank laws and monetary policy," Department of Economics, University of Western Ontario (October).

Bailey, Martin J. (1956) "The welfare cost of inflationary finance," *Journal of Political Economy*, 64, 2 (April), 93–110.

Ball, Larry (1993) "What determines the sacrifice ratio?," NBER Working Paper, number 4306.

Ball, Larry N., Gregory Mankiw, and David Romer (1988) "The new Keynesian economics and the output-inflation trade-off," *Brookings Papers on Economic Activity*, 1, 1–65.

Barro, Robert J., and David Gordon (1983) "A positive theory of monetary policy in a natural rate model," *Journal of Political Economy*, 91, 4 (Aug), 589–610.

Blanchard, Olivier (1986) "The wage-price spiral," *Quarterly Journal of Economics*, 101, 3 (Aug), 543–565.

Blanchard, Olivier, and Stanley Fischer (1989) *Lectures on Macroeconomics*. MIT Press: Cambridge MA.

Blanchard, Olivier, and Lawrence H. Summers (1986) "Hysteresis and the European unemployment problem," *NBER Macroeconomics Annual*, 15–78.

Burns, Arthur F. (1978) *Reflections of an Economic Policy Maker*. Washington, D.C.: American Enterprise Institute.

Capie, Forrest, Charles Goodhart, and Norbert Schnadt (1994) "The development of central banking," Cambridge University Press, 1994.

Caplin, Andrew, and John Leahy (1991) "State-dependent pricing and the dynamics of money and output," *Quarterly Journal of Economics*, 106, 3 (Aug), 683–708.

Caplin, Andrew, and Daniel Spulber (1987) "Menu costs and the neutrality of money," *Quarterly Journal of Economics*, 102, 4 (Nov), 703–726.

Chari, V. V., Lawrence J. Christiano, and Patrick J. Kehoe (1991) "Optimal fiscal and monetary policy: Some recent results," *Journal of Money, Credit and Banking*, 23, 3 (Aug, Part 2), 519–539.

Cooley, Thomas F., and Gary D. Hansen (1991) "The welfare costs of moderate inflation," *Journal of Money, Credit and Banking*, 23, 3 (Aug, Part 2), 483–503.

Cukierman, Alex (1992) *Central Bank Strategy, Credibility, and Independence: Theory and Evidence*. MIT Press: Cambridge MA.

Cukierman, Alex, Steven B. Webb, and Bilin Neyapti (1992) "Measuring the independence of central banks and its effect on policy outcomes," *World Bank Economic Review*, 6, 3 (Sept), 353–398.

Cukierman, Alex, Pantelis Kalaitzidakis, Lawrence Summers, and Steven Webb (1993) "Central bank independence, growth, investment, and real rates," *Carnegie-Rochester Conference Series on Public Policy*, 39 (December), 95–140.

Dawe, S. (1990) "Reserve Bank of New Zealand Act 1989," *Reserve Bank Bulletin*, 53, 1, 21–27.

Debelle, Guy (1994a) "Central bank independence: A free lunch?," mimeo, MIT, February.

Debelle, Guy (1994b) "The ends of three small inflations: Australia, New Zealand and Canada," mimeo, MIT, February.

Debelle, Guy, and Stanley Fischer (1994) "How independent should a central bank be?," mimeo, MIT, April.

de Kock, M. H. (1974) *Central Banking*, 4th edition. St Martin's Press: New York.

Dornbusch, Rudiger, and Stanley Fischer (1994) *Macroeconomics*, 6th edition. McGraw Hill: New York.

Driffill, John, Grayham E. Mizon, and Alistair Ulph (1990) "Costs of inflation," in B. M. Friedman and F. H. Hahn (eds.), *Handbook of Monetary Economics*, Volume 2. North-Holland: Amsterdam.

Duguay, Pierre (1993) "Some thoughts on price stability versus zero inflation," mimeo, Bank of Canada.

Eijffinger, Sylvester, and Eric Schaling (1993) "Central bank independence: Theory and evidence," Tilburg University, The Netherlands, February.

Faig, Miguel (1988) "Characterisation of the optimal tax on money when it functions as a medium of exchange," *Journal of Monetary Economics*, 22, 1 (July), 137–148.

Fischer, Stanley (1977) "Long term contracts, rational expectations, and the optimal money supply rule," *Journal of Political Economy*, 85, 1 (Feb), 163–190.

Fischer, Stanley (1981) "Towards an understanding of the costs of inflation: II," in Karl Brunner and Allan H. Meltzer (eds.) *The Costs and Consequences of Inflation*, Carnegie-Rochester Conference Series on Public Policy, Vol. 15, North-Holland, 5–42. (Reprinted in Fischer (1986).)

Fischer, Stanley (1983) "Welfare aspects of government issue of indexed bonds," in R. Dornbusch and M. H. Simonsen (eds.) *Inflation, Debt, and Indexation*. MIT Press: Cambridge MA. (Reprinted in Fischer (1986).)

Fischer, Stanley (1986) *Indexing, Inflation, and Economic Policy*. MIT Press: Cambridge MA.

Fischer, Stanley (1990) "Rules versus discretion in monetary policy," in B. M. Friedman and F. H. Hahn (eds.) *Handbook of Monetary Economics*, Volume 2. North-Holland: Amsterdam.

Fischer, Stanley (1993) "The role of macroeconomic factors in growth," *Journal of Monetary Economics*, 32, 3 (Dec), 485–512.

Fischer, Stanley, and John Huizinga (1982) "Inflation, unemployment, and public opinion polls," *Journal of Money, Credit and Banking*, 14, 1 (Feb), 1–19. (Reprinted in Fischer (1986).)

Fischer, Stanley, and Franco Modigliani (1978) "Towards an understanding of the real effects and costs of inflation," *Weltwirtschaftliches Archiv*, 114, 810–832. (Reprinted in Fischer (1986).)

Fischer, Stanley, and Lawrence Summers (1989) "Should governments learn to live with inflation?" *American Economic Review, Papers and Proceedings*, 79 (May), 382–387.

Friedman, Charles (1993) "Designing institutions for monetary stability: A comment," *Carnegie-Rochester Conference Series on Public Policy*, 39 (December), 85–94.

Friedman, Milton (1959) *A Program for Monetary Stability*. Fordham University Press: New York.

Friedman, Milton (1968) "The role of monetary policy," *American Economic Review*, 58, 1 (March), 1–17.

Freedman, Milton (1969) "The optimum quantity of money," in M. Friedman, *The Optimum Quantity of Money and Other Essays*. Aldine Publishing Company: Chicago.

Grilli, Vittorio, Donato Masciandaro, and Guido Tabellini (1991) "Political and monetary institutions and public financial policies in the industrial countries," *Economic Policy*, 13 (October), 341–392.

Hall, Peter A. (1994) "Central bank independence and coordinated wage bargaining: Their interaction in Germany and Europe," forthcoming, *German Politics and Society*.

Havrilesky, Thomas, and James Granato (1993) "Determinants of inflationary performance: Corporatist structures vs. central bank autonomy," *Public Choice*, 76, 249–261.

Huizinga, John (1993) "Inflation uncertainty, relative price uncertainty, and investment in U.S. manufacturing," *Journal of Money, Credit and Banking*, 25, 3 (Aug, Part 2), 521–549.

Hume, David (1955) "Of Money," in D. Hume, *Writings on Economics*, E. Rotwein (ed.). University of Wisconsin Press: Madison.

Jarrett, J. Peter, and Jack G. Selody (1982) "The productitivity-inflation nexus in Canada, 1963–1979," *Review of Economics and Statistics*, 64 (Aug), 361–367.

Keynes, John Maynard (1924) *Monetary Reform*. Harcourt, Brace and Company: New York.

Kydland, Finn, and Edward S. Prescott (1977) "Rules rather than discretion: The inconsistency of optimal plans," *Journal of Political Economy*, 85, 3 (June), 473–492.

Lohmann, Susanne (1992) "Optimal commitment in monetary policy: Credibility versus flexibility," *American Economic Review*, 82, 1 (March), 273–286.

Lucas, Robert E. (1973) "Some international evidence on output-inflation tradeoffs," *American Economic Review*, 63, 3 (June), 326–334.

Lucas, Robert E. (1994) "On the welfare cost of inflation," mimeo, University of Chicago.

McCallum, Bennett T. (1994) "Monetary policy rules and financial stability," National Bureau of Economic Research Working Paper No. 4692, April.

Mishkin, Frederic S. (1983) *A Rational Expectations Approach to Macroeconomics.* University of Chicago Press: Chicago.

Persson, Torsten, and Guido Tabellini (1993) "Designing institutions for monetary stability," *Carnegie-Rochester Conference Series on Public Policy*, 39 (December), 53–84.

Phelps, Edmund S. (1967) "Phillips curves, expectations of inflation, and optimal unemployment over time," *Economica*, 34, 3 (August), 254–281.

Phelps, Edmund S. (1972) *Inflation Policy and Unemployment Theory.* Norton: New York.

Phelps, Edmund S. (1973) "Inflation in the theory of public finance," *Swedish Journal of Economics*, 75, 1, 67–82.

Phillips, A. W. (1958) "The relation between unemployment and the rate of change of money wages in the United Kingdom, 1861–1957," *Economica*, 25, 4 (Nov), 283–299.

Posen, Adam (1993) "Central bank independence does not cause low inflation: The politics behind the institutional fix," mimeo, Harvard University, December.

Reagan, Patricia, and Rene M. Stulz (1993) "Contracting costs, inflation, and relative price variability," *Journal of Money, Credit and Banking*, 25, 3 (Aug, Part 2), 585–601.

Rogoff, Kenneth (1985) "The optimal degree of commitment to an intermediate monetary target," *Quarterly Journal of Economics*, 100, 4 (November), 1169–1190.

Roll, Eric et al. (1993) "Independent and accountable: A new mandate for the Bank of England." London: Centre for Economic Policy Research, October.

Romer, Christina, and David Romer (1989) "Does monetary policy matter? A new test in the spirit of Friedman and Schwartz," *NBER Macroeconomics Annual*, 121–170.

Rudebusch, Glenn D., and David W. Wilcox (1994) "Productivity and inflation: Evidence and interpretations," mimeo, Federal Reserve Board, Washington, D.C., April.

Samuelson, Paul A., and Robert M. Solow (1960) "Analytical aspects of anti-inflation policy," *American Economic Review*, 50, 2 (May), 177–194.

Sayers, Richard S. (1958) *Central Banking After Bagehot.* Reprinted. Oxford: Clarendon Press.

Summers, Laurence H. (1991) "How should long-term monetary policy be determined?," *Journal of Money, Credit and Banking*, 23, 3 (Aug, Part 2), 625–631.

Sidrauski, Miguel (1967) "Rational choice and patterns of growth in a monetary economy," *American Economic Review, Papers and Proceedings*, 71 (May), 534–544.

Taylor, John B. (1981) "On the relation between the variability of inflation and the average inflation rate," in Karl Brunner and Allan H. Meltzer (eds.), *The Costs and Consequences of Inflation*, Carnegie-Rochester Conference Series on Public Policy, Vol. 15, North-Holland, 57–85.

Tommasi, Mariano (1994) "The consequences of price instability in search markets: Towards understanding the effects of inflation," forthcoming, *American Economic Review*.

Vibert, Frank (1993) "The independence of the Bank of England and the Maastricht Treaty." London: European Policy Forum, May.

Walsh, Carl (1993) "Optimal contracts for independent central bankers: Private information, performance measures and reappointment," Working Paper 93–02, Federal Reserve Bank of San Francisco, May.

Wicksell, Knut (1965) *Interest and Prices*. Augustus M. Kelley: New York. Reprints of Economic Classics.

Almost every emerging market financial crisis during the period I was in the IMF occurred in a country that had formally or informally pegged its exchange rate. And in every post-crisis program, the country operated a flexible exchange rate regime. But in no case was the post-crisis flexible rate allowed to float freely.

As a result of these experiences, and of the earlier transition from the Bretton Woods system to the flexible rate system among the industrialized countries, the view developed that pegged rate systems were not sustainable—meaning they would eventually have to be given up, either in a collapse or voluntarily—and that countries with open capital markets had to choose either a very hard peg or a flexible rate regime. "Exchange Rate Regimes: Is the Bipolar View Correct?," which I presented at the annual meeting of the American Economic Association in January 2001, seeks to make sense of that view and uses a new categorization of exchange rate regimes produced by the IMF staff. This chapter shows that countries have been moving away from soft-pegged exchange rate regimes, towards hard pegs (including currency unions, most prominently the European Monetary Union) or more flexible rate regimes. It explains that development as a result of the impossible trinity, which says that a country cannot simultaneously run a monetary policy aimed at domestic objectives, a pegged exchange rate, and an open capital account.

I made two terminology mistakes in this chapter. The first was to use the word "bipolar," for some have interpreted the paper as arguing that the only viable exchange rate regimes are either hard pegs or those in which the exchange rate floats freely, without intervention. The second was to use the word "floating" instead of "flexible" in describing the flexible alternative to a softly pegged exchange rate. The chapter summarizes its thesis as *"for countries open to international capital flows*: (i) soft exchange rate pegs are not sustainable; but (ii) a wide variety of flexible rate arrangements remains possible; and (iii) it is to be expected that policy in most countries will not be indifferent to exchange rate movements" (italics in original). It then goes on to make the same point in terms of an imagined diagram, in which exchange rate arrangements are arrayed along a line from hard pegs on the left to freely floating on the right: "the intent of the bipolar view is not to rule out everything but the two corners, but rather to pronounce as unsustainable a segment of that line representing a variety of soft pegging exchange rate arrangements."

This is the view I still hold, and I believe both theory and evidence support it. Let me make just four comments. First, the paper only touches on the sort of flexible exchange rate regime that should be adopted.[1]

Second, speaking as an IMF official in January 2001—a time when the Argentine hard peg was under attack—I had to be very cautious in what I said about hard pegs. As it was, I referred several times to the adjustment difficulties that could face a country that was unable to use the exchange rate to adjust to economic shocks. The Argentine experience shows that even a very hard peg is not immune to adverse economic shocks and poor policies. Put differently, the impossible trinity argument seems to imply that a pegged exchange rate system can work provided monetary policy is dedicated to maintenance of the peg. The Argentine experience shows that this is not sufficient, that fiscal policy too may be needed to defend the peg in the face of extreme shocks, and that under such circumstances the country simply may decide that maintenance of the peg is too costly.

Another unfortunate lesson reinforced by the Argentine case is how quickly a financial system can be weakened in the face of a crisis. At the beginning of 2000, the Argentine banking system was extremely strong. Less than two years later, after the authorities had imposed a series of measures on the banking system in attempts to keep servicing the debt, and as depositors began to lose faith in the peg, the banking system had become severely weakened.

Third, the paper contains a short discussion of the use of the exchange rate as a nominal anchor during disinflation from high inflation. When the capital account is open, even a temporary peg of this type is dangerous, as the recent Turkish experience shows. I would now emphasize that any such temporary peg needs to be short-lived, lasting less than a year.

Fourth, the paper emphasizes that while a flexible rate reduces the probability of the type of external financial crisis suffered by so many pegged-rate countries in the 1990s, it does not prevent external crises caused by adverse debt dynamics. That lesson has unfortunately been driven home by the crisis in Brazil in 2002.

Note

1. Jeffrey Frankel, "No Single Currency Regime is Right for All Countries or At All Times," Princeton: Essays in International Finance, no. 215 (1998) describes a range of flexible rate arrangements.

8   Exchange Rate Regimes: Is the Bipolar View Correct?

Stanley Fischer

Each of the major international capital market-related crises since 1994—Mexico in 1994, Thailand, Indonesia, and Korea in 1997, Russia and Brazil in 1998, and Argentina and Turkey in 2000—has in some way involved a fixed or pegged exchange rate regime. At the same time, countries that did not have pegged rates—among them South Africa, Israel in 1998, Mexico in 1998, and Turkey in 1998—avoided crises of the type that afflicted emerging market countries with pegged rates.

Little wonder, then, that policymakers involved in dealing with these crises have warned strongly against the use of adjustable peg and other soft peg exchange rate regimes for countries open to international capital flows. That warning has tended to take the form of the bipolar, or corner solution, view, which is that countries need to choose either to peg their currencies hard (for instance, as in a currency board), or to allow their currencies to float, but that intermediate policy regimes between hard pegs and floating are not sustainable.[1]

Figure 8.1 shows the change in the distribution of exchange rate arrangements of the IMF's member countries between 1991 and 1999. The three categories shown are derived from a more detailed classification of de facto exchange regimes that is presented in the *Annual Report 2000* of the International Monetary Fund (pp. 141–143).[2] The arrangements described as "hard pegs" in figure 8.1 include currency boards and situations where countries have no national currency, either because they are in a currency union or because they have dollarized by formally adopting the currency of some other country. The floating group contains economies whose systems are described either as independently floating, or as a "managed float," which means that while the central bank may intervene

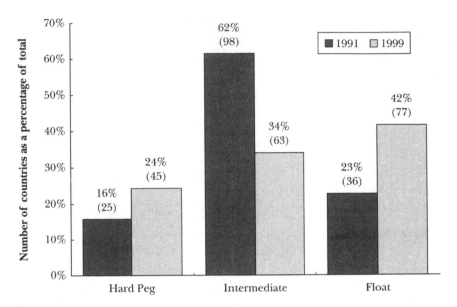

Figure 8.1
All countries: exchange rate regimes, 1991 and 1999. Source: IMF. Note: The number of countries is in parentheses.

in the exchange market, it has not committed itself to trying to bring about a particular exchange rate or exchange rate range. The "intermediate" group consists of economies with a variety of soft peg currency arrangements: these include a conventional fixed exchange rate peg; a crawling peg, in which the peg is allowed to shift gradually over time; an exchange rate band, in which the central bank is committed to keeping the exchange rate within a specified range; and a crawling band, which allows the exchange rate band itself to move over time.[3]

As figure 8.1 shows, there has since 1991 been a thinning out of the middle or intermediate range, and increases in the percentage of countries having either hard pegs or floating.[4] The percentage of countries with hard pegs increased from 16 to 24 percent; the percentage with floating rate regimes increased from 23 to 42 percent. Correspondingly, whereas 62 percent of economies had intermediate regimes in 1991, only 34 percent did in 1999. Thus, it does appear that during the 1990s, countries were moving away from the intermediate arrangements and toward either hard pegs or floating exchange rate regimes. But the significance of this movement and the specific conditions under which it makes economic sense need to be spelled out and refined.

In seeking to refine the analysis, I will argue that proponents of what is now known as the bipolar view—myself included— probably have exaggerated their point for dramatic effect. The right statement is that *for countries open to international capital flows*: (i) soft exchange rate pegs are not sustainable; but (ii) a wide variety of flexible rate arrangements remain possible; and (iii) it is to be expected that policy in most countries will not be indifferent to exchange rate movements. To put the point graphically, if exchange rate arrangements lie along a line connecting hard pegs like currency unions, currency boards, and dollarization on the left, with free floating on the right, the intent of the bipolar view is not to rule out everything but the two corners, but rather to pronounce as unsustainable a segment of that line representing a variety of soft pegging exchange rate arrangements.[5]

This version of the bipolar argument accepts that countries are likely to be concerned about the level of their exchange rate. In particular, countries will often have what Calvo and Reinhart (2000) term a "fear of floating," because they are not willing to accept the extent of exchange rate fluctuations generated by a totally free float of the exchange rate. In this case, monetary policy and possibly foreign exchange intervention policy will respond to exchange market pressures.[6] The formulation also leaves open a variety of exchange rate arrangements. For countries open to international capital flows, it includes as sustainable regimes both very hard pegs and a variety of floating rate arrangements, including managed floats. For countries not as yet open to international capital flows, it includes the full gamut of exchange rate arrangements.

The question that then arises is what exchange rate arrangements are excluded by the bipolar view. The answer is: for countries open to international capital flows, exchange rate systems in which the government is viewed as being committed to defending a particular value of the exchange rate, or a narrow range of exchange rates, but has not made the institutional commitments that both constrain and enable monetary policy to be devoted to the sole goal of defending the parity. In essence, the excluded arrangements are fixed exchange rate pegs, adjustable exchange rate pegs, and narrow band exchange rate systems.

I will start this chapter by focusing on the critical point that for developed and emerging market countries, adjustable peg exchange rate systems have not proved to be viable for the long term, and should not be expected to be viable. I will then take up a set of other issues: the "fear of floating" argument, and monetary policy under floating rate regimes; the nature of the hard peg arrangements that may be expected to be viable; the use of the exchange rate as a nominal anchor in disinflation; the behavior of exchange rates among the United States, Europe, and Japan; and what can be said about exchange rate arrangements for developing countries that are not open to international capital flows.

Exchange Rate Regimes for Developed and Emerging Market Countries

The fresh thinking about exchange rate regimes that has followed the crises of the last seven years centers on exchange rate systems for countries integrated or integrating into global capital markets.

Two groups of countries can be considered as integrated or integrating into international capital markets: the advanced countries, and emerging market countries. For the advanced countries, I draw on the list of "developed market" economies produced by Morgan Stanley Capital International (MSCI). This contains 22 economies, listed in table 8.1. The emerging market group is defined as the 33 economies contained in the union of the 27 economies that are in the MSCI emerging markets index and the 17 economies that are in the Emerging Markets Bond Index Plus (EMBI+), which is from J. P. Morgan. These are listed in table 8.2. Tables 8.1 and 8.2 also list exchange rate arrangements in place at the end of 1999.[7]

Figure 8.2 shows the development of exchange rate regimes among the developed and emerging market countries listed in tables 8.1 and 8.2. In these cases, too, there has been a shift in the bipolar direction, away from the soft peg center, towards harder pegs on one side, and floating arrangements on the other.

Of the 22 developed market economies in table 8.1, all of which have complete or nearly complete capital mobility, 10 are in the euro area and are listed as having no separate legal tender.[8] Another 10 countries are listed as having floating rates, either independently floating or managed floating. The other two countries are Hong Kong SAR, with a currency board arrangement, and Denmark, which has

Table 8.1
Developed market economies (as of December 31, 1999)

	Euro area		Other
	Exchange arrangement		Exchange arrangement
Austria	No separate legal tender	Australia	Independent float
Belgium	No separate legal tender	Canada	Independent float
Finland	No separate legal tender	Denmark	Pegged rate in
France	No separate legal tender		horizontal band
Germany	No separate legal tender	Hong Kong SAR	Currency board
Ireland	No separate legal tender	Japan	Independent float
Italy	No separate legal tender	New Zealand	Independent float
Netherlands	No separate legal tender	Norway	Managed float
Portugal	No separate legal tender	Singapore	Managed float
Spain	No separate legal tender	Sweden	Independent float
		Switzerland	Independent float
		United Kingdom	Independent float
		United States	Independent float

Source: IMF, Annual Report 2000.
Note: Economies listed in the MSCI Developed Markets index.

Table 8.2
Emerging market countries grouped by exchange rate arrangement (as of December 31, 1999)

Exchange rate regime (Number of countries)	Countries
No separate legal tender/Currency board (3) (*3)	*Argentina, *Bulgaria, *Panama
Other fixed pegs (7) (*2)	*China, Egypt, Jordan, *Malaysia, Morocco, Pakistan, Qatar
Pegged rate in horizontal band (1) (*1)	*Greece
Crawling peg (1)	Turkey
Rates within crawling bands (5) (*2)	Hungary, *Israel, Poland, Sri Lanka, *Venezuela
Managed float (3) (*1)	Czech Republic, Nigeria, *Taiwan POC
Independent float (13) (*7)	*Brazil, *Chile, Colombia, Ecuador, *India, Indonesia, *Korea, *Mexico, Peru, *Philippines, Russia, *South Africa, Thailand

Source: IMF, Annual Report 2000.
Note: * indicates country whose weight in either the EMBI+ or MSCI index is 2% or greater. Numbers in parenthesis indicate number of countries in each group; asterisked numbers are self-explanatory.

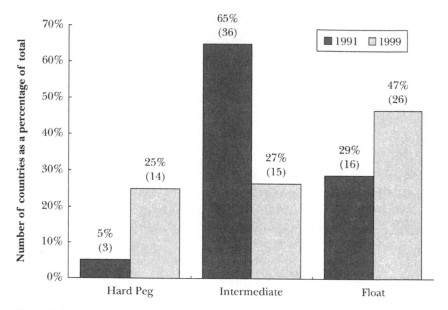

Figure 8.2
Developed and emerging market countries: exchange rate regimes, 1991 and 1999.
Source: IMF. Note: The number of countries is in parentheses.

not agreed to join the euro zone but is officially still pegging its exchange rate within a band to the other European currencies. *Thus,
among the developed economies listed in table 8.1, and depending on how
the euro zone countries are regarded, half the economies have established
very hard pegs, and nearly half the countries float.*

A decade ago, table 8.1 would have looked quite similar for the
non-euro area countries. However, the European countries were at
that time operating under the European Monetary System (EMS),
a set of adjustable exchange rate pegs operating within horizontal
bands. Part of the belief in the nonrobustness of adjustable pegs
derives from the manner in which EMS currencies were attacked in
1992 and 1993. It proved impossible to hold the adjustable pegs
within the EMS after the rise in German interest rates necessitated by
Germany's unification had imposed a domestically inappropriate
monetary policy on the other EMS members. This example is particularly telling since the attack on the EMS was successful despite the
political commitment to it by the system's members, who saw the
adjustable peg system within the EMS as a stepping-stone towards
the goal of monetary union. Part of the empirical support for the

view that countries will move away from soft peg exchange rate mechanisms to hard pegs or fixed exchange rate mechanisms is based on the creation of the euro as a single currency for Europe.

The 33 emerging market economies are grouped by exchange rate arrangement in table 8.2. The largest group of countries (13) consists of those described as independently floating. Six of those countries (Indonesia, Korea, Thailand, Russia, Brazil, and Mexico) became floaters after the major crises of the last decade, while Colombia joined the group in 1999. This is the set of transitions that has most influenced the view that soft pegs are not viable for sustained periods—and it includes many of the largest emerging market economies. Three economies are described as having managed floats. Thus, half the emerging market group of countries has some form of floating rate arrangement. While there is room for judgment over whether these countries should be listed in the "managed" or "independent" floating group, there should be no dispute that all 16 belong in one or other of those categories. Furthermore, there has during the last decade been a significant shift among these emerging market economies from various forms of pegged arrangements towards floating.

Of the remaining 17 countries listed in table 8.2, at the end of 1999 three had either currency boards or no independent legal tender. Ecuador and Greece have subsequently joined this group: Ecuador (an independent floater in December 1999) by dollarizing and Greece by joining the European Monetary Union. Eight countries had fixed or adjustable pegs at the end of 1999. Turkey had just instituted a crawling peg regime, which has now given way to a float. Five countries—Hungary, Israel, Poland, Sri Lanka, and Venezuela—had crawling bands, which in the cases of both Israel and Poland have been widening over the years, to the point of considerable flexibility.

The pattern is similar if one looks at the 16 larger emerging market economies, which are identified with asterisks in table 8.2. Half of these larger emerging market economies are floaters. Three have hard pegs, a number that by now has risen to four. Two have crawling bands. Only two of the countries in this group of larger emerging market economies have soft pegs: China and Malaysia.

Within the emerging market economies, the number of intermediate exchange rate arrangements declined in the 1990s and the number of floating and fixed regimes has increased.[9] This shift appears likely to continue. Looking ahead from the end of 1999, Greece has joined the euro zone, and Hungary and Poland are likely to. Israel is likely to move to an independently floating rate regime; Turkey is scheduled to move in that direction too, with possible membership in the euro zone a more distant prospect.

It is thus reasonable to say that economies open to international capital flows have been and are in the process of moving away from adjustable peg exchange rate systems, some towards harder pegs and more fixed exchange rates (especially in the creation of the euro zone), more towards systems with greater exchange rate flexibility. But why? *The reason is that soft peg systems have not proved viable over any lengthy period, especially for countries integrated or integrating into the international capital markets.* The fact that pegged exchange rates have a short life expectancy whether the economy is open to international capital flows or not was emphasized by Obstfeld and Rogoff (1995). But the collapse of the Bretton Woods system in the late 1960s and early 1970s, the repeated crises of the European Monetary System in the 1980s and the successful attacks on currencies within the system in 1992 and 1993, and the emerging market crises of 1994–2000 all drive home the lesson that this problem is especially intense for countries that are more open to international flows of capital.[10]

In several countries, extensive economic damage has been caused by the collapses of pegged rate regimes that had lasted for a few years. After a few years of exchange rate stability under a pegged regime, a belief gradually arises that the exchange rate will never change, which reduces perceptions of the risk of borrowing in foreign currencies and removes the need to hedge. Then, when an exchange rate crisis does strike, it is exceptionally damaging in its effects on banking systems, corporations, and government finances. In principle, it should be possible to reduce the potential damage through prudential regulations that limit the open foreign exchange positions of banks. But it is harder to control corporate sector international financing through such regulations. Moreover, it is in any case probably unwise to rely too heavily on regulatory supervision to prevent transactions that would otherwise be highly profitable.[11]

The concept of the "impossible trinity" points out that no economy can simultaneously have a fixed exchange rate, capital mobility, and a monetary policy dedicated to domestic goals. The major explanation for the nonviability of soft pegs is that they are an attempt by a country open to international capital flows to have both a fixed exchange rate and a monetary policy directed at domestic goals—

and sooner or later, an irreconcilable conflict arises between these goals. But this insight leaves open three questions. First, if the impossible trinity is correct, why did soft peg arrangements survive for so long, and why did their vulnerability become so much more apparent only in the 1990s? The second question is one of political economy: Why can't domestic monetary policy be directed credibly solely towards maintenance of the soft peg exchange rate? The third question is whether to seek to combine a fixed exchange rate and a domestically-oriented monetary policy by using capital controls to limit the mobility of foreign capital.

The evidence shown in figures 8.1 and 8.2 raises the question of what happened in the 1990s to cause exchange rate arrangements to shift in a bipolar direction. The beginnings of that move can be dated much earlier, to the breakup of the Bretton Woods system in the early 1970s. In the 1990s, the creation of the European Monetary Union accounts for much of the shift towards hard pegs. Among emerging market countries, the growing openness of capital accounts, combined with the associated development of private sector capital flows towards the emerging markets, made the force of the inconsistency expressed in the impossible trinity much more apparent and led to the collapse of several important soft pegged exchange rate arrangements in major crises.

The answer to the second question, the political economy question of why it is difficult for macroeconomic policy to protect a soft peg, must be that if the option of changing the exchange rate is open to the political system, then at a time when the short-run benefits of doing so appear to outweigh the costs, that option is likely to be chosen. Both foreign and domestic economic shocks (including policy actions) may move the equilibrium nominal exchange rate away from the official rate. If the official or pegged exchange rate is overvalued, then a government that wishes to prevent a devaluation typically has to raise interest rates. As long as the extent of the disequilibrium is small, and the requisite policy actions are taken in time, they can be expected to stabilize the situation. But if the disequilibrium has become large, either because policy was slow to react or because the country has been hit by a strong and longlasting shock, the required high interest rates may not be viable—either for political reasons or because of the damage they will inflict on the banking system or aggregate demand. Under those circumstances, speculators can be expected to attack the currency, selling it in the anticipation that the government will be forced to devalue. If the disequilibrium is large, such a speculative attack on the exchange rate is likely to succeed.

Third, why not impose capital controls to protect the exchange rate from the effects of unwanted capital flows?[12] Among the 16 larger emerging market economies identified in table 8.2, China successfully maintained its pegged exchange rate through the Asian crisis with the assistance of long-standing capital controls, providing an important element of stability in the regional and global economies. Malaysia's imposition of capital controls and pegging of the exchange rate in September 1998 has attracted more attention. However, evaluation of the effects of the Malaysian controls has been difficult since they were imposed after most of the turbulence of the first part of the Asian crisis was over—that is, after most of the capital that wanted to leave had done so—and when regional exchange rates were beginning to appreciate.[13]

In discussing capital controls, I shall assume that countries will in the course of their development want to liberalize the capital account and integrate into global capital markets. This view is based in part on the fact that the most advanced economies all have open capital accounts, which suggests that this is an appropriate goal for emerging market economies. It is also based on the view that the potential benefits of integration into the global capital markets—importantly including the benefits obtained by allowing foreign competition in the financial sector—outweigh the costs.[14]

It is necessary to distinguish between capital controls on outflows and on inflows. For controls on capital outflows to succeed, they need to be quite extensive, to cover potential loopholes. Even so, experience shows that controls on capital outflows cannot prevent a devaluation of the currency if domestic policies are fundamentally inconsistent with maintenance of the pegged exchange rate. Some countries have attempted to impose controls on outflows once a foreign exchange crisis is already underway. It is generally believed that this use of controls has been ineffective (Ariyoshi et al., 2000, pp. 18–29; Edwards, 1999, pp. 68–71). In addition, the imposition of controls on capital outflows is likely to have an effect on capital inflows to the country, since investors who are concerned about not being able to withdraw their capital from a country may respond by not sending it there in the first place.

Moreover, as an economy develops and experiences a growing range of contacts with foreign economies, controls on capital outflows are likely to become both more distorting and less effective. At some point the controls will need to be removed. Where controls on capital outflows are reasonably effective, they would need to be removed gradually, at a time when the exchange rate is not under pressure. The removal of controls on outflows sometimes results in a capital inflow, a result of either foreigners and/or domestic residents bringing capital into the country in light of the greater assurance it can be removed when desired. If the country is moving from a fixed exchange rate regime with controls on capital outflows to floating exchange rates, it is desirable to begin allowing some flexibility of exchange rates as the controls are gradually eased. Moreover, prudential controls that should be put in place for the efficient operation of the financial system often have a similar effect to some capital controls—for instance, limits on foreign exchange positions taken by domestic institutions. More generally, to reduce the economy's vulnerability to crises, a strong domestic financial system should be in place when capital controls are removed.

The IMF has supported the use of market-based capital inflow controls: for example, those that impose a tax on capital inflows. The typical instance occurs when a country is trying to reduce inflation using an exchange rate anchor. For anti-inflationary purposes, the country needs interest rates higher than those implied by the sum of foreign interest rates and the expected rate of currency depreciation. In such circumstances, the high interest rate will attract an inflow of foreign capital, which will tend to cause an exchange rate appreciation; alternatively, the country can permit the inflows and try to sterilize their monetary impact, but this typically becomes costly. A tax on capital inflows can in principle help a country maintain a high domestic interest rate without experiencing a substantial inflow of capital. In addition, by taxing short-term capital inflows more than longer-term inflows, capital inflow controls can also in principle influence the composition of inflows.

Evidence from the Chilean experience with controls on capital inflows suggests that controls on capital inflows were for a time successful in allowing some monetary policy independence, and also in shifting the composition of capital inflows towards longer-term investment. However, the Chilean controls eventually seemed to lose their effectiveness (Edwards, 2000), and they have recently been removed.

Direct controls on inflows are also used by some countries. These may be aimed at specific types of inflows, for instance, short-term (hot money) flows, or sometimes foreign direct investment. Direct investment inflows are typically quite stable, and indeed at the aggregate level continued rising even during the Asian crisis; they also bring advantages in the form of new technology. Most countries that seek to control inflows prefer long-term direct investment to short-term inflows. Nonetheless, some countries have liberalized short-term flows, while seeking to keep long-term flows out, thereby exacerbating the volatility of short-term capital flows as market uncertainties increased.

There is little question that capital controls—whether on outflows or inflows—can for some time help a country sustain a soft peg exchange rate regime. Nonetheless, such controls tend to lose their effectiveness over time. Moreover, as countries develop, they are likely to want to integrate further into global capital markets. Countries in these circumstances would be well advised to move away from a soft peg exchange rate, typically towards a more flexible exchange rate regime.

Fear of Floating

Many countries that claim to have floating exchange rates do not allow the exchange rate to float freely, but rather deploy interest rates and intervention policy to affect its behavior. As long as such interventions are not undertaken to defend a particular exchange rate, or narrow range of exchange rates, this chapter has categorized such behavior as a managed float. But such fear of floating behavior has been described as demonstrating that many—particularly emerging market—countries are not willing to allow their exchange rates to float.

It is hardly a surprise that most policymakers in most countries are concerned with the behavior of the nominal and the real exchange rates. Changes in the nominal exchange rate are likely to affect the inflation rate. Changes in the real exchange rate may have a powerful effect on the wealth of domestic citizens, and on the allocation of resources, which may have not only economic but also political effects—especially in the case of currency appreciations, in countries where exporters matter.

Thus in most countries, even those with floating exchange rate regimes, monetary policy is likely to respond to some extent to movements of the exchange rate. The United States is one of the few examples of a country that largely ignores its exchange rate in the conduct of monetary policy. But most of the other G-7 countries (Canada, France, Germany, Italy, Japan, and the United Kingdom) and emerging market economies do pay attention to exchange rates in the conduct of monetary policy. Canada, for example, until recently used a monetary conditions index to guide monetary policy, which was based on movements in both the exchange rate and the interest rate.

Many of the recent converts to floating exchange rates (several of whom were forcibly converted) have opted for inflation targeting, and that system seems to be working well and has much to commend it. With the inflation targeting approach to monetary policy, movements in the exchange rate will be taken into account indirectly in setting monetary policy, because the exchange rate affects price behavior. This will generally produce a pattern of monetary tightening when the exchange rate depreciates, a response similar, but not necessarily of the same magnitude, to that which would be undertaken if the exchange rate were being targeted directly.

Why should monetary policy not target both the nominal exchange rate and the inflation rate? Central banks may face this issue with particular force in a situation with an appreciated real exchange rate and the current account in large deficit. The first answer must be that monetary policy fundamentally affects the nominal exchange rate and not the real exchange rate, and that if any part of macroeconomic policy should take care of the current account balance by redressing an imbalance between domestic savings and investment, it is fiscal policy.

However, there is an unresolved issue about whether monetary policy in a floating rate system should be used in the short run to affect the real exchange rate. If the nominal exchange rate moves faster than the real exchange rate, then monetary policy can influence the real exchange rate in the short run. In many respects, this issue is similar to that of how monetary policy in an inflation-targeting framework should respond to movements in output and unemployment. There is almost certainly a short-run tradeoff between the real exchange rate and inflation, analogous to the Phillips curve, although it has not received much empirical attention.[15] This is not the place to pursue the issue, but just as answers have been developed to how to deal with the short-run Phillips curve in an inflation-targeting framework, so that a central bank can take into account the short-run impact of its actions on output and unemployment while recognizing that the long-run effects are negligible, it remains necessary to answer the question of how to deal with the short-run tradeoff between the real exchange rate and inflation, recognizing that in the long run greater inflation will not affect the real exchange rate.

Beyond the use of interest rates, some countries intervene directly from time to time in the foreign exchange markets to try to stabilize the exchange rate. So long as they are not perceived as trying to defend a particular rate, such interventions can be useful in reducing the degree of volatility in exchange rate markets. This is one of the remaining areas in which central bankers place considerable emphasis on the touch and feel of the market, and where systematic policy rules are not yet common. There is of course controversy over whether exchange rate intervention works at all—and even if it does, whether it is wise to use it. The Banco de Mexico has developed a method of more-or-less automatic intervention designed to reduce day-to-day movements in exchange rates, which could provide lessons in this area.

Recognizing the difficulty for an emerging market country of defending a narrow range of exchange rates, John Williamson (2000) proposes alternative regimes. He calls these BBC arrangements: basket (that is, a peg to a basket of currencies rather than a single currency), band, and crawl. He also recommends that countries if necessary allow the exchange rate to move temporarily outside the band, so that speculators cannot predict with certainty when the central bank is going to intervene. In these circumstances, a moving and elastic band would be serving as a weak nominal anchor for the exchange rate, but it is not at all clear why such a system is preferable to an inflation-targeting framework. Possibly the exchange rate band could be thought of as a supplement to an inflation-targeting framework, but it would need to be demonstrated what benefits that brings, if any. One possibility—which is not very plausible—is that by committing weakly to some range of exchange rates, the authorities make it more likely that fiscal policy will be brought into play if the real exchange rate moves too far from equilibrium.

Viable Hard Pegs

At the end of 1999, 45 of the IMF's then-182 members had hard peg exchange rate systems, either with no independent legal tender, or a currency board. Except for the 11 countries in Europe, all of the 37 economies with no independent legal tender were small. But the exception of the European single currency, the euro, is a very big one. Argentina and Hong Kong SAR are the biggest economies with currency boards. Since the end of 1999, Ecuador and El Salvador have dollarized, so that over a quarter of the IMF's 183 members have very hard pegs; the proportion in terms of GDP is similar.

At the end of 1990, plans for a single European currency did not yet exist, and there were only three currency board economies. The appraisal of the performance of currency boards, once regarded as a historical curiosity, has undoubtedly changed, as a result of several factors: the tireless proselytizing by Steve Hanke and others (for instance, Hanke and Schuler, 1994); examination of their historical record; and their performance in a number of economies, including Hong Kong SAR, Argentina, and the transition economies of Estonia, Lithuania, Bulgaria, and Bosnia-Herzegovina. Ghosh, Gulde, and Wolf (2000, p. 270) provide a balanced summary:

First, the historical track record of currency boards is sterling ... Countries that did exit ... did so mainly for political, rather than economic reasons, and such exits were usually uneventful.... Second, modern currency boards have often been instituted to gain credibility following a period of high or hyper-inflation, and in this regard have been remarkably successful. Countries with currency boards experienced lower inflation and higher (if more volatile) GDP growth compared to both floating regimes and simple pegs.... The GDP growth effect is significant, but may simply reflect a rebound from depressed levels. Third,... the successful introduction of a currency board ... [is] far from trivial ... Moreover, there are thorny issues, as yet untested, regarding possible exits from a currency board ...

The great strength of the currency board arrangement, the virtual removal of the nominal exchange rate as a means of adjustment, is also its principal weakness. In the case of an internal or external macroeconomic shock, the economy can adjust via a change either in exchange rates or domestic prices and wages. The nominal exchange rate adjustment is typically much quicker, and that via wages and prices more prolonged and, certainly in the case of the need for a decline in the real exchange rate, more difficult. In late 2000, this difficulty was evident in Argentina, where a currency board arrangement prevents the nominal exchange rate from moving, but even in Argentina, the adjustment *is* taking place as domestic prices and costs decline relative to foreign prices and costs.

It is difficult to make a general evaluation of the benefits and costs of the constraints imposed by the commitment to a currency board. For a country with a history of extreme monetary disorder, a currency board appears to be a means of obtaining credibility for a low-inflation monetary policy more rapidly and at lower cost than appears possible any other way. For a country like Argentina, with a long and unhappy inflationary history, the society may be willing to accept the occasional short-run costs of doing without the exchange rate as a means of adjustment in exchange for lower inflation, just as the memory of the German hyperinflation in the 1920s has colored German attitudes to inflation ever since.

The extensive discussion leading up to the European single currency emphasized how member countries, when deprived of exchange rate flexibility, would need to adjust to shocks with wage and price flexibility, the mobility of labor and capital, and fiscal compensation. A currency board country is unlikely to have access to fiscal compensatory measures from abroad, and nor is its labor likely to be as mobile internationally as that in the European Union will be—but we should not exaggerate the role of geographical labor mobility as a means of short-run adjustment to shocks even in large national economies. For such a country, the emphasis has to be on wage and price flexibility as well as internal labor market mobility. Domestic fiscal policy can play a countercyclical role in a currency board economy, provided the fiscal situation is strong enough in normal times for fiscal easing during a recession not to raise any questions about long-term fiscal sustainability.

Policies to this end—to encourage internal factor mobility, wage and price flexibility, and fiscal prudence in normal times—are entirely possible, and can help ensure the sustainability of a currency board over time. Such policies are of course generally desirable in *any* economy, but the need for them is greater if the exchange rate is not available as a tool of adjustment.

Another disadvantage sometimes cited for a currency board arrangement is that since the central bank cannot create money, it may not be able to act as lender of last resort. However, the circumstance envisaged by the classic argument for lender of last resort—a pure panic-based run on banks into currency—is rare. Most often financial crises have a real basis, and take real resources to resolve, as Goodhart and Schoenmaker (1995) have shown. One way or another, these resources come from the fiscal authority. The absence of a central bank capable of acting as lender of last resort can be compensated for in various ways: by the creation, typically with fiscal resources, of a banking sector stabilization fund (as has been done in Bulgaria); by setting up a deposit insurance scheme, financed by the banks and if necessary in the final resort by the treasury; by strengthening financial sector supervision and prudential controls; by allowing foreign banks to operate in the economy; and by lining up contingency credits for the banking system.

The discussion so far has implicitly centered on how the goods and factor market and the current account would adjust in world of floating or fixed exchange rates. Those who strongly favor hard pegs, such as Calvo and Reinhart (2001) or Eichengreen and Hausmann (2000), tend to focus on international flows of capital and on asset markets. Their argument is that with respect to asset markets, a country obtains essentially no benefit—seigniorage aside—from exchange rate flexibility. For example, emerging market economies cannot borrow abroad in their own currencies, and so the exchange rate creates a source of additional risk and higher interest rates for all foreign borrowing. Given this, they argue for going beyond currency boards to dollarization and perhaps in the longer run to wider currency unions.

If a country intends never to use the exchange rate as a mechanism of adjustment, then retaining exchange rate flexibility is clearly counterproductive. Hence the argument for dollarization relative to a currency board must turn on an appraisal of the gains from dollarization that would be obtained in the capital markets, for example in the reduction of spreads between domestic and foreign interest rates and by the strengthening of the financial system, versus the losses implied by forgoing both seigniorage and the option of changing the exchange rate in extremis by giving up a national currency. The balance of the argument would be tilted if a politically acceptable means could be found of transferring seigniorage to dollarizing countries; the Mack bill in the previous Congress would have done that, suggesting that, at least in the case of the dollar, some means of transferring seigniorage from the use of the dollar could eventually become politically feasible.

Both Ecuador and El Salvador dollarized in 2000, but under very different circumstances. Ecuador's decision was essentially one of desperation (Fischer, 2001); El Salvador's was based on careful consideration. The Ecuadorian case provides much food for thought about what it takes for dollarization to succeed. It was implemented without many of what were thought of as the prerequisites for success, such as a strong banking system, being in place. Much work remains to be done, particularly in the banking sector, to ensure the long-term success of Ecuador's dollarization. But at least in its first year, it has worked reasonably well.

Hard peg exchange rate systems have become more attractive than had been thought some years ago. For a small economy, heavily dependent in its trade and capital account transactions on a particular large economy, it *may* make sense to adopt the currency of that country, particularly if provision can be made for the transfer of seigniorage. While the requirements for the effective operation of such a system are demanding, in terms of the strength of the financial system and fiscal soundness, meeting those requirements is good for the economy in any case. To be sure, careful consideration needs to be given to the nature of the shocks affecting the economy. For example, even though the Canadian economy is closely connected to the U.S. economy, Canadian policymakers regard their country as benefitting from the shock-absorber role of the floating exchange rate with the U.S. dollar. But there is clearly a trend, which can be expected to accelerate if the euro zone succeeds, in the direction of hard pegged exchange rate regimes. This trend is already reducing the number of currencies in existence, and further reductions should be expected in future.

The Exchange Rate as a Nominal Anchor for Disinflation

The benefits and risks of using the exchange rate as a nominal anchor to disinflate from triple-digit inflation, as well as the real dynamics associated with such stabilizations, have been extensively studied (for a summary, see Mussa et al., 2000, Appendix III, pp. 44–47; Calvo and Végh, 1999). There are few instances in which a successful disinflation from triple-digit inflation has taken place without the use of an exchange rate anchor, particularly in countries that have suffered from chronic monetary instability. The exchange rate anchor in such disinflations sometimes takes the form of a very hard peg, for instance a currency board, but is more often a softer peg, often a crawling peg regime.

Of the eleven major exchange rate-based stabilizations since the late 1980s studied in Mussa et al. (2000), four of them—Argentina in 1991, Estonia in 1992, Lithuania in 1994, and Bulgaria in 1997—entered currency boards and disinflated successfully. The other seven countries (and Israel in 1985 could be added to this sample) generally either undertook exchange rate devaluations a step at a time, or introduced crawling exchange rate bands, which in many cases have widened over time. The disinflations of three countries—Mexico in 1994, Russia in 1998, and Brazil in 1999—ended in a currency crash, though in each case low inflation was preserved or rapidly regained following the crisis.

Countries which disinflate using a soft peg exchange rate strategy must consider their exit strategy from the pegged arrangement. An IMF study of exit strategies in this case showed that exit is best undertaken when the currency is strong, something which is quite likely to happen as the stabilization gains credibility and capital inflows expand (Eichengreen et al., 1998). This was the pattern for instance in Poland and Israel, where the band was widened as pressure for appreciation mounted. However, the political economy of moving away from a peg is complicated, even in this case. When the currency is strong, the authorities generally see no reason to move off the peg; when it is weak, they argue that devaluation or a widening of the band under pressure would be counterproductive. But the longer the peg continues, the more the dangers associated with soft pegs grow. In some cases in which the currencies of disinflating countries crashed, the IMF had been pushing unsuccessfully for greater exchange rate flexibility.

The need to move away from a soft peg is one of the reasons an exit mechanism was built into the Turkish stabilization and reform program that began in December 1999. Nonetheless, as a result of unresolved banking sector problems, the failure to undertake corrective fiscal actions when the current account widened, and political difficulties, the crawling peg failed to hold and in February 2001, Turkey was forced to float its exchange rate.

Big Three Exchange Rates

The remarkable instability of exchange rates among the major currencies is a perennial topic of concern and discussion. Movements in exchange rates among the big three—the United States, Europe, and Japan—can create difficulties for other countries, particularly for those that peg to one of those currencies. Thus the exports of east Asian countries were adversely affected by the appreciation of the dollar that began in 1995, and the strengthening of the dollar was also a factor in the difficulties faced by Argentina and Turkey in 2000.

There have been frequent proposals for target exchange rate zones among the dollar, the euro and the yen. If the target zones were to be narrow, monetary policy in each currency area would have to be dedicated to maintenance of the exchange rate commitment. There is no political support for a commitment to narrow target zones; it is not clear that monetary policy could maintain the desired exchange rate commitment; and there is not a persuasive case that the gains from maintaining a narrow commitment would be large. But given the extent of exchange rate movements among the major currencies, even wide target zones could be stabilizing.

In practice, something akin to such a system appears to operate, informally and loosely. When exchange rates get far out of line with fundamentals, two or three countries of the big three agree to intervene in the currency markets. This happened in mid-1995 when the yen-dollar exchange rate reached 80, implying a yen that was significantly appreciated relative to estimates of its equilibrium value, and in the fall of 2000, when the euro was significantly depreciated relative to its estimated equilibrium value.[16]

This informal system differs from a formal target zone system in three important ways. First, there are no preannounced target zones, and so no commitment to intervene at any particular level of exchange rates. This removes the possibility of one-way bets for speculators, but of course also removes the certainty about future exchange rates that a credible target zone system would provide—if such a system were possible. Second, the informal system operates more through coordinated interventions in the foreign exchange market than through coordinated monetary policy actions. While exchange rate movements may influence interest rates in the big three, both through their implications for inflation, and probably

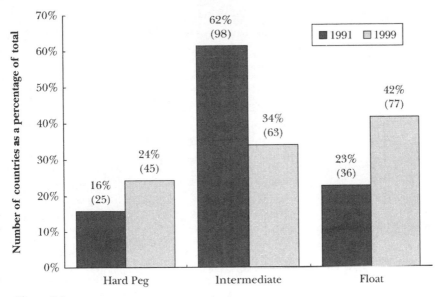

Figure 8.3
All other countries: exchange rate regimes, 1991 and 1999. Source: IMF. Note: The number of countries is in parentheses.

more directly in the cases of the Bank of Japan and the European Central Bank, coordinated interest rate changes with the sole purpose of affecting exchange rates do not appear to be on the current agenda. Third, such interventions are rare.

All of which is to say that the system is indeed informal and loose. Nonetheless it provides some bounds on the extent to which exchange rates among the United States, Europe and Japan are likely to diverge from equilibrium.

Exchange Rate Regimes for Other Countries

I have focused so far on exchange rate regimes for 55 developed and emerging market economies, which account for the bulk of global GDP, trade, and international capital flows. Figure 8.3 shows the distribution of exchange rate arrangements among the other members of the IMF as of end-1999 and end-1991, respectively. Table 8.3 groups these countries by their exchange rate regime at the end of 1999. The pattern is a familiar one: There has been a mild shift towards hard pegs on one side and a stronger shift to more flexible exchange rate regimes on the other.

Table 8.3
All other countries grouped by exchange rate arrangements (as of December 31, 1999)

Exchange rate regime (Number of countries)	Countries
No separate legal tender/ Currency board (31)	Antigua and Barbuda, Benin, Bosnia and Herzegovina, Brunei Darussalam, Burkina Faso, Cameroon, Central African Rep., Chad, Congo (Rep. of), Côte d'Ivoire, Djibouti, Dominica, Equatorial Guinea, Estonia, Gabon, Grenada, Guinea-Bissau, Kiribati, Lithuania, Luxembourg, Mali, Marshall Islands, Micronesia, Niger, Palau, San Marino, Senegal, St. Kitts and Nevis, St. Lucia, St. Vincent and the Grenadines, Togo
Other fixed pegs (38)	Aruba, Bahamas, Bahrain, Bangladesh, Barbados, Belize, Bhutan, Botswana, Cape Verde, Comoros, El Salvador, Fiji, Iran, Iraq, Kuwait, Latvia, Lebanon, Lesotho, Macedonia FYR, Maldives, Malta, Myanmar, Namibia, Nepal, Netherlands Antilles, Oman, Samoa, Saudi Arabia, Seychelles, Solomon Islands, Swaziland, Syrian Arab Republic, Tonga, Trinidad and Tobago, Turkmenistan, United Arab Emirates, Vanuatu, Zimbabwe
Pegged rate in horizontal band (4)	Cyprus, Iceland, Libya, Vietnam
Crawling peg (4)	Bolivia, Costa Rica, Nicaragua, Tunisia
Rates within crawling bands (2)	Honduras, Uruguay
Managed float (23)	Algeria, Azerbaijan, Belarus, Burundi, Cambodia, Croatia, Dominican Rep., Ethiopia, Guatemala, Jamaica, Kenya, Kyrgyz Republic, Lao PDR, Malawi, Mauritania, Paraguay, Romania, Slovak Rep., Slovenia, Suriname, Tajikistan, Ukraine, Uzbekistan
Independent float (29)	Afghanistan, Albania, Angola, Armenia, Congo (Dem. Rep.), Eritrea, Gambia, Georgia, Ghana, Guinea, Guyana, Haiti, Kazakhstan, Liberia, Madagascar, Mauritius, Moldova, Mongolia, Mozambique, Papua New Guinea, Rwanda, São Tome and Príncipe, Sierra Leone, Somalia, Sudan, Tanzania, Uganda, Yemen, Zambia

Source: IMF, Annual Report 2000.

These countries represented in figure 8.3 are developing economies that are not classified as emerging market, which means that they typically have low per capita incomes. Many of them are also small economies and not very well integrated into the world economy. Such countries will display a wide range of situations and experiences, which makes it hard to make any definite recommendations on what exchange rate regimes would work best for countries in this group. In a review of exchange rate arrangements in these economies, Mussa et al. (2000, p. 31) state:

Reflecting wide differences in levels of economic and financial development and in other aspects of their economic situations, no single exchange rate regime is most appropriate for all such countries, and the regime that is appropriate for a particular country may change over time.[17] Because of their limited involvement with modern global financial markets, some form of exchange rate peg or band or highly managed float is generally more viable and more appropriate for them than for most of the emerging market countries. Even this conclusion, however, leaves a wide range of possible regimes—for a diverse range of developing and transition countries.

They add: "IMF advice to members ... reflects this ambiguity and diversity. Consistent with the Articles of Agreement, the IMF generally respects the member's choice of exchange rate regime and advises on policies needed to support that choice."

There is room for further research on the characteristics of exchange rate systems and accompanying financial sector structural policies most suited to particular types of countries that are not yet integrated into the global financial system, taking into account the likelihood that as the country develops, it will want to open up its capital account.

Summary and Conclusions

In the last decade, there has been a hollowing out of the middle of the distribution of exchange rate regimes in a bipolar direction, with the share of both hard pegs and floating gaining at the expense of soft pegs. This is true not only for economies active in international capital markets, but among all countries. A look ahead suggests this trend will continue, certainly among the emerging market countries. The main reason for this change, among countries with open capital accounts, is that soft pegs are crisis-prone and not viable over long periods.

A country's choice between a hard peg and floating depends in part on the characteristics of the economy, and in part on its inflationary history. The choice of a hard peg makes sense for countries with a long history of monetary instability, and/or for a country closely integrated in both its capital and current account transactions with another or a group of other economies. However, countries with a historical tradition of monetary stability, or no obvious subset of other countries with which to form a monetary union, or a belief that a flexible exchange rate helps their economy adjust to the sorts of macroeconomic shocks that it experiences, may be better off with a floating exchange rate.

As more countries adopt very hard exchange rate pegs of one sort or another, including dollarization and currency unions, there will in the future be fewer independent national currencies. Exchange rates among the remaining independent currencies will mostly be floating, and for all but the biggest countries, monetary policy—and occasionally exchange market intervention—will react to and sometimes seek to affect the nominal exchange rate.

In the medium term, as in recent years, as the center of the distribution of exchange rate regimes hollows out, the shift will likely be more towards the floating than the hard peg end of the spectrum. However, over the longer term, and depending on how well the euro area and dollarized economies operate, the trend could well be to move from the floating to the hard peg ends of the spectrum.

Notes

This paper is an edited version of a lecture delivered to a joint session of the Society of Government Economists and the American Economic Association at the meetings of the Allied Social Science Associations in New Orleans, Louisiana, on January 6, 2001. I would like to thank Timothy Taylor for his excellent editing. I am grateful to my colleagues at the IMF for continuing discussion of these issues, and, in the preparation of this paper, particularly to Ratna Sahay and Grace Juhn for their assistance, Shogo Ishii, Barry Johnson, Nadia Malikyar, and Inci Otker for their work in classifying exchange rate regimes, and many other colleagues for further information regarding those classifications. Thanks, too, to Stanley Black, Olivier Blanchard, Robert Chote, Dan Citrin, Stijn Claessens, Brad De Long, David Goldsbrough, Taka Ito, Mohsin Khan, Louis Kuijs, Jaewoo Lee, Eduardo Levy-Yeyati, Paul Masson, Paolo Mauro, Sandy McKenzie, Jacques Polak, Dani Rodrik, Federico Sturzenegger, Gyorgy Szapary, Teresa Ter-Minassian, Michael Waldman, John Williamson, and Holger Wolf for their comments. Views expressed are those of the author, not necessarily of the International Monetary Fund.

1. Exchange rate regimes will be defined more precisely below: soft pegs are exchange rates that are currently fixed in value (or a narrow range of values) to some other

currency or basket of currencies, with some commitment by the authorities to defend the peg, but with the value likely to change if the exchange rate comes under significant pressure. The adjustable peg exchange rates of the Bretton Woods regime were typically soft pegs.

2. Until recently the IMF's categorization of exchange rate regimes was based on self-descriptions by member countries, which are presented in the IMF's *Exchange Arrangements and Exchange Restrictions* (EAER) publication. The categorization used in this paper, taken from the *Annual Report 2000*, is based on the IMF staff's evaluation of the de facto arrangements actually in place, rather than what the authorities say the regime is. Several authors, including Ghosh et al. (1997) and Levy-Yeyati and Sturzenegger (2000), have wrestled with the difficulty that the authorities' own description of exchange rate regimes in *EAER* is patently inaccurate for some countries, and Levy-Yeyati and Sturzenegger have developed their own categorization, based on aspects of exchange rate and reserve variability. The staff of the IMF is currently developing data for earlier years on de facto exchange rate regimes corresponding to the information provided in the *Annual Report 2000*.

3. Classification of the exchange rate regime may be difficult in marginal cases; for instance, whether a very broad exchange rate band should be classified as a soft peg or a managed float.

4. The exchange rate classifications for 1991 used in figure 8.1 were provided by the staff of the IMF, on the same basis as those for 1999—that is, using their judgment of the de facto exchange rate arrangements actually in place in member countries.

5. For analyses of exchange rate systems, see Mussa et al. (2000), Calvo and Reinhart (2000), Edwards (2000), Frankel (1999), Summers (2000), and Velasco (2000).

6. Several colleagues who commented on the first draft of this paper emphasized that monetary and exchange rate policy should not be regarded as separate, and that the key issue in choosing an exchange rate policy is the consistency of the overall macroeconomic policy framework. This perspective is of course correct, but for expositional reasons I focus more narrowly on the choice of exchange rate regime, taking it for granted that no exchange rate regime can be sustained if it is inconsistent with overall macroeconomic policy.

7. For further information on indexes from Morgan Stanley Capital International, see ⟨http://www.msci.com⟩. For a general discussion of EMBI+, which tracks total returns for traded external debt instruments in the emerging markets, see ⟨http://www.jpmorgan.com/MarketDataInd/EMBI/embi.html⟩. The MSCI list of developed market economies excludes six that are included in the IMF listing of "Advanced Economies": Greece, Iceland, Israel, Korea, Luxembourg, and Taiwan POC. Except for Iceland and Luxembourg, these are included in the emerging market economies listed in table 8.1. The description of the exchange rate regime for Taiwan POC, which is not listed in the original source, is provided by the author.

8. Technically, the national currencies for the euro area countries are scheduled to continue as legal tender within each country through the first half of 2002.

9. Fischer and Sahay (2000) document a very similar pattern over time among the transition economies in the 1990s.

10. John Williamson (2000) offers an alternate argument for the movement away from soft pegs, suggesting that it is because of pressure from the IMF and U.S. Treasury.

11. I return to a closely related point below in discussing the potential use of capital controls.

12. This question is examined by Edwards (2000), Mussa et al. (2000), and Williamson (2000). For more detailed discussion of experience with capital controls, see Ariyoshi et al. (2000).

13. See Kaplan and Rodrik (2000) for a relatively positive appraisal of the Malaysian controls.

14. The argument is developed at greater length in Fischer (1998). The point has been much disputed, including by Jagdish Bhagwati (1998).

15. Cushman and Zha (1997) contain vector autoregressions from which the implied tradeoff can be calculated in the Canadian case. See also Calvo, Reinhart, and Végh (1995).

16. For the IMF's methodology for estimating equilibrium exchange rates, see Isard and Faruqee (1998). These estimates come with a wide confidence interval, but from time to time discrepancies between actual and estimated equilibrium exchange rates can be clearly identified. Several private sector financial institutions also estimate equilibrium exchange rates; see Edwards (2000) for discussion of the methodologies and the range of estimates provided by different sources.

17. At this point the authors note that this is the conclusion reached by Frankel (1999).

References

Ariyoshi, Akira, Karl Habermeier, Bernard Laurens, Inci Ötker-Robe, Jorge Iván Canales-Kriljenko, and Andrei Kirilenko. 2000. *Capital Controls: Country Experiences with Their Use and Liberalization*, IMF Occasional Paper 190.

Bhagwati, Jagdish. 1998. "The Capital Myth." *Foreign Affairs*. May/June, 77:3, 7–12.

Broda, Christian. 2001. "Coping with Terms of Trade Shocks: Pegs vs. Floats," in Alberto Alesina and Robert Barro, eds. *Currency Unions*. Stanford: Hoover Institution Press.

Calvo, Guillermo A. 2000. "Capital Markets and the Exchange Rate, with Special Reference to the Dollarization Debate in Latin America," University of Maryland, April.

Calvo, Guillermo A., and Carmen M. Reinhart. 2000. "Fear of Floating," NBER Working Paper 7993, November.

Calvo, Guillermo A., and Carmen M. Reinhart. 2001. "Reflections on Dollarization," in Alberto Alesina and Robert Barro, eds. *Currency Unions*. Stanford: Hoover Institution Press.

Calvo, Guillermo A., Carmen M. Reinhart, and Carlos A. Végh. 1995. "Targeting the Real Exchange Rate: Theory and Evidence." *Journal of Development Economics*, 47, pp. 97–133.

Calvo, Guillermo A., and Carlos Végh. 1999. "Inflation Stabilization and BOP Crises in Developing Countries," NBER Working Paper 6925.

Chang, Roberto, and Andres Velasco. 2000. "Exchange Rate Policy for Developing Countries." *American Economic Review, Papers and Proceedings*. May, 90:2, pp. 71–75.

Cushman, David O., and Tao Zha. 1997. "Identifying Monetary Policy in a Small open Economy under Flexible Exchange Rates." *Journal of Monetary Economics*. 39, pp. 433–448.

Edwards, Sebastian. 1999. "How Effective Are Capital Controls?" *Journal of Economic Perspectives*. Fall, 13:4, pp. 65–84.

Edwards, Sebastian. 2000. "Exchange Rate Regimes, Capital Flows and Crisis Prevention," NBER, December.

Eichengreen, Barry, and Ricardo Hausmann. 1999. "Exchange Rates and Financial Fragility," NBER Working Paper 7418, November.

Eichengreen, Barry, Paul Masson, Hugh Bredenkamp, Barry Johnston, Javier Haman, Esteban Jadresic, and Inci Ötker. 1998. *Exit Strategies: Policy Options for Countries Seeking Greater Exchange Rate Flexibility*, IMF Occasional Paper 168.

Fischer, Stanley. 1998. "Capital-Account Liberalization and the Role of the IMF," in *Should the IMF Pursue Capital-Account Convertibility*? Princeton University, International Finance Section, Essays in International Finance, May, 207, pp. 1–10.

Fischer, Stanley. 2001. "Ecuador and the IMF," in Alberto Alesina and Robert Barro, eds. *Currency Unions*. Stanford: Hoover Institution Press.

Fischer, Stanley, and Ratna Sahay. 2000. "The Transition Economies after Ten Years," IMF Working Paper, WP/00/30, International Monetary Fund, Washington, D.C., February.

Frankel, Jeffrey A. 1999. *No Single Currency Regime Is Right for All Countries or at All Times*. Princeton University, International Finance Section, Essays in International Finance, August, 215.

Ghosh, Atish R., Anne-Marie Gulde, Jonathan D. Ostry, and Holger C. Wolf. 1997. "Does the Nominal Exchange Rate Regime Matter?" NBER Working Paper 5874, January.

Ghosh, Atish R., Anne-Marie Gulde, and Holger C. Wolf. 2000. "Currency Boards: More Than a Quick Fix?" *Economic Policy*. October, 31, pp. 270–335.

Goodhart, Charles, and Dirk Schoenmaker. 1995. "Should the Functions of Monetary Policy and Bank Supervisor Be Separated?" *Oxford Economic Papers*. 47, pp. 539–560.

Hanke, Steve H., and Kurt Schuler. 1994. *Currency Boards for Developing Countries*. International Center for Economic Growth. San Francisco: ICS Press.

Hausmann, Ricardo, Michael Gavin, Carmen Pages-Serra, and Ernesto Stein. 1999. "Financial Turmoil and the Choice of Exchange Rate Regime." Inter-American Development Bank, Working Paper 400.

International Monetary Stability Act of 2000. 106th Congress, 2nd Session, S. 2101.

Isard, Peter, and Hamid Faruqee, eds. 1998. *Exchange Rate Assessment: Extensions of the Macroeconomic Balance Approach*, IMF Occasional Paper 167.

Kaplan, Ethan, and Dani Rodrik. 2000. "Did the Malaysian Capital Controls Work?" Kennedy School of Government, December.

Kenen, Peter. 2000. "Currency Areas, Policy Domains, and the Institutionalization of Fixed Exchange Rates." Princeton University, April.

Levy-Yeyati, Eduardo, and Federico Sturzenegger. 2000. "Exchange Rate Regimes and Economic Performance," paper presented at IMF First Annual Research Conference, November.

Mussa, Michael, Paul Masson, Alexander Swoboda, Esteban Jadresic, Paolo Mauro, and Andrew Berg. 2000. *Exchange Rate Regimes in an Increasingly Integrated World Economy*, IMF Occasional Paper 193.

Obstfeld, Maurice, and Kenneth Rogoff. 1995. "The Mirage of Fixed Exchange Rates." *Journal of Economic Perspectives.* Fall, 9:4, pp. 73–96.

Summers, Lawrence H. 2000. "International Financial Crises: Causes, Prevention, and Cures." *American Economic Review, Papers and Proceedings.* May, 90:2, pp. 1–16.

Velasco, Andres. 2000. "Exchange Rates in Emerging Markets: Floating Toward the Future," Egyptian Center for Economic Studies, Cairo, Working Paper 46, November.

Williamson, John. 2000. *Exchange Rate Regimes for Emerging Markets: Reviving the Intermediate Option.* Washington, D.C.: Institute for International Economics, September.

9 Modern Hyper- and High Inflations

Stanley Fischer, Ratna Sahay,
and Carlos A. Végh

1 Introduction

In his classic work, Phillip Cagan (1956) studied seven of the eight hyperinflations that took place between 1920 and 1946.[1,2] Cagan defined a hyperinflation as beginning in the month inflation first exceeds 50 percent (per month) and as ending in the month before the monthly inflation rate drops below 50 percent for at least a year. Although he did not specify a minimum span of time for an inflationary episode to qualify as a hyperinflation, none of the Cagan seven lasted less than ten months.

Hyperinflations are largely a modern phenomenon. While the data must be highly imperfect, the evidence (table 9.1) indicates that many of the famous pre-twentieth-century inflations were modest by present standards: the inflation associated with the Black Death was less than 50 percent per annum, and the Spanish inflation resulting from the discovery of the New World averaged less than 2 percent and probably never exceeded 15 percent per annum. Inflation in the Roman empire in the fourth century, following Diocletian,[3] may in some years have reached triple-digit levels measured in the prices of *denarius* (a small—and getting smaller—coin) but was very low measured in terms of the gold *solidus* (a larger coin).[4] The more recent inflations summarized in table 9.1, associated with wars and paper money, did on occasion reach triple-digit per-annum levels.

The first recorded inflation that meets Cagan's definition of a hyperinflation appears to be the *assignat* inflation of revolutionary France, during which there were at least five months in 1795–1796 in which inflation exceeded 50 percent (see Forest Capie 1991; and Thomas Sargent and Francois Velde 1995). The link with the French Revolution supports the view that hyperinflations are a modern

Table 9.1
Historical episodes of high inflation

Country/Episode	Dates of episodes	Duration	Cumulative inflation[1]	Geometric annual rate of inflation	Max. annual inflation	Source(s)
Ancient Rome/Diocletian	151–301	150 years	19,900.0	3.6	n.a.	Paarlberg (1993)
China/Sung Dynasty	1191–1240	50 years	2,092.6	6.4	18.0	Lui (1983)
Europe/Black Death[2]	1349–1351	3 years	138.5	33.6	56.3	Paarlberg (1993)
Spain	1502–1600	99 years	315.2	1.4	14.6	Hamilton (1965), Paarlberg (1993)
France/John Law[6]	Feb. 1717–Dec. 1720	47 months	55.2	11.9	1,431.3	Hamilton (1936), Paarlberg (1993)
American Revolution[3,6]	Feb. 1777–Jan. 1780	36 months	2,701.7	203.7	16,098.7	Fisher (1913), Paarlberg (1993)
French Revolution[4,6]	Feb. 1790–Feb. 1796	73 months	26,566.7	150.5	92,067.6	Capie (1991)
U.S. Civil War/North	1862–1864	3 years	116.9	29.4	45.1	Paarlberg (1993),
Confederacy[6]	Feb. 1861–Apr. 1865	51 months	9,019.8	189.2	5,605.7	Lerner (1955)
Mexican Revolution[5,6]	Feb. 1913–Dec. 1916	47 months	10,715.4	230.6	7,716,100.0	Cardenas and Manns (1989), Kemmerer (1940)
China	1938–1947	10 years	2,617,681.0	176.6	612.5	Huang (1948)

1. Inflation expressed in percentage terms.
2. Price of wheat in England.
3. Depreciation of the continental currency (in units per Spanish Dollar), based on prices of beef, Indian corn, wool, and sole leather.
4. Value of assignat.
5. Pesos per U.S. dollar.
6. Maximum annual inflation based on annualized maximum monthly inflation rate.

phenomenon related to the need to print paper money to finance large fiscal deficits caused by wars, revolutions, the end of empires, and the establishment of new states.

Between 1947 and 1984 there were no hyperinflations. Since 1984, there have been at least seven (in six countries) in the market economies—with the Nicaraguan hyperinflation the worst among the seven. By the same Cagan definition, there were also in the past decade hyperinflations in transition economies, particularly the countries of the former Soviet Union. Table 9.2 shows hyperinflations during 1956–1996, as defined by Cagan, but excluding episodes that lasted less than two months.[5] The Serbian case stands out as the worst among recent hyperinflations, with a peak monthly inflation rate that exceeds those in all the Cagan seven except the post-World War 2 Hungarian hyperinflation.[6]

Interwar controversies over hyperinflation centered on the question of whether the process was driven by monetary expansion (for example Constantino Bresciani-Turroni 1937, and Frank Graham 1930) or the balance of payments.[7] The latter view accorded a major role in the inflationary process to the assumed exogenous behavior of the exchange rate. According to Bresciani-Turroni, this view was held throughout the German hyperinflation by the Reichsbank, bankers, industrialists, much of the press, and most German economists. Cagan advanced the analysis within a monetary framework by including the role of expectations, asking whether the process of expectations formation itself might have caused hyperinflation, and concluding—assuming adaptive expectations—that underlying monetary growth was instead responsible.

Since 1956, the formal analysis of hyperinflations has advanced in a number of directions, each of which brought in its train a large literature.[8] First, with the development of the theory of rational expectations, the notion that expectations alone could have caused hyperinflation became more difficult to sustain, except if there were multiple equilibria, some of them hyperinflationary and others not. Such an outcome is possible, for instance, if the inflation tax is subject to the Laffer curve, as is implied by the demand for money function assumed by Cagan (Michael Bruno and Stanley Fischer 1990).[9] The introduction of rational expectations also led to a more sophisticated econometric treatment of the demand for money, and therefore to attempts to estimate money demand functions in hyperinflations under the constraint of rational expectations (for example, Thomas Sargent and Neil Wallace 1973).

Table 9.2
Hyperinflations, 1956–1996 (Cagan definition)[1,2]

| Countries | Dates of episode | During hyperinflation | | Monthly inflation rate | | | | | |
| | | Duration (in months) | Cumulative inflation | During hyperinflation | | | Twelve months after hyperinflation | | |
				Geometric average	Median	Highest	Geometric average	Median	Highest
Angola[3]	Dec. 1994–Jun. 1996	19	62,445.9	40.3	36.0	84.1	9.5	5.3	38.1
Argentina	May 1989–Mar. 1990	11	15,167.0	58.0	61.6	196.6	12.0	11.2	27.0
Bolivia	Apr. 1984–Sep. 1985	18	97,282.4	46.6	51.8	182.8	5.7	2.7	33.0
Brazil	Dec. 1989–Mar. 1990	4	692.7	67.8	70.2	80.8	14.8	14.4	21.5
Nicaragua	Jun. 1986–Mar. 1991	58	11,895,866,143	37.8	31.4	261.2	1.8	0.8	20.3
Congo, Dem. Rep.	Oct. 1991–Sep. 1992	12	7,689.2	43.8	35.2	114.2	15.9	12.6	40.9
Congo, Dem. Rep.	Nov. 1993–Sep. 1994	11	69,502.4	81.3	65.0	250.0	12.9	12.8	26.2
Armenia	Oct. 1993–Dec. 1994	15	34,158.2	47.6	44.5	437.8	2.4	2.0	7.8
Azerbaijan	Dec. 1992–Dec. 1994	25	41,742.1	27.3	23.1	64.4	5.2	3.3	27.8
Georgia	Sep. 1993–Sep. 1994	13	76,218.7	66.6	66.3	211.2	0.4	0.9	13.0

Tajikistan	Apr. 1993–Dec. 1993	9	3,635.7	49.5	36.4	176.9	0.1	3.3	6.6
Tajikistan	Aug. 1995–Dec. 1995	5	839.2	56.5	63.0	78.1	2.9	2.1	19.6
Turkmenistan	Nov. 1995–Jan. 1996	3	291.4	57.6	55.7	62.5	11.2	9.7	25.0
Ukraine	Apr. 1991–Nov. 1994	44	1,864,714.5	25.0	14.9	285.3	10.9	7.7	28.4
Serbia	Feb. 1993–Jan. 1994	12	156,312,790.0	228.2	54.2	175,092.8	1.0	-0.2	12.4

Sources: IMF, *International Financial Statistics*; national authorities, and IMF staff estimates.

1. Cagan defines hyperinflation "as beginning in the month the rise in prices exceeds 50 percent and as ending in the month before the monthly rise in prices drops below that amount and stays below for at least a year. The definition does not rule out a rise in prices at a rate below 50 percent per month for the intervening months, and many of these months have rates below that figure."

2. Excludes the following one- and two-month episodes. In the market economies, Chile (Oct. 1973) and Peru (Sep. 1988, July–Aug. 1990). In the transition economies, Estonia (Jan.–Feb. 1992), Latvia (Jan. 1992), Lithuania (Jan. 1992), Krygyz Republic (Jan. 1992), and Moldova (Jan.–Feb. 1992). In addition, we also excluded Belarus (April 1991, Jan.–Feb. 1992), Kazakstan (April 1991, Jan. 1992), Russia (April 1991, Jan. 1992), and Uzbekistan (April 1991, Jan.–Feb. 1992) even though by Cagan's definition these episodes lasted more than two months, as they appear related to two price jumps (April 1991, and Jan.–Feb. 1992).

3. Period after hyperinflation is from July–Dec. 1996.

Second, consideration of inflation as a tax, formalized for instance in Martin Bailey (1956), implied a change in emphasis from monetary to fiscal factors as the root cause of hyperinflations—with the complication that in the presence of the Keynes-Tanzi effect (whereby, due to lags in tax collection, higher inflation reduces the real value of government tax revenues), an initially money-driven inflation could generate a growing fiscal deficit in an unstable feedback process.[10]

Third, in a famous article, Sargent (1982) studied the process of ending hyperinflations, emphasizing that a credible change in policies, preferably embedded in legal and institutional changes, could bring a hyperinflation to an end at essentially zero cost. Along similar lines, the notion that higher inflation reduces the normal policy lags meant that there could be scope for heterodox policies, involving for instance temporary wage and price controls, that would make it possible to move from a high inflation to a low-inflation equilibrium very rapidly and at low output cost.

Fourth, and closely related to Sargent's approach, the development of the game-theoretic approach to policy made it possible to analyze the concept of *credibility* (Torsten Persson and Guido Tabellini 1990), thus providing analytic content for a concept frequently invoked by central bankers and other policy makers.

In addition to the deepening understanding of hyperinflation, the period since 1956 has also seen the introduction of the important concept of chronic inflation by Felipe Pazos (1972). Pazos emphasized that the inflationary problem in many countries, especially in Latin America, was not so much one of occasional outbursts of hyperinflation followed by stability, but rather that of an ongoing process of double-digit (per annum) inflation, rising occasionally to triple digits.[11] Institutional mechanisms created to protect against the effects of inflation make the problem more deep-seated and difficult to deal with. In particular, Pazos emphasized the difficulties for disinflationary policies caused by overlapping, often indexed, wage contracts. Devastating as hyperinflations are when they occur, the problem of moderate or chronic inflation better describes the form in which inflation confronts most countries that have suffered the effects of inflation in the last half-century.

Increasing evidence on the real effects of inflation-stabilization programs in chronic-inflation countries brought to the forefront the possibility that—contrary to conventional wisdom—disinflation may lead to an initial expansion in economic activity—particularly in GDP and consumption—as argued by Miguel Kiguel and Nissan Liviatan (1992) and Carlos Végh (1992). The recession typically associated with disinflation appears to occur later in the programs. Interestingly, the initial expansion appears to be related to the use of the exchange rate as the main nominal anchor. Several types of models have been developed to explain these puzzling stylized facts, which emphasize the role of inflation inertia, lack of credibility, purchases of durable goods, and supply-side effects (see Guillermo Calvo and Végh, 1999, for a critical review).

Cagan (1956, p. 25) justified treating hyperinflations separately on the grounds that they permit "relations between monetary factors ... to ... be studied ... in what almost amounts to isolation from the real sector of the economy." In this chapter, we follow Cagan's approach of studying inflationary episodes, but rather than confine ourselves to hyperinflations strictly defined—which are quite rare— we examine the still relatively rare episodes of very high inflation, defined as inflations in excess of 100 percent per annum (an exact definition is provided below).

We do this for four main reasons. First, inflations in this range are sufficiently disruptive that in practice virtually no country has been willing to live with them for more than a few years. Second, both popular usage—which often refers to triple digit inflation as hyperinflation—and the literature have tended to treat 100 percent as a distinguishing line between high and extraordinary inflations. Third, in studying episodes of extreme inflation, it is useful to have the extra statistical degrees of freedom offered by the larger sample of countries that have experienced very high inflation, rather than hyperinflations. Fourth, as it turns out, certain simple economic relationships stand out more clearly in high inflations than they do in normal conditions.

We start by characterizing in section 2 the dynamic behavior of inflation in different ranges, first by listing the frequency of inflationary episodes in different ranges, and then by using transition matrices to assess, in particular, whether inflationary dynamics are different at high inflation rates. For the remainder of the chapter we concentrate on episodes of *very high inflation*. In our definition (formally stated in section 2), a "very high-inflation episode" takes place when the twelve-month inflation rates rises above 100 percent. Based on this formal definition, we identify 45 such episodes in 25 countries.

In section 3, we proceed to examine several mechanisms that are basic to the analysis of inflation such as the relationship between money growth and inflation on the one hand and among fiscal deficits, seigniorage, and inflation on the other. We also examine the causal relations among money, inflation, and exchange rates, as well as the concept of inflation inertia. In section 4, we shift gears and focus on (i) the behavior of macroeconomic variables during high-inflation periods compared with low-inflation periods and (ii) the real effects of disinflation. Section 5 concludes by summarizing the results and, in the process, identifying ten key stylized facts associated with very high inflation.

2   Characteristics of High Inflation

2.1   Inflationary Episodes and Dynamics

Table 9.3a presents data for 133 market economies on the frequency of inflationary episodes for specified ranges of the inflation rate in the period 1960–1996 (or, if data were not available, the longest available subsample). An inflationary episode is defined as taking place when the twelve-month inflation rate rises above the lower bound of the specified range. In that case, we take the start of the episode to be the first month of that twelve-month period, and the last month to be the first month before the twelve-month inflation rate falls below the lower bound and stays there for at least twelve months.[12] For example, take the 100-percent threshold, and imagine a country whose twelve-month inflation rate is above 100 percent only in, say, June 1970. Then, under our definition, this country ex-

Table 9.3A
Market economies: Frequency of episodes by level of inflation, 1960–1996[1] (monthly data)

Range of annualized inflation[2]	Number of episodes[3]	Number of countries	Duration (in months)		
			Average	Minimum	Maximum
25 and above	212	92	41.0	12	313
50 and above	87	49	43.4	12	216
100 and above	45	25	40.0	12	208
200 and above	17	13	47.2	15	106
400 and above	13	11	43.9	17	98

perienced a 100-percent inflationary episode from July 1969 to June 1970. Notice that, under this definition, the minimum duration of an episode is twelve months.

Although a variety of adjectives have been used to categorize inflationary episodes, for instance moderate, high, extreme, and hyper- (Rudiger Dornbusch and Fischer 1993), there is as yet no agreed convention.[13] Seen in international perspective, the ranges in the table can be regarded as "moderate to high" (for the 25–50 percent range), and "high" (for the 50–100 percent range), with the remaining categories constituting at the least "very high" inflation rates— although 25 percent per annum would not be regarded as moderate in many countries.

Table 9.3a tells us that most countries, most of the time, experience inflation of less than 25 percent per annum.[14] However, over two-thirds (92) of the countries in the sample experienced an episode of more than 25-percent per-annum inflation. Over half (49) of those countries in turn suffered from an episode in excess of 50 percent per annum, while 25 experienced an inflationary episode of more than 100 percent and eleven countries suffered from at least one episode of more than 400-percent per-annum inflation. The average duration of the inflationary episodes is remarkably similar—and, at three–four years, surprisingly long—while the maximum duration declines as the inflation rate rises. Only one country (Argentina) that experienced an inflationary episode in excess of 400 percent per annum repeated the experience.

Data on inflationary episodes in 28 transition economies are presented in table 9.3b. All of these economies experienced an episode of inflation of more than 25 percent; indeed most of them (19 out of 28) suffered from an inflationary episode in excess of 400 percent per annum. Most of the extreme inflations in these countries were at the start of the transition process when, in light of large monetary overhangs, the price level jumped in response to price liberalization. For this group of countries, over the period since prices were freed,[15] monthly inflation was generally above 25 percent per annum,[16] although inflation in most of them is now into the low double- or even single-digit annual rates.

In table 9.4, we present related (to table 9.3a) information on the statistical properties of inflation in the market economies, in the form of a transition matrix. Categorized by the inflation rate in year T (rows), these matrices show the frequencies with which the inflation

Table 9.3B
Transition economies: Frequency of episodes by level of inflation, 1987–1996[1] (monthly data)

Range of annualized inflation[2]	Number of episodes[3]	Number of countries	Duration (in months) Average	Minimum	Maximum
25 and above	30	28	56.5	16	104
50 and above	25	25	53.0	14	103
100 and above	25	23	45.9	12	100
200 and above	24	22	40.6	13	59
400 and above	20	19	39.7	13	59

Sources: IMF, *International Financial Statistics*, national authorities, and IMF desk economists.
1. The starting period for market economies (133 in total) was determined by data availability, while for transition economies (28 in total) by the period in which prices were freed on a large scale.
2. 25% per annum = 1.9% per month; 50% per annum = 3.4% per month; 100% per annum = 5.9% per month; 200% per annum = 9.6% per month; 400% per annum = 14.4% per month.
3. See text for definition of an inflationary episode.

Table 9.4
Market economies: Transition matrix[1]

Range of inflation	Year T + 1 <25	25– 50	50– 100	100– 200	200– 400	>400	Probability Will rise	Will fall	Number of observations
Year T									
<25	95.4	4.1	0.4	0.1	0.0	0.0	4.6	0.0	3343
25–50	46.5	38.4	13.3	1.4	0.4	0.0	15.1	46.5	279
50–100	10.6	23.0	47.5	14.8	1.6	2.5	18.9	33.6	122
100–200	10.1	11.9	18.6	42.4	15.3	1.7	17.0	40.6	59
200–400	11.7	5.9	5.9	11.8	17.6	47.1	47.1	35.3	17
>400	2.7	0.0	8.1	13.5	8.1	67.6	0.0	32.4	37
Total									3857

Source: IMF, *International Financial Statistics*.
1. Calculated as number of observations in year T + 1 in the corresponding column range as a percentage of numbers of observations in the corresponding row range in year T. (Rows add up to 100.) Based on pooled, cross-section annual data 1960–1996, from 133 countries.

rate in the subsequent year $(T + 1)$ is in different ranges.[17] For instance, if the inflation rate in year T is in the range of 25–50 percent, the probability that it will be less than 25 percent in the following year is 46.5 percent (corresponding to the entry in the second row, first column).

Three features of table 9.4 are noteworthy. First, when the inflation rate is less than 25 percent, it is very likely (95.4 percent probability) to be in that range in the following year. In contrast, for all higher inflation ranges (excluding the last range which has no upper bound), the probability that inflation will stay in its current range is less than 50 percent.[18] Second, consider the columns labeled "Probability will rise" and "Probability will fall." The probability that inflation will rise to a higher range increases from 4.6 percent in the lowest range to 47.1 percent in the next-to-last range.[19] This captures the idea that higher inflation is more explosive. Third, until inflation reaches the 200-percent level, it is still more likely to fall than rise.

Finally, combining table 9.2 with information in table 9.3a, we see that of the eleven market economies that experienced episodes of inflation of more than 400 percent,[20] more than half (six) also had a hyperinflation as defined by Cagan. This certainly suggests that extreme inflations carry with them a high danger of hyperinflation.

2.2 Very High Inflations

In the remainder of this chapter, most of our attention will focus on episodes of very high inflation as defined in section 2. This definition does not require the monthly inflation rate to be within the range every month, nor does it imply that the average inflation rate within an episode necessarily exceeds 100 percent per annum.[21]

Detailed data on the 45 episodes of very high inflation in 25 countries are presented in table 9.A.1 (in the appendix). Twelve of the countries (eighteen episodes) are in South America or the Caribbean (Argentina, Bolivia, Brazil, Chile, Costa Rica, Jamaica, Mexico, Nicaragua, Peru, Suriname, Uruguay, and Venezuela), nine countries (nineteen episodes) are in Africa (Angola, Democratic Republic of the Congo, Ghana, Guinea-Bissau, Sierra Leone, Somalia, Sudan, Uganda, and Zambia) with Afghanistan (two episodes), Israel (one episode), Lebanon (three episodes), and Turkey (two episodes) completing the list. The longest episodes were in Argentina (over seventeen years) and Brazil (over fifteen years); the Democratic Republic of the Congo (formerly Zaire) suffered from six episodes totaling fifteen years. The surprise in these data is the number of very high-inflation episodes in African countries, whose inflationary experience has been studied much less than that of many other countries in the group, particularly a number of Latin American countries and Israel.[22]

Bruno and Easterly (1995) present data suggesting that 40 percent per annum is a critical inflation threshold, above which the probability of inflation rising to 100 percent per annum becomes much larger. Table 9.5, which uses more finely defined inflation ranges than table 9.4, shows that the probability of annual inflation rising increases as the inflation rate rises toward 100 percent. These data confirm the impression that inflation tends to become more unstable as it rises. Even so, there is no inflation range in table 9.5 for which inflation is more likely to rise than fall. Nor does there seem to be a significant discontinuity at 40-percent inflation.

Tables 9.2 through 9.5 present useful characterizations of different aspects of the inflationary process, with an emphasis on high inflations. In summary, most of the time, in most countries, inflation is low, and low inflation is stable. However, since 1960, most countries have suffered from at least one episode of inflation of more than 25

Table 9.5
Market economies: probability of inflation being above 100 percent next year depending on inflation in the current year[1]

Range of inflation	Probability that inflation next year			Number of observations
	Will be above 100 percent	Will rise	Will fall	
Current year				
<20	0.1	6.0	0.0	3171
20–40	1.0	12.6	41.8	388
40–60	7.5	25.2	41.1	107
60–80	15.7	29.4	41.2	51
80–100	37.0	37.0	48.1	27
>100	71.7	0.0	28.3	113
Total				3857

Source: IMF, *International Financial Statistics*.
1. Calculated as number of observations in a given range followed by observations in the 100% and above range, next range, and range below, respectively, as percentage of observations in the initial range (pooled, cross-section annual data 1960–1996, from 133 countries).

percent per annum, and as many as 25 (out of 133) market economies have experienced an episode of very high inflation (i.e., twelve-
month inflation above 100 percent). Further, the data suggest that
inflation is more likely to increase the higher it is or, equivalently,
that higher inflation is relatively more unstable than lower inflation.

3 Inflationary Mechanisms

Having documented the dynamic behavior of inflation, the natural
next step is to try to determine what are the key macroeconomic
variables that underlie inflationary processes.[23] To that effect, this
section first revisits and confirms a basic tenet of monetary economics: in the long run, money growth and inflation are highly correlated.
In this (admittedly narrow) sense, therefore, "inflation is always and
everywhere a monetary phenomenon," as famously argued by Milton
Friedman (1963). While a useful starting point, the high correlation
between money growth and inflation actually raises more questions
than it answers. The first question is causation: does money cause
inflation? Or is there reverse causation from inflation to money/
exchange rate? Our basic finding is that, more often than not, causation (in the Granger sense) runs from exchange-rate changes and
inflation to money growth. We interpret this result, however, as
saying that once inflation has been triggered, monetary policy has
typically been accommodative, thus allowing inflation to be driven
by temporary shocks and by its own dynamics (i.e., inflation persistence). This leads to the next question: what triggers inflation to
begin with? The standard explanation is fiscal imbalances. By and
large, we find that fiscal deficits indeed explain high inflation using
standard regression techniques. Finally, we tackle the issue of inflation persistence by providing two definitions based on autoregressive
processes, which allow us to quantify persistence and examine how
it varies with the level of inflation.

3.1 Data and Methodology

Since several of the econometric exercises in this section rely on a
common data set and regression techniques, we first describe the
sample and the common methodology behind them. We used as
large a sample as possible with regard to both the number of
countries and the time period covered. However, both the quality

and availability of data on several macroeconomic variables varied widely across countries. To maintain consistency across all the panel regressions that were run and to maximize the number of countries included in the sample, we imposed the condition that a country be included in the sample only if there were at least ten annual observations during the 1960–1995 period for each of the five variables—inflation, reserve money, broad money (including foreign currency deposits), fiscal balance, and nominal GDP—that were needed for running the regressions. Consequently, 94 countries were selected (all market economies), each with at least ten annual observations.

For each type of regression reported below, we allowed for different coefficients for high- and low-inflation countries, where the high-inflation countries were the 24 in this sample that experienced at least one episode of very high inflation (as described in the previous section).[24] In the panel regressions, we also allowed for lags of the independent variables to affect the dependent variable of interest. In addition, subsamples that included only the high-inflation countries were tested to see whether the coefficients during their high-inflation episodes differed from their low-inflation episodes. In all panel regressions we allowed for country and period-specific effects.

To set the stage, figure 9.1 shows the averages of inflation, money growth (M2), seigniorage (as percent of GDP), and fiscal balance (as percent of GDP) for high-inflation countries (24 countries) and low-inflation countries (70 countries). As is evident from figure 9.1, high-inflation countries also exhibit high levels of money growth, seigniorage, and fiscal deficit. The remainder of this section will formally examine these relationships.

3.2   Money and Inflation

Figure 9.2 and table 9.6 show the cross-sectional (long-run) relationship between inflation and money growth, with each observation representing the simple average over the sample period of the inflation and the money growth rates, each defined as $ln(1 + x/100)$ where x is the corresponding annual rate. As shown, the relationship between money growth and inflation is extremely strong and close to one-to-one.[25] The regression coefficient is in fact 1.115 and highly significant (table 9.6, column 1). Furthermore, the relationship holds even when the sample is broken up into high- and low-inflation countries (table 9.6, column 2). In the long run, therefore, the

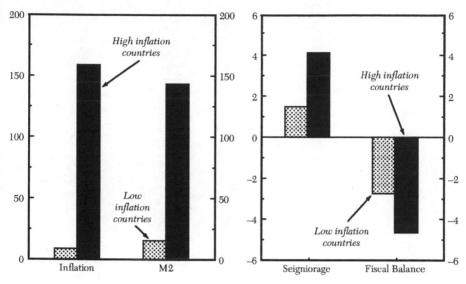

Figure 9.1
Inflation, money growth, seigniorage, and fiscal balance. Note: High-inflation countries as defined in text. Each bar is calculated by taking the average for all countries in that group for each year, and then averaging over all the years; 94 countries in total, each with 10 or more observations.

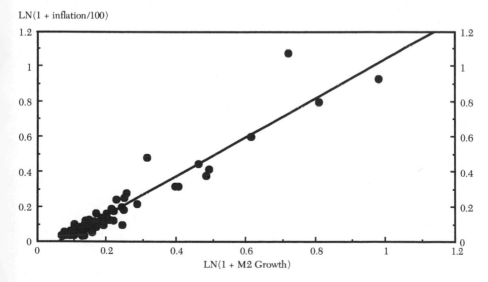

Figure 9.2
Inflation and money (M2) growth, 1960–1995 averages. Note: Slope of regression line is 1.115 with a t-statistic of 12.13; 94 countries in total, each with 10 or more observations.

Table 9.6
Inflation and money growth. Dependent variable: inflation rate[1,2] (T-statistics in parentheses)

Independent variables	Cross-section		Annual panel			Annual panel high inflation countries	
	OLS (1)	OLS (2)	OLS (3)	Fixed[4] (4)	Fixed[4] (5)	OLS[6] (6)	Fixed[4,7] (7)
Intercept	−0.069*** (−4.96)		−0.047*** (−8.19)				
Intercept/hi[3]		−0.041 (−0.87)				0.100** (2.10)	
Intercept/low[3]		−0.028*** (−3.13)				0.059*** (4.26)	
M2[1]	1.115*** (12.13)		0.972*** (30.64)				
M2/hi[1,3]		1.091*** (8.160)		1.011*** (109.70)	0.886*** (74.75)	0.978*** (21.86)	0.881*** (17.30)
M2/low[1,3]		0.804*** (11.92)		0.219*** (7.50)	0.165*** (5.57)	0.513*** (9.97)	0.421*** (6.37)
M2/hi(−1)[1,3,5]					0.242*** (16.33)	0.228** (3.89)	
M2/low(−1)[1,3,5]					0.190*** (6.40)		0.152*** (2.57)
M2/hi(−2)[1,3,5]					−0.078*** (−6.54)		−0.085 (−1.17)
M2/low(−2)[1,3,5]					0.111*** (3.78)		−0.022 (−0.98)

R-squared	0.917	0.925	0.855	0.902	0.922	0.919	0.937
Adj. R-squared	0.916	0.923	0.855	0.897	0.917	0.918	0.933
Observations	94	94	2318	2318	2130	410	380

Sources: IMF, *International Financial Statistics*; authors' estimations.

Note: Significance at the 10-, 5-, and 1-percent level is indicated by one, two, and three stars, respectively.

1. Inflation rate if defined as ln(1 + inflation/100), money growth as ln(1 + M2 growth). Minimum of 10 observations per country.

2. All results corrected for heteroskedasticity if it existed.

3. Hi and low refer to coefficients for high- and low-inflation countries or high- and low-inflation episodes.

4. Fixed refers to a fixed-effects model with both country and time dummies, both of which are significant unless otherwise indicated.

5. The number in parentheses next to the independent variables refers to the number of lags.

6. Fixed effects model of this regression was not significant.

7. Time dummies not significant.

data show a very strong relationship between money growth and inflation.

Does the money-inflation link remain valid in the short run? To answer this question, we ran a panel regression with annual data in which, in addition to allowing for different coefficients on money growth in the low- and high-inflation countries, we also allow for two lags of money growth. We then take a subsample that includes only high-inflation countries and test for different coefficients on high- and low-inflation episodes.

We find that while the relationship between money and inflation remains highly significant (table 9.6, columns 4 and 5) for both groups of countries, the coefficient for low-inflation countries is much lower, a result that is perhaps not surprising given that we are looking at a short-run relationship and the fact that GDP growth is not taken into account in the regressions. When two lags on money growth are included in the panel regression (table 9.6, column 5), the coefficients on both contemporaneous and lagged money growth are significant and different across high- and low-inflation countries. The contrast between high- and low-inflation countries in the speed with which the effects of money growth are transmitted is quite dramatic: the bulk of the inflationary effects of money growth occurs remarkably early in the high-inflation countries; in contrast, in low-inflation countries the effects are distributed evenly across the current and previous periods. In the panel subsample with only high-inflation countries (table 9.6, columns 6 and 7), the previous results of a strong effect of money growth on inflation carry through. We also find a differential effect during high- and low-inflation episodes within high-inflation countries, which is likely to be due to (i) GDP growth being more important relative to the inflation rate during low-inflation years, and (ii) the negative impact of high inflation on the demand for money.[26] In line with our previous findings, adding lags shows that the bulk of the effects takes place contemporaneously (table 9.6, column 6).

In sum, the data show that the inflation-money growth link is exceptionally strong, both in the long and short run. While the relationship may not necessarily be instantaneous nor precisely one-for-one, there can be no doubt that inflation can be ended if the monetary taps are turned off.[27,28] In this sense, therefore, our evidence overwhelmingly confirms what every schoolchild knows: inflation is always and everywhere a monetary phenomenon. This, however, is only the beginning of wisdom.

3.3   Money, Exchange Rates, and Inflation

With the money-inflation link established, there remains the question: What drives money growth? The question is relevant because high inflations are not popular, and it is reasonable to believe that it is rare for governments to take a deliberate policy decision to have a high inflation—even if a set or sequence of policy decisions produces a high inflation.[29] The usual answer to the question of what drives money growth is fiscal deficits: in this view, inflation is a fiscal phenomenon. We shall turn to this view shortly.

An alternative answer to what drives money growth is that rapid money growth, and hence high inflation, is the unintended consequence of inappropriate monetary policies, for instance policies directed at producing real outcomes that are inconsistent with the real equilibrium of the economy, be it for unemployment, the real exchange rate, real wages, or the real interest rate.[30] For instance, as noted in the introduction, there was an active controversy during and after the German hyperinflation over whether inflation was caused by money growth or the balance of payments. The latter view can be made consistent with the evidence that inflation is a monetary phenomenon by thinking of monetary policy as seeking to maintain a constant real exchange rate in circumstances where the nominal exchange rate is being moved by exogenous forces (e.g., speculation, access to external loans, terms of trade shocks, reparation payments, and so forth).

An examination of the short-run dynamics of money, inflation, and the exchange rate should shed light on the issue of whether monetary policy reacts to or leads inflation and the exchange rate. To try to disentangle the dynamic relationships—in particular to see whether money growth leads or lags inflation—we conducted Granger-causality tests by running vector autoregressions (VARs) in a three-variable system containing the inflation rate, nominal exchange rate (percentage change), and money growth. The results are based on data from only eight of the 24 market economies. The data consisted of quarterly series for the longest sample period for which data were available for each country (see table 9.7 for details).[31] An analysis of the remaining seventeen very high-inflation countries was not conducted because of large gaps in the availability of time-series data.

For each country, we first ran an unrestricted VAR. We then ran a series of restricted VARs by excluding each variable, one at a time,

Table 9.7
VAR-Based Granger Causality tests in selected high-inflation countries

Country	Years and quarters	Annualized average inflation	Seasonal dummies[1]	Appropriate lag length (in quarters)[2]	Money growth[3]	Inflation[3]	Exchange rate change[3]
Argentina	1967:1–1991:1	191.8	No	1	—	—	**
Ghana	1966:1–1996:4	32.6	Yes	3	*	**	*
Jamaica	1970:3–1996:4	20.7	Yes	1	—	—	**
Peru	1967:1–1996:4	99.1	Yes	5	**	**	**
Somalia	1967:1–1989:3	26.2	Yes	2	—	**	—
Sudan	1966:1–1994:2	32.6	Yes	3	**	**	**
Turkey	1970:1–1996:4	46.0	Yes	1	**	—	—
Uruguay	1967:1–1996:4	59.3	Yes	2	—	**	**

Sources: *International Finance Statistics*, International Monetary Fund; and authors' calculations.
1. Seasonal dummies were used in the VAR regressions when they were jointly significant at the 5-percent level.
2. Lag length determined by the one that was most significant.
3. ** = significant at 5-percent level.
   * = significant at 10-percent level.
   — = not significant at 5-percent or 10-percent levels.

from the equations for the other two variables (still in the three-variable system) and conducted chi-squared tests to see whether the exclusion of these variables is rejected. Table 9.7 presents the results of the three-way Granger causality tests. Seasonal dummies were used only if they were jointly significant at the 5-percent level in the unrestricted VAR regression. The most appropriate lag length was chosen on the basis of statistical significance.[32]

The last three columns in table 9.7 report whether a chi-squared test rejects the exclusion of the variable of interest from the VAR regressions at the 5-percent level (two stars), the 10-percent level (one star), or does not reject the exclusion (a dash). For example, in the case of Argentina, the results indicate that exchange-rate movements Granger-cause money growth and inflation, while inflation and money growth do not Granger-cause each other or changes in the exchange rate. The overall picture that emerges is that Granger causality appears to run more often from exchange-rate changes or inflation to money growth than vice versa.[33]

These regression results should not be interpreted as implying that, in some circumstances, inflation is not caused by money growth, or that inflation could not be stopped if monetary policy changed and money growth was reduced to a very low level.[34] One explanation for the creation and persistence of very high inflation which we find plausible is that inflation initially emerges as an undesired result of other policy decisions (the obvious candidate being fiscal imbalances), and continues because policymakers often tend to accommodate shocks (the shocks-and-accommodation view mentioned above)—thus allowing inflation to be driven by exogenous shocks and its own dynamics—and/or are reluctant to incur the costs needed to get rid of chronic inflation. There may be several reasons for such reluctance. First, once the public expects high inflation to continue, it may become too costly for the government not to validate the public's expectations (see, for instance, Calvo 1988a). Second, even if the mechanisms were found to credibly commit to low inflation, political battles over the distribution of the required fiscal adjustment may lead to a period of inaction that will erode the political support to proceed further (Alberto Alesina and Allan Drazen 1991). As a result, things often need to get worse (in the form of outbursts of extremely high inflation as in Argentina and Brazil in the late 1980s) before they get better (Drazen and Vittorio Grilli 1993).

3.4 Fiscal Deficits, Inflation, and Seigniorage

As mentioned above, the most commonly held view about the ultimate origins of inflation is that it results from fiscal imbalances. But does the data bear this out? To answer this question, we turn to an empirical analysis of the relationship between fiscal deficits, seigniorage, and inflation. These links derive from the flow fiscal identity:

$$fiscal\ deficit = seigniorage + borrowing \tag{1}$$

with the inflation-deficit link emerging from the link between seigniorage and inflation. In addition, there is an associated intertemporal fiscal constraint which requires that the present discounted value of primary deficits (i.e., deficits net of interest payments) plus the government's initial debt be equal to the present discounted value of seigniorage.[35] As a result of the restrictions imposed by this intertemporal constraint, there may be complicated dynamic relationships among the terms within the fiscal budget identity (1). For instance, for a given present discounted value of primary deficits, less use of seigniorage today will necessarily require the use of more seigniorage tomorrow, as shown by Sargent and Wallace's (1981) monetarist arithmetic.[36]

Fiscal Deficits and Seigniorage. We start by exploring the relationship between seigniorage and fiscal deficits. Even though in the short run, higher fiscal deficits may be financed by borrowing, the intertemporal budget constraint and optimal tax arguments suggest a positive association between seigniorage (as a financing source) and the deficit. Hence, we expect a negative relationship between seigniorage and the fiscal balance (which is the variable used in the econometric analysis).[37]

Figure 9.3 shows the cross-sectional relationship between seigniorage and the fiscal balance, each expressed as a share of GDP, for 94 market economies. Seigniorage was computed as the increase in the nominal stock of high-powered money in a given year, divided by nominal GDP in that year. A negative relationship is visible (figure 9.3 and table 9.8, column 1): a ten-percentage-point reduction in the fiscal balance leads on average to a 1.5-percent increase in seigniorage revenues (both as a share of GDP), with the highest levels of seigniorage (more than six percent of GDP) recorded for Israel, Chile, Argentina, Malta, and Nicaragua.

Seigniorage
(Change in high powered money in percent of GDP)

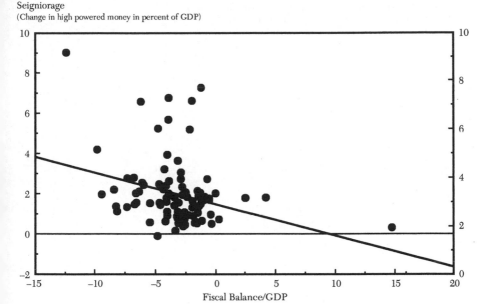

Figure 9.3
Seigniorage and fiscal balance, 1960–1995 averages. Note: Slope of regression line is
−0.152 with a t-statistic of −2.30; 94 countries in total, each with 10 or more observations.

When panel regressions with annual data are run, the coefficient
on the fiscal balance becomes even more significant but remains
unchanged quantitatively as compared to the results obtained in the
cross-section regressions (compare columns 1 and 2, table 9.8). When
different coefficients are allowed for the high- and low-inflation
countries (table 9.8, column 3), the coefficient for high-inflation countries rises sharply while that for the low-inflation countries falls and
becomes insignificant. The difference between the coefficients of the
high- and low-inflation countries is statistically significant. A ten-
percentage-point reduction in the fiscal balance in the high-inflation
countries leads, on average, to a 4.2-percentage-point increase in
seigniorage (both as a share of GDP). Allowing for separate coefficients (and constant terms) raises the adjusted R-squared from 0.048
to 0.334 (table 9.8, column 3).

When panel regressions for the subsample of high-inflation economies are run, the simple OLS yields, as expected, a much higher
coefficient than that obtained for all market economies (compare column 4 to column 2, table 9.8). The largest effects of the fiscal balance

Table 9.8
Seigniorage and fiscal balance. Dependent variable: seigniorage[1,2] (T-statistics in parentheses)

Independent variables	Cross-section OLS (1)	Annual panel		Annual panel high inflation countries	
		OLS (2)	Fixed[4] (3)	OLS (4)	Fixed[4] (5)
Intercept	1.455***	1.626***		2.77***	
	(6.48)	(17.27)		(8.13)	
Fiscal[1]	−0.152**	−0.152***		−0.376***	
	(−2.30)	(−5.33)		(−4.72)	
Fiscal/hi[1,3]			−0.420***		−0.627***
			(−14.52)		(−5.84)
Fiscal/low[1,3]			0.007		−0.041
			(0.36)		(−0.52)
R-squared	0.085	0.048	0.371	0.137	0.416
Adj. R-squared	0.075	0.048	0.334	0.135	0.392
Observations	94	2318	2318	410	410

Sources: IMF, *International Financial Statistics*; authors' estimations.
Note: Significance at the 10-, 5-, and 1-percent level is indicated by one, two, and three stars, respectively.
1. Seigniorage is defined as $[RM - RM(-1)]/GDP$, where RM is reserve money in current period, $RM(-1)$ is reserve money in last period and GDP is output in current period, and fiscal is defined as the fiscal balance in percent of GDP.
2. All results corrected for heteroskedasticity if it existed.
3. Hi and low refer to coefficients for high- and low-inflation countries or high- and low-inflation episodes.
4. Fixed refers to a fixed-effects model with both country and time dummies, both of which are significant.

on seigniorage revenues are obtained during the high-inflation periods: a ten-percentage-point reduction in the fiscal balance leads to a 6.27-percentage-point increase in seigniorage revenues, both as a share of GDP (table 9.8, column 5). On the other hand, the effect of the fiscal balance on seigniorage revenues during the low-inflation years is small and statistically insignificant.

The data thus show that the relationship between the fiscal deficit and seigniorage is strong only in the high-inflation countries. Moreover, even in these countries, the fiscal deficit-seigniorage relationship is strengthened during periods of high inflation compared to low-inflation years.

Inflation and Seigniorage. Even though in the high-inflation countries seigniorage rises as a share of GDP as the deficit increases, the

Seigniorage
(Change in high powered money in percent of GDP)

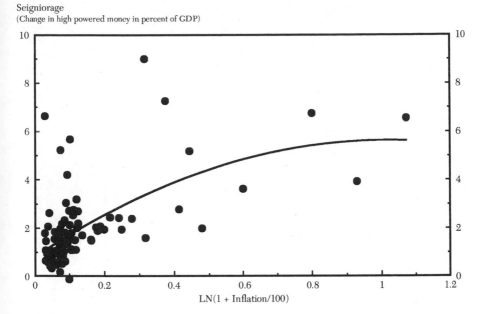

Figure 9.4
Seigniorage and inflation, 1960–1995 averages. Note: Regression line is 0.806 + 9.563*LN(1 + inflation/100) − 4.691*(LN(1 + inflation/100)^2; t-statistics on the coefficients are 2.65 and −1.31 respectively; 94 countries in total, each with 10 or more observations.

relationship between inflation and seigniorage is likely to be more complicated because seigniorage revenues may eventually decline as inflation rises; that is, there may be a Laffer curve effect as inflation continues to rise. The reason for the fall in seigniorage revenue at high rates of inflation is that the tax base—real money balances—may fall more, in proportional terms, than the growth rate of the money base, thus leading to a fall in seigniorage.[38]

Working with the same samples as those used for seigniorage and fiscal deficits, we estimate a nonlinear relationship between seigniorage and inflation of the following form:

$$Seigniorage = \alpha + \beta \; inflation + \gamma \; (inflation)^2,$$

where we expect β to be positive and γ to be negative, that is, seigniorage revenues rise as inflation rises, reaching a maximum and then declining with further increases in the inflation rate. The cross-sectional plot is presented in figure 9.4 (table 9.9, column 2), which

Table 9.9
Inflation and seigniorage. Dependent variable: seigniorage[1,2] (T-statistics in parentheses)

Independent variables	Cross-section		Annual panel		Annual panel high inflation countries	
	OLS (1)	OLS (2)	Fixed[4] (3)	Fixed[4] (4)	Fixed[4] (5)	Fixed[4,5] (6)
Intercept	1.157***	0.806**				
	(7.15)	(2.51)				
Inflation[1]	5.44***	9.563***				
	(5.81)	(2.65)				
Inflation/hi[1,3]			4.246***	9.775***	3.950***	9.938***
			(17.55)	(15.52)	(8.00)	(5.19)
Inflation/low[1,3]			3.342***	2.013	4.474**	10.85*
			(2.83)	(0.74)	(2.13)	(1.89)
Infsq[1]		−4.691				
		(−1.31)				
Infsq/hi[1,3]				−1.586***		−1.628***
				(−9.47)		(−2.94)
Infsq/low[1,3]				5.006		−1.655
				(0.73)		(−0.17)
R-squared	0.339	0.361	0.397	0.421	0.425	0.398
Adj. R-squared	0.332	0.347	0.361	0.386	0.343	0.370
Observations	94	94	2318	2318	410	410

Sources: *International Financial Statistics*; authors' estimations.
Note: Significance at the 10-, 5-, and 1-percent level is indicated by one, two, and three stars, respectively.
1. Seigniorage is defined as [RM − RM(−1)]/GDP, where RM is reserve money in current period, RM(−1) is reserve money in last period and GDP is output in current period, inflation is defined as ln(1 + inflation/100) and infsq is the square of the ln(1 + inflation/100).
2. All results corrected for heteroskedasticity if it existed.
3. Hi and low refer to coefficients for high- and low-inflation countries or high- and low-inflation episisodes.
4. Fixed refers to a fixed-effects model with both country and time dummies. Results indicate the significance of both unless otherwise specified.
5. Period effects not significant.

LN(1 + Inflation/100)

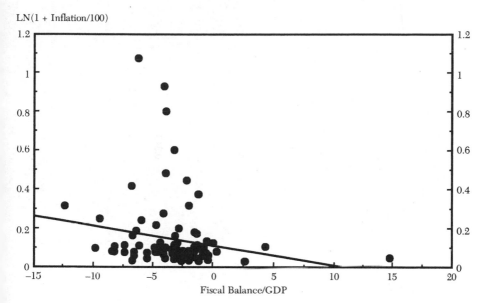

Figure 9.5
Fiscal balance and inflation, 1960–1995 averages. Note: Slope of regression line is −0.010 with a t-statistic of −2.45; 94 countries in total, each with 10 or more observations.

shows the estimated nonlinear relationship.[39] Seigniorage revenues are maximized when inflation reaches 174 percent.

The main message to emerge from table 9.9 in that a Laffer curve is visible and significant in high-inflation countries (table 9.9, column 4) and in high-inflation episodes for the sub-sample with the high-inflation countries only (table 9.9, column 6). These findings are consistent with the notion that a Laffer curve is more likely to emerge the higher is the level of inflation.

In terms of the linear regressions, table 9.9 indicates that, as expected, the coefficient on the inflation rate is significant for both high- and low-inflation countries (table 9.9, column 3) and for both high- and low-inflation episodes for the subsample of high-inflation countries (table 9.9, column 5).

Fiscal Deficits and Inflation.   Figure 9.5 shows the deficit-inflation link for the whole sample. As shown in table 9.10, column 1, the relationship is significant in the cross-section regression. This relationship, however, becomes insignificant when different constant

Table 9.10
Inflation and fiscal balance. Dependent variable: inflation rate[1,2] (T-statistics in parentheses)

Independent variables	Cross-section		Annual panel		Annual panel high inflation countries	
	OLS (1)	OLS (2)	Fixed[4] (3)	Fixed[4] (4)	Fixed[4] (5)	Fixed[4] (6)
Intercept	0.113*** (7.26)					
Intercept/hi[3]		0.447*** (4.16)				
Intercept/low[3]		0.083*** (13.16)				
Fiscal[1]	−0.010** (−2.45)					
Fiscal/hi[1,3]		−0.00001 (−0.001)	−0.042*** (−17.49)	−0.016*** (−5.63)	−0.063*** (−11.23)	−0.024*** (−3.38)
Fiscal/low[1,3]		−0.001 (−1.43)	0.000 (−0.19)	−0.001 (−0.54)	−0.005 (−0.77)	−0.012 (−1.32)
Fiscal/hi (−1)[1,3,5]				−0.028*** (−8.51)		−0.014 (−1.27)
Fiscal/low (−1)[1,3,5]				−0.001 (−0.54)		−0.012 (−1.34)
Fiscal/hi (−2)[1,3,5]				−0.032*** (−11.08)		−0.057*** (−5.52)
Fiscal/low (−2)[1,3,5]				0.002 (0.76)		−0.007 (−1.07)

R-squared	0.032	0.556	0.442	0.542	0.543	0.644
Adj. R-squared	0.021	0.541	0.408	0.512	0.478	0.586
Observations	94	94	2318	2130	410	380

Sources: IMF, *International Financial Statistics*; authors' estimations.

Note: Significance at the 10-, 5-, and 1-percent level is indicated by one, two, and three stars, respectively.

1. Inflation rate is defined at $\ln(1 + \text{inflation}/100)$ and fiscal is defined as the fiscal balance in percent of GDP.

2. All results corrected for heteroskedasticity if it existed.

3. Hi and low refer to coefficients for high- and low-inflation countries or high- and low-inflation episodes.

4. Fixed refers to a fixed-effects model with both country and time dummies. These results indicate the significance of both unless otherwise specified.

5. The number in parentheses next to the independent variables refers to the number of lags.

terms and coefficients are allowed for in the high- and low-inflation market economies (table 9.10, column 2).

When annual panels are considered, the relationship between the fiscal balance and inflation becomes significant for the high-inflation countries but does not for the low-inflation countries (table 9.10, column 3). A reduction in the fiscal balance by 1 percent of GDP in the high-inflation countries leads to an increase in the inflation rate by 4.2 percent. The introduction of lags (table 9.10, column 4) improves the fit substantially, with all the lags being significant for high-inflation countries but not low-inflation countries.

The basic results from the annual panels carry through in the subsample of high-inflation countries in the sense that the relationship between inflation and the fiscal balance is significant for high-inflation episodes but not for low-inflation episodes (table 9.10, column 5). In high-inflation periods, a 1-percentage-point reduction in the fiscal balance leads to a 6.3-percent increase in the inflation rate. It is also the case that the introduction of lags improves the fit substantially with the second lag for high-inflation episodes being statistically significant (table 9.10, column 6).[40]

In sum, no obvious long- or short-run relationship between inflation and fiscal balance is found for the low-inflation countries or during the low-inflation episodes in the high-inflation countries. The relationship, however, is quite strong in the high-inflation countries during the high-inflation episodes.[41] Lags in the fiscal balance are important in explaining inflation in the high-inflation countries and episodes.

3.5 Inflationary Persistence

As argued above (and consistent with our findings so far), we believe that inflation is typically caused by fiscal imbalances and is perpetuated by monetary accommodation to real shocks and by its own dynamics. We now explore the issue of inflation's own dynamics, which we will refer to as inflation persistence. Our aim is twofold: first, to come up with a quantitative measure of persistence and, second, to test if inflation persistence falls as the level of inflation rises. The latter point is relevant because, according to conventional wisdom, the inflationary inertia that is present at low inflation rates is responsible for the Phillips curve-related output costs of reducing inflation. Sargent (1982), however, argued that several hyper-inflations have been eliminated at no cost by a credible change in policy. A common interpretation of Sargent's views is that the shortening of contracts that takes place in high-inflation episodes reduces inflationary inertia, thereby making it less costly to stabilize from high than from moderate inflation.

In an attempt to examine this argument empirically, let the inflationary process take the following autoregressive (AR) form:[42]

$$\pi_t = \sum_{i=1}^{n} \alpha_i \pi_{t-i} + u_t \tag{2}$$

where π_t is the inflation rate at time t, i is the lag length, n is the maximum lag length, and u_t is an error term which is i.i.d. We then define two indices of inflation inertia, the mean lag and the median lag. The mean lag is defined as follows:

$$Mean\ lag = \frac{\sum_{i=1}^{n} i|\alpha_i|}{\sum_{i=1}^{n} |\alpha_i|} \tag{3}$$

This index is an average of the n lags, weighted by the coefficient, α_i, associated with each lag, i. If n equals zero, the mean lag is simply defined to be zero. Otherwise, the index has a lower bound of unity, which occurs for the case in which $n = 1$.

The median lag, m, is chosen such that it divides the sum of the coefficients, $\sum_{i=1}^{n} \alpha_i$, (the total frequency) equally before and after this lag. That is, we chose the smallest integer m such that:

$$\frac{\sum_{i=1}^{m-1} |\alpha_i|}{\sum_{i=1}^{n} |\alpha_i|} \leq 0.5 \leq \frac{\sum_{i=1}^{m} |\alpha_i|}{\sum_{i=1}^{n} |\alpha_i|} \tag{4}$$

If m equals zero, the median lag is also defined to be zero.

The hypothesis that the mean and the median lag lengths are higher in low-inflation episodes than in high-inflation episodes is now examined in the high-inflation countries that were identified in section 2.2 using quarterly data. Unfortunately, the duration of several very high-inflation episodes was far too short to lend itself to econometric estimation. To increase the number of countries in our sample, however, we combined some of the episodes identified in table 9.A.1 (as in Democratic Republic of Congo, Ghana, Mexico, Sierra Leone, Uganda, and Uruguay) when subsequent episodes were adequately close (less than ten quarters). The sample of countries was thus reduced to sixteen, with the revised high- and low-inflation episodes reported in table 9.11.[43]

Table 9.11
Inflation inertia in high-inflation countries

Country	Episodes	Average annual inflation	α_1	α_2	α_3	α_4	α_5	α_6	α_7	α_8	Appropriate lag length[1]	Mean lag	Median lag	R-squared
Argentina	1959:2–1974:2	28.0	0.46	0.06	−0.07	0.34	0.05	−0.37			6	3.4	4.0	0.369
	1974:3–1991:3	310.6	0.47								1	1.0	1.0	0.220
	1991:4–1997:1	6.2	0.30	0.12	0.11	−0.22	0.10	−0.02	−0.03	0.06	8	3.2	3.0	0.916
Bolivia	1959:2–1981:2	12.5	0.49	0.14	−0.29	0.24	0.27	−0.26			6	3.3	3.0	0.412
	1981:3–1986:3	789.3	0.58								1	1.0	1.0	0.337
	1986:4–1997:1	12.3	0.28	−0.13	−0.30	0.27	0.04	−0.08			6	2.9	3.0	0.346
Brazil[2]	1959:2–1980:2	38.0	0.85	−0.19	0.13	0.39	−0.28				5	2.5	2.0	0.753
	1980:3–1997:2	357.6	0.81								1	1.0	1.0	0.652
Chile	1959:2–1971:3	24.7	0.34	0.05	0.04	0.29	0.11	−0.33			6	3.7	4.0	0.324
	1971:4–1977:2	229.9	0.56								1	1.0	1.0	0.333
	1977:3–1997:2	19.4	0.50								1	1.0	1.0	0.610
Congo, Dem. Republic of	1968:2–1977:4	26.1	0.07	0.04	0.00	0.19	−0.12	−0.31	0.47		7	5.6	6.0	0.783
	1978:1–1997:3	281.8	0.94	−0.66	0.80	−0.67	0.56	−0.47	0.36		7	3.5	3.0	0.656
Ghana	1963:3–1976:1	13.3	0.14	−0.10	0.29	0.16	0.13	−0.49			6	4.2	4.0	0.524
	1976:2–1984:1	72.2									0	0.0	0.0	0.00
	1984:2–1997:1	27.7	0.76	−0.54	0.33	0.18	−0.33				5	2.4	2.0	0.664
Israel	1959:2–1978:3	14.3	0.51	−0.16	0.26	0.18	−0.08	0.31			6	3.1	3.0	0.738
	1978:4–1986:3	139.9	0.22	0.34	0.04	0.10	−0.90	0.05	0.05	−0.90	8	5.3	5.0	0.773
	1986:4–1997:2	14.1									0	0.0	0.0	0.00
Mexico	1959:1–1981:4	10.1	0.30								1	1.0	1.0	0.647
	1982:1–1988:3	90.6	0.69								1	1.0	1.0	0.555
	1988:4–1997:4	20.6	0.53								1	1.0	1.0	0.278

Nicaragua	1959:2–1984:1	15.3	0.75	0.11	−0.01	−0.07	−0.03	0.06	0.00	0.36	8	3.4	1.0	0.847
	1984:2–1992:1	54.3	0.89								1	1.0	1.0	0.771
	1992:2–1997:2	19.2	0.58								1	1.0	1.0	0.335
Peru	1959:2–1982:2	22.2	0.34	0.13	−1.08	0.30	−0.56	0.31			6	3.6	3.0	0.739
	1982:3–1992:1	413.0	0.54	0.14	−0.11	−0.50	0.08	−0.05	−0.05		7	2.4	1.0	0.458
	1992:1–1997:4	19.4	0.88	−0.36	0.30						3	1.6	1.0	0.925
Sierra Leone	1961:1–1986:3	17.9	0.13	−0.01	0.09	0.43	0.34				5	3.8	4.0	0.478
	1986:4–1991:4	90.0									0	0.0	0.0	0.000
	1992:1–1997:1	23.0									0	0.0	0.0	0.000
Sudan	1959:2–1989:4	16.7	0.04	−0.18	0.04	−0.02	−0.06	0.05	−0.21		7	4.5	5.0	0.582
	1990:1–1997:1	102.7									0	0.0	0.0	0.000
Suriname	1959:2–1991:4	9.3	0.05	0.22							2	1.8	2.0	0.129
	1992:1–1995:4	177.4	0.66	0.76	0.14	1.03	−0.54	−1.98			6	4.2	4.0	0.892
	1996:1–1998:2	8.0									0	0.0	0.0	0.000
Uganda[3]	1981:2–1988:4	99.0									0	0.0	0.0	0.000
	1989:1–1997:4	19.5	0.53	−0.16	−0.11	−0.16	0.11	0.20	−0.30		7	3.6	3.0	0.720
Uruguay[3]	1959:2–1974:4	49.2	0.39	0.37							2	1.5	1.0	0.436
	1975:1–1997:2	56.0	0.50	0.22							2	1.3	1.0	0.457
Zambia	1988:3–1994:1	127.8									0	0.0	0.0	0.000
	1994:2–1997:4	31.4									0	0.0	0.0	0.000

Source: IFS; authors' calculations.

1. Model reduction by F-tests (successively dropping lags and stopping when dropping the last is significant compared to the next to last).

2. Last period ignored because sample size is too small.

3. Some high- and low-inflation periods have been combined to allow sufficient sample period.

The empirical procedure employed in computing the lag lengths was as follows. Since unit roots were present in several episodes, the regressions were run in first differences, following Hamilton (1994, p. 528). Specifically, equation (2) can be rewritten as:

$$\pi_t = \rho\pi_{t-1} + \sum_{i=1}^{n-1} \beta_i \Delta\pi_{t-1} + u_t, \tag{5}$$

where the coefficients in (5) are related to those in equation (2) as follows:

$$\alpha_1 = \rho + \beta_1,$$

$$\alpha_2 = \beta_2 - \beta_1,$$

$$\alpha_n = -\beta_{n-1}.$$

Following the determination of the appropriate model,[44] the βs in equation (5) were estimated and the αs in equation (2) were calculated. Finally, using equations (3) and (4), the mean and the median lag lengths were calculated for each episode in each country. These results are reported in table 9.11. By and large, inflation persistence seems to be important. With some exceptions, the hypothesis that inertia is lower during high-inflation episodes than during low-inflation episodes is confirmed by the results for the mean lag length. The four exceptions are Israel, Mexico, Suriname, and Zambia. In Israel and Suriname, the indices of inertia appear to have increased during the high-inflation episodes, while in Mexico and Zambia, there was virtually no evidence of inertia in either the high- or the low-inflation episodes. In three other countries—Chile, Nicaragua, and Sierra Leone—the degree of inertia in the economy appears not to have increased during their last post-stabilization period. By and large, similar conclusions can be drawn from the median lag length.

To formally test for the relationship between inflation inertia and the level of inflation, we pooled the sample of 42 episodes for the sixteen countries and ran an OLS regression. Since institutional arrangements regarding indexation often differ markedly across countries, country dummies were introduced in the regression. The results were:

$$mean\ lag = -0.54 \log(\pi) \quad \text{Adj. } R^2 = 0.63,$$
$$(-2.21)$$

median lag $= -0.58 \log(\pi)$ Adj. $R^2 = 0.60$,
         (-2.43)

where the t-statistic is reported below the regression coefficient. All country dummies, with the exception of Zambia's, were significant at the 5-percent level. The regression results support the view that inflation inertia falls as the level of inflation rises.

What do we make of these results? Several remarks are in order. First, while the measures of inflation persistence defined above have the virtue of simplicity, it is not entirely clear that measures based on univariate autoregressive processes will indeed be capturing "inertia." To the extent that some underlying policy variable (i.e., the money supply in Cagan's model) is highly persistent, inflation will be equally "persistent" (in an autoregressive sense) even in a model that completely abstracts from expectational and/or nominal frictions. Hence, as argued by Leonardo Leiderman (1993), testing for inflation inertia would require estimating a structural model that embodies it in a falsifiable manner. In spite of this obvious shortcoming, we still believe that AR-based measures of persistence are useful, since, in addition to the persistence of fundamentals, they will also capture indexation and institutional practices that tend to give inflation a life of its own.

Second, our result that, on average, higher inflation exhibits less persistence is consistent with our priors. The main reason is that, as inflation increases, the length of contracts becomes shorter and/or more contracts and prices are denominated in foreign currency. In the extreme case (a full-blown hyperinflation à la Cagan), all prices are expressed in foreign currency which, by construction, should completely eliminate inflation inertia. In fact, it is the disappearance of inflation inertia in full-blown hyper-inflations that makes begging the exchange rate so effective in stopping inflation in its tracks.

Finally, to put the issue of inflation persistence into perspective, it is useful to relate our findings to an ongoing debate on U.S. inflation persistence. The conventional wisdom within the Federal Reserve is that inflation persistence increased with the rise in inflation in the 1970s and has been falling ever since (see John Taylor 1998). This belief receives support from a sophisticated multivariate procedure carried out in Timothy Cogley and Sargent (2001). In this view, therefore, the relation between the level and persistence of U.S. inflation would be positive. In his discussion of Cogley and

Sargent, however, Stock (2001) argues—based on an univariate AR representation—that inflation persistence in the United States has not changed over the past forty years.[45,46] Stock attributes the Cogley and Sargent finding to the fact that, in his view, their specification tends to confuse volatility with persistence. Whatever the merits of the argument, the fact that AR-based measures of persistence are not unduly influenced by inflation volatility is a particularly important feature when it comes to analyzing this phenomenon in developing countries. All in all, our reading of this debate is that there is much to be learned from simple AR representations, as more sophisticated techniques do not seem to necessarily translate into a cleaner measure of inflation persistence.

4   Real Effects of Inflation and Stabilization

This section focuses on the very high-inflation countries identified above and examines the behavior of key macroeconomic variables during high inflation and disinflation. Two main exercises are carried out. The first one compares the average behavior of the main macroeconomic variables during periods of very high inflation—as defined in previous sections—with periods of low inflation. This exercise is thus related to the effects of high inflation on macroeconomic performance. The second exercise deals with the real effects of disinflation from high inflation by looking at the behavior of the main macroeconomic variables just before and after a disinflation process is under way. The main issue related to this exercise is whether stabilization from high inflation may be expansionary and whether the nominal anchor matters; that is, whether exchange rate-based stabilizations are more likely to be expansionary than money-based stabilizations.

4.1   Very High- versus Low-Inflation Periods

Figure 9.6 summarizes the differences in behavior of the main macroeconomic variables during episodes of very high inflation using annual data for eighteen of the 25 market economies identified in the previous sections.[47,48] Specifically, figure 9.6 presents the averages for the different variables for very high-inflation years and low-inflation years. Average inflation was 739 percent during years of very high inflation and 22.4 percent during low-inflation years. (For

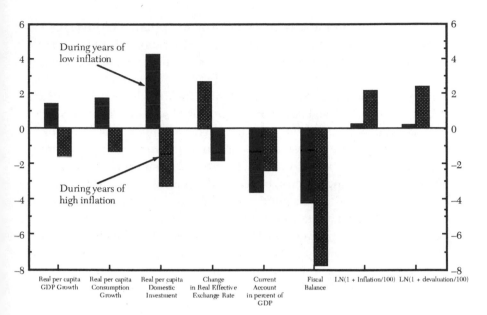

Figure 9.6
Macroeconomic performance in high-inflation countries.

scaling purposes, figure 9.6 shows the figure for $log(1 + x/100)$, where x is either the inflation rate or the devaluation rate in percentage terms.) The average rate of devaluation/depreciation is 984 percent during high-inflation periods and 16.7 during periods of low inflation.

There are few surprises. Real GDP per capita fell on average by 1.6 percent per annum during the very high-inflation episodes, and rose by 1.4 percent during years of low inflation. The same pattern holds for private consumption per capita, which fell on average by 1.3 percent during very high-inflation episodes, and rose by 1.7 percent during low-inflation years. Investment growth per capita fell by 3.3 percent during high-inflation years, while it increased by 4.2 percent during low-inflation periods. The domestic currency appreciated, in real terms, at a rate of 2.7 percent during high-inflation years and depreciated at a rate of 1.8 percent during low-inflation years. The current account deficit, as a proportion of GDP, is higher in low-inflation years (3.6 percent) than in high-inflation years (2.4 percent). The average fiscal deficit is higher during high-inflation years (7.8 percent of GDP) than during low-inflation years (4.2 percent). In sum, on average, periods of high inflation are characterized by a contraction in the levels of GDP, consumption, and investment per capita, an appreciating currency (in real terms), and higher fiscal deficits. High inflation is thus associated with bad macroeconomic performance.[49]

In particular, figure 9.6 is consistent with the view that inflation is bad for growth (see Fischer 1996 for a brief survey). The literature on this topic is unanimous in finding that very high inflation is bad for growth.[50] There is, however, controversy over the nature of the relationship at low inflation rates. Bruno and Easterly (1995) point to 40 percent as a danger point, beyond which increases in inflation are very likely to lead to a growth crisis. In the case of the transition economies, Fischer, Sahay, and Végh (1996) find that this cutoff point occurs at about 50 percent. Michael Sarel (1996) searches for a break-point in the relationship between inflation and growth, and locates it at an annual rate of 8 percent. A more recent paper (Mohsin Khan and Abdelhak Senhadji 2000) analyzes this relationship separately for industrial countries and developing countries and finds that "the threshold level of inflation above which inflation significantly slows growth is estimated at 1–3 percent for industrial countries and 7–11 percent for developing countries." Above that rate, inflation and growth are negatively related; below it, the relationship is not statistically significant. In summary, the literature finds that high inflation is bad for growth; the relationship is weaker or nonexistent at low rates of inflation; but there is no evidence that inflation is good for growth.[51]

Figure 9.6 also suggests that high inflation is bad for consumption and for investment, with changes in consumption growth of roughly the same order of magnitude as those in GDP growth and changes in investment of about twice that magnitude. If one accepts the notion that inflation is bad for growth, the behavior of investment is hardly surprising. Based on the business-cycle literature, the higher volatility of investment growth is also to be expected.

What are the specific mechanisms that could be at work in explaining the stylized fact that inflation is bad for growth? Any model in which the inflation rate adversely affects the allocation of resources is bound to generate a negative correlation between inflation and growth. Consider, for instance, a model in the spirit of Alan Stockman (1981) in which the inflation rate acts as a tax on investment (through a cash-in-advance on the purchase of capital goods). In this context, periods of high inflation will lead to lower investment and, hence, a lower capital stock. This reduces the demand for labor and leads to lower employment, output, and real wages. On the demand side—and assuming a cash-in-advance for the purchase of consumption goods—higher nominal interest rates will lower consumption by making consumption more expensive during high-inflation periods. These results are general to the extent that any model in which the inflation rate distorts both investment and consumption will generate a negative correlation between inflation on the one hand, and investment, output, and consumption on the other.[52]

Finally, while the behavior of the current account captured in figure 9.6 is consistent with the theoretical predictions, the behavior of the real exchange rate appears to be at odds. Specifically, in an open-economy version of the simple model just described, the lower demand for non-tradables that would result from higher inflation should lead to a fall in the relative price of non-tradables (i.e., a real depreciation of the currency) since the supply response is relatively inelastic in the short run. On the other hand, the lower demand for tradable goods would translate into a lower current-account deficit. We thus conjecture that the behavior of the real exchange rate, which in our sample appreciates during high-inflation years, might be explained by numerous episodes in which nominal exchange rates have been kept more or less fixed in spite of ongoing inflation.[53,54]

4.2 Real Variables in Disinflation

Conventional wisdom—based on the experience of industrial countries—holds that disinflation is costly in terms of output for-gone. In fact, the notion that disinflation is contractionary is so entrenched in the literature that the question has typically been not *if* but by *how much* output would fall in response to an inflation sta-bilization program. To answer this question, a large literature has computed the so-called "sacrifice ratio" associated with disinflation, defined as the cumulative percent output loss per percentage reduc-tion in inflation (see, for instance, Arthur Okun 1978; Robert Gordon 1982; and Fischer 1986). Laurence Ball (1994) examined 28 disin-flation episodes in nine OECD countries using quarterly data and found that, with one exception, disinflation is always contractionary, with the sacrifice ratio ranging from 2.9 for Germany to 0.8 in France and the United Kingdom. While Ball's (1994) estimates are somewhat lower than those in the earlier literature, they continue to support the notion that disinflation in industrial countries is costly in terms of output. This stylized fact is, of course, consistent with closed-economy, staggered-contracts models à la Fischer (1977) and Taylor (1979, 1980) and other models that generate a short-run Phillips-curve (Robert Lucas 1972).

The Phillips-curve-based conventional wisdom has not gone unchallenged. In an influential paper, Sargent (1982) examined the behavior of output in four classical hyperinflations and argued that stabilization was achieved at small or no output cost.[55] More recently, and for the case of much more mundane inflationary processes, Kiguel and Liviatan (1992) and Végh (1992) have argued that stabilization programs in chronic-inflation countries based on the nominal exchange rate (exchange rate-based stabilization) have actually led to an initial expansion in output and consumption, with the conventional contraction occurring only later in the programs.[56] Fischer, Sahay, and Végh (1996, 1997) also find evidence for the transition economies in favor of expansionary stabilizations, with the expansions being more pronounced for the case of exchange rate-based stabilizations. Easterly (1996), however, has argued that expansionary stabilization is a more general feature of stabilization from high-inflation countries, and occurs irrespective of whether the nominal anchor is the exchange rate or not.[57] We now proceed to revisit these important issues.

4.2.1 Stabilization Time Profiles

We first compute the time profiles for the main macroeconomic variables in "stabilization time."[58] Stabilization time is denoted by $T + j$, where T is the year in which an episode of very high inflation ends, and j $(=-3, \ldots, 3)$ is the number of years preceding or following the year of stabilization.[59] The average paths of variables are then calculated relative to year T.[60]

Consider first figure 9.7. Inflation falls sharply in the year before stabilization and continues to fall in the year of stabilization, but then stabilizes at around 25 percent. Real GDP per-capita growth is basically zero in the year before stabilization and turns positive (at around 1 percent) in the year of stabilization, peaking at more than 3 percent in year $T + 2$. A similar profile holds for per-capita consumption growth: it is essentially zero in the year before stabiliza-

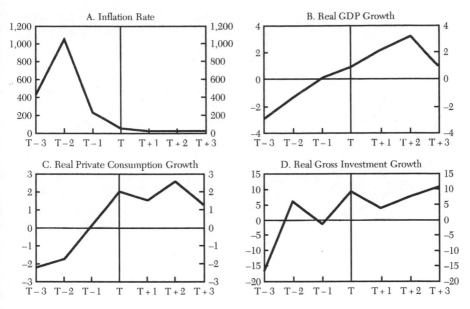

Figure 9.7
Inflation, GDP, consumption, and investment.

tion and jumps to around 2 percent in the year of stabilization, peaking at 2.6 percent in year $T + 2$. While exhibiting more variability, the behavior of real per-capita domestic-investment growth fits the same pattern. It jumps from -1.2 percent in the year before stabilization to more than 9 percent in the year of stabilization, to end with a rate of growth above 10 percent in year $T + 3$. This preliminary evidence is therefore consistent with the idea that, contrary to what happens in low-inflation countries, stabilization from high inflation appears to be associated with an expansion in output, consumption, and investment.[61]

Figure 9.8 shows the behavior of other macroeconomic variables. As expected, the rate of growth of the nominal exchange rate exhibits a similar pattern to the inflation rate. The real exchange rate, which is appreciating until year $T - 2$, begins to depreciate in the year before stabilization and continues to do so throughout the stabilization. The current account balance worsens throughout the stabilization, reaching a trough of 4 percent of GDP in year $T + 2$. Finally, the fiscal deficit falls from more than 8 percent of GDP in year $T - 3$ to close to 2 percent in $T + 3$.

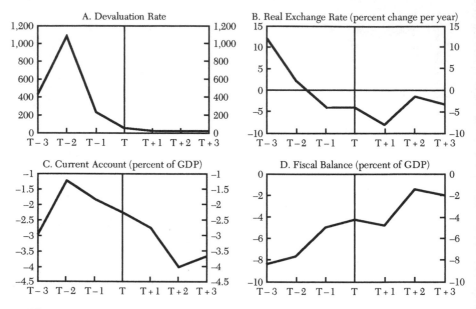

Figure 9.8
Devaluation, real exchange rate, current account, and fiscal balance.

While figure 9.7 is consistent with the idea that stabilization from high inflation may be expansionary, it offers no sense of the statistical significance, if any, of the time profile, nor does it address the question of whether factors other than the disinflation process itself may be causing such behavior. To address these questions, table 9.12 presents regressions of the main macroeconomic variables on the stabilization time dummies, controlling for three external factors: OECD growth, terms of trade shocks, and LIBOR (in real terms).[62]

Consider the first three columns, which show the results for GDP, consumption, and investment. Note that the control variables appear to play an important role in explaining these variables. In the case of GDP, for instance, all three control variables are highly significant and, at least for OECD growth and real LIBOR, with the expected sign.[63] Consumption growth is affected positively by terms of trade and negatively by real LIBOR, whereas investment growth is only affected significantly by changes in real LIBOR.

With respect to the stabilization time dummies, the results are somewhat mixed. There is evidence of an expansionary response in output growth, as shown by the significance of the coefficients on

Table 9.12
Real variables during stabilization

	Dependent variables				
	Growth in real GDP (1)	Growth in real private consumption (2)	Growth in real gross investment (3)	Current account (as % of GDP) (4)	Change in real exchange rate (5)
T − 3	−2.80	−2.48	−17.06***	0.14	11.03**
	(2.67)	(−1.85)	(−3.14)	(0.11)	(2.02)
T − 2	−1.05	−1.97	5.96	2.21	−1.88
	(−1.01)	(−1.25)	(1.10)	(1.70)	(−0.35)
T − 1	0.24	0.03	−1.17	0.93	−4.39
	(0.24)	(0.02)	(−0.22)	(0.74)	(−0.87)
T	0.71	1.85	9.45*	0.55	−3.42
	(0.68)	(1.18)	(1.71)	(0.44)	(−0.69)
T + 1	2.07*	1.20	3.64	0.02	−8.75
	(1.75)	(0.71)	(0.61)	(0.01)	(−1.62)
T + 2	2.92**	2.07	7.24	−1.48	−1.52
	(2.28)	(1.13)	(1.11)	(−1.01)	(−0.24)
T + 3	0.77	0.67	9.99	−1.18	−4.07
	(0.59)	(0.34)	(1.37)	(−0.74)	(−0.65)
OECD growth	0.60***	0.26	0.31	−0.04	−1.00
	(5.45)	(1.18)	(0.42)	(−0.25)	(−1.05)
Terms of trade	−0.004***	0.011*	0.024	0.015***	0.070***
	(−4.00)	(1.83)	(1.20)	(3.75)	(3.68)
Real LIBOR	−0.40***	−0.49***	−1.06*	−0.29**	−1.17*
	(−4.00)	(−3.27)	(−2.00)	(−2.42)	(−1.92)
Number of observations	428	355	365	395	285

Note: T-statistics in parentheses. The first three dependent variables are expressed in per capita terms. Method of estimation was OLS. Significance at the 10-, 5-, and 1-percent level is indicated by one, two, and three stars, respectively.

$T + 1$ and $T + 2$. There is, however, no evidence of any significant response in consumption growth. In the case of investment growth, the coefficient on T is significant. As to the other two variables—current account and the real exchange rate—the stabilization time dummies are, by and large, not significant.

4.3 Does the Nominal Anchor Matter?

The results so far provide only weak evidence in favor of the hypothesis that stabilization may be expansionary. Since, as mentioned above, it has been argued that the real effects of disinflation may depend on the nominal anchor, it is worth examining this issue with the sample at hand. To that effect, we selected nine out of the 27 episodes of stabilization in our sample, which can be classified as exchange rate-based stabilizations (ERBS).[64] The rest of the episodes are classified as non-exchange rate based stabilizations and include an assorted combination of other types of stabilization.[65] This two-way classification is sufficient for our purposes.

We focus on GDP growth, consumption, and investment, since we are mainly interested in the expansionary effects of stabilizations. Figure 9.9 shows the stabilization time profiles for these three variables for both exchange rate-based episodes (nine) and non-exchange rate-based episodes (eighteen). For ERBS, GDP growth rises very sharply upon stabilization—from an already positive value in the year before stabilization—and then stays high until $T + 2$ only to fall sharply in year $T + 3$. This finding is in line with other studies (see Calvo and Végh 1999). In sharp contrast, the stabilization time profile for non-ERBS stabilizations shows no discernible pattern. The profiles for consumption growth fit exactly the same pattern. With respect to investment growth, the stabilization time profiles for ERBS and non-ERBS look qualitatively similar, in that they both show a jump in investment at time T but, quantitatively, the change for ERBS is much stronger. This evidence thus seems to indicate that the profiles for the whole sample shown in figure 9.7 are basically driven by these nine episodes of exchange rate-based stabilization.

To look further into this issue, table 9.13 presents the same type of regressions as before for the two subsamples: ERBS and non-ERBS stabilizations. As column (1) shows, in ERBS real GDP growth in the two years before stabilization ($T - 2$ and $T - 1$) is not significantly different from average growth in the sample. In the first two years of the stabilization, however, growth is indeed significantly different. In contrast, as shown in column (2), in non-ERBS growth after the stabilization is never significant. As before, the three controls variables are highly significant. A similar story holds for consumption growth (columns 3 and 4). For ERBS, consumption growth in the year of stabilization is highly significant, whereas for non-ERBS no coefficient is significant after the stabilization. For investment growth (columns 5 and 6), there is no difference between the ERBS and non-ERBS sample. It should be said, however, that the coefficient on T for the ERBS sample is significant at the 11-percent level, whereas

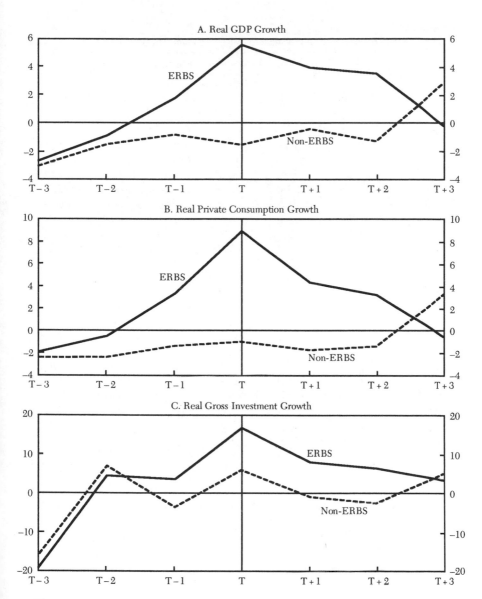

Figure 9.9
ERBS and non-ERBS stabilizations.

Table 9.13
Exchange-rate-based versus non-exchange-rate-based stabilization

	Dependent variables					
	Growth in real GDP		Growth in real private consumption		Growth in real gross investment	
	ERBS (1)	Non-ERBS (2)	ERBS (3)	Non-ERBS (4)	ERBS (5)	Non-ERBS (6)
T − 3	−2.94*	−2.93**	−1.51	−3.22	−18.87**	−16.97**
	(−1.70)	(−2.25)	(−0.59)	(−1.74)	(−2.04)	(−2.56)
T − 2	−0.79	−1.37	−0.49	−3.02	4.26	6.08
	(−0.46)	(−1.06)	(−0.19)	(−1.58)	(0.46)	(0.92)
T − 1	1.56	−0.60	3.28	−1.83	2.85	−3.86
	(0.90)	(−0.48)	(1.29)	(−0.99)	(0.31)	(−0.59)
T	5.34***	−1.55	8.98***	−1.48	16.14	5.81
	(2.90)	(−1.23)	(3.28)	(−0.80)	(1.63)	(0.88)
T + 1	3.60*	−0.07	3.62	−2.00	6.54	−0.74
	(1.65)	(−0.03)	(1.20)	(−0.63)	(0.60)	(−0.06)
T + 2	3.02	−1.04	2.65	−1.08	5.35	−1.87
	(1.52)	(−0.62)	(0.97)	(−0.46)	(0.54)	(−0.22)
T + 3	−0.09	2.37	−0.90	2.98	2.14	4.35
	(−0.04)	(1.35)	(−0.27)	(1.15)	(0.02)	(0.43)
OECD growth	0.59***	0.64***	0.26	0.28	0.38	0.46
	(5.36)	(5.82)	(0.85)	(1.27)	(0.50)	(0.62)
Terms of trade	−0.005***	−0.004***	0.009	0.012**	0.023	0.026
	(−5.00)	(−4.00)	(1.50)	(2.00)	(1.15)	(1.30)
Real LIBOR	−0.39***	−0.36***	−0.52***	−0.44***	−1.00*	−1.04*
	(−3.90)	(−3.60)	(−3.47)	(−2.93)	(−0.52)	(−1.96)
No. of observations	428	428	355	355	365	365

Note: T-statistics in parentheses. All dependent variables are expressed in per capita terms. Method of estimation was OLS. Significance at the 10-, 5-, and 1-percent level is indicated by one, two, or three stars, respectively.

that for non-ERBS is highly insignificant. Hence, whatever effects we found for investment growth in the full sample are also coming from the ERBS sample.

In sum, the evidence shown here suggests that the expansionary effects of stabilization—which are mostly evident in GDP and consumption—are due essentially to the ERBS present in our sample. This is consistent with the idea that the nominal anchor matters for the real effects of disinflations, with ERBS leading to an initial boom in output and consumption.[66,67]

4.4   In Search of an Explanation

The evidence reviewed above suggests that inflation stabilization is expansionary in the short run, particularly when based on the use of the exchange rate as the nominal anchor. Why would that be the case?

To early observers of many of these programs, the most conspicuous feature was the sharp increase in private consumption, particularly of durable goods.[68] We thus view demand-side considerations as the most plausible explanation for the observed short-run expansions. The most popular demand-side explanation (often referred to as the "temporariness hypothesis") is predicated on the idea that, in light of a rich history of failed stabilization attempts, most stabilization programs in chronic inflation countries are bound to suffer from lack of credibility.[69] Following Calvo (1986), lack of credibility has typically been formalized by positing that agents expect the program to be temporary. In the typical model, cash is needed to purchase goods (via a cash-in-advance constraint) so that a lower nominal interest rate reduces the "effective price" of consumption.[70] Then, a non-credible (i.e., temporary) stabilization induces consumers to switch future consumption toward the present, thus resulting in a consumption boom. If, in addition, prices were sticky, this consumption boom cannot take place under a money-based stabilization because the nominal money supply cannot increase endogenously to accommodate the higher consumption expenditures.

There are two potential problems with the temporariness hypothesis. First, by construction, it can only explain consumption booms in episodes in which the program was non-credible in its early stages. However, since no program in chronic inflation countries is likely to be viewed as fully credible, this is perhaps not a very damaging criticism. More important is the fact that, at a quantitative level, this hypothesis relies critically on a large intertemporal elasticity of substitution. Since estimates of this parameter are typically low, the quantitative explanatory power of this hypothesis is rather limited (Reinhart and Végh 1995b). It should be noted, however, that the formal introduction of durable goods should improve the quantitative performance of this hypothesis for two reasons. First, there is some evidence to suggest that, if durable goods consumption is taken into account, estimates of the intertemporal elasticity of substitution become higher (see Yvon Fauvel and Lucie Samson 1991). Second, in the presence of durable goods, households will also engage in intertemporal *price* speculation (Calvo 1988b). Unfortunately, the additional quantitative power brought about by these additional considerations has not yet been established.

A related, demand-side explanation has been offered by Jose De Gregorio, Pablo Guidotti, and Végh (1998). In their model, consumers follow inventory-type rules (i.e., (S,s) rules) for the purchase of durable goods. While purchases of durable goods are "lumpy" at an individual level (since any given individual consumer only buys/replaces his/her durable good every once in a while), they are initially smooth in the aggregate (as consumers buy/replace durables at different times). Consider now a stabilization that generates some sort of wealth/income effect. In response, some consumers that were not planning to buy/replace their durable good today will decide to bring forward their purchases and perhaps even upgrade (i.e., next year's Toyota becomes today's Mercedes Benz). The resulting "bunching" produces a boom in durable-goods consumption. This boom is necessarily followed by a slowdown because all the consumers that brought forward their purchases of durable goods will not want to replace them for a while. In the presence of idiosyncratic shocks, consumers would "de-bunch" over time until a new steady state is reached in which aggregate purchases are constant over time. This mechanism is thus capable of generating a consumption boom-bust cycle without having to resort to lack of credibility.[71]

Yet another and early demand-based explanation of the boom-bust cycle in consumption, originally due to Carlos Rodriguez (1982), was based on backward-looking inflation expectations, in the spirit of Cagan.[72] Specifically, Rodriguez (1982) presents a model in which, due to the interest parity condition, the nominal interest rate falls one-to-one with the rate of devaluation. Since expected inflation is backward-looking, the real interest rate falls, thus expanding aggregate demand on impact. The excess demand for home goods leads to a real appreciation of the domestic currency, which eventually throws the economy into a recession. This model thus provides a coherent and plausible explanation for episodes in which there is an early fall in the domestic real interest rate (as happened in the Argentine 1978 program, which inspired Rodriguez's contribution). It cannot, however, explain programs in which the real interest rate increased on impact, as in many heterodox programs in the mid-1980s (see Calvo and Végh 1999).

Finally, another strand of the literature has focused on the supply-side responses that may be unleashed by stabilization.[73] The main idea is that inflation acts as a "tax" either on labor supply (by distorting the consumption-leisure choice) or on investment (by making it more expensive to hold readily-available working capital). Hence, the removal of such a distortion would lead to a higher labor supply and more investment, resulting in a permanently higher level of output. While such supply-side responses are likely to be a major factor in the long-run (in line with the inflation and growth literature examined above), we remain skeptical about their ability to explain *short-run* expansionary effects. The main problem with this hypothesis is that, empirically, the short-run response of investment seems to be, at best, weak.[74] Also, if true, one should see a short-run expansion in any stabilization, regardless of the nominal anchor.

Which of the above models does better when confronted with the data? Sergio Rebelo and Végh (1995) nest most of the above explanations into a single model and compare their qualitative and quantitative power. In line with the simple models described above, they conclude that only the temporariness and sticky wages models are capable of replicating the key empirical regularities. Quantitatively, however, supply-side effects are key in helping the model account for any sizable fraction of the observed magnitudes. Still, the model has problems in accounting for the large real appreciation observed in most of these programs. Further progress on this quantitative front has been recently made by Ariel Burnstein, Joao Neves, and Rebelo (2000), who show how, by introducing distribution costs into the picture, the model can explain a much more sizable fraction of the observed real exchange rate appreciation.

4.5   In Sum

There is by now abundant evidence that high inflation is bad for growth. While the debate over the mechanisms and causality are far from being resolved, the negative correlation between high inflation and macroeconomic performance is clearly there. So, at the very least, the old idea that in some sense inflation may be good for growth or is perhaps an inevitable part of the growth process should remain buried in the cemetery of harmful policy ideas.

There is also increasing evidence that stabilization from high inflation is expansionary. While not everybody would accept this notion, different researchers with different methodologies seem to be arriving at similar conclusions. It is at least safe to say that the idea is to be taken seriously and that it is no longer a heresy to think of an expansionary inflationary stabilization program.

We also believe that the evidence supports the idea that the nominal anchor matters and that, other things being equal, exchange-rate-based stabilizations are more likely to be expansionary. This idea also makes sense theoretically: unlike a money-based stabilization which—by its very nature—reduces inflation by inducing a liquidity crunch, in exchange-rate-based stabilizations the money supply is endogenous and will accommodate whatever increase in money demand results from real channels. This why exchange-rate-based stabilizations are so attractive as a means of reducing inflation form very high levels—even though the issue of how to exit from a peg before the advent of a potential crisis remains unresolved.

5   In Conclusion: Top Ten List on High Inflation

What have we learned after our long journey through the world of high inflation and stabilization? While the sample of 161 countries (133 market economies and 28 transition economies) offers very rich and diverse experiences, some general conclusions can still be drawn. Here, in our judgment, are the ten most important stylized facts related to high inflation and stabilization:

1. Since 1957, inflation has been commonplace throughout the world. Based on a sample of 133 countries (for a total of close to 45,000 observations), we find that more than two-thirds of the countries have experienced an episode of more than 25-percent per-annum in-

flation; more than one-third has experienced episodes in excess of 50 percent per annum; close to 20 percent of countries have experienced inflation in excess of 100 percent; and around 8 percent have experienced episodes of more than 400-percent per-annum inflation. The average duration of high-inflation episodes at different levels of inflation is remarkably similar and, at 3–4 years, surprisingly long.

2. In contrast to the market economies, all 28 transition economies experienced at least one episode of inflation above 25 percent per annum. Indeed, almost 80 percent suffered inflation in excess of 400 percent. Most of the extreme inflations in these economies were related to price liberalization.

3. Higher inflation tends to be more unstable. By constructing transition matrices, we find that, as inflation rises, the probability of inflation staying in the same range decreases and the probability that inflation will rise above its current level increases.

4 Since 1947, hyperinflations (meeting Cagan's definition) in market economies have been rare (a total of seven). Much more common have been longer inflationary processes with inflation rates above 100 percent per annum. We define an episode of "very high inflation" as taking place when the twelve-month inflation rate rises above 100 percent. In that case, we take the start of the episode to be the first month of that twelve-month period and the last month to be the first month before the twelve-month inflation rate falls below the lower bound and stays there for at least twelve months. We identified 45 such episodes in 25 countries. Thirty-seven of these very high-inflation episodes took place in either Latin America or Africa. The duration of these episodes ranges from the minimum possible (twelve months) to 208 months (Argentina 1974–1991). Monthly average inflation rates during these episodes vary from 3.6 percent to 27.4 (Democratic Republic of Congo 1989–1996).

5. As expected, the long-run (cross-section) relationship between money growth and inflation is very strong. When the sample is divided between low- and high-inflation countries, the relationship is found to be stronger for high-inflation than for low-inflation countries. In the pooled, cross-section time-series panels, we find that the money-inflation link remains strong for the sample as a whole. When the sample is divided, however, the relationship for high-inflation countries is basically unchanged compared to the long

run, whereas that for the low-inflation countries becomes much weaker.

6. The long-run relationship (based on cross-section data) between fiscal balance and seigniorage is significant and negative. In the short run, the relationship is strong for high inflation countries but insignificant for low inflation countries.

7. The expected positive relationship between fiscal deficits and inflation cannot always be detected in the data. We find no significant long-run (cross-section) relationship between fiscal deficits and inflation. In the annual cross-section time series panels, the relationship is significant for the high inflation countries but not for the low inflation countries.

8. Inflation inertia—defined either as the mean lag length or the median lag length of an autoregressive inflation process—falls as the level of inflation rises. This evidence supports the notion that nominal rigidities are weakened as inflation reaches higher levels.

9. Periods of high inflation are associated with bad macroeconomic performance. In particular, high inflation is bad for growth. The evidence is based on a sample of eighteen countries that have experienced very high inflation episodes. During such periods, real GDP per capita fell on average by 1.6 percent per annum (compared to positive growth of 1.4 percent in low inflation years); private consumption per capita fell by 1.3 percent (compared to 1.7 percent growth in low inflation years) and investment growth fell by 3.3 percent (compared to positive growth of 4.2 percent in low inflation years).

10. Exchange rate-based stabilizations appear to lead to an initial expansion in real GDP and real private consumption. Stabilizations which were not based on the exchange rate do not appear on average to have had a significant effect on output, consumption, or investment.

Appendix

Table 9.A.1
Inflationary episodes in high-inflation market economies

| Country | Date of episode | | During high inflation | | Monthly inflation rate | | | | |
| | Start | End | Duration (in months) | Cumulative inflation | During high inflation | | | Twelve months after high inflation | |
					Geometric average	Arithmetic average	Highest	Geometric average	Highest
Afghanistan	July 1988–June 1989		12	109	6.3	6.5	25.6	2.9	19.8
Afghanistan	Feb. 1985–Oct. 1986		21	109	3.6	n.a.	3.9	1.4	6.4
Angola	Jan. 1991–June 1997		78	287,726,172	21.0	22.3	84.1	1.8	3.0
Argentina	July 1974–Oct. 1991		208	3,809,187,961,396	12.4	13.5	196.6	1.4	3.0
Bolivia	Aug. 1981–Aug. 1986		61	5,220,261	19.5	22.1	182.8	0.7	2.4
Brazil	Apr. 1980–May 1995		182	20,759,903,275,651	15.4	16.1	80.7	1.7	4.4
Chile	Oct. 1971–May 1977		68	127,958	11.1	11.6	87.5	3.0	4.2
Congo, Dem. Rep.	Dec. 1989–Dec. 1996		85	88,510,051,965	27.4	32.0	250.0	n.a.	n.a.
Congo, Dem. Rep.	Feb. 1988–July 1989		18	202	6.3	6.4	20.4	3.1	5.9
Congo, Dem. Rep.	July 1986–Dec. 1987		18	146	5.1	5.2	16.6	5.5	20.4
Congo, Dem. Rep.	Oct. 1982–Jan. 1984		16	146	5.8	5.9	25.1	0.8	3.8
Congo, Dem. Rep.	Feb. 1978–Aug. 1980		31	317	4.7	5.8	76.5	2.8	8.4

Table 9.A.1
(continued)

| Country | Date of episode | | During high inflation | | Monthly inflation rate | | | | |
| | Start | End | Duration (in months) | Cumulative inflation | During high inflation | | | Twelve months after high inflation | |
					Geometric average	Arithmetic average	Highest	Geometric average	Highest
Congo, Dem. Rep.	Mar. 1967–Feb. 1968		12	101	6.0	6.1	18.2	–0.1	5.7
Costa Rica	Sept. 1981–Oct. 1982		14	120	5.8	5.8	10.7	1.0	2.6
Ghana	May 1982–Feb. 1984		22	243	5.8	6.0	23.4	0.3	4.9
Ghana	Feb. 1980–Dec. 1981		23	257	5.7	5.7	13.2	1.3	7.9
Ghana	May 1976–Feb. 1979		34	567	5.7	5.9	22.8	1.1	8.9
Guinea-Bissau	Sept. 1986–Feb. 1988		18	146	5.1	5.5	25.0	4.6	12.6
Israel	Dec. 1978–Mar. 1986		88	109,187	8.3	8.4	27.5	1.7	3.3
Jamaica	Apr. 1991–May 1992		14	124	5.9	5.9	10.2	1.1	2.5
Lebanon	Aug. 1991–Dec. 1992		17	118	4.7	5.0	22.6	–0.1	1.9
Lebanon	Mar. 1990–Feb. 1991		12	100	5.9	6.2	17.7	1.3	10.3
Lebanon	Aug. 1985–Aug. 1988		37	2,345	9.0	9.6	50.1	4.4	14.2
Mexico	Dec. 1985–Aug. 1988		33	724	6.6	6.6	15.5	1.3	2.5
Mexico	Feb. 1982–July 1983		18	180	5.9	5.9	11.2	4.2	6.4
Nicaragua	May 1984–Feb. 1992		94	288,735,412,719	26.1	30.3	261.1	1.6	9.3
Peru	Dec. 1986–Mar. 1992		64	25,392,223	21.5	25.9	397.0	3.5	4.8
Peru	June 1982–Apr. 1986		47	1,953	6.6	6.7	13.9	4.6	6.6

Sierra Leone	Feb. 1989–Dec. 1991	35	689	6.1	6.2	19.9	2.5	5.9
Sierra Leone	Nov. 1986–Dec. 1987	14	144	6.6	6.9	24.1	2.7	16.1
Somalia	Oct. 1987–Nov. 1989	26	388	6.3	6.4	16.8	n.a.	n.a.
Somalia	Mar. 1983–June 1984	16	140	5.6	5.8	19.6	2.7	9.0
Sudan	Feb. 1990–June 1994	53	2,715	6.5	6.7	28.3	n.a.	n.a.
Suriname	Apr. 1992–Oct. 1995	43	4,559	9.3	9.7	40.7	−0.3	3.3
Turkey	May 1993–Mar. 1995	23	269	5.8	5.9	24.7	5.0	8.3
Turkey	Mar. 1979–Sept. 1980	19	199	5.9	6.0	21.5	2.4	8.1
Uganda	Feb. 1984–Dec. 1988	59	9,071	8.0	8.3	37.9	3.8	6.9
Uganda	Feb. 1981–Apr. 1982	15	160	6.6	7.0	43.8	1.5	5.3
Uruguay	June 1989–Aug. 1991	27	414	6.2	6.3	14.7	4.4	6.5
Uruguay	Jan. 1974–Dec. 1974	12	107	6.3	6.3	16.8	4.4	11.4
Uruguay	Dec. 1971–Sept. 1973	22	256	5.9	6.1	20.3	4.5	16.8
Uruguay	Oct. 1966–Oct. 1968	25	336	6.1	6.2	17.9	1.2	2.7
Venezuela	July 1995–Dec. 1996	18	161	5.5	5.5	12.6	n.a.	n.a.
Venezuela	June 1988–May 1989	12	103	6.1	6.2	21.3	2.4	3.3
Zambia	Aug. 1988–Mar. 1994	68	11,713	7.3	7.4	29.5	2.4	7.7

Sources: IMF, *International Financial Statistics*, national authorities, and IMF desk economists.

Notes

1. We thank Mary Hallward-Driemeier of the World Bank for her contributions at an early stage in the writing of the paper; Leonardo Bartolini, Peter Doyle, Bob Flood, Javier Hamann, Esteban Jadresic, Prakash Loungani, Peter Montiel, Maansi Sahay Seth, Murat Ucer, two anonymous referees, and seminar participants at the IMF, World Bank, and AEA meetings for helpful comments and discussions; and Claire Adams, Manzoor Gill, Nada Mora, Prachi Mishra, and Kartikeya Singh for excellent research assistance. The views expressed in this paper are those of the authors and not necessarily those of the IMF.

2. The seven hyperinflations were: Austria, Oct. 1921–Aug. 1922; Russia, Dec. 1921–Jan. 1924; Germany, Aug. 1922–Nov. 1923; Poland, Jan. 1923–Jan. 1924; Hungary I, March 1923–Feb. 1924; Greece, Nov. 1943–Nov. 1944; and Hungary II, Aug. 1945–July 1946. In addition, there was, by Cagan's definition, a hyperinflation in China from Oct. 1947 to March 1948 (Andrew Huang 1948).

3. Inflation in the century leading up to Diocletian's price control edict in 301 AD appears to have averaged under 4 percent per annum (Don Paarlberg 1993).

4. This appears to have been an early example of the adage that inflation is a regressive tax, for the solidus was reportedly too valuable to be held by the poor.

5. We exclude episodes lasting less than two months because many transition economies, especially those in the former Soviet Union, suffered at least one month of more than 50-percent inflation when price controls were lifted. Since these episodes were more in the nature of a price-level adjustment than an ongoing process of high inflation, we have changed the definition to exclude them.

6. The peak monthly rate in the post-World War 2 Hungarian hyperinflation was 41.9×10^{15}.

7. It should be noted that, at the time, some analysts also emphasized the role of expectations; see David Laidler and George Stadler (1998).

8. Of course, the verbal accounts of some of the inter-world war authors contain many of the mechanisms and subtleties developed more formally in the later literature.

9. In the presence of multiple equilibria, the key question becomes whether "learning" (or any other convergence process) will lead the economy to the "good" (i.e., non-explosive) Laffer curve equilibrium. While, theoretically, learning does not rule out the possibility of convergence to sunspot equilibria (Michael Woodford 1990), experimental evidence suggests that the economy will tend to converge to a low inflationary steady-state (Ramon Marimon and Shyam Sunder 1993). Also, as pointed out by Woodford (1990), there are many different ways—all equally plausible and satisfying some weak criteria for rational decision-making—of specifying a learning process. For the case of linear rational expectations models, Albert Marcet and Thomas Sargent (1995) analyze the speed of convergence in a setting in which agents learn by fitting ARMA models to a subset of state variables. For details on learning and its relation to the rational expectations hypothesis, see the excellent review by George Evans and Seppo Honkapohja (2001).

10. However, high inflation could actually reduce the fiscal deficit if the real value of government expenditure falls by more than real tax revenues. Eliana Cardoso (1998) points to the so-called Patinkin effect, the converse of the Tanzi effect, which could arise if, for instance, nominal government spending is fixed and its real value reduced

by inflation—an equilibrating mechanism that was operative during Brazilian high inflations.

11. Marcet and Juan Pablo Nicolini (1998) study a model with learning that can explain sudden outbursts of high inflation in chronic inflation countries. In a similar vein, see Carlos Zarazaga (1993).

12. Although our definition is modeled on that of Cagan (1956) in his classic article, it differs in one important respect from his: namely, Cagan based his definition on *monthly* rates of inflation whereas ours is based on twelve-month inflation rates.

13. The ranges used in this paper draw largely from previous work. One way to proceed would be to look for breaks in the transition probabilities. If any were found, this would suggest that inflation behaves differently in different ranges. We follow this approach only in examining some results of Michael Bruno and William Easterly (1995) discussed later in this section.

14. The total number of country-months in the sample included in table 9.3a is 44,910. For 80.1 percent of those months, the monthly inflation rate is less than 1.9 percent (corresponding to an annual rate of 25 percent).

15. The starting dates selected depend on when prices were freed and on data availability. Thus, they tend to vary across the transition economies, being 1991 for most of Eastern Europe and Mongolia, 1992 for the former Soviet Union, 1988 for Poland, 1990 for the former Yugoslavian states and Vietnam, 1986 for China, and 1986 for Hungary.

16. Of a total sample of 2,023 monthly inflation rates, only 37 percent were below 1.9 percent.

17. We have also calculated a transition matrix for the corresponding monthly rates of inflation. For all but the 200–400 percent per-annum range, the probability of inflation remaining in a given range is smaller with monthly than with annual data. Further, the probability that the inflation rate will fall is uniformly higher for the monthly than the annual data. These results are due mainly to the greater variability in monthly inflation rates compared to annual rates.

18. In discussing tables 9.4 and 9.5, we refer to frequencies and probabilities interchangeably.

19. However, there are relatively few observations in the higher inflation ranges.

20. The eleven countries are Angola, Argentina, Bolivia, Brazil, Chile, Democratic Republic of Congo, Israel, Lebanon, Nicaragua, Peru, and Suriname.

21. This is because of the end-point requirement in the definition; namely, that the twelve-month rate stay below 100 percent for at least twelve months for an episode to end. It can be seen from table 9.A.1 that in thirteen of the 45 episodes, the (geometric) average inflation rate within an episode is less than 100 percent per annum. Note also that the end of two episodes (in Congo and Venezuela) is dictated by the end of the sample period (December 1996).

22. See Carmen Reinhart and Kenneth Rogoff (2002) for a recent analysis of high inflation in Africa.

23. From this point onwards—and since we will be mostly looking at long-run relationships—we will restrict our attention to market economies.

24. The only high-inflation country not included (due to lack of data) is Afghanistan.

25. The outlier in figure 9.1 is Nicaragua (the furthermost from the regression line).

26. We could not reject the OLS model in favor of a fixed-effects one, indicating the overwhelming effect of money growth on inflation that is common across the high-inflation countries.

27. We are aware that in talking about causation we have taken a step that goes beyond the inflation-money growth correlations. But it is a short step, since money growth is always potentially controllable—if necessary with a change in monetary operating practices.

28. Naturally, for the government to be able to turn off the monetary taps permanently, the underlying fiscal problems must be addressed. Otherwise, low inflation will only be purchased at the cost of future high inflation (i.e., Sargent and Wallace's 1981 celebrated unpleasant monetarist arithmetic).

29. It is sometimes argued that the Soviet inflation of the early-1920s was a deliberate act of policy; it has also been argued that the German hyperinflation was an attempt to demonstrate that reparations could not be paid.

30. This is the so-called "shocks and accommodation" view of monetary policy in chronic inflation countries; see, among others, Charles Adams and Daniel Gros (1986), Bruno and Fischer (1986), Bruno and R. Melnick (1994), and Calvo, Reinhart, and Végh (1995).

31. The sample period is not confined to very high-inflation episodes.

32. We also ran the VARs imposing a uniform three-quarter lag length. The results on the statistical significance of the exclusion restrictions were unchanged, except in the case of Somalia.

33. Our results are thus broadly consistent with the conclusions of Montiel (1989) and Dornbusch, Federico Sturzenegger, and Holger Wolf (1990). They are also consistent with earlier analysis of the classical hyperinflations by Frenkel (1977, 1979) and Sargent and Wallace (1973). In particular, Sargent and Wallace (1973) conclude, based on Cagan's seven hyperinflations, that the causality from inflation to money is typically stronger than from money to inflation. (See also Beatrix Paal 2000.)

34. In fact, as shown by Sargent and Wallace (1973), causality from inflation to money is entirely consistent with a model in which inflation is driven by the need to finance a fixed real amount of government spending. In such a model, the "causality" from inflation to money growth emerges because the public's expected rate of inflation influences future money growth through the government budget constraint.

35. Naturally, this formulation presupposes that the fiscal authority is solvent in an intertemporal sense.

36. In a similar vein, Drazen and Elhanan Helpman (1990) show how the anticipation of future policies may trigger inflation today.

37. The public finance perspective that treats seigniorage as another form of taxation may suggest that seigniorage revenue should be more closely associated with the level of government spending rather than with the deficit (see, for example, Végh 1989).

38. The Laffer curve shape emerges from the steady state relationship between the inflation rate and seigniorage. If, for instance, expectations lag behind actual inflation, it may be possible for a time to increase seigniorage by accelerating inflation even beyond the steady state revenue maximizing rate.

39. As before, the inflation rate is defined as $ln(1 + inflation/100)$ and seigniorage as the change in high-powered money as a share of GDP.

40. Notice that since the relevant variable for determining inflationary finance is the present discounted value of primary deficits, *a priori* one would indeed expect additional lags to improve the fit.

41. Catao and Terrones (2001), however, find a statistically significant positive long-run relationship between fiscal deficits and inflation for a panel of 23 emerging market countries during 1970–2000, using an estimator that distinguishes between short-run dynamics and equilibrium relationships in heterogeneous panels.

42. Using univariate autoregressive processes to measure inflation persistence has a long tradition in the literature; see, in particular, Bruno and Fischer (1986), Bruno (1993), and James Stock (2001).

43. While the high-inflation episodes in Angola and Suriname were not short in themselves, they were preceded and followed by low-inflation episodes of limited length due to lack of data.

44. We estimated equation (5) with a maximum of seven lags, seasonal dummies, and a trend for each episode. Using the F-test, the model was reduced to determine the appropriate lag length and to see whether seasonal dummies and the trend belonged to the model. If the seventh lag was significant, we included more lags in the model.

45. Stock (2001) measures persistence by the largest root of an AR representation of inflation.

46. See also Christopher Sims' (2001) comments on Cogley and Sargent.

47. If a high inflation episode begins in the second half of the year, or ends in the first half of the year, that year is taken as a low-inflation year.

48. Due to lack of data, we excluded Afghanistan, Angola, Guinea-Bissau, Jamaica, Lebanon, Nicaragua, and Somalia. The sample consists of annual data, 1960–1995 (or longest available sub-period). Note that the total number of observations varies according to the variable considered. There are 647 observations for the nominal exchange rate, 590 observations for inflation, 533 for real per capita GDP growth, 355 for real per capita consumption growth, 365 for real per capita investment growth, 285 for the change in the real exchange rate, 407 for the current account, and 499 for the fiscal balance.

49. Benedikt Braumann (2001) also documents a sharp decline in real wages during periods of high inflation, based on an analysis of 23 episodes.

50. See, for example, Fischer (1993), De Gregorio (1993), and Bruno and Easterly (1995).

51. We find it quite plausible to believe that deflation is bad for growth, and thus would not be surprised if further research showed that inflation and growth are positively related for extremely low and negative inflation rates, for example up to 2 percent per annum.

52. Steve Ambler and Emanuela Cardia (1998) calibrate a richer model along these lines. They conclude that the model does indeed predict a negative correlation between inflation and growth (both for time series and, in the long-run, for a cross section). Since both variables are endogenous, the size of this correlation will depend on the size of the underlying exogenous shocks. The authors also offer an insightful

analysis of the pitfalls associated with interpreting standard inflation and growth regressions.

53. Notice that the real exchange rate appreciates during high inflation periods even though the average nominal depreciation (984 percent) is higher than the average rate of inflation (739 percent). This is related to the fact that the samples are not the same; that is, the number of observations for the real exchange rate is much lower than that for the nominal devaluation/depreciation and the inflation rate.

54. With a smaller sample (23 episodes), Braumann finds the expected results: during high inflation periods, a real depreciation goes hand in hand with an improvement in the external trade accounts.

55. Sargent's (1982) analysis has itself been challenged; most notably by Peter Garber (1982) and Elmus Wicker (1986); see also Végh (1992) and Bruno (1993).

56. For econometric evidence in favor of this hypothesis, see Reinhart and Végh (1994, 1995a), De Gregorio, Guidotti, and Végh (1998) and Calvo and Végh (1999). David Gould (1996) and Federico Echenique and Alvaro Forteza (1997) take issue with some of the econometric findings. At a more fundamental level, Finn Kydland and Zarazaga (1997) argue against the view that stabilizations necessarily have important real effects in high inflation countries.

57. It should be noted that none of this evidence on the relationship between inflation and growth bears on the optimal speed of disinflation. David Burton and Fischer (1998) discuss several cases of extremely rapid and successful (growth-increasing) disinflation from triple digit rates; they also show that in other cases, starting at moderate rates of inflation, disinflation has been very slow, for fear that more rapid disinflation would show output growth.

58. In selecting the stabilization episodes, we take as our starting point the episodes of very high inflation defined above (45 episodes in 25 countries, as listed in table 9.A.1). In our definition, when a very high inflation episodes ends, a stabilization starts. Due to (i) lack of data, (ii) instances in which very high inflation episodes separated by less than 12 months were consolidated into one, and (iii) instances in which the very high inflation episode is ongoing as of 1995 (the end of our sample for stabilization purposes), we end up with 27 stabilization episodes in 18 countries: (Argentina (1), Bolivia (1), Brazil (1), Chile (1), Congo (3), Costa Rica (1), Ghana (2), Israel (1), Mexico (2), Peru (1), Sierra Leone (2), Sudan (1), Suriname (1), Turkey (2), Uganda (2), Uruguay (3), Venezuela (1), and Zambia (1).

59. If the episode of very high inflation ends in the second half of the year, we take T to be the following year.

60. Notice that the number of observations for each year in stabilization time may differ. The number of observations for a given $T + j$ may also differ across variables.

61. See Peter Henry (2002) for an analysis of the effects of stabilizations on the stock market. Based on a sample of 81 episodes, he finds that, when stabilizing from inflation rates higher than 40 percent per year, the domestic stock market appreciates on average by 24 percent in real dollar terms.

62. The variable terms of trade is defined in such a way that a rise in the index denotes a terms of trade improvement.

63. The sign on the terms of trade is somewhat unexpected as it implies that a positive terms of trade shock leads to lower output. Interestingly enough, the same shock does

lead to a significant increase in consumption and an improvement in the current account, as one would expect.

64. These include (initial year of the stabilization episode according to our criteria in parenthesis) Turkey (1995), Argentina (1992), Brazil (1995), Chile (1977), Mexico (1989), Peru (1986), Uruguay (1969 and 1992), and Israel (1986).

65. We purposely choose to refer to the remaining episodes as "non-exchange rate based stabilizations" (as opposed to "money-based stabilizations") because they include not only episodes which can be characterized as money-based stabilization (i.e., stabilizations carried out under floating or dirty floating exchange rates) as, for example, Uruguay (1975), but also other episodes which defy a clear classification. An example of the latter is Turkey (1981) which relied on a PPP-type rule that aimed at keeping the real exchange rate more or less constant (see Rodrik 1991). It should also be noted that most stabilization episodes in Africa were carried out under dual exchange rates (official and unofficial). With few exceptions, however, the important characteristic of these non-exchange-rate based stabilizations is that, to at least some extent, the money supply was under the control of the monetary authorities (as is the case under dirty floating or dual exchange rates). As argued by Calvo and Végh (1999), *some* control over the money supply is enough to make these episodes formally resemble a "pure" money-based stabilization.

66. This contrasts with Easterly's (1996) results which suggest, based on a sample of 28 stabilization episodes, that there is no difference between the behavior of ERBS and non-ERBS. In the same spirit, see Javier Hamann (2001).

67. Note that figure 9.9 is also suggestive of the late contraction in ERBS discussed in the literature. This feature, however, does not show as significant in the regressions shown in table 9.13. In this study, we do not make an attempt to focus on these late real effects, for which more observations after the stabilization and perhaps a slightly different methodology would be called for (see Calvo and Végh 1999, and Braumann 2001).

68. This is supported by data provided in De Gregorio, Guidotti, and Végh (1998) for a small group of countries. For instance, in the 1978 Chilean ERBS, durable goods consumption more than doubled from the beginning of the program to the year in which consumption peaked, while total private consumption increased by only 26 percent. During the 1985 Israeli stabilization (and for the analogous period), durable goods consumption rose by 70 percent compared to 25 percent for total consumption. In the first four years of the Argentine 1991 Convertibility plan, car sales (a good proxy for durable goods consumption) rose by a staggering 400 percent, compared to 30 percent for total private consumption.

69. See Calvo (1986), Calvo and Végh (1993, 1994a,b), Enrique Mendoza and Martin Uribe (1999), and Francisco Venegas-Martinez (2001), among others.

70. In a cash-in-advance setting, the "effective price of consumption" is an increasing function of the nominal interest rate.

71. Again, if some liquid assets were needed to purchase durable goods, this boom could not happen under a money-based stabilization.

72. See also Dornbusch (1982), Fernandez (1985), Calvo and Végh (1994c) and Ghezzi (2001). Notice that, as shown in Calvo and Végh (1994c), Rodriguez's story can be reinterpreted as applying to a model with rational expectations and sticky wages (reflecting backward looking wage indexation).

73. See Amartya Lahiri (2000, 2001), Rebelo (1997), Rebelo and Végh (1995), Jorge Roldos (1995, 1997), and Uribe (1997).

74. Also, at a theoretical level, a somewhat unsatisfactory aspect of some of these models is that they rely on a number of features—gestation lags, adjustment costs, and particularly the assumption that the investment good is a "cash good"—which do not have a clear economic interpretation. In particular, there is no evidence that would seem to tie investment to the level of cash transactions. While, from a qualitative point of view, the assumption that investment be a "cash good" is not necessary to generate the desired results (as made clear by Lahiri 2001), such an assumption is essential from a quantitative point of view if this type of models is to have any chance of replicating the actual orders of magnitudes observed in the data (see Rebelo and Végh 1995).

References

Adams, Charles, and Daniel Gros. 1986. "The Consequences of Real Exchange Rate Rules for Inflation: Some Illustrative Examples," *IMF Staff Pap.* 33, pp. 439–476.

Alesina, Alberto, and Alan Drazen. 1991. "Why Are Stabilizations Delayed?" *Amer. Econ. Rev.* 81, pp. 1170–1188.

Ambler, Steve, and Emanuela Cardia. 1998. "Testing the Link between Inflation and Growth," in *Price Stability, Inflation Targets, and Monetary Policy.* Ottawa: Bank of Canada, pp. 89–116.

Bailey, Martin J. 1956. "The Welfare Cost of Inflationary Finance," *J. Polit. Econ.* 64, pp. 93–110.

Ball, Laurence. 1994. "What Determines the Sacrifice Ratio?" in *Monetary Policy.* N. G. Mankiw, ed. Chicago: U. Chicago Press, pp. 155–182.

Braumann, Benedikt. 2001. "High Inflation and Real Wages," work. paper 01/50, IMF.

Bresciani-Turroni, Constantino. 1937. *The Economics of Inflation.* NY: Augustus Kelley. Third impression 1968. Original Italian ed. 1931.

Bruno, Michael. 1993. *Crisis, Stabilization, and Economic Reform: Therapy by Consensus.* Oxford: Oxford U. Press.

Bruno, Michael, and William Easterly. 1995. "Inflation Crises and Long-Run Growth," work. paper 5209, NBER, Cambridge.

Bruno, Michael, and Stanley Fischer. 1986. "The Inflationary Process: Shocks and Accommodation," in *The Israeli Economy: Maturing through Crises.* Yoram Ben Porath, ed. Cambridge, MA: Harvard U. Press, pp. 347–371.

———. 1990. "Seigniorage, Operating Rules, and the High Inflation Trap," *Quart. J. Econ.* 105, pp. 353–374.

Bruno, Michael, and R. Melnick. 1994. "High Inflation Dynamics: Integrating Short-Run Accommodation and Long-Run Steady-States," mimeo, World Bank.

Burnstein, Ariel T., Joao Neves, and Sergio Rebelo. 2000. "Distribution Costs and Real Exchange Rate Dynamics during Exchange-Rate-Based-Stabilizations," work. paper 7862, NBER; forthcoming *J. Monet. Econ.*

Burton, David, and Stanley Fischer. 1998. "Ending Moderate Inflations," in *Moderate Inflation: The Experience of Transition Economies*. C. Cottarelli and G. Szapary, eds. Washington DC: IMF and National Bank Hungary, pp. 15–96.

Cagan, Phillip. 1956. "The Monetary Dynamics of Hyperinflation," in *Studies in the Quantity Theory of Money*. Milton Friedman, ed. Chicago: U. Chicago Press, pp. 25–117.

Calvo, Guillermo A. 1986. "Temporary Stabilization: Predetermined Exchange Rates," *J. Polit. Econ.* 94, pp. 1319–1329.

————. 1988a. "Servicing the Debt: The Role of Expectations," *Amer. Econ. Rev.* 78, pp. 641–667.

————. 1988b. "Costly Trade Liberalizations: Durable Goods and Capital Mobility," *IMF Staff Pap.* 35, pp. 461–473.

Calvo, Guillermo A., Carmen M. Reinhart, and Carlos A. Végh. 1995. "Targeting the Real Exchange Rate: Theory and Evidence," *J. Devel. Econ.* 47, pp. 97–133.

Calvo, Guillermo A., and Carlos A. Végh. 1993. "Exchange Rate-Based Stabilisation under Imperfect Credibility," in *Open-Economy Macroeconomics*. Helmut Frisch and Andreas Worgotter, eds. London: MacMillan, pp. 3–28.

————. 1994a. "Credibility and the Dynamics of Stabilization Policy: A Basic Framework," in *Advances in Econometrics*, vol. II, Christopher Sims, ed. Cambridge: Cambridge U. Press, pp. 377–420.

————. 1994b. "Inflation Stabilization and Nominal Anchors," *Contemp. Econ. Pol.* 12, pp. 35–45.

————. 1994c. "Stabilization Dynamics and Backward-Looking Contracts," *J. Devel. Econ.* 43, pp. 59–84.

————. 1999. "Inflation Stabilization and BOP Crises in Developing Countries," in *Handbook of Macroeconomics*. John Taylor and Michael Woodford, eds. Amsterdam: North Holland, pp. 1531–1614.

Capie, Forrest H. ed. 1991. *Major Inflations in History*. Aldershot, Hants, England: Edgard Publishing.

Cardenas, Enrique, and Carlos Manns. 1989. "Inflacion y Estabilizacion Monetaria en Mexico durante la Revolucion," *El Trimestre Econ.* 56, pp. 57–79.

Cardoso, Eliana. 1998. "Virtual Deficits and the Patinkin Effect," work. paper 98/41, IMF.

Catao, Luis, and Marco Terrones. 2001. "Fiscal Deficits and Inflation: A New Look at the Emerging Market Evidence," work. paper 01/74, IMF.

Cogley, Timothy, and Thomas J. Sargent. 2001. "Evolving Post-World War II U.S. Inflation Dynamics," forthcoming in *NBER Macroeconomics Annual*.

De Gregorio, Jose. 1993. "Inflation, Taxation, and Long-Run Growth," *J. Monet. Econ.* 31, pp. 271–298.

De Gregorio, Jose, Pablo E. Guidotti, and Carlos A. Végh. 1998. "Inflation Stabilization and the Consumption of Durable Goods," *Econ. J.* 108, pp. 105–131.

Drazen, Allan, and Elhanan Helpman. 1990. "Inflationary Consequences of Anticipated Macroeconomic Policies," *Rev. Econ. Stud.* 57, pp. 147–164.

Drazen, Allan and Vittorio Grilli. 1993. "The Benefits of Crises for Economic Reforms," *Amer. Econ. Rev.* 83, pp. 598–607.

Dornbusch, Rudiger. 1982. "Stabilization Policies in Developing Countries: What Have We Learned?" *World Devel.* 10, pp. 701–708.

Dornbusch, Rudiger, and Stanley Fischer. 1993. "Moderate Inflation," *World Bank Econ. Rev.* 7, pp. 1–44.

Dornbusch, Rudiger, Federico Sturzenegger, and Holger Wolf. 1990. "Extreme Inflation: Dynamics and Stabilization," *Brookings Pap. Econ. Act.* 2, pp. 1–84.

Easterly, William. 1996. "When Is Stabilization Expansionary? Evidence from High Inflation," *Econ. Pol.* 22, pp. 67–107.

Echenique, Federico, and Alvaro Forteza. 1997. "Are Stabilization Programs Expansionary?" mimeo, U.C. Berkeley and Universidad de la Republica Uruguay.

Evans, George W., and Seppo Honkapohja. 2001. *Learning and Expectations in Macroeconomics.* Princeton: Princeton U. Press.

Fauvel, Yvon, and Lucie Samson. 1991. "Intertemporal Substitution and Durable Goods: An Empirical Analysis," *Can. J. Econ.* 24, pp. 192–205.

Fernandez, Roque. 1985. "The Expectations Management Approach to Stabilization in Argentina, 1976–1982," *World Devel.* 13, pp. 871–892.

Fischer, Stanley. 1977. "Long-Term Contracts, Rational Expectations, and the Optimal Money Supply Rule," *J. Polit. Econ.* 85, pp. 191–205.

———. 1986. "Exchange Rate versus Money Targets in Disinflation," in *Indexing, Inflation, and Economic Policy.* S. Fischer, ed. Cambridge, MA: MIT Press, pp. 247–269.

———. 1993. "The Role of Macroeconomic Factors in Growth," *J. Monet. Econ.* 32, pp. 482–512.

———. 1996. "Why Are Central Banks Pursuing Long-Run Price Stability?" in *Achieving Price Stability.* Fed. Reserve Bank Kansas City, pp. 7–34.

Fischer, Stanley, Ratna Sahay, and Carlos A. Végh. 1996. "Stabilization and Growth in Transition Economies: The Early Experience," *J. Econ. Perspect.* 10, pp. 45–66.

———. 1997. "From Transition to Market: Evidence and Growth Prospects," in *Lessons from the Economic Transition.* Salvatore Zecchini, ed. Norwell, MA: Kluver Academic Pub., pp. 79–102.

Fisher, Willard C. 1913. "The Tabular Standard in Massachusetts History," *Quart. J. Econ.* 27, pp. 417–420.

Frenkel, Jacob A. 1977. "The Forward Exchange Rate, Expectations, and the Demand for Money: The German Hyperinflation," *Amer. Econ. Rec.* 67, pp. 653–670.

———. 1979. "Further Evidence on Expectations and the Demand for Money during the German Hyperinflation," *J. Monet. Econ.* 5, pp. 81–96.

Friedman, Milton. 1963. *Inflation: Causes and Consequences.* Bombay: Asia Pub. House.

Garber, Peter M. 1982. "Transition from Inflation to Price Stability," *Carnegie-Rochester Conf. Ser. Public Pol.* 16, pp. 887–912.

Ghezzi, Piero. 2001. "Backward-Looking Indexation, Credibility, and Inflation Persistence," *J. Int. Econ.* 53, pp. 127–147.

Gordon, Robert J. 1982. "Why Stopping Inflation May Be Costly: Evidence from Fourteen Historical Episodes," in *Inflation: Causes and Effects*. Robert E. Hall, ed. Chicago: U. Chicago Press, pp. 11–40.

Gould, David M. 1996. "Does the Choice of Nominal Anchor Matter?" work. paper 96–11, Fed. Reserve Bank Dallas.

Graham, Frank. 1930. *Exchange, Prices, and Production in Hyperinflation: Germany, 1920–1923.* Princeton: Princeton U. Press.

Hamann, Javier. 2001. "Exchange-Rate-Based Stabilization: A Critical Look at the Stylized Facts," *IMF Staff Pap.* 48, pp. 111–138.

Hamilton, Earl. 1936. "Prices and Wages at Paris under John Law's System," *Quart. J. Econ.* 51, pp. 42–70.

———. 1965. *American Treasure and the Price Revolution in Spain, 1501–1560.* Cambridge, MA: Harvard U. Press.

Hamilton, James D. 1994. *Time Series Analysis.* Princeton: Princeton U. Press.

Henry, Peter. 2002. "Is Disinflation Good for the Stock Market?" *J. Finance* 57:4, pp. 1617–1648.

Huang, Andrew C. 1948. "The Inflation in China," *Quart. J. Econ.* 62, pp. 562–575.

Kemmerer, Edward. 1940. *Inflation and Revolution, Mexico's Experience of 1912–1917.* Princeton: Princeton U. Press.

Khan, Mohsin S., and Abdelhak S. Senhadji. 2000. "Threshold Effects in the Relationship between Inflation and Growth," work. paper 00/110, IMF.

Kiguel, Miguel, and Nissan Liviatan. 1992. "The Business Cycle Associated with Exchange Rate-Based Stabilization," *World Bank Econ. Rev.* 6, pp. 279–305.

Kydland, Finn E., and Carlos E. Zarazaga. 1997. "Is the Business Cycle of Argentina Different?" *Econ. Rev.* 4th quarter, Fed. Reserve Bank Dallas, pp. 21–36.

Lahiri, Amartya. 2000. "Disinflation Programs under Policy Uncertainty," *J. Int. Econ.* 50, pp. 351–373.

———. 2001. "Exchange Rate Based Stabilization under Real Frictions: The Role of Endogenous Labor Supply," *J. Econ. Dynam. Control*, 25, pp. 1157–1177.

Laidler, David E., and George W. Stadler. 1998. "Monetary Explanations of the Weimar Republic's Hyperinflation: Some Neglected Contributions in Contemporary German Literature," *J. Money, Credit, Banking*, 30, pp. 816–831.

Leiderman, Leonardo. 1993. *Inflation and Disinflation: The Israeli Experiment.* Chicago: U. Chicago Press.

Lerner, Eugene M. 1955. "Money, Prices and Wages in the Confederacy, 1861–1865," *J. Polit. Econ.* 62, pp. 562–575.

Lucas, Robert E. 1972. "Expectations and the Neutrality of Money," *J. Econ. Theory* 4, pp. 3–24.

Lui, Francis T. 1983. "Cagan's Hypothesis and the First Nationwide Inflation of Paper Money in World History," *J. Polit. Econ.* 91, pp. 1067–1074.

Marcet, Albert, and Juan Pablo Nicolini. 1998. "Recurrent Hyperinflations and Learning," CEPR discus. paper 1875.

Marcet, Albert, and Thomas J. Sargent. 1995. "Speed of Convergence of Recursive Least Squares Learning with ARMA Perceptions," in *Learning and Rationality in Economics*. Alan Kirman and Mark Salmon, eds. Oxford: Basil Blackwell, pp. 179–215.

Marimon, Ramon, and Shyam Sunder. 1993. "Indeterminacy of Equilibria in a Hyperinflationary World: Experimental Evidence," *Econometrica* 61, pp. 1073–1107.

Mendoza, Enrique, and Martin Uribe. 1999. "Devaluation Risk and the Syndrome of Exchange-Rate-Based Stabilizations," work. paper 7014, NBER.

Montiel, Peter. 1989. "Empirical Analysis of High-Inflation Episodes in Argentina, Brazil, and Israel," *IMF Staff Pap.* 36, pp. 527–549.

Okun, Arthur M. 1978. "Efficient Disinflationary Policies," *Amer. Econ. Rve. Pap. Proceed.* 68, pp. 348–352.

Paal, Beatrix. 2000. "Measuring the Inflation of Parallel Currencies: An Empirical Reevaluation of the Second Hungarian Hyperinflation," mimeo, Stanford U.

Paarlberg, Don. 1993. *An Analysis and History of Inflation*. Westport: Praeger.

Pazos, Felipe. 1972. *Chronic Inflation in Latin America*. NY: Praeger.

Persson, Torsten, and Guido Tabellini. 1990. *Macroeconomic Policy, Credibility and Politics*. Chur, Switzerland: Harwood Academic Pub.

Rebelo, Sergio. 1997. "What Happens When Countries Peg Their Exchange Rates? (The Real Side of Monetary Reforms)," work. paper 6168, NBER.

Rebelo, Sergio, and Carlos A. Végh. 1995. "Real Effects of Exchange Rate-Based Stabilizations: An Analysis of Competing Theories," *NBER Macroeconomics Annual*, pp. 125–174.

Reinhart, Carmen M., and Carlos A. Végh. 1994. "Inflation Stabilization in Chronic Inflation Countries," mimeo, IMF.

———. 1995a. "Do Exchange Rate-Based Stabilizations Carry the Seeds of Their Own Destruction?" mimeo, IMF.

———. 1995b. "Nominal Interest Rates, Consumption Booms, and Lack of Credibility: A Quantitative Examination," *J. Devel. Econ.* 46, pp. 357–378.

Reinhart, Carmen M., and Kenneth S. Rogoff. 2002. "FDI to Africa: The Role of Price Stability and Currency Instability," mimeo, IMF.

Rodriguez, Carlos A. 1982. "The Argentine Stabilization Plan of December 20th," *World Devel.* 10, pp. 801–811.

Rodrik, Dani. 1991. "Premature Liberalization, Incomplete Stabilization: The Ozal Decade in Turkey," in *Lessons of Economic Stabilization and Its Aftermath*. Michael Bruno, Stanley Fischer, Elhanan Helpman, and Nissan Liviatan, eds. Cambridge, MA: MIT Press, pp. 323–358.

Roldos, Jorge. 1995. "Supply-Side Effects of Disinflation Programs," *IMF Staff Pap.* 42, pp. 158–183.

———. 1997. "On Gradual Disinflation, the Real Exchange Rate, and the Current Account," *J. Int. Money Finance* 16, pp. 37–54.

Sarel, Michael. 1996. "Nonlinear Effects of Inflation on Economic Growth," *IMF Staff Pap.* 43, pp. 199–215.

Sargent, Thomas J. 1982. "The Ends of Four Big Hyperinflations," in *Inflation: Causes and Consequences.* Robert E. Hall, ed. Chicago: U. Chicago Press, pp. 41–97.

Sargent, Thomas J., and Francois R. Velde. 1995. "Macroeconomic Features of the French Revolution," *J. Polit. Econ.* 103, pp. 474–518.

Sargent, Thomas J., and Neil Wallace. 1973. "Rational Expectations and the Dynamics of Hyperinflation," *Int. Econ. Rev.* 14, pp. 328–350.

———. 1981. "Some Unpleasant Monetarist Arithmetic," *Fed. Reserve Bank Minnesota Quart. Rev.* 5, pp. 1–17.

Sims, Christopher. 2001. "Discussion of Cogley and Sargent's 'Evolving Post–World War II Inflation Dynamics'," forthcoming in *NBER Macroeconomics Annual.*

Stock, James H. 2001. "Discussion of Cogley and Sargent's 'Evolving Post–World War II Inflation Dynamics'," forthcoming in *NBER Macroeconomics Annual.*

Stockman, Alan. 1981. "Anticipated Inflation and the Capital Stock in a Cash-in-Advance Economy," *J. Monet. Econ.* 8, pp. 387–393.

Taylor, John B. 1979. "Staggered Wage Setting in a Macro Model," *Amer. Econ. Rev. Pap. Proceed.* 69, pp. 108–113.

———. 1980. "Aggregate Dynamics and Staggered Contracts," *J. Polit. Econ.* 88, pp. 1–23.

———. 1998. "Monetary Policy Guidelines for Employment and Inflation Stability," in *Inflation, Unemployment, and Monetary Policy.* Robert M. Solow and John B. Taylor, eds. Cambridge: MIT Press, pp. 29–54.

Uribe, Martin. 1997. "Exchange-Rate-Based Inflation Stabilization: The Initial Real Effects of Credible Plans," *J. Monet. Econ.* 39: 197–221.

Végh, Carlos A. 1989. "Government Spending and Inflationary Finance: A Public Finance Approach," *IMF Staff Pap.* 36, pp. 657–677.

———. 1992. "Stopping High Inflation: An Analytical Overview," *IMF Staff Pap.* 39, pp. 629–695.

Venegas-Martinez, Francisco. 2001. "Temporary Stabilization: A Stochastic Analysis," *J. Econ. Dynam. Control* 25, pp. 1429–1449.

Wicker, Elmus. 1986. "Terminating Hyperinflation in the Dismembered Hapsburg Monarchy," *Amer. Econ. Rev.* 76, pp. 350–364.

Woodford, Michael. 1990. "Learning to Believe in Sunspots," *Econometrica* 58, pp. 277–307.

Zarazaga, Carlos. 1993. "Hyperinflations and Moral Hazard in the Appropriation of Seigniorage," work. paper 93–26, Fed. Reserve Bank Philadelphia.

Following the period of high inflations in the 1970s and 1980s, many countries that succeeded in reducing inflation rates from more than 50 percent per annum became stuck with moderate inflation—defined as an inflation rate in the 15–30 percent per annum range. These moderate inflations seemed particularly difficult to end, possibly because they represented a political economy equilibrium in which the major distortions of high inflation had been removed, and the costs of moving to single digit inflation were feared to be too high.

Rudi Dornbusch and I worked on the topic of moderate inflations soon after I had left the World Bank in 1990. Our paper, published in the *World Bank Economic Review* in January 1993, examined experiences through 1990. After I arrived at the IMF, it became clear that policymakers in a number of countries experiencing moderate inflations—including the transition economies, particularly Hungary—were anxious to learn more about the phenomenon. Consequently David Burton of the IMF and I were asked to present a paper on moderate inflations at a conference organized by the National Bank of Hungary and the IMF in June 1997.

The paper is built around the conclusions of the Dornbusch-Fischer paper and twenty case studies of moderate inflation economies.[1] The twenty cases are summarized in table 10.2. They are categorized into four groups of five countries each: countries that ended moderate inflation; countries with continued moderate inflation; transition countries with moderate inflation; and countries that succeeded in stabilizing from high inflation without getting stuck in the moderate range.

The eight main lessons drawn from these experiences are summarized in the concluding section of the paper. Taken together they argue that moderate inflation can be overcome but that there is no single magic formula for doing so—perseverance in the application of reasonable macroeconomic policies, combined with attention to structural factors, and taking advantage of favorable shocks when they occur, all help.

Rather than revisit each of the lessons, let me briefly look at the subsequent experiences of the ten countries that were then—in late 1996—still undergoing moderate inflations. Four of the five countries described in table 10.2 as experiencing "Continued Moderate Inflation"—Colombia, Costa Rica, Israel, and Mexico—now have inflation in the single digits or around 11–12 percent per annum and no longer suffer from moderate inflation. Perhaps most striking, Colombia, which had been in the moderate inflation range for nearly three decades, ended its double-digit inflation in 2000.

In each case the inflation rate came down as a result of sustained anti-inflationary policies, rather than an attempt at shock therapy. The fifth country that fell in that category in 1996, Ecuador, went the other way, with inflation rising each year between 1996 and 2000, as the government's ability to control the economy diminished and macroeconomic instability increased. In January 2000, in desperation, Ecuador instituted a currency board. Because the initial exchange rate was heavily undervalued, inflation continued at high rates for over two years, but is expected to decline to single digits in 2003.

The five transition economies listed in table 10.2 as suffering from moderate inflation in 1996—Estonia, Hungary, Latvia, Moldova, and Poland—had all reached single digit inflation by 2001. Impressively, the transition economies had vanquished moderate inflation within little more than a decade of setting out to become market economies. No doubt the global decline in inflation in the late 1990s helped.

Thus the problem of moderate inflation, which seemed so intractable in 1996, no longer besets most of the countries that were then concerned about it. Most of those countries ended their moderate inflations rather quickly. But the problem has not disappeared; a few countries still are struggling with moderate inflation rates that they want to end. Among them is Russia, which, because of its large current account surplus, has in essence to deal with the capital inflows problem described in chapter 10.

Given the virtual disappearance of the moderate inflation problem, I considered whether to omit this paper from the volume. It is included because the political economy argument that says a little more inflation is relatively costless is still potent, and we could see pressures to allow more inflation recurring in a slow-growth environment. I hope that the experiences studied in this paper would help prevent acceptance of the inflationary route—and that if the phenomenon of moderate inflation nonetheless reoccurs, the paper may prove useful to countries that decide later (and it will be all of them) that they want to go back to low inflation.

Note

1. Appendix 1 of the original paper, "Background Notes on Country Experiences," which provides details on economic developments in the twenty cases, is not reproduced here but is available in the original publication, Carlo Cottarelli and Gyorgi Szapary (eds.) *Moderate Inflation: The Experience of Transition Economies*, Washington, D.C.: IMF and National Bank of Hungary, 1998.

10   Ending Moderate Inflations

David Burton and Stanley Fischer

Many countries have had great difficulty reducing inflation from moderate (low double-digit) rates to single-digit rates. Dornbusch and Fischer (1993) studied moderate inflation, which they defined as an inflation rate that remains in the range of 15–30 percent a year for at least three years. They analyzed the mechanisms that permit such inflations to continue and make them difficult to end while also examining—including in a number of case studies—the policies needed to end them.

In this paper, we update their results and focus on the question of how to end moderate inflations. Dornbusch and Fischer listed 55 episodes of moderate inflation, on the basis of inflation data for 131 countries listed in the IMF's *International Financial Statistics*, with data ending in 1989 or 1990 and generally going back to the 1960s, but in some cases to the 1950s.[1] They then presented case studies for eight countries—Chile, Colombia, Mexico, Brazil, Indonesia, Ireland, Korea, and Spain—of which the first three were suffering from moderate inflation, and the last four had experienced moderate inflation and had succeeded in reducing inflation to low levels. At that time, Brazil had moved from moderate to high inflation.

There have been 13 episodes of moderate inflation, as defined by Dornbusch and Fischer, over the period 1990–1996 (table 10.1). Only 5 (Haiti, Honduras, Kenya, Tanzania, and Zimbabwe) were in countries that had not previously experienced moderate inflations. The most persistent moderate inflations in this decade have been in Colombia and Hungary; the most persistent moderate inflation in the past half-century has been in Colombia, where inflation was in that range from 1973 to 1996 except for two years (1977 and 1991) in which it rose marginally above 30 percent. Slightly easing the definition of an episode of moderate inflation, table 10.1 shows 19

Table 10.1
Episodes of moderate inflation, 1990–1996

Country	Period	Number of years	Period-average inflation Two years before	During	Two years after[1]
			(Episodes of three or more years)		
Africa					
Kenya	1990–92	3	12.1	21.7	37.4
Sierra Leone	1993–96	4	84.1	23.9	...
Tanzania	1991–93	3	30.8	25.3	30.8
Zimbabwe	1993–96	4	32.7	23.5	...
Western Hemisphere					
Colombia	1992–96	5	29.8	22.9	...
Ecuador	1994–96	3	49.7	24.9	...
Haiti	1990–93	4	5.5	19.7	34.0
Honduras	1994–96	3	9.8	25.0	...
Paraguay	1991–94	4	32.3	19.6	11.6
Other					
Greece	1990–92	3	13.6	18.6	12.7
Hungary	1992–96	5	31.6	23.2	...
Iran, Islamic Rep. of	1991–93	3	15.0	21.3	40.6
Myanmar	1994–96	3	26.9	21.9	...
			(Two-year episodes)		
Africa					
Algeria	1990–91	2	7.6	21.3	26.1
	1993–94	2	28.8	24.8	32.2 (1)
Burundi	1995–96	2	12.3	22.9	...
Central African Rep.	1994–95	2	−2.2	21.9	...
Ghana	1993–94	2	14.1	24.9	54.2
Lesotho	1991–92	2	13.2	17.4	10.7
Malawi	1992–93	2	12.2	21.2	59.0
Tanzania	1995–96	2	29.7	24.2	...
Zimbabwe	1990–91	2	10.2	20.4	34.8
Asia					
China	1994–95	2	10.5	20.6	8.3 (1)
Nepal	1991–92	2	8.5	16.4	7.9
Western Hemisphere					
Costa Rica	1995–96	2	11.7	20.4	...
Haiti	1995–96	2	32.6	21.3	...
Nicaragua	1992–93	2	5,215.2	22.0	9.4
Suriname	1990–91	2	4.0	23.9	93.6

Table 10.1
(continued)

			Period-average inflation		
Country	Period	Number of years	Two years before	During	Two years after[1]
Countries in transition					
Estonia	1995–96	2	68.3	26.0	. . .
Latvia	1995–96	2	72.5	21.9	. . .
Moldova[2]	1995–96	2	558.9	26.9	. . .
Poland	1995–96	2	35.1	23.9	. . .

Source: IMF, *International Financial Statistics*.
Note: In this table, an episode of moderate inflation is defined as a period of at least two consecutive years of inflation between 15 percent and 30 percent.

Length of Spell	Number of Spells	Percent
2	19	59.4
3	7	21.9
4	4	12.5
5	2	6.3
Total	32	100.0

1. Number in parentheses represents number of years (if less than two) for which a period average is computed.
2. Moldova's inflation during 1995 and 1996 was 30.2 and 23.5, respectively.

episodes in 17 countries between 1990 and 1996 in which the inflation rate was in the 15–30 percent range for two years. Five of these episodes took place in transition countries (including China).

In the group of eight countries for which Dornbusch and Fischer presented case studies, Brazil and Chile have now succeeded in reducing inflation to the single-digit range, Brazil in spectacular fashion from a very high inflation rate without a prolonged period in the moderate range. Of that group, only Colombia continued to experience moderate inflation; in Mexico, inflation was moderate in 1990 and then declined to single digits, and is now back in the moderate range as a result of the inflation following the devaluation and stabilization since 1995. In addition, Costa Rica, where inflation was in the moderate range in 1990, has not yet succeeded in reaching single digits. Other countries that were suffering from moderate inflation at that time have succeeded in reducing it below that range, often with great difficulty and, in some cases—such as Israel—with inflation

Table 10.2
Countries studied

Ended moderate inflation	Continued moderate inflation	Transition countries with moderate inflation	Stabilized from high inflation without getting stuck
Chile	Colombia	Estonia	Argentina
Egypt	Costa Rica	Hungary	Brazil
Iceland	Ecuador	Latvia	Croatia
Kenya	Israel	Moldova	Peru
Paraguay	Mexico	Poland	Slovenia

not yet safely in the single-digit range. Yet other economies, including some transition economies, succeeded in stabilizing from high inflations without getting stuck in the moderate inflation range.

In the first section, we review the theoretical framework set out by Dornbusch and Fischer, singling out elements that deserve emphasis in analyzing the problem of ending moderate inflations. In the second section, we very briefly discuss the economic costs of moderate inflation. In the third section, we present data and background information on the 20 country case studies examined in this paper, attempting to draw the lessons from these country experiences. The countries are grouped into four categories, listed in table 10.2: those that ended moderate inflations; those in which moderate inflations continue; transition economies with moderate inflation rates; and countries that reached the single-digit range without getting stuck.[2] The main lessons and conclusions about the roles of different factors in the moderate inflation process are summarized in the final section. (Background notes summarizing economic developments for the 20 countries studied are available in Appendix 1 of Burton and Fischer (1998).)

Analytic Framework

Dornbusch and Fischer classified theories of persistent inflation into those that emphasize seigniorage as a source of government revenue and those that emphasize the costs of ending inflation. They included among the seigniorage models game theory models of inflation, in which the motive for inflation may be interpreted either as seigniorage or as an attempt (which in equilibrium cannot succeed) to use surprise inflation to drive unemployment below the natural rate. They placed relatively little weight on the seigniorage motive for inflation, even though in several cases studied seigniorage amounted to over 2 percent of GDP and about 10 percent of total government revenues.

At the least, these cases suggest that the seigniorage motive should not be ignored, both because it typically takes a major effort to raise revenues by even 1 percent of GDP and even more because financing budget deficits has been problematic, especially in economies without developed capital markets. Furthermore, the notion of seigniorage should be broadened to include other benefits that inflation may provide for the government. For instance, in some countries, inflation appears to subsidize a politically powerful financial sector.[3] Or, credits supplied at the direction of the government might not appear explicitly in the government accounts, even though they are an inflationary element in the economy.[4] Experience in many economies certainly points in the direction of a credit-creation motive for inflation where the provision of subsidized credit is not recognized in the budget.

In discussing the approach according to which inflation continues because it is too costly to end, Dornbusch and Fischer present a simple Phillips curve-cum-markup-pricing-based model. With some manipulation, the pricing equation presents a useful way of thinking about the disinflation process:

$$\pi = \pi_{-1} + \alpha(w - \pi_{-1}) + (1 - \alpha)(e - \pi_{-1}) + \psi, \tag{1}$$

where π is the inflation rate, w is the rate of change of wages, e is the rate of depreciation, and ψ is an adverse supply or productivity shock (which can also be interpreted as the markup of prices over the costs of labor and imported inputs).

We take each element in turn:

• The rate of wage inflation can be reduced below lagged inflation through restrictive macroeconomic policy—that is, by using the Phillips trade-off to force wage reductions through higher unemployment. Alternatively, to the extent that wages are based on expected inflation and policymakers' announcements are credible, the rate of wage inflation could be reduced without creating higher unemployment by the announcement of a policy designed to reduce inflation. But in the situation in which moderate inflation has continued for some time, the credibility of policymakers' announcements is likely to be low.

• Equation (1) also shows the importance of wage indexation for inflationary inertia. If wages are fully indexed to past inflation—explicitly or implicitly—disinflation will get no leverage from wage behavior. This suggests the importance of finding a method of ending backward wage indexation if it does exist, possibly through incomes policy.

• The rate of inflation can be reduced to the extent that the rate of depreciation of the exchange rate falls below the lagged inflation rate. This route suggests the possibility of exchange-rate-based stabilizations.

• The last term, ψ, represents a supply shock. Favorable supply shocks have often played a useful role in disinflations, and adverse supply shocks have sometimes led to the failures of stabilization attempts.

Equation (1) may make it seem that either a real wage increase or a real appreciation is inevitable in a disinflation. Those tendencies are indeed present, but they are not inevitable. If a disinflation is pre-announced and fully credible and if wages are set in a forward-looking manner, both the rate of wage change and the rate of depreciation can be reduced to the same extent as the inflation rate. This points to the possible gains from a fully coordinated approach to disinflation.

Nonetheless, given that inflations rarely decelerate instantly, the use of a fixed exchange rate anchor is likely to be accompanied by an appreciation during the stabilization process. This is the reasoning behind the argument that the exchange rate should be over-depreciated at the start of an exchange-rate-based stabilization. It also means that countries in which the equilibrium real exchange rate is appreciating over time—as it typically is in transition economies—should be able to use the appreciation to help speed disinflation.

Aggregate Demand: Getting the Fundamentals Right

Equation (1) represents only one equation on the cost side of the inflationary process. However, it is probably necessary to state the obvious: that the other blade of the scissors, the determinants and dynamics of aggregate demand, is no less important in determining the rates of inflation and growth. In particular, no amount of credibility, incomes policy, de-indexation, exchange rate pegs, or any other device will succeed in bringing down inflation over a sustained period if the fundamentals of the budget and money growth are not consistent with a low-inflation equilibrium.

The Problem of Capital Inflows

In the presence of inflationary inertia, a country trying to disinflate will generally need a nominal interest rate higher than that implied by nominal interest rate parity. As the country's stabilization gains credibility, it is likely to suffer from a capital inflow problem, which tends to create appreciation and may push the current account to what markets view as an unsustainable level. The problem is likely to be exacerbated when the country is using a nominal exchange rate peg, be it a fixed or a crawling rate. This is one of the classic dilemmas of stabilization policy and one of the potentially adverse consequences of sticking too long to an exchange rate peg when inflation is slow to decline.

The policy dilemmas posed by the capital inflow problem are well known. If, as in many countries, the current account deficit is already large, allowing a real revaluation may lead to a larger current account deficit than appears sustainable; or it may provide disincentives to exporters that are not consistent with export-led growth. But continuation of the capital inflow leads to inflationary pressures that hinder the disinflation process.

The classic and fundamental prescription is to tighten fiscal policy. This is the preferred approach because it will make it possible to operate with both lower interest rates and a less appreciated currency. However, governments may find it politically difficult to tighten fiscal policy and will seek other solutions. Sterilization of the inflows is often effective for a short period, but, absent a more fundamental policy correction, may become increasingly expensive and therefore nonsustainable. Market-based measures to discourage capital inflows—for instance, special reserve requirements against short-term external-inflow-based deposits in the banking system—may also be effective for short periods, but the incentives to circumvent such regulations often lead to the need for continued tightening of the regulations over time. However, some countries that never fully liberalized the capital account, such as Chile, have used such controls to good effect over quite long periods.

It is often suggested that a country using an exchange rate anchor facing a capital inflow problem should widen its exchange rate band to increase uncertainty for short-term investors. To the extent that the capital inflows reflect long-term investments and fundamentals, such a broadening will likely lead to an appreciation. However, if the inflows are short-term "hot money," benefiting from the one-way bet offered by high domestic interest rates and the exchange rate peg, then a broadening of the band *could*, by increasing uncertainty about the dollar rate of return on the inflow, reduce the inflows and even lead to a depreciation.

Relative Price Adjustments

The Dornbusch and Fischer model does not explicitly include relative price changes, an element that has been important in the inflationary process especially in transition economies (see Coorey, Mecagni, and Offerdal, 1996; and Halpern and Wyplosz, 1996). In the presence of downward wage and price inflexibility, raising the relative prices of hitherto underpriced goods and services, particularly energy, has contributed to inflation. Such price changes could be interpreted in equation (1) as adverse supply shocks, but in a fuller model the budgetary consequences of the failure to raise these prices would be taken into account.

Credibility and Institutions

Dornbusch and Fischer discuss game theory models of inflation as belonging to the seigniorage (broadly defined) class of models. However, the models to which they refer may more accurately be regarded as a blend of two categories: seigniorage and "inflation too costly to end," because they include a seigniorage motive for inflation along with an expectational Phillips curve that can make it costly to end an inflation. In some cases, the game theory models do not include an explicit seigniorage motive but, along Barro-Gordon lines, attribute inflation to the government's attempts to maintain output at a level above the natural rate; in these cases, the game theory models belong to the too-costly-to-end category.

The various game theory models of inflation all have an important role for private sector expectations of inflation and thus for the credibility of government announcements. Some models include dual equilibria, one with low inflation. All these models point in the direction of policies or institutional changes (such as central bank independence) that will increase the credibility of government promises of low inflation.[5]

This discussion points to the following key factors to consider in pursuing disinflation:

• the need for the underlying macroeconomic policies to be consistent with a low-inflation equilibrium;

• the need to reduce seigniorage, broadly defined as the benefits to the government from inflation;

• the behavior of wages and other costs;

• indexation and other sources of inflationary inertia, pointing to a possible role for incomes policy and a coordinated attempt to reduce inflation;

• the behavior of the exchange rate and the possibility of an exchange rate peg;

• the capital inflow problem;

• the role of relative price adjustments; and

• possible institutional measures to increase the credibility of macroeconomic policy.

To conclude this section, we return to a point implied by Dornbusch and Fischer's categorization of theories according to the motive for inflation. Inflation does not happen out of a clear blue sky. It is serving some political economy purpose in each country where it continues. In seeking to end inflation, policymakers should try to understand what purpose its continuation serves and try to reduce or resist the pressures coming from that source.

The Costs of Inflation

Dornbusch and Fischer do not explicitly discuss the costs of moderate inflations; rather, they take for granted that such inflations should eventually be ended. The costs of inflation are extensively discussed in Fischer (1994). They include a variety of allocative costs, starting from those represented by the area under the demand curve for money, and including distortionary costs that arise from the failure to index tax and other laws and regulations for inflation. These costs are all present in an economy suffering from moderate inflation; and they imply social costs that could amount to several percentage points of GDP if inflation is in the moderate range.[6] These costs are reason enough to seek to end inflation.

The alternative of pervasive indexation of the economy is less attractive, both because the mechanisms of indexation are cumbersome and are a burden on resources and because some types of indexation operating in an economy that already includes distortions may lead to a worse equilibrium, with higher inflation and higher social costs.[7] Of the two economies that in the 1970s were thought to have been most successful in using indexation to reduce the costs of inflation, Brazil later succumbed to hyperinflation, and in Israel inflation rose to very high levels. Both subsequently had to implement stabilization programs to reduce inflation to more manageable rates.

The relationship between inflation and growth has been the subject of many studies. There is no disagreement that high rates of inflation are bad for growth. There is also general agreement that no statistically significant relationship exists between inflation and growth at low inflation rates. The question is where the break is located. Most studies find the negative relationship between inflation and growth continuing as long as inflation remains in the double-digit range, that is, including moderate rates of inflation. Sarel (1996) locates the break at an annual inflation rate of 8 percent. Bruno and Easterly (1995) are often taken to imply that the break is at 40 percent a year; however, a careful reading of their work suggests rather that the negative relationship is much stronger when inflation is higher than 40 percent and that the break may well be at a lower inflation rate. Neither they nor anyone else has presented reasons for thinking that double-digit inflation is good for growth.

Our conclusion is that there is no evidence to support the view that maintaining moderate (low double-digit) rates of inflation is good for growth and that the weight of the evidence is that double-digit rates of inflation are bad for growth.[8]

Case Studies

In this section, we summarize the information on the inflationary process in the 20 case study countries on which this paper is based, and that are summarized in Appendix 1 of Burton and Fischer (1998). In so doing, we attempt to draw out common features and lessons from experience. Annual inflation rates for the 20 countries over the past 12 years are shown in the figures in the appendix.

Countries That Ended Moderate Inflation

The most important point established by these case studies is that it is possible to end moderate inflations, and decisively so—for in four of the five countries, 12-month inflation in early 1997 was well below 10 percent (table 10.3).[9] The disinflation process in these countries varied widely: in Egypt, Iceland, and Paraguay, inflation declined from 20 percent to single digits within two to three years; the process in Chile was more gradual, while in Kenya the inflation rate rose above the moderate range to 46 percent in 1993 and then fell rapidly to 1 percent by 1995. There is no obvious growth cost of disinflation in these countries, with average growth in the last two years being above the average for the past 12 years.

Kenya appears to be different from the other countries in this group. The moderate inflation does not appear to have been deep-seated, with both annual and monthly inflation rates being far more variable than in the other four countries. Indeed, early in 1997, the 12-month inflation rate moved back above 15 percent, reflecting the effects of drought on food prices; the underlying inflation rate remained well below 10 percent. The greater variability in inflation evident in Kenya is present in several other African countries that have experienced moderate inflations. It appears to be the result of the heavy weight of agricultural products in the price basket. It may also result from the relatively low weight of the wage bill in the modern sector in GDP.

The fiscal situation in each of the countries in this group has been at least reasonably strong in recent years. The government budget deficit was decisively reduced over the period 1985–1997 in Chile, Egypt, and Kenya, but no clear pattern of deficit reduction emerged in Iceland and Paraguay. There have been budget surpluses in recent years in Chile and Paraguay. Seigniorage in Egypt was very high in 1985, but average direct seigniorage revenues in the last two years amounted to less than 1 percent of GDP for this group of countries. In Chile, Egypt, Kenya, and Paraguay, the stabilization from moderate inflation was accompanied by an appreciation of the real effective exchange rate, which was particularly marked for Chile and Egypt.

Exchange rate management also played an important part in the policy mix in these countries (see table 10.4). The exchange rate

Table 10.3
Macroeconomic performance in countries that ended moderate inflation

	Annual percent change				Percent of GDP			Exchange rates	
		CPI							
	Real GDP	Annual average	End of period	M1	General government balance[1]	Current account balance	Seign-iorage[2]	Real effective (1990 = 100)	Nominal vis-à-vis U.S. dollar (percent change)
Chile									
1985	3.5	30.7	26.4	22.7	-3.6	-8.2	0.7	136.9	63.3
1986	5.6	19.5	17.4	40.7	-1.6	-6.7	0.9	115.6	19.9
1987	6.6	19.9	21.5	25.2	0.0	-3.6	0.7	107.1	13.7
1988	7.3	14.7	12.7	22.4	4.0	-1.0	0.8	100.8	11.7
1989	9.9	17.0	21.4	17.5	6.1	-2.5	0.7	103.2	9.0
1990	3.3	26.0	27.3	22.6	3.5	-1.8	0.6	100.0	14.2
1991	7.3	21.7	18.7	44.3	2.5	0.3	0.8	102.8	14.5
1992	11.0	15.5	12.7	29.7	3.0	-1.6	1.1	108.7	3.8
1993	6.3	12.7	12.2	20.6	2.2	-4.5	0.2	110.9	11.5
1994	4.2	11.4	8.9	20.6	2.2	-1.2	0.4	113.2	4.0
1995	8.5	8.2	8.2	23.5	4.0	0.2	0.5	119.6	-5.6
1996	5.8	7.4	6.6	11.8	2.8	-3.5	0.5	123.8	3.9
Egypt[3]									
1985	4.8	16.9	11.4	17.7	-22.8	-13.7	6.1	143.9	0.0
1986	4.2	25.1	28.0	4.6	-17.1	-10.1	2.0	138.4	0.0
1987	4.0	14.2	13.5	2.5	-19.9	-17.9	-0.4	129.9	0.0
1988	3.0	20.2	21.9	10.2	-18.1	-14.3	2.3	97.0	0.0

1989	2.4	21.2	28.5	6.0	-18.4	-12.5	1.1	103.4	23.8
1990	2.1	19.5	7.2	17.0	-15.2	-7.9	2.8	103.0	78.8
1991	0.3	21.1	25.8	10.8	-4.2	-2.8	3.2	96.6	102.5
1992	0.5	11.2	9.3	20.2	-3.5	-8.9	4.8	102.0	5.9
1993	2.9	9.0	9.7	8.9	-2.1	-6.3	1.9	117.0	0.9
1994	3.2	9.4	12.0	16.8	-1.3	-4.6	3.1	121.2	1.0
1995	4.2	7.2	13.1	8.4	-1.3	-5.8	1.6	120.0	0.2
1996	5.0	6.2	5.4	6.7	-0.8	-6.2	1.2	128.3	0.0
Iceland[4]									
1985	3.3	31.7	35.9	33.7	-1.7	-3.9	1.7	98.2	31.0
1986	6.2	21.9	13.6	42.2	-4.0	0.6	2.2	97.9	-1.0
1987	8.6	17.7	24.3	40.4	-0.9	-3.4	0.7	105.8	-5.9
1988	-0.1	25.8	20.6	16.6	-2.0	-3.5	0.7	110.8	11.2
1989	0.2	20.8	25.2	27.6	-4.6	-1.4	1.6	101.1	32.6
1990	1.2	15.5	7.2	35.8	-3.3	-2.2	-1.1	100.0	2.2
1991	1.2	6.8	7.5	13.8	-2.9	-4.7	0.4	102.4	1.2
1992	-3.4	4.0	1.5	13.8	-2.8	-3.1	-0.5	102.8	-2.5
1993	0.9	4.1	4.7	0.5	-4.5	0.1	-0.5	95.3	17.5
1994	3.5	1.6	0.5	10.5	-4.7	1.9	0.1	89.4	3.5
1995	1.2	1.7	2.0	6.0	-3.0	0.8	-0.2	89.0	-7.5
1996	5.7	2.3	2.6	11.1	-1.5	-1.9	0.8	89.3	2.8
Kenya[5]									
1985	4.3	13.0	10.2	-1.3	-5.4	-1.5	1.0	142.9	14.0
1986	7.1	4.8	6.0	35.6	-6.6	-1.0	2.5	124.8	-1.3
1987	5.9	7.6	8.3	8.0	-4.2	-6.4	1.5	115.5	1.4

Table 10.3
(continued)

| | Annual percent change | | | | Percent of GDP | | | Exchange rates | |
| | Real GDP | CPI | | M1 | General government balance[1] | Current account balance | Seign-iorage[2] | Real effective (1990 = 100) | Nominal vis-à-vis U.S. dollar (percent change) |
		Annual average	End of period						
1988	6.2	11.2	13.0	1.3	−4.7	−5.5	0.2	110.5	7.9
1989	4.7	12.9	12.9	13.0	−4.5	−7.6	1.2	108.8	15.9
1990	4.2	15.6	20.6	27.2	−5.7	−5.5	1.6	100.0	11.4
1991	1.4	19.8	14.4	15.0	−2.9	−1.8	1.3	98.0	20.0
1992	−0.8	29.5	37.4	47.1	−9.6	−1.3	4.3	102.6	17.1
1993	0.4	45.8	52.1	27.4	−6.4	2.8	5.1	89.4	80.0
1994	2.7	28.8	6.6	12.6	−1.1	0.9	2.8	112.2	−3.4
1995	4.9	1.5	6.7	3.8	−0.2	−4.4	3.9	111.1	−8.2
1996	4.2	9.0	11.0	13.9	−0.2	−0.4	…	108.6	11.1
Paraguay[6]									
1985	3.5	25.2	23.1	30.8	−2.9	−8.1	1.8	151.8	52.6
1986	0.0	31.8	24.1	27.7	0.3	−9.7	3.0	152.9	10.6
1987	4.3	21.8	32.0	42.5	0.7	−7.1	3.4	123.0	62.2
1988	6.4	23.0	16.9	25.2	1.0	−5.0	2.3	127.5	0.0
1989	5.8	26.0	28.5	46.7	3.1	0.4	3.0	97.6	92.0
1990	3.1	38.2	44.1	30.3	3.7	0.8	2.1	100.0	16.4
1991	2.5	24.9	11.8	28.6	1.0	−2.0	2.6	113.2	7.8
1992	1.8	15.5	17.8	28.4	−0.5	−2.2	3.3	109.6	13.2

1993	4.1	18.3	20.4	19.7	0.8	−1.1	2.0	110.1	16.3
1994	3.1	20.6	18.3	32.3	1.2	−3.5	2.6	112.9	9.6
1995	4.2	13.4	10.5	21.0	0.7	−4.1	2.0	113.8	3.1
1996	1.5	9.8	8.2	2.2	0.8	−3.0	0.4	118.8	4.7

Sources: National authorities; IMF, *International Financial Statistics*, and staff estimates.

1. Excludes municipal governments in Chile.
2. Defined as the first difference of reserve money over nominal GDP.
3. Data based on annual fiscal years; data for 1996/97 are projections; deposits at central bank are unremunerated.
4. Seigniorage is poor indicator of Iceland's seigniorage revenue because of the remuneration of deposit money bank reserves at the central bank and because of various changes in the mode of this remuneration (including interest and indexation) over the 1980s.
5. General government and current account balances are based on annual fiscal years.
6. Seigniorage not adjusted for remuneration of reserves.

Table 10.4
Selected countries: policy and other factors in inflationary process

	Fiscal policy	Exchange rate policy	Monetary policy	Capital inflows	Indexation	Incomes policy	Relative price adjustment	Other
Countries That Reduced Moderate Inflation								
Chile	Budget surplus since late 1980s.	Real rate rule; band appreciated on several occasions to help reduce inflation.	Targets real interest rates to control domestic expenditures. Policy generally directed toward reducing inflation.	Large throughout 1990s.	Wages, financial instruments, and exchange rate indexed.	Not a factor.	Not a significant factor.	Price- and non-price-based controls on capital inflows; shocks to terms of trade influenced inflationary process.
Egypt	Major fiscal adjustment underpinned stabilization.	Pegged throughout as nominal anchor.	Supporting role.	Episodes of large inflows; offset with sterilized intervention.	Not a factor.	Not a factor.	Not a factor.	Controls on capital inflows.
Iceland	Little change in fiscal position during stabilization; central bank financing curtailed.	Used as an anchor.	Supporting role.	Not a factor.	Not a significant factor.	Wage moderation through national agreements.	Not a significant factor.	Exogenous shocks important factor in inflationary process.

	Fiscal	Exchange rate	Monetary	Capital flows	Wage indexation	Incomes policy / social pact	Price liberalization	Other
Kenya	Substantial fiscal adjustment following external crisis of 1993; low deficit since then.	Flexible; financial policies at times directed to stabilizing rate.	Primary role in disinflation.	Erratic capital inflows; substantial sterilized intervention at times.	Not a factor.	Not a factor.	Price liberalization in maize market a factor.	Weather and terms of trade shocks significant factors. Reforms, including external liberalization, helped raise economic growth.
Paraguay	Budget in balance or surplus throughout 1990s.	Significant reduction in rate of depreciation in 1995 an important factor.	Tightening contributed to reduction in inflation in 1995.	Not a major factor in 1995–96.	Backward-looking wage indexation a factor.	Minor role in 1995–96.	Not a major factor in recent years.	Exogenous shocks, especially in agriculture, helped lower inflation.

Countries with Persistent Moderate Inflation

	Fiscal	Exchange rate	Monetary	Capital flows	Wage indexation	Incomes policy / social pact	Price liberalization	Other
Colombia	Not a major factor; some loosening in 1995–96.	Crawling band, with preannounced rate of crawl.	Supporting role; affected by inflows.	Important factor affecting monetary policy and current account.	Backward-looking wage indexation a major factor.	Social pact introduced in 1995—limited effectiveness.	Not a major factor.	Deeply entrenched inflation expectations.
Costa Rica	Unstable and relatively weak fiscal position; deteriorations linked to electoral cycle.	Real exchange rate rule.	Hampered by fiscal deficit and inflows.	Significant factor; partially sterilized.	Informal wage indexation in public and private sectors.	Not a factor.	Not a major factor.	Increase in value-added tax rate a factor in 1995.

Table 10.4
(continued)

	Fiscal policy	Exchange rate policy	Monetary policy	Capital inflows	Indexation	Incomes policy	Relative price adjustment	Other
Israel	Expansionary fiscal policy starting in 1994 hindered reduction in inflation.	Nominal anchor: first as peg, later as crawling band.	Tightened to fight inflation in 1994; sterilized intervention to counter inflows.	Large inflows starting in 1994.	Indexation contributed to inertia.	Not a factor.	Not a major factor.	Wages and housing prices affected by immigration; food prices affected by security situation.
Ecuador	Major reason for changes in inflation.	Generally flexible—used partially as an anchor in 1993–94.	Strongly influenced by fiscal policy.	Minor factor.	Secondary role.	Secondary role.	Administered price increases at times a factor.	Fiscal policy affected by exogenous shocks.
Mexico	Major factor behind initial stabilization; influenced later changes in inflation performance.	Used as nominal anchor through end-1994; flexible since.	Main tool for reducing inflation in 1995–96.	Inflows major factor in early 1990s; outflows triggered crisis.	Important factor prior to 1987.	"Social pact," which replaced indexation, important in controlling inflation.	Administered price increases minor factor.	Weak banking sector.
Countries That Reduced High Inflation Rapidly								
Argentina	Fiscal position strengthened over two years prior to Convertibility Plan.	Currency board.	Supporting role; remonetization and fall in interest rates as inflation declined.	Reflows of capital as confidence restored.	Indexation of austral-denominated contracts made illegal.	Freeze on public sector wages and prices.	Corrective price adjustments prior to stabilization.	Structural reforms to improve competitiveness.

Brazil	Small operational surplus at time of stabilization; fiscal stance subsequently weakened.	Anchor role following introduction of new currency.	Loosening in fiscal stance placed increasing burden on monetary policy.	Substantial inflows; exacerbated by imbalance between monetary and fiscal policy.	Backward indexation effectively eliminated prior to stabilization by denominating wages, prices, and financial transactions in new unit of account.	Following introduction of new currency, wages to remain fixed during contract period. Public prices fixed.	Prior denomination of prices and wages in unit of account designed to avoid relative price misalignments.	Most prices implicitly indexed to exchange rate before stabilization.
Croatia	Fiscal policy geared to avoiding domestic financing of budget.	Anchor role.	Supporting role.	Significant factor affecting monetary policy.	Abolished in 1993 in state sector.	Applies to government- and state-owned enterprises—important role.	Not a major factor.	
Peru	Substantial adjustment prior to stabilization, with need for domestic financing of public sector eliminated.	Floating; also unified. Initial real appreciation.	Anchor role, with sharp initial increase in real interest rates; substantial remonetization subsequently accommodated.	Large inflows; intervention, partially sterilized.	With hyperinflation, backward-looking indexation not viewed as a problem for stabilization.	Direct government intervention in wage setting eliminated.	Prices substantially liberalized at start of stabilization, causing surge in inflation.	Stabilization supported with substantial liberalization and reform; economy highly dollarized.
Slovenia	Restrained, with budget in overall balance since monetary independence.	Mostly flexible; used as anchor for short period.	Main anchor for much of the time.	Substantial at times, reflecting large interest differential.	Economy highly indexed.	Significant since 1994.	Significant effect at times.	Capital controls introduced in 1995.

Table 10.4
(continued)

Transition Economies

	Fiscal policy	Exchange rate policy	Monetary policy	Capital inflows	Indexation	Incomes policy	Relative price adjustment	Other
Estonia	Low deficit supported currency board.	Currency board.	Not a factor.	Primarily accommodative.	Not a factor.	Not a factor.	Major factor.	
Hungary	Important factor: first loosened, then tightened.	Shift from ad hoc adjustments to crawling band as anchor in 1995.	Supporting role.	Hindered disinflation in 1995–96.	Minor factor; no formal wage indexation.	Restriction of wages in state enterprises important in 1995.	Important factor.	
Latvia	Generally restrained— not a major factor.	Initially floating; pegged as anchor since 1994.	Initially, main anti-inflation instrument.	Not a major factor	Not a factor.	Not a factor.	Major factor.	Banking crisis in 1994–95 affected money demand and financial policies.
Moldova	Fiscal adjustment crucial for reduction in reliance on central bank financing.	Initially flexible, but increased weight given to exchange rate stability since 1995.	Stabilization money based, particularly until 1995.	Not a major factor.	Not a factor.	Not a significant factor.	Important factor.	Price level affected by drought in 1994.
Poland	A relatively weak fiscal position in early 1990s hampered disinflation.	Anchor role: peg replaced by crawling band.	Supporting role—evidence of independent effect on inflation.	Important factor— hampered monetary policy.	De facto wage indexation important factor.	Important factor, particularly in early 1990s.	Important factor.	

served as a nominal peg, or anchor, in all the countries except Chile and Kenya; in Chile, exchange rate management was directed at the real exchange rate. Indexation was widespread in Chile and insignificant in Egypt, and backward-looking wage indexation was a factor in Paraguay. Incomes policy played an important role in Iceland, but not elsewhere. It is significant that major relative price changes appear not to have been an important factor,[10] for their absence may well facilitate disinflation from a moderate level.

The Chilean case deserves special attention among this group of countries, for Chile apparently disinflated without a nominal anchor. As the more detailed description in appendix 10.1 makes clear, this is only partially true, for the inflation target was the nominal anchor. Chile actively used aggregate demand policy, particularly fiscal policy, but also monetary policy, to ensure that inflation kept on declining. It is this focus that enabled Chile to bring its inflation down from the moderate range while following a real exchange rate rule, and in the presence of pervasive indexation.

The experience of this group clearly illustrates that capital inflows can complicate matters for policymakers trying to stabilize. Inflows were a problem in four of the five countries, particularly so in Chile and Egypt. While Egypt managed to rely on sterilized intervention, this approach was expensive and generally cannot be the sole defense when the inflows are large. Chile also used capital controls, a widening of the exchange rate band, and appreciations of the band to cope with inflows. Strong fiscal positions helped both countries cope with the pressure of inflows.

Exogenous shocks played an important role in the inflationary process in several of these countries, for example, changes in agricultural prices in Kenya. In Paraguay, a fall in food prices, as a result of a good harvest, was a major factor in reducing inflation in 1995. In Chile, an improvement in the terms of trade in 1994 helped in managing exchange rate policy and with disinflation. These examples show that it is important to capitalize on favorable exogenous shocks, including through exchange rate appreciation. Iceland's experience in the 1970s and 1980s illustrates what happens when negative shocks are too freely accommodated.

Table 10.5 summarizes the behavior of macroeconomic variables in these five countries before and after their stabilization from moderate inflation. The only significant changes are in the fundamentals— the budget deficit and money growth. There was surprisingly little

Table 10.5
Macroeconomic performance of countries that ended moderate inflation (period averages)

	Before stabilization	After stabilization
Real GDP (percent change)	4.0	3.8
Inflation (period average)	21.0	7.5
Inflation (end of period)	20.2	8.1
M1 (percent change)	24.4	11.8
Government balance (ratio to GDP)	−4.0	−0.3
Current account balance (ratio to GDP)	−4.6	−3.0
Seigniorage (ratio to GDP)	1.8	1.5
Real effective exchange rate (1990 = 100)	111.2	111.9
Nominal exchange rate (percent change)	20.2	2.4

Sources: National authorities; IMF, *International Financial Statistics*, and staff estimates.
Note: The countries are Chile, Egypt, Iceland, Kenya, and Paraguay.

change in seigniorage. The real effective exchange rate did not change on average, but the current account improved slightly.

Nontransition Countries with Continued Moderate Inflation

Four Latin American countries—Colombia, Costa Rica, Ecuador, and Mexico—plus Israel make up this group of countries. Only Colombia and Ecuador are defined in table 10.1 as having experienced three-year episodes of moderate inflation, but the others have been fighting low double-digit inflation for some time.

As time goes by, Colombia is increasingly seen as the quintessential moderate-inflation country. Colombia's moderate inflation is into its third decade, and the expectation of its continuing is deeply ingrained despite the government's declared intention to the contrary. There has been some success in reducing inflation from just below 30 percent at the end of the 1980s to about 20 percent more recently. In comparison with other Latin American countries, GDP growth has been strong in Colombia, especially during the years of the debt crisis and into the first half of this decade. The budget deficit was small over most of the last decade, although it has begun to increase in the last year. Seigniorage revenue averaged about 2 percent of GDP for most of the last 12 years, but in the last 2 years has declined to less than 1 percent of GDP (tables 10.6 and 10.7). Inflation in Colombia therefore seems to be essentially inertial.

Inflation inertia stems both from expectations and from the indexation of labor contracts, which typically cover two years, with the second year's increase linked to the previous year's inflation. Labor contracts are not synchronized. Colombia has operated a crawling peg exchange rate system since 1967. It introduced a formal crawling band in 1994, with a width of 14 percent and a rate of crawl set on the basis of expected inflation differentials. Capital inflows began on a significant scale early in this decade, responding in part to financial liberalization. They have increased more recently: for much of 1996, the exchange rate was at the most appreciated part of the band, reflecting both short-term capital inflows based on high dollar rates of return and the implications for the country's economic prospects of major oil finds. The real effective exchange rate has appreciated substantially since 1990, and the current account has shifted to a deficit of more than 5 percent of GDP. A variety of restrictions have been imposed on capital movements since 1993.

Although policy has had the goal of gradually moving to low inflation, and monetary policy has been exercised to that end, Colombia's good growth performance has no doubt reduced the pressure for fighting inflation. That Colombia's inflation performance was better than that of many of its neighbors for a long time must also have made it easier to accept that living with inflation was the right choice, especially as it was combined with a better growth record. Improved growth and inflation performance in Argentina and Chile, as well as the superior inflation performance in Brazil, is most likely changing this evaluation.

Inflation in Costa Rica has fluctuated more than in Colombia, reflecting in part a four-year electoral cycle. Both fiscal and monetary policies have varied because of the accommodation of election-related spending, and seigniorage revenues have been large in some years. The current account deficit has also fluctuated widely. Costa Rica succeeded in reaching single-digit inflation in 1993, but the achievement was not cemented, and the budget deficit and money growth increased sharply in 1994.

Fiscal policy changes, responding in part to external shocks, have played a significant role in the inflationary process in Ecuador. Inflation was moderate in 1985–1987, but then rose to close to 100 percent as a result of policy changes driven by adverse oil price movements and an earthquake. Inflation stayed at about 50–60 percent through 1992, when renewed efforts were made to stabilize. These efforts brought inflation into the moderate range from 1994–

Table 10.6
Macroeconomic performance in countries with continued moderate inflation

| | | Annual percent change | | | Percent of GDP | | | Exchange rates | |
	Real GDP	CPI Annual average	CPI End of period	M1	General government balance[1]	Current account balance	Seign-iorage[2]	Real effective (1990 = 100)	Nominal vis-à-vis U.S. dollar (percent change)
Colombia									
1985	3.1	24.0	22.5	10.7	-4.2	-5.0		183.5	41.2
1986	5.8	18.9	20.9	43.5	-0.3	1.5	1.8	136.8	36.5
1987	5.4	23.3	24.0	30.3	-1.4	-0.2	1.9	122.0	24.9
1988	4.1	28.1	28.2	25.7	-1.8	-0.7	1.7	117.6	23.3
1989	3.4	25.9	26.1	23.4	-2.0	-0.4	1.7	113.4	27.9
1990	4.3	29.1	32.4	33.8	-0.7	1.4	1.6	100.0	31.3
1991	2.0	30.4	26.8	31.7	-1.0	5.4	3.1	102.9	26.0
1992	4.0	27.0	25.1	44.3	-0.6	1.8	3.1	112.0	19.9
1993	5.4	22.6	23.0	27.7	-0.8	-4.0	2.5	118.4	13.7
1994	5.8	23.8	23.4	27.4	-0.5	-4.7	2.1	132.7	-2.1
1995	5.4	21.0	19.5	23.1	-1.2	-5.4	0.9	134.5	8.0
1996	2.1	20.2	21.3	23.3	-2.6	-5.5	0.4	144.0	13.6
Costa Rica[3]									
1985	0.7	15.0	10.9	12.7	-2.7	-3.3	3.2	116.4	13.3
1986	5.5	11.8	15.4	37.7	-3.4	-1.7	2.8	107.3	11.0
1987	4.8	16.8	16.4	0.8	-2.0	-5.1	0.0	102.9	12.1
1988	3.4	20.8	25.3	36.6	-2.6	-3.5	2.5	96.6	20.8
1989	5.6	16.5	10.0	8.4	-4.1	-7.3	2.1	101.9	7.5
1990	3.6	19.0	27.3	4.4	-4.4	-7.8	-0.9	100.0	12.4

1991	2.3	28.7	25.3	30.2	−3.1	−1.3	4.0	92.7	33.7
1992	7.7	21.8	17.0	35.4	−1.9	−5.5	3.0	98.1	9.9
1993	6.3	9.8	9.0	8.5	−1.9	−8.3	1.5	101.0	5.7
1994	4.5	13.5	19.9	27.7	−5.0	−3.2	2.8	99.7	10.5
1995	2.5	23.2	22.6	0.9	−5.0	1.1	−0.1	101.4	14.4
1996	−8.0	17.6	13.8	6.9	−5.2	1.8	0.6	102.2	15.6
Ecuador									
1985	4.4	28.0	24.4	25.5	1.9	1.0	1.5	203.9	11.2
1986	3.2	23.0	27.3	18.7	−5.1	−5.7	1.8	164.2	76.5
1987	−5.2	29.5	32.5	32.3	−9.6	−11.9	2.1	126.3	38.8
1988	10.5	58.2	85.7	53.8	−5.8	−5.5	2.8	94.8	76.9
1989	0.2	75.7	54.2	38.1	−3.5	−5.3	1.9	109.7	74.5
1990	2.3	48.4	49.5	51.7	0.6	−1.6	2.4	100.0	45.9
1991	5.0	48.8	49.0	47.0	−2.0	−6.1	1.9	106.2	36.3
1992	3.6	54.6	60.2	44.5	−2.9	−1.7	2.2	106.5	46.6
1993	2.0	45.0	31.0	49.4	−0.5	−4.7	1.6	124.3	25.1
1994	4.4	27.3	25.4	35.6	0.4	−4.1	0.7	132.0	14.5
1995	2.3	22.9	22.7	12.7	−2.5	−3.6	1.2	129.5	16.7
1996	2.0	24.3	25.5	35.5	−3.2	−1.9	1.1	128.8	24.4
Israel									
1985	4.0	304.6	185.2	245.7	1.2	4.8		97.1	302.0
1986	3.6	48.2	19.7	112.8	3.8	4.9	1.3	94.7	26.2
1987	6.3	19.9	16.1	49.5	−0.3	−3.0	3.9	92.4	7.2
1988	3.6	16.3	16.4	11.3	−2.8	−0.9	1.3	101.4	0.3
1989	1.2	20.2	20.7	44.4	−5.8	2.8	1.7	102.4	19.9
1990	6.1	17.2	17.6	30.6	−4.5	0.9	2.2	100.0	5.2
1991	6.3	19.0	18.0	13.7	−4.4	−0.7	1.2	101.6	13.0
1992	6.6	11.9	9.4	32.0	−3.1	0.3	0.9	99.2	7.9

Table 10.6
(continued)

| | Annual percent change | | | | Percent of GDP | | | Exchange rates | |
| | Real GDP | CPI | | M1 | General government balance[1] | Current account balance | Seign-iorage[2] | Real effective (1990 = 100) | Nominal vis-à-vis U.S. dollar (percent change) |
		Annual average	End of period						
1993	3.5	10.9	11.3	27.9	-2.3	-1.7	3.3	98.1	15.1
1994	6.8	12.3	14.4	7.7	-1.2	-3.1	-0.8	99.1	6.4
1995	7.1	10.0	8.1	15.1	-3.1	-4.5	-2.7	99.9	0.0
1996	4.4	11.3	10.6	0.5	-4.2	-5.2	2.2	105.5	6.0
Mexico									
1985	2.2	57.7	63.7	49.5	-7.6	0.4	1.8	113.8	53.1
1986	-3.1	86.2	105.7	67.2	-12.9	-1.0	3.4	79.5	138.2
1987	1.7	131.8	159.2	129.7	-15.0	2.9	3.0	73.3	125.3
1988	1.3	114.2	51.7	58.1	-11.6	-1.3	1.4	90.7	64.9
1989	4.2	20.0	19.7	40.7	-5.2	-2.6	0.4	97.5	8.3
1990	5.1	26.7	29.9	60.3	-3.6	-2.8	1.0	100.0	14.3
1991	4.2	22.7	18.8	118.3	-0.6	-4.7	0.9	109.8	7.3
1992	3.6	15.5	11.9	15.1	1.6	-6.7	0.5	118.8	2.5
1993	2.0	9.8	8.0	17.7	0.7	-5.8	0.3	127.7	0.7
1994	4.5	7.0	7.1	3.8	-0.1	-7.0	0.7	122.8	8.3
1995	-6.2	35.0	52.0	7.0	0.1	-0.6	0.5	82.0	90.2
1996	5.1	34.4	27.7	39.6	-0.1	-0.5	0.7	92.6	18.4

Sources: National authorities; IMF, *International Financial Statistics*, and staff estimates.
1. Central government deficit for Costa Rica.
2. Defined as the first difference of reserve money over nominal GDP.
3. Seigniorage does not include adjustments for remunerated reserves.

1996, but recent political instability has caused inflation to rise above this range.

Ecuador has not generally relied on an exchange rate anchor, although it did so for a time in 1993–1994. Neither indexation nor incomes policy has been important, but relative price changes have been—including recently when they also contributed to political instability.

Inflation in Israel came down to the moderate range in 1985 and dropped to less than 15 percent a year in 1992 at the start of a sustained period of growth. Growth was propelled both by the major immigration that gradually increased aggregate supply and helped keep wage growth low and by the peace process. Inflation has mostly fluctuated in the range of 10–15 percent, occasionally dropping into the single-digit range.

Israel has used an exchange rate peg of some type since 1985, originally a fixed rate and more recently a crawling band. The rate of crawl has been gradually reduced, and the width of the band increased, over time. Increasing emphasis has been placed on inflation targeting, which is possible if consistent with the parameters of the exchange rate system. However, significant fiscal expansion at the end of 1994, as well as—for a time—confidence about the peace process, has made it more difficult to reconcile the exchange rate band with the inflation target. As a result, the exchange rate has been at the most appreciated point of the band, and monetary policy has had to sterilize on a massive scale to prevent rapid monetary growth. This sterilization has had significant fiscal costs and, in the context of disagreement on the strategy between the treasury and the central bank, has increasingly limited the central bank's room for maneuver.

Wage indexation remains important, indexation is pervasive in the financial system, and the tax system is highly indexed. Indexation has certainly contributed to the inflationary inertia, as has the public perception that there are few costs to inflation. This perception may appear surprising in light of triple-digit inflation in the first half of the 1980s, but that was not a period of sustained recession; nor was there much output cost of stabilizing.[11]

Mexico's inflation was in the moderate range from 1989 to 1991; stabilization to this range from triple digits was assisted by a major fiscal tightening. A crawling peg exchange rate system served as the anchor for monetary policy through 1994, with the *Pacto*—an

Table 10.7
Macroeconomic performance of moderate-inflation countries

| | Annual percent change | | | | Percent of GDP | | | Exchange rates | |
| | | CPI | | | | | | | |
	Real GDP	Annual average	End of period	M1	General government balance	Current account balance	Seign-iorage	Real effective (1990 = 100)	Nominal vis-à-vis U.S. dollar (percent change)
Countries That Ended Moderate Inflation									
1985	3.9	23.5	21.4	20.7	-7.3	-7.1	2.3	134.7	32.2
1986	4.6	20.6	17.8	30.2	-5.8	-5.4	2.1	126.0	5.7
1987	5.9	16.3	19.9	23.7	-4.9	-7.7	1.2	116.3	14.3
1988	4.6	19.0	17.0	15.2	-4.0	-5.9	1.2	109.3	6.2
1989	4.6	19.6	23.3	22.2	-3.6	-4.7	1.5	102.8	34.7
1990	2.8	23.0	21.3	26.6	-3.4	-3.3	1.2	100.0	24.6
1991	2.6	18.9	15.6	22.5	-1.3	-2.2	1.7	102.6	29.2
1992	1.8	15.2	15.7	27.8	-2.4	-3.4	2.6	105.2	7.5
1993	2.9	18.0	19.9	15.4	-2.0	-1.8	1.7	104.5	25.2
1994	3.4	14.4	9.3	18.6	-0.7	-1.3	1.8	109.8	2.9
1995	4.6	6.3	8.1	12.5	0.0	-2.7	1.6	110.7	-3.6
1996	4.4	6.9	6.8	9.2	0.2	-3.0	...	113.8	4.5
Countries with Continued Moderate Inflation									
1985	2.9	85.9	61.3	68.8	-2.3	-0.4	...	143.0	84.2
1986	3.0	37.6	37.8	56.0	-3.6	-0.4	2.2	116.5	57.7
1987	2.6	44.3	49.6	48.5	-5.7	-3.5	2.2	103.4	41.7
1988	4.6	47.5	41.5	37.1	-4.9	-2.4	2.0	100.2	37.2

1989	2.9	31.7	26.1	31.0	−4.1	−2.6	1.6	1C5.0	27.6
1990	4.3	28.1	31.3	36.2	−2.5	−2.0	1.2	100.0	21.8
1991	4.0	29.9	27.6	48.2	−2.2	−1.5	2.2	102.6	23.3
1992	5.1	26.2	24.7	34.2	−1.4	−2.4	1.9	106.9	17.4
1993	3.8	19.6	16.5	26.3	−1.0	−4.9	1.9	113.9	12.1
1994	5.2	16.8	18.0	20.4	−1.3	−4.4	1.1	117.3	7.5
1995	2.2	22.4	25.0	11.8	−2.3	−2.6	−0.1	109.5	25.9
1996	1.1	21.6	19.8	21.2	−3.1	−2.3	1.0	114.6	15.6

Transition Countries with Moderate Inflation

1992	−17.2	673.0	...	...	−8.0	0.8	...	...	...
1993	−4.5	209.2	193.5	...	−3.3	−2.5	5.0	...	...
1994	−4.0	93.0	46.9	40.6	−4.2	−4.8	2.8	122.0	...
1995	1.8	28.1	24.7	...	−3.3	−3.9	...	124.1	...
1996	1.0	21.8	16.3	...	−2.4	−7.0	...	128.5	8.9

Sources: National authorities; IMF, *International Financial Statistics*, and staff estimates.
Note: See table 10.2 for a list of the countries in the three groups.

agreement among government, business, and labor—playing a central role in the disinflation. With sustained fiscal discipline,[12] and continuing real exchange rate appreciation through 1993, inflation fell to single digits.

However, with the support of large capital inflows, the current account deficit was mounting during this period, and, after a series of adverse shocks, the famous devaluation took place at the end of 1994. While many important lessons are to be learned from this difficult experience, we emphasize here only the simplest: large current account deficits should be avoided, especially when financed by short-term flows, and, if they do materialize, it is essential to correct the situation before the market forces a disorderly correction.

From the viewpoint of the moderate inflation issue, there is an important contrast between Mexico's disinflation at the start of this decade and the current disinflation. There has been no official exchange rate target, the exchange rate has been flexible, and the rate of disinflation has been rapid, helped by both remarkable wage flexibility and a very strong fiscal performance. Although the government has consulted with the private sector in formulating its annual budget and economic plan, there is no formal incomes policy. The authorities intend to move gradually to the single-digit inflation range. Despite occasional rumblings, there appear to be no plans to move to a different exchange rate system.

The contrast between the first and second Mexican disinflations gives cause for reflection. In the profoundly depressed economy of 1995–1996, when there was little pressure from wages, it was possible to disinflate rapidly without the use of an exchange rate anchor. If the process stays on track, Mexico will achieve single-digit inflation with a monetary rather than an exchange rate anchor.

Colombia, Israel, and Mexico are the largest economies in this group, and their experience is worth summarizing. Each used a pegged exchange rate as an essential element in the fight against inflation, and, although none succeeded fully in this effort, use of an exchange rate anchor in Israel and Mexico was an important element of the disinflation. Each of these countries had to deal with major capital inflows, and none found an easy solution. Colombia and Mexico experienced a substantial real appreciation while using the exchange rate as an anchor, and the current account deficits in all three countries have at times been larger than the authorities were comfortable with. In its 1985 stabilization, Israel used an incomes policy, which has since become less important; the *Pacto* played an important role in the first Mexican disinflation of the 1990s; and Colombia has tried a social pact without a great deal of success. Indexation is important in both Colombia and Israel. Fiscal policy has been reasonable in all three countries in the 1990s, but fiscal easing in both Colombia and Israel has complicated the task of inflation reduction in the last few years, and quasifiscal operations contributed to the crisis in Mexico in 1994.

Transition Economies with Moderate Inflations

The initial disinflation patterns seem to be very similar for Estonia, Latvia, Moldova, and Poland, where triple-digit inflation declined rapidly to about 20 percent in 1996 (tables 10.7 and 10.8). Hungary, whose inflation level was similar in 1996, looks more like the classic moderate-inflation countries, such as Colombia. While the recent inflationary experiences of these five countries are even more similar, disinflation has been faster in Estonia, Latvia, and Moldova than in Hungary and Poland. In recent months, 12-month inflation in Estonia and Latvia has declined to less than 10 percent. There are thus significant differences in the pattern of inflation within this group of countries.

In Estonia, Latvia, and Moldova, an initial burst of inflation was caused by price liberalization in the presence of a large overhang of rubles. Inflation declined to double digits after the initial adjustment, but then was relatively slow to decline further as a result of (1) an initial undervaluation of the currency relative to its medium-term equilibrium value, which could be attributed to uncertainty about the future development of policies and the economy; (2) domestic relative price adjustment, particularly of administered prices[13]; and (3) the Balassa-Samuelson effect of differential productivity growth between the traded and nontraded goods sectors. Inflation in Poland followed a similar path, particularly in the early years of stabilization, reflecting the same forces at work. Because Hungary started its reform effort earlier, it did not experience a major inflationary burst in the early 1990s.

While Estonia moved early to a currency board, Latvia pegged to the SDR only in 1994. Moldova was formally floating, but has increasingly been operating an undeclared managed float that seeks to maintain exchange rate stability. Thus, in these three countries, as

Table 10.8
Macroeconomic performance in transition countries with moderate inflation, 1985–1996

| | | Annual percent change | | | Percent of GDP | | | Exchange rates | |
| | | CPI | | | | | | | |
	Real GDP	Annual average	End of period	M1	General government balance	Current account balance	Seigniorage[1]	Real effective (1990 = 100)	Nominal vis-à-vis U.S. dollar (percent change)
Estonia									
1991	−7.9	...	...	...	5.2	55.8	...	...	...
1992	−21.6	1,069.3	...	...	−0.3	3.4	...	...	...
1993	−8.4	89.0	37.9	83.1	−0.7	1.4	10.0	74.6	...
1994	−0.1	47.7	41.6	20.9	1.3	−7.5	1.5	85.4	−1.8
1995	2.9	28.9	26.5	29.8	−1.2	−5.1	2.0	100.0	−11.8
1996	3.1	23.1	14.8	31.5	−1.5	−10.4	2.2	108.1	5.0
Hungary									
1985	−0.3	7.0	8.6	19.3	0.2	−3.4	4.0	114.6	4.3
1986	1.5	5.3	5.4	11.2	−1.7	−6.0	2.0	103.1	−8.6
1987	4.1	8.6	10.9	15.1	−2.0	−2.8	−3.2	93.1	2.5
1988	−0.1	15.7	14.8	−1.5	0.9	−2.3	−1.0	95.2	7.3
1989	0.7	16.9	18.1	25.8	−0.8	−2.3	3.4	96.4	17.2
1990	−3.5	29.0	34.6	26.4	2.0	0.7	8.0	100.0	7.0
1991	−11.9	34.2	31.0	16.9	−3.0	0.8	11.0	111.6	18.2
1992	−3.1	23.0	24.7	31.0	−6.1	0.9	3.0	120.9	5.7
1993	−0.6	22.5	21.1	10.4	−6.3	−9.0	3.7	132.1	16.4
1994	2.9	18.8	21.2	9.5	−7.6	−9.5	3.4	131.1	14.4
1995	1.5	28.2	28.3	...	−3.6	−5.7	...	125.8	19.5
1996	1.0	23.6	19.8	...	−0.2	−4.0	...	128.0	21.5

Latvia									
1991	−8.0	...	...	...	6.3	...	...	...	...
1992	−35.0	951.2	...	...	−0.8	1.8	...	...	...
1993	−16.1	109.1	34.9	...	0.6	7.0	5.3	86.6	−8.3
1994	2.2	35.9	26.3	19.9	−4.0	−2.4	3.4	98.2	−17.1
1995	0.4	25.1	23.1	2.5	−3.3	−3.5	2.5	100.0	−5.7
1996	2.8	18.8	13.2	19.0	−1.3	−6.8	1.5	97.9	4.4
Moldova									
1992	−29.1	1,276.0	2,198.4	540.3	−26.2	−3.8	9.3	...	...
1993	−1.2	788.5	836.0	287.9	−7.4	−11.7	4.4	...	...
1994	−31.2	329.6	116.0	112.9	−8.7	−6.9	4.1	115.0	...
1995	−3.0	30.2	23.8	76.5	−5.7	−8.6	3.8	100.0	...
1996	−8.0	23.5	15.1	18.3	−6.7	−12.9	0.9	97.6	2.4
Poland									
1985	5.1	15.1	...	20.4	...	−6.7	...	201.7	29.9
1986	4.2	17.8	...	21.9	...	−5.7	...	158.2	19.1
1987	2.0	25.2	...	25.9	...	−6.4	...	115.1	51.2
1988	4.1	60.2	...	51.3	...	−6.4	...	105.1	62.4
1989	0.2	245.4	639.6	253.7	−7.4	−2.8	...	118.8	234.3
1990	−11.6	600.0	225.9	401.1	3.1	1.1	...	100.0	560.1
1991	−7.0	76.4	60.3	14.4	−6.7	−1.2	...	155.7	11.3
1992	2.6	45.3	44.4	38.8	−6.6	1.9	3.1	166.0	28.8
1993	3.8	36.9	37.7	31.3	−2.9	−0.1	1.6	178.6	32.9
1994	6.0	33.2	29.4	39.7	−2.0	2.3	1.7	180.2	25.4
1995	7.0	28.1	21.9	36.4	−2.7	3.3	3.1	194.7	6.7
1996	6.0	19.8	18.7	31.8	−2.1	−1.0	1.6	211.0	11.2

Sources: National authorities; IMF, *International Financial Statistics*, and staff estimates.
1. Defined as the first difference of reserve money over nominal GDP.

in Hungary and Poland, an exchange rate peg of some type has been an essential element of monetary policy.

Both Estonia and Latvia have had very small budget deficits in recent years, whereas the initial Moldovan stabilization was accompanied by a big fiscal tightening. Seigniorage has been quite large in these economies in some years. Neither wage indexation nor incomes policies played an important role in the two Baltic countries and Moldova, and none of them suffered significantly from the capital inflow problem (but this became a major issue in 1997 in Estonia).

Disinflation in Estonia, Latvia, and Moldova was largely a process of getting the macroeconomic fundamentals right and allowing relative price adjustments to take place. The recent rapid declines in inflation in these three countries testify to the absence of strong forces of inertia in the system, beyond the need for a real appreciation of the exchange rate. Nevertheless, it will be important to be vigilant for any signs of overvaluation.

It has been argued that the nominal exchange rate peg in the Baltic countries contributed to inflation, for with nominal appreciation ruled out, the only way for a real appreciation to take place was through domestic inflation. There is no doubt about the arithmetic, but there is a question of whether a steady appreciation would have encouraged problematic capital inflows, as well as the issue of whether the real exchange rate would have appreciated more rapidly, at a cost in terms of exports, had the nominal rate been appreciating. We see no decisive arguments on either side. The experience of the Russian appreciation in the spring of 1995 that led the authorities to introduce their exchange rate band is not necessarily relevant, because that appreciation and the accompanying speculative capital flows took place within a floating exchange rate regime.

The experiences of Hungary and, to some extent, Poland are more like those of nontransition countries with moderate inflation in several respects. Both have operated a crawling peg exchange rate regime and have had to deal with a capital inflow problem, in the process confronting the same policy dilemmas as the other countries with moderate inflation. A tightening of the fiscal position in each country furthered the disinflation process. While wage indexation has not been an important factor in Hungary, policymakers have had to deal with entrenched inflation expectations; de facto wage indexation has been a significant element in the inflationary process in Poland.

An important difference between these two countries and non-transition countries with moderate inflation, however, is that relative price changes have been more important in Hungary and Poland. Another difference is the still relatively large size of the state enterprise sector and the weak corporate governance even in some newly privatized enterprises, which make it hard to control wage growth. These are common features of all transition economies. Incomes policy was an element of the early disinflation efforts of most of this group, although it applied only to state enterprises and was generally phased out as privatization proceeded. In Hungary, wage discipline in state enterprises was central in helping achieve the stabilization of the external balance in 1995.

Last, the fiscal stance has been as important in all five of these economies as elsewhere; indeed, because domestic bond financing of deficits is generally more difficult in these economies, especially soon after transition begins, the fiscal situation is likely to be more important than in nontransition economies. Weak fiscal positions and reliance on seigniorage slowed the early stages of disinflation for several countries in this group. Quasi-fiscal activities by the banking system were also a feature of early stages of reform in all these countries, later reflected in problems in the banking system—Latvia experienced a major banking crisis, and all these countries have had to restructure their banking systems.

Countries That Stabilized from High Inflation without Getting Stuck

The countries that stabilized successfully from triple-digit inflation rates in the mid- to late 1990s, including Bolivia, Israel, and Mexico, all appeared to get stuck subsequently in moderate inflation. However, in the 1990s a number of countries stabilized (Argentina, Brazil, Peru, and Slovenia) from very high rates of inflation to single-digit inflation without remaining long in the moderate range (table 10.9).

The disinflation was especially rapid in Croatia, while Slovenia shows a pattern more similar to that of the 1980s stabilizers. For the last two years, Argentina and Croatia have been operating in the low single digits, while Brazil, Peru, and Slovenia have only recently

Table 10.9
Macroeconomic performance in countries that stabilized from high inflation

| | Annual percent change | | | | Percent of GDP | | | Exchange rates | |
| | | CPI | | | | | | | |
	Real GDP	Annual average	End of period	M1	General government balance[1]	Current account balance	Seigniorage[2]	Real effective (1990 = 100)	Nominal vis-à-vis U.S. dollar (percent change)
Argentina[3]									
1985	−7.0	628.6	385.4	583.6	−6.2	−1.1	7.7	91.0	789.6
1986	7.1	92.2	81.9	89.7	−4.0	−2.7	1.8	90.8	56.7
1987	2.5	130.6	174.8	113.6	−6.4	−3.9	2.8	84.1	127.4
1988	−2.0	342.5	387.8	351.5	−4.8	−1.2	5.1	77.3	308.2
1989	−7.0	3,193.4	4,923.3	4,987.7	−15.8	−1.6	11.2	67.8	4,736.7
1990	−1.3	2,314.9	1,343.9	887.6	−2.7	3.4	4.7	100.0	1,051.8
1991	10.5	171.7	84.0	174.4	−2.5	−0.1	2.3	136.6	95.6
1992	10.3	24.9	17.5	48.8	−0.2	−2.8	1.4	154.7	3.9
1993	6.3	10.6	7.4	31.0	0.9	−3.1	1.5	172.1	0.8
1994	8.5	4.1	3.9	13.5	−0.5	−3.7	0.4	169.7	0.0
1995	−4.6	3.4	1.6	0.5	−1.4	−1.4	−0.1	160.6	0.1
1996	4.4	0.2	0.1	18.5	−2.0	−1.9	0.3	160.3	0.0
Brazil									
1985	7.9	227.0	248.6	334.3	−4.3	−0.1	2.7	68.1	235.5
1986	7.6	145.2	63.5	330.1	−3.6	−2.1	4.2	63.9	120.2
1987	3.6	229.7	432.3	215.4	−5.5	−0.5	8.1	64.0	187.3
1988	0.3	682.3	1,006.4	401.0	−4.8	1.3	4.0	69.5	568.2

1989	3.3	1,287.0	1,759.2	1,337.0	−6.9	0.2	10.2	86.0	981.6
1990	−3.1	2,937.8	1,657.7	2,333.6	1.6	−0.9	7.1	100.0	2,310.1
1991	0.3	440.8	493.8	429.4	1.5	−0.4	7.1	79.2	495.3
1992	−0.8	998.7	1,156.4	981.8	−2.2	1.6	9.1	72.4	1,009.9
1993	4.2	2,169.2	2,828.7	2,017.8	0.2	−0.1	10.5	81.9	1,859.9
1994	6.2	2,695.1	1,258.6	2,098.7	0.5	−0.3	9.6	97.6	1,887.7
1995	4.2	82.6	25.9	31.2	−4.8	−2.5	0.7	110.7	43.5
1996	...	18.2	11.3	22.2	...	...	...	112.2	9.5
Croatia[4]									
1993	−4.2	1,516.6	1,122.6	...	−0.8	0.9	1.6	85.6	...
1994	1.1	97.5	2.4	111.9	1.5	0.7	0.1	98.1	67.6
1995	2.5	1.6	4.6	24.6	−1.0	−9.5	0.1	100.0	−12.8
1996	4.7	3.5	3.7	37.9	−0.5	−7.7	0.1	98.9	3.9
Peru									
1985	2.8	163.4	158.3	251.6	−4.0	0.6	9.9	41.4	216.6
1986	10.0	77.9	62.9	102.6	−4.6	−5.6	4.2	46.2	27.1
1987	8.4	85.8	114.5	137.0	−6.9	−5.5	5.8	52.4	20.7
1988	−8.8	667.0	1,722.1	491.5	−5.4	−7.0	7.9	47.6	665.2
1989	−11.7	3,398.6	2,775.3	1,805.7	−7.2	−0.7	7.2	76.0	1,969.5
1990	−3.8	7,481.8	7,649.7	4,627.4	−5.7	−3.4	6.5	100.0	6,947.0
1991	2.9	409.5	139.2	124.6	−1.4	−3.1	1.3	119.7	311.2
1992	−1.8	73.5	56.7	71.3	−2.8	−4.5	1.0	123.5	61.3
1993	6.4	48.6	39.5	48.1	−2.6	−5.2	0.6	115.2	59.6
1994	13.1	23.7	15.4	57.7	−2.3	−5.1	0.8	122.9	10.4
1995	7.0	11.1	10.3	23.6	−2.7	−7.2	0.7	123.0	2.7
1996	2.8	11.5	11.8	18.0	−0.8	−5.8	0.2	125.7	8.9

Table 10.9
(continued)

	Annual percent change				Percent of GDP			Exchange rates	
	Real GDP	CPI		M1	General government balance[1]	Current account balance	Seign-iorage[2]	Real effective (1990 = 100)	Nominal vis-à-vis U.S. dollar (percent change)
		Annual average	End of period						
Slovenia									
1992	−5.5	202.6	88.2	136.0	0.3	7.4	...	91.3	194.8
1993	2.8	31.9	22.9	41.0	0.3	1.5	1.0	82.3	39.3
1994	5.3	19.8	18.3	43.5	−0.2	3.8	1.6	93.1	13.7
1995	3.9	12.6	8.6	25.8	−0.03	−0.2	0.9	100.0	−8.0
1996	3.1	9.7	8.8	14.4	0.3	0.3	0.6	94.2	14.2

Sources: National authorities; IMF, *International Financial Statistics*, and staff estimates.

1. Central government deficit for Argentina; privatization is considered a financing item in Peru.
2. Defined as the first difference of reserve money over nominal GDP.
3. From February 1995 onward, banks' reserve deposits at the Central Bank of Argentina began to be remunerated and so were excluded from the monetary base.
4. Seigniorage for Croatia is defined as the first difference of reserve money, adjusted for remuneration of reserves, over the price level.

Table 10.10
Macroeconomic performance of countries that stabilized from high inflation (period averages)

	Before stabilization[1]	After stabilization
Real GDP (percent change)	0.3	4.5
Inflation (period average)	1,369.7	223.4
Inflation (end of period)	1,456.2	102.5
M1 (percent change)	1,112.0	182.3
Government balance (ratio to GDP)	−1.2	−0.2
Current account balance (ratio to GDP)	−1.6	−2.6
Seigniorage (ratio to GDP)	6.5	2.0[2]
Real effective exchange rate (1990 = 100)	74.0	115.8
Nominal exchange rate (percent change)	1,227.5	154.7

Sources: National authorities; IMF, *International Financial Statistics*, and staff estimates.
1. Excludes Croatia and Slovenia.
2. Excludes Croatia.

moved into the single-digit range inflation—inflation in Peru and Slovenia registering about 10 percent in 1995 and then moving slightly higher.

In the countries that stabilized from very high inflation, a major fiscal tightening was involved. In Brazil, the tightening came well before the stabilization.[14] The budget deficit remains well within the Maastricht limits in all these countries, except Brazil, where the fiscal deficit actually increased after stabilization. As can be seen in table 10.10, there has on average been a significant improvement in the fiscal situation in these countries since stabilization. Seigniorage was very large on average before the stabilizations and declined to more normal levels following stabilization (table 10.10).

A nominal exchange rate anchor was central to the stabilization strategy in Argentina, Brazil, and Croatia, with Argentina taking the step—extraordinary for a large country—of instituting a currency board while permitting the circulation of both the U.S. dollar and the peso. The Brazilian disinflation was particularly skillful in unraveling the inflationary inertia implied by the existing structure of labor contracts: the dollar was essentially allowed to serve as numeraire before the introduction of a new currency, which was then tied to the dollar. In Croatia, the currency was allowed to float at the start of the stabilization program, but was soon fixed against the deutsche mark, with the implicit indexation of most prices to the deutsche mark helping bring rapid price stability. During most of its disinflation, Slovenia had a floating exchange rate, but it did use an exchange rate anchor in 1994–1995, a period in which it made significant gains on the inflation front. Peru undertook a money-based stabilization with a floating exchange rate.

Because fiscal policy in Brazil weakened after the stabilization, a heavy weight was placed on monetary policy to control aggregate demand. High real interest rates attracted capital inflows, even though the authorities had capital inflow controls in place. The other countries in the group have also experienced periods of rapid capital inflows, while Argentina in 1995 had to battle hard (and successfully) against the capital outflows caused by the "tequila" effect. Peru, too, has had to face both significant capital inflows at times and tequila effect pressure in the opposite direction. Slovenia introduced some capital controls in 1995.

Wide-ranging structural reforms that tackled the underlying causes of lax fiscal policies and slow growth were critical elements of several of the stabilizations from high inflation, especially those in Argentina and Peru. These reforms were crucial for ensuring that low inflation could be sustained and, hence, also for the initial credibility of the stabilization program.

Wage indexation was pervasive in Brazil before the stabilization, but was used to help bring about a coordinated disinflation. Slovenia has also had widespread indexation, as did Argentina before it stabilized. Argentina, Brazil, and Croatia have all tried to discourage indexation. However, the Brazilian and Croatian cases suggest that indexation can also further disinflation—provided it is virtually instantaneous. Incomes policy has not been an important factor in these countries since 1994 except in Slovenia.

The stabilizations from high inflation had no output cost; rather, output growth was significantly higher after stabilization than before (table 10.10). This is a common result in such stabilizations.

The lessons of these stabilizations from high inflation may be quite limited for moderate-inflation countries. The breakdown in the structure of contracts during hyperinflation, particularly their shortening and growing indexation to a foreign currency, makes stabilization in some ways easier.[15] The disorganization of a hyperinflation may also build political support for stabilization that is harder to gather when the economy is still functioning reasonably well.

If there is one lesson, it is probably that there is no point in stopping prematurely in the stabilization process. Each of the countries in this group could undoubtedly have declared victory when its inflation reached the moderate range. But by using the political support generated by the ending of the scourge of hyperinflation, they were able to press inflation lower, at no cost in terms of output.

Growth and Disinflation

The output costs of disinflation have been extensively studied. They are not obvious in the two categories studied in this paper in which inflation has been reduced to below the moderate range, that is, the moderate-inflation countries that have stabilized (table 10.5) and the high-inflation countries that have stabilized without getting stuck (table 10.10). We have not made a careful study of the sacrifice ratio or the output costs of disinflation, if any. However, we do note that there is a significant negative correlation between growth and inflation in the sample of 20 countries, for 1985–1996, presented in tables 10.3, 10.6, 10.8, and 10.9. The negative correlation is much stronger when the high-inflation countries that have stabilized are excluded from the sample.

Overall Lessons

Although we have been drawing lessons from the case studies as we have proceeded, it is useful to set out the most important conclusions:

(1) Moderate inflation can be beaten, but there is no single magic formula: various monetary and exchange rate strategies can be effective. Nonetheless, most of the successful stabilizers have used an exchange rate anchor. Regardless of approach, perseverance is a key to success.

(2) A strong fiscal position consistent with only a small reliance on seigniorage and a reduction of the government debt burden if it is high is a critical element of successful stabilization from moderate and high inflations.

(3) Structural reforms that take on the underlying causes of weak fiscal discipline and low growth are critical for the credibility and sustained success of stabilization programs.

(4) Capital inflows can confront policymakers with uncomfortable choices among fiscal tightening, relaxing monetary policy, allowing the exchange rate to appreciate, and costly and possibly ineffective sterilized intervention. Fiscal tightening can lead both to lower interest rates and to a real depreciation. In addition, the appropriate response will most likely involve some sterilized intervention, a degree of exchange rate flexibility, and, possibly, monetary accommodation (if there is reason to believe that money demand is increasing). Sterilized intervention on a large scale, however, can store up problems for the future by causing a buildup of short-term debt and imposing a heavy interest bill on the central bank. Certainly, any relaxation of fiscal policy can exacerbate the problem of capital inflows. Price-based controls on capital inflows may be effective in the short term, particularly in extending the maturity of inflows. But over time they are likely to be circumvented.

(5) It is important to capitalize on favorable exogenous shocks and resist the effects of adverse shocks on inflation.

(6) Policymakers, especially under an exchange-rate-based stabilization, must constantly guard against significant overvaluation and the emergence of a large current account deficit, because such circumstances can lead to an external crisis and destroy the framework for stabilization. The surest way to deal with a real overvaluation and reduce the current account deficit is through a tightening of fiscal policy.

(7) Relative price adjustment has played a central role in the inflationary process in transition economies. Real appreciations are to be expected in these economies, but it is necessary even in these countries to be on the alert for overvaluation as relative price adjustment runs its course.

(8) Stabilization from high inflation is clearly good for growth, and there is little evident output cost of disinflation in the stabilizations from moderate inflation either.

Appendix: Inflation Data

Annual inflation rates for the 20 countries over the past 12 years are shown in the following figures, as are 12-month inflation rates over the past 2 years. Table 10.11 lists 64 episodes of moderate inflation between 1950 and 1996.

Table 10.11
Episodes of moderate inflation, 1950–1996[1]

Country	Period	Number of years	Period-average inflation		
			Three years before[2]	During	Three years after[2]
Africa					
Ghana	1973–75	3	7.6	21.9	81.9
Kenya	1990–92	3	10.6	21.7	25.2
Seychelles	1972–75	4	14.6(1)	20.6	13.9
Sierra Leone	1993–96	4	93.1	23.9	...
South Africa	1985–87	3	12.9	17.0	14.0
Sudan	1973–75	3	6.3	21.8	12.7
	1980–82	3	22.5	25.2	36.7
Swaziland	1979–81	3	12.0	18.4	11.8
Tanzania	1981–83	3	16.6	27.2	34.0
	1991–93	3	31.0	25.3	27.5
Congo, Dem. Rep. of	1972–75	4	6.7(2)	22.4	66.0
Zambia	1976–78	3	8.2	18.3	11.4
Zimbabwe	1993–96	4	27.6	23.5	...
Asia					
Korea	1974–76	3	9.4	21.6	14.3
	1979–81	3	13.3	22.8	4.3
Myanmar	1987–90	4	7.0	21.4	28.7
	1994–96	3	28.7	21.9	...
Pakistan	1973–75	3	5.1(1)	23.6	7.8
Western Samoa	1981–83	3	15.4	18.4	8.9
Industrial countries					
Greece	1979–87	9	12.7	20.7	15.9
	1990–92	3	14.5	18.6	11.4
Iceland	1986–90	5	48.4	20.3	5.0
Ireland	1974–76	3	9.7	18.6	11.5
	1980–82	3	11.5	18.6	8.2
Italy	1974–77	4	7.2	17.6	16.0
	1980–82	3	14.7	18.5	11.6
New Zealand	1980–82	3	13.4	16.2	9.7
Portugal	1974–85	12	8.9	22.8	10.2
Spain	1975–80	6	11.6	18.5	13.7
United Kingdom	1974–77	4	8.6	18.1	13.2

Table 10.11
(continued)

Country	Period	Number of years	Period-average inflation		
			Three years before[2]	During	Three years after[2]
Middle East and Europe					
Bahrain	1974–78	5	8.4	19.3	5.8
Egypt	1986–91	6	15.1	19.8	11.3
Iran, Islamic Rep. of	1980–83	4	16.5	20.8	11.8
	1986–89	4	12.2	24.5	16.8
	1991–93	3	19.6	21.3	36.7
Israel	1987–91	5	242.2	18.5	11.7
Turkey	1956–59	4	12.9(2)	19.1	1.6
	1973–77	5	11.5	19.0	71.4
Western Hemisphere					
Argentina	1962–65	4	51.5	25.8	25.8
Bolivia	1988–91	4	4,013.5	17.4	9.5
Brazil	1968–72	5	45.8	20.8	23.1
Chile	1951–53	3	14.5(1)	23.3	67.8
	1965–68	4	34.7	24.3	27.7
	1989–92	4	18.0	20.1	10.8
Colombia	1973–76	4	9.8	22.1	25.2
	1978–90	13	25.4	23.6	26.7
	1992–96	5	28.5	22.9	...
Costa Rica	1987–92	6	13.0	20.6	15.5
Ecuador	1985–87	3	32.0	26.8	60.8
	1994–96	3	49.4	24.9	...
El Salvador	1987–90	4	21.9	21.6	14.7
Grenada	1977–81	5	...	19.6	6.5
Haiti	1990–93	4	−0.1	19.7	28.4
Honduras	1994–96	3	17.8	25.0	...
Jamaica	1973–75	3	8.5	20.7	18.6
	1984–86	3	10.3	22.9	9.8
Mexico	1974–81	8	7.4	21.7	75.4
	1989–92	4	110.7	21.2	17.2
Paraguay	1954–57	4	73.0	22.4	8.2
	1987–89	3	25.8	23.6	25.9
	1991–94	4	29.1	19.6	11.6(2)
Uruguay	1969–71	3	96.0	20.4	83.6

Table 10.11
(continued)

			Period-average inflation		
Country	Period	Number of years	Three years before[2]	During	Three years after[2]
Countries in transition					
Hungary	1988–90	3	7.0	20.6	26.5
	1992–96	5	26.7	23.2	...

Source: IMF, *International Financial Statistics*.

Length of Spell	Number of Spells	Percent
3	29	45.3
4	20	31.3
5	8	12.5
6	3	4.7
7	0	0.0
8	1	1.6
9	1	1.6
10–13	2	3.1
Total	64	100.0

1. An episode of moderate inflation is defined as a period of at least three consecutive years of inflation between 15 and 30 percent. This table updates an earlier table in Dornbusch and Fischer (1993), which used data that ended in 1989 or 1990 depending on the country. Small differences between the two tables are due to a more stringent application of the 15 to 30 percent criteria in the current table to define a moderate-inflation episode.

2. Number in parentheses represents number of years (if less than three) for which a period average is computed.

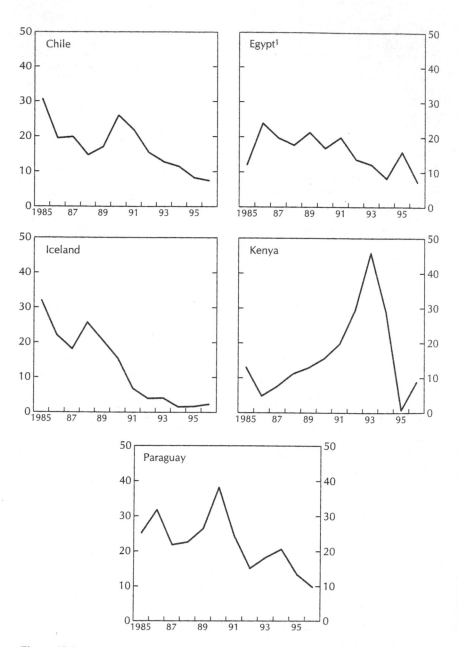

Figure 10.1
Countries that ended moderate inflation (percent change in the annual consumer price index). Sources: IMF, *International Financial Statistics*, and staff estimates. 1. Based on fiscal years.

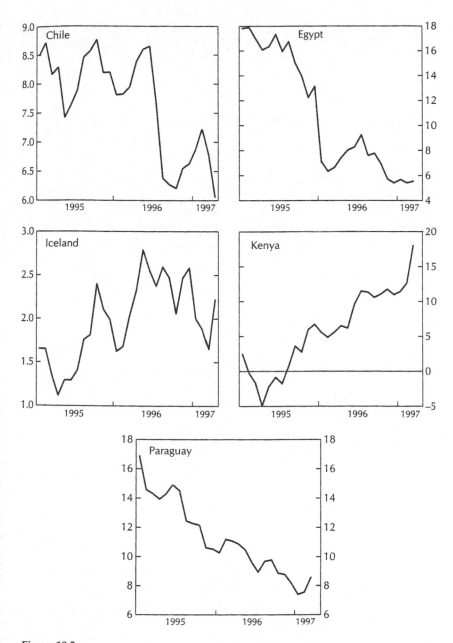

Figure 10.2
Countries that ended moderate inflation, January 1995 through April 1997 (twelve-month percent change in the consumer price index). Sources: IMF, *International Financial Statistics*, and staff estimates.

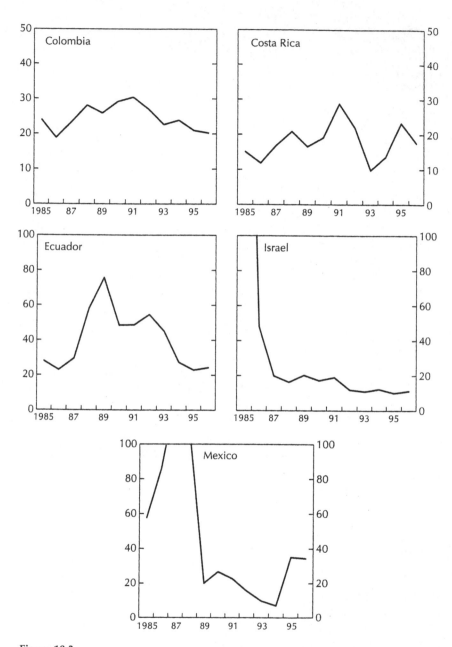

Figure 10.3
Countries with continued moderate inflation (percent change in the annual consumer
price index). Sources: IMF, *International Financial Statistics*, and staff estimates.

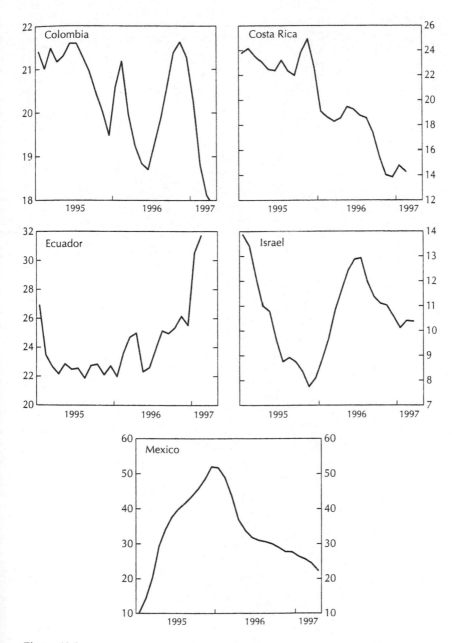

Figure 10.4
Countries with continued moderate inflation, January 1995 through April 1997 (twelve-month percent change in the consumer price index). Sources: IMF, *International Financial Statistics*, and staff estimates.

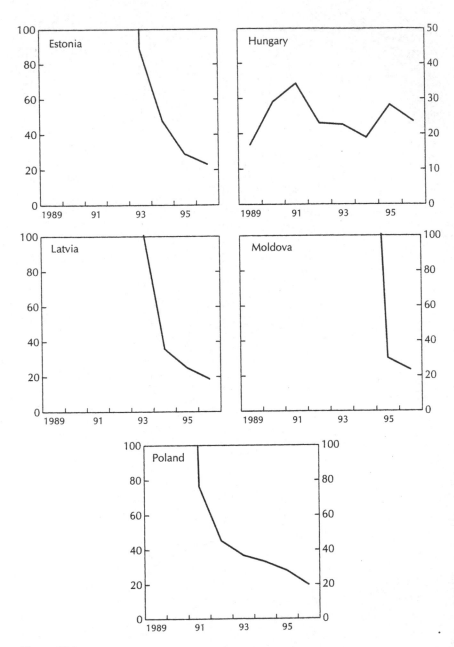

Figure 10.5
Transition countries with moderate inflation (percent change in the annual consumer price index). Sources: IMF, *International Financial Statistics*, and staff estimates.

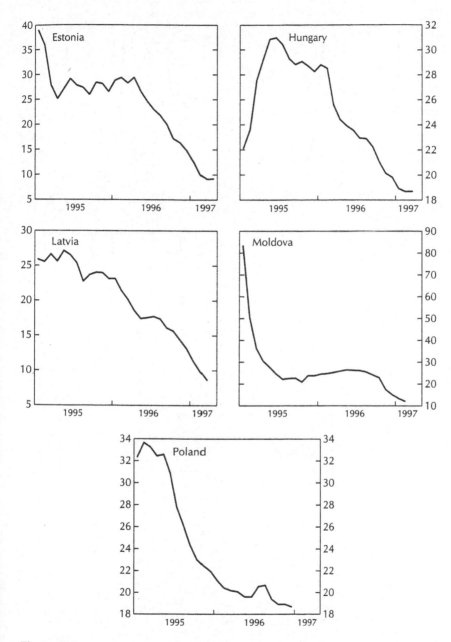

Figure 10.6
Transition countries with moderate inflation, January 1995 through April 1997 (twelve-month percent change in the consumer price index). Sources: IMF, *International Financial Statistics*, and staff estimates.

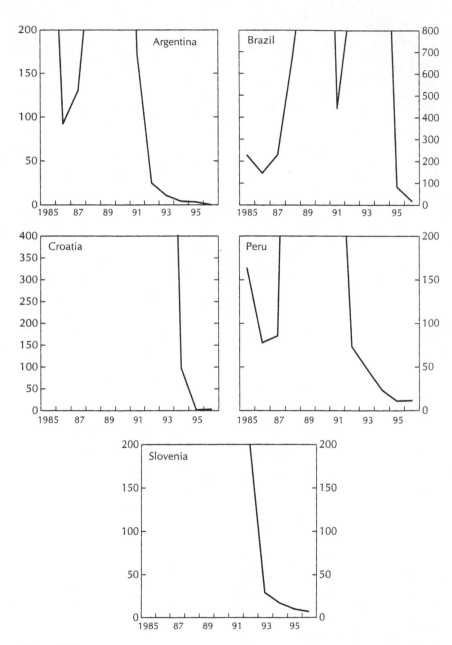

Figure 10.7
Countries that stabilized from high inflation (percent change in the annual consumer price index). Sources: IMF, *International Financial Statistics*, and staff estimates.

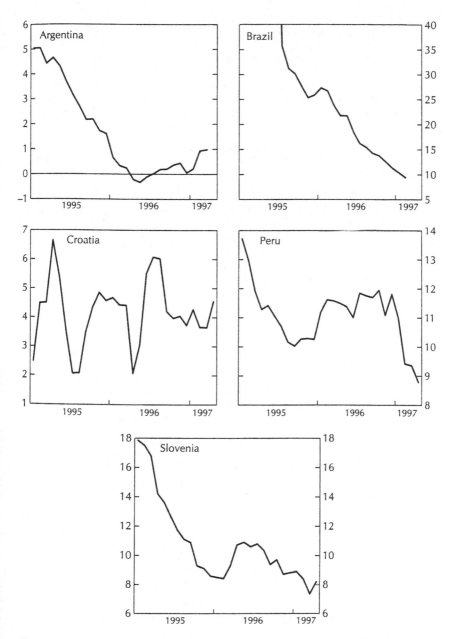

Figure 10.8
Countries that stabilized from high inflation, January 1995 through April 1997 (twelve-month percent change in the consumer price index). Sources: IMF, *International Financial Statistics*, and staff estimates.

Notes

We are grateful to our discussant at the seminar, André Icard of the Bank for International Settlements, for his comments and to Claire Adams for excellent research assistance. Views expressed are those of the authors. The developments described in the paper cover the period through May 1997. Since then, inflation in Kenya and Israel has declined to the single-digit range, and the rate in Latvia continues in the single digits. Inflation in Costa Rica and Mexico has declined significantly.

1. An updated version of Dornbusch and Fischer's table 10.5 is presented in table 10.11, which appears at the end of this chapter; through 1996, there were 64 episodes of moderate inflation.

2. Countries in table 10.2 are categorized according to their current rates of inflation, and some of the moderate inflation countries in table 10.2 are accordingly not experiencing a moderate inflation episode as defined in table 10.1.

3. Posen (1995) emphasizes the role of the financial sector in determining the extent of public support for anti-inflationary policies.

4. Direct credit creation by the central bank would appear in the calculation of seigniorage, though not necessarily in the measured budget deficit; inflationary credit creation by, for example, development banks would not show up directly in either seigniorage or the budget.

5. Cukierman and Liviatan (1992) present a model in which the imperfect credibility of the policymaker leads to a gradual stabilization being optimal. There is no stabilization without pain in this model, as the policymaker has to create a low level of activity to establish his or her reputation as a serious stabilizer; they contrast this result with that in models with backward-looking nominal contracts where it is generally possible to devise a path for inflation (albeit often one that is quite complicated and that would likely suffer from credibility problems) that stabilizes without pain.

6. Feldstein (1996) has recently presented an estimate that the benefits of reducing inflation from 2 percent a year in the United States would amount to about 1 percent of GDP a year. Extrapolating to moderate inflation rates, his analysis would imply very large costs, which, in his model, derive largely from the distortionary impact of inflation on capital taxation.

7. This is demonstrated in Fischer and Summers (1989): indexation that reduces the costs of inflation for society at a given inflation rate may lead to an equilibrium with higher inflation and higher social costs; in their model, indexation that affects the slope of the Phillips curve does not necessarily produce this result.

8. Some empirical work finds a strong negative relationship between rates of productivity growth and inflation, even at the very low rates of inflation prevailing in the United States and other leading industrial countries. However, it is not clear whether this relationship is causal or cyclical (this work is reviewed in Fischer, 1996).

9. We have also studied Bolivia, another country that successfully reduced inflation to single digits after a long period of moderate inflation, which began in 1985 with a radical decline in inflation from hyperinflationary levels. Bolivia's policy approach in recent years has been similar to Chile's, involving the use of a real exchange rate rule combined with monetary and fiscal policies directed at reducing inflation.

10. Because the Kenyan inflation rate is heavily affected by changes in agricultural prices, relative price changes could be said to have played an important role in this case.

11. The stabilization in mid-1985 was followed by a short slowdown, but growth picked up at the beginning of 1986. A recession that began in 1987 should probably be attributed to the need to establish the credibility of the new inflation range. It is also likely that the fact that Israel received financial aid to support the stabilization from the United States in the form of a US$1.5 billion grant rather than a loan affected public perceptions of the costs of inflation.

12. As noted in appendix 10.1, the quasi-fiscal deficit did rise in 1994, particularly as a result of lending by development banks.

13. As described in the note on Estonia in appendix 10.1, between July 1992 and April 1996, the price of traded goods rose threefold; nonadministered, nontraded goods prices rose fivefold; and administered nontraded goods prices rose more than ninefold. This is typical of the adjustments that have had to be made in many of the transition economies.

14. Brazilian fiscal deficit data are for the operational deficit; that is, the deficit includes only real interest on the debt.

15. This comment was of course frequently made in discussions of the applicability of Sargent's famous paper (1982) to industrial country inflations.

References

Bruno, Michael, and William Easterly, 1995, "Inflation Crises and Long-Run Growth," NBER Working Paper No. 5209 (Cambridge, Massachusetts: National Bureau of Economic Research).

Burton, David, and Stanley Fischer, 1998, "Ending Moderate Inflations," in *Moderate Inflation: The Experience of Transition Economies*, ed. by C. Cottarelli and G. Szapáry (Washington: IMF and National Bank of Hungary).

Citrin, Daniel A., and Ashok K. Lahiri, eds., 1995, *Policy Experiences and Issues in the Baltics, Russia, and Other Countries of the Former Soviet Union*, IMF Occasional Paper 133 (Washington: International Monetary Fund).

Coorey, Sharmini, Mauro Mecagni, and Erik Offerdal, 1996, "Designing Disinflation Programs in Transition Economies: The Implications of Relative Price Adjustment," IMF Working Paper 96/138 (Washington: International Monetary Fund).

Cukierman, Alex, and Nissan Liviatan, 1992, "The Dynamics of Optimal Gradual Stabilizations," *World Bank Economic Review*, Vol. 6 (September), pp. 439–458.

Dornbusch, Rudiger, and Stanley Fischer, 1993, "Moderate Inflation," *World Bank Economic Review*, Vol. 7 (January), pp. 1–44.

Feldstein, Martin, 1996, "The Costs and Benefits of Going from Low Inflation to Price Stability," NBER Working Paper No. 5469 (Cambridge, Massachusetts: National Bureau of Economic Research).

Fischer, Stanley, 1994, "Modern Central Banking," in *The Future of Central Banking: The Tercentenary Symposium of the Bank of England*, ed. by F. Capie and others (New York: Cambridge University Press).

———, 1996, "Why Are Central Banks Pursuing Long-Run Price Stability?" in *Achieving Price Stability: A Symposium* (Kansas City, Missouri: Federal Reserve Bank of Kansas City).

———, and Lawrence Summers, 1989, "Should Governments Learn to Live with Inflation?" *American Economic Review, Papers and Proceedings*, Vol. 79 (May), pp. 382–387.

Halpern, László, and Charles Wyplosz, 1996, "Equilibrium Exchange Rates in Transition Economies," IMF Working Paper 96/125 (Washington: International Monetary Fund).

International Monetary Fund, *International Financial Statistics* (Washington), various years.

Loser, Claudio L., and Eliot Kalter, eds., 1992, *Mexico: The Strategy to Achieve Sustained Economic Growth*, IMF Occasional Paper 99 (Washington: International Monetary Fund).

Posen, Adam, 1995, "Central Bank Independence and Disinflationary Credibility: A Missing Link?" Staff Report No. 1, Federal Reserve Bank of New York (New York).

Pujol, Thierry, and Mark Griffiths, 1996, "Moderate Inflation in Poland: A Real Story," IMF Working Paper 96/57 (Washington: International Monetary Fund).

Sarel, Michael, 1996, "Nonlinear Effects of Inflation on Economic Growth," *Staff Papers*, International Monetary Fund, Vol. 43 (March), pp. 199–215.

Sargent, Thomas, 1982, "The Ends of Four Big Inflations," in *Inflation: Causes and Effects*, ed. by R. Hall (Chicago: University of Chicago Press).

11   *Introduction*

Chapter 11, "Recollections," describes my initiation into the real world of policymaking and inflation stabilization. It was a privileged beginning, for among other skilled and experienced policymakers and economists, I worked with Secretary of State George Shultz and Herb Stein on the American side, and Shimon Peres and Michael Bruno on the Israeli side.

From late 1983 the U.S. government pressed the Israeli government to stabilize its economy. Inflation was well into the triple digit range, and the budget and balance of payments deficits were too large to be sustainable. Nonetheless it was not until mid-1985 that the Israeli government put in place the comprehensive program that turned out to be one of the most successful stabilizations in history.

This chapter tells part of the American side of that story. In one sense, as outsiders trying to help a country stabilize its economy, we were acting much like the IMF does when it works with a country suffering from severe macroeconomic problems. But the differences are also striking. In particular, the paper tells a story about Herb Stein's and my desire to put conditions on the provision of U.S. financial assistance in support of the stabilization. For good reasons, George Shultz did not want to impose formal conditionality. But he did allow us to say that he would be "disappointed" if Israel accepted, without implementing a stabilization plan, the $1.5 billion grant (not a loan) that Congress was willing to provide. Many times in later years I wished that IMF "disappointment" would have sufficed to ensure that agreed conditions were carried out.

In recent years the IMF has emphasized that a program is more likely to succeed if it is "owned" by the country, in the sense of being in part designed locally, at least being accepted by the government as making economic sense, and being willingly implemented by the country. The success of the Israeli program appears to confirm the importance of ownership. For this was an Israeli program, almost entirely designed by Israelis, and accepted by the cabinet after a prolonged and tough debate. But we need to understand also that ownership is a complex concept, for the program was not widely accepted until it began to succeed, and that the American pressure helped ensure its acceptance. Indeed, some time after the program had succeeded, then Prime Minister Peres said he had not been convinced the program would work, and that he had been operating on the basis of his faith in the advice of Secretary of State Shultz and the Israeli and American economists who were advising him.

"Recollections," as befits its title, is long on anecdotes. Let me conclude with one more, which illustrates another key lesson I learned, this one from Herb Stein. Over dinner one night in 1984, Herb asked what was happening in the Israeli economy. I replied with a lengthy analysis of the state of the economy, the role of the budget deficit, of indexation, of monetary policy, and the balance of policy views among the various participants—in short, a very good exam answer. When it was over, Herb asked me: "Well, but what do we want them to *do*?" That is the bottom line question that a policy adviser has to answer—but he or she also has to explain in comprehensible terms why those are the right policies to choose.

11

Recollections of the United States' Role in the Israeli Stabilization Program

Stanley Fischer

The Israeli stabilization program had many very interesting economic aspects, some of them—the heterodox elements—novel at the time, though less so now.[1,2] Its lessons will continue to be drawn and redrawn as long as stabilizations are studied.[3] The key economic aspects have already been discussed by others, and especially by Michael Bruno, whose role in the formulation and execution of the program was critical.[4]

Rather than focus on the economics, I will talk mainly about the American role in the stabilization. My memory has been reinforced by detailed notes that I kept at the time. I will also talk about one or two underemphasized economic elements in the program, and will conclude by reflecting on the current economic situation in Israel.

George Shultz

The key American figure in the Israeli stabilization was then Secretary of State George Shultz. My own formal involvement began at the end of 1983 when Shultz put together a group of American economists to advise him on the Israeli economy. The original group of four academic advisers consisted of Paul McCracken, former Chairman of the Council of Economic Advisers (CEA) and then at the University of Michigan; Abraham (Abe) Siegel, then Dean of the Sloan School at MIT and a longtime friend of Shultz's;[5] Herbert Stein, also a former Chairman of the CEA and longtime friend and colleague of Shultz's, then at the American Enterprise Institute; and myself, a Professor at MIT.

I had studied the economy of Israel for some time, originally informally during sabbaticals at the Hebrew University from the University of Chicago in 1972 and from MIT in 1976–1977, then more systematically starting in January 1980, which I spent as a visiting scholar in the Research Department of the Bank of Israel.[6] That visit to the Bank of Israel resulted in a paper with Jacob Frenkel on stabilizing the economy, which was discussed at a seminar in the Bank and later published (1982). In the United States, it was probably a paper on the Israeli economy written for a 1983 Carnegie-Rochester conference that received most notice around the time I was asked to join the State Department team.[7]

I was initially reluctant to join the State Department group, partly because I thought I knew too much about the stabilization plans that were then being entertained by Israeli policymakers, and partly because the State Department had an anti-Israel reputation at the time. After a conversation with Abe Siegel that concluded with his telling me "Fischer, when the Secretary of State asks you to do something, you do it!", I joined up—for what turned out to be one of the most interesting and meaningful experiences of my life, and one which helped shape my future career.

It did not strike me in 1983 that there were several odd things about Shultz's advisory group. For one thing, it is not normal that the Secretary of State deals with the economies of other countries. Normally it is the Treasury.[8] And even if it had been the State Department, the Secretary surely would not normally have spent so much time on a problem of this type. For another, now that I have worked inside bureaucracies, I realize how unusual it is for outside advisers to be given as active a role in the formulation of policy as we eventually had, and also how impressive the State Department's cooperation with the group was. Under-Secretary for Economic Affairs, Allan Wallis, who headed the U.S. side of our talks with the Israelis, was especially generous in this respect.

Shultz opened the first meeting of the advisory group with the Israelis, which took place in Washington early in 1984. Emanuel Sharon, then Director-General of the Treasury, headed the Israeli delegation, which also included the late Eytan Berglas, Nissan Liviatan, and Eytan Sheshinski. Speaking quietly, Shultz said it was not good for the United States to have the economy of its most dependable ally in the Middle East be weak, and that its problems could not be solved by throwing more money at them. He said he intended to try to help the Israeli government strengthen its economy, by giving advice in whatever ways might be possible.

The advisory group met either with other members of the U.S. government, or with visiting Israelis, in a series of meetings through the middle of 1984. But because of the Israeli elections, nothing came of those meetings. I did however see how effectively Paul McCracken used his ignorance of the Israeli economy: whenever a particularly complicated explanation of some Israeli problem came forth—and they were typically very complicated, often built on a firm belief that the Israeli economy was immune to the laws of economics and sometimes logic—Paul would say, pulling the hayseeds out of his hair, that he didn't really understand the Israeli economy, and perhaps someone could explain why something which worked one way in the United States worked the opposite way in Israel.

Prime Minister Peres

The group came back to life in October 1984, when Shimon Peres visited Washington as the new Prime Minister. He arrived with the newspapers saying that he was not coming to ask for aid. I was teaching and couldn't make it to the meeting, but Herb Stein, with whom I had the pleasure of working throughout this period and from whom I learned a great deal, was there.[9] Herb called later to report on the meeting and said, "You know, for a guy who didn't come to ask for aid, he did pretty well."

Mr. Peres asked for an additional four billion dollars of aid over the next two years, as a safety net to support stabilization; he also asked for a ten billion dollar investment fund to help support entrepreneurs, and a few other things. But I guess what you learn watching Shimon Peres is that if you don't ask, you don't get—and that some of the impossible things you ask for and dream about actually happen.

As a result of the Peres visit in October 1984, the Joint Economic Development Group (JEDG) was set up. The idea was the same as that underlying the Joint Military Working Group between Israel and the United States, that people from each government meet with their opposite numbers to review current problems. But there was an important variation, namely that there would be private economists, both American and Israeli, together with government officials, in the working group. The idea, almost certainly George Shultz's, was that there were people in Israel, professional economists, who knew what needed to be done, but who were not succeeding in influencing their government's policy. The JEDG would help provide a forum for them, and in turn help the Israeli government think its way through the issues.

The JEDG played an important role in the stabilization process from the time of its setting up until the day the program was decided on, June 3, 1985. The JEDG worked primarily because of the importance that George Shultz assigned to it, and to a considerable extent because of Emanuel Sharon, Director-General of the Israeli Treasury, who headed the Israeli team for the negotiations. His counterpart was Allan Wallis, Under-Secretary of State for Economic Affairs.

Sharon, who was determined to deal with Israel's economic problems, played a central and vital role in the stabilization. He understood how to use the JEDG, both the advice that came from it, and the fact that it was the channel to the United States. Many outside economists believed there was no-one in government who had the technical and political skills to bring about stabilization. I don't know how many such people there were, but there was at least one, Emanuel, who acted as the conductor of the stabilization orchestra, calling forth the right notes and even occasional harmony from the many players involved in the program, politicians and bureaucrats on the Israeli side, the administration and the legislature on the United States side.

After an abortive two visits to Washington in November 1984 and January 1985 by Israeli economists, to explore U.S. support for a program that would start with a pegging of the exchange rate and controls on some prices, with fiscal action being deferred until later, there was not much work until March. In March, George Shultz sent Herb and me to Israel, to try to figure out what needed doing.[10] We met with the relevant policymakers in the Treasury and the Bank of Israel, with academics, and with the Secretary-General of the Histadrut. At the end of this visit Herb pulled out of his pocket a list of ten points, ten actions the Israelis needed to take in order to stabilize the economy. The ten points were a bit heavier on the monetary aggregates than I might be today, and some Israeli friends told me there was too little on the fiscal side, but they were the essential components of a stabilization program.

Supplemental Aid

There were intensive contacts between the Israelis and the U.S. side in the first half of 1985. By that stage Israel's request for a safety net for stabilization had taken shape as a proposal for a $1.5 billion grant that the United States would provide to Israel when it stabilized.

From the time of Herb's and my visit to Israel in March, until the end of July 1985, much of the attention of the U.S. side was focused on, first, encouraging the Israeli government to stabilize, and second, making sure that the supplementary aid was not disbursed to the Israelis before they had taken action to stabilize the economy. The problem was that Congress was so favorably disposed towards Israel at that time, it was difficult for the administration to keep them from giving money to the Israelis no matter what their economic policy.

With the permission of both Herb Stein and George Shultz, I want to tell two stories, which illustrate both the Congressional pressure to give the money to the Israelis, and the subtlety of the Israel–U.S. relationship.

First, a story about Herb. In April 1985, after our visit to Israel, the two of us were called to testify to a subcommittee of the House Appropriations Committee, chaired by Congressman David Obey. This was supposedly a secret meeting, but Danny Halperin, the Economic Attache at the Israel Embassy in Washington, was there.

We explained what we hoped would happen, and how the U.S. aid would be used. Congressman Jack Kemp, who came in late, looked at us and said, "You are worse than the IMF; all you're going to do is to create a recession. What Israel needs to do is to cut taxes, not to go in for austerity." Then he turned to Herb Stein and said, "Professor, how much aid would it take Israel to stabilize the economy?" And Herb replied without missing a beat, "Congressman, it will take exactly as much money as you are willing to give them. It's called supply side economics."

The second story took place at the end of May 1985, just before the U.S. team went to Israel for what we were sure was going to be the critical meeting with the Israeli government. At that time, there were many signs that the Israeli government was trying to get the money without agreeing to a program.

Further, George Shultz did not like the idea of conditionality. All along his idea had been that the Israeli government would set out a program with their own "markers," actions that they would set as their own conditions so that both sides could monitor the program. Neither Herb nor I thought that this generous approach would work, and so Herb visited George Shultz to ask him if we could impose conditions on the aid. Shultz said no. Herb called me in Boston and said, "Well, why don't you try?"

I was, as usual, staying up late to try to finish a paper for a conference[11] but managed to fit in a six hour trip to Washington on the day I was supposed to depart from Boston for our Israeli visit. I arrived at the State Department with a speech all ready to deliver to Secretary Shultz. As I was winding up to deliver my speech, he said, "You want me to tell the Israelis that they are not going to get the money unless they do a program, is that right?" And I said yes. He said, "Well, I won't say that." I asked why not, and he said, "Because they will get the money even if they don't carry out the program, and I don't make threats that I can't carry out."

So I said "Well, this is awkward. We are going to Israel to say you have to carry out this program, or else. What is the or else?" Mr. Shultz thought about it for a while and he said, "You can tell them I will be very disappointed if they get the aid without carrying out the program."

Before coming to this tenth anniversary conference, I wrote to George Shultz to ask if he would mind my telling this story. He wrote back and said it would be fine to tell the story, but that I should understand that the word "disappointed" carried a lot of weight under those circumstances. He must have meant that the U.S.–Israeli relationship is multidimensional, and that his goodwill was needed across the board. Besides, there was an extraordinary degree of trust between the Israelis and George Shultz.

Jerusalem, June 1985

The U.S. delegation for the JEDG meeting in Jerusalem in June 1985 was headed by Allan Wallis. The key meeting took place on June 3 between the U.S. side and the Israeli economic team, headed by Prime Minister Peres and including, of course, Finance Minister Modai. I am sure Mr. Modai will confirm that the U.S. side did not go beyond its brief on conditionality.

Under-Secretary Wallis opened for the U.S., and he was followed by Herb Stein. They made very strong presentations, emphasizing among other things that the monthly inflation rate in April had been 19.4 percent. When my turn came, I started with two general comments: first, that working with the State Department, I had been astonished by the depth of support for Israel, and that the proposals that were being made came from friends of Israel. And second, that there were many excellent economists in Israel who had been thinking about how to do a stabilization, on whom the Prime Minister could draw. Further, that although views on what had to be done might seem to differ among these economists, there was virtually total agreement on the essentials, including the need for a large budget cut and for a devaluation.[12]

Among other things, I said that no economic program has succeeded without a small team that runs the intellectual part of it and that is responsible for the coherence of the program and for following its execution.[13] At that point Mr. Peres turned to Emanuel Sharon and said in Hebrew, "Who will we put on the team?"—and that was the moment that I knew that this time the Israeli government would actually undertake a serious stabilization program.

After that, the team of Emanuel Sharon, Mordecai Fraenkel[14] (Research Director of the Bank of Israel), and Amnon Neubach (Economic Adviser to the Prime Minister) as the insiders, and Michael Bruno and the late Eytan Berglas as the outside academics, was appointed, and the hard work began. They worked intensively, together and with the Prime Minister, and on July 1, after an all-night cabinet meeting, the historical stabilization program was adopted. The American role was much less significant after that.

Economic Aspects of the Program

It is important to recall that this was a heterodox program, orthodox in the massive (about 8 percent of GDP) cut in the budget deficit, brought about mainly through a cut in subsidies, the fixing of the exchange rate[15] and the tightening of monetary policy, but decidedly not orthodox in freezing prices and originally wages. The heterodox elements played an important part in bringing inflation down almost immediately, after the initial price shock associated with the devaluation, and were certainly critical to the political acceptability of a very tough program.

I am sure that George Shultz did not like the heterodox parts of the program, nor did Herb Stein; they had both been in the Nixon administration when it imposed wage-price controls, and they thought that had been a mistake. But as long as the fundamentals, particularly the budget deficit, were taken care of, they were willing to go along—the very tough budget correction made everything else in the program possible. I don't underestimate the importance of the heterodox elements. Nor should one underestimate the role of the pegged exchange rate: I believed then, and believe now, that pegging to the exchange rate in a situation when you have very little idea what will happen to money demand, is the right strategy.

I would like also to reflect on a few aspects of the program that have been underemphasized. One, which I largely missed at the time, and that George Shultz emphasized from the beginning, was the Bank of Israel Law. From 1984, at every meeting with the Israelis, Shultz kept asking when that law was going to be passed.[16] Believing in those days that if you are going to do the right thing you will do it with or without a law, I couldn't understand his insistence. However, the law was extremely important: it freed up the Bank of Israel to do what had to be done to assure the success of the stabilization program.

The second element that I would like to mention is that every program is tested at some point. Exchange-rate based stabilizations are easy in the beginning. Countless exchange-rate based stabilizations have reduced inflation early. It is the next two or three years that the program succeeds or fails.

That is what happened in Israel. It took a big battle between the Bank of Israel with its newly appointed governor, Michael Bruno, and populist pressures to cut interest rates and devalue, to ensure the success of the stabilization program. The battle was concentrated in 1986 and 1987, but guerilla warfare continued afterwards.

There are two types of economies. In some economies people are always pushing for an appreciation; those economies are in real trouble, because there are no exporters. In other economies people are always pushing for a depreciation; they are in better shape because the export interests dominate, but they are bound to have a serious problem with inflation. The predominance of the devaluation school in Israel is exaggerated to a remarkable degree. The unremitting pressure in this country for devaluation no matter what, for lower interest rates no matter what, was dealt with by a newly independent central bank and by a tough governor with the courage to use the legal independence he had been given.

Those were difficult times for the Bank of Israel. It took a recession in 1988–1989 to bring about the stabilization after all. Miguel Kiguel and Nissan Liviatan (1990) have argued that you always get a recession in a stabilization program, it is just that with an exchange-rate based stabilization, the recession comes later. However, I don't think it was inevitable that there be a stabilization-related recession in the

Israeli case. Rather, I believe that the recession can be traced to a very specific mistake that was made early in the program.

The stabilization program assumed a cut in real wages that was supposed to accompany the reduction of absorption in the domestic economy produced by the budget-cutting exercise. After a one-time nominal wage increase, there was a wage freeze at the beginning, and a cut in real wages as a result of the larger price level change associated with the devaluation. The wage freeze generated pro-tests and strikes. Just when the government was winning that battle, it signed a very generous wage deal with the Histadrut, which I believe led eventually to the recession. The deal raised real wages by a cumulative 12 percent in the first three months of 1986, totally undoing the real wage decline at the beginning of the program. Consumer demand rose and the economy grew rapidly. The Bank of Israel had to put on the interest rate brakes to prevent a recurrence of inflation. That led to a recession—but not one that was inevitable from the beginning.

I made at least one other mistake at the time, in underestimating the importance of structural reforms. My colleagues on the U.S. team, particularly Martin Bailey, economic advisor in the State Department, were pushing hard for structural reform from the beginning. As a good macroeconomist I said rightly that this doesn't have much to do with stabilization. That's true. But given the need for structural reforms in Israel, including privatization, and the resistance of the political system to making them, the pressure for structural reform should have been much greater from the American side which was then at its time of maximum leverage; it should be greater now; and it should be much greater from Israeli economists.

If there is a real failure in the stabilization program, this was it: the second stage, the structural reforms, either didn't happen or have taken place very slowly. There have been some reforms in the capital markets, and trade liberalization is continuing. But the privatization debate is much the same now as it was ten years ago. Relatively little has been privatized, and the same reasons are given for not privatizing: the stock market is either too high or too low, it is necessary to put a regulatory framework in place, the investors are unwilling, and so forth. The first time you hear why privatization is going slowly you are very impressed. You are less impressed hearing the same stories ten years later. Similarly, progress in re-ducing the role of government in the economy, and in removing a variety of price and non-price barriers to competition, has been extremely slow.

Growth after the stabilization was disappointing, and it should have been possible to make progress with structural reform more rapidly. Of course, with growth now at 6 percent, the perceived need for reform has been reduced, but those reforms—including the need to cut the size of government—would still raise the growth rate.

Concluding Comments

I am surprised to come to Israel every few months and hear the same arguments that were made more than ten years ago and that led to the high inflation: we need a devaluation, we need lower interest rates, and a little more inflation doesn't hurt. Today the Israeli economy is overheating, growth is rapid, unemployment is below the natural rate—and there is pressure for lower interest rates. To be sure, the argument is that the interest rate should be cut to produce a devaluation, which is needed because the current account deficit is large. But in these conditions, cutting interest rates through monetary expansion will lead very rapidly to inflation. The right cure is a tightening of fiscal policy, which will reduce aggregate demand and make it possible to reduce interest rates and depreciate without increasing inflation.

It was relatively easy to get inflation down to the 20 percent range in the stabilization program. It was much more difficult to get it down to the single digit range. Inflation is finally within that range now. It is tempting to say that a small incease in inflation wouldn't make a difference, so interest rates should be cut whether or not there is a fiscal contraction. But without a fiscal contraction, inflation will show up very quickly, and then there will be the same argument, that another few percent on the inflation rate doesn't matter. In fact, a percent or two more of inflation never does matter much. It's just that these things add up. That is how you get to higher and higher inflation—and we should not need to be reminded that inflation is very costly to the economy and the society.

Let me sum up with a true story. In December 1984, since George Shultz had appointed us to work on stabilizing the Israeli economy, and I had never before been involved in such an exercise except in the text books, I went to see a very senior IMF official, to ask him how to stabilize an economy. He had been studying the Israeli economy and he said, "Forget it. They are not going to stabilize now. They don't have enough of a crisis. It's true the inflation rate is 500 percent, and there has been pressure on the reserves, but the economy is still growing a bit. They have a guarantee of U.S. assistance if there is a run on the reserves. You will not persuade them to undertake a stabilization until the crisis gets much worse."

Well, we are all very grateful that he was wrong. You did stabilize earlier than other economies would have, the stabilization was skilfully carried out, and it has been extremely successful. George Shultz helped make that happen. But U.S. assistance also made it a relatively costless stabilization. Unlike stabilizations from hyperinflation, like the German hyperinflation, or the Argentinian hyperinflation of 1990, this inflationary episode did not leave enough antibodies to inflation in the system. In that respect, this was a stabilization that came too easily.

Notes

1. This is an edited and extended version of a lecture given at the Israel Economic Association's Conference on the 10th Anniversary of the Israeli Stabilization Program. Although the lecture has been rewritten, I have tried to retain its informal tone. The conference took place in Jerusalem in June 1995, and this paper will appear in the Hebrew language *Economic Quarterly*, vol. 42, no. 4, Dec. 1995. I am grateful beyond words to the late Don Patinkin, who had taken a keen interest in the stabilization program, and who managed despite his terminal illness to attend the lecture. I am grateful also to George Shultz and Herbert Stein, both for permission to quote from conversations, and for their extraordinary cooperation during the period we worked together on Israeli stabilization.

2. The views expressed are those of the author, and not necessarily of the International Monetary Fund.

3. For instance in the volumes edited by Bruno *et al*, 1988, and 1991.

4. Bruno (1993) presents the most complete account of the stabilization program.

5. Shultz started his academic career as an Assistant Professor at MIT.

6. I was invited by Mordecai (Meme) Fraenkel, then Director of the Research Department, who had spent the academic year 1978–1979 as a Visiting Scholar at MIT.

7. The paper was published in 1984.

8. Representatives of other interested U.S. government agencies, including Treasury and OMB, attended meetings of the advisory group and meetings with representatives of the Israeli government throughout. Shultz took over formal control of the U.S. role in the Israeli stabilization program at a meeting in March 1985 attended by Secretary of Treasury Baker, White House Chief of Staff McFarlane, OMB Director Stockman, Richard Murphy and Tim Hauser from the State Department, and Herb Stein and myself.

9. The original group of four private economists gradually became two, Herb and I. Herb Stein (1990) has published his own brief account of the stabilization.

10. Of course, there had been much thinking by Israeli and other economists about Israeli stabilization; several of the plans are described in Bruno (1993).

11. This paper, "Exchange Rate versus Money Targets in Disinflation," later published in my book, *Indexing, Inflation, and Economic Policy* (MIT Press 1986), was written to analyze the basic choice between a fixed exchange rate and money targets that would have to be faced in the Israeli stabilization.

12. I was covering many of the same points as Herb Stein.

13. Emanuel Sharon and I had discussed this and other details of the possible stabilization program the day before.

14. Meme and I worked closely together during the stabilization. His good judgment could be relied on for an accurate reading of what was happening and what would happen.

15. Successful stabilizations from high inflation have generally operated with a fixed exchange rate. Only in recent years, in some of the transition economies, have there been successful money-based stabilizations.

16. The law removed the obligation for the Bank of Israel to finance the government deficit.

References

Bruno, Michael (1993). *Crisis, Stabilization, and Economic Reform*. Oxford: Clarendon Press.

———, Guido Di Tella, Rudiger Dornbusch, and Stanley Fischer (1988). *Inflation Stabilization*. Cambridge, MA: MIT Press.

———, Stanley Fischer, Elhanan Helpman, and Nissan Liviatan, with Leora Meridor (1991). *Lessons of Economic Stabilization and Its Aftermath*. Cambridge, MA: MIT Press.

Fischer, Stanley (1984). "The Economy of Israel," in *Carnegie-Rochester Conference Series on Public Policy*, Vol. 20, Spring.

———, and Jacob Frenkel (1982). "Stabilization Policy for Israel" *Economic Quarterly*, (Hebrew) 29, 114 (Sept.), 246–255.

Kiguel, Miguel, and Nissan Liviatan (1990). "The Business Cycle Associated with Exchange Rate Based Stabilization," mimeo, World Bank.

Stein, Herbert (1990). "Israel's Economy: Observations of an Adviser," *American Enterprise*, 1 (May–June), 12–18. (American Enterprise Institute).

12 *Introduction*

When I joined the IMF in September 1994, the attention of the institution was focused on the transition process in the more than thirty countries that were formerly in the Soviet bloc. Inflation remained high in all the countries of the former Soviet Union, and growth had barely begun in any of the transition economies.

Controversies abounded: shock therapy versus gradualism; whether inflation stabilization was necessary before growth could begin, or whether instead growth was impossible unless inflation was in the 40 percent range; whether the exchange rate should be fixed or flexible; how rapidly to liberalize prices and trade; whether, how, and how rapidly to privatize; the right sequencing of structural reforms; and more.

At the same time, the fact that so many economies were attempting to make the transition offered an unparalleled opportunity for econometric analysis, despite the very few observations available on individual economies. When Ratna Sahay, Carlos Vegh, and I started work on this chapter, transition in Poland was only six years old, and most countries of the former Soviet Union had started their transition only three years before, in 1992. Nonetheless, by using a panel of the twenty-six transition countries for which data were available, and by deploying the indices of the extent of structural reforms in these economies developed by the EBRD, we were able to extract some conclusions from the early experience.

Our basic conclusion was that rapid macroeconomic stabilization was conducive to growth. So too were structural reforms. These conclusions were broadly supportive of the conventional wisdom, which was embodied in the approach to transition being followed by the IMF and the other international agencies. However, the data and the methods of analysis were not sufficiently refined for us to be able to answer some of the more difficult questions then being discussed, for instance those on the desirable speed of privatization or on the sequencing of reforms.

The broad conclusions we drew have stood up to the further experience of the transition process. Indeed, they may seem obvious by this stage. But they were not obvious at the time, partly because many argued that China's experience provided a different lesson, namely that reforms should be gradual, particularly price and trade liberalization. As Sachs and Woo (1994) and others have emphasized, the structure of the Chinese economy was very different from that of the countries in the former Soviet bloc when they began their respective reforms. The Chinese economy was far more heavily agricultural than nearly all the former Soviet economies—and transition in agriculture in China was very rapid. Thereafter growth in China took place in the context of rapid industrialization. In Russia and the former Soviet bloc, the need was to reduce the size of the heavy industries and develop a more modern industrial structure. Ironically one or two articles have now appeared tentatively asking whether Russia's more rapid approach to industrial restructuring might in the end turn out to be more successful than China's gradualist strategy, for China still faces the formidable problem of reforming the state-owned industrial enterprises.

Just over a decade after the start of the transition experience, the transition countries are no longer treated as a single group. Nearly all of the twenty-six countries studied in this paper have achieved macroeconomic stabilization, and despite the similarities among them, each has to contend with its own structural problems. Structural reforms in the countries that are candidates for entering the European Union are being powerfully driven by the accession process. Reforms in the other transition economies are at different stages of progress, with the attainment of macroeconomic stability and the revival of the structural reform process in Russia the most important development among those countries.

Looking back, what should we say about the transition process? First, overall the process has been a remarkable political success, in that most of the countries that set out on the road to a market economy, turning their backs on communism and central planning, retain that orientation. That is no small achievement. Second, the Baltics and the countries that are closest to Western Europe have by and large done better than those farther away. This second result reflects the importance of a political consensus on the political and economic direction in which the country should move. Third, the process was more costly than it had to be in some countries, in which reforms were halting—thus delaying the return of growth—and in which the most vulnerable members of the population were not protected during the transition.

A great deal has been made by some who were not involved in the transition process about the failure to recognize the need for institutional reform and an appropriate legal framework for the private economy. The failure was not one of recognition, as a look at the literature at the start of the reform process will confirm (for example, Fischer and Gelb 1991). Nor was there any lack of trying to build the legal and institutional frameworks. Rather the failure was one of execution, for a great deal of advice and detailed technical assistance was offered in these areas, and many laws were passed. The key question then became whether to move ahead with other structural reforms or to wait for the right institutional framework to be developed. That was a question to which there was no general answer, but rather the need to examine each issue separately.

Finally, after 1998 a debate developed on "Who lost Russia?" The answer is that Russia was not lost, but rather continues down the reform path towards a market economy, in a basically democratic political system. To be sure, the process could have been more direct, and the 1998 crisis could have been avoided had Russia been able to pursue the policies laid out in its agreements with the IMF, and had it moved away from its exchange rate peg at an earlier stage.[1] But Russia has made the fundamental political decision to join the rest of the industrialized world. This has happened even though there was relatively little financial aid from the West to Russia. And that reflects the critical point: the Russian reform process was driven largely by Russia and Russians. We outsiders did as much as we could to support the reformers. That is what we should have done, and we probably had some influence at some times. We could have done more, particularly earlier. But Russia is too big, too powerful, and too complex for outside advisers and the international financial institutions to have been able to determine the outcome in Russia.

Note

1. Of course, some argue that it took the shock of the 1998 crisis to persuade Russia to become serious about stabilization and reform.

12

Stabilization and Growth in Transition Economies: The Early Experience

Stanley Fischer, Ratna Sahay, and Carlos A. Végh

More than 30 countries that were in the Soviet orbit or in the former Yugoslavia are currently in the process of economic transition from a centrally planned to a market-based system. A complete list of countries in such a transition would also include Cuba, Vietnam, China, and even certain African countries like Angola, Ethiopia, and Mozambique. The focus of this paper, however, will be on the nations of eastern Europe and those that were effectively part of the former Soviet Union.

The transition can be said to have begun in 1989, with Poland inaugurating its big bang stabilization and reform program on January 1, 1990. There were, of course, earlier attempts at reform among the transition economies: Yugoslavia in the 1950s, Hungary in 1968, and even the former Soviet Union at various times, including the attempts by Gorbachev. These attempts, however, did not have the explicit goal of making the transition to a market economy. At the time the transition began, there was thus little direct experience of the process of economic transformation, and those advising on and designing the reforms had to draw on general principles and related experiences—the lessons from structural reforms in developing countries in the 1980s and earlier, the experience of China since the late 1970s, and previous reform efforts in the transition economies themselves.

Mainstream analyses of the transition process generally emphasized the need for action in six areas (for example, Lipton and Sachs, 1990; Fischer and Gelb, 1991): macroeconomic stabilization; price liberalization; trade liberalization and current account convertibility; enterprise reform (especially privatization); the creation of a social safety net; and the development of the institutional and legal framework for a market economy (including the creation of a market-based financial system). Price and trade liberalization would reinforce each other in permitting international competition to affect domestic prices.

Given the goal of moving to a market economy, there could not be much disagreement over the general proposition that reform was needed in these areas. However, major controversies arose over the speed and sequencing of reforms and the strategy to be followed in each area. The debate over the speed of reform was frequently cast in terms of "big bang" or "shock therapy" versus gradualism.[1] In practice, the big bang could apply only to certain aspects of the reform process—macroeconomic stabilization and price and trade liberalization—for the other three elements of the reform process inherently take time. However, decisions to initiate action and proceed in the other three areas could be taken earlier or later.

Interesting and critical as the answers to the questions of the optimal speed and sequencing of reform are, it was necessary to make decisions on how to proceed well before the evidence could be gathered. As time has passed, the experiences of individual countries and groups of countries have been examined and lessons drawn. More recently, as data have become available, more quantitative analyses of the experience of the transition economies have become available through the European Bank for Reconstruction and Development (EBRD) in its 1994 and 1995 *Transition Reports*, De Melo, Denizer, and Gelb (1995), Havrylyshyn and Botousharov (1995), and Sahay and Végh (1996), among others.

The focus of this paper is on the relationship between stabilization and growth. There are essentially two views on this issue. The first is that stabilization is necessary for the resumption of growth. This view draws on a priori arguments that inflation is bad for growth as well as evidence that inflation is negatively associated with growth (Fischer, 1993; De Gregorio, 1993). Recent work by Bruno and Easterly (1995), which argues that 40 percent per annum inflation is a red line beyond which growth will not be sustained, is particularly convincing in this regard, though it does not draw on the experience of the transition economies.

The alternative view is that the transition economies are not like market economies, and that inflation in transition economies therefore cannot be reduced to below the 40–50 percent per annum range without adversely affecting growth, unless key structural reforms

—particularly privatization and demonopolization—have already been implemented.[2] While no one argues that hyperinflation is good for growth, there are some who assert that, because firms need access to easy credit, inflation rates much below 10 percent per month are simply impossible if the economy is to grow.

In this paper, we first present and summarize data on the experience of growth and stabilization in 26 transition economies in eastern Europe, the former Soviet Union, and Mongolia for the period 1989–1994. When the average performance for this group is profiled, a rather bleak picture emerges: real GDP has fallen uninterruptedly since reforms began, while inflation has been high and rising, fueled by fiscal deficits averaging more than 6 percent of GDP. Such profiles in *chronological time*, however, hide a simple but key fact: countries started their inflation stabilization programs at different points in time. A brighter picture emerges when the data are rearranged in *stabilization time*: in the year of stabilization, inflation falls substantially and continues to fall thereafter, as fiscal deficits are brought under control. More remarkably, output quickly begins to recover and after two years growth is positive. These results strongly suggest that reducing high inflation is a precondition for the revival of growth.

After establishing the typical patterns of inflation and growth, we conduct an econometric analysis of the main short-run determinants of growth and inflation. As expected from the stabilization time profiles, we find that lower fiscal deficits have led to lower inflation and higher growth. Moreover, pegged exchange rate regimes appear to have been more effective in reducing inflation and thus raising growth. This evidence is consistent with the idea that while the reduction of fiscal deficits is a key precondition for disinflation, a pegged exchange rate may help in bringing about a more rapid disinflation from high inflation. Structural reforms also appear to have played a vital role in reviving growth and reducing inflation.

Recent Experience in Transition Economies

This section examines patterns of GDP growth, inflation and fiscal deficits for 26 economies in transition in eastern Europe, the former Soviet Union, and Mongolia. Warnings about the data are essential before proceeding.

Data Caveats

Most of the data used in this paper, which are available on request from the authors, have been provided to us by IMF (International Monetary Fund) economists working on these countries. They are based on estimates by national authorities or made by IMF economists for working purposes before official estimates become available. Given the often fragmentary information with which the IMF has to work and the differences in definitions of variables across countries, the country economists would put wide confidence intervals around the data. Thus, while it is customary when using data to issue warnings and then proceed, it is important in this case to emphasize that the biases in the data—particularly in output data—may well be very large and may affect some of the reported results.

There are two broad sets of qualifications. First, the output data are likely to be seriously biased, for both conceptual and measurement reasons. At a conceptual level, the prices at which goods were valued before the transition process began were out of line: the quality of goods was typically very poor and even purchasing power parity calculations are unlikely to capture the quality differences; goods were frequently not available at any price; and relative prices were different from world prices. The combined impact of these factors is likely to overstate the decline in output and the increase in prices that have been such an extraordinary feature of the transition process. To understand why, imagine the extreme hypothetical situation where goods had a positive price in the base period according to the national accounting system, but had zero value on the world market. Then, it could easily occur that output declines in terms of base period prices, but rises in terms of world market prices.[3]

Second, there is a serious measurement problem. Many of the republics of the former Soviet Union have had to build new independent statistical services, an inevitably slow process. Where earlier statistical systems did exist, they had been set up to measure output from the state sector. As the state sector output declines and private sector output rises, an increasing share of output is not recorded. Although no comprehensive re-estimates of GDP exist, Berg and Sachs (1992) provide a detailed analysis of the decline in Polish output between 1989 and 1990. They favor a demand-based estimate (that is, one based on consumption, investment and net exports), which suggests a decline of 4.9 percent over a supply-based estimate (that is, one based on sectoral shares of output in agriculture, industry and services) of a decline of 8.7 percent; both to be compared with a 12 percent decline in the official data. In general, in transition economies, official statistical reports place greater reliance on supply-based estimates. Dobozi and Pohl (1995) estimate the drop in GDP using power consumption as a proxy for changes in output. They argue not only that output declines are much smaller than official estimates for virtually all transition countries, but also that official underreporting in the countries of the former Soviet Union has been much higher than in eastern Europe.[4] Kaufmann and Kaliberda (1995) present calculations of the size of the unofficial economy, also based in large part on electricity consumption. Their preliminary conclusions are that on average the growth of the unofficial economy reduces output declines for countries of the former Soviet Union by about half, but with wide variations across countries.

Some of the measurement problems related to output data also apply to inflation. Since price increases in the previous controlled price regime may have been disguised as quality improvements and inflation in the black markets simply ignored, inflation during the transition may have been overestimated. Furthermore, during a period of price liberalization, both base-year weighted (Laspeyres) and current-year weighted (Paasche) price indices are likely to be biased upward (Osband, 1991). The mismeasurement of inflation is likely to have been greater in the initial stages of the transition process when prices were freed than in later stages when relative prices better reflected the scarcity of goods.

Basic Information and Indicators

Table 12.1 lists the 26 countries in eastern Europe, the former Soviet Union, and Mongolia, for which we have comprehensive data for the period 1989–1994.[5] In the judgment of the IMF economists working on those countries, stabilization plans have been implemented in 25 of the 26 countries, with Turkmenistan being the exception. For each country, we list the date on which the stabilization program was implemented. The date given is the starting date of a country's *inflation* stabilization program and not necessarily the starting date of

Table 12.1
Initial conditions and stabilization programs in transition economies

Country	Stabilization program date	Exchange regime adopted	CMEA exports to total GDP (1990)[a]	GNP/ Capita at PPP (US$ 1988)[b]
Albania	August 1992	Flexible	2.3	1386
Armenia	December 1994	Flexible	21.3	4923
Azerbaijan	January 1995	Flexible	33.1	4456
Belarus	November 1994[c]	Flexible	44.5	7218
Bulgaria	February 1991[c]	Flexible	15.3	5968
Croatia	October 1993	Fixed	5.6	NA
Czech Republic	January 1991	Fixed	9.8	NA
Estonia	June 1992	Fixed	27.2	9078
Georgia	September 1994	Flexible	19.1	6390
Hungary	March 1990	Fixed	9.8	6569
Kazakhstan	January 1994	Flexible	17.8	4666
Kyrgyz Republic	May 1993	Flexible	21.3	3244
Latvia	June 1992	Flexible/Fixed[d]	31.3	7911
Lithuania	June 1992	Flexible/Fixed[d]	33.7	6816
Macedonia, FYR	January 1994	Fixed	5.6	NA
Moldova	September 1993	Flexible	24.8	4596
Mongolia	October 1992[c]	Flexible	17.3	NA
Poland	January 1990	Fixed	16.5	4941
Romania	October 1993[c]	Flexible	3.3	3722
Russia	April 1995[c]	Flexible	17.9	7519
Slovak Republic	January 1991	Fixed	9.8	NA
Slovenia	February 1992	Flexible	4.6	10663
Tajikistan	February 1995[c]	Flexible	22.1	2730
Turkmenistan	Not started	Not applicable	33.6	3825
Ukraine	November 1994	Flexible	24.6	5536
Uzbekistan	November 1994	Flexible	24.0	3046

Sources: IMF staff estimates; national authorities; De Melo, Denizer, and Gelb (1995).
a. CMEA stands for the Council for Mutual Economic Assistance—a regional trading arrangement comprising the former USSR and nine other Soviet bloc countries. In the case of FSU countries, the ratios are FSU exports to GDP.
b. As currencies have generally been undervalued during the transition, the PPP measures are far higher than measures in U.S. dollars based on market exchange rates.
c. These countries had more than one stabilization attempt.
d. The Latvian currency was pegged to the SDR in February 1994; Lithuania adopted a currency board in April 1994. Both countries had flexible exchange rate regimes prior to these dates.

an IMF program.[6] When several stabilization attempts have been made (which was the case in six countries), we take the most serious attempt (as of mid-1995) as the reference date.[7]

The third column of table 12.1 indicates the exchange rate regime adopted during the stabilization program. Countries that announced an exchange rate peg, including a crawling peg, are classified as having a fixed rate regime.[8] In two cases—Croatia and the former Yugoslav Republic of Macedonia (FYRM)—the exchange rate regime is classified as a peg on the basis of the policies actually implemented, even though the authorities did not explicitly announce it as such. Of course, many countries, in particular Azerbaijan and the Kyrgyz Republic, that are listed as having adopted a flexible exchange rate regime have often intervened in foreign exchange markets to stabilize the exchange rate.

The last two columns in table 12.1 relate to initial conditions of the economy: estimates of per capita GNP in 1988, on a purchasing power parity basis and the ratio of CMEA exports to GDP in 1990— both these measures are taken from De Melo, Denizer, and Gelb (1995). (CMEA stands for Council for Mutual Economic Assistance, a trading arrangement among the economies in the Soviet orbit.) The purchasing power parity GNP data provide a pretransition estimate of the relative income levels of the transition economies; current estimates, in dollars, would be *far* lower. The ratio of CMEA exports to GDP is an indicator of the extent of the shock the Soviet bloc countries suffered as their previous trading arrangements collapsed in the early 1990s. In the absence of data on CMEA exports for countries of the former Soviet Union, exports within the former Soviet Union are reported for these countries.

Table 12.2 provides information on inflation and output performance in all 26 economies during 1989–1994. The inflation rate is based on the consumer price index (CPI) when available; when the CPI was not available or the series was too short, the retail price index was used. Depending on whether inflation (or any other variable) is measured within a particular period (an "end-period" measure) or as an average in a particular period as compared to a previous period (an "average" measure), comparisons across countries or across time within the same country are likely to differ, particularly when inflation rates are high and variable. It is more common to report average measures, as these are more useful in studying and comparing the evolution of inflation over time. On the

Table 12.2
Inflation and output performance in transition economies, 1989–1994

Country	Year in which inflation was highest[a]	Maximum annual inflation[a]	Year in which inflation fell below 50%[a,b]	Year in which output was lowest[c]	Cumulative output decline (1989 = 100)[c]	Cumulative output growth since lowest level[d]
Albania	1992	236.6	1993	1992	39.9	19.9
Armenia	1993	10896.2	—	1993	66.8	5.4
Azerbaijan	1994	1788.0	—	1994	59.0	—
Belarus	1993	1994.0	—	1994	39.3	—
Bulgaria	1991	338.8	—	1993	27.4	1.4
Croatia	1993	1149.7	1994	1993	36.9	1.1
Czech Republic	1991	52.1	1992	1993	21.4	2.5
Estonia	1992	946.7	1993	1993	34.9	3.0
Georgia	1994	8273.5	—	1994	74.6	—
Hungary	1990	34.6	NA	1993	18.3	2.1
Kazakhstan	1992	2566.6	—	1994	51.2	—
Kyrgyz Republic	1993	1365.6	—	1994	50.6	—
Latvia	1992	958.2	1993	1993	52.0	2.8
Lithuania	1992	1162.6	1994	1993	61.1	1.7
Macedonia, FYR	1992	1927.3	—	1994	45.2	—
Moldova	1992	2198.4	—	1994	60.6	—
Mongolia	1992	325.0	1992	1993	22.3	2.1
Poland	1989	639.6	1992	1991	17.8	13.0
Romania	1993	295.5	—	1992	26.4	4.8

Russia	1992	2510.4	—	1994	48.3	—
Slovak Republic	1991	58.3	1992	1993	25.1	4.8
Slovenia	1991	246.7	1993	1992	16.8	6.9
Tajikistan	1993	7343.7	1994	1994	61.3	—
Turkmenistan	1993	9743.0	—	1994	36.5	—
Ukraine	1993	10155.0	—	1994	52.1	—
Uzbekistan	1994	1232.8	—	1994	15.6	—
All transition economies[e]		2632.2			40.8	
Eastern Europe and Baltics[e]		619.0			32.6	
FSU and Mongolia[e]		4645.6			49.1	

Sources: IMF staff estimates and national authorities.

a. Inflation calculated from December to December.

b. A dash indicates that inflation was above 50% during the transition years, as of 1994. In the case of Hungary, this criterion is not applicable, because inflation was below 50% even before 1989.

c. Output decline from 1989 to the year in which output was lowest. For countries in which output has not begun to grow, 1994 is taken as the year of minimum output. GDP measured on an annual average basis.

d. Lowest level refers to the lowest output level reached during 1989–1994. A dash indicates that no positive growth has been recorded as of 1994.

e. Simple average.

other hand, end-period measures are likely to convey more information if the focus is on developments *within* a particular period or on the response to policy variables within a short time period. Accordingly, average measures are reported in profiling the time path of inflation, while end-period measures are used in documenting extreme annual values and in conducting the econometric exercises.

Inflation has been extremely high in the transition economies. Of the 26 countries listed in table 12.1, 22 experienced at least triple-digit annual inflation in the 12 months preceding the month the stabilization program was implemented. The remaining four countries—the Czech Republic, the Slovak Republic, Hungary, and Tajikistan—had double-digit inflation. By the end of 1994, however, over half the countries had reduced inflation to the double-digit range, with Croatia having moved all the way to deflation. The maximum inflation rate was typically recorded at the start of the transition process, when price and, in most cases, trade controls were lifted. A qualification to these high inflation numbers is in order, as part of the recorded inflation during the year in which prices were freed was accounted by one-time price jumps that eliminated the monetary overhang from previous years (Sahay and Végh, 1996). Table 12.2 shows the year in which inflation was highest and the annual rate of inflation in that year.

Inflation in the transition economies often met Cagan's (1956) definition of a hyperinflation: inflation exceeding 50 percent in at least one month. The classic hyperinflations studied by Cagan took place in the aftermath of the First and Second World Wars. Although inflation exceeded 50 percent in at least one month in 17 out of the 26 countries in our sample, it persisted at this rate for more than four months in only two countries, Armenia and Georgia.[9] In most countries, the brief hyperinflationary outburst reflected the elimination of the monetary overhang upon price liberalization.

The reported cumulative output declines in the transition economies range from a minimum of 15.6 percent in Uzbekistan to an almost incredible 74.6 percent in Georgia. Table 12.2 shows the year in which output was lowest and the cumulative output decline in these 26 economies.[10] As already noted, these data are certainly inaccurate, perhaps highly so, with some estimates suggesting that output in the countries of the former Soviet Union decreased on average by about one half the reported amounts. Some of the largest output declines were recorded in countries that experienced civil

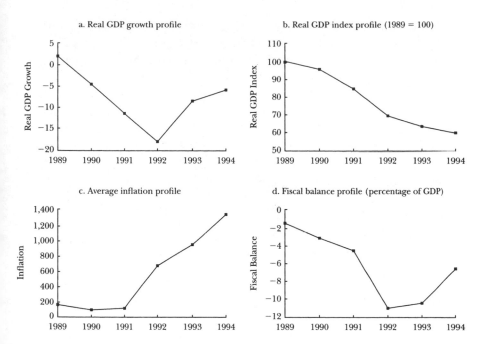

Figure 12.1
Growth, inflation, and fiscal balance profiles in calendar time: all transition economies.

war or trade embargoes, like Croatia, FYRM, Armenia, Georgia, Azerbaijan, and Tajikistan. From a welfare point of view, the significance of aggregate output measures should also be qualified in the light of the massive redistribution of income that is taking place during the transition process.

The overall picture of poor economic performance conveyed by the indicators just discussed is summarized in figure 12.1.[11] Panel *a* shows the (unweighted) average growth rate of measured real GDP since 1989—which we take to be the year in which the transformation process began—until 1994. Measured growth has on average been negative in every year. The growth rate reached a trough in 1992, reflecting the effects of the breakup of the Soviet Union and the collapse of CMEA trade. The growth rate then increased, but remained negative. The corresponding plot for the *level* of real GDP in panel *b* shows that, on average, GDP in 1994 was about 60 percent of its initial level. Despite the gloom of the aggregate output data, it should be noted that output growth was positive in more than half of the 26 economies in 1994. The story on inflation since the start of the transition process, presented in panel *c*, appears equally disturbing, with average inflation rising markedly since 1991. Panel *d* in figure 12.1 profiles the fiscal balance of the government as a percentage of GDP; the data are official estimates, based mainly on IMF staff discussions with the national authorities. An attempt was made to define the fiscal balance on a commitment, rather than a cash, basis; when not available, the fiscal balance was reported on a cash basis. Also, the general government budget figures are reported; when not available, central government data are used. Panel *d* highlights the large fiscal deficits during the transition.

Stabilization Time

The picture conveyed by the data just presented is obscured by looking at profiles in chronological time. As table 12.1 indicates, countries started their stabilization programs at different points in chronological time. An alternative way of looking at the data is to compute the profiles in "stabilization time." Stabilization time is denoted by $T + j$, where T is the year in which the stabilization program was implemented and j is the number of years preceding or following the year of stabilization. In the case of Poland, for instance, which stabilized in 1990, the year 1990 takes the value T in stabilization time, and a year such as 1994 takes the value $T + 4$. We then compute the average value for each variable in stabilization time. For example, GDP growth in the stabilization year is averaged for all countries, and this average is graphed at time T in panel *a* of figure 12.2. The average for GDP growth one year after stabilization is graphed at time $T + 1$ in that panel, and so on. Note that the number of observations for each year in stabilization time may differ. For example, there are only two observations relating to year $T + 4$ —those for Hungary and Poland, whose stabilizations started in 1990. For the purposes of the time profiles shown in the paper, we report averages only for those years in stabilization time for which there are at least three observations.

The shift from chronological time in figure 12.1 to stabilization time in figure 12.2 changes the picture dramatically. Panel *a* in figure 12.2 shows real GDP growth falling until the year of stabilization, but then recovering, with growth on average becoming positive in year $T + 2$. Panel *b* shows correspondingly that, in terms of levels, real GDP begins to increase two years after stabilization. Panel *c*

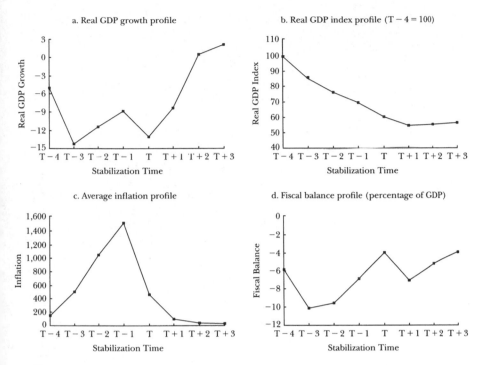

Figure 12.2
Growth, inflation, and fiscal balance profiles in stabilization time: all transition economies. Notes: Stabilization time T is defined as the year the stabilization program started. For details, see text.

shows that inflation, in turn, peaks in the year before stabilization, comes down very sharply when the stabilization plan is implemented and remains low thereafter.[12] The behavior of fiscal balances roughly mirrors the behavior of inflation. Panel d in figure 12.2 shows very large average fiscal deficits before stabilization—around 8–10 percent of GDP—followed by a significant improvement in the year of stabilization and, with a brief interruption, continued improvement.[13] The message that emerges from figure 12.2 is that real GDP rebounds following inflation stabilization, which in turn appears highly correlated with the improvement in the public finances.

Since there were systematic differences in the date of stabilization between the countries of the former Soviet Union and those of eastern Europe, the stabilization time profiles in figure 12.2 represent a changing population of countries. In particular, the observations for $T + 2$ and $T + 3$ come from eastern Europe and the Baltics, rather

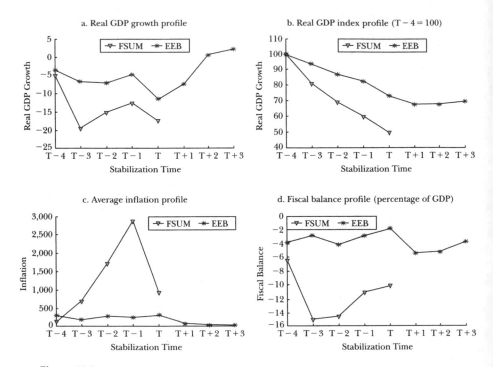

Figure 12.3
Growth, inflation, and fiscal balance profiles in stabilization time.

than from the other republics of the former Soviet Union. Therefore, we divided the sample into two groups: the first group comprises all countries of the former Soviet Union (excluding the Baltics) and Mongolia, referred to as FSUM in figure 12.3; the second group includes all eastern European countries and the Baltics, referred to as EEB in figure 12.3.

Figure 12.3 presents profiles in stabilization time for the two groups of countries. Since we do not show data points for which there are less than three observations, no poststabilization experience is shown for the FSUM group. For this group, panels *a* and *b* show that the level of output has been declining continuously. Inflation, however, declined sharply in the year of stabilization, as shown in panel *c*, helped by a significant improvement in the public finances, as shown in panel *d*, albeit to an average deficit close to 10 percent of GDP.

As in the FSUM countries, figure 12.3 shows that growth in eastern Europe and the Baltics is negative up to the year of stabilization. Real GDP growth turns positive two years after stabilization. Indeed, output has begun to grow in all these countries except FYRM, which was subject to a trade embargo. In terms of levels, average GDP for the EEB countries never fell as low as it did for the FSUM countries. Also, inflation in these economies never reached the levels that it did in the former Soviet Union, reflecting the fact that fiscal deficits were relatively lower. After stabilization, the average rate of inflation quickly fell below 100 percent, and then below 50 percent, although the scale of the chart makes this difficult to discern.

Inflation and Growth

The time profiles of figures 12.2 and 12.3 suggest that growth follows stabilization: inflation falls sharply in the year of stabilization and then growth revives. It is also apparent that much higher fiscal deficits are associated with higher inflation and thus lower growth.

We now report some efforts to investigate the growth-inflation association in more detail. In figure 12.4 we plot the average (logarithmic) inflation and growth rates for each country during the period 1992–1994. The relationship is negative and statistically significant ($R^2 = 0.63$), which confirms the existence of a negative correlation between inflation and growth for the countries in this sample.

We also examine the relationship between inflation and growth by asking whether there are individual country counterexamples to the negative association found in the regression. First we consider the 14 countries among the 26 where output growth had begun by 1994 (as shown in table 12.2). In 10 of these countries, annual inflation fell below 50 percent in the same year as growth began, or in an earlier year. The 10 countries are Albania, Croatia, Czech Republic, Estonia, Hungary, Latvia, Lithuania, Poland, Slovak Republic, and Slovenia. Of the four remaining countries in which growth has begun, inflation in Mongolia was just above 60 percent in 1994, the year growth began. In the case of Armenia, inflation was reduced more or less simultaneously with the recovery of output, and inflation was running at an annual rate of just above 50 percent in Armenia in the first six months of 1995. Bulgaria and Romania were the only two countries where growth was recorded as positive one or two years prior to inflation being reduced to below 50 percent. However, in the first

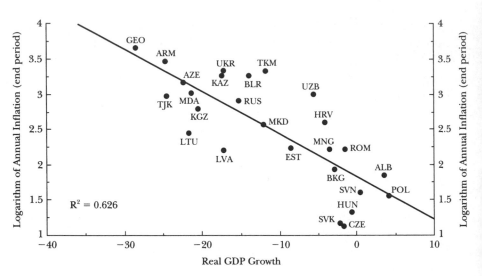

Figure 12.4
Transition economies: inflation-growth correlation, average of 1992–1994. Source: IMF staff estimates and national authorities. Notes: ALB: Albania; ARM: Armenia; AZE: Azerbaijan; BLR: Belarus; BGK: Bulgaria; HRV: Croatia; CZE: Czech Republic; EST: Estonia; GEO: Georgia; HUN: Hungary; KAZ: Kazakhstan; KGZ: Kyrgyz Republic; LVA: Latvia; LTU: Lithuania; MKD: Macedonia; MDA: Moldova; MNG: Mongolia; POL: Poland; ROM: Romania; RUS: Russia; SVK: Slovak Republic; SVN: Slovenia; TJK: Tajikistan; TKM: Turkmenistan; UKR: Ukraine; UZE: Uzbekistan.

half of 1995, both countries were still growing and inflation was reduced to an annual rate of less than 35 percent (annualized).

Examining the preliminary data for the first half of 1995 more systematically, there are now 15 economies that have begun to grow—the additional country is the Kyrgyz Republic, which also reduced its inflation rate sharply. In each of these economies, annualized inflation was around 50 percent or less in the first six months of 1995. These figures tend to support the view that low inflation—below 50 percent in annual terms—is a necessary condition for growth to begin.

There is also the question of whether countries that have low inflation are growing. As of 1994, 11 countries had reduced annual inflation below 50 percent. In 10 of these countries, growth revived either in the same year or with a lag of one to two years. The only exception is Tajikistan, which had very low inflation but negative growth in 1994. In this case, the low inflation was apparently due to an outright shortage of bank notes and not a result of a deliberate anti-inflation policy. Preliminary data show that Tajikistan returned to high inflation in the first six months of 1995. In addition, as of mid-1995, two other countries—Georgia and FYRM—have brought annualized inflation below 50 percent, but growth has not yet revived. As mentioned earlier, FYRM still faced trade embargoes during this period.

In conclusion, there are only two countries in this sample that were able to grow before inflation was reduced to an annual rate below 50 percent per annum. Conversely, countries that succeeded in reducing inflation also began to grow, typically with a lag. For this group of countries, therefore, stabilization appears close to being both a necessary and sufficient condition for growth.

Determinants of Growth and Inflation

The previous section documented the time patterns of GDP, inflation and the fiscal balance in the transition economies during the period 1989–1994. In this section, we use some simple econometric analysis to examine the determinants of growth and inflation. We run two sets of regressions, the first with the average annual rate of growth of real GDP as the dependent variable and the second with the annual end-period inflation rate, expressed as a logarithm, as the dependent variable. As explanatory variables, we considered: macro-economic policies (exchange rate and fiscal policy); the extent of structural reforms; and initial conditions—such as the initial level of per capita GDP, dependence on CMEA trade (or trade within the former Soviet Union) and the effects of the CMEA collapse in 1991 and the breakup of the Soviet Union in January 1992.

Data Definitions and Methodology

The growth rate data are the same as those presented in the previous section; the inflation rate data are based on end-period prices, as compared with annual averages in the time profiles. The figures for the fiscal balance of the government (measured as a percentage of GDP) are also the same as those used in the previous section. The effects of the exchange rate regime (as listed in table 12.1) were captured by a dummy variable, which takes on a value of one when the exchange rate was fixed, and zero otherwise. If the exchange rate regime changed during the sample period 1992–1994 (as in Latvia and Lithuania), we adopted the procedure of assigning the value of one (zero), if the exchange rate regime was fixed (flexible) for more than six months in that year.

The extent of structural reforms in each year was measured as an economic liberalization index (as computed by De Melo, Denizer, and Gelb, 1995, for the period 1989–1994, based on information presented in the 1994 and 1995 *Transition Reports*), where zero represents an unreformed planned economy and one represents a fully reformed economy. This index is a weighted average of three indices: price liberalization and competition (with a weight of 0.3), trade and foreign exchange regime (with a weight of 0.3), and privatization and banking reform (with a weight of 0.4). On the basis of the yearly liberalization index, De Melo, Denizer, and Gelb (1995) construct a cumulative liberalization index (CLI) to capture the depth of reforms over the 1989–1994 period. For econometric purposes, we used the CLI.

We experimented with two different ways of capturing the effects of the trade disruptions caused by the breakups of the CMEA and the Soviet Union. The first was to use a dummy variable ($Y92$), which takes a value of one for the year 1992 and zero otherwise; the second was to use the ratio of CMEA exports to GDP, presented in table 12.1. For countries formerly within the Soviet Union, we use exports within what used to be the Soviet Union. To the extent that exports within the former Soviet Union are an underestimate of CMEA exports for these countries, the estimated coefficient associated with the ratio of exports within the former Soviet Union to GDP will provide a lower bound of the impact of the breakup of the CMEA trade for these countries. Finally, World Bank estimates of per capita purchasing power parity income figures for 1991 were used.

To carry out the econometric analysis, we pooled the cross-section and time series data for all 25 countries for three years, 1992–1994. The main reason for excluding the period 1989–1991 is that macroeconomic policy as commonly understood in market economies simply did not exist in more than half the countries before 1992, especially in the former Soviet Union and Albania. In particular, it is difficult to define the exchange rate regime as either fixed or flexible during the pre-reform period.

Estimation was carried out using annual data for the three years for the 25-country sample.[14] We allowed for the intercept to vary across countries (to capture fixed effects), except when the CMEA exports to GDP variable (*CMEAGDP*) or initial income (*LCPWB*91) were included in the regression since the regressors become collinear (in that case, a common intercept was assumed). This formulation enables us to test whether there are differences across countries (presumably reflecting omitted variables), modeled as parametric shifts in the regression function.

The role of the exchange rate regime in stabilization and growth has been a subject of controversy for some time. Based on our reading of previous experience, we expected growth to be higher and inflation lower in countries with a fixed exchange rate. Stabilizations from high inflation have typically relied on a nominal exchange rate anchor, which tends to allow for a rapid remonetization of the economy (Sargent, 1982; Végh, 1992). But such stabilizations are not sustainable unless fiscal deficits are reduced. In the context of the transition economies, the benefits of pegged exchange rates have been stressed by Hansson and Sachs (1994) and Sahay and Végh (1996). In addition, stabilization from high inflation has typically been associated with growth rather than recession (Rebelo and Végh, 1995; Easterly, 1995).

We also expected inflation to be higher and growth lower the larger the fiscal deficit, the smaller the extent of market-oriented reforms and the higher the ratio of CMEA exports to GDP (because the breakup of the CMEA would then have a greater impact on the economy). Given the short time period, we did not have a firm expectation on whether initial per capita GDP would matter nor, if it did, in which direction. Endogenous growth theory predicts a negative relationship between the initial per capita income and the growth rate over some subsequent period in the long run. In the short run, however, it is quite possible that the quality of economic management may have been positively associated with income, in which case higher income would be associated with more rapid growth during the transition.

Of course, since our regressions are not based on a particular structural model, causation is in some cases not self-evident, and given that the data are sparse and preliminary, the empirical analysis should be viewed as exploratory and the results merely indicative of the relative importance of some key policy and structural variables.

Output Estimation Results

The first three columns in table 12.3 report the output growth results obtained from the fixed effects model. In all cases, country-specific effects turned out to be highly significant (using a likelihood ratio test), indicating that there were some differences across countries that are not captured by the explanatory variables. Column 1 shows that a pegged exchange rate regime and tighter fiscal policy were conducive to higher growth.

However, when further explanatory variables are added (regressions 2 and 3 in table 12.3), the fiscal variable loses significance. These additional variables—Y92, the time dummy intended to capture the effects of the trade disruptions, and CLI, the cumulative liberalization index—are highly significant. These results thus seem to confirm our prior that the CMEA collapse and the breakup of the Soviet Union had a major negative impact on growth across countries in 1992.[15] The state of market-oriented reforms, as reflected in the liberalization index CLI, appears to have been critical in spurring

Table 12.3
Fixed Effects Model for 25 Transition Economies, 1992–1994
(*t-statistics in parenthesis*)

	Dependent Variable: GDP Growth			Dependent Variable: Log of Inflation		
	(1)	(2)	(3)	(4)	(5)	(6)
FIXED	18.10	15.77	11.35	−2.72	−2.55	−1.84
	(3.04)	(3.10)	(2.00)	(−3.03)	(−2.90)	(−2.08)
FISCAL	0.53	0.30	0.30	−0.09	−0.07	−0.06
	(2.31)	(1.48)	(1.42)	(−2.47)	(−1.96)	(−1.68)
CLI			7.42			−0.97
			(3.54)			(−2.97)
Y92		−9.28			0.69	
		(−4.41)			(1.90)	
R-squared	0.64	0.75	0.72	0.71	0.73	0.75
Adjusted R-squared	0.45	0.60	0.55	0.55	0.57	0.61
Likelihood ratio	56.61	70.00	53.98	54.61	57.00	46.53
Probability value	0.00019	0.00000	0.00043	0.00035	0.00017	0.00382
Total observations	75	75	75	75	75	75

growth (regression 3). This is an important result from the policy viewpoint. In other analysis, not reported in table 12.3, we found that countries with lower initial per capita income had lower output declines.

The regressions thus suggest that countries that achieved macroeconomic stabilization (through the use of fixed exchange rates) and undertook deeper reforms grew faster. The results also point to the importance of initial conditions—trade dependency and initial per capita income—in influencing the growth rate during the transition.

Inflation Estimation Results

As in the growth regressions, we found the country-specific effects to be highly significant in the inflation regressions (as indicated by the likelihood ratio tests reported in table 12.3). Our most prominent finding, looking at the last three columns of table 12.3, was that the pegged exchange rate dummy and the measure of the fiscal position of the government are highly significant and, when used together, as in regression 4, explain more than 70 percent of the time series cross-country variation in inflation. The negative shock associated with Y92 is only marginally significant (at the 10 percent level, column 5). In contrast, and somewhat surprisingly, the liberalization index CLI turns out to exert a strong downward effect on inflation, as shown in column 6. The inclusion of CLI, however, improves the fit only marginally. We also found (but do not report in table 12.3) that countries that started with higher per capita incomes and those that suffered a larger CMEA shock had higher inflation rates during the transition.

The results thus strongly suggest that, in addition to addressing the fundamental fiscal disequilibria, a pegged exchange rate has been a key component of successful inflation stabilization packages. Moreover, structural reforms and initial conditions influenced the inflationary process during the transition.

Policy Lessons and Conclusions

As of the first half of 1995, growth had revived in 15 of the 26 transition economies studied here. With the exception of the former Yugoslav Republic of Macedonia, all eastern European countries are growing, and so are some countries in the former Soviet Union. Considering the extent of the transformations taking place in these economies, the decline in inflation and the return of positive growth within a few years has to be regarded as a major and striking achievement. The evidence discussed in this paper strongly suggests that growth requires stabilization and that stabilization leads to growth. Moreover, it appears that for growth to begin, annual inflation should be less than 50 percent. A fixed exchange rate and smaller fiscal deficits seem especially important in reducing inflation and raising growth rates.

However, there are alternative interpretations of the connection between inflation and growth. For instance, it may be that stabilizations succeed only if growth follows. If growth does not follow stabilization, then governments may find it impossible to sustain the stabilization. While this could be true, it is nonetheless striking that there are only two cases in which growth has taken place without inflation having been reduced to less than 50 percent per annum; moreover, even in these two cases inflation was on its way down and had declined to less than 35 percent soon after growth revived.

Alternatively, it could be argued that there is no inherent link between inflation and growth in these economies but, rather, that the link is forced by the policy conditionality of international financial institutions, which accompanies the access to external financing that is necessary for growth. A variant of this view would be that it is the benefit from foreign technical assistance provided by an IMF/World Bank program that produces growth, rather than the financing by itself. In most transition economies, inflation has been reduced in the context of explicit IMF stabilization programs with two exceptions, Croatia and Slovenia, which still received technical assistance from the IMF.[16] Thus, the idea that the stabilization-growth link is a product of IMF program design cannot be dismissed. However, the fact that the inflation-growth results for the transition economies so closely resemble those for other economies reported by Bruno and Easterly (1995)—in their case that countries in which inflation exceeds 40 percent per year get into trouble, and that countries that stabilize from high inflation typically experience growth—leads us to doubt that the results in this paper merely reflect IMF program design.

Yet another hypothesis is that countries that want to reform undertake a whole set of actions, of which inflation stabilization is one, but that the other components may be more important. The correlation between the index of structural reforms and stabilization is high, and would thus support this view. While the results in table 12.3 strongly support the view that structural reforms also promote growth, we do advance the hypothesis—based on prior results and those reported in this paper—that stabilization to an inflation rate of below 4 percent per month is a necessary condition for sustainable growth. We also regard the evidence as supporting the notion that transition countries that stabilize inflation will begin to grow within two years, though this assumes that governments that stabilize have a proclivity to reform, for one could imagine a country that stabilized inflation but undertook no structural measures and failed to grow. An additional aspect to keep in mind is that the stabilization efforts in all these countries are also likely to be mutually reinforcing to the extent that these economies initially depend on each other for export markets.

It could also be argued that the results on stabilization and growth presented in this paper reflect what has happened in the more advanced, more market-oriented economies of eastern Europe, and that they are not applicable to the other economies in transition—those of the former Soviet Union and Mongolia. That could be, but we doubt it. For one thing, the Baltics were in most respects deeply integrated into the economy of the former Soviet Union, but they stabilized early and began to grow just as the leading countries of eastern Europe. For another, in Albania, one of the least developed economies of eastern Europe, growth revived soon after a radical stabilization program.

While it is not possible to settle the issue of causation with the data available so far, we venture a prediction that is implied by the hypotheses we are advancing. The prediction is that the profile for the countries of the former Soviet Union and Mongolia will follow the pattern seen in figure 12.3 in the next few years. In other words, growth in these countries will on average increase in 1995 and will turn positive in most of these countries by 1996 or 1997.

Notes

We are grateful to our IMF colleagues for making data available and helping us in their interpretation. We received valuable comments from Alan Auerbach, Gérard Bélanger, Christopher Browne, Eric Clifton, Robert Corker, Cevdet Denizer, Alan Gelb, James Haley, Ishan Kapoor, Peter Keller, Alan Krueger, Christopher Lane, Henri Lorie, Neven Mates, Peter Murrell, Hiroki Owaki, Assaf Razin, Anthony Richards, Markus Rodlauer, Massimo Russo, Miguel Savastano, Mark Stone, Jeromin

Zettelmeyer, and, in particular, Paul Cashin and Sunil Sharma. Timothy Taylor offered extensive and very helpful suggestions on an earlier draft. We are thankful to Manzoor Gill and Ximena Cheetham for extremely efficient research assistance. The views expressed are those of the authors and do not necessarily represent those of the International Monetary Fund.

1. See Aslund (1995), Balcerowicz and Gelb (1994), and Sachs (1993) for arguments favoring speedy reform strategies; see also Klaus (1994). For theoretical analyses of the speed of transition, see Aghion and Blanchard (1994), Castanheira and Roland (1995), and Cohen (1995). Kornai (1993) presents a more gradualist view of optimal reform strategy. See also the interviews with policymakers in Blejer and Coricelli (1995).

2. This latter argument has been strongly propounded by Grigory Yavlinsky. Yavlinsky and Braguinsky (1994), for example, argue that de-monopolization needs to precede stabilization. The view that a tight monetary policy will not reduce the inflation rate in a monopolistic economy is an old one, though there is nothing in the quantity theory of money that requires a competitive economy for its operation. The familiar counterargument is that the existence of monopolies affects the level of prices, rather than their rate of change.

3. The opposite phenomenon happened in the Soviet Union in the 1930s, when growth in base year prices far exceeded that in later period prices (Fischer, 1994).

4. Dobozi (1995) presents further estimates. In a letter to the editor of *Transition* (April 1995, p. 11), Koen criticizes the method, pointing to several implausible results, for instance that output in Poland fell more in 1992 than indicated by the official data.

5. We exclude Serbia for lack of sufficient data, and East Germany because of the special circumstances of its transition—namely, reunification with a wealthy and industrialized West Germany. While our study excludes China, Cambodia, Laos, and Vietnam, we do believe that there is much to be learned from the experience of these countries: the interested reader might begin with Gelb, Jefferson, and Singh (1993) and Sachs and Woo (1994).

6. In practice, however, most stabilization dates coincide with the starting date of an arrangement with the Fund.

7. In principle, for the quantitative exercises undertaken below, all stabilization attempts should be included in the sample. However, due to the short sample period, these data points would not be statistically independent, which would imply "double counting" for the purposes of quantitative analysis. The choice of a particular stabilization program—when there have been multiple attempts—necessarily involved a judgment call on our part. We should stress though that the judgment about the seriousness of the stabilization attempt was not based on eventual inflation performance, but rather on an evaluation of the policy package associated with the stabilization attempt.

8. Latvia and Lithuania had flexible rate regimes at the time of stabilization but later moved to a fixed rate and hence are listed as flexible/fixed. We include Russia in the category of flexible since it moved to an exchange rate band only in July 1995.

9. Serbia, which is not in our sample, also experienced hyperinflation—by Cagan's definition—during 1993 and part of 1994 (Bogetic, Dragutinovic, and Petrovic, 1994; IMF staff estimates). All three countries—Armenia, Georgia, and Serbia—were affected by war.

10. For countries in which output has not begun to grow, we take 1994 as the year of minimum output. This means that the eventual recorded maximum output decline for some of the economies is likely to exceed the level reported in table 12.2.

11. Of the 26 countries in the sample, Turkmenistan is excluded from the time profiles in all figures and from the econometric analysis, because there had been no stabilization attempt as of mid-1995.

12. We do not show profiles of money growth, which would look very similar to the inflation profiles. Havrylyshyn and Botousharov (1995) present evidence showing a strong positive correlation between money growth and inflation for the transition economies.

13. The temporary deterioration in the fiscal balance a year after stabilization appears to be associated with the initial large expenditures needed for structural reforms (for example, creating social safety nets and cleaning up bad loans in the banking system).

14. To be specific, the estimated equation for the pooled cross-section time series regressions takes the form

$$DEPVAR_{it} = \alpha_i + \beta_1 FIXED_{it} + \beta_2 FISCAL_{it} + \beta_3 CLI_{it} + \beta_4 Y92_{it}(\beta_5 CMEAGDP_{it})$$
$$+ \beta_6 LPCWB91_{it} + u_{it},$$

where $DEPVAR$ is either log inflation or GDP growth, as defined above; i $(= 1, \ldots 25)$ indexes the country; t $(= 1992, 1993,$ and $1994)$ indexes time; and u is an error term assumed to be $i.i.d$ over i and t and uncorrelated with the explanatory variables. $FIXED$ is the exchange rate dummy; $FISCAL$ is the government balance variable (thus, a fiscal deficit would take on a negative value); CLI is the cumulative value of the liberalization index; $Y92$ is the time dummy for 1992; $CMEAGDP$ measures the exports going to other CMEA or FSU countries; and $LPCWB91$ is the log of per capita income in 1991, from World Bank data.

15. We also found (but do not report) that countries with larger shares of CMEA exports in total exports (or exports within the former Soviet Union) suffered larger output declines.

16. The Serbian stabilization program, not part of this study, was also highly successful in reducing inflation in early 1994 (Bogetic, Dragutinovic, and Petrovic, 1994) without an explicit IMF arrangement.

References

Aghion, Philippe, and Olivier Blanchard, "On the Speed of Transition in Central Europe," *NBER Macroeconomics Annual*, 1994, 9, 283–320.

Aslund, Anders, *How Russia Became a Market Economy*. Washington, DC: Brookings Institution, 1995.

Balcerowicz, Leszek, and Alan Gelb, "Macropolicies in Transition to a Market Economy: A Three-Year Perspective," *Proceedings of the World Bank Annual Conference on Development Economics*, 1994, 21–44.

Berg, Andrew, and Jeffrey Sachs, "Structural Adjustment and International Trade in Eastern Europe: The Case of Poland," *Economic Policy*, April 1992, 14, 118–155.

Blejer, Mario, and Fabrizio Coricelli, *The Making of Economic Reform in Eastern Europe.* Aldershot, Engl.: Edward Elgar, 1995.

Bogetic, Zeljko, Diana Dragutinovic, and Pavle Petrovic, "Anatomy of Hyperinflation and the Beginning of Stabilization in Yugoslavia 1992–1994," mimeo, World Bank and CES MECON, Belgrade, 1994.

Bruno, Michael, and William Easterly, "Inflation Crises and Long-Run Growth." NBER Working Paper No. 5209, 1995.

Cagan, Phillip, "The Monetary Dynamics of Hyperinflation." In Friedman, M., ed., *Studies in the Quantity Theory of Money.* Chicago: University of Chicago Press, 1956, pp. 25–117.

Castanheira, Micael, and Gerard Roland, "Optimal Speed of Transition: A General Equilibrium Analysis," mimeo, University of Bruxelles, 1995.

Cohen, Daniel, "The Transition in Russia: Successes (Privatization, Low Unemployment …) and Failures (Mafias, Liquidity Constraints …). A Theoretical Analysis." Centre for Economic Policy Research, London, Discussion Paper 1224, August 1995.

De Gregorio, José, "Inflation, Taxation, and Long-Run Growth," *Journal of Monetary Economics,* June 1993, *31,* 271–298.

De Melo, Martha, Cevdet Denizer, and Alan Gelb, "From Plan to Market: Patterns of Transition," mimeo, World Bank, September 1995.

Dobozi, Istvan, "Electricity Consumption and Output Decline: An Update," *Transition,* September/October 1995, *6,* 19–20.

Dobozi, Istvan, and Gerhard Pohl, "Real Output Decline in Transition Economies: Forget GDP, Try Power Consumption Data!" *Transition,* January/February 1995, *6,* 17–18.

Easterly, William, "When is Stabilization Expansionary?" mimeo, World Bank, 1995; forthcoming in *Economic Policy.*

European Bank for Reconstruction and Development, *Transition Report.* London: EBRD, October 1994.

European Bank for Reconstruction and Development, *Transition Report Update.* London: EBRD, April 1995.

Fischer, Stanley, "The Role of Macroeconomic Factors in Growth," *Journal of Monetary Economics,* December 1993, *32,* 485–512.

Fischer, Stanley, "Russia and the Soviet Union Then and Now." In Blanchard, Olivier, Kenneth Froot, and Jeffrey Sachs, eds., *The Transition in Eastern Europe.* Vol. 1, Chicago: University of Chicago Press, 1994, pp. 221–257.

Fischer, Stanley, and Alan Gelb, "The Process of Socialist Economic Transformation," *Journal of Economic Perspectives,* Fall 1991, *5:*4, 91–105.

Gelb, Alan, Gary Jefferson, and Inderjit Singh, "Can Communist Economies Transform Incrementally? The Experience of China," *NBER Macroeconomics Annual,* 1993, *8,* 87–133.

Hansson, Ardo, and Jeffrey Sachs, "Monetary Institutions and Credible Stabilization: A Comparison of Experience in the Baltics," mimeo, Harvard University, 1994.

Havrylyshyn, Oleh, and Peter Botousharov, "Five Years of Transition: Just the Facts," mimeo, IMF, 1995; forthcoming in *Bulgarian National Bank Review*.

Kaufmann, Daniel, and Aleksander Kaliberda, "Integrating the Unofficial Economy into the Dynamics of Post-Socialist Economies: A Framework of Analysis and Evidence," mimeo, World Bank, Kyiv office, 1995.

Klaus, Vaclav, *Rebirth of a Country: Five Years After*. Prague: Ringier, 1994.

Kornai, Janos, "Transformational Recession: A General Phenomenon Examined Through the Example of Hungary's Development," *Economie Applique*, 1993, 46:2, 181–227.

Lipton, David, and Jeffrey Sachs, "Creating a Market Economy in Eastern Europe: The Case of Poland," *Brookings Papers on Economic Activity*, 1990, 1, 75–133.

Osband, Kent, "Index Number Biases During Price Liberalization." IMF Working Paper 91/76, International Monetary Fund, 1991.

Rebelo, Sergio, and Carlos A. Végh, "Real Effects of Exchange Rate–Based Stabilization: An Analysis of Competing Theories," *NBER Macroeconomics Annual*, 1995, 10, 125–174.

Sachs, Jeffrey, *Poland's Jump to the Market Economy*. Cambridge, Mass.: MIT Press, 1993.

Sachs, Jeffrey, and Wing Thye Woo, "Structural Factors in the Economic Reforms of China, Eastern Europe and the Former Soviet Union," *Economic Policy*, April 1994, 18, 101–145.

Sahay, Ratna, and Carlos A. Végh, "Inflation and Stabilization in Transition Economies: An Analytical Interpretation of the Evidence," *Journal of Policy Reform*, forthcoming 1996.

Sargent, Thomas J., "The Ends of Four Big Inflations." In Hall, Robert E., ed., *Inflation: Causes and Effects*. Chicago: University of Chicago Press, 1982, pp. 41–97.

Végh, Carlos A., "Stopping High Inflation: An Analytical Overview," *IMF Staff Papers*, September 1992, 39, 629–695.

Yavlinsky, Grigory, and Serguey Braguinsky, "The Inefficiency of *Laissez-Faire* in Russia: Hysteresis Effects and the Need for Policy-Led Transformation," *Journal of Comparative Economics*, August 1994, 19:1, 88–116.

13   *Introduction*

This chapter was presented at a conference entitled "Quo Vadis Europe?" The question raised by the title of the chapter is how far the transition countries of Central and Eastern Europe (CEE) are from those of Western Europe in terms of time and economic development. The key question is how long it will take the CEE countries to reach the income levels of the poorer West European countries.

The chapter focuses on the thirteen transition economies in CEE. It is an interesting fact, and not a coincidence, that the income levels of the former transition economies on average decline the farther east and south they are—and that countries' economic development compared to that of Brussels decreases along with their geographical distance from Brussels. The countries of central Europe, the Czech and Slovak Republics, Hungary, and Poland, are closer to the industrial heartland of Europe, which must be an important factor accounting for their relatively high incomes among the transition economies.

The chapter includes data (table 13.2) on the PPP income levels relative to the average of other European countries of six of the CEE countries for 1937 and for 1992. Every one of the six—Bulgaria, Czechoslovakia, Hungary, Poland, Romania, and Yugoslavia—lost significant ground relative to the average of the other European countries during those 55 years. Interestingly, the relative positions among the six, with Czechoslovakia in the lead, did not change during that period. And while there was convergence among the income levels of the West European countries during that period, there was none among the socialist bloc six.

The chapter shows considerable policy convergence among the CEE countries. Already in 1995, most of them were close to meeting the macroeconomic Maastricht criteria, except on inflation and the exchange rate. By now most of them have achieved low inflation. Their indices of structural reform are impressive, with only privatization and banking reform falling significantly behind (table 13.4). No doubt the prospect of entering the European Union has provided a critical incentive to the reform process in most of the countries.

We then ask how long it will take the 13 CEE countries to reach the income levels of the low-income European countries (Spain, Portugal, and Greece). Using standard growth regressions, the estimated answer varies from 11–15 years for the Czech Republic, to over 60 years for Albania. These are optimistic estimates of the transition time, for they assume good policies by the 13 CEE countries, and only 2 percent per capita growth in the low-income EU members. The results for the richest of the then transition countries are encouraging. But, as we note at the end of the chapter, the length of time it will take is not predetermined. It depends on the shocks— positive and negative—that will affect those economies. Even more, it depends on the policies those economies follow, which in turn depends on the extent of the domestic consensus on the political and economic direction in which the country should move.

At the end of the chapter (table 13.10), we estimate how much income per capita each of the six countries for which 1937 income data were available lost during the subsequent 55 years. And we then ask how long it will take to make up the gap for each country, assuming that growth from 1992 is determined by a standard growth regression. The estimate is that it would take about 23 years, or close to a generation. "In other words, the cost of the socialist experiment—which lasted roughly two generations—was, in terms of lost income, equivalent to about one generation."

13

How Far Is Eastern Europe from Brussels?

Stanley Fischer, Ratna Sahay, and Carlos A. Végh

Introduction

At the end of the 1930s, today's transition countries in Central and Eastern Europe (CEE) were at very different levels of development.[1] Starting at different times, and to differing extents, all these countries were in the Soviet economic orbit until 1990. With the transition process now well under way, the question is where they are heading and how far down the road they are.

The present destination, explicitly for some, implicitly for all, is Brussels.[2] The concept of the distance from Brussels is multidimensional. One simple measure, not without theoretical and empirical justification, is physical distance. The interest in this measure comes from the well-known work of Giersch (1979), which relates the level of economic development in Europe to distance from Düsseldorf (for other measures, see Gros and Steinherr [1995]).

Figure 13.1 shows the geographical distance from Brussels of the capital of each of the thirteen CEE countries included in this paper. Relative to countries already in the European Union (EU), CEE is not geographically far from Brussels. While no CEE capital is as near as that of most of the Western European countries, most are closer than Helsinki and Lisbon, and all are closer than Athens. By this distance standard, the CEE countries meet EU norms.

But, of course, the distances in which we are most interested are in time and in economic space. In this paper, we first compare income gaps between the countries of CEE and those of the EU, then evaluate recent economic performance in CEE in light of EU standards, and finally address the question of how long it will take the CEE countries to close the income gap with EU countries.

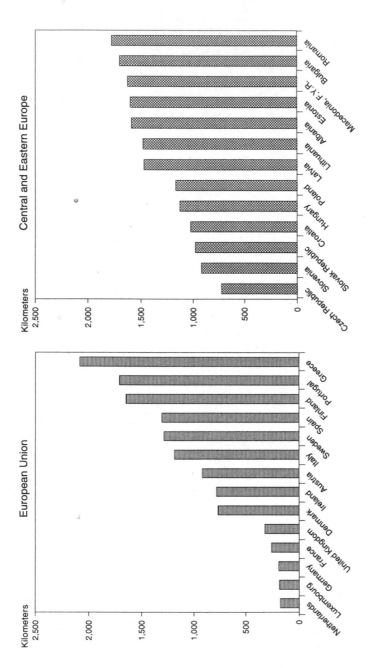

Figure 13.1
European Union, Central and Eastern Europe: distance of capital from Brussels (in kilometers).

A disclaimer and word of warning are in order before we begin. Forming an adequate judgment on how close a country is to Brussels requires detailed and sophisticated knowledge of the structure of the economy and its current and likely economic performance. We could not, even if we wanted to, form such a definitive judgment at this time. Rather, we seek here to provide a basis for further discussion by presenting various distance measures and relating them to economic performance and growth potential.

We present three different concepts of distance from Brussels: income gaps between CEE and EU countries, relative macroeconomic performance, and CEE's progress in adopting market-based systems. We find that, while income gaps are still large, the richer CEE countries are not far from the low-income EU countries. Recent macroeconomic performance in CEE has been quite impressive and several important indicators are, by and large, close to the Maastricht criteria. Structural transformation towards a market-based system has been fairly rapid, with privatization and financial sector reforms lagging behind. We also try to quantify the notion of distance from Brussels by asking how long it will take for CEE countries to catch up with EU countries. Based on long-run growth projections, we find that, on average, it may take about 30 years for CEE to catch up with the income levels in low-income EU countries.

Income Gaps

Table 13.1 shows income levels of CEE countries. These are PPP estimates for 1995, from the IMF's *World Economic Outlook* (WEO) database. While there is no overlap between the per capita income levels of CEE and the EU, it is worth noting that the levels in the more advanced CEE countries are quite close to those of some countries already in the EU. The highest 1995 PPP per capita income level in the CEE countries, that of the Czech Republic, was seven percent below that of Greece, the lowest per capita income country in the EU. The gap between the poorest country in CEE, Albania, and the richest in the EU, Luxembourg, is enormous: per capita real GDP in Albania is shown as less than two percent that of Luxembourg.[3]

Table 13.2 compares levels of per capita income in several EU and CEE countries in 1937 and 1992; that is, before the rise of socialism in CEE and soon after its fall. The most striking observation is that the per capita income of each of the six CEE countries relative to the

Table 13.1
1995 per capita income (in dollars, PPP-based)

European Union		Central and Eastern Europe	
Belgium	19,928	Czech Republic	8,173
Netherlands	19,376	Slovenia	6,342
Luxembourg	30,063	Slovak Republic	6,671
France	20,829	Croatia	4,142
Germany	18,988	Hungary	6,211
United Kingdom	18,857	Poland	6,364
Denmark	20,737	Latvia	5,002
Ireland	15,611	Lithuania	3,035
Austria	19,922	Albania	538
Italy	19,745	Estonia	7,203
Sweden	18,712	Macedonia, F.Y.R.	1,628
Spain	14,408	Bulgaria	5,132
Finland	17,433	Romania	3,542
Portugal	11,935		
Greece	8,727		

Source: IMF *World Economic Outlook* database.

Western European average worsened during this period. Hence, rather than converging towards Western European levels, the CEE countries diverged considerably. For example, with a per capita income of 72 percent of the Western European average in 1937, Czechoslovakia was very close to Austria, Greece, and Ireland. By 1992, with a per capita income of only 44 percent of the Western European average, Czechoslovakia had fallen way behind all three countries. On the other hand, a cursory look at the relative position within Western Europe suggests that income gaps have narrowed over the last 40 years.[4]

Interestingly, and in sharp contrast to Western Europe, the relative per capita income levels *within* CEE remained largely unchanged, with Hungary and Czechoslovakia leading both in 1937 and in 1992. This suggests that the predominant factor determining growth during this period was the common effect of socialism rather than country-specific policies, shocks, or initial conditions.

Tables 13.1 and 13.2 raise the question of whether the divergence of income levels of the transition economies from those of Western Europe that occurred during the communist period will now be reversed, and if so, at what speed. We approach the question by first

Table 13.2
Selected European countries: comparison of per capita income (PPP-based, in 1990 Geary–Khamis dollars)

	1937		1992	
	GDP per capita	Relative to Western European average	GDP per capita	Relative to Western European average
Austria	3,177	0.79	17,160	1.11
Belgium	4,915	1.22	17,165	1.11
Denmark	5,453	1.36	18,293	1.18
Finland	3,342	0.83	14,646	0.95
France	4,444	1.11	17,959	1.16
Germany	4,809	1.20	19,351	1.25
Italy	3,247	0.81	16,229	1.05
Netherlands	5,301	1.32	16,898	1.09
Norway	3,871	0.96	17,543	1.13
Sweden	4,664	1.16	16,927	1.09
Switzerland	6,087	1.51	21,036	1.36
United Kingdom	5,870	1.46	15,738	1.02
Greece	2,820	0.70	10,314	0.67
Ireland	3,018	0.75	11,711	0.76
Spain	2,043	0.51	12,498	0.81
Turkey	1,271	0.32	4,422	0.29
Average	*4,021*	*1.00*	*15,493*	*1.00*
Bulgaria	1,566	0.39	4,054	0.26
Czechoslovakia	2,882	0.72	6,845	0.44
Hungary	2,543	0.63	5,638	0.36
Poland	1,915	0.48	4,726	0.31
Romania	1,130	0.28	2,565	0.17
Yugoslavia	1,284	0.32	3,887	0.25

Source: Maddison (1995).

examining policy convergence, and then considering other factors that will affect the rates at which convergence of income levels might take place.

Macroeconomic Policy Convergence

The Copenhagen Summit criteria provide a very broad guiding principle in several areas for the accession of the CEE countries to the EU. While the political, legal, and institutional criteria are of great importance, this chapter focuses on the economic aspects. With no specific guidelines on economic performance for CEE membership in the EU, we choose to use the Maastricht criteria as a guiding principle for determining policy convergence.

The Maastricht criteria specify measures of macroeconomic convergence required for EMU membership.[5] The criteria relate to inflation, long-term interest rates, the general government budget deficit, gross government debt, and exchange rates. Specifically, consumer price inflation must not exceed that of the three best-performing countries in the EU by more than 1.5 percentage points; interest rates on long-term government securities should not exceed the average of those in the same three (low-inflation) countries by more than two percentage points; the deficit to GDP ratio should not exceed three percent; the debt to GDP ratio should not exceed 60 percent; and the exchange rate should have been held within the normal fluctuation margins of the ERM for two years without a realignment.[6]

The CEE countries have made significant progress towards macroeconomic stability during the past five years. The average inflation rate in those countries declined from about 480 percent in 1992 to 23 percent in 1995. Similarly, the average fiscal deficit declined from 5.3 to 3.1 percent of GDP. Table 13.3 shows how inflation rates and fiscal deficits in the CEE countries in 1995 compare with those of EU countries. While only one CEE country, Croatia, would have satisfied these two Maastricht measures, the fiscal performance of most CEE countries compares well with that of EU countries. Inflation rates in the CEE countries are generally significantly higher than those of the EU countries, but they have been declining. It is still true, though, that inflation rates in some of the best-performing CEE countries—Poland, Hungary, and the Baltic countries—have been

Table 13.3
European Union, Central and Eastern Europe: inflation and fiscal balance, 1995 (percent)

		Percent of GDP	
	Inflation	Fiscal Balance	Public Debt[d]
European Union			
Austria	2.3	−6.1	67
Belgium	1.5	−4.5	134
Denmark	1.9	−1.7	82
Finland	1.0	−5.6	60
France	1.8	−5.0	52
Germany	1.8	−3.5	58
Greece	9.3	−9.0	113
Ireland	2.5	−2.1	85
Italy	5.4	−7.2	123
Luxembourg	1.9	0.4	2
Netherlands	2.0	−3.8	79
Portugal	4.1	−5.2	73
Spain	4.7	−5.9	65
Sweden	2.6	−6.8	80
United Kingdom	2.8	−5.1	49
Central and Eastern Europe			
Albania	7.8	−12.4	62
Bulgaria	62.1	−5.9	101
Croatia	2.0	−1.7	39
Czech Republic	9.1	−1.6	13
Estonia	28.3	−2.3	7
Hungary[a]	28.2	−6.9	86
Latvia	25.1	−1.0	16
Lithuania	36.5	2.9	12
Macedonia, F.Y.R.[b]	17.4	−0.9	40–70
Poland	27.8	−2.3	55
Romania	32.0	−2.5	21
Slovak Republic	9.9	0.6	33
Slovenia[c]	12.8	−0.3	25

Source: IMF *World Economic Outlook* database and IMF staff estimates.
a. Fiscal balance excludes privatization revenue; if included, fiscal balance would be −3.7 percent of GDP in 1995.
b. Extent of sovereign debt not clearly established after the breakup of Yugoslavia.
c. The portion of the external debt include Slovenia's estimated share of "uncollected debt" of the former Yugoslavia.
d. Preliminary estimates for Central and Eastern Europe.

declining quite slowly from the 20–40 percent range, reflecting the difficulty of reducing moderate rates of inflation to the levels of the G-7 countries.

The data on public debt that we present for CEE countries should be viewed as highly tentative.[7] Most CEE countries would appear to satisfy the Maastricht criterion on public debt, with Bulgaria and Hungary being the more noticeable exceptions. The last two criteria—on interest rates and exchange rates—are more difficult to evaluate. The interest rate criterion is hard to apply to CEE countries, since markets for long-term debt are not well developed. The criterion on exchange rates is, strictly speaking, not applicable to CEE countries, since they do not share a regional exchange rate arrangement. Judged on the basis of no realignment for two years, however, most CEE countries would not meet the criterion with the exception of Estonia and Lithuania, which have currency boards.

Structural Policy Convergence

The countries of CEE have made impressive progress in putting market mechanisms in place. This section presents evidence of the extent of structural policy reform in the CEE countries, based on indices computed by de Melo et al. (1995), who draw on qualitative indicators prepared by the European Bank for Reconstruction and Development (EBRD 1994, 1995).

Three measures of structural reforms have been produced, reflecting policies in different areas: price liberalization and competition (LII), trade and the foreign exchange regime (LIE), and privatization and banking reform (LIP). In turn, a weighted liberalization index has been constructed using these three indices, with weights of 0.3 for LII and LIE, and 0.4 for LIP. Although the work of Sachs and Warner (1995) suggests that trade and foreign exchange reform is the most critical area for growth, regression results in Fischer et al. (1997) suggest that privatization has been critical as well.

Table 13.4 presents measures of structural policy reform for the CEE countries. In principle, the indices could range from zero for a country in which no reform has taken place to one for a country which has reformed completely.[8] The remarkable aspect of the data is the extent of structural policy reforms in the CEE countries. There is no country for which both price and trade liberalization has not

Table 13.4
Central and Eastern Europe: economic liberalization indices, 1995

	Weighted economic liberalization index	Price liberalization and competition (weight: 0.3)	Trade and foreign exchange regime (weight: 0.3)	Privatization and banking reform (weight: 0.4)
Czech Republic	0.93	0.9	1.0	0.9
Slovenia	0.85	0.9	1.0	0.7
Slovak Republic	0.86	0.9	0.9	0.8
Croatia	0.85	0.9	1.0	0.7
Hungary	0.93	0.9	1.0	0.9
Poland	0.89	0.9	1.0	0.8
Latvia	0.81	0.9	1.0	0.6
Lithuania	0.86	0.8	1.0	0.8
Albania	0.74	0.9	0.9	0.5
Estonia	0.93	0.9	1.0	0.9
Macedonia, F.Y.R.	0.78	0.9	0.9	0.6
Bulgaria	0.61	0.7	0.8	0.4
Romania	0.71	0.8	0.9	0.5

Source: de Melo et al. (1995).

been substantially accomplished. There is much more variation in the extent of privatization and banking reform, with Hungary, Estonia, and the Czech Republic having achieved most by 1995, and Bulgaria, Romania, and Albania the least.

The aggregate index for each country in CEE exceeds 60 percent, and for the four countries with the highest overall index—the Czech Republic, Estonia, Hungary, and Poland—the score is 89 percent or higher. Although these countries have gone a long way in carrying out reforms needed for a market economy, the underlying economic institutions are not necessarily at the same level as those in the EU: banking systems are still weak, corporate governance inadequate, and tax collection agencies not as effective in the new environment. Moreover, the ways in which the government and individual economic agents interact in ex-socialist countries today differs in many ways from the culture in countries with a long tradition of free markets. Strong liberalization measures are muted by bureaucratic inertia, the nature of policy-making bestowed by central planning, and local political resistance (Murrell 1996:32).

Combining the Indicators

It would be convenient if the indicators presented in tables 13.1 through 13.4 could be combined to give an overall measure of economic distance from Brussels. It would also be useful if the policy-related data in tables 13.3 and 13.4 could be combined to yield an overall index of policy convergence. The creation of such indices would be easy if there were a high correlation between the different measures or indices. Table 13.5 shows correlations between the different variables, including distance and per capita income, based on data presented in tables 13.1, 13.3, and 13.4.

Distance from Brussels is generally correlated with each of the indicators, supporting the notion that physical distance is closely correlated with economic distance. Among the three policy indicators, inflation, the fiscal balance, and the liberalization index, some correlations are small, particularly the one between inflation and the fiscal balance.

Figure 13.2 combines the five indicators shown in figures 13.1 and tables 13.1–13.4: distance, income per capita, inflation, the fiscal balance, and liberalization. The countries are ranged from left to right on the horizontal axis according to distance of the capital from Brussels, that is, in the order in which they appear in figure 13.1. There are then four indices for each country: from left to right, inflation, fiscal balance, per capita income, and liberalization. Each has been transformed onto a scale that runs from zero to one, with zero indicating a value farthest from Brussels, and one closest.[9]

An overall impression given by figure 13.2 is that economic distance from Brussels increases—on average—with geographical distance from Brussels. Another is that the CEE transition countries have done exceptionally well in keeping their budget deficits down.

We now present a rank order index which combines the performance in six categories (table 13.6). The best-performing country in each category is ranked first in that category. For example, in table 13.6 Croatia is ranked first in the category "annual inflation," since it had the lowest inflation rate in 1995. When an overall index is created by assigning equal weights to each category, the Czech Republic, the Slovak Republic, and Slovenia are the best performers, in that order. The laggards are Bulgaria, Romania, and Albania. Again, table 13.6 also suggests that, with the possible exception of Estonia,

Table 13.5

Cross-correlations between different measures of economic distance

	Per capita income	Fiscal balance	Inflation	Distance	Liberalization			
					Aggregate	Price	Trade	Banking
Central and Eastern Europe								
Per capita income	1.00							
Fiscal balance	0.47	1.00						
Inflation	0.03	−0.16	1.00					
Distance	−0.62	−0.36	0.58	1.00				
Liberalization	0.56	0.33	−0.48	−0.66	1.00			
Price	0.17	0.19	−0.84	−0.52	0.72	1.00		
Trade	0.39	0.31	−0.42	−0.53	0.86	0.63	1.00	
Banking	0.64	0.33	−0.32	−0.63	0.97	0.55	0.75	1.00
European Union								
Per capita income	1.00							
Fiscal balance	0.67	1.00						
Inflation	−0.65	−0.63	1.00					
Distance	−0.72	−0.63	0.66	1.00				

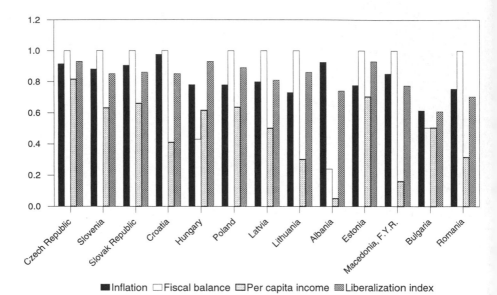

Figure 13.2
Central and Eastern Europe: combined indicators, 1995.

the distance from Brussels is, after all, a good predictor of economic distance.

Time from Brussels

The measures presented so far are suggestive of the economic distance of CEE countries from Brussels. We now ask how long it would take the CEE countries to catch up with those of the EU. We can think of the growth process in the transition economies as being driven by two forces (see Fischer et al. 1996b): first, the transition process itself and, second—and increasingly so as stabilization and structural transformations are achieved—by the typical long-run growth process of a market economy.

In Fischer et al. (1996a, 1997), we have explored the determinants of transitional growth in some detail. We find, not surprisingly, that countries that have achieved macroeconomic stabilization and undertaken deeper reforms are growing faster during the transition. More precisely, the results show that a pegged exchange rate regime, tighter fiscal policy, and most measures of structural reform (as captured by various liberalization indices), have affected growth positively.[10]

Table 13.6
Ranking of CEE countries by selected criteria[a]

	Distance from Brussels	Per capita income	Liberalization index	Annual inflation	Fiscal balance	Public debt (% of GDP)	Overall ranking[b]
Albania	9	13	11	2	13	11	11
Bulgaria	12	7	13	13	11	13	13
Croatia	4	9	7	1	6	8	5
Czech Republic	1	1	1	3	5	3	1
Estonia	10	2	1	10	7	1	4
Hungary	5	6	1	9	12	12	8
Latvia	7	8	9	7	4	4	6
Lithuania	8	11	5	12	10	2	9
Macedonia, F.Y.R.	11	12	10	6	3	9	10
Poland	6	4	4	8	7	10	6
Romania	13	10	12	11	9	5	12
Slovak Republic	3	3	5	4	1	7	2
Slovenia	2	5	7	5	2	6	3

a. The most favorably placed country ranked first.
b. Overall ranking determined by assigning equal weights to each criterion.

These transitional growth results suggest that several of the variables presented earlier in the paper as measures of policy distance from Brussels also help predict how rapidly income levels will grow during the transition period. Gradually, as macroeconomic stability is assured and structural transformation completed, the determinants of growth of typical market economies should predominate. The remainder of this section is devoted to an exploration of long-term growth prospects in transition economies.

We drew on past cross-country studies of the determinants of growth to calculate implied growth rates for the CEE transition economies. Recent work on economic growth (see Barro and Sala-i-Martin [1995] for a survey of the literature) has focused on the concept of *conditional convergence*, that is, on whether, adjusting for differences in various policies and other economic characteristics, income in poorer countries is growing more rapidly than in richer countries. Given the structural relationships estimated in previous studies, we controlled for initial levels of state variables and predicted rates of growth conditional on our expectation of the two control variables that we take to reflect government policy—investment rates and government consumption.

Table 13.7 presents information on some key state and control variables for the CEE economies.[11] We present data for the latest year available. Thus, population growth rates are for 1993 (source: World Bank 1996); primary and secondary school ratios are mostly for 1993, otherwise one or two years before 1993 (sources: World Bank 1996; Krajnyak and Zettelmeyer 1997); gross capital formation is for 1995 (source: IMF *World Economic Outlook* database), exports and government consumption (in percent of GDP) for 1995 (source: ibid.); and initial per capita income in dollars on a purchasing power parity basis is for 1995 (source: ibid.).

Given the data available for these countries, we predicted future growth prospects using an equation of the form

$$g(t) = f(Y_0, PS_0, SS_0; INV(t), GOV(t), POP(t)), \qquad [1]$$
$$\quad - \quad + \quad + \quad + \quad ? \quad -$$

where $g(t)$ is per capita growth during the time interval t, Y_0 is the per capita income in the starting year, PS_0 is the primary school enrollment rate (in percent of the total primary-school-aged population), SS_0 is the secondary school enrollment rate (in percent of the total secondary-school-aged population), $INV(t)$ is gross capital for-

Table 13.7
Factors affecting long-term growth in Central and Eastern Europe

	Population growth rate	School enrollment[a]		Gross capital formation[b]	Per capita income in dollars, PPP-based	Exports of goods and services[b]	Government consumption expenditure[b]	Inflation in 1995[c]
		Primary	Secondary					
Albania	1.19	0.96	0.79	0.17	538	0.13	0.12	7.9
Bulgaria	−0.35	0.86	0.71	0.12	5,132	0.50	0.17	62.1
Croatia	0.06	0.87	0.80	0.10	4,142	0.41	0.30	2.0
Czech Republic	−0.06	0.99	0.89	0.31	8,173	0.52	0.20	9.1
Estonia	−0.31	0.83	0.92	0.30	7,203	0.68	0.21	28.3
Hungary	−0.53	0.94	0.81	0.23	6,211	0.32	0.10	28.2
Latvia	−0.53	0.83	0.92	0.18	5,002	0.41	0.20	25.1
Lithuania	0.15	0.92	0.92	0.19	3,035	0.32	0.24	39.5
Macedonia, F.Y.R.	1.12	0.87	0.80	0.38	1,628	0.45	0.14	17.4
Poland	0.20	0.98	0.83	0.16	6,364	0.27	0.18	27.8
Romania	0.19	0.86	0.80	0.30	3,542	0.28	0.14	32.0
Slovak Republic	0.35	1.01	0.96	0.22	6,671	0.65	0.20	9.9
Slovenia	0.41	0.97	0.80	0.25	6,342	0.54	0.20	12.8
Average	0.14	0.91	0.84	0.22	4,922	0.42	0.18	23.2

Source: International Monetary Fund (*World Economic Outlook* database) for per capita income, exports of goods and services, government consumption, expenditure, and inflation; The World Bank (1996) for population growth, school enrollment, and gross capital formation; Organization for Economic Cooperation and Development (1996) for gross capital formation; and Krajnyak and Zettlemeyer (1997) for secondary school enrollment.

a. Share of school age population.
b. Share of GDP in current prices.
c. Period average.

mation (in percent of GDP) during the time interval t, $GOV(t)$ is government consumption expenditure (in percent of GDP) during the time interval t, and $POP(t)$ is the growth rate of the population during the time interval t.

The predicted signs from neoclassical and endogenous growth models are presented below the explanatory variables in equation [1]. Per capita growth, $g(t)$, is negatively related to Y_0—this follows from the neoclassical convergence hypothesis that, ceteris paribus, poorer countries tend to grow faster than richer ones. The primary and secondary school enrollment ratios represent investment in human capital. Countries investing more in human capital tend to grow faster (see Romer 1990; Grossman and Helpman 1991). Higher physical investment ratios also increase the growth rate on the path to the steady state, and if sustained will also raise the steady-state level of output. The empirical literature is not conclusive regarding the effects of government consumption on growth (see Ram [1986] and Levine and Renelt [1992] for contrasting results). The impact on growth should depend on the type of government spending, as well as on the distortions associated with its financing.

The neoclassical growth model implies that for a given saving rate, per capita income growth is reduced by population growth. Some models with endogenous population growth imply a further negative impact of population growth on per capita income growth because higher population growth rates imply that a larger amount of time is spent in raising children than in other productive activities.

As table 13.7 indicates, initial income levels in the CEE transition countries are relatively low. On this basis, one should expect these countries to grow faster than Western Europe in the future. The most impressive features in table 13.7 are the extremely high primary and secondary school enrollment ratios in the CEE countries (especially relative to other developing countries). The basic literacy that is ensured by these ratios is an important requirement for growth. Despite the high level of basic education attained in most of the CEE economies, it is likely that further human capital investment will be required to provide retraining in market-based institutions, build entrepreneurial skills, and ensure technological innovation and adaptation.[12]

Gross capital formation in the CEE transition countries amounted to an average of 22 percent of GDP in 1995, with wide variation across countries. In contrast, the fast-growing market economies in

Asia typically have an investment ratio of at least 30 percent of GDP. Government consumption in most countries declined sharply from 50–60 percent at the start of the transformation process, to an average level of 18 percent of GDP in 1995.[13] While government consumption at the previous rates was not sustainable and must have reduced growth, it is becoming increasingly clear that sharp reductions in expenditures on the scale seen in some of the transition economies may be adversely affecting reform and growth. Rapid revenue declines and the need to reduce budget deficits for various reasons (see Cheasty and Davis 1996; Haque and Sahay 1996) have often led to tax evasion, involuntary expenditure compression, sequestration, and a build-up of arrears.[14] Indeed, it is likely that growth would be enhanced by well-planned public spending on building market-based institutions, improving the quality of government administration, improving physical infrastructure, and setting up a social safety net.[15]

Population growth rates in the CEE economies are low, and in many cases negative. As the extensive state support system for dependents, particularly children, is reduced, we could expect a further decline in population growth rates. It is likely though that population growth rates will recover once the economic prospects in these economies become less uncertain.

Table 13.8 provides preliminary insights on the growth potential in CEE transition economies by comparing key determinants of growth with past averages for slow and fast-growing market economies. Human capital indicators are extremely favorable and so is the degree of openness. The inflation rate in 1995 was still quite high, but is declining rapidly.[16]

To project long-term growth in the CEE transition economies, we used the equations estimated by Barro (1991) and Levine and Renelt (1992):[17]

Barro growth equation:

per capita growth $= 0.0302^* - 0.0075^* \, Y_{1960} + 0.025^* \, PRIM$

$$+ 0.0305^* \, SEC - 0.119^* \, GOV \qquad [2]$$

Levine and Renelt growth equation:

per capita growth $= -0.83 - 0.35^* \, Y_{1960} - 0.38 \, POP$

$$+ 3.17^* \, SEC + 17.5^* \, INV. \qquad [3]$$

Table 13.8
Central and Eastern Europe in a global perspective

	Fast growers	Slow growers	Central and Eastern Europe in 1995[a]
Primary-school enrollment rate[b]	0.90	0.54	0.91
Secondary-school enrollment rate[b]	0.30	0.10	0.84
Investment/GDP[c]	0.23	0.17	0.22
Government consumption/GDP[c]	0.16	0.12	0.18
Exports/GDP[c]	0.32	0.23	0.42
Annual inflation rate[c]	12.3	31.1	23.2

Source: Levine and Renelt (1992) and table 13.7.
a. Average for 13 CEE countries.
b. 1960.
c. 1960–1989.

Here Y_{1960} is the initial level of real per capita income on a PPP basis (expressed in logs in the Barro equation and divided by 1,000 in the Levine–Renelt equation), POP is the growth rate of population, $PRIM$ is the gross primary school enrollment rate, SEC is the gross secondary school enrollment rate, GOV is the share of government consumption expenditure in GDP, and INV is the share of investment in GDP. (The stars next to the estimated coefficients indicate that they are significant at least at the 5 percent level.)

It is imperative to caution the reader about several qualifications that apply to the growth predictions below. There is a plethora of estimated growth equations available in the literature, of which we use only two. Moreover, the values of the estimated coefficients are sensitive to model specification, the countries selected, and the sample period. Thus, our projections could differ in significant ways were we to apply other studies. These projections have also abstracted from some potentially important external, political, and institutional factors. While such factors are hard to assess quantitatively (even in the existing growth literature), they could exert considerable influence on the growth process.

For all variables in equations [2] and [3]—with the exception of investment and government consumption—we used the figures presented in table 13.7. For the control variables, we assumed the same investment and government consumption ratios (in percent of

GDP) across all countries because, as table 13.7 indicates, these figures exhibit a wide range of variation (and some even seem unrealistic) at the present time. Moreover, using current figures for investment and government consumption to project growth would be equivalent to assuming that current policies will not only differ very widely across countries but also not change in the future. Hence, for the purposes of our exercise, it makes more sense to assume that all countries follow the same policies, those that constitute a "good" policy scenario. Hence, we assumed a high investment ratio (30 percent of GDP) and a low level of government consumption (10 percent of GDP).

Not surprisingly, the more optimistic scenario is obtained by using Barro's equation (table 13.9), which gives a relatively high weight to the human capital variables. The projected average per capita growth rate for the region is 5.6 percent, with all countries falling in the 4.9–7.1 percent range. In the calculations based on the Levine and Renelt equation, the average per capita growth rate declines to 5.3 percent, with all countries falling in the 4.4–6.3 percent range.

Based on initial per capita income and the projected per capita growth rates for the CEE countries, we computed the number of years it would take for each of these countries to converge to the average per capita GDP level in the low-income European Union countries (Greece, Portugal, and Spain). As indicated in table 13.9, the average per capita GDP for these three European countries ($11,690) is more than twice the average for the CEE countries ($4,922). These three European countries were assumed to grow—in per capita terms—at 2 percent per year. According to both equations, it would take, on average, about one generation to converge to the per capita level of the low-income European Union countries: the Barro equation predicts 28 years, while the alternative Levine–Renelt predicts 31 years. Among the Eastern European countries, the Czech Republic, the Slovak Republic, and Estonia are projected to take the shortest time to converge.

Drifting away from Brussels

So far, we have asked how long it may take for CEE countries to converge to the per capita GDP level of the low-income European Union countries (i.e., how long it will take to "reach" Brussels). We now ask a different question: How badly did more than 40 years of socialism hurt growth in the CEE countries? In other words, by

Table 13.9
Policy simulations for GDP convergence to low-income EU countries[a]

	Per capita income in $, PPP-based	Barro[b]			Levine–Renelt[c]		
		Projected		No. of years to converge to low-income EU levels	Projected		No. of years to converge to low-income EU levels
		growth rate	per capita growth		growth rate	per capita growth	
Albania	538	8.29	7.10	63	7.47	6.28	75
Bulgaria	5,132	4.56	4.92	29	4.65	5.01	28
Croatia	4,142	5.44	5.38	32	5.55	5.48	31
Czech Republic	8,173	5.39	5.44	11	4.34	4.40	15
Estonia	7,203	4.92	5.23	16	4.62	4.93	17
Hungary	6,211	4.75	5.28	20	4.49	5.02	22
Latvia	5,002	4.98	5.50	25	5.26	5.79	23
Lithuania	3,035	6.25	6.10	34	6.37	6.22	33
Macedonia, F.Y.R.	1,628	7.19	6.08	50	7.08	5.96	52
Poland	6,364	5.62	5.42	18	4.95	4.75	23
Romania	3,542	5.66	5.47	36	5.84	5.64	34
Slovak Republic	6,671	6.21	5.86	15	5.34	5.00	19
Slovenia	6,342	5.72	5.31	19	4.99	4.58	24
Average for transition economies	4,922	5.77	5.62	28	5.46	5.31	31
Average for low-income EU countries	11,690		2.00			2.00	

a. For illustrative purposes, the average of the three lowest-income countries in the European Union (Greece, Portugal, and Spain) is considered. These countries are assumed to grow at 2 percent per annum.
b. Government consumption/GDP = 10 percent.
c. Investment/GDP = 30 percent.

Table 13.10
Estimating income lost during the Socialist period

		GDP per capita		GDP per capita "lost" during socialism (3) minus (2)
	1937 (1)	1992 (actual) (2)	1992 (predicted)[a] (3)	
Bulgaria	1,566	4,054	14,000	9,946
Czechoslovakia	2,882	6,845	15,845	9,000
Hungary	2,543	5,638	15,448	9,810
Poland	1,915	4,726	14,584	9,858
Romania	1,130	2,565	13,102	10,537
Yugoslavia	1,284	3,887	13,446	9,559
Average	1,887	4,619	14,404	9,785

	Projected future growth (Barro)[b]	Number of years required to make up	Projected future growth (Levine–Renelt)[b]	Number of years required to make up
Bulgaria	4.92	26	5.01	25
Czechoslovakia	5.65	15	4.70	18
Hungary	5.28	20	5.02	21
Poland	5.42	21	4.75	24
Romania	5.47	31	5.64	30
Yugoslavia	5.59	23	5.34	24
Average	5.39	23	5.08	24

a. Predictions based on authors' regressions (see text).
b. Czechoslovakia's growth rate is the average of those of the Czech Republic and the Slovak Republic, while Yugoslavia's is the average of those of Croatia, Slovenia, and F.Y.R. Macedonia.

how much did CEE countries "drift away" from Brussels during that period?

Due to lack of data, we will try to answer this question only for the six CEE countries indicated in tables 13.2 and 13.10. To provide an answer, we proceeded in three stages. We first took the 12 core Western European countries (the first 12 countries listed in table 13.2), and estimated the absolute convergence coefficient (defined below) for the period 1937–1992. We then used this estimate of the convergence coefficient, together with the initial per capita GDP of the CEE countries (column 1 in table 13.10), to compute what the level of per capita GDP in these CEE countries *would have been* in the 1990s had they followed the general convergence pattern of Western

Europe. Finally, we used the projected long-term growth rates for the CEE countries from table 13.9 to calculate how long it would take to make up for the years lost under socialism.

Based on Barro and Sala-i-Martin (1992), we first estimated the following equation using a nonlinear least squares procedure:

$$\ln(y_{i,T}/y_{i,C}) = C - (1 - e^{-\beta T}) \ln(y_{i,0}) + \varepsilon_i,$$ [4]

where y is GDP per capita, i indexes the countries, T is the length of the period (55 years in this case), β is the convergence coefficient, ε is an independent error term, and C is the constant term (which is common across countries). The estimated β coefficient for the 12 Western European countries is 0.029, which is significant at the 5 percent level. This implies that these countries were converging at an average rate of about three percent per year during this period; that is, about three percent of the income gap between the richer and poorer countries was closed every year.[18]

On the basis of the estimated β coefficient for the control group (the 12 Western European countries) and the initial (1937) per capita GDP of the six CEE countries, we predicted the per capita GDP in the terminal period (1992) for the six countries. These predicted values are indicated in column (3) of table 13.10. The gap between the predicted value and the actual value in 1992 is interpreted as the "loss" attributable to the socialist experiment.[19]

Finally, we computed the number of years it would take to make up for such a loss. As shown in table 13.10, it would take 23–24 years, on average, to make up for the lost time, ranging from 15–18 years for the former Czechoslovakian republics to about 30 for Romania. In other words, the cost of the socialist experiment—which lasted roughly two generations—was, in terms of lost income, equivalent to about one generation.

Concluding Comments

Six years into the transition from socialism to a market economy, there is sufficient preliminary evidence to discuss the question, How far is Central and Eastern Europe from Brussels? We presented different measures of distance, ranging from physical distance (which, after all, turns out to be not a bad proxy for economic distance) to time distance (in terms of years needed to catch up with EU income levels). One overall conclusion is that the richest CEE countries are not that far away from Brussels; for example, it could take the Czech Republic only about 15 years to catch up with the low-income Western European countries. Naturally, the catching-up time is directly related to the time squandered during the socialist experiment. We estimate that, on average, the CEE countries gave away about one generation worth of income during the 40 or more years of socialism.

Of course, the length of time it will take any given CEE country to reach Brussels is not predetermined. Our estimates of how long it will take CEE to reach Brussels were based on the best-case scenario that policies that promote investment and improve the quality of public spending are in place. Many of the transition economies in Central and Eastern Europe have moved rapidly on several of the necessary fronts, particularly in liberalizing the price, foreign exchange, and trade regimes. However, many of the market-based institutions still have some distance to go before reaching Western European standards. In most economies, privatization of state enterprises is still far from complete and the banking system is under severe strain. Nonetheless, while not all transition economies are equally well placed, the starting conditions are favorable in most countries. The right policies will ensure a safe trip to Brussels.

Notes

We thank László Csaba, Daniel Gros, Peter Ludlow, Xavier Sala-i-Martin, and conference participants for insightful comments and suggestions. We are grateful to our IMF colleagues for making data available and for helping us interpret them, and to Claire Adams for excellent research assistance. The views expressed in this paper are those of the authors and do not necessarily reflect those of the International Monetary Fund.

1. The 15 Central and Eastern European (CEE) transition countries are Albania, Bulgaria, Bosnia-Herzegovina, Croatia, the Czech Republic, Estonia, Hungary, Latvia, Lithuania, the former Yugoslav Republic of Macedonia, Poland, Romania, the Federal Republic of Yugoslavia (Serbia-Montenegro), the Slovak Republic, and Slovenia. In 1939, there were 10 countries, with the differences resulting from the breakups of Czechoslovakia and Yugoslavia. As a result of data difficulties, FRY (Serbia-Montenegro) and Bosnia-Herzegovina have been excluded from this study.

2. Of the 13 countries discussed in the paper, 10 are currently (as of September 1996) associate members of the European Union; they are the Visegrad countries (the Czech Republic, Hungary, Poland, and the Slovak Republic), the Baltics (Estonia, Latvia, and Lithuania), and Bulgaria, Romania, and Slovenia.

3. The size of the gap reinforces our belief that available data for the transition economies underestimate GDP (see Fischer et al. 1996a).

4. A formal test of convergence is presented below.

5. For a description of the criteria, see the IMF's *World Economic Outlook* (1996:40–43).

6. As discussed in IMF (1996), the criteria leave some room for judgment.

7. Official figures are often not available; the figures in table 13.3 are estimates provided by IMF country economists.

8. Under this definition, a Western European country would have an index of one.

9. The income variable is 1995 per capita income divided by 10,000; the inflation index is $(1/(1 + \text{inflation}))$ in 1995; the fiscal index is 1 for countries with a deficit of less than 3 percent of GDP and otherwise $(3/\text{absolute value of the deficit})$, where the deficit is expressed as in table 13.3; and the liberalization index is the overall index as in table 13.4.

10. These results are based on regressions that include, in addition to CEE, the non-Baltic countries of the former Soviet Union and Mongolia.

11. Not all the variables presented in table 13.6 were used in the subsequent regression-based simulations of growth rates. We include some (such as the inflation rate) because they have been significant in several empirical studies of growth, although they do not appear in the growth regressions used below.

12. Despite consistently high human capital indicators, Easterly and Fischer (1994) show that a leading cause of economic decline in the former Soviet Union was the low elasticity of substitution between capital and labor, which they argue was, in part, explained by lack of entrepreneurial skills and the slow adaptation to imported technological progress.

13. We have to repeat the standard warning on data: data on gross capital formation as well as on government consumption are subject to a wide margin of error, primarily because the demand-based U.N. system of national income accounting is still at an early stage in most of the countries included in table 13.7.

14. In noting this point, we do not mean to imply that larger budget deficits would be desirable, but rather that both revenue collection and the quality of public expenditures need to be improved in these countries.

15. Keefer and Knack (1995) present empirical evidence from cross-country growth regressions that point to the positive impact on growth of better institutions.

16. See Fischer (1993) for evidence that inflation is negatively associated with growth.

17. We chose these equations both because they are widely quoted and because it was relatively straightforward to obtain data for the CEE transition economies matching the right-hand side variables in the Barro (1991) and Levine and Renelt (1992) regressions.

18. Barro and Sala-i-Martin (1991) find that the rate of convergence for 73 regions across seven Western European countries during 1950–1985 was about two percent per year. In our sample, if we add the four Southern European countries (Greece, Portugal, Spain, and Turkey) to the core 12 Western European countries, the rate of convergence slows down considerably to about one-half percent per year. This fall in the rate of convergence may indicate that the beta coefficient is biased when the Southern European countries, which have remained relatively poor, are included in the sample, perhaps because the latter group was converging to a lower steady-

state income level. This could be tested by controlling for other variables that affect the steady-state—i.e., by testing for conditional convergence—which lies beyond the scope of this paper.

19. It can be argued that the CEE countries were different from the 12 core Western European countries in 1937 and, therefore, would not have converged to the same steady-state. However, the hypothesis of absolute convergence appears to make sense for at least Czechoslovakia, Hungary, and Poland, which shared a common historical background and economic structures with Western Europe and were also physically close to Brussels. The answer is less obvious for the other three CEE countries listed in tables 13.2 and 13.10.

References

Barro, R. J. (1991). Economic Growth in a Cross-Section of Countries. *Quarterly Journal of Economics* 106:407–443.

Barro, R. J., and X. Sala-i-Martin (1991). Convergence across States and Regions. *Brookings Papers on Economic Activity* (1):107–158.

——— (1992). Convergence. *Journal of Political Economy* 100:223–251.

——— (1995). *Economic Growth*. New York: McGraw–Hill.

Cheasty, A., and J. Davis (1996). Fiscal Transition in Countries of the Former Soviet Union: An Interim Assessment. IMF Working Paper 96/61. Washington, D.C.

De Melo, M., C. Denizer, and A. Gelb (1995). From Plan to Market: Patterns of Transition. Mimeo. The World Bank, Washington, D.C.

Easterly, W., and S. Fischer (1994). The Soviet Economic Decline: Historical and Republican Data. Mimeo (March). The World Bank, Washington, D.C.

EBRD (European Bank for Reconstruction and Development) (1994). *Transition Report*. October. London: EBRD.

——— (1995). *Transition Report Update*. April. London: EBRD.

Fischer, S. (1993). The Role of Macroeconomic Factors in Growth. *Journal of Monetary Economics* 32:485–512.

Fischer, S., R. Sahay, and C. A. Végh (1996a). Stabilization and Growth in Transition Economies: The Early Experience. *Journal of Economic Perspectives* 10:45–66.

——— (1996b). Economies in Transition: The Beginnings of Growth. *American Economic Review, Papers and Proceedings* 86:229–233.

——— (1997). From Transition to Market: Evidence and Growth Prospects. In S. Zecchini (ed.), *Lessons from the Economic Transition*. London: Kluwer Academic Publishers.

Giersch, H. (1979). Aspects of Growth, Structural Change, and Employment—A Schumpeterian Perspective. *Weltwirtschaftliches Archiv* 115(4):629–652.

Gros, D., and A. Steinherr (1995). *Winds of Change*. London: Longman.

Grossman, G. M., and E. Helpman (1991). *Innovation and Growth in the Global Economy*. Cambridge, Mass.: MIT Press.

Haque, N. U., and R. Sahay (1996). Do Government Wage Cuts Close Budget Deficits? An Analytical Framework for Developing Countries and Transition Economies. IMF Working Paper 96/19. Washington, D.C. Forthcoming in *IMF Staff Papers*.

IMF (International Monetary Fund) (1996). *World Economic Outlook*. May. Washington, D.C.

———— *World Economic Outlook* database, Research Department. Washington, D.C.

Keefer, P., and S. Knack (1995). Why Don't Poor Countries Catch Up? A Cross-National Test of an Institutional Explanation. IRIS Working Paper. University of Maryland, College Park.

Krajnyak, K., and J. Zettelmeyer (1997). Competitiveness in Transition Economies: What Scope for Real Appreciation? IMF Working Paper, forthcoming. Washington, D.C.

Levine, R., and D. Renelt (1992). A Sensitivity Analysis of Cross-Country Growth Regressions. *American Economic Review* 82:942–963.

Murrell, P. (1996). How Far Has the Transition Progressed? *Journal of Economic Perspectives* 10:25–44.

OECD (Organization for Economic Cooperation and Development) (1996). Short-term Economic Indicators—Transition Economies 2/1996. Paris.

Ram, R. (1986). Wagner's Hypothesis in Time Series and Cross-Section Perspectives: Evidence from "Real" Data for 155 Countries. *Review of Economics and Statistics* 68:194–204.

Romer, P. M. (1990). Endogenous Technological Change. *Journal of Political Economy* 98 (Part II):S71–S102.

Sachs, J., and A. Warner (1995). Economic Reform and the Process of Global Economic Integration. *Brookings Papers on Economic Activity* (1):1–95.

The World Bank (1996). The Social Indicators of Development Database. Washington, D.C.

III

Poverty and Development

It is a staple of rhetoric against inflation to describe it as the cruelest tax of all, and to say that inflation disproportionately hurts the poor. The issue is important in judging the social costs of inflation, a topic in which I have long been interested.[1]

While there are reasons inflation is likely to be a regressive tax—for instance that the poor are less likely to own inflation-protected financial assets than the rich—I thought we lacked good evidence to go along with this view. That changed in 1994 when the Brazilian *Plan Real* stabilization clearly improved the relative incomes of the poor. Whether that was due to the effects of lower inflation per se or because of the adjustment of the real minimum wage that took place at that time, or both, was however not clear.

In this chapter William Easterly, then of the World Bank but now at New York University, and I use polling data for nearly 32,000 households from 38 countries, to see what the poor say about the extent to which inflation is a problem for them. We also look at the impacts of actual inflation on the income share of the poor.

In the poll, people are given a list of issues and asked to choose two or three they personally are concerned about most. "Inflation and high prices" is one of the issues.[2] The basic result is that the poor are more likely than the rich to list inflation as a personal problem. This result is statistically stronger in the industrialized countries than in the developing countries in the sample. The result stands up to several robustness checks.

This is what people think, and it may reflect perceptions rather than reality—though, to be sure, perceptions matter in elections. In the third section of this chapter, we also look at the relationship between inflation and direct measures or inequality, poverty, and real wages. These tend to support the view that inflation is bad for the poor, though the statistical results are surprisingly not very strong.

Thus this paper provides further evidence that inflation is bad for the poor.

An interesting feature of the data can be found in figure 14.1, which plots the probability of mentioning inflation as a top problem against average inflation over the past decade. There is a significant positive relationship, but the deviations from the average relationship are of interest. In particular China and Singapore stand out as being much more inflation averse than the average, and Brazil and Ukraine as being less inflation averse. Possible reasons for these deviations are discussed in the text of the chapter.

Notes

1. Including in work with Franco Modigliani (1978) and John Huizinga (1982) respectively, which is cited at the end of the chapter.

2. In the text we discuss whether the interpretation we put on the answer is seriously polluted by the inclusion of "high prices" and conclude probably not.

14   Inflation and the Poor

William Easterly and Stanley
Fischer

The claim that "inflation is the cruelest tax of all" is often interpreted
as meaning that inflation hurts the poor relatively more than the
rich. It could also mean that the inflation tax is particularly unfair
because, the taxing mechanism being little understood, the inflation
tax can be imposed by stealth.

The essential a priori argument is that the rich are better able to
protect themselves against, or benefit from, the effects of inflation
than are the poor. In particular, the rich and more sophisticated are
likely to have better access to financial instruments that hedge in
some way against inflation, while the (small) portfolios of the poor
are likely to have a larger share of cash. The poor may also depend
more than the rich on state-determined income that is not fully
indexed to inflation. Among the elderly poor, pensions are often not
fully indexed and so inflation will directly reduce their real incomes.
For the remainder of the poor, state subsidies or direct transfers may
also not be fully indexed.

However, these arguments are not decisive. Aside from the points
that the poor are likely to hold relatively more cash in their portfolios, and to be less sophisticated, the relative effects of inflation
on the rich versus the poor must be specific to the institutions and
histories of each economy. Certainly, study of the long list of the
potential effects of inflation on the economy outlined in Fischer and
Modigliani (1978) does not lead to a clear presumption that it is the
poor who are hurt relatively more by inflation, especially because so
many of the effects of inflation come through complicated details of
the tax system, including capital taxation. The question must be an
empirical one, and the answer may well differ among economies.

In this chapter, we examine inflation's effects on the poor in two
ways. First, we draw on the results of a global survey of 31,869

individuals in thirty-eight countries, which asked whether individuals think inflation is an important national problem. This provides an indirect way at getting at the issue of whether inflation is more of a problem for the poor than for the rich. Second, we assess the effects of inflation on direct measures of inequality and poverty in various cross-country and cross-time samples.

Our evidence supports the views that inflation is regarded as more of a problem by the poor than it is by the nonpoor, and that inflation appears to reduce the relative income of the poor. It thus adds to a growing body of literature that on balance—but not unanimously—tends to support the view that inflation is a cruel tax. We start by reviewing the literature, and then turn to the new evidence.

Literature Survey

Most of the literature deals with the United States, using annual data on poverty rates and inflation. Powers (1995) finds that inflation worsens a consumption-based poverty measure over 1959–1992, but has no significant impact on the income-based poverty rate. Cutler and Katz (1991), in contrast, find that an increase in inflation reduces the poverty rate over 1959–1989. Blank and Blinder (1986) found that inflation increased poverty rates, but also slightly increased the income shares of the bottom two quintiles (only the second quintile was significant). On balance, Blank and Blinder argue that "there is little or no evidence that inflation is the cruelest tax."

Moving to other countries, Cardoso (1992) argues that the inflation tax does not affect those already below the poverty line in Latin America because of their negligible cash holdings. However, she finds that higher inflation is associated with lower real wages in a panel of seven Latin American countries. An additional fragment of evidence comes from Rezende (1998, p. 568), who points out that the Gini coefficient in Brazil increased steadily with rising inflation in the 1980s and then declined with the successful inflation stabilization of 1994–1996. Datt and Ravallion (1996) found in a cross-time, cross-state study of India that observations with higher inflation rates also had higher poverty rates.

Romer and Romer (1998) argue that the effects of inflation on the incomes of the poor are likely to differ between cyclical and longer-term perspectives. In the short run, an increase in (unanticipated) inflation will be associated with a decline in unemployment, that may well relatively benefit the poor. Over the longer term, however, higher inflation cannot permanently reduce unemployment, and the effects of inflation on the poor could then be reversed. Even in a cyclical perspective, Romer and Romer find the effects of unemployment on the income distribution to be stronger in earlier decades than in the nineties. Using an international panel, they find that lower inflation tends to increase the income of the poor over the longer term—a result they attribute in part to the negative association between inflation and economic growth. Agenor (1998) also finds poverty rates to be positively related to inflation in cross-country data.

In our work using polling data, we will explore the impact on attitudes to inflation of factors other than relative income. The poor are less educated, and there may be an independent effect of inflation's impact on the uneducated. Our priors on the impact of education on attitudes to inflation are, like those on income, ambiguous. One consideration is that human capital may be a good hedge against inflation, so those with more human capital feel more protected (also stocks and bonds may be good hedges against inflation and they are also held disproportionately by the more educated). The uneducated probably have a lower weight of human capital relative to cash in their portfolios, and so dislike inflation more. But the more educated may know more about the damage that inflation can do to the economy as a whole and so may be more likely to mention inflation as a top concern than the less educated.

Previous literature using polling data includes Fischer and Huizinga (1982), who analyzed the relative probabilities of mentioning inflation and unemployment as a (or the most) serious problem facing the nation, in the United States over the period 1939–1978. They found that inflation was consistently more frequently cited as a serious problem than unemployment except during recessions. Apropos the question in this paper, they found a positive association between income and the probability of mentioning inflation as a serious problem ("inflation aversion"), although the relationship was sometimes nonmonotonic. Moreover, in regression analysis income was positively but insignificantly related to inflation aversion. Rose (1997) found no association between the standard of living and inflation aversion relative to unemployment aversion in a sample of polling data from ex-Communist countries.

Fischer and Huizinga (1982) also found little relationship between the level of education and inflation aversion. However, their education variable discriminated only between high school education and above.

We will control for the national averages of inflation aversion when testing the poor's relative inflation aversion. On the cross-section relationship between inflation aversion and actual inflation, Fischer (1996) found a surprisingly weak correlation using the same survey data that we use in this paper. Likewise, Rose (1997) found little association among transition countries between actual inflation and inflation aversion—inflation aversion rose relative to unemployment as inflation was falling. The Czech Republic with its low inflation had higher inflation aversion than Ukraine and Belarus with their quadruple-digit inflations (although causality is important—the Czechs' inflation aversion could be the reason they have low inflation). However, Fischer and Huizinga (1982) did find that the cross-time variation in the United States of mentioning inflation or unemployment as the most serious problem was associated with actual inflation and unemployment.

Shiller (1996) poses a question closely related to ours, "*Why* Do People Dislike Inflation?" He conducted a questionnaire survey of 677 people in the United States, Germany, and Brazil. His answer was that people perceived inflation as reducing their standard of living. In the U.S. sample, when asked what was their biggest concern about inflation, 77 percent of the sample chose the response "inflation hurts my real buying power." Only 7 percent chose the traditional view of economists—"inflation causes a lot of inconveniences: I find it harder to comparison shop, I feel I have to avoid holding too much cash, etc." When pressed further, the majority in the samples in the United States, Germany, and Brazil supported the view that their wages would not rise as fast as the price level during the process of inflation. If Shiller's results indeed reflect most people's view of inflation, than we might expect the poor and uneducated to dislike inflation more because they are probably less protected by asset income from changes in their real wages. We will find some support for the idea that inflation reduces the real wages of the poor in our empirical results.

Results on Inflation Concerns and Income

The Data

Roper Starch Worldwide, a marketing, public opinion, and advertising research firm, coordinated the survey that we use to measure inflation concerns. International Research Associates (INRA) did the actual field work with its affiliates and partner companies. The survey was undertaken by Roper Starch during February to May 1995. Table 14.1 lists the thirty-eight countries—nineteen industrialized, and nineteen developing and transition—covered in the survey.

Respondents to the survey from all countries were classified according to their standard of living (self-assessed) and level of education. The survey question on which we focus is:

Here is a list of things people have told us they are concerned about today. Would you read over the list and then tell me which two or three you personally are most concerned about today.

The economic concerns included in the list were "recession and unemployment, inflation and high prices, money enough to live right and pay bills, educational quality." There were fourteen other noneconomic concerns, and respondents could also say "other, none of these, don't know." We define a dummy variable that takes the value 1 if people mention "inflation and high prices" among the top two or three concerns (the top two or three are not ranked among themselves), and 0 otherwise.

The wording of the inflation response is unfortunate in that it also includes "high prices."[1] It is unclear how the respondent will interpret "high prices"—will it be high prices compared to the past or high prices compared to the respondent's wage? If the latter, then the respondent may simply be complaining about low real wages. Fortunately, there is another "top concern" that directly addresses the standard of living, which is "money enough to live right and pay bills." The correlation among all respondents between these two "top concerns" was only .0043, with a p-value of .437. Hence, we can be moderately reassured that the "inflation and high prices" question is really about inflation and not about real wages. Fischer and Huizinga (1982) found no difference in poll responses in the United States to questions that mentioned just "inflation" and those that mentioned "inflation and high prices."

The income question on the survey asked the respondents to classify themselves in one of seven categories: "rich, very comfortable, comfortable, average, just getting by, poor, and very poor." Thus participants are self-classifying on this question, and we should therefore interpret the answers as relating to the relative income of the participant in his or her own country. We define dummy

Table 14.1
Percentage of responses that mentioned given problem as among the top two or three problems, by country

	Inflation and high prices	Crime	AIDS	Reces- sion/ Unem- plmnt	Drug abuse	Money enough to live on	Govern- ment corrup- tion	Educa- tion quality	Immi- gration	Racial/ Ethnic rela- tions	Environ- mental pollu- tion	Reli- gious extre- mism	Foreign rela- tions	Foreign aid	Terror- ism	Other/ Don't know
Australia	4	17	6	13	6	8	8	9	6	4	12	2	1	3	1	1
Austria	7	16	10	9	8	6	6	2	6	4	11	3	1	2	7	2
Belgium	10	13	9	18	10	5	12	2	6	2	5	2	1	1	2	1
Brazil	7	17	14	10	9	8	14	10	0	1	4	1	1	2	2	0
Canada	10	18	8	17	6	10	6	7	4	3	7	1	1	1	1	1
Chile	5	10	17	8	19	9	7	13	0	0	7	1	1	1	2	0
China	25	13	1	10	1	11	15	12	1	0	8	0	1	1	1	1
Colombia	9	15	14	11	10	4	10	9	1	0	9	1	1	0	7	0
Czech Republic	14	26	7	4	7	8	11	3	1	2	12	2	0	0	2	0
Denmark	3	12	7	10	3	9	3	8	8	6	15	2	5	5	3	1
Finland	4	21	3	24	5	16	9	1	2	1	8	3	0	0	1	3
France	4	12	19	21	6	6	6	4	4	3	4	5	1	2	2	0
Germany	8	21	6	16	7	6	6	3	4	4	12	2	0	1	3	0
Greece	9	13	14	20	15	2	6	6	0	0	8	1	1	1	3	0
Hong Kong	11	12	7	14	6	8	3	5	3	1	7	2	3	4	3	9
Hungary	19	17	2	10	2	17	9	7	2	1	8	1	2	1	1	0
India	13	14	7	14	7	7	9	9	2	3	6	3	1	1	5	0
Indonesia	12	24	9	24	11	2	5	6	0	1	4	1	1	1	0	0
Ireland	4	18	10	15	17	10	6	3	3	1	5	1	0	3	3	0
Italy	6	10	12	22	2	7	13	3	3	4	11	3	1	1	1	0
Japan	6	9	6	20	2	4	21	6	0	1	17	1	4	1	0	3

Mexico	17	13	7	18	7	7	15	5	1	1	4	1	1	1	2	0
Netherlands	3	23	6	12	7	7	5	5	4	7	7	8	0	1	3	2
Norway	2	19	2	12	11	10	4	9	4	4	11	3	2	3	1	1
Philippines	12	24	4	12	10	4	10	6	0	0	9	1	1	0	6	0
Poland	11	22	6	12	7	11	11	2	0	1	10	4	1	1	3	0
Russia	22	28	1	13	1	15	8	2	1	3	5	0	0	0	1	1
Singapore	23	12	4	9	4	12	2	14	1	3	10	1	2	1	0	2
Spain	7	6	12	18	13	9	10	4	1	2	6	1	0	3	9	0
Sweden	5	20	5	15	11	3	4	3	6	6	13	3	1	1	2	1
Switzerland	6	15	11	15	10	5	5	3	4	6	10	5	2	1	3	0
Taiwan	11	13	4	8	11	4	18	12	1	1	13	0	1	0	1	2
Thailand	5	23	20	12	10	1	8	7	1	0	10	1	0	0	1	0
Turkey	19	8	5	12	4	5	11	7	1	3	8	6	1	1	10	0
Ukraine	22	26	2	9	3	19	10	2	0	2	4	0	0	0	0	0
United Kingdom	5	19	4	14	9	11	6	10	3	2	7	2	1	2	3	0
USA	7	24	12	6	11	10	6	7	3	4	4	2	1	1	1	0
Venezuela	16	16	10	11	11	5	13	12	1	0	2	0	1	1	2	0
Sample average	10	17	8	14	8	8	9	6	2	2	8	2	1	1	3	1

variables for each category that take the value 1 if the respondents self-classify in that category and zero otherwise. Similarly the education question asked the respondents to put themselves in one of the following three categories: "primary or less, secondary/technical, higher." We again code three dummy variables for each category. We will also include country dummies in our regressions, and will later review them as indicators of the underlying sensitivity to inflation in each country.

Table 14.1 shows summary statistics on the poll responses in each country. The percentages for each problem x are the number of total responses that mentioned x as among the top two or three national problems, where each respondent has two to three responses. The average across nations is for 10 percent of the responses to be "inflation." Only crime and recession/unemployment account for more responses on average.

Income and Education Results

We do a probit equation, with the dependent variable equal to one if inflation is mentioned as among the top two or three national concerns. The independent variables are the income category dummies and the education category dummies. The results are shown in table 14.2. The category "rich" is omitted from the specification, so the coefficients on the income variables measure the difference between the coefficient on that income category and "rich." Likewise, the category "higher education" is omitted, so the coefficients on the education variables measure the difference between that category and "higher education."

Table 14.2 shows the results. (Individual country effects are not shown at this point; they will be discussed below.) The likelihood of mentioning inflation as a top concern is decreasing in the standard of living of the respondent. The coefficient increases monotonically as respondents range from "very comfortable" to "very poor." The coefficients on "just getting by," "poor," and "very poor" are all statistically significant, meaning that the difference between those categories and "rich" is statistically significant. The significance is not overwhelming given the large sample, but it does pass the common statistical threshold. The very poor have a 10.5 percent higher probability of mentioning inflation as a top concern than do the rich. The poor are thus relatively more concerned than the rich about inflation.

Table 14.2
Estimated probit equation for mentioning "inflation and high prices" as a top national concern

	Observations: 31,869			
	Parameter estimate	Standard error	*t*-statistic	*P*-value
Constant	−1.09	0.14	−7.95	[.000]
Standard of living of individual ("Rich" is omitted category)				
Very Comfortable	0.03	0.14	0.25	[.801]
Comfortable	0.15	0.13	1.17	[.240]
Average	0.25	0.13	1.91	[.057]
Just Getting By	0.28	0.13	2.11	[.035]
Poor	0.31	0.14	2.30	[.022]
Very Poor	0.36	0.15	2.39	[.017]
Educational attainment ("Higher education" is omitted category)				
Primary School	0.13	0.02	5.22	[.000]
Secondary School	0.06	0.02	2.79	[.005]

Note: Country intercept dummies are included but not shown.

The pattern for the education variable is similar: the less educated dislike inflation more than the more educated. The difference between those who have a primary education or less and those with higher education is highly significant statistically, though not absolutely large. The coefficient implies that those with only a primary education have a 3.8 percent higher probability of mentioning inflation as a top concern than do those with higher education.[2] Those with a secondary education are also significantly more likely to mention inflation as a top concern than those with higher education. Recalling the possibly offsetting effects of human capital as a hedge against inflation and the greater knowledge of inflation's damage with higher education, as factors affecting the response, our results suggest that the first effect dominates the second.

Robustness Checks

Our first robustness check is to split the sample between developing and developed countries. Table 14.3a shows that the results are still very strong in the industrial country sample, but table 14.3b shows much weaker results in the developing country sample. The magnitudes of the coefficients are uniformly lower in the developing

Table 14.3A
Results for industrial economies (16,352 observations; country effects included but not shown)

	Parameter estimate	Standard error	t-statistic	P-value
Constant	−1.25	0.23	−5.56	[.000]
Standard of living ("Rich" is omitted category)				
Very Comfortable	0.16	0.23	0.69	[.391]
Comfortable	0.26	0.22	1.15	[.184]
Average	0.33	0.22	1.51	[.022]
Just Getting By	0.31	0.22	1.40	[.039]
Poor	0.49	0.23	2.13	[.004]
Very Poor	0.59	0.26	2.29	[.004]
Educational level ("Higher education" is omitted category)				
Primary School	0.29	0.04	7.97	[.000]
Secondary School	0.18	0.03	5.74	[.000]

Table 14.3B
Developing countries (15,517 observations; country effects included but not shown)

	Parameter estimate	Standard error	t-statistic	P-value
Constant	−1.20	0.17	−7.01	[.000]
Standard of living ("Rich" is omitted category)				
Very Comfortable	−0.04	0.17	−0.23	[.822]
Comfortable	0.10	0.16	0.61	[.539]
Average	0.21	0.16	1.28	[.202]
Just Getting By	0.27	0.16	1.65	[.099]
Poor	0.25	0.17	1.50	[.134]
Very Poor	0.27	0.18	1.44	[.150]
Educational level ("Higher education" is omitted category)				
Primary School	0.00	0.03	0.01	[.993]
Secondary School	−0.03	0.03	−1.20	[.230]

Table 14.4
Results with aggregated income classes

	Parameter estimate	Standard error	t-statistic	P-value
Industrial countries				
Constant	−1.11	0.08	−14.65	[.000]
Income Class ("Upper Class" is omitted category)				
Middle Class	0.15	0.06	2.52	[.012]
Lower Class	0.36	0.09	4.07	[.000]
Educational level ("Higher education" is omitted category)				
Primary Education	0.30	0.04	8.36	[.000]
Secondary Education	0.19	0.03	5.99	[.000]
Developing countries				
Constant	−1.24	0.08	−16.28	[.000]
Income Class ("Upper Class" is omitted category)				
Middle Class	0.26	0.07	3.69	[.000]
Lower Class	0.23	0.06	3.91	[.000]
Educational level ("Higher education" is omitted category)				
Primary Education	0.03	0.03	0.83	[.406]
Secondary Education	−0.02	0.03	−0.62	[.537]

country sample than in the industrial country sample. In the industrial country sample, the very poor have a 14 percent higher probability of mentioning inflation as a top concern than the rich. In the developing country sample, the very poor have a 9 percent higher probability than the rich.

The weakness of the developing country results may have to do with collinearity in discriminating among the finely defined income categories. When we aggregate the bottom two categories as "lower class," the middle three categories as "middle class," and the top two categories as "upper class," we get statistically significant differences in the developing country sample between "lower class" and "upper class," and between "middle class" and "upper class" (table 14.4). These differences are also significant in the industrial sample. The coefficient on "lower class" continues to be higher in the industrial sample than in the developing country sample.

The education variables are not robust across the two samples. They are still highly significant in the industrial country sample, but are always insignificant in the developing country sample.

Table 14.5
Robustness to age and occupation
(31,443 observations; country dummies are included but not shown)

	Parameter estimate	Standard error	*t*-statistic	*P*-value
Constant	−1.34	0.14	−9.43	[.000]
Standard of living ("Rich" is omitted category)				
Very Comfortable	0.04	0.14	0.31	[.755]
Comfortable	0.15	0.13	1.12	[.264]
Average	0.23	0.13	1.77	[.076]
Just Getting By	0.25	0.13	1.90	[.057]
Poor	0.28	0.14	2.04	[.041]
Very Poor	0.32	0.15	2.13	[.033]
Educational attainment ("Higher education" is omitted category)				
Primary School	0.10	0.03	3.69	[.000]
Secondary School	0.06	0.02	3.01	[.003]
Age Groups (14–20 age group is omitted category)				
People in their 20s	0.17	0.03	4.84	[.000]
People in their 30s	0.21	0.04	5.66	[.000]
People in their 40s	0.17	0.04	4.34	[.000]
People in their 50s	0.20	0.04	4.87	[.000]
People in their 60s	0.28	0.05	6.03	[.000]
People in their 70s+	0.26	0.06	4.60	[.000]
Occupational Groups ("Student" is omitted category)				
Professional/Executive	0.06	0.04	1.50	[.133]
White Collar	0.06	0.04	1.48	[.140]
Blue Collar	0.09	0.04	2.37	[.018]
Unemployed	0.05	0.05	1.04	[.300]
Homemaker	0.06	0.04	1.55	[.121]
Retired	0.06	0.05	1.15	[.250]

Our second robustness check is to also include age and occupational groups. The seven age groups are 14–20 (the omitted category), 21–29, 30–39, 40–49, 50–59, 60–69, and 70 and over. The occupational categories are student (the omitted category), professional/executive, white collar, blue collar, unemployed, homemaker, and retired. Table 14.5 shows the results.

The results on poverty and education are robust to the inclusion of age group dummies and occupational group dummies. The poor and very poor are still significantly more likely than the richer to mention inflation as a top concern. Primary-educated and secondary-educated respondents are still more likely to cite inflation as a concern than those with higher education.

All of the age groups are more likely to be concerned about inflation than teenagers. The age group most concerned with inflation is that of people in their sixties, followed closely by people in their seventies and above (the difference between the sixties and seventies is not statistically significant). This group is at the stage in the life cycle of consuming by running down their assets, and so may dislike the uncertainty introduced by inflation.

The occupational group most concerned with inflation is blue-collar workers. This reinforces the finding that those who are more averse to inflation are relatively disadvantaged on several different dimensions—the poor, the uneducated, and the unskilled (blue-collar) workers.

We also tried a gender dummy. Males were slightly more likely to mention inflation as a problem than females, but the difference was not statistically significant.

Other Concerns

We also examined what other economic concerns the poor had, to see how their concern with inflation compares to other problems. Table 14.6 shows which concerns are disproportionately and significantly more likely to be mentioned by the poor. The result on unemployment and recession is very surprising—the poor are more likely to mention it as a problem than the rich, but the difference is not significant.

Other concerns follow a more predictable pattern. The poor are much more likely than the rich to mention "money enough to live right" as a concern, not surprisingly. The less educated are predictably much less likely to mention quality of education as a concern than the more educated.

On a question where our priors were not so clear, we found that the poor were less likely than the rich to mention crime as a concern. The difference was not very significant, however. Confusing the picture on crime further, the primary-educated were more likely to mention crime than the college-educated.[3]

We also tried the gender dummy in the regressions for the other economic concerns. The only significant results were that females

Table 14.6
What other concerns do the poor have?

	t-statistic on income or educational level in probit regression for mentioning concern shown				
	Inflation and high prices	Recession and unem- ployment	Money enough to live right, pay bills	Educational quality	Crime
Standard of living of individual ("Rich" is omitted category)					
Very Comfortable	0.25	−0.52	0.05	0.86	−0.29
Comfortable	1.17	0.26	1.43	0.50	−0.55
Average	1.91	1.03	2.88	−0.41	−0.35
Just Getting By	2.11	1.34	4.89	−0.47	−1.43
Poor	2.30	1.51	5.27	−0.94	−2.07
Very Poor	2.39	1.04	5.81	0.54	−1.14
Educational attainment ("Higher education" is omitted category)					
Primary School	5.22	−0.43	6.01	−17.66	4.42
Secondary School	2.79	−0.05	4.04	−11.85	0.97

were more likely than males to mention "money enough to live right" and "education quality" as concerns.

Country Effects

Although not directly relevant to our main question, the pattern of country effects is interesting [as was previously noted by Fischer (1996)]. Figure 14.1 graphs the countries' propensity to mention inflation as a top national problem (from table 14.1) against the actual inflation rate in the decade preceding the survey (1985–1994). (We would get a very similar picture using the country dummies from the regression in table 14.2 for inflation preferences.) Although there is a significant positive relationship between the log of average inflation 1985–1994 and the country propensities to mention infla- tion as a top problem, there are some striking outliers. The country in which respondents were, ceteris paribus, most concerned about inflation is not Ukraine, Russia, or Brazil—in all of which the infla- tion rate shortly before the poll had been around 1000 percent or higher—but is China with its modest inflation rate of 12 percent. An even more striking outlier is Singapore, where the likelihood of mentioning inflation as a top problem is similar to those of Russia

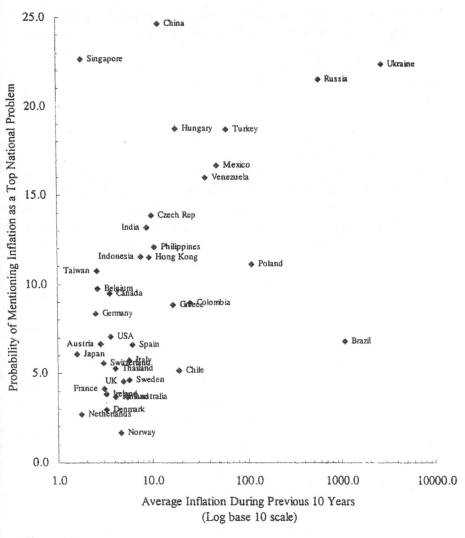

Figure 14.1
Probability of mentioning inflation as a top national problem, and average inflation during previous 10 years.

and Ukraine, even though inflation was only 2 percent, which tied with Japan and the Netherlands for lowest inflation in the entire sample! Since Singapore's population is largely of Chinese descent, we speculate that there is a Chinese dummy variable. This Chinese variable may have something to do with the memory of the hyperinflation in China after World War II. (The Taiwan and Hong Kong dummies are also at least weakly consistent with the Chinese dummy hypothesis.) It is interesting that another country that had a post-WWII (and post-WWI) hyperinflation—Hungary—also displays a high tendency to mention inflation as a top problem relative to a modest recent inflation. Perhaps surprisingly, the observation for Germany is not far out of line with the average.

Outliers in the other direction are Brazil and Chile. Brazilians are a little less likely to mention inflation as a top problem than Americans, despite having had around 1000 percent inflation in Brazil over the previous decade. It could be argued that since the survey was conducted in early 1995, Brazilians may have already incorporated favorable expectations about the success of the stabilization plan (the *Plan Real*) introduced in mid-1994. Brazilians may also have been relatively well protected from inflation by indexation—but the election results in Brazil following the success of the *Plan Real* led us to expect high Brazilian inflation aversion. Chile is a similar outlier, with low concern about inflation despite a history of high inflation—this could suggest that the Chilean inflation stabilization had great credibility by 1995, and could also reflect the extensive capital market inflation indexation in Chile.

More germane to our main question, we also relate actual country inflation to another poverty-related question asked on the Roper-Starch survey. This question asked

Do you strongly agree, mostly agree, mostly disagree, or strongly disagree with the following statement: "In our society, the rich get richer and the poor get poorer."?

In figure 14.2, we graph the percentage of respondents in each country who answer this question "strongly agree" against the actual rate of inflation 1985–1994. We see a positive association (which is highly statistically significant). Thus, not only do the poor within each society complain more about inflation, but the whole society has a perception of a growing gap between rich and poor in high-inflation societies.[4]

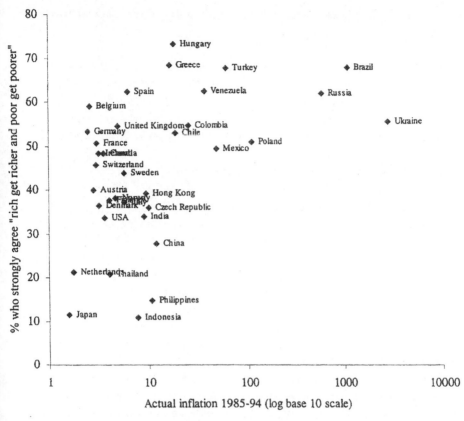

Figure 14.2
Association between perception that "rich get richer and poor get poorer" and actual inflation.

The evidence from the poll data provides very strong support for the view that the poor express relatively more dislike of inflation than the rich, and that the less educated are more inflation averse than the more educated. This provides some support for the view that inflation hurts the poor relatively more than the rich. Another interpretation would be that, whatever the facts about the damage inflation does and to whom, the poor believe it to be more damaging than do the rich. This would suggest that populist politicians are likely to pursue more anti-inflationary policies than those seeking to appeal to the middle and upper classes, which is not in accord with our ex ante beliefs. Perhaps populist politicians depend on a core group of poor supporters who receive benefits financed by inflation, even though the poor as a whole may dislike inflation.

Results Using Direct Measures of Inequality, Poverty, and Real Wages

In this section we turn to more direct evidence on the effects of inflation on the distribution of income. We use a number of different measures of the relative well-being of the poor: the share of the bottom quintile in income, the poverty rate, and the real minimum wage. All of these three indicators are correlated with inflation.

Results on the bottom Quintile in Income

We look at changes from one decade average to the next in the share of the bottom quintile of income, using the data of Deininger and Squire (1996) for the 1970s, 1980s, and 1990s. We regress the change in the share of the bottom quintile on decade average CPI inflation and real GDP per capita growth (both from the World Bank database). We use the inflation tax rate transformation $[\pi/(1 + \pi)]$ of the percent inflation rate π. This transformation reduces the extent to which extreme values of inflation will dominate the results; it is also the tax rate on money balances in discrete time, or the annual rate of loss in the value of money caused by inflation over the period being considered. However, the results shown here are robust to simply using the decade average percent inflation, or the log change in the CPI. Growth turns out not to be a statistically significant determinant of changes in the distribution of income, as other authors have found (for example, Ravallion and Chen 1997), so in table 14.7 we show only the results with the inflation tax.

Table 14.7
Dependent variable: DINCQ1 (change in the share of the bottom quintile of the income distribution)

Variable	Coefficient	Standard error	t-Statistic	Prob.
C	0.004195	0.001545	2.714256	0.0077
INFLATIONTAX	−0.017412	0.005195	−3.351531	0.0011
R-squared	0.028909	Mean dependent variable		0.002084
Adjusted R-squared	0.019918	S.D. dependent variable		0.013564

Notes: Method: Least Squares. Included observations: 110. White heteroskedasticity-consistent standard errors and covariance.

The *R*-squared is very modest, so we are not explaining much of the variation in changes in bottom quintile shares. However, the coefficient on the inflation tax rate is highly significant. We also try controlling for growth but it is not significant and does not change the significance of the inflation tax. A movement from zero inflation to hyperinflation would decrease the share of the bottom quintile by 1.7 percentage points (from the coefficient on the inflation tax). This is economically significant since the sample average share of the poor in income is just 6.2 percent.

Given the transformation of the inflation rate, the effect of changes in inflation is nonlinear: a change in the inflation rate from zero to, say, 40 percent, would reduce the share of the bottom quintile by 0.5 percent, which again is large relative to the typically small share of the bottom quintile in the income distribution. With a positive constant, implying that ceteris paribus the share of the bottom income quintile in this sample would have increased over time, we have the share of the bottom quintile increasing if the inflation tax is less than .24 (corresponding to an inflation rate of 31 percent) and decreasing otherwise.

There may be an argument for using the *change* in the inflation tax rate on the right-hand side of this equation instead of the level. We do not have clear priors on this: the level of the inflation tax is what is important if some nominal incomes of the poor are fixed. On the other hand, only "surprise" inflation may effectively tax the poor, so we would then want the change in inflation (as opposed to surprises in the price level, in which our original specification is appropriate). When we rerun the equation above with the change in the inflation tax, it is not statistically significant. Alternatively, we can run the equation in levels: the share of the bottom quintile regressed on the inflation rate (and the growth rate). The inflation tax rate is then a significant determinant of the share of the bottom quintile; an increase of the inflation tax from zero to hyperinflation would then lower the share of the bottom quintile by 1.7 percentage points.

After getting this result in an earlier version of this paper, we became aware of related results by Romer and Romer (1998). They show that the log of average income of the poorest fifth of the population is negatively related to log inflation across countries, and the Gini coefficient is positively related to log inflation.

Inflation and the Poverty Rate

We use data on poverty rates that span more than one point in time for forty-two developing and transition countries over 1981–1993, from household data collected by Ravallion and Chen (1997). For each country, they construct a country-specific poverty line linked to mean income: it is 50 percent of the initial mean income for the household survey for that country, starting with the initial year of the years included in the sample for that country. Ravallion and Chen present sixty-four episodes of changes in poverty rates using this country-specific poverty line. The median length of an episode is three years. In table 14.8 we regress the percentage change per year in the proportion below the poverty line (50 percent of initial mean income) on real GDP, per capita growth, and the inflation tax rate, over the period spanned by the change in poverty rate.

The inflation tax rate has a significant positive effect on the increase in poverty. The growth rate has a negative effect on the change in poverty, as Ravallion and Chen also found. The result on the inflation tax rate is not robust to using the percent inflation rate or the log inflation rate (they have the same sign, and log inflation is significant at the 10 percent level), but the inflation tax rate does have appeal as the most appropriate functional form.[5]

Once again, we are uncertain about whether the level of the inflation tax rate or its change is more appropriate, for the same reasons mentioned before. In any case, the change in the inflation tax rate is insignificant in the poverty change regression, although it becomes significant of the same sign as in levels when an extreme outlier (Poland 1989–1993) is omitted.[6]

Table 14.8
Dependent variable: POVERTYCH (change in percent of households below the country-specific constructed poverty line)

Variable	Coefficient	Standard error	t-Statistic	Prob.
C	7.171827	9.541762	0.751625	0.4552
GROWTH	−5.328780	1.439615	−3.701533	0.0005
INFTAX	62.54719	30.81613	2.029690	0.0468
R-squared	0.496244	Mean dependent variable		35.79547
Adjusted R-squared	0.479727	S.D. dependent variable		69.48502

Notes: Method: Least Squares. Included observations: 64. White heteroskedasticity-consistent standard errors and covariance.

Inflation and the Real Minimum Wage

The real minimum wage is not as clear an indicator of the well-being of the poor as the two previous measures. A decrease in the real minimum wage could benefit the poor by facilitating their entry into formal sector employment, and too high a minimum wage could make the poor worse off by increasing formal sector unemployment. Nonetheless, assuming the minimum wage regulations are observed, the real minimum wage *is* a welfare indicator for the group of workers that are at the bottom of the formal sector wage distribution.

How might inflation affect the real minimum wage? The government usually sets the nominal minimum wage. If there is downward nominal rigidity, the government will find it easier to lower the real minimum wage during times of high inflation. There is also the arithmetic relationship pointed out by Bacha and Lopes (1983), among others, that, given an initial real minimum wage, the average real minimum wage is lower the higher is inflation for a given indexation lag (for example, one month) from prices to wages.

We use minimum wage data collected by Rama and Artecona (1999), using a pooled sample of annual data for all years in which it is available for all countries. We use the same CPI series as before. We regress the log change in the real minimum wage on the inflation tax and on real growth per capita. High growth per capita implies rising labor productivity and so would be expected to translate into higher average real wages; if the real minimum wage is sensitive to the average real wage, we would expect it to increase also. The results are shown in table 14.9.

Table 14.9
Dependent variable: log percent change in real wage

Variable	Coefficient	Standard error	t-Statistic	Prob.
C	0.041116	0.016368	2.511911	0.0125
Inflation Tax Rate	−0.004066	0.001900	−2.140478	0.0331
GROWTH	0.004589	0.001547	2.966504	0.0032
R-squared	0.127369	Mean dependent variable		−0.000940
Adjusted R-squared	0.122048	S.D. dependent variable		0.198479

Notes: Method: Least Squares. Included observations: 331. White heteroskedasticity-consistent standard errors and covariance.

A high inflation tax rate is significantly associated with a negative percent change in the real wage. The real minimum wage change is positively associated with growth, as expected, with one percentage point more growth increasing real minimum wages by 0.4 percent. The explanatory power of the regression is again modest. The implied effect of inflation on the minimum real wage is fairly strong: an increase in the inflation tax rate from zero to, say, 20 percent would reduce the real wage by eight percentage points. This strong result depends in part on a large outlier—Nicaragua in 1987 when inflation was near 1000 percent but the nominal minimum wage only increased by 22 percent. When this outlier is omitted, the relationship between the real minimum wage change and the inflation tax is still significant, although the magnitude of the coefficient is cut in half.

We also ran the change in real minimum wage equation on the change in the inflation tax and the growth rate. The change in the inflation tax is highly significant. Thus, both the level of the inflation rate [as would be predicted by Bacha and Lopes 1983] and its change (as would be predicted by models in which only surprise inflation matters) are significantly associated with the real minimum wage.

Conclusions

This chapter presents evidence that supports the view that inflation makes the poor worse off. The primary evidence comes from the answers to an international poll of 31,869 respondents in 38 countries. These show that the disadvantaged on a number of dimensions—the poor, the uneducated, the unskilled (blue-collar) worker—are relatively more likely to mention inflation as a top concern than the advantaged on these dimensions. Each dimension is significant when controlling for the others, suggesting that the different components of being disadvantaged have independent effects on attitudes to inflation.

We also examine the impact of changes in inflation on direct measures of poverty and relate them to inflation. We found that high inflation tended to lower the share of the bottom quintile and the real minimum wage, while tending to increase poverty. Similar results on the direct effects of inflation on the per capita incomes of the poor have been found recently by Romer and Romer (1998) and Agenor (1998). This paper presents evidence from surveying the poor themselves that they suffer more from inflation than the rich.

Notes

This paper was prepared for the Annual World Bank Conference on Development Economics (ABCDE), April 1999. Views expressed here are not necessarily those of the World Bank or the International Monetary Fund. The authors are grateful for the diligent research assistance of Claire Hughes Adams and for the comments of our discussant, Martin Ravallion, other ABCDE participants, and two referees.

1. It is not uncommon in such polls for "inflation and high prices" to be classed together as one issue.

2. The coefficient estimates are not the same as the marginal probabilities, which vary with the right-hand-side variables. The marginal probabilities reported here are at the sample means.

3. Muddling the crime story further, there was only a weak statistical association between the country dummies in the crime regression and the prevalence of actual crimes.

4. This result seems to depend on the transition and developing countries, as can be seen from inspection of figure 14.2.

5. This seems to imply that some of the extreme inflation observations don't fit the regression line very well. This conjecture is confirmed: Brazil and Peru are notable outliers to the regression using log inflation as the right-hand-side variable. If Brazil and Peru are omitted, then there is a significant effect of log inflation on the change in poverty.

6. This outlier seems anomalous because it shows a large increase in poverty, while two other observations on Poland covering subperiods of this period do not show a dramatic change in poverty.

References

Agenor, Pierre-Richard. "Stabilization Policies, Poverty, and the Labor Market." Paper, IMF and World Bank, 1998.

Bacha, Edmar, and Francisco Lopes. "Inflation, Growth, and Wage Policy: A Brazilian Perspective." *Journal of Development Economics* 12 (1983).

Blank, Rebecca, and Alan Blinder. "Macroeconomics, Income Distribution, and Poverty." In *Fighting Poverty: What Works and What Doesn't*, edited by Sheldon Danziger and Daniel Weinberg, pp. 180–208. Cambridge, Mass.: Harvard University Press, 1986.

Cardoso, Eliana. "Inflation and Poverty." National Bureau of Economic Research Working Paper No. 4006, March 1992.

Cutler, David M., and Lawrence Katz. "Macroeconomic Performance and the Disadvantaged." *Brookings Papers on Economic Activity* 2 (1991).

Datt, Gaurav, and Martin Ravallion. "Why Have Some Indian States Done Better Than Others at Reducing Rural Poverty?" World Bank Policy Research Working Paper 1594. April 1996.

Deininger, Klaus, and Lyn Squire. "A New Dataset Measuring Income Inequality." *World Bank Economic Review* 10 (September 1996), 565–591.

Fischer, Stanley. "Why Are Central Banks Pursuing Long-Run Price Stability?" Federal Reserve Bank of Kansas City Symposium, *Achieving Price Stability*, 1996.

Fischer, Stanley, and John Huizinga. "Inflation, Unemployment, and Public Opinion Polls." *Journal of Money, Credit, and Banking* 14 (February 1982), 1–19.

Fischer, Stanley, and Franco Modigliani. "Towards an Understanding of the Real Effects and Costs of Inflation." *Weltwirtschaftliches Archiv* (1978), 810–823.

Powers, Elizabeth, T. "Inflation, Unemployment, and Poverty Revisited." *Economic Review*, Federal Reserve Bank of Cleveland (Quarter 3 1995), 2–13.

Rama, Martin, and Raquel Artecona. "A Data Base of Labor Market Indicators across Countries." World Bank paper, 1999.

Ravallion, Martin, and Shaohua Chen. "Distribution and Poverty in Developing and Transition Economies: New Data on Spells during 1981–1993." World Bank paper, 1995.

———. "What Can New Survey Data Tell Us about Recent Changes in Distribution and Poverty?" *World Bank Economic Review* (1997), 357.

Rezende, Fernando. "Prospects for Brazil's Economy." *International Affairs* 74 (July 1998), 563–576.

Romer, Christina, and David Romer. "Monetary Policy and the Well-Being of the Poor." National Bureau of Economic Research Working Paper 6793, November 1998.

Rose, Richard. "What Is the Demand for Price Stability in Post-Communist Countries?" University of Strathclyde, paper, 1997.

Shiller, Robert J. "Why Do People Dislike Inflation?" National Bureau of Economic Research Working Paper 5539, April 1996.

15   *Introduction*

The ABCDE, the Annual World Bank Conference on Development Economics, was set up in 1989, when I was Chief Economist at the World Bank. The Tenth Annual Conference was celebrated in April 1998, and I was very glad to be invited to speak on that occasion, for it provided an opportunity to look back and survey developments over the past ten years of development and development economics.

I chose to do that by reviewing important World Bank publications during the period, especially several of the Bank's *World Development Reports. WDR* is the Bank's flagship publication on development. Each year it focuses on a particular topic and develops it in depth. The *Report* is written by a team that typically includes outsiders, under the direction of a senior researcher, generally but not always from the Bank. *WDR* is taken very seriously by the Bank, and it can be assumed to reflect the Bank's and the profession's thinking on the topic at the time.

The *Report* for 1991, headed by Vinod Thomas, entitled *The Challenge of Development*, in effect presented a consensus view on the best development strategies.[1] Its arguments are summarized in the chapter, and they remain relevant and convincing. The *Report* devoted considerable space to the role of the state in development, recommending a general approach (quoted in this chapter) that makes eminent sense. This issue has of course been at the center of controversy on development for a very long time. The Japanese government thought that the Bank staff underestimated the importance of the role of the state in development, especially in East Asia, and helped finance a study on that question, *The East Asian Miracle*, published in 1993.[2] The study did find that in most of the eight East Asian countries studied, the state had played an important role in directing development, particularly through export promotion strategies.

I then ask how the developments of the 1990s would affect an updated version of the 1991 *WDR*, and venture guesses at the answers.

The last substantive section of the paper deals with some of the challenges of globalization—a topic that has only gained in importance as the center of controversies over development in the years since.

A final note: The 1990 *WDR* on *Poverty* was written under the direction of Lyn Squire when I was at the Bank. I took a particular interest in that *WDR* because the fight against poverty is the essential task of the World Bank, and a critical political and moral challenge facing the world then and now. The 1990 *WDR* recommended a development strategy similar to that described in the 1991 *Report* but emphasized the importance of direct anti-poverty measures, many examples of which were given in the 1990 *Report*.

A decade later, the Bank brought out another *WDR* on poverty— *WDR 2000/2001: Attacking Poverty*. The economics of this volume were similar to those of its 1990 predecessor, but it laid great stress on a point due to Amartya Sen, the need to involve civil society and the poor in making decisions on their own future. Although some controversy surrounded the writing of the 2001 *Report*, the message about the involvement of individuals in making decisions on their own future is surely right. Some elements of that approach are embodied in the design of the PRGF (Poverty Reduction and Growth Facility) of the IMF, and in the associated World Bank strategy.

Notes

1. The report was written under the general direction of Larry Summers, my successor as Chief Economist at the World Bank.

2. The team for that study was headed by Kemal Dervis, who in 2001 became Minister of the Economy in Turkey in the midst of a deep economic crisis, and who was critical in nursing the Turkish economy back toward health.

15 ABCDE: Past Ten Years, Next Ten Years

Stanley Fischer

It is a privilege to speak at this 10th Annual World Bank Conference on Development Economics (ABCDE), and I want to thank Joseph Stiglitz for inviting me to help celebrate the 9th anniversary and the 10th conference. I cannot think back to the start of these conferences without reflecting on my brief and happy years at the World Bank, and I hope you will excuse me if I start by straying from my subject to say a few words of thanks to the Bank and the people who serve in it.

Let me say first how grateful and proud I am to have served as chief economist of this remarkable institution and thus to be part of a chain that includes Hollis Chenery, Anne Krueger, Lawrence Summers, Michael Bruno, and Joseph Stiglitz, from all of whom we have all learned so much. I started learning from Joe more than 30 years ago, when I was a graduate student at the Massachusetts Institute of Technology and he was an assistant professor, back from his initial foray into the study of development in Nairobi. I would in particular like to pay tribute to my predecessor, Anne Krueger, whose then-controversial insistence on the centrality of trade liberalization in economic development has been amply borne out by subsequent research.

It was not only an education but also a pleasure to work with so many talented and devoted people in the World Bank—the dedicated leadership and staff in the Development Economics Vice Presidency and other friends and colleagues throughout the institution. Although any list is bound to be invidious, I would particularly like to thank some of my closest associates: my advisers, first Johannes Linn and then Andrew Steer; Dennis de Tray, research director and co-conspirator in setting up the ABCDE; the leaders of the *World*

Development Report teams for 1989, 1990, and 1991—Millard Long, Lyn Squire, and Vinod Thomas; and Kate Oram. Although I would like to go on and on in this vein, I shall now turn to the topic of the ABCDE.

Goals of the ABCDE

According to the introduction to the first volume of conference proceedings, the ABCDE was created to improve member country and World Bank policymaking by enhancing the knowledge base (Fischer and de Tray 1990). The goals were to open up the Bank to outside ideas and problems, and if possible to help shape the research agendas of those outside the Bank who were also thinking about development.

When the conference series was formally evaluated in 1995, after seven conferences, the goals were described more precisely as being:

• To expose World Bank economists to fresh insights and recent developments in economics that are influencing views outside the Bank and may alter Bank policy advice.

• To draw attention to issues that are of crucial interest to a wide range of development practitioners.

• To induce leading researchers to explore and account for the real-world implications of their work, and to incorporate the Bank's practical knowledge of developing and transition economies in their analyses.

• To improve policymaking in the Bank and its member countries by enhancing our understanding of economic processes.

The title assigned to this address, "ABCDE: Past Ten Years, Next Ten Years," suggests that I should review the record of the past nine conferences and then look ahead. I will look back, but not to review the record. That was done by the 1995 evaluators, who pronounced themselves on the whole satisfied. Based on a selective reading of the conference volumes, I agree with their assessment.

Instead I will reflect on the development consensus when I left the Bank in 1990 and how its focus has changed. Looking forward, the assigned title "ABCDE: Next Ten Years" violates the fundamental rule of forecasting, which is to forecast an event or a date but not both. Rather than attempt to forecast the content of future

ABCDEs, I will end by speculating on the implications of globalization for developing countries.

Development Issues at the Start of the 1990s

When the first ABCDE took place in 1989, four important developments stood out among developing countries:

• The debt crisis was on its way to resolution, and the lost Latin American decade was drawing to its end.

• The transition was beginning in Eastern Europe, though even as late as 1989 hardly anyone anticipated that the Soviet Union would soon disintegrate.

• The East Asian miracle was in full swing, with per capita growth over the previous 25 years averaging more than 6 percent, and per capita GDP in China having more than doubled during the 1980s.

• Average per capita GDP in Sub-Saharan Africa had declined during the 1980s, nearly offsetting the gains since independence. Indeed, in some African countries per capita incomes had been falling for 25 years.

In thinking about economic development, there was growing consensus about many of the policies needed to produce growth. At the time of its original presentation in 1989 John Williamson's Washington Consensus summarized views that were held in much of official Washington, including the World Bank (see Williamson 1990). But in the next few years the consensus broadened to include many researchers and policymakers in developing countries in Latin America and elsewhere.

The consensus within the World Bank, no doubt also representative of views within much of the development economics field, was best captured in *World Development Report 1991: The Challenge of Development*, which summarized its preferred approach as market-friendly. That report was preceded by *World Development Report 1990: Poverty*, which is an essential companion to its successor, and whose message—crucial to the Bank's mission—is no less relevant today than it was then. However, I will focus on *World Development Report 1991*, both because I want to examine the overall strategy for development espoused by the Bank at that time and because sustained reductions in poverty are best attained in a growing economy.

World Development Report 1991 argued that the primary responsibility for development rests with developing countries, which should emphasize:

- Investing in people.
- Improving the climate for enterprise.
- Opening economies to international trade and investment.
- Getting macroeconomic policy right.[1]

The report also argued for a reappraisal of the roles of the market and the state:

> Put simply, governments need to do less in those areas where markets work, or can be made to work, reasonably well. In many countries it would help to privatize many of the state-owned enterprises. Governments need to let domestic and international competition flourish.... [They] need to do more in those areas where markets alone cannot be relied upon. Above all, this means investing in education, health, nutrition, family planning, and poverty alleviation; building social, physical, administrative, regulatory, and legal infrastructure of better quality; mobilizing the resources to finance public expenditures; and providing a stable macroeconomic foundation, without which little can be achieved. (p. 9)

How did the messages of the report relate to the four issues—the end of the debt crisis, the start of transition, the East Asian miracle, and negative growth in Africa—then dominating the development agenda? The message was clearly relevant for all these situations, particularly Latin America. But it needed further development and specificity to provide a practical guide for action for transition economies. And what precisely the role of the state had been in East Asia and how—if at all—that fit into the paradigm so eloquently defined by *World Development Report 1991* remained as major question marks.[2]

At about the same time that *World Development Report 1991* was published, a mainstream position began to emerge on the strategy for reform in transition economies (see Lipton and Sachs 1990 and Fischer and Gelb 1991). Despite agreement on the reforms needed in different sectors, the speed and sequencing of reforms provided ample room for debate, especially over whether and in what areas of reform very rapid adjustment—shock treatment—might be preferable. This issue gained particular salience in light of the contrast between the negative growth of reforming Eastern European countries and the stellar performance of China, with its more gradualist strategy, particularly in privatization (see Sachs and Woo 1994 and World Bank 1996).

The World Bank's *The East Asian Miracle*, published in 1993, sought to answer the questions about the development strategies followed in the eight high-performing East Asian economies, a group that included Japan but not China. These economies had succeeded not only in achieving unprecedented growth rates but also in maintaining relatively equal distributions of income. In most—but not all—cases superb growth was accompanied by high rates of saving and investment.

The study concluded that these economies had succeeded first by getting the basics right, particularly in investing in human capital and in ensuring macroeconomic stability. Further, all the economies had kept price distortions within bounds, especially by limiting the bias against agriculture found in many developing countries. They had also encouraged the import and absorption of technology. But this was not the whole story, for in some of the eight economies government had intervened systematically and in many ways to foster development. The most important intervention came through various measures of export promotion. Also important were significant financial sector interventions, in some cases import protection efforts, subsidies to declining domestic industries, and investments in applied research. These interventions were more pervasive in Japan, the Republic of Korea, Singapore, and Taiwan (China) than in the other high-performing Asian economies. Indeed, one of the striking results of *The East Asian Miracle* study is how few generalizations apply to all eight economies.

The answers to questions beget further questions—in this case, what makes for successful interventions, and whether other countries can hope to succeed by pursuing a similar approach. Here the study emphasized the creation of institutions, including capable and reputable bureaucracies, whose procedures were shielded from political interference, and mechanisms of consultation among government, business, and others, including academics and journalists. In most cases these took the form of deliberation councils. Export promotion strategies generally keyed off world prices and, in some cases, used export targets and contests among local firms to provide incentives. Although all the economies except Hong Kong went through a phase of import substitution, these policies were later abandoned. Attitudes toward foreign direct investment varied, but in cases where it was encouraged the focus was on export promotion rather than import substitution. The study concluded that the promotion of specific industries generally had failed, while directed credit and the repression of financial systems had in some cases succeeded. In all cases the study emphasized that subsidies and distortions were limited—and modified or abandoned if they threatened macroeconomic stability.

The East Asian Miracle produced mixed reactions, with some complaining that it did not sufficiently emphasize the positive role of the state. But no reader could come away from the volume without a reinforced belief in the importance of getting the fundamentals right, while at the same time thinking that export promotion strategies had played an important role in development and that the quality of institutions matters a great deal.

Looking Back

If *World Development Report 1991* were to be rewritten today, its basic message probably would not change much. That is not because there is nothing new under the sun, but because most of what is in the report is analytically and empirically well founded. Although we should always emphasize the tenuous nature of our knowledge, we should also acknowledge that the field of development economics— which was born less than 60 years ago—continues to mature as the stock of theory, data, and country experiences on which it can draw increases.[3] In the characteristically measured words of Michael Bruno's (1995, p. 17) keynote address to this conference in 1994, "a hard core of knowledge—small but increasing—has been sustained and buttressed through the turbulence."

At the same time, the experiences, reflections, and research of the 1990s—much of it presented in *The East Asian Miracle* and in *World Development Reports* since 1991—should lead to some changes in emphasis and views. What are they? The experience of the transition economies, some of it studied in *World Development Report 1996: From Plan to Market* as well as in the European Bank for Reconstruction and Development's excellent *Transition Reports*, largely supports the consensus view of *World Development Report 1991*. Some controversy might remain over the speed of adjustment. I believe that it should be very fast to achieve macroeconomic stability and price and trade liberalization. Other reforms, which are bound to take longer, should proceed as quickly as possible.

In coming years we will also need to draw lessons for the development consensus from the East Asian crisis. It is far too early to tell what these lessons will be. But some elements are clear—none of them clearer than the need for a robust banking and financial system. The Basle Committee's Core Principles go a long way toward summarizing what is needed, and more details are provided in the IMF's Framework for Financial Stability (Folkerts-Landau and Lindgren 1998). Weak supervision and regulation in this area sow the seeds of future crises, underscoring the point that government needs not only to get out of certain areas of regulation but also to strengthen others. The importance of the financial sector is not a new theme for the World Bank; it was the subject of *World Development Report 1989: Financial Systems and Development*. But the devastation than has been propagated by weak banking systems in the East Asian crisis—including in Japan—would surely strengthen the emphasis on the need for healthy financial systems in any future *World Development Report* on development strategies.

It is interesting to consider whether the current crisis will lead to a modification of the agnostic views on financial repression expressed in *The East Asian Miracle*. The answer should be related to the conclusions drawn from East Asia's experience with capital account liberalization. Recent experience should reinforce the widely held view that capital accounts should not be liberalized until domestic financial systems, including their regulation, are strengthened. It should also reinforce the urgency of strengthening domestic financial systems. Given that, I doubt that there remains a strong case for financial repression. But vulnerability to short-term capital outflows should be controlled through strong prudential regulations for the financial system and close monitoring of corporate borrowing from abroad. There is also a case for using market-based measures to control the pace and volume of short-term capital inflows, as is now done in several countries.

Beyond the financial system, the East Asian crisis will lead to a reexamination of the benefits of the close relations among government, business, and the financial sector that have been practiced in several East Asian economies. We are likely to conclude that the opacity of financial relations within the corporate sector and among these three sectors should not survive. That does not necessarily rule out a continuation of close consultation among the three sectors, and with labor as well.

Let me now list a few other topics that merit more attention in a future *World Development Report* on development strategies: efficient regulation, institutional development, governance, environmental regulation, urbanization, and income distribution.

• Enough has been said about the combination of strong state intervention in some parts of East Asian economies and inadequate financial sector regulation and supervision to make the point that any future *World Development Report* on development strategies will have to identify the types of regulation that are needed to strengthen economic performance (see Stiglitz 1997, pp. 11–23). Such an analysis could draw on some of the excellent material in *World Development Report 1997: The State in a Changing World*.

• By emphasizing the need for efficient bureaucracies and human capital creation, *World Development Report 1991* directed attention to the role of institutions in economic development. The question of how to build the institutions needed for economic development should be taken further in a future *World Development Report*. Among these institutions are the education system and an efficient government. The question of institutional development is one that development economics has struggled with for some time. But there should be further insights from the experience of transition economies, many of which already possessed technically knowledgeable individuals as these economies began their transition to a market system. This human capital base made it possible to develop some institutions, such as central banks, quickly. The development of other institutions, including, in Russia, the tax system, has proved more difficult. We need to find out why and see whether it is possible to do better—especially in countries where overall technical training is much lower.[4]

• The ability to run the government well is one meaning of governance, a topic that has gained increasing attention since the early 1990s. Governance in its other meaning—as it relates to corruption—also deserves more attention in a future *World Development Report* on development strategies.

• *World Development Report 1991* wrestled with the issue of the environment, and *World Development Report 1992: Development and the*

Environment was devoted to the topic. The environment deserves more attention, and efforts could certainly draw on work done for *World Development Report 1992* and subsequently in the World Bank and elsewhere.

• Anyone who has recently visited the capitals of developing countries must have been struck by the problems of urbanization. This issue was discussed at some length in both the first and the second *World Development Reports,* for 1978 and 1979. Urbanization interacts with problems of population growth and surely deserves more attention in a future *World Development Report.*

• The distribution of income in many developing countries, especially in Latin America, is very unequal. Social justice, as well as the sustainability of the development effort, requires that we find ways of making development more equitable.

The subjects I have cited have been studied extensively in the Bank and elsewhere in the development economics field, and it is unlikely that their inclusion in an update of *World Development Report 1991* would produce major surprises or a major change in message.

Globalization

Next I turn to a subject that could produce major changes— globalization. Over the past 50 years the volume of world trade has increased more rapidly than GDP, and most economies have become ever more open to international trade. Despite the obstacles to trade against which we regularly and rightly inveigh, this trend is likely to continue—particularly since the ardor for regional trading arrangements has not diminished and as the World Trade Organization becomes more active. This trend is part of the process of globalization, including the globalization of production, which will shape the world economy in the decades to come.

At the same time, the globalization of international capital markets has accelerated at an extraordinary pace in the 1990s. If the Republic of Korea and Thailand stick with current reforms, even the East Asian financial crisis—like the Mexican peso crisis before it—will likely have only a passing effect on the volume of international capital flows. Still, increases in interest rates in industrial countries, which should not be ruled out, will probably cause a slowdown in funds flowing to emerging markets.

The Mexican and East Asian crises have demonstrated the power of international capital markets. Although some countries will conclude that they want to stay out of these markets, most will not. Two of the countries hardest hit in the tequila crisis—Mexico and Argentina—have continued to open their markets to foreign capital. Similarly, Korea and Thailand will be more, not less, open to international capital flows after this crisis.

Countries that want to participate in international capital markets will have to strengthen their macroeconomic policies and their financial systems. Capital market liberalization should be gradual and should take place only as the domestic financial system is strengthened and prudential and other controls are put in place. But most countries will liberalize, more or less gradually.

To deal with the risks posed by the globalization of capital markets, actions will be needed by industrial and developing country governments, to strengthen not only the international economic system but also their domestic economies. I will focus on one aspect of recent discussions about the strengthening of the international economic system: the notion that a variety of standards should be developed and put in place.

The Basle Committee's Core Principles provide an agreed standard for banking system behavior and supervision. Similarly, the IMF's Special Data Dissemination Standard constitutes an agreed international standard for statistical data. Codes of good practice can be envisaged for accounting standards, corporate governance, securities markets, and other aspects of private sector behavior. The IMF recently produced a code of good practices on fiscal transparency—Australia and New Zealand have already introduced their own such codes—and has been asked to develop a code of good practices with respect to monetary policies.

Such codes will provide a comprehensive set of rules that countries can implement to improve their economic performance and to guide international capital flows.[5] If bank regulators in creditor countries cooperate, a system of risk weighting for investments in developing countries could emerge based on the extent to which such standards are observed. Of course, this would require that implementation of the standards be monitored and certified. In a rational world observance of the standards would also help determine the terms on which corporations and governments would have access to international capital markets. In this way macroeconomic policy, corporate transparency, and financial market regulation in developing countries could be improved using the discipline of international capital markets.

As globalization proceeds, the question of the optimal exchange rate arrangement and of the desirability of maintaining a national currency will again come to the fore. The arguments on these issues are well known. To cut them short, let me simply predict that if the euro succeeds—and I expect it to—we will likely see the development of several large currency blocs associated with large trading areas. These in turn could eventually—in the Keynesian long run— coalesce into a single currency.

The ongoing globalization of goods and capital markets promises to bring profound changes to the global economy and to individual economies. Although most advanced economies will be well equipped to deal with these changes, even some of them will have to improve institutions and policies to meet international standards. Most developing economies will need to take actions on many fronts to meet international standards. They will need help to strengthen their institutions and build their human capital. Some that may not have access to international capital markets will need financial assistance. Here one thinks most of the needs of many Sub-Saharan African countries.

These are early days for the international economy that, spurred by the liberalization of trade and capital flows as well as by technological change in the financial sector, is continuing to emerge from the destruction wrought by the Great Depression and World War II. The system is accident-prone and lacks a regulatory authority and lender of last resort. We need to work on the architecture internationally and in individual economies to make it safer. But at the same time we should not forget that this system has brought unprecedented and sustained, though not uniformly shared, economic growth and prosperity—and that it will continue to do so for countries that follow the right policies.

Conclusion

Let me conclude with a confession. For a long time, even after *World Development Report 1991* was published, I believed that there was an elixir of growth, a magic ingredient missing from the set of policies listed in the report, that if included would make a miracle—even an

East Asian miracle—possible. I no longer believe that. Or rather, I believe that I know the missing ingredient. It is hard work. For it is a long and arduous task, a matter of many people doing many things right over many years, to make a country grow.

Notes

I am grateful to Boris Pleskovic and Vinod Thomas for helpful discussions.

1. The report also analyzed the contributions to the growth of developing countries that could be made by industrial countries and international financial institutions.

2. Amsden (1989) challenges the views of international financial institutions by arguing that in the Republic of Korea the government contributed to fast growth by systematically distorting market incentives ("getting prices wrong"). See also Wade (1990).

3. Although Adam Smith and other founding fathers of economics can be thought of as fundamentally concerned with economic growth and development, and although development economics draws on other branches of economics, especially trade theory, development economics as a field should probably be dated to the 1940s. Systematic empirical work had to wait for the development of a database, which began in the 1950s.

4. These issues are discussed in *World Development Report 1997*, which suggests focusing on the basics when the capacity of the state is limited.

5. The idea that such rules would improve economic performance is part of the German notion of *ordnungspolitik*, associated with Walter Eucken in the 1940s.

References

Amsden, Alice. 1989. *Asia's Next Giant: South Korea and Late Industrialization.* New York: Oxford University Press.

Bruno, Michael. 1995. "Development Issues in a Changing World: New Lessons, Old Debates, Open Questions." In Michael Bruno and Boris Pleskovic, eds., *Proceedings of the World Bank Annual Conference on Development Economics 1994.* Washington, D.C.: World Bank.

EBRD (European Bank for Reconstruction and Development). Various years. *Transition Report.* London.

Fischer, Stanley, and Dennis de Tray. 1990. "Introduction." In Stanley Fischer and Dennis de Tray, eds., *Proceedings of the World Bank Annual Conference on Development Economics 1989.* Washington, D.C.: World Bank.

Fischer, Stanley, and Alan Gelb. 1991. "The Process of Socialist Economic Transformation." *Journal of Economic Perspectives* (fall): 91–106.

Folkerts-Landau, David, and Carl Lindgren. 1998. "Toward a Framework for Financial Stability." World Economic and Financial Survey. International Monetary Fund, Washington, D.C.

Lipton, David, and Jeffrey Sachs. 1990. "Creating a Market Economy in Eastern Europe: The Case of Poland." *Brookings Papers on Economic Activity 1.* Washington, D.C.: Brookings Institution.

Sachs, Jeffrey, and Wing Thye Woo. 1994. "Structural Factors in the Economic Reforms of China, Eastern Europe, and the Former Soviet Union." *Economic Policy* 18 (April): 101–145.

Stiglitz, Joseph E. 1997. "The Role of Government in Economic Development." In Michael Bruno and Boris Pleskovic, eds., *Annual World Bank Conference on Development Economics 1996.* Washington, D.C.: World Bank.

Wade, Robert. 1990. *Governing the Market: Economic Theory and the Role of Government in East Asian Industrialization.* Princeton, N.J.: Princeton University Press.

Williamson, John, ed. 1990. *Latin American Adjustment: How Much Has Happened?* Washington, D.C.: Institute of International Economics.

World Bank. 1993. *The East Asian Miracle: Economic Growth and Public Policy.* A Policy Research Report. New York: Oxford University Press.

———. Various years. *World Development Report.* New York: Oxford University Press.

This chapter is included because it represents my views on the relationships between growth and poverty, and reform and poverty, in developing countries. There are two key points:

• Sustained and continuing poverty reduction requires sustained and continuing economic growth.

• There is nothing inevitable about the relationship between growth and poverty reduction; what happens to poverty and income distribution during growth is determined in large part by policy.

In the Indian context, beyond directed anti-poverty policies, in which India has done well, I identify in particular: investing in human capital; increasing labor market flexibility; agricultural reform; and inflation reduction (inflation was then running in the low double digits). The arguments are developed in greater detail in the chapter.

India achieved a great deal in the 1990s. The average growth rate of real GDP from 1991 to 1999 was 5.7% per annum, or 3.7% per capita. The inflation rate declined to the low single digits during the decade. Some deregulation of industry and of the financial system took place. Because two sets of data conflict, there has been some controversy about what happened to poverty during the decade, but increasingly the consensus is that poverty was substantially reduced.[1]

Nonetheless, India could have done better. The reform process accelerated following the balance of payments crisis of 1991 but then lost momentum in the second half of the decade. The government budget deficit remained very high throughout the decade, and the failure to reduce it is still a problem. Fortunately, deft management of monetary and exchange rate policy, along with capital controls, enabled India to avoid being dragged into the Asian crisis.

What of the future? It is in a sense encouraging that India achieved such high growth in the 1990s despite shortcomings in both its structural and fiscal policies. For it could do better yet by intensifying the structural reform process and strengthening the fiscal situation, and thereby achieve the 7–8 percent per annum growth rate to which it aspires, and which is very much in reach.

Note

1. Surjit Bhalla, *Imagine There's No Country*, Washington, D.C.: Institute for International Economics, 2002; and Angus Deaton and A. Tarrozi, "Prices and Poverty in India," Princeton, mimeo, 1999.

16   Economic Reform and the Poor

Stanley Fischer

It is a great pleasure indeed to be here again in Bombay, almost exactly five years after I had the honor of presenting a public lecture in the Reserve Bank. The topic then was the dangers of excessive budget deficits[1] and I am happy to report that the Governor of the Reserve Bank found my views on the issue to be totally sound.

A year later India was in the grip of one of the most serious financial crises in its history. Thanks to the resolute actions of the Government, which were backed by the IMF and other multilateral and bilateral creditors, India rapidly surmounted that crisis—and seized the opportunity to begin a process of change that, if sustained and deepened, will enable this country to fulfill its potential as a major economic power in the global economy. Four years since the crisis, India has emerged stronger than before. The external position is now much more robust, economic growth has been restored, industry has become more dynamic and competitive, and foreign investors have been eager to participate in India's emerging success.

If I emphasize what still needs to be done, rather than what has been achieved, you will understand that is because it may still be possible to change the future, rather than because of a lack of appreciation of the achievements of the last four years. A visitor returning after four years cannot fail to be greatly impressed by the changes in the approach to economic policy and by changes in the Indian economy that may be more evident to the outsider than those who live here.

When I was here last, I was with the World Bank. Now that I have moved to the Fund, it would be natural to re-emphasize the message of my previous lecture, that large fiscal deficits endanger macro-economic stability. Nothing I have learned in the last five years has changed my views that fiscal policy is key to macroeconomic stability, and that macroeconomic stability is essential if growth is to be sustained and permanent progress made in the attack on poverty. This time I would add that advantage should be taken of a period of sustained growth to reduce the deficit decisively, and then I would go on to describe the supporting structural policies, among them privatization, continued trade and domestic deregulation, and financial sector reform, that are needed to ensure that the growth process takes permanent hold. However, there are three reasons not to pursue this topic: first, I do not have the privilege of speaking in India often enough to justify saying the same thing again—however crucial and correct the message is; second, I suspect that the arguments are well known and increasingly accepted by most in the audience; and third, the argument was convincingly laid out in last year's Exim Bank Commencement Day Annual Lecture by Dr. Vijay Joshi.

Alternatively, at this point, three months after Mexico devalued its currency, I could use the occasion to draw the lessons of Mexico for market-oriented reform. Interesting as that might be, let me only summarize my views by stating that Mexico has been in most respects a model reformer—in balancing its fiscal accounts, in liberalizing trade and entering NAFTA, in privatization and in aspects of domestic deregulation—but that it made the critical mistake of allowing the exchange rate to become so overvalued that the current account deficit reached and was expected to remain at eight percent of GDP. The adverse effects on confidence of the devaluation that became unavoidable, in part because of the credit policies pursued in 1994, were compounded by the structure of the government debt. Despite the setback suffered by Mexico, I have no doubt that the market-oriented approach will continue to be the only road to development and growth, albeit with variations that reflect countries' individual histories and political economies.

The Mexican case also illustrates the remarkable speed and power of private capital flows in the emerging global markets. You will not be surprised to learn that the IMF is devoting a considerable amount of thinking to adapting its role and the instruments at its disposal to enable it to help its members deal with the world of the twenty first century, whose shadow has cast itself before us in Mexico.

The topic I have chosen today, "Economic Reform and the Poor," lies at the heart of the political economy of the market-oriented approach to economic reform. The question is often posed whether such reforms have benefitted, or can benefit, the common person. The concern is entirely legitimate, for the ultimate objective of growth is to raise the living standards and the well-being of virtually everyone. This is particularly so in India, which contains a substantial portion of the world's poorest people, and where literacy, sanitation, and nutrition standards rank among the world's lowest.

In talking about economic reform and the poor it is important to get the focus correct. *The prime aim of policy must be to achieve sustained growth, for there can be no permanent improvement in the living standards of the great bulk of the population without continuing growth.* When per capita GDP is as low as it is in India, no amount of redistribution can raise the living standards of most people to the levels that have been attained elsewhere in Asia by countries that at one time were as poor as India. The question is not redistribution versus growth, but rather how to ensure that growth reduces poverty, and preferably also reduces the inequality of income.

This is a complex issue, and there is much that we, in the international agencies, in governments, and in the academic world, still have to learn about the links among adjustment, growth, poverty reduction, and income distribution. Early research by Simon Kuznets and others pointed to a worsening of income distribution in the initial stages of development, leading economists to think there was a tradeoff between growth and equity. However, both East Asia's dramatic progress over the past two decades and further academic research has made it clear that there is nothing inevitable in the relationship between growth and income distribution, and that what happens to poverty and income distribution during growth is determined in large part by policy.[2]

More important, the evidence suggests that rapid growth is not only compatible with, but is likely to be enhanced by policies—such as investing in primary and secondary education—that also improve income distribution and reduce poverty.[3]

A growing body of research indicates that the key to rapid poverty reduction is high quality growth, that is, sustained, broad-based growth that generates employment, improves the quality of human capital, and is outward oriented. The challenge is to identify the right mix and sequencing of policies so that the benefits of reform are felt quickly, and by as many people as possible. The right approach improves the human resource base and brings down the rate of population increase, as well as generating support for further reforms. Thus, a virtuous circle of rapid growth and improving living standards can be created—and has been created in many countries on this continent.

Within this general framework, I will focus on four key lessons that are particularly relevant to India's reform strategy. *First*, the most important investment a country can make is in its people. This is not a slogan, but a fact that should drive policy: the development of India's human resources is key to achieving rapid, sustained growth.[4] *Second*, flexibility in labor markets helps to foster employment generation and facilitates the process of industrial restructuring. *Third*, agricultural reform is critical to boosting growth and improving living standards for the majority of the population. *Finally*—and here I turn to macroeconomics—a concerted effort should be made to establish price stability, for inflation imposes a heavy burden on the poor and saps India's growth potential.

Before moving on to these four lessons, let me note briefly that direct poverty relief schemes also play a key role in the fight against poverty, and that India has pioneered in creating many of the most successful of such schemes. Indeed, the budget for 1995/1996, announced on March 15, includes several measures aimed at poverty alleviation and spreading the benefits of reform.[5]

I will not discuss these and other direct poverty relief and social safety net measures in any detail, not because they are not important in reducing the social costs of adjustment, but because their scope is necessarily limited by the overall resource constraint on the economy, and because the focus of this chapter is those aspects of pro-growth policy that can help ensure that growth reduces poverty and improves income distribution.

Developing Human Resources

The issue of the role of government is often posed by asking whether government is too big, and the expected answer in the case of India would be yes. But that answer is at best partial, and it is certainly highly misleading. In certain areas, particularly in regulating economic activity, the tentacles of the Indian Government reach too far, and help stifle the potentially creative private sector. In other areas, including infrastructure, education and the provision of health and other social services, the Government (central and state together) is doing too little, or is misdirecting its activities.

Empirical research has consistently demonstrated the importance of accumulating human capital as a prerequisite for rapid, sustained growth in living standards. The acquisition of formal education and improvements in health standards definitely increase labor productivity. Extending educational opportunities and healthcare to the least-advantaged also empowers them to escape poverty through their own efforts. The East Asian experience shows how this can be done.

East Asian countries have devoted considerable public resources to education over a prolonged period of time. The early decision to do so was important. This is because as soon as economic growth began to take off, real spending per pupil could be increased without raising the share of such spending in GDP. Improved education and health standards also fostered a decline in fertility rates, which implied a slower growth of the school-age population, thus again allowing higher spending per pupil. In 1989, the East Asian economies spent an average of 3.7 percent of GDP on public education. Many other developing economies spent the same share or more. However, with larger and faster growing populations to provide for, and with slower economic growth, they could not achieve the levels of spending per pupil typical in East Asia.

The second principal lesson from the East Asia experience is the importance of the *structure of education spending*. Other than Singapore, all the successful East Asian economies have devoted 80–90 percent of education budgets to primary and secondary schooling. As a result, primary and secondary school enrollment rates are high and the goal of universal primary education is close to being achieved. One important benefit has been a rapid narrowing of the gender gap in education, which has not only increased the skill level of the female labor force but also has enhanced the home learning environment and helped to lower the population growth rate. These policies not only contributed to growth: they were also instrumental in promoting equality. Moreover, since education enrollment rates increase with both income and equality, the whole process has been self reinforcing. Not surprisingly, therefore, recent research in the World Bank and elsewhere has shown relatively high direct and indirect returns to women's education.[6]

India has always attached a high priority to education, and many key indicators of educational attainment have shown a sustained improvement. This year's budget—incorporating higher

outlays on education and greater emphasis on primary education—
is a further indication of the Government's commitment. Yet the
fact remains that enrollment rates and literacy lag far behind those
in East Asia. Moreover, the improvement in educational attainment
reflects mainly increased secondary education: remarkably enough,
the proportion of the population that has completed primary school
actually declined over the last 30 years. In addition, educational
opportunities are not as readily available to the poor and to women
as to others. Consequently, the better off derive much of the benefit
from public education, preserving and possibly exacerbating existing
inequalities. Part of the problem is that India spends some 15 percent
less, relative to GDP, on education compared with the East Asian
average.

Low female enrollment rates are critical not only because they
deny opportunities to individuals, but also because they deny the
country the direct economic returns of the education. Moreover, they
matter because there is a strong link between female educational
attainment and fertility rates. Per capita growth in India, and the
quality of economic growth, would benefit from lower population
growth. Both improved access to education, particularly for women,
and increased spending on family planning, would help reduce
population growth.

A similar story can be told with regard to healthcare. India has
achieved high standards in its best medical facilities. But a high
proportion of budget outlays on health are absorbed by curative
healthcare and urban hospitals, leaving inadequate allocations to
primary and preventive healthcare, including family planning.
Health standards would also benefit from increased attention to
improving nutrition, particularly for children; broadening access to
clean drinking water; and extending sanitation facilities in rapidly
expanding urban areas.

Increasing and redirecting resources to primary education and
basic healthcare will not be easy in view of both budgetary
constraints and the political economy of educational and health
reform. Moreover, reorienting spending patterns will undoubtedly
be resisted by those with a vested interest in the existing structure.
Change will also be complicated by India's federal system of government. The states are responsible for the provision of virtually all
primary and secondary public education and healthcare. Unfortunately, it is at the decentralized level that budgetary change has
proved most difficult to accomplish and pressure group politics

have their greatest influence. The wide disparities in education and healthcare spending across states are a consequence. Reforming center-state relations, and improving governance more generally, therefore have a role to play in a growth-oriented education and health strategy.

Making Labor Markets More Flexible

Flexible labor markets contribute importantly to achieving high quality growth. This point is well illustrated by the experience of the East Asian countries. Wages and employment in these countries have been largely determined by the interaction of labor supply and demand, rather than by government legislation, public sector leadership, or union pressure. The result has been a powerful virtuous circle. Flexible labor markets have encouraged efficient allocation of workers across sectors, higher investment, and use of more labor-intensive technologies. This process has contributed to more rapid output growth, which in turn has enhanced labor demand, employment, and wages. The cycle has been reinforced by high levels of education, vocational training, and healthcare that have allowed the pattern of employment to become gradually more skill-intensive, again supporting rising wages and living standards.

India's experience has been very different. Employment in the organized private sector has stagnated since the mid-1970s, while the capital intensity of production has grown rapidly. The passage of legislation in the mid-1970s (the Industrial Disputes Act), which required firms to obtain government permission before retrenching workers, has surely been an important factor behind this outcome. Firms do not want to take on new workers if they are uncertain whether and when excess labor can be cut back in response to changing market conditions. Thus, paradoxically, policies designed to protect Indian workers in fact do them a disservice by foreclosing valuable employment opportunities.

Of course, this pattern, of high firing costs generating high rates of unemployment, has also been observed in Europe, most notably in Spain where the current unemployment rate exceeds 23 percent and the natural rate of unemployment is estimated to be about 18 percent. European economists also rely on the insider-outsider model of labor markets to explain real wage rigidity and other labor market phenomena associated with high and persistent unemployment. In these models, wages and work conditions are determined mainly by the insiders whose employment is likely to continue, rather than by the outsiders who could potentially benefit from changes in the terms of employment. This pattern is visible too in India, where present policies protect a small, highly visible segment of the labor force (about 8 percent of the total). Conversely, they discriminate against the vast majority of workers who are employed in the lower wage informal sector, where they receive minimal legal protection of their working conditions.

It is sometimes argued that because the informal sector in India is so large and flexible, the costs of restrictions in the formal sector are overestimated. That is of course to some extent true. Nonetheless, restrictions in the formal sector and the segmentation of labor markets have direct economic costs. Segmented labor markets result in an inefficient allocation of resources and generate pressures on the public sector to hire more workers, resulting in substantial overmanning. Moreover, labor market rigidities interfere with the adjustment of the economy in response to changing economic conditions, technologies, and external shocks, as the European experience confirms. It is important that India avoid this European trap.

Let me venture some general suggestions on what can be done in this area. A more effective employment policy for India needs to move on two fronts simultaneously: to increase the flexibility of the employer-employee relationship, and to support the effective redeployment of labor. The key element is to change the role of government in the labor markets. It should no longer be required to vet any labor force reduction before it can occur. Instead, such decisions should be left to free bilateral negotiation between management and workers. The Government should focus on ensuring that fair labor legislation is applied uniformly and that workers who need to look for new jobs are given adequate support. In this latter respect, the minimum compensation required for laid-off workers could be raised (it is now 15 days' wages per year of service); and the funds available in the National Renewal Fund could be deployed more effectively for retraining and placement services for retrenched labor.

Reforming Agriculture

Any strategy to achieve rapid growth and make significant inroads on poverty must tackle the low productivity that continues to plague India's farm sector. The reasons are clear: some 80 percent of India's poor reside in rural areas, where they are predominantly engaged in farm activities. Farming employs 70 percent of India's labor force and accounts for 32 percent of its GDP. Thus, the most direct means of combating poverty is to boost employment, productivity, and wages in agriculture.

Further, the benefits do not end with poverty reduction. Agricultural development provides a strong foundation for growth in the rest of the economy. It is no coincidence that the most successful countries of East Asia have achieved rapid rates of farm productivity growth, generating sharp increases in agricultural output in a context of stable food prices and rising rural wages. Most notably, and notwithstanding the recent stagnation in agricultural output, China's spectacular growth in the last 15 years started with radical and extremely rapid reforms in the agricultural sector—incidentally, a fact that should qualify the common view that China has pursued a gradualist reform strategy. Because land ownership and usage patterns in India differ from those in East Asia, such rapid reforms could not be duplicated in India. But it remains true that progress in agriculture would support economic growth, reduce poverty, and could help to improve the distribution of income.

A basic reason for the successful agricultural development of the East Asian economies is that they did not promote industry at the expense of agriculture. They generally avoided the taxes, food price controls, and pro-industry allocations of credit that have been common in other developing economies. Equally important, they refrained from taxing agriculture indirectly through industrial protection and exchange rate overvaluation. Agricultural productivity was also enhanced by public sector investment in rural infrastructure, by programs to disseminate new technologies, inputs and know-how to farmers, and by effective land reform.

India has also devoted considerable resources to agricultural and rural development over the past three decades. The spread of irrigation, fertilizers, and high-yielding seed varieties across the country has boosted food production, contributing to the ending of famines in India.[7]

However, despite the success of the adoption of Green Revolution technologies, there remain significant distortions created by India's protected trade regime, industrial regulations, and controls on internal and external trade in agricultural products. Moreover, rural infrastructure remains inadequate and yields are well below international levels. In part for these reasons, labor productivity in India's farming sector has grown on average by just 1/2 percent per year over the past two decades, compared with productivity growth in East Asian farming of over 2 percent per year. Most of the increases in food production have come through the intensification of cropped areas in a few regions of the country, supported by extremely costly subsidies (for power, irrigation, and fertilizers) which are no longer sustainable. Low productivity has constrained farm wages, contributing to persistent poverty in rural areas.

What can India do to promote agricultural development and thereby tackle poverty, especially rural poverty, head on? Here I am once again at a comparative and absolute disadvantage, and I shall venture only general suggestions. The key is to untangle the complex web of distortions that reduce incentives for producers and inhibit productivity growth. There are three requirements. First, the agricultural sector should be liberalized—as was the industrial sector in 1991—by dismantling the pervasive controls on commerce in agricultural products. This would involve eliminating licensing requirements for wholesale trade and storage of virtually all commodities, phasing out the remaining elements of compulsory public procurement, abolishing the remaining controls on imports and exports of many agricultural items, ending the licensing of agro-processing industries, and—with safeguards—lifting the ban on futures and forward trading. Many of these controls were set up in the 1950s under the Essential Commodities Act, at a time when the centralized management of agricultural supply and prices was considered necessary to prevent acute shortages. Such an approach no longer seems necessary in an India where basic supply conditions are much stronger and a robust private sector exists to do the job well.

Second, the system of price incentives facing the farmer needs to be brought into line with market realities, while providing adequate infrastructural support. In recent years, progress has been made toward raising procurement prices toward international levels, but the link needs to be more systematic. In addition, the enormous distortions implied by heavily subsidized fertilizers and electricity for farmers need to be addressed. While there can be no doubting the political difficulties of dealing with this issue, it would be far more productive to phase out these subsidies and redeploy the budgetary resources toward increased investment in rural infrastructure, particularly transportation and storage facilities needed to get products to the market, and in strengthening rural credit systems.

Third, it will be necessary to look again at the public distribution system. Increasing the role of markets and international trade in agricultural supply may raise price volatility and imply significant increases in the prices of some commodities. In a country such as India, making available certain essential foodstuffs at subsidized prices does provide significant protection for the poor. However, the present public distribution system is extremely inefficient and does not do a particularly good job of delivering cheap food to the poor. The system needs to be overhauled to reduce its costs and ensure a much more effective targeting to the truly needy.

Tackling Inflation

Inflation is sometimes referred to as the cruelest tax of all, because of its heavy incidence on the poor, and because it is to a considerable extent invisible to most of those who bear its burden. The poor in India seem particularly vulnerable to inflation. Their wages are set in nominal terms in an economy with minimal indexation. Moreover, most of their limited financial savings is held in the form of currency.

Beyond its adverse distributional effects, inflation also directly reduces growth and slows the rate at which poverty is reduced. Much research, including Fischer (1993), has demonstrated the negative association between inflation and growth.[8]

There are many reasons for such a negative relationship: among them that inflation creates uncertainty, reduces the efficiency of resource allocation (in part through its interactions with the tax system), lowers investment, and thus reduces the rate of productivity growth. Inflation in the double digits, or in the upper single digits, serves no useful purpose, often threatens to rise further, and should be fought and reduced.

How can inflation be brought down while minimizing the short-term impact on growth? An effective inflation reduction program requires measures both to contain aggregate demand and to enhance aggregate supply. To complement these measures, institutional reforms to establish a policy-making framework with a clear commitment to price stability would reduce the potential costs of inflation reduction.

On the demand side, sustained fiscal adjustment supported by monetary policy is the lynch-pin of successful price stabilization. Reducing inflation without choking off growth will depend crucially upon substantial further fiscal consolidation. First, deficit reduction would reduce the pressures for monetary financing of the deficit by the RBI. The RBI has successfully resisted these pressures in recent years, but has allowed the foreign exchange inflow to affect money growth. A further reduction in the deficit would give the monetary authorities more room to offset the effects of the capital inflows. Second, fiscal adjustment would ease pressure on interest rates and allow a greater share of resources to be made available to the private sector. A tight monetary policy without supporting fiscal policy could be effective in bringing down inflation in the short run. However, it would raise real interest rates, tend to promote a real exchange rate appreciation, and thus discourage the investment and exports needed for sustained growth.

This is not the occasion to go deeply into the question of how to continue reducing the deficit and ensure that the debt-to-GDP ratio begins to decline.[9]

What is needed are measures that would unambiguously establish the direction and durability of reforms. In particular, continued tax reforms and improvements in the structure of government spending programs are essential. Well-designed expenditure reforms would leave room for necessary spending on infrastructure and human capital and help to foster confidence in the sustainability of adjustment.

On the supply side, the combination of a rapidly growing economy and a relatively inefficient distribution system is likely to lead to bottlenecks and capacity constraints in the period ahead, which would add to inflationary pressures. To relieve such pressures, high priority should be given to further import liberalization, taking advantage of the present high level of international reserves. Lifting internal restrictions on trade in agricultural products and improving facilities for the distribution and processing of foodstuffs would also help. Perhaps most importantly, India's infrastructure (particularly its power supply, ports, and roads) need to be modernized rapidly. In view of the resource constraints faced by the Government, this will require finding effective ways to involve private capital.

Finally, let me stress the importance of making inflation an explicit policy target and establishing an institutional structure for policy making that demonstrates a clear commitment to price stability. A number of countries have acted recently to achieve price stability after years of tolerating moderate rates of inflation—including Chile, Canada, New Zealand, and the United Kingdom. Innovations have included publicized "policy target agreements" between the minister of finance and the central bank governor and legislation to increase central bank autonomy. Last year's agreement between the Reserve Bank of India and the Ministry of Finance regarding the phasing out by 1997/1998 of the RBI's ad hoc financing to the Government is important in this regard. Its effective implementation—and implementation is so far on track—would enhance the central bank's ability to run an independent and anti-inflationary monetary policy.

Concluding Remarks

To sum up, the main message I would like to leave with you is that economic reform can directly and rapidly reduce poverty at the same time as it increases growth. The stabilization and reform program pursued since 1991 has provided a sound base that is beginning to transform India, but further bold steps are still required for India to emulate the rapid growth and sustained progress in poverty reduction achieved in East Asia. Continued and deepened structural reforms in the areas of trade and industrial liberalization, privatization, and financial sector reform, conducted on the foundation of macroeconomic stability, are essential to sustaining and increasing the growth rate. I do not in any way underestimate the profound political difficulties involved in effecting these changes, but their long-run benefits will be enormous.

In focusing on those policy decisions that can help ensure that growth directly reduces poverty and improves the distribution of income, I have emphasized four areas: building up human capital and in general improving the quality of government spending, encouraging employment growth by making labor markets more flexible, developing agriculture, and bringing down inflation. These reforms would all serve to strengthen the positive linkages between growth and poverty reduction. Of course, it will also be important to ensure that adequate steps are taken to protect the poor and disadvantaged who might be adversely affected in the short run, through appropriate targeting of food subsidies and the provision of effective safety nets for redeployed workers. But the essential ingredient in sustained poverty reduction is achieving high quality economic growth.

Notes

This chapter was prepared for presentation at the tenth Exim Bank Commencement Day Lecture in Bombay on March 27, 1995. I am grateful to P. R. Narvekar, Charles Collyns, Ajai Chopra, Richard Hemming, and Karen Parker of the IMF for substantial assistance, and to Guy Pfeffermann of the IFC and Roberto Zagha of the World Bank for helpful comments.

1. The substance of the lecture appears in Fischer and Easterly (1990).

2. Alesina and Perotti (1994) contains a survey of the recent literature.

3. See Persson and Tabellini (1994).

4. This point is convincingly made in Amartya Sen's 1994 Lakdawala Memorial Lecture.

5. Specific measures include a social assistance program for the poorest, larger spending on rural housing schemes, and subsidies for life insurance for poor households.

6. See Summers (1994).

7. The qualification "contributing" takes into account the striking fact made well-known by Amartya Sen that there has never been a famine in a democracy (see Dreze and Sen, 1989).

8. Based on their recent research, Michael Bruno and William Easterly (1995) claim that the negative association between inflation and growth becomes significant only at inflation rates in excess of 40 percent. This result is different from those reported in Fischer (1993), so that the issue of the inflation-growth relationship at low inflation rate remains open.

9. For an analysis of the sustainability of India's fiscal stance, see Buiter and Patel (1995).

References

Alesina, Alberto, and Roberto Perotti (1994). "The Political Economy of Growth: A Critical Survey of the Recent Literature," *The World Bank Economic Review*, 8, 3, 351–371.

Anant, T. C. A., Tamal Datta Chaudhuri, Shubhashis Gangopadhyay, and Omkar Goswami (1994). *Industrial Sickness in India: Institutional Responses and Issues in Restructuring*, New Delhi (April).

Barro, Robert, and Jong Wha Lee (1993). "International Comparisons of Educational Attainment," *Journal of Monetary Economics*, 32, 3 (December), 363–394.

Bruno, Michael, and William Easterly (1995). "Inflation Crises and Long-Run Growth," mimeo, World Bank.

Buiter, Willem, and Urjit R. Patel (1995). "Budgetary Aspects of Stabilization and Structural Adjustment in India," mimeo, University of Cambridge, Faculty of Economics and Politics (January).

Dornbusch, Rudiger, and Stanley Fischer (1993). "Moderate Inflation," *World Bank Economic Review*, 7, 1 (January), 1–44.

Dreze, Jean, and Amartya Sen (1989). *Hunger and Public Action*. Oxford: Clarendon Press.

Fischer, Stanley (1993). "The Role of Macroeconomic Factors in Growth," *Journal of Monetary Economics*, 32, 3 (December), 485–512 and William Easterly (1990). "The Economics of the Government Budget Constraint," *World Bank Research Observer*, (July), 127–142.

Joshi, Vijay (1994). "Macroeconomic Policy and Economic Reform in India," Ninth Annual Exim Bank Commencement Day Lecture Bombay: Export-Import Bank of India.

International Labour Organization (1993). *India: Employment, Poverty and Economic Policies*, Asian Regional Team for Employment Promotion (ARTEP), New Delhi (December).

Persson, Torsten, and Guido Tabellini (1984). "Is Inequality Harmful for Growth?" *American Economic Review*, 84, 3 (June), 600–621.

Pursell, Gary, and Ashok Gulati (1993). *Liberalizing Indian Agriculture: An Agenda for Reform*, World Bank, (September).

Sen, Amartya (1994). "Beyond Liberalization: Social Opportunity and Human Capability," Development Economics Research Programme, London School of Economics, Paper No. 58 (November).

Summers, Lawrence (1994). "Investing in All the People: Educating Women in Developing Countries," World Bank EDI paper number 45.

World Bank (1993). *East Asia Miracle: Economic Growth and Public Policy*, Washington, D.C.

Index